Errata

Page 131: lines 3 and 4 should read:
> Shortly before the convention, McGillivray wrote to Diefenbaker
> again with more advice:

Page 244: line 39: "natural resources" should read "national resources"

Page 260: line 37: "natural resources" should read "national resources"

ROGUE TORY

ROGUE TORY

The Life and Legend of JOHN G. DIEFENBAKER

Denis Smith

MACFARLANE WALTER & ROSS

TORONTO

Macfarlane Walter & Ross
37A Hazelton Avenue,
Toronto, Canada M5R 2E3

CANADIAN CATALOGUING IN PUBLICATION DATA

Smith, Denis, 1932–
Rogue Tory: the life and legend of John G. Diefenbaker

Includes bibliographical references and index

ISBN 0-921912-92-7

1. Diefenbaker, John G., 1895-1979.
2. Canada – Politics and government – 1935–   . *
3. Prime ministers – Canada – Biogaphy. I. Title.

FC616.D53S5 1995   971.064-2-092   C95-932462-3   F1034.3.D5S5 1995

Information on excerpts from published sources
appears in the Acknowledgments

The publisher gratefully acknowledges
the support of the
Canada Council and the Ontario Arts Council

Printed and bound in Canada

To the memory of my parents,
Doris and Bruce Smith,
who raised me as a westerner;
to my wife, Dawn;
and to Alastair, Stephen, and Andrea,
Canadians of another generation

Contents

Prologue

IN CANADA THE WINTERS ARE HARD. POLITICIANS PREFER TO CAMPAIGN IN THE temperate months of spring or autumn when travel is reliable and the public mood is not depressed by storm and winter darkness. But 1958 was an exceptional year. Prime Minister John G. Diefenbaker, who had come to power with a minority of parliamentary seats in the general election of June 1957, dissolved the House of Commons in early February and entered a winter contest in defiance of nature. On March 31, after a campaign that dazzled the electorate and dismayed his foes, Diefenbaker's Progressive Conservatives won the largest majority in the country's history: 208 of 265 seats, spread evenly across every region of the nation. The invincible Liberal Party was shattered, its front bench decimated, its treasury exhausted, its new leader humiliated by an electorate that had chosen to "Follow John." The Social Credit Party disappeared entirely from parliament, and the Cooperative Commonwealth Federation (CCF) was reduced to eight seats.

John Diefenbaker was sixty-two, yet he did not seem it. The prime minister campaigned at a frenetic pace, and with his famous victory he opened a Conservative era that might outlast the Liberal reign of twenty-two years. As expectations rose in the aftermath of victory, the prospect did not appear unreasonable. Instead, the Conservative prime minister gave the country a decade of continuous convulsion, marked by his government's defeat in April 1963 and his own forced departure from the leadership in September 1967. For a decade and more after that, the old warrior remained hovering in parliament, the scourge of Liberal governments and his own successors. But it was the tumultuous decade of leadership from 1957 to 1967 that made him a subject for the history books.

When Diefenbaker died in August 1979, he was given an extended state funeral modelled – at his own direction – on the funerals of Winston

Churchill, John Kennedy, and Robert Kennedy. It culminated in a transcontinental train journey and burial on the grassy bluffs of the South Saskatchewan River overlooking the city of Saskatoon, beside the centre that had been built to house his personal and public papers and the relics of a lifetime.

What was remembered, and buried, on those bluffs was as much a legend as a man. The man lived a long public life, but it was a life of turmoil, rebuff, failure, disappointment, and bitterness more than of triumph and satisfaction. Yet out of it Diefenbaker built the legend of a morally triumphant underdog, the representative Canadian common man. The country took to the legend even as it rejected John Diefenbaker the politician.

When he became prime minister in 1957, the country did not know him. When it came to know him and to experience his leadership, the country preferred the legend to the man. To understand him – and perhaps to understand his country as well in the twentieth century – it is necessary to know both legend and man, both myth and reality.

John Diefenbaker was born into colonial Ontario before the end of the nineteenth century. He was of German-Scots ancestry, and his name cast him and his family as outsiders in a society that was, in the twilight of the Victorian era, proudly British in its politics and imperial in its view of the world. His father – despite his German name – was an admirer of the British parliamentary model and of imperial ideals. His mother was an independent Highland Scot with scant respect for the institutions her husband revered. Young John somehow absorbed the influences of both his parents – his father's romantic imperialism and his mother's iconoclasm and driving determination – without entirely reconciling them. From both mother and father, and from the conditions of his youth, he learned about life on the margins of society in a country where most others lived on the margins too. From there, he developed a youthful ambition to move to the centre. While his ambitions were forming and deepening, he could not know the costs of achieving them.

At sixty-one, he came to power late – perhaps too late, both for his administrative capacities and for the suppleness and timeliness of his political ideals. The office of prime minister he had coveted for years seemed in some essential ways beyond his ability to master. That may have been because the country he was chosen to govern was not the country that had formed him. It was already casting off its ties of empire, just as the imperial centre had cast it off. It had achieved international maturity in a world of technology and weapons he scarcely understood. And it was subject to the dominating influence of a friendly neighbour at the very moment when Canadians had come to accept their independence in the world. At home, the western Canadian vision of the nation as a single community absorbing all its subcommunities into a greater whole – a vision Diefenbaker had embraced – came into conflict with a revived French Canadian (or Québécois) nationalism. The conflict was one that Diefenbaker could never really comprehend. As a westerner, an outsider, a romantic parliamentarian of the Edwardian era, he was a man out of time and place in late twentieth-century Ottawa.

Yet in two senses he was a perfect representative of Canadians in the post-war era. He entered parliament from a bankrupt province at the end of ten years of depression, and his belief in a compassionate social policy was shared by progressives of all parties. In 1957 he spoke for a new independence among Canadians of every region, expressing a confident sense of themselves that meant rebellion against the patronizing smugness of Liberal governments of the 1940s and 1950s. His victories of 1957 and 1958 brought to the country a brief sense of liberation and of new horizons to conquer, but the expectations could not be fulfilled.

Privately and publicly, he was never fully in control of his emotions. By 1957 – perhaps much earlier – he was scarred by his failures. He was suspicious of colleagues, unfamiliar with the play of political compromise, inexperienced in sharing tasks and authority. Probably he was too old to learn new tricks. But he was also a man of high theatrical talent, stubbornness, and pluck, who found great pleasure in the political battle. That mixture of character and circumstance produced a life of complexity both for John Diefenbaker and for his country.

CHAPTER 1

A Prairie Youth and a Curious War

1895-1919

JOHN GEORGE DIEFENBAKER WAS THE FIRST SON OF MARY AND WILLIAM Diefenbaker, born in Neustadt, Ontario, on September 18, 1895. A second son, Elmer, was born in 1897. William Diefenbaker was a public school teacher, and the family lived an itinerant life. In John's first fifteen years they occupied at least nine homes in Ontario and Saskatchewan.[1] In 1897 there was a move to Greenwood, east of Toronto; in 1900 there was another to Todmorden, slightly to the north; and in the summer of 1903 there was a trip across the continent by rail to Regina and north to Rosthern, and by box wagon to a schoolhouse home in the district of Tiefengrund (Deep Ground) near Fort Carlton. In 1905, again, there was a relocation thirty miles south to the Hague school district; in 1906, another shift to homestead land near Hoffnungsfeld; and finally in February 1910, after four hard winters on the homestead, a move to Saskatoon, where John and Elmer could complete their schooling. After a few months in a rented house, the family settled into its own home at 411 – 9th Street. Here they remained for almost four decades, until the widowed Mary Diefenbaker entered hospital as an invalid in 1957.

Not surprisingly, John Diefenbaker's memories of his early life in Ontario are sparse: a dog poisoned by unfriendly neighbours; daily prayers and Bible readings, weekly church and Sunday school; music on the family's Thomas organ; springtime lilacs around the house in Greenwood; a sledding accident involving a near-fatal collision with a milk cart; and first encounters with the automobile in Todmorden. As he recalled those events seven decades later, some revealing signs of the man were evident: a memory of childish impudence towards the privileged and a delight in the marvels of the automobile.

Our home then was on the highway taken by the aristocrats of Toronto in their newfangled electric carriages when out for a spin on a Sunday. I saw

1

practically the beginnings of this new traffic: how they travelled, looking neither to right nor left, the cynosure of all eyes, the women in big hats, with a
kind of handkerchief around their chins, and the men wearing dusters.
Sometimes these cars ran and sometimes not. When they broke down they
afforded me a great deal of enjoyment. I would ask the drivers such helpful
questions as, "Do you think it will ever start again?" This, I found, having
done it once, practically assured sharp ejaculations of annoyance, so I invari-
ably raised the question at every opportunity, just to test the reaction.
Needless to say, none of these people offered me a ride, however much I
might secretly have wished for one. Not until 1907, when on the homestead,
did we get our first ride in an automobile, in the back of a Brush one-seater,
owned by a real estate man in Radisson, Saskatchewan.[2]

In his memoirs Diefenbaker also recalled his first attendance at a "great
national event" – the victory parade past Toronto City Hall of Canadian units
returning from the Boer War in November 1900. Dressed by his mother in his
best blue velvet sailor suit and Balmoral cap, young John set off by horse and
wagon with the local garbageman, Mr Skelhorn, for the trip to city hall. As the
wagon turned onto Danforth Avenue from Don Mills Road, it hit a bump and
John was tossed into the greasy bottom of the slops tank, emerging "unhurt
but...the filthiest mess that anyone could imagine." Skelhorn soon dropped
him off, Diefenbaker claims, and John set out alone to watch the marchpast.
"There was Mayor Urquhart of Toronto along with all the other political and
military celebrities on the steps of the City Hall, and four or five feet away that
urchin covered with grease. I was such a fright that nobody dared touch me.
There I watched with wonder the returning soldiers and joined in the cheers
for the Highlanders. When my mother heard what I had done, she was
shocked."[3]

In 1902 the family made a tenting trip to Stoney Lake, north of
Peterborough. Here John's father gave him his introduction to fishing, which
became a lifelong passion and one of his few diversions.[4]

John began school in his father's classroom in Greenwood at the age of
four – the result, he suggested, of precocity and an assertion of will. "I objected
to staying home; I knew how to read, having learned in order to understand
the thermometer on page one of the *Globe*, which gave the weather forecast
each day."[5] His experience of school over the next few years was "sometimes
unpleasant." As the teacher's son, John was shown no favours: "When there
was some mischief in the class and I was blamed whether rightly or wrongly by
the other students, their word was accepted." John recalled that he was

forbidden to fight, which meant he was the loser whenever he was attacked or challenged. His German name was one subject of challenge. "I used to get quite upset when my schoolmates teased me about my name. I felt that my forbears' having been in Canada for so long a time made me a Canadian. I was just seven years old, but my ideas on that subject have not changed with the passage of time. One must remember, however, that in those days Toronto was ninety-eight per cent British."[6]

Diefenbaker's ancestors were unprivileged immigrants to North America. He describes them as "dispossessed Scottish Highlanders and discontented Palatine Germans" who arrived in Upper Canada early in the nineteenth century. On the first page of his memoirs, Diefenbaker offers an inaccurate account of the family's history on his father's side, claiming that his grandfather "was born in Upper Canada" to parents who had emigrated from the Grand Duchy of Baden early in the nineteenth century. In fact, his grandfather, George M. Diefenbacker (sometimes spelled Diefenbach or Diefenbacher), was born in Baden and emigrated to Upper Canada in the 1850s, where he married and bought land in 1858. He was a wagon-maker. After his son's move to the Saskatchewan homestead, grandson John recalled the arrival from Ontario of "a magnificent wagon of oak and maple" that was unsuitable for use on rutted prairie trails. Grandmother Diefenbacker, seen through a grandson's eyes, was "a dutiful rather than an affectionate person." Once the family left Ontario in 1903, the children had no further contact with these grandparents. At some point John's father, William, simplified the spelling and changed the pronunciation of his name to Diefenbaker.[7]

William Thomas Diefenbaker was born in April 1868, one of seven children, and educated in Hawkesville and Kitchener, then named Berlin. After high school graduation, he began a teaching career on a temporary certificate, and in 1890–91 gained his professional (or normal school) qualification at the Model School in Ottawa. In that year, his son believed, William haunted the gallery of the House of Commons, absorbing the political atmosphere in the last year of Prime Minister John A. Macdonald's life. He disliked John A. "because of his legendary capacity for drinking and because of his reputation for wiliness, although he had a considerable regard for Macdonald's capacity as a leader in Parliament."[8] William's hero was Wilfrid Laurier, and parliament was his object of veneration. "Father had...so strong an appreciation for British traditions – having no British blood in his veins – for what the British had done for freedom, that he left that with me...He knew more about Parliament than I know today as far as the formalities are concerned."[9] This was the romantic age of parliamentary government, and William passed on that romance to his son. "The House of Commons lived for him, and it lived for me when I heard him recount the events he had witnessed and stories of the parliamentary personalities he had seen."[10] From his father the boy absorbed a thoroughly whiggish sense of history as the progressive expansion of freedom, developing benevolently and inevitably under British law.

John Diefenbaker always expressed filial affection and admiration for his father, but as he grew up he came to sense in William a certain diffidence and lack of ambition. In the memoirs he notes that William "was not a driver in any sense of the word, but a dreamer who loved books...an excellent teacher...content to serve the public weal through his church, his schools, and his lodge, the Independent Order of Foresters."[11] The memoir description is brief and unreflective, but it suggests a kindly, withdrawn, perhaps shy man with a wide smattering of general knowledge in British history, languages, astronomy, and elementary mathematics, almost entirely self-taught.[12] The dreamer had a distant and resigned gaze and a slightly receding chin, which he bequeathed to his elder son. In later life he was white haired and comfortably portly.

Mary Diefenbaker was sturdy, straight-backed, and firm in expression. She was the force in the family, "the much more determined personality," in her son's understated words. To these he adds a few conventional phrases: "When I look back over my life, Mother gave me drive, Father gave me the vision to see what could be done." Mary, John tells us, was a devout Baptist, frugal, and, curiously, "a wee bit fey."[13] He leaves this ambiguous Scottish expression undefined, although it points to a certain strangeness or imbalance of character. Later evidence suggests that his mother was a dour, intimidating, prejudiced, ignorant, and wilful woman whose influence over her two sons was powerful and lifelong.[14] But in these early years the sparse documentary record permits only the occasional glimpse into the Diefenbakers' domestic history. It appears that she already regarded her husband as ineffective after a few years of marriage.[15]

As an adult – and especially after he had become prime minister – Diefenbaker demonstrated an unusual interest in the collection of family history and relics, almost exclusively from his mother's side of the family. She was a Scot, of Highland descent, a Campbell of Argyll on her mother's side, a Bannerman of Kildonan on her father's side. She had none of her husband's reverence for things English; the Bannermans had nursed resentments through the generations since 1745, and Mary passed on their defiant spirit to her son.[16] The Bannermans lost their tenancies in the great Sutherland clearances of 1811–12, and in 1813 John Diefenbaker's great-grandparents were chosen as members of the third party of Red River settlers sponsored by Lord Selkirk. They crossed the North Atlantic in the late summer of 1813 and, typhoid-ridden, were dropped at Fort Churchill, where they wintered in desolation. The depleted party reached the Red River Settlement in June 1814.

Life there was hard and contentious, and after another winter more than one hundred settlers, including the Bannermans, travelled east by canoe brigade to Upper Canada. They took land in the present Elgin County, then at the Scotch Settlement near Holland Landing, and finally in Bruce County, where John's mother was born in 1872. Family stories suggested that the Bannermans had grown prosperous; in his memoirs Diefenbaker records that "when they began their move to Bruce, Great-grandfather had five thousand dollars in gold. This they carried in the feed bag under the wagon, a place thieves were not likely to search." There is no evidence, however, that Mary Bannerman brought any significant dowry to her marriage. John Diefenbaker had no memory of his maternal grandparents, who died in his early childhood.[17]

In the first years of their married life, William and Mary Diefenbaker lived on the small and uncertain salary of a local schoolmaster – a few hundred dollars a year, some of it delivered in kind if the trustees could not muster cash. Sometimes William moonlighted for extra funds by teaching bookkeeping; but young John carried a memory of family debt into adulthood. "Father had bought things on credit and owed some three hundred dollars. The debt was not easily cleared away. As a direct result of this experience, it became a fixed rule in our family that never again would we buy anything on credit. This self-imposed ban was temporarily lifted when we moved onto the homestead, but was renewed when we moved into the city of Saskatoon in February 1910."[18]

Three hundred dollars amounted to almost a full year's salary for William, and thus was a substantial burden. In addition to that anxiety, perhaps abetted by a sense of Highland grievance passed on by his mother, the boy was beginning to feel the disparities of wealth and poverty in turn-of-the-century Ontario. The family next door in Todmorden enjoyed Quaker Oats in boxes, while the Diefenbakers bought their oatmeal in bulk; down the road the Davies family, with their racing stables, "had everything that money could buy. They had Shetland ponies and two-wheel carts in which the poor were not allowed even the shortest ride." The "consciousness of injustice which has never left me" already seemed to be developing a sharp edge.[19]

In the spring of 1903 the struggling family reached a point of crisis. William's health broke down. "The doctors," say the memoirs, "considered that he was on the verge of developing what was then described as galloping consumption. Their advice was that he leave Toronto and seek the benefits of a prairie climate." The newly settled lands of the North-West Territories were reputed to be dry, bracing, and sunny, offering just the change of air recommended for consumptive patients of the time. William applied through an Ottawa teaching agency for a prairie job, and by early summer had received and accepted an offer at Tiefengrund, near Fort Carlton, on the old cart route between Winnipeg and Edmonton.[20]

As the move west approached that summer, William came to doubt the decision. Relatives on both sides of the family recommended against it. The northwest was unknown and, so they believed, uncivilized. Mary Diefenbaker later remembered – in spirit, at least – the warning of her brother Duncan: "Well, what's the matter with you? Going to that awful country where there's nothing but bears and Indians – they'll kill you!"[21] But Mary insisted: the choice had been made, and there would be no turning back. Household furnishings were dispatched ahead, and on August 15 the Diefenbakers prepared to board the Canadian Pacific transcontinental train in Toronto despite William's reluctance.

> Of course, we did not have the money to travel in style, to sleep in elegant, comfortable carriages, or to eat in luxurious dining cars with damask curtains and gleaming silverware. We were to travel colonist class, a very basic third-class accommodation used mainly for transporting immigrants to the Prairies. Realizing that there would be no sleeping accommodation and no meals served, Mother prepared and carefully packed lunches to carry us through to Winnipeg, and put together two rolls of quilts, blankets, and pillows...The train was to leave Toronto in the late afternoon. Father went down early to put our supplies on board. Misdirected by a railway official, he placed our food and bedding on a car whose destination was *not* Winnipeg. We arrived shortly before departure time to find, too late, what had taken place. Thus, we began our journey. Could there have been a more inauspicious launching into a new country?[22]

The other passengers were immigrants of many nationalities and itinerant harvest workers, all of them accustomed to hardship. They shared blankets and food with the Diefenbaker boys, but the discomforts of crowding, heat, and hard wooden seats were real. John Diefenbaker recalled that his first substantial meal came more than twenty-four hours after leaving Toronto, when the train reached the lakehead at Fort William. There, his father suggested retreat. Mary once again insisted that the journey would go on – without William, if necessary. In his seventies, John remembered his mother's taunt: if William turned back, "the rest of us will carry on and you'll come out sooner or later." The hapless father stayed with the family, despite further protests in Winnipeg.[23]

Young John had fleeting memories of Winnipeg, Regina, and Saskatoon as the family passed through these successively smaller prairie outposts. Saskatoon was a tiny hamlet of five hundred residents on the treeless prairie, bolstered earlier that summer with the tents of the Barr colonists on their way to Lloydminster. At Rosthern station, where the family finally disembarked, a small crowd met the evening train "speaking languages we did not understand: Ukrainian, Hungarian, Polish. Many spoke in German and a few in French, both of which languages Father could speak very well." In that, at least, he had the advantage over Mary, who knew only English.[24] The family rested for two nights at the Queen's Hotel before setting out on the seventeen-mile wagon journey to William's school in a district settled by Mennonites, French Canadians, Indians, and Métis.[25]

For two winters the Tiefengrund school was the Diefenbaker home. The schoolroom and family quarters shared one building, and a separate summer kitchen stood behind. The one-storey family apartment had three modest rooms and a kitchen, and was heated by a wood stove. With new curtains, fresh wallpaper, and their Ontario furnishings, the Diefenbakers made the spare frame building comfortable enough. The schoolroom was plain, furnished with desks "made of rough two-inch lumber," and decorated with wall charts warning graphically against the evils of tobacco and alcohol.[26]

The schoolhouse was a communal gathering point as well as a home. Members of the North-West Mounted Police, Indians, Métis, homesteaders, and travellers called by regularly, among them the legendary leader of the Métis military forces in the Saskatchewan rebellion of 1885, Gabriel Dumont. As newcomers, the Diefenbakers were overwhelmed with hospitality. "Everyone tried to make us know that we were under their constant care, and this was always true as the old-timers welcomed the newly arrived. We had food in abundance, wildfowl, jack rabbits, and tame chickens. Vegetables were brought to our door. The Mennonites in the district made pork sausages and cured hams for us. In that first fall, the ratepayers brought us loads of fire-wood and helped us cut it into stove lengths. Everyone shared in the business of everyone."[27]

By late 1904 William Diefenbaker had decided to seek homestead land for himself near Borden, across the North Saskatchewan River to the northwest on virgin grasslands. The homestead had to be registered on payment of a fee of $10 at the Dominion Lands Office in Prince Albert, occupied within six months, and lived on for three years before the actual transfer of title. On December 15, 1904, after waiting outside the Lands Office all night, William managed to register his claim. But in the absence of capital he could not occupy it in 1905. Nevertheless, he broke ten acres of soil as a token of his good faith. He then successfully sought a year's relief against cancellation by swearing a declaration before a justice of the peace: "I have not had the money to make further improvements upon the said homestead up to the present. I intend, all being well, to have more breaking done upon the said homestead during the coming Spring or early Summer, and also to build a small house into which we wish to move...about July 15, 1906. I have not yet the means necessary to buy the necessary horses, implements, etc. to farm said homestead sufficiently to earn a livelihood for me and my family."[28]

Meanwhile William searched for a better-paying job that would allow him cash to move onto the property in 1906. In August 1905 he found it, in the one-room school at Hague, thirty miles south of Carlton. Hague was a thriving village of a few hundred on the rail line, with four grain elevators and various farm service companies. To supplement his income, William was also hired as village secretary, and he was able to buy a small house on a $775 mortgage. John recalled his own paying jobs that summer, at the age of ten, as a farm labourer and a local newsboy for the Saskatoon *Phoenix*.[29]

The political status of the North-West Territories was about to change. On September 1, after long pressure on Ottawa, they were transformed into the two provinces of Alberta and Saskatchewan. This mark of progress was welcomed across the prairies, and in Hague the new teacher/secretary hung out the Union Jacks and chaired a village meeting of celebration. To the south in the capital, Regina, there were grander ceremonies in the presence of Prime Minister Sir Wilfrid Laurier and Governor General Earl Grey. On September 5 the lieutenant governor appointed the new leader of the provincial Liberal Party, Walter Scott, as the province's first premier; and his easy victory in the provincial election of December 1905 began forty years of Liberal hegemony in the province.[30]

In the summer of 1906 the Diefenbakers made a doubly convenient move onto the homestead. William received a teaching appointment (paying $600 per year) at the new school in Hoffnungsfeld, three miles northeast of his land; and William's bachelor brother Edward was named teacher in the Halcyonia school, three miles to the southeast. He arrived from Ontario to claim homestead land adjoining that of the family, and began a long schoolteaching career

8

in the new province. Like William, he was thin and hollow-cheeked, largely self-educated, and constantly curious. Diefenbaker wrote that he was "wrestling with the philosophy of Kant and Schopenhauer" in his eighties.[31]

John Diefenbaker's memory of this busy summer was benign. In Hague the family rented out the house and loaded their possessions onto a haywagon for the forty-mile, two-day journey north to Borden at the Great Bend of the North Saskatchewan River. On top, the chickens were loaded in crates; behind, the family cow, Lily, followed on a tether.[32] Once on the land, William, John, and Elmer began work as carpenters. "For our house, it was decided that there should be three rooms, the largest of which would be divided into a living room and a bedroom for our parents. Elmer would bunk in the kitchen, while the third room was for storage, and was often used by overnight visitors. (I was to sleep in Uncle Ed's shack.) Father wanted Mother's kitchen to be the most attractive room. In consequence, it was lined with 'V'-joint boards, which took varnish well. (This lumber cost one hundred and twenty-five dollars a thousand, compared with shiplap at less than fifty dollars.)"[33]

The summer's labour produced house, barn, Ed's one-room shack, a vegetable garden, a flower garden, and ten more acres of broken land.[34] The Diefenbakers were prepared for winter, with spartan shelter and an adequate food supply. Mary's butter could sometimes be exchanged for groceries; otherwise there was plentiful home produce, bread, domestic chicken and turkey, prairie chicken, duck, goose, prunes, wild mushrooms, strawberries, raspberries, and saskatoons in season. The storeroom filled up with preserves. John and Elmer did the hand churning, and John acquired a lifelong addiction to buttermilk.[35]

These were the bumper years of prairie homesteading. The railway branch lines had snaked out across the province, and both the dominion government and the railways promoted settlement with glowing promise. In 1905–06 there were 30,819 homestead registrations in western Canada, two-thirds of them in Saskatchewan.[36] The lands filled up. But if the colonization posters promised "the last best west," life instead was grindingly hard. Homesteading was "a gigantic gamble," wrote John Archer, "which the nation won but which broke many an individual player."[37] Winters were brutal, and that first season of 1906–07 was one of the hardest: John remembered that blizzards and cold kept the schools closed for five weeks after Christmas, while the family struggled to cut enough firewood to keep household temperatures above freezing. In the south of the province, many large ranches were driven out of business by the loss of cattle and sheep wintering in the fields without fodder.[38] The winter of 1907–08 was equally cold and prolonged.

Sufficient supplies of firewood and water were essential. The Diefenbakers traded for firewood with Ukrainian settlers in the parklands to the north and piled their wood supply in pole-lengths, teepee-style, according to the fashion. The water supply, by contrast, was "our major problem." Every well the family sank produced undrinkable alkaline water. For three and a half years on the land the Diefenbakers hauled barrelled water by stoneboat sled twice a week from the nearest neighbour's farm – and treated it as a precious resource.[39]

In September 1906 John entered grade seven at his uncle's school in Halcyonia, while Elmer attended his father's school. John's schoolmates "were mainly old-country English, from around Birmingham," while Elmer's were German-speaking Mennonites.[40] Decades later a classmate recalled that John, "with his crop of yellow curls and his 'suit' clothes, found Halcyonia boys to be terrible teases" who made fun of him as a teacher's pet.[41]

For the first year or two John and Uncle Ed walked to school in spring, summer, and fall, conversing all the way. "The walk to school was alright," John remembered in his old age, "because we talked about things. Uncle Ed was quite a scholar in Shakespeare and he'd bring up some line in Shakespeare...and start to explain it and chat about it and then he'd get into this extrasensory perception...Ed always had ideas. He didn't have any extra-terrestrial communication, but he said as between people of similar views there is a transmission of viewpoints and we call it coincidence. He called it extra-sensory perception."[42] In this belief Edward Diefenbaker followed a popular pseudo-scientific fashion of the period.

During the winter John and Uncle Ed rode a rough-hewn horse-drawn cutter to and from school; and on March 11, 1908, they almost perished in a blizzard. There was a district concert in the school that night, and young John decided to wear his best Sunday clothes – new leather shoes, cloth coat, and woollen cap – "because," he said, "I wanted to be a sport."[43] Ed, more sensibly, wore his heavy winter garb. Blizzard snows coincided with the concert, and soon Ed decided they should leave for home to relieve John's parents of worry. Midway home the horse foundered in a snowdrift. Uncle Ed wrapped John in horseblankets and struggled to keep the boy awake during the night. In the morning the storm broke. Ed, John, and the horse stumbled home across the snow, John's legs "frozen to the knees." He remembered three weeks of convalescence, his legs at first wrapped in snow-filled blankets, then swollen and discoloured, "I suppose...gangrenous." That was an exaggeration, since he recovered without physical damage. But "for years thereafter I was afraid to go outside our house, even to the woodpile, when blizzards were blowing."[44]

The next summer William's brother Henry, a carriage-maker from Illinois, covered the cutters in canvas and equipped them with small stoves to prevent similar misfortunes. In family memory they became "Diefenbaker schooners."[45]

The summers were warmer, but still precarious. "Rainfall was always uncertain. During one year there was frost in every month. In another, we were partially hailed out. One year we experienced a prairie fire...If Father had not acted when the danger became evident, we would have lost our buildings and some forty loads of hay. He got out the team, hitched them to the plough, and turned two furrows around the haystack and buildings; then he ploughed two concentric furrows fifty or so yards away and burnt the intervening area before the prairie fire reached us."[46]

Each year a little more land was cleared and sown, but the crops of wheat, oats, and barley were small: John Diefenbaker estimated their cash value at an average of $150 a year. Mary tried to raise turkeys for sale, but lost the flocks to disease or badgers in two of three years. For a few years John and Elmer ran a modestly successful trapline for ermine, and John earned a little cash on the annual harvest.[47] Aside from the income from teaching, Mary's butter sales, and rentals from the Hague cottage to offset the mortgage, that seemed to be all.

John remembered Sunday church services in Halcyonia school or sometimes at home; often there were visitors for the Sunday meal that followed. Occasionally the family played host to a community sing-song around the Thomas organ. John and Elmer kept busy with daily chores, bareback riding, hunting, and the normal exploring and mischief-making of country youth, but outside school they spent their days alone with the family. For John, that meant dependence on his father's and uncle's conversation and on the family library, which included the adventure novels of G.A. Henty, Ridpath's *History of the World*, an encyclopedia, the Bible, Shakespeare, Gibbon's *Decline and Fall of the Roman Empire*, Herndon's *Life of Lincoln*, Macaulay's *History of England from the Accession of James II*, Darwin's *Origin of Species*, *Tom Brown's Schooldays*, *The Pickwick Papers*, and *Black Beauty*. The family's faith involved belief in the literal truth of the Bible, absolute standards of right and wrong, and the goodness of God's universe. The world beyond the homestead was dominated by the power of God, the English language, and the British connection – not always in that order.[48] Such ideals could offer a sustaining faith against the unforgiving frontier, and there was no disposition to question them in the Diefenbaker family.

What could be questioned was continued life on the land. At the end of 1909 William would acquire title after the necessary three years' occupation, but only a few acres were under cultivation, and the prospects looked bleak.

During the summer, after three years in Uncle Ed's classroom at Halcyonia, John went to Saskatoon to write the provincial examinations for grades nine and ten – and failed them. In the memoirs he explains that the disappointment arose not from Uncle Edward's teaching or his own incapacity, but from overindulgence in the pleasures of a Saskatoon ice-cream parlour.

> I had a little money given me for the week, ice cream was not expensive, and here was the opportunity to have as much as I could swallow – heaven indeed. This was the end of June, and very hot. The departmental regulations required that if a student failed on one examination he lost all of them, no matter how well or poorly he did on the rest. On Friday, the last day of the examinations, I had about a quart of ice cream for breakfast. I felt squeamish during the morning examination, but everything seemed to go well enough. At lunch I walked over to the Maple Leaf for more ice cream. I felt still less well. To make a long story short, back in the examination room, I took sick and had to leave at the end of half an hour. I lost my year.[49]

John's mother had already made known her desire to move to Saskatoon. When he returned home, his parents made the decision to leave the farm to "permit Elmer and me to get the best education within our parents' means."[50] Given their hardships, the choice was understandable: it was a common one. It was also an admission of defeat – for William's efforts as a farmer and rural schoolteacher, for Uncle Ed's tutoring of John. Henceforth the family would devote itself to the children's advancement rather than the father's.

William announced his wish to give up teaching. He went off to Saskatoon – then at the height of the urban land boom, with a growing population of more than 10,000 – to look for other work. He found it as a clerk in the provincial Land Titles Office, at a salary of $720 a year. Mary showed her disapproval – whether of the salary, or the lowly status, or both, we do not know. But the job was taken, and in February 1910, once title to the homestead had been acquired, the Diefenbakers moved to town. Despite their departure, Uncle Ed remained a rural schoolteacher until his retirement. In 1911 William took work as an inspector in the Saskatoon Customs Office, where he stayed for twenty-six years until his retirement in 1937.[51]

The family continued to live frugally in the city. They kept a cow, and for a few months the boys sold milk. Household vegetables were supplied from their own garden plots. John and Elmer sold newspapers, and John soon became a distributor, selling the Saskatoon *Phoenix*, the Winnipeg *Tribune*, and, intermittently, the Calgary *Eye-Opener* to a network of newsboys, for a weekly net income of about $20. For two summers John also worked as a janitor for $20 a month.[52]

John enrolled on arrival at the Saskatoon Collegiate Institute, and in June 1910 passed his grade nine and ten examinations on the second try, without ice-cream. During John's senior matriculation year of 1911–12, William arranged a job offer for him at the Northern Crown Bank, but "Mother, despite the fact that Father's salary was small, took a strong stand, and Father, on reflection, agreed with her that I should be given an opportunity to complete my education."[53] Once again mother's will prevailed.

That seemed to include enrolment after high school at the University of Saskatchewan, which occupied temporary space on the top floor of the Collegiate Institute and would move to its new campus in the autumn of 1912. Both mother and son already had a sense of John's mission – although its gradual emergence, and its initial substance, are difficult to trace. It certainly came early. At first Mary favoured a career for John in the Baptist Church. But John, stimulated by his father's romantic stories and his own browsing in the family library, had his eye on politics from an early age. His interest – or perhaps his identification – centred on inspiring anecdotes about two legendary radicals, one English, the other American. John Lilburne, the seventeenth-century English Leveller, had demanded equality and freedom of speech at the risk of exile and imprisonment. Abraham Lincoln, "a small-town lawyer," Diefenbaker wrote in his memoirs, "was to become the symbol of American democracy, tribune of his people, a man whose origins were those of a pioneer on the United States frontier."[54] These two, joined with the Canadians John A. Macdonald and Wilfrid Laurier, were his heroes – and they were heroes meant to serve a practical purpose.

In a long paragraph in the memoirs John Diefenbaker reflected, circumspectly but revealingly, on his life and ambition, tracing his sense of destiny back to his early years:

> Every little boy or girl has some ultimate ambition, to be a farmer or a train engineer, a nurse, a schoolteacher, or a doctor, and no doubt in every case the best possible. Some pursue their ambition with a single-minded devotion and attain it. Others, caught in the byways of life, find more attractive or more realistic goals. As one looks back over life from the vantage of many years, it is difficult not to be fascinated by the "ifs" of his experience. Perhaps it would be simpler if one's theology embraced the concept of predestination. Mine does not. It would seem to me that we are given opportunities, not guarantees, and that all we can do is to strive forward, contributing as

we can to the common good, trying to make certain that our decisions and actions are not inconsistent with our highest ambitions. Our ultimate future depends so much on character and circumstance. I was eight or nine years old when I said to my mother, "Some day I am going to be Prime Minister." She did not laugh. Always a practical woman, she pointed out the near-impossibility of anyone's realizing that ambition, and in particular one living far out on the Prairies. I was deeply concerned. Uncle Ed provided me a more sympathetic audience. As we walked or rode to and from school each day, I told him of my thoughts and ambitions, and discussed the things I had read. He was a wonderful person, with a lively, inquiring mind and all the time in the world to listen to the dreams and plans which Elmer and I might unfold. From my earliest boyhood I was given to a romanticization of the future in which I would be able to do something for my country.[55]

Was this just the old politician giving retrospective shape to his life as he fashioned a myth for the history books? Partly, no doubt. But the story of John's ambition had earlier origins and was a familiar one in the Diefenbaker family, in several variations. On June 17, 1957, for example, when Diefenbaker was about to become prime minister, Elmer cabled congratulations "on the occasion of a dream at the tender age of six at last coming true."[56] His mother told the journalist Patrick Nicholson that "when John was only six years old...he once looked up from reading about Laurier, and confided to her in all seriousness that he proposed to become prime minister of Canada too. Just as seriously she replied: 'If you work hard enough, there's no reason why you shouldn't.'"[57] At the end of his life Diefenbaker believed that he had been one of those who "pursue their ambition with a single-minded devotion and attain it," and that he had guided his life "to make certain that our decisions and actions are not inconsistent with our highest ambitions." Yet in his view the career was not simply a product of his own acts, an expression of his own character; there was a larger destiny at work, the "circumstance" within which character could play out its role. If not predestined, his goal seemed somehow to beckon him, to be available specially to him – and thus to be a source both of confidence and of justification. Diefenbaker never spoke of any ultimate ambition except to be prime minister of Canada.

That emerging sense of purpose could only have been aided by the fifteen-year-old's encounter with the prime minister, Sir Wilfrid Laurier, on July 29, 1910, when Laurier came to Saskatoon to lay the first cornerstone for the university.

His private railway car was at the station one morning when I went over to pick up our newspapers. There he was, standing on the platform, taking the morning air. This memory of him will stay with me always, his dignity, his plume of snow white hair. I sold him a newspaper. He gave me a quarter – no better way to establish an instant rapport with a newsboy. We chatted about Canada. I had the awed feeling that I was in the presence of greatness. That afternoon, when he laid the cornerstone, he included in his remarks a reference to his conversation with a Saskatoon newsboy which, he observed, had ended with my saying, "Sorry, Prime Minister, I can't waste any more time on you, I've got work to do." I took some pride in July 1957, after I became Prime Minister, in the fact that my railway car was stationed in exactly the spot where Sir Wilfrid's had stood.[58]

Whatever words may have passed between them, Diefenbaker remembered that "Sir Wilfrid inspired me with the idea that each of us, no matter who he is or what his upbringing, or however humble his parentage and home, can rise to any position in this country, provided we dedicate ourselves."[59]

For the aspiring teenager, there were two immediate goals: a mastery of public speaking and the law. Public speaking was the more difficult of the two, because "my diffidence and nervousness were hard to overcome." At Saskatoon Collegiate he took part in a special class in oratory, speaking about the great English jurists and politicians and the landmarks of English history. When it came to the annual school oratorical contest, John reached the finals but then froze and forgot his peroration.[60] There was much more agonizing practice before his fears on the platform were overcome.

What John noticed about his political heroes was that "many of them had started their careers in public life as lawyers...I was impressed by the lives of those who, in the practice of law, stood for the liberties of the individual and for the assurance that no one, however poor, should be denied justice. I decided that was the kind of lawyer I wanted to be."[61] From the beginning, he would be an advocate with a cause. The pursuit of oratory, the law, and politics were all to be explained out of duty to the voiceless, the poor, and the meek. John Diefenbaker's childhood experience – of family hardship and humiliation, a mother's will, a father's romance with whig history, a pioneer community of many origins and languages – was combining to shape his life. In June 1912 the shy and aloof sixteen-year-old graduated from high school in Saskatoon, an ambitious romantic who quietly nurtured his dreams.

IN SEPTEMBER 1912 JOHN DIEFENBAKER REGISTERED AS AN ARTS STUDENT AT THE University of Saskatchewan. Classes were held for the first time that year in the new College Building, the first of five buildings under construction on the new campus on Caswell Hill. The architects, David Brown and Hugh Vallance, had designed generously in the collegiate gothic style of Washington University in St Louis, Missouri, and the buildings taking form on the treeless prairie symbolized the province's confidence in its boundless future.[62] Since he entered university with senior matriculation standing, Diefenbaker qualified as a second-year student and managed to avoid most of the undignified hazing of freshmen. But he did recall that he was "unceremoniously heaved into the decorative pool" in front of the College Building after arriving for registration in his short pants.[63]

The first president of the university, Walter C. Murray, had recruited an able young group of faculty members, and the university's small enrolment meant that students came to know their teachers well. John Diefenbaker did not shine as a student – partly, he later believed, because "I was reluctant to accept unchallenged what I was told, and always wanted to follow propositions through to their logical conclusion," an attitude that was ahead of its time in the era of certitude before 1914 and perhaps gave hint of his later combative style.[64] He took courses in history, political science, and economics in preparation for his legal studies, but otherwise took little part in university life. "I was too shy and I had little spare time. I still had newspapers to sell, morning and afternoon." But he persisted in his struggle to master public speaking, taking part in the university's mock parliament and the first provincial Boys' Parliament in Regina in the fall of 1912.[65]

At the end of his university year, the young man gave up his newspaper business and took work for the summer as a farm labourer south of Blaine Lake. His wages of $20 a month doubled to $40 during harvest in August and September, but his savings were exhausted by medical bills to treat a carbuncle on his neck, which he blamed on the steady diet of salt ham and potatoes inflicted on him by his bachelor employer.[66]

In his second university year, 1913–14, he studied economic history and began work in law with courses in contracts and jurisprudence. For economic history – broadly defined – he wrote an essay on "The Rise of the Regal Power" in medieval Europe.[67] Beyond classes, Diefenbaker recalled that he was "a little more outgoing" as a member of the mock parliament, where he became leader of the Conservative Party and leader of the opposition, and in the Boys' Parliament, where he barely missed election as premier.[68]

Early in 1914 the Wheat Heart School District, close to the Diefenbaker land, advertised for a schoolteacher at $65 to $70 per month, to commence work on May 1. John Diefenbaker, lacking both experience and a teaching certificate, responded with an offer to serve at $63 a month. The local school board procured a provisional certificate in his name from the provincial Department of Education and signed a contract appointing him for a term of seven months at that rate, to terminate at the closing of school for the winter on December 1, 1914. (The long holiday occurred in winter to avoid heating expenses for the school building.) There is no record, beyond the contract, of whether the new teacher intended to complete the term or not; if he had done so, he would have been unable to enrol for his third year of university in early October. Diefenbaker taught school for the summer, but on September 9 he gave four weeks' notice of resignation, proposing that his uncle, Edward Diefenbaker, should finish the term in his place. The trustees agreed, provided that Edward signed a new contract.

The would-be lawyer added a further claim, citing a section of the School Act which stipulated that a contract of more than four months should be compensated on an annual basis. At the rate of $756 per year, this would amount to a salary of $75.60 per month rather than the agreed $63.00.

On October 2 Diefenbaker notified the school board that his uncle would replace him in the school that very day and would sign a new contract in the coming week. Edward did not sign a contract, but instead asked the board to continue paying the salary of $63 each month to John Diefenbaker. The board agreed, and Edward completed his nephew's term.

With his original claim unsettled, Diefenbaker increased the pressure in January 1915 with a request that he be paid a further sixty cents a day for the entire period of the contract, or a total of $84.60 per month. The Wheat Heart School Board protested to the deputy minister of education that Edward Diefenbaker's failure to sign a contract "was a trick to render the board liable to have to pay the additional salary due to the first teacher...for practically two months after his resignation had expired." Diefenbaker responded that "the Board had me for these two months and I had my substitute." The board replied that it would never have hired the teacher if his demands had been known in advance; in any case, there were insufficient funds to meet his claim. The provincial department washed its hands of the affair and told the young man to seek legal advice if he wished to pursue it. For a few months Diefenbaker threatened he would, then he dropped the matter in May.[69]

Diefenbaker's own account of his short teaching experience is different from this one, though not necessarily inconsistent. He does not mention the salary dispute but emphasizes that his own enthusiasm for the classroom was shared by his students: "They would come to school however early I was prepared to come, and stay as late as I could stay with them. Sometimes we were there from seven in the morning until six in the evening." Diefenbaker writes that he intended to carry on teaching in 1915; to do so he would require a favourable report on his work from the school inspector in order to renew his temporary certificate. On the day the inspector arrived, however, "the children were busy with their work but I was nowhere in sight. He found me at the back of the yard with a .22 shooting gophers, which were so numerous as to be almost a plague. I did not get my certificate."[70]

If this account is true, it is obviously incomplete. It suggests that when John Diefenbaker took the job in May 1914, he intended to honour the contract; otherwise he could not expect to maintain the option of teaching again in 1915. This would mean an interruption of two years or more in his university education – a possibility his financial needs might have dictated. When the inspector reported unfavourably and deprived him of a renewal, he perhaps decided to break the contract (with the aid of Uncle Ed) and return to university for his degree. The consequent loss of income might then explain his desperate appeal to the fine print of the School Act for added salary. What the memoir does not explain is the whiff of sharp practice, the "trick" complained of by the school trustees of Wheat Heart, Saskatchewan. From John's perspective it may have been simply a first, experimental use of the law that did not succeed.

There was another, infinitely greater event that summer, which altered Diefenbaker's circumstances. European mobilizations had occurred in July, and on August 4, 1914, after the German invasion of Belgium, Britain declared war. Canada automatically became a belligerent beside the imperial parent. In Saskatchewan, as elsewhere in the dominion, war against Germany was greeted with patriotic fervour, "almost with jubilation." Nightly demonstrations of enthusiasm lasted seven days in Saskatoon, and within weeks thousands of volunteers from the prairies were on their way east to the camps and overseas ports. Editorials and sermons denounced the kaiser and German militarism, and pronounced the cause a righteous one.[71] At first there was general belief that the war would be brief and victorious, but before the end of the year that faith had been drowned in the mud of Flanders.

When John Diefenbaker returned to university in October 1914 for the final year of his arts degree, he took more economics and a heavy load of courses in law.[72] He retained his position as leader of the opposition in the mock parliament, and by the time of graduation in the spring of 1915 he had gained a certain political reputation. "In the mock parliament," reported the graduation issue of *The Sheaf,* "as leader of his party, he was particularly zealous." The report concluded that he planned to remain at the university for a master's degree and to study law. Elsewhere the paper imagined him forty years on, in 1955, as leader of the opposition in the Canadian House of Commons. As Diefenbaker wryly wrote, "It was in error by one year."[73]

During the summer of 1915 Diefenbaker and his friend Stanley Mighton were employed as commission salesmen by the John A. Hertel Company of Chicago, travelling by bicycle to small towns in central Saskatchewan to hawk popular religious literature. Their leading item was a book of Bible lessons called *The Chosen Word.* The salesmen collected a deposit of $1.00 on each sale, which they kept as an interim wage; eventually they recovered a 40 percent commission on sales ranging from $2.50 to $7.95 per volume, with bonus prizes for the leading salesmen. By early July Diefenbaker and Mighton were described in the company's *Canadian Bulletin No. 10* as "Western Giants" and each had won a suitcase. They were unusually diligent.

> These men seem to have planned thoroughly their work, and then worked their plan. In a village of less than 800 people, they have already placed some 75 copies of Chosen Word. Think of it!! Why the success of these men? First, they have ability; Second, they are not afraid to use their ability – not use it for one or two hours a day, but for nine and ten hours at a stretch day in and day out. That is what counts.
>
> Mr. Diefenbaker on Saturday, June 26th, made the most remarkable record ever made by anyone selling Chosen Word. He took 9 orders out of 9 calls, 5 in the best binding. His sales for the day were nearly $60.00, his profits nearly $24.00. Think of the possibilities in this work. Let one catch THE SPIRIT OF SUCCESS, and he will get orders which otherwise would seem impossible. Mr. Diefenbaker gives as his motto for the last week, "Stop bawling, get right in and do some mauling." Go to it, Mr. Diefenbaker, that $200.00 Motor Cycle is worth the effort.[74]

The sales guidelines offered a mixture of uplift plus handy tips for success and the collection of deposits. Diefenbaker quickly mastered the slick pitch designed for use on gullible housewives. He later recalled weeks of bounty followed by weeks of poverty, and in the end he did not win the motorcycle. But he finished the summer standing fifth among all the company's North American salesmen as a "Top Notcher," with his friend not far behind. His weekly sales averaged $223.60 over the summer, for a total commission income of more than $700.[75] During the barren weeks, Mighton was said to augment their income by hustling winnings at the pool table.[76]

In July, Elmer Diefenbaker, inspired by his brother's success, took the road to Humboldt with a friend on the same mission. He wrote to John that he was "going to sell books just as you are doing now." But a week later he reported little success – and then there was silence. "Dear John – Everything's bum around here. If I don't get some decent place to work I'm going home. Mostly foreigners and Catholics around here, and you know how easy it is to sell to these darn fools. The Catholic priest is much in favour of work but if he recommends it to people he is afraid of being fired. He says they are sore at him now. If you are not going to Yorktown we would like that burg. It's a little piece of Canora. Write me as soon as you can & tell me if we can have it. Elmer"[77]

In the autumn John returned to the university for his master's degree in political science and economics, taking courses in economic history, the history of political thought, and British constitutional law. By now the war had become a horrible battle of attrition in the trenches, and the call for Canadian volunteers was growing more intense. For the able-bodied, active service was the alternative, or the sequel, to university; and in March 1916 John Diefenbaker enlisted before the academic year was finished. (He received his degree in absentia in May.) In mid-April he arrived in Winnipeg for officers' training, dressed in the peacetime scarlet and blue of his militia unit because the supplies of khaki uniforms had temporarily been exhausted. In a postcard home he reported a friend's gossip that "70 out of a class of 100 failed the last exam so I'll have to work." But after a month of elementary lectures and drill, the examinations on May 16 proved easy. On May 27 John Diefenbaker received his commission as a "Lieutenant in the Infantry of the Active Militia" attached to the 29th Light Horse.[78]

For the moment, however, he returned to Saskatoon as a civilian and in June entered the office of Russell Hartney to begin his law articles. On July 1 the British launched their great offensive on the Somme, which met immediate disaster. In August, after more than a month of merciless slaughter, the British Army called for a Canadian draft of three hundred junior officers for immediate service. On August 21 Diefenbaker wrote to the district commander in Regina requesting overseas posting.[79] His brief diary entries record the activities of the next few days:

> Tuesday August 22: Rec'd telegram of acceptance from Col. Edgar. Resigned at Russell Hartney's office.

Wednesday August 23: Accepted by telegram after a great deal of arguing with father etc.

Thursday August 24: All my time spent in preparation. Aird & McMillan accepted unofficially by 'phone message to me.

Friday August 25: Prepared to leave to Regina. Decided to stay till morning. Elmer came home from Biggar.

Saturday August 26: Left Sktoon at 12 o'clock noon CNR. Mother, Father, Aunt Sadie Oscar Elmer present Arrived Regina 6 o'clock Accepted by DOC.[80]

Three days later Diefenbaker wrote that he was "still stranded. No further word received." On Wednesday, to John's surprise, his mother arrived in Regina. The next day they returned together to Saskatoon, where Uncle Ed joined the clan for a few days more of uncertainty – perhaps dispute – over John's future. The diary notes that Aunt Sadie had become ill and that Mary Diefenbaker was "quite excited." By September 4 the young officer was at last on the road under orders to proceed to Camp Hughes in Manitoba. On September 7 he had arrived and noted: "First morning ever spent in camp most lonesome ever have been. Rifle Drill etc."[81]

Lieutenant Diefenbaker was now a member of the 196th (Western Universities) Battalion. After some cold nights under canvas at Camp Hughes, the contingent left for Halifax on September 17. Thus John Diefenbaker spent his twenty-first birthday on a troop train in northern Ontario, while his mother's birthday chocolates (which had reached Camp Hughes too late) were gratefully distributed by the chaplain to the thirty-man guard that remained behind.[82]

Because they reached Halifax after the scheduled departure of the SS *Olympic* on September 20, the contingent instead boarded the White Star Line's SS *Lapland* on September 23 and sailed four days later. The memoirs report a week's delay because "there was a submarine close at hand," but Diefenbaker nevertheless wrote a postcard home, in apparent disregard of security, announcing his imminent departure. The passenger list noted the presence of "Lieut. SR J G Diefenbaker" among a company of 138 officers, 113 NCOs, 1776 rank and file, and 16 civilians – a total of 2043 passengers. Among the civilians were Sir George Perley, the Canadian high commissioner and representative of the Borden government in London, and his wife. The young lieutenant played shuffleboard with Lady Perley, who promised him that if he ever wanted assistance in London, her husband would oblige.[83]

Off Ireland the convoy missed its rendezvous with a destroyer escort and "took precautions against 'subs,'" but without apparent danger. On October 6, after a nine-day passage, the *Lapland* docked in Liverpool. By late that night the men of the 196th were bunked down uncomfortably at Shorncliffe camp in Kent.[84] There they undertook training within sound of shellfire at the front, while more seasoned officers joked grimly about their diminished life expectancies.[85]

The next five months were a curious and puzzling interlude in John Diefenbaker's life, subsequently obscured or falsified. There are four distinct accounts of his military career, two of them retrospective and two contemporary. The memoirs were published in 1975, and a conversational version was recorded of the same story; during his months of active service in 1916 and 1917 he wrote a personal diary, while his army personnel file includes his official medical papers. In summary, after a few weeks' training at Shorncliffe and Crowborough camps, he was found medically unfit for overseas service and ordered back to Canada, where he returned in February 1917. But Diefenbaker's own recollections tell a story significantly different from that of his diary and the army records.

The memoirs offer a vivid explanation of these events.

I enjoyed army life. We worked hard. The drill was heavy, the hours long. Trench work was our forte...At the conclusion of one day's work we were cleaning up. I was at the bottom of a seven-foot trench when someone, unaware of my presence, threw in a heavy entrenching tool, a combination shovel and pickaxe. It hit me squarely on the spine and down I went. I haemorrhaged most severely. Blood always seems more than in fact it is, but I would think that I must have lost a couple of quarts. My concern at the time was that if I reported to the medical authorities I would miss my chance to go to the front with my friends. My brother officers, and in particular Hugh Aird and Allan McMillan wanted me to report but I demurred, my contention being that if I did, I would be put in hospital and everything would be over. I booked off duty for a few days. The haemorrhage eased on the second day, but on the fourth day it started again. The single line in my diary for that day reads: "Bleeding today from the mouth." Perhaps, had I immediately reported my injury, nothing would have been different, but I shall always wonder.

After being hospitalized, I was medical boarded again and again. Finally, what I had tried to avoid became a reality: I was invalided home. I did manage to get them to agree and recommend that, if I became fit again, I could return to active service. However, this was not to be, for after being boarded a number of times in Saskatoon I was put in Category E; in other words, totally unfit for further service. When it was suggested I was now eligible for a pension I refused to consider the idea, although on three occasions thereafter, over a period of twenty-five years, I haemorrhaged as a direct result of my injury. The impact on my back caused my heart to be moved out of alignment. In the early 1920s I underwent surgery. In 1925 I was still unable to get life insurance except subject to a lien of 50 per cent, reducible by 5 per cent each year for ten years, at which time the full amount of the policy would be payable.[86]

Diefenbaker offered variations on this story in interviews and campaign materials over the years from 1940 to 1970. In 1969 he said that "my heart was twisted out of place," and "I'd been losing weight very fast and I went from 180 pounds down to 130–128." In 1940 a mimeographed biographical sketch prepared for the use of newspapers in Lake Centre federal constituency said: "He sailed for France in 1916 a Lieutenant in the 1st Canadian Mounted Rifles. While on active service he was wounded and spent several months in the hospital." After interviews with John and Elmer, Patrick Nicholson wrote in 1968 that Diefenbaker had been "sent to France where, soon after landing, he suffered a severe injury in a non-combatant accident which he prefers not to describe and which confined him to hospital for four months." Peter Newman wrote more briefly, in 1963, that Diefenbaker was invalided home, but "the details of his military career are obscure. He seldom discussed his overseas experiences and consistently declined to wear his World War I service ribbons."[87]

Lieutenant Diefenbaker's military diary offers brief, virtually daily notes on his activities that seem to contradict the story of a serious – or even a minor – injury. The diary records an easier regime than the memoirs. On his second day in Shorncliffe camp, Diefenbaker dined at the Metropole Hotel in Folkestone; the following week there was musketry school in the daytime, but theatre on two evenings. After only ten days at Shorncliffe and at least one more night out, the diary notes four days' leave at the Hotel Cecil in London. During the day the young Canadian saw the obligatory sights; at night there was music hall at the Hippodrome, Drury Lane, and Empire theatres. On Sunday, October 22, Diefenbaker returned to Shorncliffe, but on October 25 he was given six days' leave while the Canadian camp was moved to

Crowborough in Sussex. Diefenbaker enjoyed another evening of music hall in London and took the overnight train to Glasgow and Edinburgh. There he saw family friends and was an enthusiastic sightseer for four days. On his return south he spent another day in London before arriving at Crowborough camp on the morning of October 31. For three days his unit engaged in "tactics and squad drills," and on November 4 the officers wrote examinations in tactics, field engineering, and law.[88]

The first real signs of discomfort appear in the diary for November 5 to 8, but they are general rather than personal. Diefenbaker writes that he was off parade, "as were nearly all the boys due to epidemic which continued for several days with greater or less results." In his case, apparently less, since a railway ticket stub and pamphlet from the Charing Cross Hotel show that Diefenbaker returned first class from London to Shorncliffe on November 8. Meanwhile the carnage on the Somme continued, and on November 10 he reports: "Several members of the 19th Class included in the draft" for the front.[89]

The crucial week appears to be the next one:

Monday, November 13: Trench digging and drill from 7.45 to 5.30. Great deal of rain.

Tuesday, November 14: Medical examination today. Passed with weak heart and defective eyesight.

Wednesday, November 15: No drill. Exempted. M.D. says I must go to Hospital to have eyes tested.

Thursday, November 16: No drill. Attend lectures merely. Went to Brighton 2nd Eastern Hospital. Spent night at hospital.[90]

On Friday, however, Diefenbaker seemed to be well. After promenading in Brighton, he travelled by train to Hastings and Dover, where he spent the weekend sightseeing and attending the movies with a Miss Thornloe. On Sunday evening he returned to camp, and during the week was engaged again in drill, muddy trench digging, and examinations. There is no hint of any accident. On Sunday, November 26, he writes: "At 11 o'clock went before Medical board pronounced unfit for further service and marked 'Canada.'"[91]

The diary reveals nothing about Diefenbaker's state of mind; the laconic record simply continues. But he now assumed, or was told, that he had no further military duties. Believing he was free to take leave, on November 29

Diefenbaker checked into the Charing Cross Hotel and filled the next day with sightseeing at the zoo, Madame Tussaud's, the House of Commons, and theatre in the evening. He may also have spent the day that followed in London. On December 2 he registered at the Bear Hotel in Lewes and undertook more sightseeing. On December 6, back in camp, there was trouble.

> Wednesday, December 6: ...After being called for some time up before orderly room to explain absence from parade O.C. and Off. excuses [sic] me on recommend. of D.H.D.M.S. Subject to slight duty alone...

> Friday, December 8: Orders out that all men unfitted for service must report to every Parade and then be dismissed. Disagreeable term begins. Warned for escort duty. Commenced at 12.30 p.m. over Desjardins in Hut 4. Lounging about...

> Tuesday, December 12: No one seems to know what is going to happen to me. But events are always going to happen the day following.[92]

On December 15 Lieutenant Diefenbaker received notice of his return to Canada, but the order still appeared imprecise. When he was listed to take examinations the next day, he noted that he "did not need it as I had been previously excused." On Monday, December 18 – three weeks after he had been declared medically unfit – the diary contains its first report of any symptoms: "Spent very sick day. Spat blood on and off and at night became very feverish." On December 19 Diefenbaker wrote: "Confined to bed today. M.O. pays visit and says my case is being dealt with now and arrangements have been made." On December 20 there was "nothing doing as usual. The usual vagueness pervades the atmosphere." Finally, on December 21 he had "escort duty for the last time" and was posted to the 196th Battalion at Seaford, Sussex. That was immediately followed by six days' leave in London and Liverpool, visits with friends, more sightseeing and theatre.[93]

After an active day in London on December 29, Diefenbaker remembered that he was due back at Seaford. He took an evening train, registered at the Bay Hotel, and reported to the medical officer, who ordered him to hospital. He entered Ravenscourt Hospital "preparatory to being boarded again," and remained there for the month of January. Two brief pages record that on January 16 his friend Allan McMillan was posted to France (he was killed on April 9), and that after mid-month the patient was allowed out each afternoon to "spend time at picture shows etc."[94]

The forgotten soldier at last received orders on February 7 to report for embarkation in Liverpool five days later. That left him time for an evening in Seaford with "Miss Bennell" and three more days of sightseeing in London. On February 12 John Diefenbaker registered at the Adelphi Hotel in Liverpool ("Best hotel I ever saw"), and next day boarded the SS *Grampian* bound for Canada. The *Grampian*, Diefenbaker wrote, was a "bum ship of 10,900 tons." The passenger list contained "about 100 officers and 200 men and a few civis." Once on board, the Canadians were informed that they would remain in dock for a week. Diefenbaker told his diary: "Nothing of interest. Dismal and dreary and everyone was fed up with the delay." At 3:50 am on February 20, 1917, the *Grampian* sailed for Canada, and the war service diary ended.[95]

From then on the invalided officer's trail appears only intermittently for several months. The *Grampian* docked in Saint John, New Brunswick, on February 28, and Diefenbaker received a rail pass, apparently home to Saskatoon. Ten days later the officer commanding the Regina military district replied to Diefenbaker's inquiry from Toronto, advising him that he should apply for home service in the 105th Saskatchewan Fusiliers "until such time as you are again fit for overseas. One company of the Battalion will be for overseas service, and if agreeable to you you might be transferred to it." Diefenbaker remained on active service until the end of June. During that time he provided the army with at least one medical certificate from a Saskatoon surgeon, who noted that he had been "invalided from France" but was now healthy and capable of return to the front, where he wished to be. The advice was rejected, however, and in late October Lieutenant Diefenbaker was formally "struck off strength" of the Canadian Expeditionary Force and posted to the CEF Reserve of Officers in order to "maintain your claim of Seniority in the C.E.F." At the same time Diefenbaker applied for appointment to the Royal Flying Corps, but was refused "on account of the Medical History Sheet submitted to them."[96]

The military story ends on a minor key in 1918. In April the Canadian Board of Pension Commissioners informed Diefenbaker: "Owing to the fact that you are suffering from no disability which was due to or was incurred during your military service it has been decided that you are not entitled to pension." Six weeks later he received a War Service Badge for "Service in England."[97]

Diefenbaker's version of the story and his own diary and documentary record are thus marked by inconsistencies, the most important of which can only be clarified by a review of the army's medical files on Lieutenant

Diefenbaker. Above all, the diaries contain no mention of an accident and no report of any internal bleeding until weeks after he was found unfit for continued service. There is no diary entry, as Diefenbaker claimed in the memoirs, that reads "Bleeding today from the mouth." The diary does not make clear what was the basis for the medical board's decision, but says only that his first stay in hospital was "to have eyes tested" because his eyesight had been found "defective." Then came the medical board's decision. After that, Diefenbaker seemed active and fit until two days in December, when he "spat blood...and at night became very feverish." Thereafter he spent several vigorous days on leave over Christmas. Although he spent some weeks in hospital in January 1917, his diary does not give the impression that he was being treated for any serious complaint, though his presence in hospital could indicate a regime of rest and diet. Almost the only certainty on which the two records coincide is that Lieutenant Diefenbaker was invalided home.

Once he was back in Canada the story remains confusing. A civilian physician certifies that the young officer is well enough to return to overseas service and he requests it, but the Canadian Army denies the appeal. After this history of rejection, there is a final, vain application for transfer to the Royal Flying Corps. The Pension Board rejects a pension claim on the ground that Diefenbaker suffers from no disability "due to or incurred during...military service." Yet Diefenbaker himself insists sixty years later that he refused to consider a pension and that his injury caused him repeated illness and surgery in the years after the war.

Why would John Diefenbaker obscure the record? There may be good reasons. Posting to the front, in late 1916, meant almost certain death, as Diefenbaker himself recalled. Without the medical disqualification, he said in 1969, "I wouldn't be here, no possibility; the possibility is so remote. We went overseas with 184 lieutenants and twelve weeks later there were 33 living. Utter slaughter. Young officers going over the top...went down and everyone in the ranks of the 196th Battalion, or practically everyone, was...wiped out, that's all." In that atmosphere of impending death, human reactions varied. But depression and psychosomatic symptoms were natural responses – even sane ones, as can now be admitted – and they were widespread in the First World War as in the Second. The army code of duty and valour, however, regarded them as signs of weakness or cowardice. In battle, they could be grounds for humiliation, court martial, or execution. Behind the lines they were treated as signs of instability unacceptable in an officer who was expected to lead his men by example.[98] The Canadian Militia, like the British Army, sought as far as possible to weed out potentially unreliable officers before testing them in combat.

If the young officer was ruled unfit because of some mild complaint with a physical origin or a psychosomatic condition – either of which might be beyond his conscious control – or because he had consciously chosen illness as a means of avoiding assignment to the trenches in France, he would undoubtedly have felt shame, embarrassment, and a desire to disguise the nature of his illness. A trenching injury could have provided the necessary cover story, for both his private self-respect and his public reputation. With time, it would be understandable if he came to believe it himself.

What does the official medical record reveal? Before his departure overseas in the officers' draft of August 1916, Lieutenant Diefenbaker was medically examined and pronounced fit for service.[99] In the decisive medical case sheet of late November 1916, however, the examining physician noted that "this officer suffered a great deal from symptoms of weakness and partial loss of compensation before enlistment. Immediately after enlistment he was given ten days leave owing to heart trouble."[100] This comment is not based on any previous record in the file and apparently repeats Diefenbaker's own testimony. The reference to "ten days leave" may explain his return to Saskatoon from Regina with his mother on August 31, although there is no indication of any further medical examination before his second departure on September 4.

The medical history confirms that Diefenbaker was treated in hospital for defective vision in mid-November.[101] On November 26, 1916, he was examined by a medical board, which diagnosed "cardiac disease" involving shortness of breath on exertion and general physical weakness that precluded physical training.[102] The medical case sheet for this date is not accompanied in the army files, as was normal, by a formal report and recommendation, but the recommendation is recorded elsewhere as "permanently unfit" on the basis of cardiac disease or "D.A.H." DAH, or "Disordered Action of the Heart," is medical shorthand for "a condition in which symptoms occur, such as palpitations and shortness of breath, which are attributed by the patient to disorder of the heart. There is no evidence, however, of heart disease, and psychological factors are thought to be of importance."[103] As in the diary, there is no mention in the case sheet of any accident or injury preceding the medical hearing.

Following his return to Canada, Diefenbaker was ordered to appear before an army medical board in Saskatoon so that a full report on his condition could be made to the Board of Pension Commissioners. The board was convened on April 27, 1917, and confirmed the previous opinion: Diefenbaker was unfit for service, suffering from "shortness of breath upon exertion, pain in pre-cordial region." The incapacity was described as "permanent but will no doubt improve under treatment," with 100 percent disability "for three months."[104] He was subsequently reported to be under outpatient treatment in the Saskatoon military hospital, where he was "receiving general tonics and rest."[105]

In August 1917, once again, Diefenbaker was summoned to a medical board hearing in Saskatoon. The board's report describes his original disability as "Mitral Incompentincy" (sic) caused by "Overwork. Entrenching while in England." The description offers a case history provided by Diefenbaker and recorded in clipped medical style:

> Was examined Nov. 1, 1916 for transfer to Reserve Battalion and was found Physically fit. Classified A1. At this time was taking instruction at Canadian Military School, was digging trenches which continued for 10 days, 7 hours each day which strenuous work he was not accustomed to, at end of this time began spitting blood which lasted 2 days, was admitted to Hospital was there for 10 days, sent to A.D.M.S. at Crowborough, examined and found Physically unfit. Suffering from present condition Mitral Incompentincy [sic], given light duty for 2 weeks, then put back on duty through orders of Colonel of school not A.D.M.S. Gradually became worse examined again and re-admitted to Hospital. He remained for 8 weeks then sent back to Canada.[106]

Besides confusing the chronology and exaggerating the length of his stay in hospital, Diefenbaker for the first time put on the official record his claim to have spat blood.

The medical examiners described his heart condition as permanent, but said that his "general weakness" was expected to disappear within two months. A treatment of "tonic with rest" was prescribed, with a recommendation for a further medical board hearing after two months.[107]

On October 10, 1917, Diefenbaker appeared before the same medical board in Saskatoon. His disability was identified in the board's report as "V.D.H." or valvular disease of the heart, and a previously unstated cause was described: "Hit in back with pick axe."[108] In the opinion of the board, the patient was now fully recovered, required no more treatment, and was described as fit for general service. But he was also recommended for discharge, as the commanding officer explained, "there being no vacancy in this District whereby his services could be utilized at present."[109] On October 25 Diefenbaker was struck off strength of the Canadian Expeditionary Force.[110] A short time later the army confirmed that his request for enrolment in the Royal Flying Corps could not be entertained.

The official record thus confirms that Lieutenant Diefenbaker was judged unfit for active service under a series of commonly used medical euphemisms: cardiac disease, general weakness, disorder affecting the heart, and valvular disease of the heart. These descriptions justified an officer's honourable discharge, while suggesting discreetly that a basic physical disability had not necessarily been demonstrated. In particular, the diagnoses did not appear to be linked to Diefenbaker's own claims to have coughed up blood or to have been injured in the back with a pick axe. Those suggestions, which Diefenbaker later emphasized as evidence of a serious physical injury, appeared on the record from his personal testimony months after the original medical ruling. The two events might have occurred, but the most plausible conclusion is that as explanations for his disability they were rationalizations, or comforting fictions, rather than the truth as army medical officers would have described it.

The symptoms John Diefenbaker spoke of during the 1920s suggested a gastric complaint consistent with a psychosomatic diagnosis in 1916. That was one common illness of soldiering in the wars of the twentieth century, although the recognition that it could be genuine and disabling came slowly even to the psychiatric medical services. The main object of the exercise, after all, was no more than to get men upright into battle where they could bravely live or bravely die – or to get them home if they could not be trusted to do so. In the First World War there was no question of treatment, little official desire for understanding, and hesitation to recognize what was later called battle exhaustion as a legitimate ground for a disability pension. Diefenbaker's actual desire for a pension based on recognition of a physical injury, and his subsequent denial of any desire for one when it could not be based on that recognition, suggest, in the circumstances, that he and the medical boards considered his complaints to be psychosomatic, or believed that was a possibility. His renewed willingness to enter battle perhaps indicated a desire to cleanse the record of any lingering blemish, to prove that he could do it after all.

For the twenty-one-year-old, this experience must have been a profoundly disturbing affair, best suppressed and forgotten. It was his first great test as a man, and, according to all the conventional standards of the time, he had failed. The evenings on the town in London would hardly compensate for the embarrassment and emotional turmoil. But at least he was alive, and able to renew his political quest once the experience was firmly behind him. By extraordinary coincidence, Diefenbaker's chief political rival as prime minister after the passage of forty years, Lester B. Pearson, was invalided home in similar circumstances just one year later. His story too was confused; but Pearson, in his maturity, came closer than Diefenbaker to an open admission of what had happened.[111]

There is another slight twist to the story. One result of the disaster on the Somme was the collapse of the Asquith government and the accession of David Lloyd George as prime minister of the United Kingdom on the evening of December 7, 1916, after a week of intrigue. He was, as A.J.P. Taylor described him, "the first son of the people to reach supreme power."[112] John Diefenbaker recalled that on the day before Lloyd George's first appearance in the House as prime minister, he went to the Canadian High Commission to claim the favour offered in September by Lady Perley. "Out came Sir George. He welcomed me and ushered me into his office and asked what he could do for me. I told him that I wanted a ticket for the gallery at Westminster the next day. He replied: 'If you came to me and wanted a promotion to the rank of Major, it would be so easy, but this can't be done.' I said to him, 'Now, you heard Lady Perley's promise.' I got my ticket and was one of a half-dozen Canadians to hear Lloyd George on that memorable day. He raised the horizons of the British people from the frightful slaughter on the Somme to the hope of ultimate victory."[113]

Lloyd George became prime minister, but did not speak in the House on December 8, when Lieutenant Diefenbaker was in Crowborough under reprimand for his previous absence from parade; on that day he recorded his first "escort duty" in the diary. The diary does mention a visit to the House of Commons one week before, on November 30. But the leadership crisis had not yet erupted, Asquith was still prime minister, and Lloyd George did not speak. His first appearance in the House as prime minister occurred on December 20, when Diefenbaker was still in camp. There is no further mention of Westminster in the diary until February 10, 1917, when Diefenbaker recorded a visit to the "Hses of Parlt etc." The Perley incident seems too specific to be imaginary, but its timing remains obscure. Diefenbaker said that after the war Perley "used to laugh about it and Lady Perley...often spoke of it." Apparently Diefenbaker did not hear Lloyd George's rallying speech on the war as he had claimed, but this was a good story – if slightly embellished – for the demobilized lieutenant to bring back from England.[114]

In April 1918 the young man returned to Russell Hartney's Saskatoon law office as an articling student. In June he shifted to another firm, Ferguson and MacDermid, but that lasted just three months. One of the partners later said, "We didn't get along too well. Any student I had, I wanted him in the office looking after business but he was always running around, into politics.

So, we soon parted ways." The student found another haven in the firm of Lynd and Yule, where he completed his articles in the spring of 1919. The routine was boring and his record indifferent.[115]

There are only traces of Diefenbaker's life in the immediate aftermath of his brief military career. One of them, written in his distinctive flowing hand, is a ten-page tribute to the poet Robert W. Service, prepared for reading at a social evening – perhaps at the First Baptist Church in Saskatoon. Diefenbaker sees Service himself as the "dreamer of dreams...player of parts" who narrates his novel, *The Trail of '98*, as "a little shy mannered lad...with healthy bright cheeks and a soul wrapped up in dreams." Service's poetry, of Yukon sourdoughs and First World War Tommies in the trenches, "which at first glance appears to be merely a conglomeration of vulgarity and blasphemy," is more than that for Diefenbaker. Rather, it is the product of rough circumstance transmuted into popular romance. "He has no real artistic finesse," writes the young man, "but he drives home eternal and dramatic truths with sledge hammer blows."

> This is the law of the Yukon
> > and ever she makes it plain
> Send not your foolish and feeble
> > send me your strong and sane.
> Strong for the red rage of battle;
> > sane for I harry them sore
> Send me men girt for the combat,
> > men who are great to the core.

Diefenbaker reads Service's works "as a biography" and judges him to be "kind, good-natured, fond of bravado and the companionship of all classes, possessed of great determination and will power together with a fervid love for his native land." What took Service into the Red Cross ambulance corps at the front, Diefenbaker insists, was a simple belief not in British power, not in the triumph of force, but in British "civilization."

For those who read Service's doggerel and doubt his religious faith, Diefenbaker responds that, despite its lack of piety, the verse is permeated with "the spirit of Christian charity." The poetry will last in Canada, Diefenbaker suggests, because "he depicts in a remarkably true manner the customs and tenets of the classes and peoples amongst whom he has lived." Service's simple, rugged, populist sentimentality suited the ex-serviceman.

The entire program was offered as a dramatic performance, with readings of illustrative verse by three young ladies – including the fifteen-year-old Olive Freeman, who would become the second Mrs Diefenbaker thirty-five years later. For his audience, the handsome war veteran with the penetrating eyes and the rolling voice must himself have seemed that dreamer of dreams and player of parts.[116]

Like other universities, the University of Saskatchewan gave academic credit for war service, allowing veterans to telescope their degree programs. Diefenbaker gained credit in the law school for his undergraduate courses in law, plus one year's credit as a soldier, and thus was eligible for graduation in the spring of 1919. The university opened late in the autumn term of 1918 because of the influenza epidemic, and Diefenbaker attended few classes during the year; but in April 1919 he wrote and passed his finals. He was evidently more mature and self-confident than in his undergraduate days. *The Sheaf* commented on his active extracurricular year, as vice president of law, associate editor of *The Sheaf*, alumni representative on the students' council, and a participant in debating and moot trials: "He has occupied a place which will be difficult to fill, and hereafter all transgressors of the Students' Code will breathe more freely when he relinquishes his position as *custodian of justice.*"[117]

In May he received his law degree. At his request, the Law Society of Saskatchewan granted Diefenbaker two years' exemption from the normal three years of articling (for "the period of your unfitness for military service"), and the same month he wrote his final bar examinations, placing seventh among thirty-nine candidates. On June 30, 1919, John George Diefenbaker signed the roll of the Law Society in Regina, and on July 1 he opened a practice in the small town of Wakaw, Saskatchewan.[118]

CHAPTER 2

Choosing a Party,
Choosing a Wife

1919-1929

ORTY MILES NORTH OF SASKATOON THE PRAIRIE GIVES WAY TO PARKLAND, A belt of rolling fields and woodland groves of poplar, birch, spruce, and pine. This was the first area of intensive homesteading in the province, settled before the First World War by immigrants from Germany, Hungary, Ruthenia, and Galicia (later Poland, Ukraine, and western Russia). By 1919, as a result of the wartime agricultural boom, the region was moderately prosperous and thriving, served by an extensive railway network and a growing system of highways, producing wheat for export and market products for the towns and cities. Midway between Saskatoon and Prince Albert in this parkland belt lies Wakaw Lake, and one mile to the west the village of Wakaw, which was established on the Grand Trunk Pacific Railway line in 1911. In 1919 Wakaw was a busy market town of slightly less than four hundred residents, surrounded by the most densely settled rural townships in the province. The skyline was dominated by three grain elevators on the east and a scattering of still-expanding one- and two-storey buildings on the two business streets running west from the railway line: a hotel, post office, town hall, mission hospital, school, Catholic and Ukrainian churches, weekly newspaper, general stores, farm suppliers, a restaurant or two, and a few business offices. To the east, at the original townsite on the shores of Wakaw Lake, there were a few more buildings, including a Baptist church. The village was on the district court circuit, with a provincial police office and a local jail, and was easily accessible to Saskatoon, Prince Albert, and Humboldt, where the high court sat.[1]

John Diefenbaker was not content to remain in Saskatoon as a junior employee of an existing law firm. He was determined to get as much courtroom experience as he could, to make his reputation, and to earn enough money to pay off his debts. That meant opening his own office in a town that needed a barrister. With the help of a lawyer friend, he reviewed the court

34

dockets for a number of places in the province and settled on Wakaw, where, he recalled, "people were particularly litigious." It was close enough to home, in familiar country, and had only one practising lawyer. During the month of June the newcomer made his preparations – with some difficulty. Local businessmen, he found, were loyal to the lawyer who was already on the scene and reluctant to rent office space to a competitor. Diefenbaker was offered the use of a vacant lot opposite the railway line. He negotiated credit purchases from a lumber company and, within weeks, he and a carpenter had built a primitive two-room frame shack for $480.08 plus labour. Here he opened for business on July 1. He was joined in the office by an articling student, Michael Stechishin, a classmate from the Faculty of Law. (The arrangement required special permission from the Law Society, since Diefenbaker had no more experience than his student.) Stechishin's fluency in Ukrainian was of significant help in dealing with clients, many of them fellow immigrants from Ukraine.[2]

The slim young lawyer now to be seen in Wakaw had an unusual presence. As Garrett and Kevin Wilson describe him, he had "an intense and serious look." "Above a frame that was tall and slender, almost slight, was a head that was arresting in its appearance. A finely-sculpted mouth and nose went almost unnoticed as the observer's attention was drawn to the strange, commanding blue eyes, piercing and questioning, that made one somewhat uncomfortable. Full black hair, receding in striking waves, unfashionable for the time, accentuated the effect of the eyes beneath. Dressed severely and formally in dark suit and vest, the lawyer was an outstanding figure as he strode the streets of Wakaw."[3] That sober presence, those intense blue eyes, were the signs of a man who did not expect to be slighted.

The new lawyer in town soon had his first client. Early in the morning of August 6 a doctor from nearby Cudworth brought a wounded youth to the Wakaw hospital and his assailant, John Chernyski, to the provincial police detachment. There Chernyski made a statement, was charged with shooting the injured boy, and was placed in the cells. Ten days later, at the request of Chernyski's wife, John Diefenbaker took on his defence at an agreed fee of $600 – a very substantial sum in 1919.[4]

Chernyski admitted to the shooting and the defence was straightforward: the young boy had been crossing Chernyski's land on his bicycle when he was set upon by Chernyski's dogs. In the twilight the farmer had mistaken the grounded intruder for a fox or a coyote and had blasted him with his shotgun. The error was immediately clear. Chernyski and his family provided first aid and sought medical help in the village of Cudworth, and Chernyski turned himself in. After a preliminary hearing in Wakaw and his counsel's successful appeal for bail to the district court in Prince Albert, Chernyski was committed for trial on a charge of wounding "in the absence of precaution and care," or criminal negligence.

The case was heard before Chief Justice J.T. Brown of the Court of King's Bench in Humboldt late in October 1919. After a two-day hearing in which the injured youth testified to bad blood between the two families, while the defence relied on testimony that the shooting was an error committed in the fading evening light, the jury found Chernyski not guilty. John Diefenbaker had been succinct in his examination of witnesses and his summing up, and he had his first victory.

In memory, he embellished events for the sake of a good story and ignored what may have been a key element in his success with the jury. In the 1960s Diefenbaker recalled that the jurors at first agreed to convict on a lesser charge than attempted murder because this was his first court case, and then decided to acquit after one of them had remarked: "But this is the kid's birthday." In fact, there had never been a charge of attempted murder, and the trial occurred more than one month after the defence lawyer's twenty-fourth birthday. Diefenbaker's successful appeal for bail in district court had been heard on the eve of his birthday in September, but that was not a jury hearing.[5]

The missing element of explanation was provided by Emmett Hall. In the autumn of 1919 he was articling in Humboldt and joined his university friend at the defence table to assist in jury selection. Afterwards he left the courtroom, and that evening he saw the judge in the dining room of the Arlington Hotel. Chief Justice Brown asked him to sit with him and told Hall that he believed, on the whole, the defence had a good case. But he thought Diefenbaker was overplaying the extent of darkness, making the scene too obscure to see any target. Hall took this as a bit of friendly advice intended for the defence lawyer, and the next morning in court he wrote a note to Diefenbaker on the back of his copy of the indictment:

> We were sitting & talking with the judge & he, in commenting on the case said that the only weakness displayed in your case so far was that you had too much stress upon the darkness. I would comment upon it, but don't paint it too black, he is somewhat suspicious of your evidence as to the darkness – He is very favourable – He doesn't believe that the injured man is telling the truth about his actions...
>
> He is very suspicious of the injured man on account of the discrepancies between his testimony here & at Wakaw. Referring to the darkness the judge

is quite impressed by this fact, the light was lit inside & when accused rushed out the darkness would appear greater.[6]

Once Diefenbaker read this missive, the darkness lightened to dusk, and the defence counsel emphasized the difficulty of sudden adjustment from a lighted room to the twilight outside. The argument for an unfortunate mistake became plausible and the case was won. When Emmett Hall met the chief justice again that evening, Brown joked about "the sudden 'enlightenment' that had struck the Chernyski trial."[7] If the freshman lawyer had a little unexpected assistance, it seemed to come from his friend and the judge, not from the jury.

That first piece of good luck in the courtroom gave Diefenbaker's career as a barrister its stimulus. Local scepticism disappeared and the office was soon busy. In his next substantial case he gained acquittals for five out of ten clients in a lawsuit for fraud in grain deliveries brought against them by the Progressive Farmers' Grain Company. The charges involved kickbacks to the grain buyer for falsifying the records of grain deliveries; Diefenbaker convinced the juries that there was insufficient evidence to convict half his clients, and he received legal fees in excess of $3000 in the case. By the summer of 1920 he was able to begin paying off his debts, move into a larger office, convert his shack into living quarters, and buy an impressive new Maxwell touring car at a price of $1764.[8]

But the bounty was temporary. The wartime wheat boom was fading by 1920 and the entire Saskatchewan economy felt the results of falling grain prices. The firm's business suffered and Diefenbaker suspected discrimination. In June, when his local bank manager wrote to inform him that his account was overdrawn by $72.80, Diefenbaker replied in a tone of aggrieved sarcasm that a personal meeting would have been preferable to a letter, but "it would appear that such course would not result in the necessary publicity... I was under the impression," he continued, "that in return for doing little favours for you, such as taking care of orders for payments etc., that I might at least be treated in as courteous a manner as others of whom I know, but in that I again must have been mistaken."[9] The firm's financial difficulties extended through most of the following year. Like other lawyers of the time, Diefenbaker supplemented his legal work by arranging mortgage loans and selling insurance, and this business helped to see him through. His annual net income, which he had estimated at $3600 in April 1920, actually amounted to $2400 for 1921.[10]

Still, John Diefenbaker was gathering valuable experience – and confidence – in the courtroom and the community. In the fall of 1920 he was elected to the village council for a three-year term. He appears in a 1919 photograph as manager of the Wakaw football team, although he wrote in his memoirs that he was "the very enthusiastic manager of the local baseball team." The young man had inherited frugal habits and his living expenses were low. He was devoted first of all to his work, and then, increasingly, to politics. The automobile seemed to be his main source of relaxation and adventure: in the summer of 1921 he drove to Vancouver and in 1923 to Los Angeles, both long trips over unpaved roads. He bought a summer cottage at Wakaw Lake, and he fished and hunted.[11]

Diefenbaker remained on close terms with his parents and made it a habit to spend weekends in Saskatoon with them. He relied particularly on his self-assured mother for advice and emotional strength. His social life seems to have been cautious; with young women he remained shy and ill at ease, although he dated with school and university friends and attended Saturday dances at the Art Academy and Teachers' Social Club in Saskatoon, or the village hall in Wakaw. Unlike his more relaxed brother, Elmer, John disliked dancing, had no sense of rhythm, and disdained small talk; he took part to keep up appearances and to avoid accusations of being a dull bookworm. One acquaintance told biographer Simma Holt: "We used to go to dances as a group...and we would see John there but did not pay much attention to him. He was always very properly dressed and stood board straight. He seemed just as inflexible. He was tall, slim, quiet, aloof, not aggressive, a very poor mixer."[12] As a young professional and politician-to-be, John planned to marry, since a wife was expected in both roles and he had no wish to buck the conventions. He also seemed very dependent on women for emotional support. But he found the social round leading to courtship and marriage a painful one.

Olive Freeman, one of the performers in Diefenbaker's tribute to Robert W. Service, was an early object of the veteran's attentions. She was the teenage daughter of the minister at First Baptist Church in Saskatoon, Dr Charles B. Freeman. Olive made an immediate impression on the young man that he did not forget; but when she moved with her family to Brandon in 1921, the two lost touch for more than twenty years.[13] Later John claimed that his infatuation led quickly to a proposal of marriage, either by mail or in person, and an implied rejection. Olive's memory, as she conveyed it to her daughter, was that the returned soldier had merely asked her for a date, but had not pressed it when she told him her age.[14]

By the early 1920s Diefenbaker was courting another young woman in Saskatoon, Beth Newell. She was as shy as he, and they carried on their romance in private, although friends were aware of it. Beth worked as a cashier at the Massey Harris Company and lived at home with her widowed, asthmatic mother, who took in boarders for income. By late 1921 or early 1922, according to Simma Holt, the couple were engaged, and soon Beth and her mother had collected linens and cottons for her hope chest and made a wedding dress. From the distance of fifty years, friends recalled Beth as John's adoring companion. "She was a good listener and loved to hear him talk about his cases. This quality was one he sought in women all his life: he needed someone to listen, react, and tell him what she thought of his actions or aspirations."[15]

Late in the autumn of 1923 Beth, who had appeared "frail and weak" in the preceding months, was apparently diagnosed with tuberculosis. There is no direct record of what followed between the two, but Holt suggests that John never saw or talked to her again. She died in May 1924.[16]

The young man's own health, which he had regarded with care since his invaliding home in 1917, suffered several lapses in these years, and his apparent break with Beth Newell may have resulted from his personal fear of tuberculosis. Pulmonary TB, like polio and scarlet fever, remained a scourge in the 1920s. Diagnosis was haphazard, treatment was inadequate, and the possibility of infection could be a source of panic. Diefenbaker was still subject to occasional internal bleeding, although the nature of his illness remained uncertain. In March 1923 he was bedridden for several days with his undiagnosed complaint, first in Wakaw and then in his parents' home in Saskatoon, where his mother could care for him. In April he spent a week at the tuberculosis sanatorium at Fort Qu'Appelle, and in November he followed the path of other Canadian pilgrims to the Mayo Clinic in Rochester, Minnesota, for examination and treatment. There he had surgery for a gastric ulcer, which led to a radical improvement in his health. But he was still not robust and continued to suffer stomach ailments for several years more.[17]

J OHN DIEFENBAKER'S FIRST WIDELY PUBLICIZED COURT CASE WAS SIGNIFICANT FOR him for at least two reasons: he won a victory against his legal competitor in Wakaw, A.E. Stewart; and he acted in the case for clients from the minority French-speaking community of Saskatchewan. The Saskatchewan School Act provided that "English shall be the sole language of instruction in all schools," but the provincial government, out of political prudence, in fact closed its eyes to infringements in some areas where there were few English-speaking settlers. In January 1922 Stewart, acting for William Mackie, an English-speaking resident of the Ethier School District, entered a complaint against two school trustees, Rémi Ethier and Léger Boutin, charging that their board had violated the School Act by permitting regular teaching in the French language. The local justice of the peace in Wakaw found Ethier and Boutin guilty, imposing a fine of $30 and costs. They asked Diefenbaker to appeal on their behalf.

The appeal was heard before district court judge A.E. Doak in May 1922. The evidence convinced the judge that the school was in fact conducting its teaching "practically entirely" in French. "I have no hesitation in coming to the conclusion," Judge Doak wrote, "that sec. 178 was being consistently and deliberately broken in this school, and that if the trustees did not know it, it was simply because they chose to ignore the fact. Indeed I am more than a little suspicious that it was being done with their connivance." Diefenbaker, however, argued the legal fine point that the trustees were not responsible for the school's internal operations. On that technical ground, the judge overturned the previous conviction. Since the judgment seemed to sustain the *de facto* right of French language instruction, the Franco-Catholic association of the province was pleased and took up a subscription to pay the lawyer's legal fees.

Diefenbaker had handled a politically sensitive brief with dexterity: without challenging the legal dominance of English in the schools, he had won a practical victory for French language teaching. The case made headlines in the province and launched his public reputation as a defender of minorities. He was proud both to have taken the appeal, despite advice that it would harm his political reputation in the anti-French, anti-Catholic atmosphere of Saskatchewan, and to have won it as he did. If he took the case because he objected to a constitutional wrong, he won it by subtle indirection. The larger, constitutional wrong was not corrected, but for the French community the local triumph was reason enough for gratitude.[18]

By Christmas 1922 John Diefenbaker had won two more criminal jury trials as a defence lawyer in Humboldt and Prince Albert, as well as handling many other criminal cases in the local police court. Although the volume of his civil work was increasing, his growing reputation was based on his talents in criminal defence. He found the role congenial and honed his skills in the courtroom with every case. On stage for the defence, he discovered his special dramatic genius. By the use of his voice, his penetrating eyes, his raised arm and accusatory finger, his sense of the ridiculous, his edge of sarcasm, his command of the fine points of law and evidence, he became a master of his juries. As defence counsel his role was not to prove a case but to raise doubts, to act on his instinctive feel for the mood of the jury. The man seemed made for the part and grew naturally into it. He could identify easily with the unfortunate, the dispossessed, the poor, with all those who lacked the birthright and assumed superiority of wealth, power, language, and education of the British Canadian mainstream; and he could argue with passion. In Saskatchewan there was fertile ground for his talent.[19]

During the Christmas holiday in 1922, while John Diefenbaker was at home in Saskatoon, a fire destroyed his Wakaw office along with several other buildings. In his memoirs he said of Wakaw that "for a while arson seemed the favourite local sport" and that he was twice burnt out by "fires set in buildings farther up the street. When the insurance companies finally stopped making cash settlements in fire claims and began to replace burnt-out buildings, arson somehow ceased to be an important item on the calendar of local crime." But the setback was a minor one. For Diefenbaker, records were not vital to his practice, and within two weeks he had reopened in new offices without apparent harm.[20]

Now John Diefenbaker dominated legal business in Wakaw. A.E. Stewart departed early in 1923, and Stewart's successor, Thomas Paterson, could not maintain the practice. The Prince Albert firm of Halliday and Davis opened a branch office in 1923, but they too failed locally – in part because Diefenbaker challenged the right of an articling student, Clifford Sifton Davis, to run the office in defiance of the rules of the Law Society. The Davis firm was run by Clifford's brother, T.C. Davis, the mayor of Prince Albert and chief, by inheritance, of the Liberal Party organization in northern Saskatchewan. The episode, Diefenbaker recalled, "did not augur well for our future relations."[21] His triumph complete, Diefenbaker now planned to move on himself. He made Alexander Ehman his Wakaw partner, and on May 1, 1924, he went north to establish his practice in Prince Albert.[22]

JOHN DIEFENBAKER'S FATHER WAS A LIBERAL SUPPORTER OF SIR WILFRID LAURIER. He maintained that loyalty during the federal election of 1911, the first one to leave a marked impression on his politically ambitious son, although he doubted the wisdom of Laurier's commitment to reciprocity with the United States. John remembered that his father was impressed by the defection of the western Liberal minister Clifford Sifton in opposition to reciprocity, but he was also suspicious that "the powerful Eastern financial interests" supporting Conservative leader Robert Borden's campaign against reciprocity "were more concerned with selfish ends than with national welfare."[23] His father's ambiguity held some of the seeds of John's own political vision.

"The election," said Diefenbaker, "had a profound influence on me, and perhaps more than anything else made me a Conservative. I attended all the meetings in Saskatoon."[24] Despite the strong desire for free trade in the west, John was impressed by Conservative warnings that reciprocity would lead to economic and political union with the United States. He was stirred by the Conservative brand of Canadian nationalism, with its still-heady mix of local and imperial sentiments. "The Tories," he recalled, "had a marvellous campaign. They didn't have any arguments but they raised the flag and we'd sing...'We're soldiers of the King.' 'Rule Britannia' had its place in those programmes as we cleaved to our British heritage in defiance of American manifest destiny and Grit continentalism. The result was a tremendous revelation of Canadian determination to be Canadian. This impressed me greatly."[25]

Borden triumphed and reciprocity was dead. But Saskatchewan remained Liberal. The next federal election, in December 1917, split the conventional mould when Borden's Conservatives were joined by pro-conscription English-speaking Liberals across the country campaigning as Unionists against Laurier's Liberal rump from Quebec. For the returned soldier, support for the Unionists was automatic and did not require a decisive choice between Liberals and Conservatives. Diefenbaker campaigned in Saskatoon for the Union candidate, even though he opposed the government's Wartime Elections Act, which had removed the vote from those naturalized Canadians who had arrived from enemy nations any time after 1902. This piece of crass demagogy was anathema in the prairies and could only deepen the young man's sense of alienation from the leadership of the Conservative Party. As a poll worker, he was also aware of the government's manipulation of soldiers' votes to assure that they were applied to constituencies where they were most needed.[26] Diefenbaker took to the hustings during the campaign, but his timidity as a speaker kept his remarks short.[27]

Diefenbaker's political attitudes were being formed, it seemed, through neither his brief wartime experience of the larger world nor any deep historical reflection, but through absorption of his father's attitudes and his own direct experience of Saskatchewan life. He left no record of his views on the Russian revolution, the peace settlement of 1919, the creation of the League of Nations, the postwar eruption of radicalism in the Progressive movement, the Winnipeg General Strike, or the conservative reaction that was labelled "the Red scare."

By 1921 John Diefenbaker's political affiliation was not yet entirely clear. This was the year of the Progressive Party sweep against both the old parties in the west and Ontario; in Prince Albert constituency the sitting Unionist member, Andrew Knox, had gone over to the Progressives and was re-elected easily. Diefenbaker admired him and respected his political strength. In Wakaw the young lawyer apparently kept a low profile during the campaign. He suggests, however, that the Liberal Party approached him "to enlist me for party work and as a possible candidate" for both the provincial and the federal elections of 1921. The invitations were declined, but with sufficient ambiguity to prompt his election as secretary of the Wakaw Liberal Association one weekend in his absence. "I returned on the Tuesday from Saskatoon and was amazed to find the Liberal Association minute books and paraphernalia in my office. I immediately delivered them back to the local Liberal president, Mr. J.H. Flynn."[28] Four years later, in March 1925, the Wakaw Liberal Association discussed a motion to nominate him as Liberal candidate for the provincial constituency of Kinistino – a discussion that took place in the presence of his Wakaw law partner, Alexis Etienne Philion, "one of several who surely would have known if they were putting their man into the right pew but the wrong church."[29] But the motion was defeated. (Diefenbaker wrote of this incident as an "approach" to be the Liberal candidate, but dates it the year before, when he was still a resident of Wakaw, and does not mention the motion's defeat.) These repeated Liberal soundings were flattering acknowledgment of his political ambition, his growing reputation, and perhaps of the skill with which Diefenbaker withheld commitment while awaiting the right opportunity. Were they also indications of his leanings? The record is not clear. In retrospect, he believed that the reigning Saskatchewan Liberals were eager to catch him: "There were suggestions...that came to me that if I would go over to the Liberal Party there was no position that would be denied me in the province...but I was never keen."[30] During the period in Wakaw, however, neither the Conservatives nor the Progressives made any overtures to the aspiring politician.

In Prince Albert, Mayor T.C. Davis was chosen as Liberal candidate for the June 1925 provincial election. Davis and others claimed that Diefenbaker was one of his supporters in that campaign.[31] Davis won his seat in Prince Albert, as the Liberal Party again swept the province with its apparently invincible machine. Just three weeks later, on June 19, Diefenbaker finally revealed his Conservative colours by addressing a small organizing meeting for the federal Conservative campaign in Prince Albert; and on August 6, 1925, a nominating meeting declared him the party's federal candidate by acclamation.[32]

In a province dominated both federally and provincially by the Liberal Party, the decision was Diefenbaker's Rubicon. He seemed to be committing himself to political oblivion. "For me," Diefenbaker wrote, "the election campaign was a test involving more than votes. I passed my thirtieth birthday during the contest. I had come of age politically, and my candidacy was a public declaration of my political faith."[33] From the start, his faith was a peculiarly personal one that did not wholly fit the party to which he now gave his permanent allegiance. He had decided to make his own way – slowly if necessary – without the patronage of the Liberal Party that had sought him, and within a party so lacking in local strength that it seemed open to his own shaping influence. Its very weakness would allow him his freedom and nurture his eccentricity.

The decision was not made alone. When John Diefenbaker moved to Prince Albert, he grew close to Sam Donaldson, the leading local Conservative. Donaldson, a wealthy former livery stable owner and land speculator, had been mayor of Prince Albert before the turn of the century, a member of the provincial legislature, and briefly (from 1915 to 1917) member of parliament for Prince Albert. He was a colourful character, wise in the political rough-and-tumble of Saskatchewan's early days. He had engaged the Liberal Party in combat as it built its pervasive provincial machine, and he had won his first legislative election in 1905 only after a series of court cases and a decision of the legislature to overturn the official – and corrupted – result favouring the Liberal candidate. Diefenbaker saw "pluck and courage and character" in that story and in Donaldson's political career; it was the kind of high-spirited knight errantry that struck romantic chords and recalled his own youthful heroes. As a defence counsel, Diefenbaker had already begun to shape himself in the same anti-establishment mould. In Saskatchewan politics, it was clear, to be anti-establishment was to be anti-Liberal. When Donaldson suggested that the young man should enter politics as a Conservative because Davis would always stand in his way as a Liberal, Diefenbaker saw the point. But he baulked at the suggestion that he might contest the provincial election in Prince Albert against Davis. A few weeks later, Donaldson made a more compelling offer of the federal candidacy and promised Diefenbaker that he would organize the nomination. The bait was taken.[34]

The election was called for October 29, 1925. There was little chance of a Conservative victory in Prince Albert, where the party had lost its deposit in 1921. But this was an occasion for the budding politician to establish his reputation and his federal party credentials and to practise his platform style. Diefenbaker faced the sitting Progressive member, Andrew Knox, and the Liberal, Charles McDonald. The Progressives were fading before Mackenzie King's blandishments, and the Liberals were his real opponents. They managed to get under his skin when Davis mocked him as "a fallen-away Liberal." Diefenbaker replied with an admission: "T.C. Davis seems to think that the fact I was once a Liberal is an offence. Well, as I get older I see the indiscretions of my youth. I'm not here to tell falsehoods. I *was* a Liberal, but I could not help but see the failures of the Liberal Government in carrying out their promises. He says I sought a Liberal nomination; that's an unqualified falsehood. It is true that certain persons wanted me to accept nomination. But that I sought it, is false."[35]

His Conservative faith was, from the beginning, a blend of conventional British Canadian loyalty and western recalcitrance. "I haven't spent a lifetime with this party," he reflected in 1969. "I chose it because of certain basic principles and those...were the empire relationship of the time, the monarchy and the preservation of an independent Canada. None of these things I thought the Liberal party could support."[36] He added to that general disposition two other elements: a distrust of the Ontario-centred policies of the Conservative leader, Arthur Meighen; and a personal response to the dilemmas of cultural assimilation that were especially acute in the racially diverse prairie provinces.

The candidate disagreed publicly with his leader on two matters of western concern: the inviolability of low Crow's Nest Pass freight rates on the movement of prairie grain and the completion of the Hudson Bay Railway as an alternative outlet to the sea for grain exports. To Diefenbaker's horror, Meighen warned voters that a Conservative government might alter the statutory Crow rates and persisted in his opposition to the railway. Diefenbaker, in response, promised a public meeting on October 7 that, if elected, he would resign his seat in two years if the railway was not then under construction.[37] His opponents pointed out the disagreement with Meighen, but Diefenbaker held his ground. As he later wrote: "My position was difficult. It need not have been. But I chose to speak for myself."[38]

From the time of the German war, if not before, John Diefenbaker had been sensitive about his name and ancestry, eager to assert his native-born Canadian status and his British loyalties. Canada was a country still uncertain of its own character, divided by distinct social rankings and widespread prejudices in which persons of British lineage were top of the heap. That was evident in the legislatures and cabinets outside Quebec, in business, in local councils, in the grain growers' associations. Politicians and educators on the prairies puzzled over the problems of asssimilation created by the vast immigration of the previous three decades, and in the communities there were dark gusts of exclusion and discrimination. They touched Diefenbaker personally. In the 1925 campaign he heard himself described, in the old wartime pejorative, as a "Hun." He confronted the insult in his speech at the Orpheum Theatre in Prince Albert on October 7:

They call me a Hun! Probably the opposing candidates do not, but their minions most certainly do, and one of the leading Liberals has publicly apologized for this serious allegation. The only crimes they can pin upon me are those of youth and of German ancestry. Am I a German? My great-grandfather left Germany to seek liberty. My grandfather and my father were born in Canada. It is true, however, that my grandmother and my grandfather on my mother's side spoke no English: being Scottish, they spoke Gaelic. If there is no hope for me to be Canadian, then who is there hope for?[39]

The claims about his grandparents stretched the truth for the sake of effect: his Diefenbaker grandfather was German-born and his Bannerman grandparents spoke English. But the candidate struck a theme that endured for his long political career. In his ideal Canada, there would be no distinctions of race or national origin, no hybrid collection of minorities, visible or invisible, but instead a "united nationality" of equals. His vision was expressed with feeling, and Diefenbaker saw no paradox in it. He simply took for granted that the emerging common nationality would absorb the dominant British heritage of values and institutions – and discard the rest. In western Canada that would become a potent dream.[40]

The young Conservative campaigned vigorously. "I carried my message to village and town throughout my constituency, to Domremy and Wakaw, to Rosthern, to Blaine Lake, Marcelin, Leask, and Shellbrook, to Briarlee, Wild Rose, and Honeymoon."[41] His courtroom reputation was growing and his platform style reflected the defence counsel's persuasive skills. A Progressive supporter warned that he should not be underestimated: "He takes himself very seriously and you will all do well to take him the same way. He has any amount of ability and has distinguished himself in his profession by his hobby of taking tough cases. He can take an out and out rascal and describe him with such wonderful oratory that one may almost see a halo around the rogue's head."[42]

But in Saskatchewan the task was hopeless. The Conservative Party picked up seats elsewhere and returned the largest group to parliament, although it did not get a clear majority. In Saskatchewan, however, the party faced defeat across the board. Diefenbaker ran third behind McDonald and Knox in Prince Albert and lost his deposit. He blamed Arthur Meighen squarely for Conservative losses on the prairies; he was convinced that Meighen's rigidity on freight rates and the Hudson Bay Railway had cost him a parliamentary majority.[43]

The candidate's disappointment was mollified by the encouraging editorial judgment of the Liberal Prince Albert *Herald*: "There are many today ready to prophesy that the last has not yet been heard of him in the political life of this country." In early December the constituency party held a banquet in Diefenbaker's honour attended by 250 supporters in celebration of his fighting spirit. "No community can defeat such a man as J.G. Diefenbaker," said the Reverend R.F. Macdougall in his toast to the guest; Diefenbaker responded that the occasion marked not defeat but rededication.[44]

Prime Minister King had lost not only his plurality but his own seat in North York. Yet he clung to power, delayed the opening of the House, and accepted Charles McDonald's offer to resign his seat to allow for a by-election in Prince Albert. The local Conservatives did not nominate against him, although Diefenbaker says in his memoirs that, on the suggestion of the national party office, he privately encouraged a Conservative to contest the seat as an independent.[45] On February 2, 1926, King easily won election as the new member for Prince Albert. Almost immediately afterwards he persuaded Premier Charles Dunning of Saskatchewan to enter the federal cabinet, and Dunning was succeeded as premier by James G. Gardiner. Gardiner appointed his Prince Albert member, T.C. Davis, as minister of municipal affairs, and Davis also took charge of Prime Minister King's constituency affairs. John Diefenbaker, having cast his lot with the Conservative Party, now found himself facing the formidable Gardiner-Davis-King organization in the riding of his choice.[46]

The Conservative newcomer was beginning to attract notice beyond his own province. In 1926 he accepted an invitation to address the convention of the British Columbia Conservative Party, where another young political devotee, the reporter Bruce Hutchison, found him a compelling presence on the platform. "He was tall, lean, almost skeletal, his bodily motions jerky and spasmodic, his face pinched and white, his pallor emphasized by metallic black curls and sunken, hypnotic eyes. But from this frail, wraithlike person, so deceptive in his look of physical infirmity, a voice of vehement power and rude health blared like a trombone."[47]

Another federal election was expected soon. On February 16, 1926, a Conservative nominating meeting – much larger than that of the previous year – unanimously reaffirmed Diefenbaker as the party's Prince Albert nominee. During the next few months the King government faced the rapidly blossoming scandal over corruption in the customs department, and at the end of June King resigned as prime minister when the governor general refused to grant him a dissolution of parliament. Arthur Meighen became prime minister, was defeated at once in the House, and was granted a dissolution for a general election on September 14.[48]

Meighen and the Conservatives thus went into the campaign with what should have been the advantages of office. The previous King government, however, had gained extensive goodwill – and further undermined support for the Progressives – by adopting the old age pension proposal of two independent labour MPs, J.S. Woodsworth and A.A. Heaps. During the campaign King managed to obscure the issue of the customs scandal by charging that the governor general, Lord Byng, had improperly reduced Canada to colonial status by refusing his request for a dissolution, while Meighen had connived in the affair by accepting office. Technically the charges were absurd, but they had emotional power. Meighen bore the added electoral burden of leading a government defeated on its first vote in the House. In Quebec he was still reviled for his imposition of wartime conscription, while in English-speaking Canada he had lost some of his previous pro-British support after his nationalist speech of November 1925 in Hamilton.[49]

Although Diefenbaker regarded Meighen as "a man of integrity and principle, and of powerful intellect,"[50] he found him, once again, an infuriating party leader in an election campaign. For one thing, Meighen chose to ignore King's "constitutional issue," while King exploited it. For another, Meighen insisted on his vehement opposition to the old age pension. Diefenbaker, among others, recalled that he argued with Meighen over the pension, which he saw as a matter of decency rather than the first stage of socialist decadence; but the leader would not be moved. Meighen maintained his unpopular views on the Crow's Nest Pass rates and the Hudson Bay Railway as well.[51]

In Prince Albert there was a straight, two-way contest between Mackenzie King and John Diefenbaker. Diefenbaker did his best to "explain matters that were unexplainable" in Meighen's platform. But as much as possible, and with fresh confidence, he fought his own local campaign against the Liberal leader. He found attack more congenial than defence. Mackenzie King, he charged, was an interloper in Prince Albert, an absentee leader who had jumped from constituency to constituency and had "never yet been elected twice in the same riding. Let him be elected and defeated in the same riding in the same year." King, said Diefenbaker, rewarded criminals by appointment to the Senate, lied about Senate reform, and had clung stupidly to office after his party's 1925 electoral defeat.[52]

In the east, several Conservatives publicly ridiculed King for his flight to a Saskatchewan constituency in terms that were acutely embarrassing to the local Conservative candidate. The Saskatoon *Phoenix* commented that R.J. Manion, one of Meighen's ministers, had made a base appeal to "racial" prejudice by claiming that 99 percent of the Prince Albert voters' list consisted of "names...such that you and I couldn't pronounce," and adding that "I welcome them. We need them. But the fact still remains that they don't know Canadian problems as Canadians do."[53] In late August the Toronto *Telegram* reported the jibe of a speaker at a Conservative rally in North York: "Mackenzie King has gone to Prince Albert, has left North York. He doesn't like the smell of native-born Canadians. He prefers the stench of garlic-stinking continentals, Eskimos, bohunks, and Indians."[54] Liberal pamphlets appearing in the riding in the last week of the campaign made similar claims: "The Conservative candidate in North Grey, speaking on Mr. Meighen's platform at Owen Sound, hurled insult at the electors of Prince Albert. 'Mr. King' he said, 'is running in a riding among the Doukhobors, up near the North Pole where they don't know how to mark their ballots.' Citizens of Prince Albert: Mark your ballot for Mackenzie King and reject this insult!"[55]

For John Diefenbaker such taunts were doubly painful. They reflected racial prejudices in a party that, in the west, was struggling unsuccessfully to build links with non-British voters; and they touched his personal sensitivity about both his name and his own uncertain attitudes. The confusion of Diefenbaker's position on the social question was illustrated in a Roman Catholic parish newsletter, *St. Peter's Messenger*, of Meunster, Saskatchewan, that reported on his participation in the annual Orangemen's celebrations in MacDougall in July 1926. Diefenbaker, said the newsletter, had appeared on the platform with the Reverend Canon Strong and the Reverend R.F. MacDougall, "two veteran advocates of bigotry and fanaticism." In his address, he had appealed for a Canada that would be "all Canadian and all British" – an imperialism, in the *Messenger*'s eyes, that was "a strictly Orange principle" – and he had taken the Orange line in opposing a distinctive Canadian flag. Both these attitudes, the *Messenger* suggested, were coded expressions of prejudice against Catholicism and French-speaking Canadians. Instead, it called on the electors of Prince Albert "– Catholics and Protestants, French and English – to show that they are entirely out of sympathy with those who either directly or indirectly advocate religious intolerance in our country." Diefenbaker would discover "that to ride the stormy seas of politics to Ottawa in a rickety Orange tub is an impossible task in Saskatchewan."[56] While Diefenbaker deplored prejudice when it took the form of insults against European names and origins, he was still prepared to seek support among Saskatchewan's anti-Catholic and anti-French-speaking voters – without, apparently, noticing the inconsistency.

Diefenbaker was now refining a talent for turning grievance back upon his accusers. He responded to renewed rumours that he was a German by asserting that only his great-grandfather was German and adding: "Suppose I was a German, does it make for a united Canada to knock settlers?" And he threw another charge at the King campaign. On September 4 he told an election meeting: "Representatives of Mr. King are going through this constituency telling the non-English speaking people that, if the Conservative Government is returned, they will all be deported one by one without trial."[57] That, he said, was a falsehood. Yet Diefenbaker did not respond to a challenge from Dr Robert Scott of Wakaw to prove his claim of Liberal scare-mongering.[58]

Mackenzie King's campaigns, both local and national, were triumphant. The Liberal Party won a parliamentary majority, Meighen lost his seat in Portage la Prairie, and the Conservatives returned only one candidate – the millionaire tycoon from Calgary, R.B. Bennett – from all three prairie provinces. "I still think," Diefenbaker wrote in his memoirs, "that I might have overcome the constitutional issue, the Hudson Bay Railway, the Crow's Nest rates controversy, and even the old age pension question, had it not been for the offensive racial comments of those Ontario Conservatives...Despite this, I put on a good fight in the city; King's lead in the rural polls, however, was unassailable." Even in Wakaw the local boy's vote was overwhelmed, as it had been the previous year.[59]

In October 1926 Diefenbaker attended a post-mortem meeting of elected and defeated Conservative candidates and senators held in the great Railway Committee Room of the House of Commons. There, in orotund language, he lamented the loss of votes suffered "as a result of indiscretions and unsound judgement of individuals whose verbosity had been detrimental to the interests of the Conservative party" – a reference, apparently, to the crude remarks about the race, odour, and literacy of the voters of Prince Albert constituency. But there was enough ambiguity in his words that they could also be taken as a reflection on the wisdom of Arthur Meighen. Meighen had come to the meeting carrying his resignation as leader, and after long debate it was accepted. Following departure of the defeated candidates, Conservative MPs chose Hugh Guthrie as interim leader in the House.[60] Diefenbaker returned to Prince Albert to nurse his wounds and prepare to fight another day.

The federal Conservative caucus decided that the party would choose its new leader, for the first time, in a national convention, to be held in Winnipeg in October 1927. When that meeting opened in the drafty atmosphere of the Amphitheatre Rink on October 10, John Diefenbaker was present as a Saskatchewan delegate and supporter of Guthrie's candidacy. But Bennett's advocates had made thorough preparations, and there was little doubt that their man would win the leadership. He did so easily, on the second ballot, against Guthrie and four other candidates.[61]

Bennett's acceptance speech was an oratorical triumph. It impressed the young lawyer from Prince Albert, who noted above all Bennett's words about destiny and service.

> One night long ago I had a dream – I don't believe in dreams because they usually indicate only a bad digestion – but I thought I was here in my dreams: that I had been called upon to say something to this vast audience, and I am going to say it to you now, what that something was, because it was very real. They were not the words of a human person; they were the words of the Man of Galilee: I looked it up the next day because it stayed with me. "And whomsoever of you will be the chiefest, shall be the servant of all."
>
> . . .
>
> Men and women, you have honored me beyond my deserts, beyond any deserts I ever may have, you have made me, for the moment, the chiefest among you, and please God I shall be the servant of all.[62]

This was an ingenious bit of mock humility, identifying himself at the same moment with Christ and Everyman. The image stuck with John Diefenbaker.

For the next two years the new leader devoted his abundant energies and wealth to the revival of the Conservative Party following its demoralizing defeat of 1926. Diefenbaker had not supported Bennett in 1927 "because of his close identification with the established economic interests," but he soon admitted he was mistaken in that judgment. Bennett revealed himself, in Diefenbaker's eyes, as a man of independent character and strong Methodist conscience. He quickly severed his business ties and showed that he would not accept dictation from "the self-appointed Eastern bosses of the Party." That spirit of defiance, in a western Conservative leader, provoked the young man's increasing admiration. Bennett's political instincts seemed to be Diefenbaker's own.[63]

Meanwhile, the Conservative Party of Saskatchewan was preparing itself for renewed assault on the local Liberal government and its formidable machine. The Liberal Party had held power since 1905 by careful management of its relations with the grain growers' associations, the federal Progressive Party, and the immigrant communities; now there were signs of decay in its alliances and popular resentment over the excesses of its patronage practices. And there were whiffs, as well, of an unpleasant fever in the prairie air, an epidemic of hatred that might also be turned to Conservative advantage.

In December 1926 three self-seeking commercial agents of the racist "Invisible Empire of the Knights of the Ku Klux Klan" arrived in Saskatchewan in search of profit and acclaim. They found a ready audience among elements of the English-speaking Protestant community who were uneasy about – or unreconciled to – life with large numbers of non-English-speaking and mostly Catholic neighbours. In recent years, substantial flows of European immigration had been renewed to the province. The Klan's agents, flaunting the mumbo-jumbo, paraphernalia, and exotic appeal of the American Klan, adjusted its targets and methods to local circumstances. There were a few midnight parades and cross-burnings, but no lynchings. Usually, the Klan devoted itself to public meetings denouncing the influences of the Catholic Church, the French language, and continental immigration, and the organizers pocketed the substantial takings from membership fees. In October 1927 they absconded with the funds. The self-styled Canadian head office of the Klan in Toronto dispatched a replacement to Saskatchewan in the person of another itinerant American, J.H. Hawkins, who attracted fresh converts with his carnival oratory. He was soon joined by a genuine Canadian anti-Catholic bigot, the ex-seminarian John James Maloney. A raucous series of organization meetings swept the province in late 1927 and 1928, and by the end of that year there were more than one hundred local branches of the Klan boasting executives and members from all levels of society and including a sprinkling of doctors, lawyers, clergymen, village councillors, and mayors.[64]

For the provincial Liberals, the school system was central to its policies of cultural balance and accommodation. For Anglo-Saxon nativists and anti-Catholics, in contrast, it was the sacred source of cultural purity. In 1928 the Klan focused its attentions on Protestant fears about the school system. As Martin Robin writes:

> Klansmen, throughout 1928 and 1929, pressed the education issue with an enthusiasm – and venom – seldom witnessed before in the province. When it came to education, Klansmen – like Orangemen – had their strong likes and dislikes. Dear to their patriotic hearts was the public school, free of sinister sectarian or foreign-language influences, an institution mandated to preserve Protestant Anglo-Saxon culture and to Americanize, or Canadianize, the uninvited alien who had slipped by the immigration sentries. Among Klansmen's favourite dislikes were separate Catholic schools, sectarian influences in public schools, and, in the case of Canada, subversive French-language provisions thrust on the public schools by a conniving Catholic minority.[65]

Although there were only a handful of separate schools in the province, few nuns among schoolteachers, and less than 3 percent of schools offering

French to the intermediate level, the Klan encouraged repeated protests among Protestant ratepayers in those districts.[66] In one celebrated case in the Gouverneur school district, the Klan encouraged Protestant families to withdraw their children from school over French language teaching and the presence of crucifixes in the classrooms. When truancy charges were laid, the Klan employed a leading Conservative lawyer and Orangeman, J.F. Bryant, in their defence. He argued that the school had ceased to be a public school by its practices, and the presiding justices of the peace, both members of the Klan, dismissed the charges.[67]

Premier Gardiner watched the grassfire spread of the Klan with concern and in August 1927 told Mackenzie King: "It would appear...that the main object of the organization is to spread propaganda which will be of benefit to the opponents of the Government, both Provincial and Federal, at the time of the next election."[68] King replied to him: "What you are face to face with is, I think, only the spreading to Western Canada of the influence of the Orange Order as the electioneering nucleus of the Tory Party. You cannot, I think, do a better thing than to expose as quickly and completely as possible tactics such as those which your letter describes."[69] Gardiner set about gathering materials for his file. In January 1928, when the provincial Conservative leader told the legislature that "all the forces of the province opposed to the present government" should unite to defeat it, Gardiner erupted in a bitter condemnation of the Klan.[70] The Klan's links to the Conservative Party had previously been the subject of gossip; now they were the leading issue of partisan debate. Gardiner made sure of that.

When the provincial Conservative Party held its leadership convention in Saskatoon in March 1928, the Klan's activities and the premier's denunciation promised a volatile occasion. Some delegates were members of the Klan, many were sympathetic with its intolerant aims, and most sensed that the party might ride to power in the wake of the Klan's campaign against foreigners and Catholics. Indeed, only three among the three hundred convention delegates were Roman Catholic. As delegates entered the hall, J.H. Hawkins and his aides distributed Klan pamphlets. The convention's policy resolutions coincided precisely with the Klan's views on secular public schools, the promotion of patriotism, and selective immigration – with the exception of a single resolution that made a bow towards racial tolerance but seemed intended as much to throw racist accusations back at the Gardiner government.

Whereas certain unscrupulous members of the Saskatchewan Government are making use, in remote districts of the Province, of statements made by certain Eastern Conservatives and certain irresponsible individuals reflecting on our non-English electors, and are endeavouring thereby to incite racial hatred against the Conservative party: We hereby declare that these parties do not represent the Conservative policy or the Conservative attitude towards our immigrants of non-English extraction and we deplore the use of such language by such individuals and hereby repudiate it. We stand for fair and square treatment of all our citizens irrespective of race or creed.[71]

J.F. Bryant, the party's vice president, told R.B. Bennett that "we have a splendid platform and...not a single word...used in the convention or in any resolution can in any way embarrass our Conservative friends in other parts of Canada." Even the few Catholic delegates, he insisted, approved the resolutions, although he admitted that they were "very sore in that there were none of them elected to any of the Executive offices."[72]

These Roman Catholic delegates, along with several sympathizers, warned Bennett in a thick flurry of letters after the convention that the national party would be grievously damaged by the Saskatchewan's party's links to the Klan and repudiation of Catholic support.[73] They noted above all that two Catholic delegates, J.J. Leddy and A.G. MacKinnon, had been nominated to the executive but excluded from it by manipulation, and that the party's leaders, J.T.M. Anderson and J.F. Bryant, were both promoters of the Klan if not actual members. Another leader, Dr W.D. Cowan, was an admitted member. Bennett quickly expressed his sadness, concern, and embarrassment at the behaviour of the Saskatchewan party. But Anderson and Bryant reassured him that all was well, while others counselled that the party could keep a discreet distance and still benefit from the Klan's political aid. Bryant concurred in that view in a letter to Bennett at the end of May 1928: "They are...going very strong and will be of great assistance in defeating the present Government, and I do not think that we should throw any stones at them any more than we should expect that the Liberals should throw stones at the Knights of Columbus or any other similar organization that is so strongly supporting them."[74]

Despite his show of concern, Bennett eventually recognized his limited power, took the safe line of non-interference, and counselled Catholic Conservatives in Saskatchewan to shelter behind the barricades while letting the dirt fly, since it could result in a Conservative victory. The Klan would be neither formally embraced nor repudiated.[75]

John Diefenbaker attended the Saskatoon convention as a delegate from Prince Albert and may have played a role in the removal of the name of one Catholic delegate, A.G. MacKinnon, from the official slate of nominees for the executive. According to Bryant, Diefenbaker typed the list of nominees from which MacKinnon's name mysteriously disappeared, and the secretary of the nominating committee who dictated the names to Diefenbaker insisted that the change occurred – if at all – at the typing stage.[76] Diefenbaker himself left no record of the events. But clearly, as one delegate wrote to Bennett, "it was considered inexpedient that any Catholic should hold office in the organization."[77]

As the popular tide swept with them, the Conservatives hoped for a provincial election during 1928. Gardiner held off, however, and instead tested the waters with a by-election in Arm River constituency in October. It became "the most vicious in Saskatchewan's history."[78] The issues were already in the air, and all of them put the Liberal government on the defensive: French language teaching, an improper Catholic presence in public school classrooms, and corruption in the Liberal patronage system. Bryant added an anti-Semitic tinge to the package by charging that Harry Bronfman had paid off the Liberal Party to avoid prosecution on liquor smuggling charges. The Conservative candidate in Arm River was Stewart Adrain, a Regina lawyer and Grand Master of the Saskatchewan Orange Association.[79]

Bryant dominated the Conservative campaign with his corruption charges, his accusations of a vast conspiracy to turn Saskatchewan into a French-speaking and Catholic province within ten years, and his open sympathy for the Ku Klux Klan. Party leader Anderson echoed Bryant with more restraint, while other Conservative leaders kept their distance and declined any role in the campaign. But Diefenbaker shared the stage with Bryant on several nights in late October.[80]

On the last weekend of the campaign, Diefenbaker accepted Anderson's request that he attend a Gardiner meeting in order to challenge "any statements of questionable truth."[81] When Diefenbaker repeatedly interrupted, Gardiner invited him to come to the platform to address the meeting. Diefenbaker told the audience that he wished to ask the premier "some questions in connection with education." But he began with a disclaimer: "As it appears to be the custom for speakers in this campaign to indicate their religious beliefs, I hereby state that I am a Baptist and I am not a member of the Ku Klux Klan." He then challenged the premier to state his position on "sectarian influences which we in the northern part of the province find pervading the entire education system." In Wakaw, for example, he asserted that "nuns in religious garb teach in what is a public school and the crucifix is hung on the wall." Diefenbaker spoke ominously of Gardiner's recent travels in the east. "Do you know also where he went?" Clutching and quoting from a French language newspaper, Diefenbaker told the audience: "He went into Quebec province." When Gardiner replied, he asked reporters to keep his remarks about the Wakaw case off the record for the sake of social harmony; for Diefenbaker, that became a cowardly evasion and a subject of ridicule.[82] Whatever spirit of tolerance John Diefenbaker had claimed when he defended Boutin and Ethier in 1922 had disappeared later in the decade.

On polling day in Arm River there was an extraordinary turnout of 91 percent. The Liberal Party won the by-election, but with a tiny margin of fifty-nine votes.[83] For the Conservatives, the message was that excess would be rewarded. The 1929 campaign was under way. Bryant, Diefenbaker, and others maintained their attacks on the corruption and religious bias of the Gardiner regime, and they were joined by the fresh newspaper voice of the Conservative Party, the Regina *Daily Star*. Diefenbaker told an audience in North Battleford in November: "I do not believe in bigotry. I would not like to see the Conservative Party go into power on a religious question. I do not wish to hurt the religious feelings of any, but in the face of danger it is necessary to speak frankly." It was no more fair, he suggested, for Protestant children to be forced into a school presided over by nuns and decorated with altars and crucifixes in every room than it would be to force Catholic children into a school "presided over by an Orangeman in regalia or a Klansman in a nightshirt." Yet Protestants, he claimed, were being coerced in that way.[84]

After a turbulent spring session of the legislature, the provincial election was at last called for June 6, 1929. The Liberal Party stood on its progressive record, while the Conservative and Progressive opposition emphasized the emotional issues of race, religion, language, and immigration familiar from Arm River. In a number of ridings Conservatives and Progressives made informal agreements not to nominate against each other. The Conservatives, especially, were confident that they could undermine the pluralist coalition that had sustained Liberal governments since 1905. Against this disturbing current of emotionalism the Liberal Party did little except to plead for tolerance.[85]

In Prince Albert, Diefenbaker decided at the last possible moment to seek the provincial nomination. He defeated one of his mentors, Mayor Samuel Branion, in a contested meeting at the end of April. He faced the attorney general, T.C. Davis, in the campaign, and was himself promised the attorney generalship if he and the party won the election. Diefenbaker, like his leader, Anderson, denied any anti-Catholic sentiments, but his election literature called for a vote "for the Conservative candidate, J.G. Diefenbaker, if you believe in a public school free from sectarian influences." Diefenbaker's old legal competitor from Wakaw, C.S. Davis, his opponent's brother, claimed that "Mr. Diefenbaker is hand in hand with the Ku Klux Klan, and if elected he would be directly answerable to it...it is only necessary to go into Mr. Diefenbaker's committee rooms and you will find the heads among them there." Diefenbaker did not respond to the charge.[86] In his memoirs he noted the accusation, suggested that James Gardiner had raised the Klan from obscurity by his attacks upon it and thus had made it "a recognizable centre of opposition to his government and its policies," and concluded that "everyone who opposed Gardiner, his policies, and the viciousness of his machine was tarred with the dirty brush of Klan fanaticism." This was not an admission of fellow-travelling with the Klan, but it was something less than a denial. The record made that difficult.[87] Whatever his private preferences might have been, Diefenbaker – like many other Saskatchewan Conservatives in 1929 – found himself tempted into an unspoken and unsavoury alliance by the prospect of victory. Diefenbaker succumbed.

On election day there was a major realignment of the vote, as the Conservatives had hoped. Areas with high Catholic and European immigrant populations overwhelmingly returned Liberals, while the Conservatives made gains in regions of Protestant and Anglo-Scandinavian settlement. The Liberal Party lost 6 percent of the popular vote, while the Conservative Party gained 13 percent. Gardiner lost half his seats in the legislature. Anderson won twenty-four seats to Gardiner's twenty-six, but five Progressives and six Independents held the balance of power. In Prince Albert T.C. Davis held his seat by several hundred votes against John Diefenbaker.[88] Afterwards, Davis wrote privately that Diefenbaker's "proper place would be as a third-rate vaudeville performer in a four-a-day vaudeville house."[89] For the moment, Gardiner retained power, but that was unlikely to last beyond the first meeting of the new legislature in September.

SINCE HIS ARRIVAL IN PRINCE ALBERT IN THE SUMMER OF 1924, JOHN DIEFENBAKER had become more and more immersed in politics. Despite – perhaps partly because of – the indifferent economic state of the city in the mid-1920s, his legal practice grew steadily but slowly from its foundations in Wakaw. Much of his work involved minor civil and criminal matters, "a potpourri of disputes from a very fractious society," in the words of Wilson and Wilson.[90] Diefenbaker never attracted major business clients in the city; bad debts, estates, minor thefts, assault, insurance claims, and slander were the firm's mainstays. As he had learned in Wakaw, judicious publicity was useful to a criminal lawyer. In the age before television, criminal trials offered the newspapers a steady diet of sensation, and Diefenbaker was careful to encourage press coverage of his court cases.[91]

In Wakaw, Diefenbaker maintained his office for five years after his departure, first in the hands of Alec Ehman, then Alexis Philion, and finally R.B. Godfrey, until it was closed in 1929. In Prince Albert, Frank C. Cousins joined the partnership in 1925. He died suddenly in June 1927 of a heart attack, "the victim," Diefenbaker wrote, "of an attack of delayed shell shock."[92] For the next two years Diefenbaker ran the Prince Albert practice alone, until William G. Elder joined the firm in the autumn of 1929. From early 1927 Diefenbaker shared the office with his amiable but feckless brother, Elmer, who had taught school for a few years before drifting into the insurance business. Elmer performed routine chores for John, both business and political, while John treated him indulgently as a dependent child. That relationship would continue throughout Elmer's life.[93] Since his arrival in Prince Albert in 1924 John had lived an austere bachelor's life in the Avenue Hotel; now the brothers took rooms in the Donaldson home, where they stayed for the next two years.[94]

The law firm was located prominently on Central Avenue, upstairs in the red-brick Bank d'Hochelaga building. The strikingly erect young lawyer in his three-piece suits and black homburg was soon a familiar figure on the streets of the frontier town. So were his automobiles: at first the Maxwell, then a 1927 Chrysler Sedan, then a 1929 Chrysler 75. Diefenbaker maintained the various Masonic Lodge attachments he had made in Wakaw, with the Ancient Free and Accepted Masons (Scottish Rite), the Elks, the Loyal Orange Lodge, and later the Shriners. He became a director of the Prince Albert Canadian Club, the Kinsmen, the Prince Albert City Band, and a member of many other local societies. Although law and politics had made him a public figure, and his rhetorical skills were growing remarkable, Diefenbaker remained socially awkward and never penetrated the inner circles of local power. Partly, of course – but not entirely – that was a political matter. Until 1929 he was shut out of provincial rewards and frustrated by the dominance of the Davis family in public life. Not only did T.C. Davis manage legal patronage as attorney general of the province, but he owned the Prince Albert *Herald* and used it shamelessly for the promotion of Liberal causes. In the memoirs Diefenbaker suggested, with some exaggeration, that when he began practice in Prince Albert, the newspaper refused to use his name when reporting his cases.[95]

Soon after arriving in Prince Albert, John met Emily Will, the daughter of a prominent local real estate agent, George Will. For several months they courted and friends began to assume that the couple would marry. But the courtship faded. John was still making his weekend trips to Saskatoon to stay with his parents, and there, apparently, he met Edna May Brower – perhaps through his brother, or perhaps crossing paths at the railway station. Edna's family, like John's, had homesteaded near Saskatoon, and after high school and normal school she had become a teacher, first in Rosetown and then at Mayfair school in Saskatoon. Edna had a long-term engagement with a Langham farmer and car dealer who was twenty years her senior, but by the summer of 1927 her interest was shifting to John Diefenbaker. Edna was slight, pretty, full of high spirits, outgoing, and had inherited a notable eye for fashion from her mother, Maren Brower. She enjoyed a busy social life in Saskatoon, and as her romance with the Prince Albert lawyer grew, acquaintances wondered what the attraction could be. "Whatever the reason, Edna's photograph album, which is filled with pictures of herself and her many swains – a passing parade of young men with her in buggies, on horseback, beside airplanes, and in cars – suddenly begins to show pictures of only two people, herself and John, nuzzling, snuggling, swimming, laughing, picnicking. This pictorial record did not match the impression other people had of John as a cold, introverted loner."[96]

Even in the midst of courtship, Edna's friends could not see the affectionate man that Edna saw. A teaching colleague, Molly Connell, visited John in Prince Albert with Edna in 1928 and recalled: "His eyes, they just bored right through you. They were like steel; hard eyes. There was never any tenderness or warmth about John Diefenbaker. I felt it then, but one does not say that to a good friend who may be in love with him."[97]

Edna was introduced to John's parents, realized John's dependence on his mother, and saw that Mary Diefenbaker was "a strong and rigid woman, single-minded in her possessiveness towards her son." Edna was attracted to William Diefenbaker, whom she viewed as a victim of Mary's harsh contempt. Mary could show little more than bare toleration for the young woman, "sometimes stilling the effervescence and enthusiasm that poured from John's lady friend." She extolled the brilliance of her son to Edna, and made clear that she expected always to retain John's first loyalty.[98]

Despite Mary's thinly veiled hostility, Edna and John drew closer: two opposites attracting in mysterious and not-so-mysterious ways. They were young people in love, but they engaged also in the calculations of ambition. John told Edna of his political desires, of his awkwardness in personal relations, of the pain of defeat, of his wish to be prime minister. It was, he said, "more than a goal; it is my destiny." She encouraged him, perhaps realizing this was a fate she could share.

In her heart she knew that the John Diefenbaker she knew had no hope of becoming the prime minister of Canada: She was not so blindly in love that she could not see he lacked the essential qualities for a successful public figure, except for his driving ambition and his showmanship. But she knew that she was a good teacher, and that she and her family in the West and in Toronto, and all the family's friends would help him. She had no illusions; her brothers were popular and building a name in sports circles (particularly in curling) and her oldest brother Edward was now a prominent eastern lawyer with many highly placed political and business friends.[99]

By the summer of 1928 John and Edna were close enough for John to invite Edna to join him and his family on an auto trip to California. Little record of the vacation remains, beyond a postcard from Yellowstone Park, a photograph of John, Mary, and Edna, and John's rankling memory of a traffic violation in California. Apparently William stayed behind in Saskatoon, while Elmer and his mother chaperoned the couple.[100] Soon after their return, John and Edna began planning for a wedding, and Edna gave notice that she would give up her teaching job at Christmas.

A few days after the Arm River by-election, Edna's father, Chauncey Brower, died in Victoria, where he had gone with Edna's mother and sister-in-law for comfort in the last stages of a long illness. Maren Brower took charge of the wedding arrangements and proposed that the couple should marry in Toronto from the home of Edna's prosperous brother, Edward. For Edna that was an appealing prospect. Edward gave her a gift of $5000 to buy her dress and trousseau, and in the spring of 1929 he, his wife, Mabel, Maren, and Edna took off for New York City to outfit the bride. There she indulged herself in a wedding dress by the fashionable French couturier Lucien Lelong, an extensive wardrobe, and linen, towels, sterling silver, and Crown Derby china for her new home.[101] While Edna devoted herself excitedly to preparations for the wedding, John stayed behind in Prince Albert to fight the provincial election campaign – a division of labour that suited both John's temperament and the manners of the time.

Just three weeks after his latest election defeat, John Diefenbaker and Edna Brower were married in Walmer Road Baptist Church in Toronto. A wedding announcement appeared in the Toronto papers.

The bride, who was given in marriage by her brother, Mr. E.H. Brower, was dressed in a Lelong frock of white tulle over white satin, with a tight-fitting bodice and bouffant skirt, hat of tulle to match and silver brocade shoes. She carried a shower bouquet of Ophelia roses, orchids and lilies of the valley. After the ceremony a reception was held at 34 Kilbarry Rd., the home of the bride's brother. After a buffet lunch had been served, the bride and groom left for the west via boat, the bride wearing an ensemble of Madeline blue georgette with hat, shoes and bag to match and carrying a white fox fur. Mr. and Mrs. Diefenbaker will reside in Prince Albert, Sask., where Mr. Diefenbaker is well known in political circles.[102]

Thus Diefenbaker, thrice defeated but "well known," identified himself in the social columns as a politician rather than a criminal lawyer. For him, the Toronto wedding perhaps gave promise of an entrée into the Ontario world of power and influence in which his new brother-in-law moved – a world that had always beckoned but now seemed unexpectedly closer.[103] Thanks to Edward and Mabel's hospitality, John and Edna had a small taste of that in the days before the wedding.

But above all John was in love, and the elixir worked wonders. Simma Holt describes the transformation as the wedding guests remembered it. "At the wedding reception they saw the stiff and stodgy John come out of his shell to laugh openly, even uproariously, at his bride's antics and to produce brilliant, though often cutting comments. This was not the dull man they thought they had known or the family friends at the functions had heard about in gossip about Edna's choice. He moved through the crowd, with Edna at his side, talking, joking, hugging her, praising her, seeming able to be gregarious with her. He even danced with her."[104] And before the newlyweds left on the boat, they visited Edward and Mabel's son Ted, who was bedridden in hospital and later recalled the occasion with affection.[105]

Following their Great Lakes trip, the Diefenbakers settled temporarily into the Avenue Hotel in Prince Albert while their new house was being finished. Edna was soon friendly with their fellow residents, entertaining the women with coffee and bridge games, but John found relaxation more difficult. "John just never seemed to bend or get the starch out," one of Edna's close friends remembered.[106] But he was besotted with Edna. In her company he beamed, kissed, whispered, and ignored his surroundings. Edna's niece, Sheila, who visited on weekends and holidays and was treated as a daughter, was embarrassed by this constant "smooching around": "Aunt Edna used to call Uncle John 'Donny Boy,' and this man, who was so articulate in the public arena, reverted to baby talk in private. In the evening they relaxed and were playful; he pulled her down on his knee and she would just sit there and they would neck, and hug and kiss as though they had just discovered smooching."[107]

During the day, John telephoned Edna frequently to tell her about his work or to seek her advice and comfort. At a reception for the newlyweds given by the local Conservative Party, Edna captivated the guests, who saw her instantly as a political asset for the still-dour and unsuccessful candidate. Once the couple moved into their home, a stucco bungalow with two bedrooms on 20th Street West, Edna and her mother decorated and furnished it with slightly flowery taste and great enthusiasm. As the customs of professional life dictated, Edna would be the homemaker and loyal spouse, standing in the background to sustain and encourage her husband's career with total dedication. She would be unusually close in that background, softening, reassuring, urging on, indulging his fancies and his ambitions. Edna hoped there would be children and decorated the second bedroom in yellow as a nursery. John's natural ease and generosity with Sheila suggested that he would make a good father. But there would be no children. That absence was almost certainly a factor in the strains of discord that soon entered the Diefenbaker home.[108]

JOHN DIEFENBAKER'S FIRST DEFENCE IN A MURDER TRIAL CAME IN 1927, WHEN HE appeared as junior counsel in *R. v. Bourdon*, a case involving drinking, mutual threats, and a shotgun killing. The accused offered a confused story that mixed claims of self-defence and accident during a struggle at his farmhouse. There were no witnesses and there was no solid evidence to undermine the defendant's claims. At the preliminary hearing Diefenbaker raised doubts about the competence of the police investigation, but at trial, senior counsel chose to emphasize the defendant's story instead. That was enough, in the end, to bring a jury decision of not guilty. But the successful defence did not quite fit Diefenbaker's combative style, and he never again served as a junior in a criminal trial.[109]

The Prince Albert lawyer's second involvement in a murder trial came at the appeal stage of *R. v. Olson*, late in 1928. Ernest Olson, a farm labourer who had been charged with the murder of William Robson, was defended at trial by H.E. (Bert) Keown, a political friend of Diefenbaker. Olson, who had left Robson's employment taking Robson's wife with him two years earlier, was convicted of murder and sentenced to death on the sole evidence of Mrs Robson that he had confessed the murder to her. The trial jury had rejected medical evidence that the accused was too "feeble-minded" to stand trial. Keown had appeared without any opportunity to prepare his case, and there were questions about the trial judge's impartiality. Keown gave notice of appeal and called in his associate John Diefenbaker.

At the appeal hearing, Diefenbaker accepted the original jury decision to allow Olson to stand trial. But he argued that the judge had improperly told the jury that Mrs Robson was a credible witness; Mrs Robson herself might have committed the murder and falsely accused her former lover. He asked that the conviction be quashed in favour of a new trial.

The Court of Appeal ruled that, on balance, there had been no miscarriage of justice. The conviction was sustained, but the court recommended that the medical evidence on Olson's mental capacity should be brought to the attention of the minister of justice. Diefenbaker did so, and in February 1929 the federal cabinet commuted the death sentence to life imprisonment.[110]

The young lawyer's next murder case – the first that he handled through all stages of trial himself – occurred in the late summer and early autumn of 1929. This one exemplified his courtroom style and added to his popular reputation as a defender. Nevertheless, it was anything but a model victory.

Early in August Constable L.V. Ralls of the RCMP detachment at Foam Lake, Saskatchewan, was called to investigate the death, by shooting, of a prosperous farmer, Nick Pasowesty, on his land near Sheho. Nearby Constable Ralls found one shotgun shell and one empty casing; police later found the family weapon that had fired the fatal shell. Under questioning, Nick's two sons, his third wife, Annie, and the hired help all confessed ignorance of the shooting; they had dispersed to work in several directions that morning. Further investigation revealed some conflict with a neighbour and tension between husband and wife. But suspicion soon focused on the seventeen-year-old younger son, John, a spendthrift whom Nick had recently bailed out of a car purchase and a bad debt. When a friend of John's told Ralls that John had boasted of shooting his father on the day of the killing, Ralls took the boy into custody.

After a night in the cells, John Pasowesty told Ralls he was ready to confess and, in the presence of a witness, he said he had killed his father in self-defence after Nick had fired first at him. When Ralls pointed out that only one shell had been used, John altered his confession, admitting that he had hidden in the brush and ambushed his father. He was charged with murder and quickly committed for trial. One week later, in Prince Albert jail, he changed his account again. The real story, he said, was that his mother had shot her husband and "told me that I should say that I have killed my old man because I might get out of it somehow because she would get some lawyers for me." On that basis another charge of murder was laid, against Annie Pasowesty. She consulted John's lawyer, G.T. Killam, who shifted to her defence and suggested John Diefenbaker as her son's new defence counsel.

Diefenbaker could not be present for Annie's preliminary hearing on September 6 in Sheho, but instructed his replacement that John Pasowesty should refuse to testify. Since John's evidence was the sole basis for the charge, the hearing was brief. John was called to the witness stand but refused to identify himself. Annie's lawyer asked for dismissal of the charge and, after a week's adjournment, it was dropped. Once again there was a single defendant.

The case came to trial on November 19, 1929, before Mr Justice George E. Taylor of the Court of King's Bench at Wynyard. He was, in the words of Garrett and Kevin Wilson, "a prosecution-minded martinet" who habitually intimidated defence lawyers in his courtroom.[111] Diefenbaker knew and disliked him.

The defence counsel's hope was to make the case for Annie Pasowesty's guilt and to challenge the admissibility of his client's confession on the ground that it was coerced by the police. That meant getting John's statement about his mother into evidence, preferably by her own admission or in police testimony in order to avoid calling the accused to the stand. But when Diefenbaker questioned Annie, the judge brusquely barred any reference to her arrest. Next Diefenbaker called Constable Ralls and led him firmly through the events leading to John's arrest. Despite eliciting evidence that the youth had been driven "somewhere up the road" by the police for questioning, that they had told him his boots seemed to match the prints at the murder scene, that he had been arrested without any chance to speak to his family, and that he had acted strangely – perhaps out of fear – in custody, Diefenbaker could not convince the judge that the confession was inadmissible. Mr Justice Taylor cut him short and allowed it.

Now Diefenbaker could only try to get his client's accusation into evidence and convince the jury that it might be true. Believing that the Crown would call the RCMP constable who took down the accusation, Diefenbaker had not subpoenaed him; but Crown counsel did not call him. As the prosecution's summing up began, Diefenbaker asked that the officer be called. The judge intervened. "You know how to get them; to subpoena them and bring them here."

"But the deputy attorney general was down here," Diefenbaker responded.

"Do not make any more statements about that," said the judge. "There is a legal way in which you can get witnesses, and do not start giving evidence in this case yourself."

"With all due diffidence," Diefenbaker replied, "I was told that all I had to do was to give them the names and they would arrange for subpoenas and everything."

Mr Justice Taylor rebuked Diefenbaker before the jury: He had no right to "make statements by way of evidence" or to entangle the case in cross-trails, and the failure to call the witness was his own responsibility.[112] The rebuke may have been deserved, but it was crude, and it inevitably tipped the psychological balance against the defence. Diefenbaker was now forced to call the accused in order to get John Pasowesty's story about his mother into evidence. But putting the accused on the stand was something Diefenbaker sought always to avoid.

Under oath, Pasowesty insisted that he had confessed to the murder to protect his mother. He identified his Prince Albert statement naming her as the murderer, and Diefenbaker was then able to read it into the record. But the fact that a charge had been laid against her could still not be mentioned. Perhaps most damaging to the Crown, Pasowesty recalled that his mother had spoken to him in Ukrainian in the presence of a police matron at the Prince Albert jail. When the matron had asked him what she said, he had replied: "My mother said, 'John, you say you did this, you say you did it, and I will see you get free.'"

When cross-examination began the next morning, the prosecutor carefully and politely revealed the weaknesses in the boy's story. He elicited further admissions that John Pasowesty had planned to leave home for Alberta and had recently attempted to buy poison for an uncertain purpose. On re-examination, Annie Pasowesty admitted that on the day her husband's body was discovered she had ordered ten gallons of cider and invited the neighbours to drink it. Diefenbaker wondered whether this was custom or celebration.

In his final argument to the jury, Diefenbaker insisted that the accused had no motive for murder, nothing that could weigh against "the great love of a son for his father, the respect and veneration in which we human beings hold our parents." Instead, he suggested, "Annie Pasowesty committed this crime. A schemer, a plotter, she contrived an arrangement where she could kill her husband and throw suspicion upon her son. And worse. Then she induced this boy to confess to the crime, to take that responsibility upon himself and steer all suspicion away from her." She had motives: her unhappiness in marriage, her husband's estate. "The truth in this case lies in the statements the boy gave to the police in Prince Albert, the statements he made when at last he realized he was being used."

The prosecutor, Herb Sampson, concluded instead that the son was the callous schemer who could not be believed. The judge's summing up – although it was phrased more obliquely – left the same impression of distrust: John Pasowesty was "the kind of person that he demonstrated himself to be in the witness box." The jury, the judge reminded them, was obliged to consider the facts "uninfluenced by any consideration of sympathy whatever."

Four hours after they retired, the jury returned to the courtroom to request a review of evidence about the family's movements on the morning of the killing. Since the record had not been transcribed, the judge offered to read his notes of the evidence. The jury concurred and the judge proceeded. When he was questioned about the accuracy of Diefenbaker's suggestion that the accused had not been away from the house long enough to commit the murder, the judge made a crucial suggestion: "I am satisfied that I have taken down what was said correctly as to that, but while they put it that way, ten to fifteen minutes, still I would suggest to you that was not meant for any accurate statement at all. It is just a statement that men estimate about a thing afterwards, that they have kept no track of." After further glossing of the record, the jury once again retired. An hour later they returned with a verdict of guilty. Mr Justice Taylor commented that the verdict was "the only reasonable conclusion that could have been arrived at upon the evidence," and sentenced John Pasowesty to be hanged at Prince Albert jail on February 21, 1930.

Diefenbaker's appeal, on the ground that the court should not have allowed the boy's confession into evidence, was summarily dismissed by the Court of Appeal on January 15, 1930. Now the defence was reduced to petitioning the federal cabinet for clemency – and assuring that the press was well supplied with sensational leads. Although he had not raised the issue of mental capacity at any earlier stage of the case, Diefenbaker now gained the evidence of two "alienists" or psychiatrists who judged that Pasowesty had a mental age of nine or ten years. That was enough to convince the cabinet and, after one stay of execution, the boy's sentence was commuted to life imprisonment on March 3, 1930. At the end of a harrowing ordeal, that could almost be counted a victory.[113]

While awaiting the appeal hearing in the Pasowesty case, the firm of Diefenbaker and Elder took on another murder defence without fee. The case was an equally sordid affair of family violence, *R. v. Wysochan*.[114] The murder victim was Antena Kropa; her husband Stanley was the only witness. The accused, Alex Wysochan, had attempted to run off with the victim a few weeks earlier, but they had been intercepted by the police and Antena had returned to her husband. On Christmas Day, 1929, Stanley Kropa arrived bleeding at a neighbour's home claiming that Alex Wysochan had broken into his house while drunk and brandishing a revolver, threatening to shoot him. Stanley claimed to have escaped out a window, and then to have heard four shots and his wife's anguished cry. When the police arrived, they found Antena dying with three gunshot wounds, while Wysochan lay beside her in a drunken stupor, suffering from a superficial flesh wound. As she was carried to hospital,

Antena reached out to her husband and cried, "Stanley, help me out because there is a bullet in my body."

The case seemed straightforward: Alex Wysochan was charged with murder. But the defence, too, seemed clear: if counsel could convince a jury that Wysochan was too drunk to form an intent to kill, the offence would be reduced to manslaughter and the accused man's life would be saved. Instead, Diefenbaker chose to reject the claim of drunkenness and to assert that Stanley Kropa was the murderer. This was risky, even foolhardy. It meant that Diefenbaker would have to put his client onto the witness stand to challenge Kropa's story with his own. Wysochan could not claim, as he had already told friends, that he had been too drunk to remember anything.

The trial was called for March 18 in Humboldt. For much of January and February Diefenbaker had been bedridden with a revival of his old gastric ulcer and, after the first day's hearing, the Regina *Morning Leader* commented that "Mr. Diefenbaker is recovering from a long illness and the strain of the trial is telling severely on him."[115] But he had Edna in the audience for support, primed to watch the jury's reactions as an aid to her husband.

The prosecution made a tightly woven case. Stanley Kropa told of his wife's affair and his willingness to have her return to his home. He repeated the story of Wysochan's drunken invasion and his own escape; other witnesses testified to Wysochan's heavy drinking that day; the revolver was identified as Wysochan's; police evidence showed that all four bullets had been fired at close range; and there were no identifiable fingerprints on the weapon. The prosecutor suggested that Wysochan must have fired all the shots after Kropa had dived out the window. The case rested.

Diefenbaker called Alex Wysochan, who testified through a Polish interpreter. He admitted his affair. Wysochan claimed that when he and Antena were found by the police during their attempted flight a few weeks before the murder, Stanley Kropa had taken his clothes and the revolver home with him and had kept them. Wysochan said that the affair had continued after Antena's return home. On Christmas Day Kropa had found him drinking at the Windsor Hotel and invited him home; after his arrival, Kropa had set upon him, Antena had tried to separate them, and he had heard shots. Struggle and drink had left him confused, but he knew he had not used the gun. The story complete, Diefenbaker ended with a flourish. He asked Wysochan to bare his chest and reveal his wound to the jury.

In cross-examination the prosecutor, Frank Clayton Wilson, sought to emphasize Wysochan's brazen act of wife-stealing. For a prairie jury in 1930, that would be strong evidence of general depravity and untrustworthiness.

Under questioning, Wysochan admitted that Kropa was a good man. Which one of these two was more likely to tell the truth?

Diefenbaker's concluding argument to the all-male, all-English-speaking jury came on the morning of the third day. Edna maintained her jury watch while he spoke, telegraphing messages to him by her expressions as he glanced now and then in her direction. Although strained and weak, Diefenbaker called forth his energies and riveted the attention of his audience. Alex Wysochan was a bad man, but the issue was not immorality; it was murder, and Wysochan had no motive for murder. He loved Antena Kropa. Stanley Kropa, on the other hand, had a motive. He had been wronged and he had killed in revenge. That was the only believable story.

The prosecutor rose to drown the defence in invective. Wysochan was a "dirty little coward," a "little rat," a "reptile," a drunkard who had gone to the Kropa house to kill his mistress's husband. If Kropa had shot the couple, would he have left the house through a broken window? Would his wife have appealed to him as she lay dying?

Mr Justice Bigelow, in his charge to the jury, commented carefully on the law, the evidence, and the arguments, but inclined towards the case for the prosecution. He disagreed with Diefenbaker on the question of motive. If the jury believed Stanley Kropa had told the truth, then a motive was unnecessary. Wysochan had come to kill Antena's husband, and then for some reason – impossible to discover but perhaps related to the love triangle – had turned on the wife when her husband had escaped. Kropa was only likely to leave through a window if his life was threatened. If he had used the gun, wouldn't he have done a better job on Wysochan? It seemed more likely that Wysochan had shot Antena as Stanley escaped and then attempted to kill himself. Bigelow agreed with the prosecutor that the dying woman would hardly have called for her husband's help if he had shot her. The jury, he said, could dismiss the charge if they doubted Wysochan's guilt; they could convict him of murder; or they could convict him of manslaughter if they judged him too drunk to form an intent to kill. At 4:30 pm the jury retired.

For five and a half hours they deliberated without conclusion, until the case was adjourned overnight. In the cells the guards heard Wysochan sing "Nearer My God to Thee" in Polish. Next morning, after a brief session, the jury returned with a verdict of guilty. Mr Justice Bigelow concurred in the verdict, offered no hope of clemency, and sentenced Wysochan to the gallows on June 20, 1930. Then, to John Diefenbaker's distress, the judge immediately called another case for sentencing, in which Diefenbaker represented the defendant. This was a hard day.[116]

At the appeal hearing before Chief Justice Haultain on May 26, Diefenbaker challenged the admissibility of Antena Kropa's last words as hearsay evidence and argued that the judge's charge to the jury had been unfairly biased against the accused. On June 10 Haultain upheld the conviction. The dying woman's words were admissible as "evidence more or less strong of a certain feeling or attitude of mind" that the jury had been free to weigh as it chose; and the judge's charge, while it was "on certain points...not favourable to the accused," had adequately pointed out to the jury that it was the sole judge of fact. The federal cabinet refused to grant a reprieve and, on June 20, Alex Wysochan was hanged in Prince Albert penitentiary, still protesting his innocence.[117] Whatever the truth of the case, Diefenbaker's gamble at long odds had failed. By denying the crime and seeking acquittal, he had lost the chance to argue for a reduced charge of manslaughter that might have saved his client's life. The burden of that knowledge could not have eased Diefenbaker's stomach pains. By the date of Wysochan's execution, John was away from Prince Albert, recuperating from his illness at Edward Brower's home in Toronto.

CHAPTER 3

A Provincial Life

1929-1938

Twenty-four years of Liberal dominance came to an end in Saskatchewan in September 1929. Following the provincial election, the three opposition groups agreed to join forces to form a "cooperative government" under Conservative leadership, but Premier Gardiner chose to remain in power until his government could be tested in the legislature. It was defeated at once in a vote of confidence on September 6, and three days later J.T.M. Anderson became premier of the province. At last the Liberal machine's challengers would have their revenge. Official patronage was in their hands, and the records of the previous regime were available to the Anderson ministry for scrutiny. But the government also had the energy and the reforming commitment of a new administration, and for two years it was active and ingenious. Negotiations were quickly completed to transfer jurisdiction over natural resources from Ottawa to the province; a public service commission was created to establish a merit system of appointment and promotion in the civil service, thus undermining the Conservative Party's ability to build its own machine; a royal commission examined the problems of immigration and settlement in the province; legislation was adopted to ban religious symbols, religious dress, and French language instruction in the public schools; and a program of mechanized highway construction replaced the old system of labour-intensive roadwork favoured by the Liberals.[1] The racial and religious fanaticism of the months leading to the election miraculously faded away, as the new government responded moderately to the anti-Catholic and anti-immigrant prejudices it had helped to arouse.

John Diefenbaker benefited at once by the change of government. As defeated Conservative candidate in Prince Albert, he assumed control of provincial patronage in the constituency and recommended the appointment, among others, of Mayor Samuel Branion as the local crown prosecutor. On

January 1, 1930, both Diefenbaker and Branion were named King's Counsel in the annual provincial honours list.[2]

Diefenbaker's feisty participation in the 1928 Arm River by-election had drawn the attention of Conservatives in the federal riding of Long Lake, whose boundaries contained the provincial constituency, and as a federal election approached in 1930 the local party association sought him out. After the strains of his winter murder trials, Diefenbaker continued to suffer internal bleeding, and in June 1930, on medical advice, he and Edna went east on holiday. The Conservative association reached him by telegram in Toronto, asking whether he would accept nomination; Diefenbaker replied that his illness made that impossible. For a young man of such intense political ambition, the choice forced upon him must have been painful. Long Lake offered his first real prospect of victory after three electoral defeats: Arm River had fallen easily to the Conservatives in the provincial election, and the Anderson government was still enjoying its honeymoon in power. The signs of economic decline in the country were obvious after the Wall Street crash of the previous October, and the outlook for the King government was not good. But when the general election was called for July 28, 1930, John Diefenbaker was not on the candidates' list.[3]

Instead, the Conservatives in Long Lake nominated Dr W.D. Cowan – the former, perhaps continuing, member of the Klan – who won the seat. In Prince Albert, Diefenbaker took to the platform in support of his successor candidate, George Braden. Otherwise, the Prince Albert lawyer's activity in the campaign was restricted to persuading Robert Weir to contest Melfort, with the assistance of Diefenbaker's friend David Burgess as campaign manager. Weir was also successful in R.B. Bennett's sweeping victory and became minister of agriculture in the new government. On July 28 the Conservative Party increased its vote in Saskatchewan by 36 percent, taking eight seats in a province where it had held none since 1917. Mackenzie King held onto Prince Albert with a reduced margin, but his government was finished. Nationally, Bennett found himself with a comfortable parliamentary majority of thirty-four.[4]

For Diefenbaker, the political climate was at last favourable, but his role remained a limited one. J.F. Bryant, who was now minister of public works in the Anderson cabinet, continued to harass the former government with accusations of political interference in provincial police operations. The charges were old ones, since Gardiner had transferred jurisdiction to the RCMP and wound up the force in 1928. In February 1930 Bryant offered his evidence to the legislature; the result was the appointment of a royal commission of investigation subsequently known as the Bryant Charges

Commission. Diefenbaker assisted Bryant in planning for the commission's hearings, and in August 1930 he was appointed junior counsel to the commission, along with Colonel C.E. Gregory, acting on behalf of the Conservative government. For fifty-five days of hearings that autumn, Gregory and Diefenbaker made headlines as they teased away at a parade of witnesses testifying to the blatant use of the police force to promote the Liberal cause. At least two potential witnesses disappeared, and plentiful evidence went into the record of a shabby exercise in low politics. Although T.C. Davis was shown to have used the police force to seek evidence linking the Ku Klux Klan to the Conservative Party (a subject of sensitivity that threatened to backfire on the Conservative investigators), nothing tied James G. Gardiner directly to any improprieties. Once the possibilities of political gain began to fade, the Conservative government lost interest in the inquiry and halted testimony in time for a report to the legislature in the spring of 1931.[5]

The commission recommended total fees of $30,500 for the four counsel, including $6500 for Diefenbaker – a substantial sum in 1931, which the government refused to pay. Diefenbaker and the others eventually received payment when one of them sued, but for several years the Liberal Party used the figures freely in the legislature in the hope of embarrassing the partisan from Prince Albert.[6]

On the prairies the economic boom began to weaken in the summer of 1929, well before the Wall Street crash of October 29. The price of wheat in world markets was falling, and the size of the Canadian crop was reduced by drought. For the time being, the wheat pools set an optimistic interim price for 1929 wheat of $1 per bushel and borrowed funds for advance payments to farmers. The full impact of depression came in 1930 and 1931. As world grain prices continued to drop, the pools found themselves overburdened with debts, sought emergency government support, and before long surrendered their marketing role to a makeshift federal agency. The downward spiral of drought, falling grain prices, debt, foreclosure, unemployment, tight money, and rising tariffs hit the agricultural economy with special intensity, and by mid-1931 the prairie provinces were mired in the depths of a ten-year crisis. Crop failure throughout the whole of southern Saskatchewan in 1931 led the Anderson government to create the Saskatchewan Relief Commission to coordinate the distribution of rural relief payments. Depression now distracted and preoccupied governments at all levels, as the costs of relief exploded and revenues evaporated. The provincial government, like others, found itself the confused and unwitting victim of economic catastrophe.[7] As Saskatchewan lost its livelihood, confidence in government disappeared.

Diefenbaker's legal practice had grown steadily since his arrival in Prince Albert in 1924. By 1929 he employed two lawyers and eight secretaries, and enjoyed a comfortable personal income, after expenses, of $4573. Because he had no investments beyond his local real estate, and no debts, Diefenbaker was unaffected by the stock market crash and the initial losses of the great depression. His income held up through the first six years of depression and declined only modestly to about $3500 per year in 1936, 1937, and 1938.[8] The decline was at least partially due to his political preoccupations. He took pride in claiming to be one of Saskatchewan's most prosperous lawyers, billing only those clients who could afford his fees; others he took on without charge. Yet his papers reveal that he pursued the collection of legal fees with great persistence in this period.[9] In 1933, with reduced billings and a smaller office staff, Diefenbaker wrote to his landlord requesting a rent reduction from $60 to $50 monthly, or to $40 with less space. "I have endeavoured," he explained, "to carry on during the past six months according to the strict letter of the agreement but I realize now very clearly that I cannot continue on this basis and that to do so would be ruinous to me." The Banque Canadienne Nationale refused to consider a reduction in 1933, although it did later allow Diefenbaker a $5 monthly saving.[10]

Diefenbaker's partner, William Elder, left Diefenbaker alone in practice when he departed from the firm in mid-1932. The parting was bitter; the issues, in Elder's eyes, were finances and ethics. Diefenbaker made no comment.[11] The following year Diefenbaker took on John M. Cuelenaere as an articling student when he turned up to remind Diefenbaker of a promise he had made six years earlier after a political meeting in Leask. Cuelenaere stayed on as a partner and valued associate for more than twenty years, complementing Diefenbaker's courtroom talents with his own skills in legal research. In the memoirs, Diefenbaker generously concedes that "this was one of the best things I have ever done." Cuelenaere turned out to be "a hard worker" and "an excellent counsel." He was an active Liberal who later served as mayor of Prince Albert, member of the provincial legislature, and provincial cabinet minister.[12]

The early glow of John Diefenbaker's marriage to Edna lasted into 1930 and 1931. She made a comfortable home for him, graciously hosted his dinner parties, for a time coaxed John out to weekend dances, and projected her warmth easily into the community in a way that John had never been able to accomplish. The young lawyer continued to show her off and to appreciate her as his public ornament. The couple surmounted an initial confrontation in the autumn of 1929 when Elmer arrived with John at their new home, intending – at John's invitation – to take up residence with them. Edna responded that she was moving out to her mother's home and would return only when Elmer had another place to live. After a few days Elmer left for lodgings, and John brought Edna home.[13]

The family triangle perplexed and troubled Edna. She was genuinely sorry for Elmer, slow Elmer, "poor Elmer," the ne'er-do-well who was protected, abused, and manipulated by his domineering brother. Members of the family recalled that Edna was repeatedly distressed by John's tirades against Elmer, delivered in person and on the telephone. Often, Elmer sought Edna's protection as an intermediary, reporting his mishaps to her rather than directly to John. Among other things, there were frequent car accidents. Edna would then – sometimes successfully – seek to soften her husband's anger before it descended on his hapless brother.

But her most difficult problem was always with John's mother, Mary. She treated Edna with cool and haughty reserve, and expected that John's first loyalty would always be to her rather than to his wife. This was a loyalty imposed and enforced from above, and never repudiated by the son. John talked daily with his mother by telephone – often more than once – and rushed off to Saskatoon at short notice when she sought his presence. That happened regularly, whatever previous plans John and Edna might have made. Soon Edna came to dread the last-minute cancellation of engagements following the latest phone call from Saskatoon. When John himself was committed in court, Edna would be dispatched unwillingly to her mother-in-law's aid. Sometimes John's parents arrived in Prince Albert – inconveniently and with little warning – and Edna would dutifully entertain her ungrateful visitor while John went fishing with his father. By the mid-1930s Edna reconciled herself to playing third fiddle for John: she knew that mother and politics would take precedence forever. For the sake of peace she accepted the arrangement, but she confided to friends that it was a heavy burden.[14]

In the early 1930s Diefenbaker's political ambitions were in suspense while his public life focused on his legal career. By her husband's choice, Edna was more and more involved in that life. John telephoned home several times each day, seeking advice and reassurance or relaying gossip. Edna inspected and approved John's courtroom wardrobe, tidied up and calmed his younger clients before trial, and held a watching brief on his courtroom performance and the reactions of judges and juries.[15]

In return for his unusual emotional dependence, Diefenbaker took care that Edna enjoyed solid material comfort. She dressed well, kept open charge accounts at local department stores, and always had household help. She travelled regularly to trials, political meetings, and bar conventions with her husband, and shared John's pleasure in a series of fancy automobiles – new Chryslers in 1930 and 1931, Buicks in 1934 and 1936.[16]

Nevertheless it was soon clear to Edna that John would maintain his own rhythm of life, distinct from her own. While Edna enjoyed evenings out and often could not sleep until the early hours of morning, John preferred an early bedtime, sometimes by 8 pm, and an early rise. John's routine departure from the dinner table for the bedroom left Edna with lonely hours to fill each evening. The young lawyer was active in the clubs and formal social activities that were congenial and helpful to his career in law and politics, but he frequently opted out of engagements accepted by Edna. Aside from Edna's devoted and invaluable role as his legal and political aide and his tutor in manners, the social lives of the couple were scarcely compatible. Edna was an attractive and outgoing social butterfly; John was narrowly dedicated to the pursuit of his own ambitions. But the customs of the time in small-town Saskatchewan meant that Edna could only live in John's shadow.[17]

In 1933 Diefenbaker was ready to renew his political life. Although it was obvious that the provincial Conservative Party was failing, Diefenbaker attended the annual convention in Saskatoon in October to seek election as vice president of the party. He was victorious on the third ballot, joining his legal colleague J.A.M. Patrick, who had been elected president. But the party came out of the convention demoralized and divided.[18]

By autumn 1933 the endless depression had sapped the budgets of every Saskatchewan municipality. Almost half of Prince Albert's revenue was consumed by interest on the city's debt. As relief support and debt payments grew, civic services languished. In November, when it appeared that the Prince Albert mayoralty would be filled by acclamation, Diefenbaker put himself forward at the last moment on a populist platform of interest reduction and an appeal for federal public works. The public responded enthusiastically, but the civic establishment, business, the *Daily Herald*, and the Liberal Party raised the alarm of debt cancellation. After one hectic week of campaigning, Diefenbaker came within forty-eight votes of victory in a record poll, 1068 to 1020. His post-election statement hinted ominously at major civic improprieties:

> The determination with which the financial magnates of the city fought my candidature yesterday is convincing evidence that they were fearful and alarmed at the prospect of the investigation into city finances which would have been made had I been elected mayor.
>
> But even as a private citizen it is not my intention to give up the fight. I

shall make every effort during the next few months to ascertain the entire and exact financial set-up of the city and the connection with and participation therein of certain people and interests in this city.[19]

As he soon revealed when he sought information from the city council on all transactions in civic debentures since 1919, Diefenbaker suspected that the unnamed "financial magnates" were undermining Prince Albert's financial condition in order to buy existing civic debentures at discounted prices. When the council made available its records, they showed few debenture purchases, none of them by anyone connected with the city. Diefenbaker gave up on the subject, but cultivated his suspicions.[20] He was inclined to fight elections in a mood of righteous grievance, a mood which, in defeat, could slide over into bitter charges of conspiracy. Diefenbaker was drawn compulsively to the flame of politics, and it had already burned his soul.

Early in the new year, the Conservative Party in Prince Albert nominated Samuel Branion as its candidate for the forthcoming provincial election. Branion then resigned as the local crown prosecutor and was succeeded in the position by John Diefenbaker. That was a curious role for "Prince Albert's pre-eminent defence counsel" to accept; perhaps, as the Wilsons conclude, "Diefenbaker had...obviously decided that the modest fee tariff of the attorney general's department was more attractive than the generally unpaid glamour of the defence."[21]

The prospects of his Conservative patrons did not, in any case, show much promise for the long term. The government had lost a by-election decisively to the Liberals in Kinistino in 1933, and the Conservative Party was now openly divided between moderate supporters of the Anderson government and a "true blue" right wing. The depression doomed governments everywhere. Jimmy Gardiner's Liberals were well prepared for a contest, but they patiently prolonged the agonies by avoiding votes in the legislature that might defeat the coalition. The government held on grimly to the end of its five-year term and went to the polls on June 19, 1934.

As vice president of the provincial party, Diefenbaker campaigned loyally in what was clearly a desperate cause. The party lacked money, spirit, organization, and program. It fought a three-way campaign against the Liberals and the new Farmer-Labour Party (soon to become the Cooperative Commonwealth Federation), and was undermined from both right and left. The former party president and true blue Tory, Dr D.S. Johnstone, campaigned for the Liberals, and former coalition allies defected wholesale to Farmer-Labour. On election day the government found itself without a single seat. Gardiner took fifty seats and Farmer-Labour, five. Six days later Diefenbaker resigned as crown prosecutor in Prince Albert, and a month later James Gardiner resumed office as premier of the province. T.C. Davis of Prince Albert was once again attorney general. The Conservatives returned to the provincial wilderness, with a federal election still to come.[22]

Diefenbaker's regard for R.B. Bennett was sustained by Bennett's record in office after 1930. It was not just that Bennett was a winning Conservative leader: so, too, was J.T.M. Anderson, but Diefenbaker never showed great admiration for him. For one thing, Diefenbaker's focus was on Ottawa rather than Regina. For another, Diefenbaker saw Bennett as a politician on the grand scale and an object of emulation: independent, dignified, dominant, brusque, defiant, harsh, and unsociable, yet, behind the mask, loyal, generous, and sentimental. More than any other politician, the prime minister in the wing collar became his model.

In his willingness to finance the Conservative Party after 1927, Bennett showed that he would not be managed, in Diefenbaker's words, by "the self-appointed Eastern bosses of the Party."[23] Once the Conservative Party had come to power, Diefenbaker admired Bennett's dramatic – if unsystematic – lunges against the forces of the depression and his willingness, eventually, to use the power of the state without the restraints of dogma. Bennett's ministry, Diefenbaker later wrote, "was not a government that sat on its hands."[24] Diefenbaker praised the Farmers' Creditors Arrangement Act of 1934 for saving "tens of thousands of farmers from bankruptcy and ruin," and took satisfaction in the thought that "this was not a measure to which the banking and mortgage institutions were particularly favourable."[25] Yet he also recalled approvingly that the Bennett cabinet had come quietly to the aid of the Royal Bank and Sun Life, thus saving "a wholesale crash of corporations."[26] Diefenbaker had no coherent economic framework of his own against which to judge Bennett's erratic policies. It was their political – or perhaps even their theatrical – impact that interested him. Bennett was certainly theatrical.

Diefenbaker's memory of R.B. Bennett went back to the turn of the century at Tiefengrund: "I first saw Bennett as a boy when he came to my father's school. The living quarters were attached to part of the school building. In the election of 1904 he was Richard Bonfire Bennett. He had a reputation for speaking two hundred and twenty words a minute. I think the audience did not exceed sixteen, but he spoke for hours."[27] After Bennett had become prime minister, he showed unfailing courtesy towards the young acolyte from Prince Albert. When Diefenbaker visited Ottawa he was welcomed in the prime minister's office; and more than thirty years later Diefenbaker had vivid recollections of those visits. What stuck notably in his memory were the moments of partisan point-scoring. For example:

> I was here in Ottawa the morning in 1933 when the revelations came out concerning King having had his expenses paid – $4,500 – by Beauharnois Company in the Caribbean, or in the Bahamas. I came to see him about 8.30 in the morning. Bennett was in his office. He said, "Frightful! Frightful exhibition here this morning! Young man, frightful!"
>
> "What happened?"
>
> He said, "That weasely King came in crying. He said, 'Please, Mr. Bennett, call off your dogs. They're destroying me. Don't press this.' And I said, 'King, go and weep no more.'"[28]

Bennett, in his generosity, called off the assault. "And then a year and a half later when Chubby Power and the others brought out the fact that Bennett wore shoes that cost $25 and had a suite in the Chateau that cost so much, they smeared him all up. King rubbed his hands in unholy glee."[29]

In 1934 Bennett's minister of trade and commerce, H.H. Stevens, became chairman of the muckraking Royal Commission on Price Spreads. Stevens's purpose was to apply his Methodist conscience to the exposure of price gouging and harsh labour practices in the retail trade of the big department stores. The commission's public hearings through late summer and autumn were a righteous sideshow that proved highly embarrassing for Eaton's and Simpsons, and brought Stevens into conflict with Bennett and other members of the cabinet, especially C.H. Cahan. In October, Stevens resigned from cabinet and commission – not so much, it soon became clear, because he disagreed with Bennett over policy, but because Bennett saw in him a challenge to his own dominance. Diefenbaker watched the inquiry in admiration and urged Bennett to make peace with his outspoken minister. Bennett would not do so.[30]

Diefenbaker could not claim presence at the birth of Bennett's New Deal, but he wrote that Bennett told him, during a visit to Ottawa in the summer of 1934, that "something has to be done. These conditions cannot be permitted. I have tried, but no one seems to have an overall plan." Six months later, said Diefenbaker, "when every traditional method of government had been exhausted to meet the depression, and time had provided no respite, he shocked the great interests in Eastern Canada with legislation that could never have been expected from one of their own."[31]

Bennett proclaimed his New Deal in a series of six radio broadcasts in January 1935. The speeches were a dramatic last effort to save the failing administration, prepared by Bennett's brother-in-law and minister in Washington, W.D. Herridge. Bennett proposed a program of economic reform modelled on the American National Industrial Recovery Act and the preliminary recommendations of the price spreads inquiry, designed, like Roosevelt's New Deal, to remedy abuses in the capitalist system rather than to destroy it. There would be a national trade and industry commission to suppress unfair business practices; a national employment and social insurance commission; regulation of wages and hours of work; an advisory economic council; heavier capital gains taxes; and extended low-cost farm credits. Bennett's rhetoric echoed the populism of his discarded minister, Stevens, in its attacks on the avarice of big business.[32]

Although the need for radical responses to the economic disaster was more and more widely admitted, Bennett's own cabinet received the proposals with as much surprise as the public. Mackenzie King greeted Bennett's initiative coolly and made no effort to outbid him. Although there was widespread popular scepticism about the prime minister's death-bed conversion to economic reform, Diefenbaker professed new hope in a letter to his friend Robert Weir, the minister of agriculture.

> You will be pleased to know that Mr. Bennett's speeches are being enthusiastically received in this Province. I have spoken with large numbers of farmers during the past few days and their attitude (almost without exception) has been one of unstinting praise.
>
> A Liberal today paid our leader a real compliment – "Mr. Bennett has not been a timeserver" he said. The Party has been broken and discouraged since the June debacle in Saskatchewan and needed a tonic – the radio speeches have provided just that, and have given our rank and file something to enthuse over – a new hope and a new spirit.
>
> I have often spoken to you about the fact that in my opinion the Conservative Party appeared to live in the past. If there was any substance in that view it now no longer holds true.[33]

In Saskatchewan, the province most devastated by drought and depression, Bennett's measures may have received widespread approval. But that did not necessarily translate into votes for a discredited government. Although the party had perhaps received "a tonic," Diefenbaker concluded realistically that "the reaction of the electorate is evident, but in my opinion the election should be held off to the very latest possible date."[34]

It was already too late for the Bennett government to recover lost ground; instead, it displayed signs of terminal confusion. For three months after his new deal speeches, Bennett was ill and did not appear in the House of Commons, while talk swirled on the back benches about a change of leadership. One faction favoured Stevens, but Bennett and others opposed him for his ambition. Bennett was said to prefer the return of Arthur Meighen if illness forced his own retirement. The conflict seemed irreconcilable, and by June 1935 party leaders were pleading with Bennett to remain as leader whatever his health.[35] Stevens drifted closer to a definitive break with the party.

Throughout the Western world, 1935 was a time of political as well as economic desperation. In Britain the breadlines were long; in Germany the Nazi party was consolidating its domestic power by brutal use of the mailed fist; in Spain the Second Republic was lurching towards disaster. The times gave birth to wild dreams and demagogues. Next door in Alberta, William Aberhart had launched Social Credit from the radio microphones of the Prophetic Bible Institute; and across the border in the United States Father Coughlan preached a similar, confused message of hatred, revenge, and hope. In Washington, Senator Huey Long of Louisiana was beginning to mount a populist challenge to President Roosevelt. Diefenbaker was fascinated, and in January, soon after Bennett's radio speeches, he wrote to the senator.

> As a Canadian admirer of yours and of the great fight you are putting up for the under dog, I take the advantage of every opportunity offered to hear you over the air.
>
> I recall a very striking speech made by you in one of the Western States in the Fall of 1932 during the fight waged by you against the then President in his campaign for re-election – your attitude with regard to wealth inheritance and distribution impressed me greatly, and was far in advance of political thought at the time.
>
> Today public opinion is demanding the carrying out of your ideas regarding wealth, and this applies not only in the United States but also in Canada.
>
> The other evening I listened to your broad-cast over the Columbia network. Your subject-matter was striking in its breadth of vision and persuasiveness, and I am writing you to ask that you favor me with a copy of that speech if you have any available for distribution.
>
> With every good wish for your success in your campaign to make the lot of the unprivileged a better and a happier one, I am,
>
> Yours respectfully,
>
> John G. Diefenbaker[36]

There is no record of a reply. Diefenbaker continued to ruminate on such populist-radical ideas, and in March he was gathering materials for a speech to be entitled "Capitalism Controlled."[37]

The face of Canada was transformed by the depression. Thousands of the unemployed, young men and old, traversed the country on freight trains in search of jobs. The Bennett government established a system of relief camps for single men, offering bed, board, and manual labour without wages. These spartan conditions stimulated a relief camp union, organized with communist influence, which sought minimal pay for the inmates of the camps. At the end of May 1935, in the face of Ottawa's indifference, the Vancouver branch of the union announced an "On-to-Ottawa" journey, and on June 3–4 about one thousand men took to the freight cars for the journey east. Initially the CPR cooperated, and the demonstration gathered public support as it moved eastwards. Crowds gathered in sympathy at railway stations, and in Calgary, Swift Current, and Moose Jaw local governments welcomed and fed the destitute travellers, now numbering two to three thousand. The policy of the Gardiner government was to assist the trekkers on their way, but when the trains arrived in Regina the railway company stopped further trespassing and the RCMP, under federal orders, halted the cavalcade. At that point, in Gardiner's view, Ottawa had assumed responsibility for public order, and thus was also responsible for feeding the men. Tense days passed while federal and provincial ministers met the protest leaders, and a delegation travelled to Ottawa to meet Prime Minister Bennett. But Bennett rejected their demands, and Ottawa gave directions for dispersal of the men through a temporary internment camp in Lumsden, Saskatchewan. The strike leaders agreed to disperse, but on their own terms. On July 1, in the course of urgent negotiation, police and trekkers clashed violently in Regina's market square, resulting in one police death and many injuries. Following the violence, the province reasserted its supervision over public order, and Gardiner and Davis arranged for special trains to take the men out of the province. Gardiner was convinced that Bennett, with support from the CPR, intended to picture the march on Ottawa as a communist-inspired insurrection, and then to put it down in a Liberal province for political gain. If that was the federal government's intention, it turned out to be misguided. The events deepened political division in the country and did nothing for the reputation of the Conservative regime.[38]

Bennett finally dissolved parliament on August 15 and called a general election for October 14, 1935. Diefenbaker was directly affected in two ways by the dying government's last dispersal of patronage. In August the provincial party president, J.A.M. Patrick, was appointed to a district court judgeship, leaving Diefenbaker as acting president of the party; and in September he was appointed Prince Albert lawyer for the Canadian Farm Labour Board.[39] Two months earlier, on July 22, Diefenbaker had declined federal nomination for the party in Prince Albert. The prospects were hopeless, and this was obviously no time for another futile battle. Diefenbaker told the nominating meeting: "I think this is a time for us to have a farmer as a candidate. A farmer might unite us and then we could get some place." He was half right: the meeting nominated a farmer.[40]

As party president, Diefenbaker was obliged to show the flag in the campaign, no matter how bleak the prospects. He did so for Bennett's appearances in the province during the campaign in September.

> It was in this capacity that I chaired a public meeting for Bennett shortly after the 1 July 1935 riots in Regina when the Communist-led Ottawa trek was broken up. It was as big a meeting as any hall in Regina could accommodate. To the left of the platform was a large group of those who had taken part in the riots: noisy, vociferous, offensive, and profane. There had been threats that the Prime Minister would be shot. The Regina Conservative Association took those threats seriously; the rostrum had been turned into a bullet-proof shield which came up to my shoulders. Mr. Bennett was sitting directly behind me in the cover of the rostrum. During my opening remarks I turned to him and he wasn't there; he had taken his big chair out in front. His courage calmed the audience. The speakers preceding him had a fairly rough time. Mr. Bennett just sat there. When he got up to speak, he was cheered. Courage, Barrie said, is the greatest attribute of all. That is, next to integrity. Bennett had both.[41]

Across the prairie border in Alberta, Aberhart and his Social Credit evangelists swept into provincial power on August 22 with fifty-six of sixty-three seats, wiping out the United Farmers government as Gardiner had decimated the Saskatchewan Conservatives in 1934. In the enthusiasm of victory, the new party's agents were soon nominating for the federal election throughout the prairies, or proposing alliances with the CCF against the parties of finance capital. Eventually all four parties in Saskatchewan refused alliances, but the public was left in unusual confusion. The disorder was compounded when Stevens proclaimed his own Reconstruction Party at the end of August, campaigning on a reform platform that hit many chords of prairie protest. In Saskatchewan Stevens managed to make only three nominations, but the break with Bennett further undermined Conservative morale. Gardiner devoted his usual close attentions to the Liberal cause as the campaign progressed. The only real uncertainty concerned the extent of Conservative devastation and the division of the spoils among so many contenders.[42]

On October 14 Mackenzie King's Liberals won a landslide victory, with 173 seats to the Tories' forty. Social Credit elected seventeen members, the CCF seven, and Reconstruction only one. In Saskatchewan the Liberals took sixteen seats, Social Credit and the CCF two each, and the Conservatives one. Mackenzie King once again won Prince Albert with ease, while the Conservative candidate ran third behind Social Credit. The Conservative popular vote in Saskatchewan slid by almost half to 19 percent, just behind the CCF and just ahead of Social Credit. Diefenbaker's chosen vehicle to Ottawa had again been shunted to the sidelines.[43]

Jimmy Gardiner's ambitions, like those of John Diefenbaker, always reached beyond Saskatchewan. The election of 1935 gave him his opportunity, and two weeks after the Liberal victory he was sworn into the new King cabinet as minister of agriculture.[44] He held that portfolio for twenty-two years, as prairie baron of the federal party, until the Liberal government's defeat in 1957. At the end of October, W.J. Patterson succeeded Gardiner as premier of Saskatchewan.

Bennett returned to the House of Commons as leader of the opposition, with a dispirited and divided party behind him. For two years he maintained his position while discord mounted – some of it, inevitably, in public. Finally Bennett faced a private meeting of national party delegates in March 1938 and announced his resignation as leader, to take effect after a leadership convention in July. Diefenbaker attended the March meeting and was impressed by Bennett's bitter leavetaking. In his papers Diefenbaker preserved a copy of that speech and later extracted from it Bennett's concluding words: "Every time you publicly criticise anyone in your Party you do a great harm to your Party and every time you publicly criticise the leader of your Party you add fuel to the fires of opposition that must always burn against him...I ask you – why assist the enemy? Surely my successor will receive better treatment than did I...As for me, my task is done...Give to my successor loyalty. By loyalty I mean loyalty – true loyalty, not loyalty that will destroy."[45]

Diefenbaker and his friend Jack Anderson spent the evening of Bennett's resignation with the leader in his parliamentary office. It was apparently a boozy session – for Bennett at least – as telegrams of regret and praise began to come in. Diefenbaker recalled that one wire read: "History will give you a large place. Deeply regret your resignation. Suggest the Conservative Party will now need a leader and that you get behind George Drew. He's going places."

Bennett fumed and dictated a reply: "Thank you. Stop. Do not intend to get behind George Drew. Conservative Party and Drew not going same places."[46]

The same evening, after learning that Diefenbaker had been married for almost nine years, Bennett apologized for not sending him a wedding present. On his return to Prince Albert, Diefenbaker found that Bennett had transferred a gift of $2500 into his trust account.[47] Ten months later, when Bennett left Canada to live in England, Diefenbaker wired Bennett as he boarded the SS *Montcalm* in Saint John, New Brunswick: "I wish to extend to you sincere good wishes coupled with expression of the hope that you may be long spared to serve the Empire."[48]

JOHN DIEFENBAKER'S REPUTATION AS A DEFENCE COUNSEL BROUGHT HIM FOUR more murder cases from 1930 to 1936. In October 1930 Diefenbaker and Bill Elder opposed crown attorney Samuel Branion in defence of Nadia Bajer of Wakaw on a charge of murdering her newborn daughter by suffocation a few weeks earlier. Bajer was a penniless mother of two young children who had been abandoned three years before by her husband. She lived in the village as an occasional house-cleaner and laundress, and in 1930 found herself pregnant by one of her customers. The man urged her to abort the child, and left her when she refused. In early September the local RCMP detachment received a report that, although Bajer was no longer pregnant, there was no baby in the house. When Corporal DesRosiers investigated, Bajer said that she had given birth, but that the baby had fallen to the floor and died. She had buried the body in the garden in a shoebox.

The child's body was exhumed and examined by the coroner and a second doctor, who found a bruise on its head and a small piece of cotton cloth in its mouth. Bajer told the police corporal that she had used the cloth to stop the baby's crying, "as I did not want anyone to know that I had had a baby." Both doctors concluded that the child had died by suffocation, and Nadia Bajer was charged with murder.

The trial opened before a crowded Prince Albert courtroom on October 9, 1930. Diefenbaker and Elder raised reasonable doubts over the crown's medical testimony about the probable cause of death, and in defence brought four witnesses to the stand. The first, A.E. Danby, was a former Prince Albert chief of police who was then Wakaw's justice of the peace. He had conducted the preliminary inquiry, and testified that the body showed none of the signs usual in cases of suffocation or strangulation. The revered director of the Wakaw hospital, Dr Robert G. Scott, who was also a political opponent of Diefenbaker, testified to the same effect. Two more doctors confirmed his judgment.

By late afternoon, with the courtroom audience now overflowing from the building, Diefenbaker rose for his summation of the case for the defence. As the accused woman sobbed uncontrollably in the background, Diefenbaker described her painful life, her courage in rejecting an abortion, her fear of ostracism in the tiny town. This was a case to tug the heartstrings, and Diefenbaker knew it.

She had the courage to refuse, the courage to admit her sin, the courage to confess her wrong. Would such a woman then take the cowardly course of murdering her own child and covering up the crime?

This is not a case of trying to cover up murder, but of a woman trying to hide her shame. Yes, Nadia Bajer buried a body. Early in the morning she laid her child away, but not a child taken by her hands.

Scientific medical evidence has shown that the prosecution has not proven that the child died because of a rag in its mouth, a rag placed there to stop the child from crying. Nadia Bajer's child died from natural causes.[49]

Bajer's crying alone broke the silence of the courtroom as Diefenbaker resumed his seat.

Samuel Branion offered a brief and subdued closing for the prosecution, and the trial judge, Mr Justice H.Y. MacDonald, asked the jury to rule on three questions: Had the child been murdered? Had Nadia Bajer borne a baby? And had she concealed its birth? The jury took only fifteen minutes to reach its verdict. Nadia Bajer was not guilty of murder, but guilty of concealing a birth. Diefenbaker and Branion agreed that the accused had suffered enough, and MacDonald imposed a suspended sentence. The distraught woman was free. Diefenbaker and his partner accepted the praises of the crowd. "It was doubly satisfying," wrote the Wilsons, "to have won at home in Prince Albert. The glory lasted for weeks down on Central Avenue."[50]

In September 1933 Diefenbaker defended nineteen-year-old Steve Bohun on a charge of murdering Peter Pommereul, a general store keeper and postmaster in the village of Redberry, near North Battleford. Faced by the police with strong evidence of his complicity, Bohun had confessed to shooting and robbing Pommereul of $324 in postal funds. The cash, which was found in his possession, gave him a stake to elope with his pregnant girlfriend, Annie Barchuk. Motive, footprints, murder weapon, and confession all pointed to Bohun's guilt. But when his parents visited him in jail, Steve Bohun claimed that the RCMP had beaten him into a false confession. Diefenbaker entered a plea of not guilty when the case opened in the Court of King's

Bench in North Battleford before Chief Justice J.T. Brown.

Almost at once, the jury was excluded for forty hours while Brown heard argument on whether to allow evidence of Bohun's confession and his other admissions of guilt. Eventually the judge admitted the statements. When the jury returned, the prosecution called Constable Arthur Cookson, the investigating detective. In all the formality of the courtroom, before robed and high-collared judge and counsel, Cookson appeared equally impressive in his RCMP dress uniform of redcoat, breeches, high boots, and spurs. But as he faced cross-examination from the formidable John Diefenbaker, he recalled that "I was anything but the serene and confident Mountie I appeared to be...It was his eyes, most of all."[51]

The police officer knew that the original defence lawyer had taken possession of one of Bohun's shirts, bloodied by a self-inflicted nosebleed after the young man had retracted his confession. Cookson dreaded Diefenbaker's use of that evidence to suggest police intimidation. The defence counsel, after a calculatedly slow opening, moved towards Cookson.

> Arriving at the witness box, Diefenbaker rested his right arm on its railing, and, now only a couple of feet from Cookson, fixed him with a piercing glare.
>
> "Do you understand the nature of an oath?" he demanded loudly. It was one of his standard opening gambits, almost certain to unnerve any witness.
>
> And then it began. For an hour and a half, John Diefenbaker paced slowly up and down before Arthur Cookson, penned in the witness box, probing, attacking, pleading, criticizing and confusing, trying to create the impression that Steve Bohun had been manhandled and threatened from the moment of his arrest.
>
> "His eyes were steely, his lips somehow became firm, and his jaw jutted out at me. He was very fierce and intimidating. And all the while I was waiting for that damn shirt to jump out at me," Cookson remembers.[52]

Diefenbaker pressed his questions about police intimidation of the suspect. "Using a technique he had learned in this very courtroom from a Winnipeg lawyer who beat him in a contested divorce case, John Diefenbaker stood facing the rapt spectators. With his back to Cookson, he continued to throw questions at him, increasing his psychological mastery of the situation."[53]

Diefenbaker took Cookson through the details of his first, night-time encounter with Bohun, ending with a visit to the Pommereul store. "And there," Diefenbaker suggested, "you showed him the blood stains still upon the floor, the blood of the dead Peter Pommereul, didn't you?" Cookson agreed that he had done so.

"And then, Constable Cookson, then you tried to force this young boy to put his hands upon those blood stains. What do you say to that?" Diefenbaker whirled and pointed a long finger and arm at the investigator.

"I did no such thing." The policeman was vehement in denial and he rose from his seat in indignation.

But the accusation itself left a vestige of doubt. Of course, the police would deny any such action. But there was an intriguing element to the suggestion. Might it have happened? It was a very clever ploy by the defence lawyer.[54]

There was no mention of the bloodied shirt.[55] Cookson finished his examination under strain, but with his essential story undamaged. Diefenbaker put the other police witnesses through the same daunting tests, and then asked the judge once again to consider ruling Bohun's statements out of court. This time Chief Justice Brown accepted Diefenbaker's request. Just one of the defendant's statements remained in evidence: His assertion that "I didn't shoot the old man," made at the moment of his arrest but before Cookson had told him of any killing. Sample plaster casts of Bohun's footprints were also excluded on the ground that they, too, might have been obtained by coercion.

The last witness for the prosecution was a doctor who had treated Bohun for a head injury seven years earlier. He conceded in cross-examination that Bohun had probably suffered "a serious and permanent impairment of his mental processes" as a result of the accident.

Diefenbaker's only witness for the defence was Dr S.R. Laycock, a prominent educational psychologist from the University of Saskatchewan. He had tested Steve Bohun, and said that Bohun was "high-grade feeble minded." He doubted that the accused could understand "the nature and quality of the act which he was alleged to have committed."

In his summing up, Diefenbaker made a double claim for the defendant. There was reasonable doubt that he had committed the crime, but if the jury decided he had done it, the professional evidence pointed to insanity. "Mentally crippled as a boy, distraught over the pregnancy of his young love, in his mind abandoned by his father, Steve Bohun could not appreciate the action he took, in the legal sense. Neither did he really know it was wrong," Diefenbaker concluded.

The prosecutor, R.B. Mills, made his own careful review of the evidence, suggesting that it pointed beyond reasonable doubt to the accused. On the issue of insanity, he insisted that the defence had provided insufficient evidence to accept such a claim. The judge agreed that the jury could not properly find Bohun not guilty by reason of insanity.

The jury retired at 7 pm on a Saturday evening and returned only three hours later with a verdict of guilty, adding "a strong recommendation to mercy on account of his age and inferior mentality." One week later Steve Bohun was sentenced to hang in Prince Albert jail on February 23, 1934. The chief justice noted that the recommendation for mercy would be drawn to the attention of the minister of justice.[56]

As in the Pasowesty case five years earlier, John Diefenbaker inexplicably waited until after a conviction before seeking adequate psychiatric assessment of his client. Now he arranged for examination of Bohun by two physicians and another specialist in intelligence testing. The doctors reported that Bohun had "low mentality" or "feeble mentality" and could not distinguish right from wrong. The educational psychologist placed his mental age at nine years, and said that "he had no conception whatever that he is under sentence of death...and...cannot in his own mind associate any connection between the crime for which he was convicted and the punishment he is to receive."[57]

When Ottawa refused clemency on the jury's recommendation for mercy, Diefenbaker went to court on February 22, 1934, to seek a stay of execution so that the minister of justice could examine the new evidence of mental incapacity. The court granted a two-week stay until March 9. Within a few days, petitions from two hundred residents of Prince Albert also arrived in Ottawa pleading for mercy.[58]

Early in March the superintendent of the Homewood Sanatorium in Guelph, Ontario, the psychiatrist Dr Harvey Clare, examined Bohun, acting, apparently, on behalf of the minister of justice. On March 7 John Diefenbaker was informed that the cabinet would not halt the execution, and on March 9 at 6 am the Canadian hangman, Arthur Ellis, pulled the trap in Prince Albert jail. Bohun showed no emotion as he went to the gallows.[59]

Seventeen months later a violent murder occurred in John Cuelenaere's home town of Leask, fifty miles from Prince Albert. The victim was Ernest Fouquette, a sixty-two-year-old farmer whose badly beaten body was found in a downtown alley after a normally raucous Saturday night in the farming community. One year before, Fouquette's wife, Annie, had separated from him and moved into town with the couple's nine children. Diefenbaker had acted for Annie in a successful lawsuit for family support, but Fouquette had refused payment. When the court seized Fouquette's goods and arranged to auction them to enforce payment, Fouquette's friends rallied to him. They arrived at the sale towing a dead and tarred steer, and warned that successful bidders would win a free ride. The auction sale collapsed. Subsequently, Fouquette's farm was vandalized, and the tense affair remained unsettled until his murder. Now it had become a prairie gothic horror story.

The RCMP conducted an exhaustive investigation, which placed Annie Fouquette, her son Napoleon, Annie's two brothers, and her brother-in-law in Leask that evening. All of them claimed to have left town before the killing, and no evidence emerged to connect them with the crime. In frustration, the RCMP decided to conduct a fishing expedition at the inquest, in the hope that something incriminating might slip out in testimony under oath. For a full week in November 1935, forty-two witnesses were called before the coroner and jury in the Leask Legion Hall. What emerged was a great confusion of memory loss and contradiction among members of the family, but no direct evidence about the crime. Two witnesses claimed they had heard Ernest Fouquette and his son Napoleon talking in the lane just before the murder, but no one had seen them.

Finally, Annie Fouquette's brother-in-law, Nick Grovu, told the coroner that he had something to add to his testimony. He paused nervously on the stand, but eventually claimed that his wife was providing a false alibi for Napoleon Fouquette. Anne Grovu shouted a denial, and the Legion Hall erupted in disorder. The coroner wrestled the hearing to a close and sent out the jury. It returned with the expected verdict of "murder by a person or persons unknown," and general suspicions of perjury.

The coroner requested that the police arrest Annie Fouquette, Anne Grovu, and one of their brothers on charges of perjury. Although the RCMP suspected Annie Fouquette of the crime, they lacked any evidence to justify a charge against her. Instead, in a further attempt to force the issue, they charged her son Napoleon with murder. Annie Fouquette called in her lawyer, John Diefenbaker, for the defence.[60]

On November 26, 1935, the preliminary hearing opened to another packed house in the Leask Legion Hall. It too lasted five days. The *Star-Phoenix* noted dryly that "reports indicate the village was as busy as on sports days."[61]

Knowing the crown had a dubious case against his client, Diefenbaker gambled that he could expose enough weaknesses in the evidence to have the charges thrown out before trial. As the prosecution introduced its witnesses, Diefenbaker toyed mischievously with them in cross-examination, to the delight of the audience and the annoyance of the crown attorney. Tony Verrault, who claimed to have heard father and son in heated discussion just before the murder, admitted under relentless questioning that he had once proposed marriage to a Fouquette daughter, "but had not been very serious." He had not volunteered his evidence to the RCMP at the beginning because, he said, he was afraid of "Mrs. Fouquette and her relations." Nick Grovu, whose accusation had probably precipitated the charge against Napoleon, testified uneasily that he had left for Saskatoon after the inquest, "to be away from my wife's relatives." Diefenbaker soon had him tied up in knots.

Despite the defence lawyer's unusual efforts to prevent an indictment, the magistrate committed Napoleon Fouquette to trial for murder and commended the police for a fair investigation in the face of "a solid wall of opposition in their efforts to solve this mystery." The wall of silence held. When the case came up for trial in Prince Albert in February 1936, the crown still lacked sufficient evidence and argued for an adjournment until April. In that event, Diefenbaker called for the release of his client on bail. The judge set over the case as requested and granted bail of $20,000 – an amount far beyond the capacity of the destitute family. When the trial opened again on April 28, the police had no more evidence to offer. The crown attorney conceded defeat and entered a stay of proceedings. Napoleon Fouquette went free, the case remained unsolved, and John Diefenbaker had a victory by default.[62]

Meanwhile Diefenbaker – his sensational courtroom skills now widely renowned – was involved in another front-page murder trial. This one involved a cast drawn from the depression's refugees who had wandered north to Lake Athabasca seeking a livelihood in the bush. Winter darkness, isolation, and loneliness added to the normal burdens of poverty in these empty lands. John Harms, an American from Colorado, had been in the area since 1932, running a trapline out of cabins at Spring Point and Scorched Dog Island. He often carried a Smith & Wesson .38 Special in a shoulder holster. In the summer of 1935 a young Albertan, John Anthony, who had left his family in the dustbowl while he searched for income in the north, made a partnership agreement with Harms and joined him at Spring Point. Within a few months the pair were quarrelling over their take, and in November, while drinking homebrew beer in Harms's cabin, they argued and fought. In the course of a struggle Harms drew his gun, fired once, and Anthony fell dead. What followed, Harms claimed, was lost in an alcoholic fog. After a drunken encounter with a frightened woman neighbour who saw the corpse and escaped, Harms retreated to his Scorched Dog Island hut by dogsled and awaited the arrival of the RCMP. Nine days after the killing, an RCMP officer from Fort Chipewyan, Alberta, flew in with a Canadian Airways bush pilot and arrested Harms. He surrendered willingly, signed a statement, and was flown to

Goldfields on Lake Athabasca, where he was charged with murder. There, in the bar-room of the Goldfields Hotel, a preliminary hearing sent John Harms for trial at the Court of King's Bench in Prince Albert.

When he reached Prince Albert jail, Harms sought out the celebrated defence counsel John Diefenbaker. Diefenbaker could see that acquittal was unlikely: There were no other suspects, and Harms had told his story of the argument and shooting to the arresting officer. But the conviction might be reduced to manslaughter if the defence could demonstrate provocation or drunkenness. Diefenbaker decided to call no witnesses and to present no evidence for the defence; instead, he would rely on his skills in cross-examination and rhetoric to convince the jury that John Harms had not intended to kill John Anthony.

The trial took place before Mr Justice H.V. Bigelow and a six-man jury on February 4, 1936, providing melodramatic copy for the local press. "The court heard...of an orgy in Athabasca homebrew that left its victim crazed, and of the suspicion engendered in the lonely cabin, that suddenly blazed into hatred and spent itself in a single puff of revolver smoke as the drink-mad Harms faced his partner in a last man-to-man struggle for mastery."[63]

The crown called nine witnesses. Diefenbaker, in a mood of relaxation or carelessness, allowed all the technical evidence and Harms's statement to go into the record without challenge. He cross-examined only the police officer, Sergeant Vernon, who had made the arrest, and the woman, Micky Lindgreen, who had confronted Harms on the day of the murder. Lindgreen conceded that Harms had a bad temper and was easily provoked when drinking. She testified to his drinking that day; and after the killing, she agreed, he had behaved for an instant "in a very wild manner" towards her and her child and had frightened her. But Lindgreen's responses to Diefenbaker's questions were careful and laconic. With Sergeant Vernon, Diefenbaker concentrated on Harms's precise words at the time of his arrest. Vernon insisted that Harms had not said that he had been drinking heavily before the crime; only that "he had got pretty drunk afterwards and he doesn't remember a thing. His mind is a blank."

"As to what took place at the time of the shooting," Diefenbaker asked, "he made the statement, 'I don't know what I did'?"

"No, he didn't say," Vernon replied. "I remember asking if he aimed and how many shots he fired, and he said only one shot. And with regard to aiming, he said, 'I don't know what I did.'"

Diefenbaker could squeeze nothing more from the witness, and by mid-afternoon the case had reached final arguments. In his closing address, the defence counsel offered his reconstruction of the incident to the jury. Harms had been drinking heavily, had acted in self-defence under provocation, and had not been able to appreciate his act when he shot John Anthony. The statement made by the accused to Sergeant Vernon was the only evidence before the jury of what had happened, and that, Diefenbaker claimed, supported his argument. He called for a verdict of manslaughter.

In his brief summing up, Mr Justice Bigelow threw doubt on most of Diefenbaker's argument without offering clear guidance to the jury. He pointed out that Harms was a partial witness in his own defence, whose statement could be accepted or rejected in whole or in part. Claims that he had killed in self-defence or under provocation had to be judged according to ordinary standards of reasonableness, and drunkenness was irrelevant to such claims. But drunkenness might be taken into account in considering whether Harms was able to form an intention to kill, and thus could possibly justify a reduced conviction for manslaughter. At this point in his charge to the jury, Bigelow noticed that the dinner hour had come and he suddenly concluded. He neglected any effort to review the evidence, asked the jury to consider a verdict, and adjourned the court until the following morning. The jury returned at ten o'clock the next day with a verdict of guilty. Mr Justice Bigelow immediately imposed the death sentence.[64]

Harms had been able to pay his lawyer only $35 as a retainer to take his case and he remained without funds. Nevertheless, Diefenbaker filed notice of appeal, at the same time requesting appointment by the court as counsel for the defence, which would provide him with transcripts of the trial and a small fee for services of $75. The Court of Appeal obliged.

The appeal was heard in Regina on April 6 and 7, 1935, with Chief Justice Haultain presiding. By now, thanks to the work of John Cuelenaere, Diefenbaker was meticulously prepared to challenge the propriety of Mr Justice Bigelow's charge to the jury. He presented several grounds of appeal, essentially claiming that Bigelow had failed to explain the defence's case fairly to the jury. The court was sympathetic – although Diefenbaker was discomfited by a remark of Chief Justice Haultain: "In Milwaukee," he commented, "people drink sixty or seventy bottles of beer a day." On April 20, just eighteen days before the date of execution, the Court of Appeal found Bigelow's charge to the jury unacceptable and ordered a new trial.[65]

The trial took place in early June before Mr Justice H.Y. MacDonald. John Diefenbaker was accompanied at the defence bench by John Cuelenaere, and this time all parties made patient efforts to explain the legal complexities of the case to the jury. The hearing took two days rather than one. Again,

Diefenbaker called no witnesses, but he emphasized in much greater detail the evidence of Harms's intoxication. The judge, too, reviewed the evidence and the law with care. The jury took less than two hours to return a verdict of manslaughter with a recommendation for mercy, and "a haggard but obviously grateful John Harms gazed adoringly upon his defence counsel, John Diefenbaker."[66] Harms, now saved from hanging, was sentenced to a penitentiary term of fifteen years.

AFTER THE ELECTORAL DEFEATS OF 1934 AND 1935, THE SASKATCHEWAN Conservative Party was orphaned and impoverished, existing as scarcely more than a paper organization. Its active membership had been reduced to a handful of lawyers scattered across the province and a few hundred volunteers who might be rallied reluctantly for the next campaign. J.T.M. Anderson remained as lame duck leader of the provincial party, but he was prepared to resign at any time. John Diefenbaker, as acting president, held the loose strings of the party in his hands; he alone enjoyed sufficient income to devote time to the party's affairs. Once Anderson was gone, the leadership seemed there for the taking. It was puzzling why anyone would want it.

By the spring of 1936 the local remnants of the party began to call for a leadership convention, without any signs of enthusiasm for the obvious candidate. We do not know how much Diefenbaker coveted the leadership; for months he neither rejected nor asserted his candidacy. His silence suggested either genuine indecision or a cautious desire to avoid another humiliating rebuff. A press report in May suggested that he was "making a strong bid for provincial leadership of the party," although there were few overt signs of it. Diefenbaker told his correspondents vaguely that he knew nothing about the leadership except that the choice would occur at a convention sometime in the autumn.[67] As late as October 2 he wrote to his friend Dinny Hanbidge that "I have not, nor do I now seek that leadership, nor have I at any time intimated to anyone that I was a candidate for the leadership, and my own impression is that the item that appeared in the Press some months ago...was put there by someone desirous of doing me harm."[68] How that could do him harm if he did not in fact seek the leadership remains obscure. The remark may have hinted inadvertently at his real intention. In the meantime, Diefenbaker used two devices of delay. He called on the constituency parties to begin a utopian effort to create "completely new organizations" before the still-unscheduled provincial convention. The call to that leadership convention would have to come from the party president himself. Perhaps judging that the easiest way to avoid premature pressure for the call would be to make himself scarce,

Diefenbaker decided to travel. He would join the "Vimy Pilgrimage" in July 1936 to attend the dedication of the great Canadian war memorial in France. He had had an exhausting few years in the courtroom and on the hustings, and could certainly justify a holiday. So on July 13 he sailed for Europe on the SS *Montcalm* from Montreal, leaving Edna behind in Prince Albert. He remained away until the end of August.

John Diefenbaker was not a reflective writer and he left little on the record about this journey. It began with the unveiling of the memorial at Vimy Ridge on July 26, continued with four days in England, then six days in France under official French government patronage, and ended with a private trip lasting one week to the Olympic Games in Berlin. Diefenbaker had a friendly contact in Berlin, and after three days on his own he was given tickets to the Olympic stadium and discussed Hitler's regime with his host. But there is no documentary evidence of Diefenbaker's firsthand reactions to Nazi Germany.[69] In a speech in 1937 he referred with distaste to his experience of Nazi propaganda. And in 1940 he wrote to an acquaintance with a touch of hyperbole that "no foreigner without an official position could have had a better opportunity of seeing the Nazi system in operation, and I concluded, during my trip, that Hitler was determined to destroy the liberty of the individual of his Nation and of the entire world." In a brief correspondence with his Berlin friend after the games, Diefenbaker exchanged postage stamps, tourist pamphlets, and an Olympic Games publication, without any reflections on politics.[70]

Back in Prince Albert in early September, Diefenbaker continued to hedge about the date of a leadership convention, but by the end of the month he had called it for October 28 in Regina. Various candidates for the leadership were being canvassed, but no one had come forward with any enthusiasm and there was no sign of a draft. Hanbidge wrote to Diefenbaker on September 25 suggesting that there was support in the south both for Diefenbaker and for M.A. MacPherson. The party was still divided between the "true blues," who had abandoned Anderson's cooperative government, and the loyalists. "The position of the leadership in the Province," Hanbidge admitted, "is a mighty difficult one...and one of our big problems will be to try to choose a man as leader who can bring all these more or less combative groups into a harmonious organization, fighting together for one cause."[71]

Diefenbaker, in response, wrote on October 2 that he could support either Anderson or MacPherson as leader, but knew that neither one would accept. In a show of humility that neatly echoed Hanbidge's desire for unity, he offered himself for the job. "I have been asked over and over again whether I will let my name stand at the Convention, and I have decided to do so providing that there is a substantial request from Conservatives in the Province that I do so. I would sooner stay at my profession as I know what a sacrifice it will be on my part, but I am prepared to take a try at it if, and only if the Party would unite behind me."[72] One week before the convention, Diefenbaker set out, belatedly, to solicit that "substantial request" for his own nomination. He wrote to friends in a number of constituencies urging them to attend the convention, to encourage others to come, and to give him their support if they could. He asked his legal colleague H.E. Keown of Melfort to nominate him, but Keown declined.[73]

More than five hundred delegates gathered in the Regina city hall on October 28. As acting president of the party, John Diefenbaker took the chair. J.T.M. Anderson offered his formal resignation as leader, and Diefenbaker rose to invite nominations for vice president of the party. A delegate asked why, if the president was in the chair, the meeting needed to name a vice president. Diefenbaker – still playing coy – would not say that he would be forced to vacate the chair in order to accept nomination, but instead remained silent and embarrassed for a few awkward moments. Then a discerning delegate stepped forward as substitute chairman, and the meeting proceeded.

One after another the nominations for leader came forward; one after another they were declined: Anderson, MacMillan, MacPherson, Perley. Then came Diefenbaker, who did not decline. Then there were more: Craig, Weir, Hanbidge, Keown, Sallows, Lynd, Turnbull. All declined; only Diefenbaker remained. He stepped up and said that he would accept the nomination: "If you think I can lead this party to victory, I'll lead the party. If you think I'm not the man, then I'll get behind the man you choose, and give him my whole-hearted support." There was no one else. Diefenbaker promised a platform that would honour the party's traditions but would be radical enough to meet the unusual needs of the day, "radical in the sense that the reform program of the Honourable R.B. Bennett was radical."

The Regina *Leader Post* said: "He carries his forty years lightly, is darkly slim and erect, and thunders forth his convictions and ideas in resonant tones of purposeful youth." The Conservative Regina *Daily Star* called him "one of Saskatchewan's most able young criminal lawyers. He has figured in some exceptionally remarkable court cases and his powers of speech are well known." The Saskatoon *Star-Phoenix* noted that "there has been little doubt these last few months as to who would get the bid to lead the Conservative forces in Saskatchewan," but warned that he had inherited a party "little inclined to follow any single lead...There seems to be another division in the party as well. This one is over matters of change in policy. There is a general feeling that the party must shift its ground considerably to the left of traditional Conservatism. The question which will bother the convention and the leader is: How far to the left?"[74]

No one, with the possible exception of Edna, believed that Diefenbaker could make much of the moribund provincial party. She told a reporter: "His heart is in his work. He will try even harder now that he has been chosen leader. I know he will be happy at it...I am happy, of course I am. His happiness is mine too...He will succeed, I know it."[75]

Diefenbaker could expect about eighteen months to prepare for the next provincial election in 1938. During that time he would have to reunite the party, attract enough funds to finance a campaign, seek out candidates, and decide how to confront the new and burgeoning forces of the CCF and Social Credit. These were complex and not altogether distinct problems. In the absence of a staff or a leadership team, they fell almost exclusively into Diefenbaker's hands, and he dealt with them out of his Prince Albert law office. This dictate of necessity probably suited his own taste as well: He had never before managed an organization or delegated authority, and his habits as a courtroom lawyer inclined him to keep all the strings in his own hands. As leader, he never let them go. His only active companion in the discouraging struggle was Keown, who had succeeded him as president of the party. Diefenbaker's partner Jack Cuelenaere took over most of the office's legal business.

The key to solving the party's dilemmas, Diefenbaker believed, was cash. Money would permit the hiring of regional organizers, the nomination of candidates, and the conduct of a campaign. Since the province's residents were insolvent, that cash would have to come from elsewhere – from the national party organization and its fundraisers in Ottawa, Toronto, and Montreal. Diefenbaker set out, by letter, telephone, personal visits, and approaches through intermediaries, to solicit funds for the Saskatchewan party. R.B. Bennett was a friend and potential ally, but he was handicapped by his own declining authority in the defeated national party. When Bennett expressed his intention to remain as party leader in August 1937, Bennett's and Diefenbaker's mutual friend Jack Anderson wrote to congratulate him and to plead that the national party should now come to the aid of the provincial party.[76] Simultaneously Diefenbaker set out for Ottawa, via the Canadian bar convention in Toronto, "to see whether something can be done." But as he left Saskatchewan, one of the party's chief Ontario fundraisers, J. Earl Lawson, MP, told Keown: "If there was anything in the world I could do to assist Mr. Diefenbaker I should be only too anxious to do so. It is impossible for me, however, at this time to suggest any way in which you could secure funds."[77]

Aside from Bennett's unexpected personal gift of $2500 to Diefenbaker in March 1938 – which may or may not have been intended for partisan uses – the national party contributed nothing to the provincial party until after the 1938 Saskatchewan election.[78]

Diefenbaker persisted in his lonely task, criss-crossing the province to encourage local Conservative nominations well before an election call. By the spring of 1938, on paper, he seemed to have about forty candidates ready to share his martyrdom. But when Premier Patterson called the election for early June 1938, the party's bank accounts were still empty. "One by one," Diefenbaker recalled, "my candidates drifted away. They had lived through the drought, and the vast majority of them did not have enough money to pay their deposits, let alone to fight an election. With a personal loan from the bank I covered the election deposits of twenty-two of our candidates."[79] In a legislature of fifty-two members, this meant that Diefenbaker could not hope to form a government even if he won all his seats.

The Conservative campaign was submerged and virtually invisible. Three parties dominated the contest: the governing Liberals, the CCF, and Social Credit. Only the Liberals nominated a full slate. Social Credit came closest to that, with forty-one candidates, and the CCF named thirty-one. The Liberal Party could count on the assistance of its pervasive provincial organization and generous federal patronage under the guidance of Jimmy Gardiner. Since 1934 the CCF, with five seats, had formed the official opposition. Its prospects grew as the depression continued, and its organizations blossomed in rural districts throughout the province. Perhaps out of insecurity, perhaps out of a sense that the Conservatives were a waning force, the party offered confusing signs that it would cooperate with Conservatives in saw-off nominations in some constituencies. Diefenbaker recoiled from such links, but could not prevent the nomination of three "Unity" candidates who stood with local support from both CCF and Conservative associations.[80]

For Diefenbaker, the most annoying competition came from Social Credit, because it upstaged his campaign, gave the Liberal incumbents a handy focus, and assured that corporate funding from the east would flow to the Liberals rather than the Conservatives. Although the Aberhart government in Alberta had already lost momentum, it made an aggressive thrust into the Saskatchewan campaign. The party barely existed outside a few local associations; decisions and management came from Alberta. Aberhart's deputy in religion and politics, Ernest Manning, was made chief organizer in Saskatchewan, and candidates were chosen by the executive of the Western Canada Social Credit League, which was established in Edmonton a few weeks before polling day. Aberhart himself made an imperial progress through Saskatchewan, addressing one mass meeting after another about the crimes of finance capital and creating enough uncertainty to allow the Liberal Party to campaign as though it faced only a single challenger.[81] In a year when international aggression was in the headlines, Aberhart's peaceful invasion was alarmingly compared with Japanese, German, and Italian conquests in Manchuria, Austria, and Ethiopia. "Upon the result of this election," Liberals intoned, "will depend whether or not Canada is to continue as a united British nation."[82]

In this four-party turmoil, the Conservative Party's modestly progressive program was lost. Diefenbaker, like the CCF, criticized the Liberal government for its failure to deal with the weight of farm debt, but insisted that a Conservative government would not spend beyond its means. The party program called for refinancing of the provincial debt, "equitable adjustment" of farm debts, a study of crop insurance or guaranteed acreage payments, and a commitment in principle to public health insurance. Diefenbaker was attacked from the right by some Tory true blues, but was generally ignored in the din of overheated rhetoric. As usual, he complained about the Liberal machine. In his own riding of Arm River, he said, "Government inspectors...are so thick they have been ordered to wear a distinctive ribbon in their lapels so they will not go around asking each other for their vote."[83]

The outcome was devastating, though predictable. The Patterson government was returned with thirty-eight seats; the CCF elected ten members; Social Credit and Unity each won two seats; and the Conservatives failed across the board. In Arm River, John Diefenbaker lost a two-way contest against the incumbent Liberal. The Conservative popular vote fell to 12 percent, less than half that of 1934. Social Credit proved to be a thirty-day wonder, and the CCF emerged as the clear alternative to the provincial Liberal Party.[84]

The leader's bitter reaction combined complaint with self-justification. He wrote a few days after the election to a Winnipeg friend:

I have never passed through difficulties the like of which I experienced during the four months preceding the election. Without funds it was impossible to get candidates in the field...

In the latter days of the campaign Social Credit did the Party much harm. Almost all Eastern Financial concerns instructed their employees to vote Liberal in order to withstand Social Credit, and while much is made of the fact of the falling away of about 50% of the vote as compared with the 1934 election figures, the comparisons are not fair because in that year the co-operative party (Conservatives, Independent, etc.) received 114,000 votes with every seat contested. In the last Provincial election the vote received was only 50% of this total with only twenty-three seats contested, and the situation was, therefore, that in twenty-seven seats Conservatives had to cast their votes for C.C.F., Social Credit or Independent candidates. As a matter of fact the vote cast for Conservative candidates in this election was greater than the number cast for Conservative candidates in the last Federal election. So much for the past.[85]

Diefenbaker complained to E.E. Perley of Liberal vote-buying and Conservative miserliness, and warned of his own disenchantment.

Eastern Canada certainly let me down badly...Relief was distributed in a way that was never equalled in this Province. I know of instance after instance where distribution of seed oats and wheat was made a day or two before the election in excess of the allotments allowed, and in some cases after the recipient had completed his seeding. Bribery by relief and direct was practised on every hand, and the only salvation for the Conservative Party is to start in organizing now.

If Eastern Canada will not give us assistance, then I do not know how the Conservative Party in this Province can ever hope to get any where. If, on the other hand, they give us assistance, I will continue to do my part in building up the organization.[86]

The provincial party, in its disarray, did not blame John Diefenbaker for the loss. From its perspective, his performance had been an act of valiant self-sacrifice. Despite the defeat, he was reinforcing a small provincial network of loyalists who expected to fight again at his side. One of them, the Saskatoon lawyer John Hnatyshyn, a candidate in Touchwood constituency, wrote to say: "I only wish to reaffirm my admiration and confidence in you as leader. I will always be proud to be a member of the party and hope that I can be of some assistance to you in the future."[87] At a post-election meeting in Moose Jaw in October, Diefenbaker's resignation as party leader was unanimously refused. He was the only leader they had. In 1939 he was still paying off provincial electoral debts from his own pocket.[88]

CHAPTER 4

Seats of the Mighty

1940-1945

JOHN AND EDNA SHARED THE DISAPPOINTMENT OF THE SASKATCHEWAN election, his fifth personal defeat. Despite all the signs that the cause was lost before the campaign began, Diefenbaker had thrown himself into it without reserve. Edna had been at his side as he toured the province, offering advice and comfort, tirelessly gracing his presence with her engaging smile and her capacity for friendship. They were both demoralized. But if John Diefenbaker suffered the public loss, his position also allowed him to compensate for disappointment in ways unavailable to his wife. As provincial leader he was inexorably bound up in the party's national activities. That meant he had both a potential scapegoat for local failure and an arena for continuing activity. The burden of defeat could be lessened and some dignity restored by blaming the eastern party establishment for its indifference and by stoically holding onto his presence in the national organization. By 1938 he was too much a politician simply to drop out and make his career as a criminal lawyer.

At first the thought certainly passed through his mind. He wrote later: "What I wanted to do was gradually and responsibly to relinquish my political obligations, and to devote the rest of my life to the practice of law."[1] Alvin Hamilton, who acted as Diefenbaker's organizer in northern Saskatchewan for the disastrous campaign, recalled: "Up until the 1938 defeat John was determined to go on. But this one was the hardest yet, and he made up his mind to drop it and just concentrate on the law."[2] The law office did indeed offer an immediate refuge, but so did the political timetable. Diefenbaker did not have to rush into any decisive acts of renunciation that he might later regret. "Gradually and responsibly" stepping back could as easily mean waiting for the next opportunity while the wounds gradually healed.

For Edna, there was no public activity to absorb her energy or comfort her distress. Sometime after the strenuous campaign had ended, she began to show worrying symptoms of stress.[3] To relieve the strain of the couple's incompatible night-time routines, Edna had moved into the spare bedroom in 1937 or 1938. Now her insomnia was growing worse, and her physician, Dr Humphreys, recommended "a small glass of beer at bedtime." When that seemed inadequate, he prescribed the mild sedative phenobarbitol. Edna's niece Sheila Brower believed that she took the pills reluctantly and often too late, which meant that she was frequently drowsy or confused in the mornings, or when John returned for lunch. Her maid Florence Pelletier encouraged Edna to get out and walk, but she refused. Her lethargy and inactivity increased. She knew, at thirty-nine, that she would not have children, and she knew too that she was the prisoner of her husband's political addiction. The 1938 campaign had sharpened her distaste for the abrasion, hypocrisy, and cruelty of politics, yet she could think of no other life beyond the one she shared with John. In these months his own pain meant that he was unusually brusque and testy with her. Relief for both of them, in the form of totally distracting activity, would only come when John plunged into his next campaign.[4]

Almost immediately after the Saskatchewan election, on July 5–7, the national Conservative Party held its leadership convention in Ottawa. Diefenbaker complained vigorously about the failure of eastern financial support for the Saskatchewan campaign and hinted that he and others might boycott the leadership convention in protest. At the same time he sought reservations at the Château Laurier for the convention period, and applied pressure from several directions when a room was denied him.[5] The hints of boycott prompted a quick and appeasing response from John R. MacNicol, MP, joint chairman of the forthcoming meeting. MacNicol congratulated Diefenbaker on his "splendid effort" in the provincial campaign, insisted that his presence in Ottawa would be important, and offered to send a cheque for $125 to cover his rail fare and expenses.[6]

At the same time Diefenbaker urged Murdoch MacPherson to attend the convention so that MacPherson might be nominated for the leadership. Diefenbaker told others that he had "received so many requests to attend that I have decided to do so providing my health will permit." In mid-June he asked for, and received, complimentary railway passes to Ottawa for himself and Edna from a supporter in Regina. On June 27 he wired MacNicol to say that he could not accept the offer of party funds, but when MacNicol replied that the money had already been sent by cable, he relented and two days later acknowledged its receipt. Diefenbaker did not report that he had already received free rail passage, and must have regarded the cash as slight but deserved recompense for his personal spending in the provincial campaign.

As provincial leader he was an ex officio convention delegate, but when invited to represent Lake Centre (or Arm River) he replied that he would do so. There may have been fleeting thoughts of withdrawal, but Diefenbaker was not yet closing any doors.[7]

In Ottawa he was shown the ritual honours of a provincial party leader, and his resentments softened. But the Saskatchewan chief played no part in the manoeuvres preceding the selection of a new national leader. The leading candidate was Dr Robert Manion, an Irish Roman Catholic of pleasing disposition from Fort William, Ontario, and a former minister in the Bennett administration. Manion had the support of most Quebec delegates to the convention and seemed to offer the prospect of Conservative revival in Quebec in alliance with the Union Nationale government of Premier Maurice Duplessis. But Manion was opposed by the influential president of the CPR, Sir Edward Beatty, because he had persistently rejected Beatty's campaign for amalgamation of the two national railways. In the weeks before the convention various alternative candidates were promoted in Toronto and Montreal, but Manion remained the favourite.

The 1938 convention was, by later standards, a loosely organized affair to which many delegates came uncommitted. MacPherson's stirring speech in acceptance of his nomination made him an instant challenger to Manion. Suddenly the other three candidates – Ontario's Joe Harris, J. Earl Lawson, and Denton Massey – saw their support drain away as the dark horse from the prairies became the choice of the eastern party establishment. But Manion's support held, and on the second ballot he was elected leader by a margin of less than two hundred votes over MacPherson.[8] Although Diefenbaker had supported MacPherson, he was satisfied with the choice of Manion and he came home encouraged.

By the spring of 1939 Diefenbaker was discreetly preparing the ground for a federal nomination in Lake Centre, while continuing to hold the lame duck position of provincial leader. He was concerned to avoid public rebuff and embarrassment, and wanted the nomination only if it was a sure thing. He would need assurances of adequate financing for a campaign and promises that no local candidates would challenge his nomination. Arthur Kendall, the national organizer for Saskatchewan, assured him in May that unusual efforts were under way to clear his path to the nomination. Once the date for a nominating convention was set, Kendall said, "I have made sure that you will receive many invitations to become the candidate...Several key men will take care of the build up." What was more, Kendall wrote that secret efforts were under way to arrange for withdrawal of the CCF candidate, Ross Fansher, from the race. If that "saw off" could be achieved, "everyone agreed that you could win hands down in a straight fight." Kendall advised Diefenbaker, in the meantime, to make no public commitments.[9]

The local executive set a convention date for mid-June in the village of Imperial and wrote formally to ask whether Diefenbaker would allow his name to go into nomination. Diefenbaker took Kendall's advice and replied non-committally on June 6: "This letter came to hand only today, and I am giving the question every consideration, and will let you know in a few days." Writing the same day to his adviser Jack Anderson, Diefenbaker displayed his calculated indecision. He had "not definitely decided yet," and was "very much in doubt as to what I should do." He thought he should go no further than saying "I will accept nomination provided that no local candidate is in the field." His health required an early visit to the Mayo Clinic – and that, he implied, might rule out his candidacy altogether. On the other hand, he asked Anderson whether he could obtain promises of national financial support for his candidacy "before the Convention."[10] He was hedging, he was overtly reluctant – but he was inviting nomination on the right terms. He wanted a unanimous convention and the appearance of a draft.

After some last-minute juggling of court dates with his partner Jack Cuelenaere, Diefenbaker cleared his calendar to attend the nominating convention and, on June 15, he drove down from Prince Albert to Imperial with Edna. Diefenbaker's name was the first in nomination, followed by six others, including three from Regina and that of the local president, W.B. Kelly. Diefenbaker spoke first: "I stated that, in my opinion, they should have a local candidate. I stated that if it had not been for the number of excellent local candidates whose names had been placed in nomination, I would have welcomed the opportunity to stand as their candidate. My mover and seconder accepted my disclaimer," and Diefenbaker formally withdrew.[11] A small fire interrupted proceedings, but balloting then went ahead without his name on the list. In what appears to have been an elaborate and prearranged charade, W.B. Kelly was victorious, but immediately withdrew in favour of Diefenbaker, who had left the hall and was sitting in his car with Edna while engaged in conversation with another delegate. Diefenbaker was called back – with apparent surprise – to hear the convention join in unanimous support for his nomination. "So there I was," he would recall with a smile, "caught right by the ears."[12]

In the memoirs Diefenbaker writes that he returned to the car, and Edna, in silence. When he finally confessed that he had been nominated, "We decided that I had somehow to get out of it." Diefenbaker says that he telephoned Kelly the next day to withdraw, but was told – and agreed – that he could only do so at the next meeting of the constituency executive in February 1940. This was an unlikely part of the larger charade: it may have been the means of dealing with Edna's opposition. If he really did intend to withdraw, and if Kelly knew it, the local association would not have delayed a fresh nomination for eight months. The national office had been urging a series of early nominations. The next day Diefenbaker commenced intensive efforts, by telephone, letters, and meetings, to organize his constituency campaign in every town, village, and hamlet in the riding. He never stopped, until the declaration of war in September put a temporary halt to all partisan political activity. On July 4 he wrote to Anderson that "I had my medical examination and the doctor reports on a very distinct improvement in my condition, and no necessity of an operation at this time. The blood report was exceptionally good, and I am, therefore, all ready to get started." With the nomination in his pocket, Diefenbaker revealed himself as anything but a reluctant candidate.[13]

Beyond his intensive work over the summer to build a campaign organization in Lake Centre, Diefenbaker faced two tactical issues, one national and one local. R.B. Bennett's brother-in-law, W.D. Herridge, had left the Conservative Party after Bennett's resignation to join with the editor of the Ottawa *Citizen*, Charles Bowman, in forming the New Democracy Party – a heterodox splinter on the centre-right of a confused political spectrum. Herridge claimed that it would adopt and build upon Bennett's New Deal policies to offer a radical alternative to the Liberals, and he sought Diefenbaker's allegiance. Diefenbaker met Herridge in 1938 and again after his own nomination in 1939, each time rejecting the invitation on the practical ground that breakaway third parties never succeeded in Canada. But Herridge persisted. He gained the national support of Social Credit, whose candidates ran under the name of New Democracy in 1940, and Herridge himself ran in Kindersley, Saskatchewan.[14]

Meanwhile, discussions continued in Ottawa and Regina about the CCF candidate in Lake Centre. "I have some encouragement...that there is a possibility of the CCF candidate being withdrawn," E.E. Perley wrote to Diefenbaker on June 23, "and I want to advise you to be very careful in the first few speeches you make not to attack Fansher personally or go after him too strong...Keep this in the strictest confidence and await developments." On July 20 Arthur Kendall reported that Fansher was unlikely to withdraw, but offered no serious threat because he had "neither organization, nor finances, nor hopes of securing them...I honestly believe you can win this Seat in a three cornered fight." By that time Diefenbaker had decided not only that the party should avoid any arrangements with the CCF, but that "the chances are better for our candidates in this Province when there are three or four opposing candidates in the field." That was a dictate of realism in Lake Centre, where he expected five contestants.[15]

In late August, as the European situation moved towards war, John and Edna made a ten-day trip to Ottawa – where Diefenbaker met Robert Manion and John Robb, the party's dominion organizer – and then on to Quebec City, where they holidayed briefly. Diefenbaker returned to Prince Albert expressing confidence in the party's prospects, but all expectations were suspended with the German invasion of Poland and the outbreak of war in early September. Faced with that calamity, Canadian politicians temporarily put their partisan ambitions aside. In Ottawa there was press speculation about a coalition government, while the Conservative Party postponed its election planning and closed its national offices. The moratorium was both an expression of national solidarity and a political necessity, since party fundraising dried up with the declaration of war.[16] Mackenzie King promised another session of parliament before an election, and the country settled uneasily into an autumn of phoney war and partial mobilization. Manion, in his delicate effort to build party strength in both English-speaking Canada and Quebec, gave his party's support to the King government in its declaration of war and its commitment not to conscript Canadians for overseas service. But his electoral hopes in Quebec were shattered when Premier Duplessis unexpectedly dissolved the legislature for an October campaign directed against the centralizing effects of a federal Liberal war effort. King's Liberal ministers from Quebec campaigned for Duplessis's defeat on patriotic grounds, and the Conservative Party found itself voiceless. Faced with his own pro-British party outside Quebec, Manion could not possibly endorse the nationalist and isolationist premier. Duplessis was overwhelmingly defeated by the Quebec Liberal Party under Adélard Godbout.[17]

Duplessis's opportunist misstep – and a defiant challenge from Premier Hepburn of Ontario, who had joined with the provincial Conservatives to denounce the weakness of Ottawa's war effort – now tempted King into his own act of opportunism. When parliament reconvened on January 25, 1940, the opposition parties expected a regular session that would permit debate on Canadian policy in the war. Instead, the prime minister announced that the House had been abruptly dissolved for a general election on March 26. King hoped to consolidate his power before the expected outbreak of European fighting in late spring. In surprise and frustration, MPs returned to Union Station and the trains homeward, to face a brutal winter campaign. Mackenzie King had caught the opposition disorganized and unprepared, at a moment when appeals to patriotism meant support for the party in power.

When parliament was dissolved, John Diefenbaker was about to leave Prince Albert by train for Ottawa, anticipating his first appearance before the Supreme Court of Canada in early February.[18] For ten days the candidate was caught in limbo for the court case, unable to recommence his campaign when it mattered most.

When he did reach home in February, he was plunged at once into another murder trial, as court-appointed counsel for the defence of Isobel Emele. The case was a bit of rare good fortune for the politician – and he knew it. Diefenbaker defended a woman accused of murdering her pro-Nazi tyrant of a husband, and he used on her behalf all the appeals to sympathy, decency, and patriotism he could muster in the early months of war against Germany. "I...put on trial the influence of the German-American Bund in Saskatchewan politics," Diefenbaker conceded frankly in his memoirs.[19] As in 1914, the family name was a potential source of embarrassment, but this time there was political risk for the candidate as well. The trial offered an unexpected chance to display his own loyalty to Canada despite his German name and ancestry. To Diefenbaker's relief, news reports of the case made him an anti-Nazi defender of the helpless.[20]

Isobel Emele had married Henry Emele in the mid-1920s. She was an Ulsterwoman and a proud British imperialist; he was a German-American admirer of Adolf Hitler. In the early years of their marriage Emele was twice convicted of assaulting his wife, and since 1931 the couple and their four children had lived in discord on their farm north of Prince Albert. On September 18, 1939, Isobel, distraught and half-dressed, confronted an off-duty RCMP officer near her home with the claim that her husband had shot himself. The officer found Emele lying wounded outside the house, with no sign of a weapon nearby. Before he died on the way to hospital, Emele told the constable: "She gave me the works." His wife denied the claim: "He is out of his mind. He does not know what he is saying." Isobel repeated later to the investigating officer that her husband had gone mad and killed himself.

The police kept her overnight at the farm, took her to Prince Albert the next day to identify her husband's body, removed her children, and then detained her for another day at the farm under supervision – all without access to a lawyer. On the third day she confessed that, in a rage at Emele's antagonism, she had shot him through a hole in the kitchen door with a .30 calibre Remington rifle. She produced the gun, and the police found that the hole in the door was smudged with carbon and matched the height of the wound in her husband's chest. Only then, after being charged with murder, was she able to talk with Diefenbaker's articling student Russell Brownridge.

She told Brownridge her story. Henry Emele had bullied and abused her for years, withheld money, and flaunted his pro-Nazi sentiments as an organizer for the Bund. When Germany invaded Poland he grew more boastfully arrogant: "Hitler will run this country and you'll learn to like it," he insisted. After the shooting she had been held incommunicado by the RCMP for two days until the confession. When Diefenbaker read her statement, he smiled and said to Brownridge, "I shouldn't have much trouble crying our way out of this."[21]

Following the preliminary hearing, the case was set for trial in the Court of King's Bench in Prince Albert on February 13, 1940. Diefenbaker and his partner John Cuelenaere did not call the defendant, but instead built their case in cross-examination. They carefully revealed Emele's sentiments and his bullying. They challenged the admissibility of his wife's confessions, on the ground that they had been extracted under "a subtle third degree," and of the dying man's words as hearsay. And they suggested a careless police investigation at the location. The judge accepted Diefenbaker's arguments and refused to allow the confessions or Emele's reported words to go into the record.

Diefenbaker rose for his summing up at 5 pm on Saturday, February 17, and turned to the jury. "Fully alert, his voice charged with dedicated purpose, it was his eyes that commanded the attention of the six listening men as they fixed each one in turn."[22] Diefenbaker picked up the Remington from the exhibit table, turned the barrel to his chest, and showed how Emele might have shot himself. "The length of the arms is what counts," he insisted. "And there is no evidence before this court as to the length of that man's arms." Nor were there fingerprints to link Mrs Emele to the weapon. The onus of proof, he reminded the jury, was with the crown. "They have not proved one thing that can tie the accused up with the death of her husband." The evidence about the direction of the bullet, he insisted, was inconsistent; Isobel Emele could not have shot him through the door as the prosecution claimed. And she had just prepared and cooked a noonday dinner for two. "That," Diefenbaker declared, "does not look like premeditated murder to me."

The judge added two further reasons for doubt in his own charge to the jury and sent them out early in the evening to consider the verdict. They were back in a short time with a verdict of not guilty. The courtroom erupted in applause.

Isobel Emele was free and John Diefenbaker was launched in triumph into his election campaign. He recounts the sequel in his memoirs. "The outcome of the trial was considered harmful to the Liberal Party in the election.

Strong representations were made and the Crown appealed, I suspect for the wrong reasons. The Court of Appeal ruled that the second alleged confession should have been admitted as evidence by the trial judge; my client's acquittal was set aside and a new trial ordered. I defended her a second time in June 1940, with both confessions in evidence, and the jury brought in a verdict of acquittal. Years later, she sent me one hundred dollars to buy a watch."[23]

WHEN THE ELECTION WAS CALLED AT THE END OF JANUARY, THE CONSERVATIVE leader, Robert Manion, had asked for a wartime coalition government and announced that his party would campaign as the National Government party. Diefenbaker wired Manion: "Your statement regarding National Government has general appeal and was a master stroke."[24] But Mackenzie King had the advantage of wartime incumbency and campaigned confidently for a renewed Liberal mandate. Both the Liberals and the CCF undercut Manion's call for a coalition government by announcing that they would not serve in it; and within the Conservative Party the idea offered the pretext for secret but inconclusive discussions about Manion's own removal.[25] The Conservative Party remained disorganized and underfinanced throughout, but this time Diefenbaker was well prepared. His Lake Centre organization sprang back to life, and the candidate set out on a chilly odyssey in late February and March. Edna often accompanied him, opening paths for the candidate with her easy warmth. On the platform his skills needed no guidance. In five weeks he packed in fifty-seven meetings, as well as a fifteen-minute radio broadcast once a week. He had little outside help, aside from one speech at Lumsden by the maverick Conservative H.H. Stevens, who had returned to the fold after his disastrous 1935 campaign as leader of his own Reconstruction Party.[26]

The thumbnail biography prepared for distribution to the press by Russell Brownridge described Diefenbaker as

> probably the most colourful figure in Saskatchewan seeking election...Possessed of a brilliant intellect and an unusual capacity for hard work...With a gift for lucid and forceful expression, he presents a striking personality both in Court and on the platform...Veteran of many political battles, and always against great odds, he launches into each new effort with the courage and confidence of one who believes wholeheartedly in the justice of his cause...He sailed for France in 1916 a Lieutenant in the 1st Canadian Mounted Rifles. While on active service he was wounded and spent several months in the hospital...Though a Baptist in belief, he supports numerous religious and charitable organizations.[27]

Diefenbaker had decided on his political strengths: he was "a striking personality" with a reputation for battle "against great odds"; he was a champion of justice and a patriot. Those were the characteristics that moved his audiences, the qualities that would make – or break – his career in politics. They were the stuff of legend. He hoped they would finally carry him upwards.

With the national party's limp and self-effacing appeal for a national coalition, Diefenbaker was able, in effect, to make up his own platform. He called for a legislated floor price for wheat to satisfy prairie farmers. He revived the old charges that Liberals were spreading fear among immigrants that a Manion government would deprive them of their naturalized status as Canadians. He accused the King government of "a marked tendency towards dictatorship." He attacked the pacifism of CCF leader J.S. Woodsworth. And in his closing broadcast he accused his Liberal opponent of "a deliberate lie" in claiming that he, Diefenbaker, had been a First World War conscript. He was a volunteer. "Johnston's statement," Diefenbaker said with a certain sweep, "reflects on everyone who enlisted in the twenty months preceding conscription." This claim of youthful patriotism, he was later convinced, brought him "quite a number of votes."[28] There was no harm in emphasizing his own loyalty in two world wars and displaying his talent for righteous indignation.

On election night, during a spring blizzard, John and Edna were at home in Prince Albert with their close friends Lorne and Mabel Connell and Diefenbaker's partner Jack Cuelenaere. The national results, reported on CBC radio, were depressing. Manion himself was defeated, and the Conservative Party returned just forty members – exactly as in 1935. King's Liberals elected 181 members, for a gain of eight seats. On the prairies, the Liberals elected thirty-one and the Conservatives only three. But John Diefenbaker was in, by a slim margin of 280 votes. He discovered his victory only after radio reporting had closed down for the night, when Jack Cuelenaere called Liberal headquarters in Regina for their latest count. Diefenbaker joined Ernest Perley as the second Saskatchewan Conservative in the new parliament, an MP at last.[29]

From Victoria, where his parents had been wintering with Elmer, Mary Diefenbaker wrote to express a mother's pride – and to offer a bit of homely advice. She saw the world from the point of view of an honest and unprivileged outsider, acknowledged her son's ambition, and urged her values on him.

The Battle is over and the victory won, and I bet you feel pretty proud of your self. Well I feel that way myself, so do we all! you put up a good fight and you must be very tired. I can see by your letter that the aim of your ambition is to fill Kings chair. well I think you will get there some day, if you work hard enough. There is a lot of hard work ahead, for there has to be some changes in this old world of ours. The rich have to live on less and the poor have more than they have to day, and I hope you will be one of them that will work for those changes, what ever they may be. and I want you to be honest and upright in all you do, and dont try and get rich on other peoples money. you will find that it pays in the end, to be honorable and just at all times. I dont want to preach to you. but I mean all I say, and I think you will do just what I want you to do.[30]

In a letter written the same day, John's father also looked ahead: "As to leadership...I am exceedingly well pleased that you have got on to a foundation...where you can no longer be prevented to show what you can do...Edna's natural ability to be bright and polite should add materially in the advancement of your future political successes."[31]

SPRING ARRIVED ON THE CANADIAN PRAIRIES AS THE BUOYANT COUPLE PREPARED TO depart for Ottawa and John's first session of parliament. Their personal fortunes had been revived in electoral victory, but this was otherwise a time of profound and deepening anxiety. The phoney war of winter gave way, on May 10, to the German invasion of Holland, Belgium, and Luxembourg, a vast blitzkrieg aimed at the heart of France by a flanking attack around the defences of the Maginot Line. The same day Winston Churchill replaced Neville Chamberlain as prime minister of Britain in a wartime coalition government. That night the Diefenbakers boarded the train for Ottawa, and by their arrival on May 13 German armies had crossed the River Meuse and entered France. Soon Panzer divisions were sweeping towards the Channel ports in a daring effort to encircle large parts of the French and British armies. Remnants of the French forces were retreating south in disarray, and in Paris official documents were being burned in ministry courtyards. On May 20 German tanks reached the mouth of the Somme and cut off the allied armies to the north. From May 27 to June 4 England's little ships and sailboats took off 337,000 soldiers from the beaches of Dunkirk, two-thirds of them British and one-third French.[32] These momentous events overshadowed preparations for the opening of the nineteenth Canadian parliament.

When John Diefenbaker sat down for breakfast in the CNR dining car on May 11, he was joined accidentally at the table by another freshman member of parliament, the Liberal James Sinclair from Vancouver. Soon Edna, "a vivacious, attractive redhead," came to breakfast as well. She announced to

Sinclair that her husband was a new Conservative MP whose acquaintance would be helpful "because he is going to be prime minister." Sinclair asked: "Didn't your husband run quite often?" "Five times," she replied. "Just like Robert the Bruce! The spider, up and down, up and down. But my husband will help you." Sinclair doubted that, "because I am a Liberal MP." The conversation broke up in laughter.[33]

Sinclair was an immediate friend. Edna's charm, he remembered, helped him to decide that he should no longer postpone his own wedding. After breakfast John returned to his compartment to read, while Sinclair and Edna carried on their conversation in the parlour car. "I was very attracted to her personality. I remember she had deep dark red hair and great blue eyes. We were sitting side by side talking and John came in. He said he worked so hard, that was why he had stayed back there alone. We got quite a relationship going. Four or five times a day she would remind John he was going to be prime minister."[34]

As the Diefenbakers travelled back and forth between Ottawa and Prince Albert over the next five years, this pattern of easy acquaintanceship in the dining and observation cars was maintained. Edna usually made the relaxed initial contacts, always preparing the way admiringly for her husband. "During these encounters," wrote Simma Holt, "John was humorous and friendly and people never forgot him; they talked about those train meetings years later. In the parlour car the routine would continue in the same manner. Edna had set the stage; now John took over. They both enjoyed this teamwork and knew they were good at it. They were proud of each other and of the way they worked together so effectively." On the trains, in the early 1940s, the couple showed the same open affection for each other that had been so evident in Prince Albert ten years before.[35]

Diefenbaker's new role as an MP meant a great expansion of his home neighbourhood. For John and Edna, Prince Albert and Saskatoon were now linked by two thousand miles of steel to Ottawa's Union Station, the Château Laurier, Wellington Street, and the Parliament Buildings. John maintained his partnership in Prince Albert with John Cuelenaere and returned home for Christmas, Easter, and the summer recess, shipping boxes of legal files relentlessly in both directions as he travelled.[36] But his focus was on the House of Commons. The Diefenbakers took a room in the Château (like many other MPs, including R.B. Bennett before them), and lived their life out of John's parliamentary office in the Centre Block. Edna acted as John's unpaid assistant, sat above him in the members' gallery, and spread her network of friendship and information-gathering quickly into the press gallery and across to the government benches. The journalist Patrick Nicholson recalled that Edna's "radiance...bubbling with joie de vivre" brought light to John's "gloomily barren little back-bencher's office on the fifth floor of the Parliament Building."[37] The Diefenbakers' close political partnership was unusual in Ottawa, and Edna's enthusiastic support for her husband did much to cement his valuable attachments in the press gallery. The only common criticism of Edna in the parliamentary community of the early 1940s was that she talked too much about "my Johnny" and his brilliant prospects. The Liberal MP Paul Martin, who was soon a friend, said: "I have my ambitions too, but I have my wife better trained."[38] Along with Edna's infectious spirits, there was a shade of gaucherie as well.

When John Diefenbaker entered the House of Commons, it was a small, exclusive, staid, slightly shabby but comfortable men's club. Its members still gloried in the reflected aura of the Westminster Parliament and took for granted that they were participants by adoption in mankind's highest, most sophisticated political institution, the shining product of centuries of political evolution. This was not an altogether vain belief, for it had the effect of raising standards of decorum and debate in this outpost of empire – as did the impressive mass of the buildings, halls, and debating chambers themselves, in grand imitation of Westminster's own parliamentary gothic. For Diefenbaker, privileged entry into the House his father had extolled to him as a child was a dream achieved. Once he was there, the House became his second and true home, and he stayed in it until his death thirty-nine years later. His attachment to parliament always remained with him, even as Canadian politics swirled and shifted around him. By the end, he was the last parliamentary romantic in the chamber.

Within days of his election victory, Diefenbaker received letters from the party's national organizer, J.M. Robb, and the defeated leader's private secretary, R.A. Bell, about planning for the forthcoming session. Bell noted that in Manion's absence a House leader would have to be chosen by the caucus and that Manion had asked him to say Diefenbaker was one of the prospects. He should therefore prepare a speech for the opening debate, in expectation that he might be chosen.[39] Robb ventured further: "A House Leader will have to be selected. In looking over the list, I can see no one any stronger than yourself. I hope you will not take offense if I just give you my opinion that if this matter of House Leader should be presented to you, I would give it very great care. It might be better to be patient and abide [sic] your time."[40]

Diefenbaker was daunted. He copied the letters and sent them to his mother in Victoria:

Personally I do not know, even if it is offered to me, that I will accept it, as it seems too great a responsibility to be assumed, and I do not think that I have the necessary ability to fill the position. However, I intend to go ahead and prepare a speech which will have to be delivered early in the session. I had intended not to say anything at all for the first two or three months, but, in view of the lack of debating strength in the House, it seems that I will have to alter my intention, and that I will have to speak.[41]

His mother offered cautionary words a week later:

How does it feel to be member of Parliament? how about the leadership. you should think it over very carefully. There is no doubt about your having the abality, to fill the position you know the jealousy there is in this world, and you must think about your health. not having had experience and the responsibility will so great and enother thing. the ones that has been there for years will be wild and might not work with you as they should when you get to Ottawa you will know what is best.[42]

The Conservative caucus met on the day of John Diefenbaker's arrival in Ottawa, choosing R.B. Hanson as House leader from a field of six.[43] Soon afterwards the new member wrote proudly to Mary Diefenbaker on his first sheet of House of Commons letterhead. He seemed content that he had not sought the House leadership, although he explained that the decision of caucus had been prearranged in any case.

Well, I have my seat – third row on the right in the same column as Hanson and the whip, – I have been sworn in and am now a full-fledged member.

I refused to let my name stand for the leadership as I couldn't hope to get anywhere as everything was pretty well cut and dried...

Between ourselves there is more log-rolling and back-biting here in one day than there is elsewhere in a year...

The war situation makes us all very fearful and there will be no functions after the opening...[44]

In his first experience of the parliamentary caucus, as in the leadership convention of 1938, Diefenbaker kept his distance from the internal scramble for influence and advantage. Whether out of naivety, indifference, or incapacity, he established a pattern of aloofness that he later maintained. Others might intrigue; he would hold himself above or beyond

113

that battle with a certain sense of his own dignity.

With John in Ottawa, his mother now became an intermittent correspondent, offering her son a flow of family gossip, complaint, advice, strangled emotion, and prejudice in her semi-literate hand. On May 24 she wrote:

> How does it feel to be setting in the seats of the mighty? hope you are enjoying yourself and that you like it at Ottawa. You know John ambition is a funny thing and whn you get it, it means nothing, at least you are never satisfied.
>
> Well I hope you will do good work down there. The war comes first of all. The British needs all Canada can give her in evrything I am afraid we are going to have a bad time fighting those devils The loss of life has been terrible one wonders why it should be. One thing I know that cruel, bloodthirsty nation will get what is coming to her in the end...
>
> Elmer came home this afternoon he is all het up about the hunks, and Grits, with him they are all in the same class. he has been working hard, and has done very well...How does Edna like it there? she must get fed up sometimes she has a lot of time to put in.[45]

When parliament opened on May 16, 1940, John Diefenbaker was in his place, "somewhat overawed at taking my seat in the House after all those years of trying." Despite his rhetorical talent, he decided to give himself a few weeks, "until I was at ease in my new surroundings," before venturing on his maiden speech.[46] But on May 27 he was on his feet with his first questions demanding protection for northern Saskatchewan "against enemy activities." He held up a handful of resolutions "from various bodies in Saskatchewan demanding that the government do something toward controlling the nazi influence within their province." He referred to "the critical situation – I call it critical advisedly – arising from subversive activities in Saskatchewan," the result, he claimed, of the recent release from detention of enemy aliens. He asked for "the immediate recruitment to full strength of the Prince Albert infantry and artillery units" as a means of restoring public confidence. He offered no evidence to support his alarmist claims of Nazi subversion on the Canadian prairies. The minister, in reply, pointed out that aliens under detention were only released after examination by special tribunals. Other members echoed Diefenbaker's alarm as the police made emergency arrests across Canada; the Conservative member for Toronto-Parkdale, Dr H.A. Bruce, warned that there were "thousands of Quislings" awaiting the moment to betray the country.[47] Within days, Diefenbaker was appointed to the House Committee on the Defence of Canada Regulations, which henceforth met in secret to consider the emergency rules and review cases of wartime arrest and internment.[48]

The all-party committee, under the chairmanship of the minister of national revenue, J.L. Ilsley, held twenty-five meetings between June 13 and August 1, 1940. It then reported unanimously, with a series of modest proposals for amendments to the defence regulations.[49]

John Diefenbaker rose to deliver his maiden speech in the House of Commons on June 13, 1940 – "an awesome ordeal," as he recalled the occasion. He had roused himself to an unusual pitch of nervous preoccupation. "I felt that I was in a great vacuum, surrounded by a material of one-way transparency: I could see the others in the House, but they could not see me; and perhaps they could not hear me. Never before or since have I experienced anything like it."[50]

Diefenbaker explained to the House that he was speaking in debate on the emergency regulations, following the minister of justice (Ernest Lapointe), because he had been named to the special committee to examine those rules. The speech was a short and emphatic declaration of patriotism. The new member supported the government in its wartime restriction of liberty, repeated his concern that potential subversives had been released from detention in Saskatchewan and Manitoba, asserted the loyalty of most Canadians of German descent, and called for an end to census statistics based on country of origin: "Let us build up in this country an unhyphenated Canadianism that is dominant, proud and strong." His extreme but vague condemnation of "the trade of treachery and of traitors, the undermining of the country from within," was explicitly linked to his belief in general loyalty: "There are those who are disloyal; and in the interests of the majority of loyal citizens of various national strains, those who are treasonable must be shown their place, so that those who are loyal and patriotic shall not be denied the fruits of their loyalty."

Diefenbaker warned that in Saskatchewan there was "an ever rising body of opinion" that subversives were still at liberty. He called for creation of a national home defence corps to pre-empt the formation of vigilante committees in the west, and urged an immediate national registration of adult males. This would not only provide the names of "men all over the dominion who want to serve," but "would bring to light the names of many who are to-day in Canada without having complied with the immigration regulations and who are in position to carry on subversive activities."

Finally, Diefenbaker called for the rigid suppression of unpatriotic writing: "Why should such anti-British publications as the *Saturday Evening Post* and the Chicago *Tribune* be allowed to enter the country? What is the use of having a department of information to furnish dependable information to the people if such information is neutralized, if not completely destroyed, by malicious articles appearing in these particular papers?" Prosecutions under the war regulations, he noted, could only be carried out against newspapers or magazines published in Canada.

In his peroration Diefenbaker asserted that while the armed forces defended Canada abroad, parliament had the parallel task of waging war against "malicious disaffection" within. Just as "our gallant boys" would not fail Canadians overseas, parliament "must not fail them" at home.

The atmosphere of war and the member's uneasiness about his German name and ancestry had produced a curiously ambiguous opening for John Diefenbaker's parliamentary career. The prime minister must have felt some relief that the gadfly from Prince Albert had been tamed by taking him at once into the government's confidence on the special committee.[51] One of the first acts of the committee was to recommend passage of a sweeping treachery bill, providing for the death penalty for conviction on charges of giving assistance to the enemy. It reflected, and may have been partly inspired by, the new member's opening remarks in the House. The bill was quickly introduced and passed third reading on July 25.[52]

John Diefenbaker was not the only MP disoriented by the early and disastrous months of war. With the fall of France on June 16, the Conservative House leader R.B. Hanson reversed his party's position on compulsory military service. He approached Mackenzie King to ask for full conscription for overseas service, and renewed the Conservative appeal for a coalition government to enforce it. King responded the next day by introducing the National Resources Mobilization Act, which authorized national registration and conscription for home defence, but he maintained his commitment against compulsory overseas service. King rejected Hanson's request for coalition as a veiled attempt to remove him from power, but did offer a merely consultative role in the War Committee of cabinet to the leader of the opposition. Hanson refused, and King noted complacently in his diary that the Tories "can say nothing more from now on about every effort not having been made to meet their wishes for inside knowledge."[53]

On declaration of war in September 1939 the government had proclaimed a state of emergency under the War Measures Act. This proclamation effectively suspended both the federal constitution and the normal lawmaking and critical roles of parliament, allowing the cabinet to govern by fiat. A mounting stream of wartime orders-in-council and regulations – cabinet decrees with the force of law and unchallengeable in the courts – were issued under the authority of the act, dealing with all aspects of Canadian life. Consumer prices, industrial production and marketing, rationing, transportation, wages and employment, internment, press censorship, and free speech all fell under the arbitrary rule of the wartime cabinet and the federal bureaucracy. The House of Commons was left with no more than a vestigial role, approving taxes and annual spending estimates, examining those few bills the King government chose to submit to parliament, and seeking information about the nature and extent of the national war effort – but always within the limits of a self-imposed commitment to sustain Canada's war. For five years Mackenzie King and his cabinet colleagues were the country's benign dictators.

In these circumstances, the Conservative Party was triply handicapped. The emergency constitution deprived parliament of a central role; the Conservative opposition had only forty seats in the House; and the party benches conspicuously lacked brilliance. House leader Hanson was a former minister and a competent debater, but he had only two other members with ministerial experience, Earl Rowe and Grote Stirling. Hanson could be silenced, apparently at will, by Mackenzie King's intimidation. The party's most trenchant debater, Arthur Meighen, was harmlessly isolated in the Senate. There were a few colourful eccentrics like Tommy Church, the former mayor of Toronto, on the back bench, but the party depended on its slim crop of newcomers to give it strength. Among them, Howard Green of Vancouver, Gordon Graydon of Peel, and Art Smith of Calgary made favourable impressions.[54] Dr Herbert A. Bruce, a distinguished surgeon and former lieutenant governor of Ontario, represented the traditional conscriptionist sentiments of the *Globe and Mail* and the Toronto Tory establishment. Despite his nervousness, the new member from Lake Centre, Saskatchewan, soon established himself as the party's most theatrical critic in the House. The tall, erect lawyer had a dominating presence: he could strike a compelling phrase, he was indefatigable, and he revealed a talent – sometimes mischievous, sometimes portentous – for getting under the skin of any minister who showed signs of self-importance.

During the 1940 and 1941 sessions of parliament, John Diefenbaker's interventions in the House were relatively infrequent and cautious. In November 1940 he asked for, but was refused, a parliamentary inquiry into reports that CBC radio had banned broadcasts by members of the parliamentary opposition. He made passing suggestions for the inclusion of a Canadian member in an imperial war cabinet (on Borden's First World War model) and for the return of R.B. Bennett to Canada as coordinator of air-craft production, in emulation of Lord Beaverbrook's role in the United Kingdom.[55] But most of his questions and comments were routine references to the domestic effects of war, relating to farm prices and marketing, defence contracts, or national registration and enlistments. They were carefully placed within a framework of patriotic admiration for the Canadian armed forces, the British people, and the Churchill government. His most persistent themes were that the Canadian government had neglected the interests of prairie farmers and had failed to mobilize Canada's resources, both material and human, with sufficient dedication.[56] These were part of the opposition's stock-in-trade, reflecting English-Canadian interests and anxieties.

By 1942 Diefenbaker had identified himself with two general lines of criticism, one relating to conscription, the other to the processes of government. Call-ups and exemptions for service within Canada, he claimed, were being unequally and unfairly applied, and conscription for overseas service was required. The King government faced growing complaints in English-speaking Canada during 1941 that its promise to Quebec not to send conscripts abroad was wrong. After the overwhelming Japanese attacks on Pearl Harbor, the Philippines, Indochina, Hong Kong, Singapore, and the Dutch East Indies in December 1941 – and surrender of the Canadian contingent at Hong Kong – the domestic political pressures obliged Mackenzie King to seek some respectable way out of his commitment. In January 1942 the government announced that it would seek release, by plebiscite, "from any obligations aris-ing out of past commitments restricting the methods of raising men for mili-tary service." Diefenbaker responded for the Conservatives that a decision in favour of full overseas conscription should be taken by the House of Commons in a free vote without regard for "political considerations."[57]

When Mackenzie King presented his plebiscite legislation to the House in February, he argued on the high ground of moral principle that his solemn promise to the public could only be revoked with the public's consent. Diefenbaker led off for the opposition by conceding that "I am not now oppos-ing the plebiscite to release the government from its pledge." Instead, he chided the government for undermining the supremacy of parliament by appealing beyond it, called for "a one hundred per cent vote" of the public in favour of the plebiscite question, and challenged the prime minister to say what his government would do once it received that public consent. The campaign period should be minimal, and voters should be promised immediate mobilization after the vote. "Where shall we be in ten weeks?" he worried. "Only on Thursday last we read in the press that if Java falls and Australia be attacked, the next places on the Japanese time-table to be attacked are Hawaii and Alaska in April."[58] The dominos were falling while Mackenzie King dithered.

The plebiscite gave the prime minister a strong English-speaking majority in favour of release from his promise, but a majority against release in Quebec. King had appeased English-speaking sentiment and bought some time, but he dared not confront Quebec voters, who remained overwhelmingly opposed to conscription. In June 1942 his government made the next move in its skilful game of ambiguity by repealing the legal limitation on overseas service for conscripts, without actually drafting anyone for service abroad. Diefenbaker protested that "the government cannot forever procrastinate; it cannot forever fight this delaying action, if the morale of the people of Canada is to be maintained."

When Paul Martin asked whether Diefenbaker wanted immediate conscription for overseas service, he replied that "the time has come when there is only one mobilization that will assure equality, and fairness, and unity in Canada." To his French Canadian friends, he appealed for "unity of effort" – something, if it were granted, that would permit King to proceed with compulsory service overseas. The appeal for fairness and unity was Diefenbaker's way of opposing French-speaking attitudes without overtly opposing French Canadian voters. He perceived the whole Canadian war effort as something beyond calculation of merely Canadian interests. There was now a higher duty to Britain and the empire which should transcend all domestic divisions. If Diefenbaker did not understand that many French Canadians could never share that belief, he did know the political realities: his arguments would not persuade the House. King's ambiguity won the day.[59]

The Saskatchewan member's second general criticism of the King government concerned its wartime usurpation of parliamentary authority. It was a strong traditional – and populist – theme, which Diefenbaker had first used in the 1940 campaign. By 1942 it was fully developed. In the budget debate that July he made his case for the prosecution.

> I intend to discuss a trend which is gradually becoming more pronounced as the war goes on and is against the full operation of our parliamentary institutions and all that they stand for in the democratic way of life...This parliament represents the people of Canada; it is the repository and trustee of their hopes of survival...I have no apologies to offer for speaking on this subject; for this is the only place, the only forum, where one can express one's views, where one can make one's criticisms, where one can advance

constructively such ideas as one believes are in the interests of the country as a whole.[60]

Diefenbaker's touchstone was a speech that day in the British House of Commons by Prime Minister Churchill, in which he had pointed to free parliamentary debate as the very purpose for which the war was being fought. In Mackenzie King's parliament, Diefenbaker saw but a poor shadow of Churchill's Westminster.

> There is a tendency on the part of this government not to give the attention to parliament that it should, and we are approaching a state where parliament need not be called together except for the purpose of voting supply.
> ...I refer...to the attitude of the government in continuing in ever-increasing measure to govern by order in council, with the result that we in this parliament are denied the opportunity of debate on matters which affect the welfare of the people as a whole.

The member's charges were wide. Price, trade, and agricultural regulations had been imposed by order-in-council during a parliamentary sitting; not all regulations had been made public; private members' days in the House had been suspended; and the government responded to more and more questions with the answer that "it is not in the public interest to reveal information." Canadian newspapers had been prosecuted under the defence regulations for what he saw as "fair and constructive criticism."

Diefenbaker noted that the Canadian emergency regulations permitted prosecution for making statements "likely to prejudice" the war effort, regardless of intent. In Britain, by contrast, the rules prohibited only false statements intended to prejudice national defence; in other words, an intention to deceive was required for conviction. The Canadian rules were potentially "an instrument of tyranny."

> These are extraordinary sections. They were never intended to be used for the prosecution of political opponents. Their use should be circumscribed...There is not a member of this house, there is not an honourable, patriotic citizen anywhere in Canada who may not be convicted of an offence under these sections if they are used against him...I say the time has come...to stand up for...the rights of loyal citizens all over this dominion, and to secure from the government the assurance that these sections will no longer be used against loyal citizens of proven patriotism.

Diefenbaker closed with another reference to the words of Churchill, who had encouraged critics to speak out "in driving forward our war effort and trying to gain an earlier inch or a more fruitful hour whenever it may be possible."[61]

Next to Arthur Meighen, no politician more easily annoyed Mackenzie King than John Diefenbaker. The member for Lake Centre knew it. He sensed the points of weakness in the prime minister's vanity and took pleasure in plunging the knife. But his mischief was accompanied by covert admiration: Diefenbaker could see, and would himself emulate, King's political skills. In the memoirs Diefenbaker wrote:

> King had an infinite capacity to express one view and within five minutes to express the reverse. In debate, if you quoted some statement of his which you believed to be irregular, he would always clear it up by saying: "Read on." He knew that sooner or later in the speech from which you were quoting he would have said the very converse. He also had a talent for a lachrymose performance when he believed this tactic to be to his advantage. Or, he could wrap himself in the garments of righteousness, quote scripture, and condemn the Tories as apostles of darkness. Throughout the years, he did all he could to destroy his political opponents, sometimes not excluding those within his own party, while all the time clasping his hands in pretence that he would never do anything unfair or unjust. No more sublime actor have I ever known.[62]

For the jealous prime minister, Conservative allusions to Winston Churchill were always odious. In May 1941, Diefenbaker recalled, when he accompanied R.B. Hanson and Grote Stirling to a private briefing on the war effort, King had exploded at his presence: "What business have you to be here? You strike me to the heart every time you speak. In your last speech who did you mention? Did you say what I've done for this country? You spoke of Churchill. Churchill! Did he ever bleed for Canada?"[63]

"There were tears in King's eyes. There was rage on his face," Diefenbaker wrote. But suddenly he became calm and reported that the British battleship *Hood* had been sunk; he was in despair. The embarrassment passed. A few days later the scene became the subject of gossip in the House, and King accused Diefenbaker of breaching confidence. Diefenbaker demanded a withdrawal. "I had not spoken to anyone about it. King withdrew, but only after he realized that I would reveal his inane conduct at the inter-party meeting. His outburst about Churchill, however, told me something important about King's normally well hidden nature. Indeed, neither liked the other.

Churchill disliked the political opportunism of King. King envied the popularity of Churchill."[64] Henceforth, Diefenbaker used the words and example of the British prime minister frequently in the House. For him, in King's presence, the image of Churchill was both talisman and weapon.

Diefenbaker knew, too, of King's peculiar sensitivity about the reputation of his grandfather, the rebel William Lyon Mackenzie. When Diefenbaker was called upon, without notice, to second Howard Green's motion of censure over the Hong Kong inquiry in July 1942, he had no notes on the subject of the motion. Instead, he diverted attention and disconcerted the prime minister by reading from army lectures on the sources of political freedom prepared for Canadian officers. Along with the Spartans at Thermopylae, the Barons at Runnymede, and Bishop Latimer, the lectures listed the brave William Lyon Mackenzie. "It was obvious to all that I found it passing strange that he should have been included along with the greats. Imagine, William Lyon Mackenzie! Well, King lost his customary sense of proportion. I have never seen him more annoyed, and his voice rose to a level that I imagine has only been equalled in the days when the buffalo roamed the Western plains."[65] Diefenbaker was temporarily shouted down. When he continued, he goaded the prime minister further with the tale that his own great-grandfather Bannerman had followed Mackenzie to the United States border – but in pursuit, as a loyal militiaman. "Well, if anyone thought there had been a noisy, uncontrolled, raucous House before, it was silence beside what happened afterwards. King was completely out of control; he screamed and referred to the Conservative Members as a 'mob,' a term he later had to withdraw."[66]

During the lunchtime adjournment, Diefenbaker writes, King somehow persuaded Hanson that the entire exchange should be edited out of Hansard. King, however, tells a different story to his diary:

> Shortly before noon...there was quite a scene when I began taking Diefenbaker, of Lake Centre, and Hanson, to task over some of the insinuations they were trying to make, and the effort to prevent me from speaking. I referred to the tactics as being typically Tory and that they were actions of a mob. Diefenbaker had sought to have it appear I was responsible for some references to my grandfather, in his struggle for freedom, in some book of instructions for the training camps...The whole thing was more of an emotional outburst...I think the incident rather pleased our men, but after lunch Hanson brought the matter up as a question of privilege. I quickly withdrew the remark about the "mob" and agreed to have the whole incident

expunged from Hansard. I was not in any way ashamed of it, but realized that, as Prime Minister, I should not have used that particular expression.[67]

What remained in the official record were Diefenbaker's mischievous references to the prime minister's grandfather, minus the claims about his own loyal ancestor and King's cries about the Conservative mob. But press stories the next day recounted the full exchange, without the offstage byplay.[68] Diefenbaker's show had amused the galleries, but perhaps distracted attention from the opposition's more serious complaints about the secrecy of the Hong Kong inquiry.

JOHN DIEFENBAKER'S HISTRIONIC SKILLS BROUGHT HIM IMMEDIATE PROMINENCE IN the House. But that was not all gain. In letters to his parents he spoke of jealousy in the caucus and slights involving the pronunciation of his name. For the family, the matter of the name always involved Diefenbaker's ambition for the leadership. "Do try and forget that name of yours," wrote his mother in March 1941. "Surely you have lived that down. It is not your friends, but your enemy's that talk that way...Some day you will get where you want to be, if not now later."[69] His father wrote twice on the subject in the same week. "Your name? Well, I imagine, in the end...any opposition will disappear from the very fact, that they are making so much of your being able to qualify as leader. Already, I should judge, the people are beginning to get used to it...Then too, possibly the best thing for you to do in the matter of jealousy, is to strive unnoticed to hide any feelings of dislike for such apparent attitude on the part of any of your party or other fellow members."[70] William was pleased that a radio reporter from Ottawa got the name right: "I am still glad when I think of how nicely he pronounced your name."[71]

John conscientiously sent Hansard to his parents and maintained a flow of press clippings about his political activities. In 1942 the Diefenbaker name still troubled him. "And such publicity of late," exclaimed his father in May.

> The *Globe and Mail* are not speaking Conservative. But when they tell about your parliamentary stand in certain things – editorially – when it is in an approving way, to my notion, they are backing you.
>
> Even the *Financial Times*. Well! They spoke of "Campbell-Bannerman." What a nice name it would be and what it might mean to you.[72]

His mother responded, apparently, to the same article: "That about changing your name. I think its crazy would that make you a better Canadian than you are? I dont think it would help you to change your name now. If it had been done years ago it would have been all right."[73]

THESE CONCERNS REFLECTED WHAT JOHN DIEFENBAKER SENSED AS AN EARLY CHANCE to seek the leadership of the Conservative Party. With the wartime suspension of most political activity, the party limped through 1940 and 1941, its prospects bleak and its treasury nearly empty. In June 1940, when Hanson made a desperate appeal to MPs and senators for funds to keep a small central office in Ottawa open, contributions of $50 each brought in $3350. That made up the budget for the rest of the year.[74] In 1941, thanks to initiatives taken at an informal national meeting in January, the party raised $36,000 through solicitation of traditional business sources in Montreal and Toronto. Diefenbaker attended that meeting as the lame duck leader of his provincial party, and $9000 of the total was eventually contributed to the Saskatchewan wing.[75]

Hanson's role as House leader was temporary, and he carried on desultory discussions about the choice of a permanent leader. Conservative loyalists talked gloomily of the party's displacement by the CCF at the next general election if the party could not renew itself. Hanson led the parliamentary party with modest efficiency, but there were growing strains in the caucus over the party's attitudes on overseas conscription. In a war for British survival, this was bound to be the fundamental issue in the party of Robert Borden and Arthur Meighen. Hanson, however, was sensitive to the memories of national conflict in the First World War and to the party's rural supporters who opposed conscription; he did not press the issue so long as voluntary recruitment satisfied military needs, as it did through 1940 and 1941. But others in the party, and much of the English language press – moved by a sense of fairness, or convictions of principle, or anti-French prejudice, or anger at Mackenzie King's political shrewdness on the issue – believed that the Conservatives should reject King's caution and declare unambiguously for compulsory overseas service. Meighen, with his "measureless contempt" for the prime minister, was one of them, but for months he kept a frustrating silence.[76] Once the caucus had decided in May 1941 to hold a party conference in the autumn to discuss a leadership convention, he was determined to see the leader chosen quickly so that the party could "get into action on strong British total war lines without delay." That would mean a direct challenge to the King government. When Hanson still insisted on restraint in an address at the Albany Club in Toronto just before the autumn conference, Meighen and the proconscription lobby were moved to immediate action.[77] Despite his own genuine fears about a return to the electoral wars, Meighen seemed the obvious candidate.

The Dominion Conservative Association – a gathering of about two hundred persons made up, in Diefenbaker's words, of the parliamentary caucus and "the Warwicks or king-makers of the Party...the Toronto and Montreal groups" – met in the Railway Committee Room of the House on November 7, 1941. After Hanson's opening remarks, Meighen made a fighting speech about the government's inadequate war effort. The meeting fell into bickering over whether it had the authority to choose him as leader, or only to set the time and place for a convention. A subcommittee eventually voted overwhelmingly to invite Meighen to take the leadership, but the next day he declined and left the meeting. Debate continued through the day, until a unanimous motion in favour of Meighen was adopted. Diefenbaker initially opposed Meighen, warning that "if you resign to seek a seat in the House of Commons, King, who hates you...will destroy you." But in the end Diefenbaker voted for him.[78]

After days of painful reflection, Meighen reluctantly gave in to the pressure and told the party that he would lead it on a platform of coalition and conscription reminiscent of 1917. This was a heady and divisive mix that was certain to rouse old Canadian demons. A House of Commons seat was opened for him by the resignation of the Conservative member for York South, and Prime Minister King set the by-election for February 9, 1942. King promised, out of conventional courtesy, that the government would not nominate against Meighen, but privately he was horrified. If Meighen led the Conservatives in the Commons, "it would be helping to break up our Dominion."[79]

Meighen meant to fight the by-election on the issue of conscription. He had the backing of a Committee for Total War organized by a group of Toronto businessmen with the aid of George McCullagh's *Globe and Mail,* but the King government undercut Meighen by its announcement in late January of the forthcoming plebiscite on whether to release it from its pledge against compulsory overseas service. The CCF candidate, J.W. Noscworthy, and his party fought a vigorous campaign of personal invective, labelling Meighen as the stooge of the "Conservative old guard," the voice of the war profiteers, a leader who had been chosen improperly to protect their privileges. Noseworthy called vaguely for the conscription of wealth as well as manpower. Editorials in the *Financial Post* and the Winnipeg *Free Press* gave credence to rumours that Meighen's selection had been rigged by the "big interests"; and Meighen was distracted by what he described as "a ruthless and dishonest campaign all through Canada." Despite Mackenzie King's avowal of neutrality, Meighen believed that local Liberals were active in the CCF campaign.

Meighen was disgusted and exhausted by the whole affair. "It was partly," wrote Roger Graham, "that he had lost his liking for this kind of warfare and had been projected into the leadership against his will, partly the odiousness of the CCF's propaganda, partly the hypocrisy of the Liberals, as he regarded it, in first announcing that they would not oppose him and then combining with the CCF." On election day both Meighen and King expected defeat: Meighen with more than a hint of relief, King with dread for himself and the country.[80]

Meighen's intuition was the correct one: he lost to Noseworthy by more than 4000 votes. That evening the drama centred in the House of Commons, and Diefenbaker was in his place to experience it. King's Liberals had won three other by-elections, and his arch-enemy had been vanquished. King wrote: "When I went in I was given a tremendous ovation, which kept up for a considerable time and was renewed after the Speaker had mildly called order to enable the debate to proceed. When I sat down, I looked straight across at the Tories – Hanson, Diefenbaker and a few others – as much as to say: 'You have got now pretty well what you deserve.' To our own men in different parts of the House I turned with a pretty happy countenance, and was given a great cheer. When Coldwell came into the House I nodded him congratulations across the floor. He too looked supremely happy."[81] Diefenbaker recalled that King "laughed uproariously," pointed across the chamber to the Conservative benches, and cried "Diefenbaker and Hanson, you have your answer."[82]

Despite being singled out as an object of King's gloating, Diefenbaker's response to the defeat was not one of complete despair. The by-election stew of truth and falsehood, rumour and accusation enriched his special vision of Canadian politics. It affected his perception of all three parties. The performance of the CCF confirmed the threat offered to the old parties by this band of apparently reckless extremists. The behaviour of the Liberal Party sustained the worst claims about King's limitless hypocrisy. And Meighen and his Ontario supporters – seen partly through the eyes of his accusers – left the image of a party still managed by an old, élitist clique. All three parties, as John Diefenbaker glimpsed them through the prism of York South, were more or less foreign to him. Instead, he began to see the possibility of another political realm, the product of his party's failure and his own western experience, in which he might feature as symbol and inspiration. In early 1942 he could scarcely articulate this vision and he had scant evidence that it was widely shared, but that was soon to come. The immediate reality was the defeat of Arthur Meighen.[83]

The rejection of Meighen and his campaign for overseas conscription left the Conservative Party in disarray. Late in February Meighen told the parliamentary caucus that he would not try to enter the House again, but would retain the leadership for an indefinite time. He urged them to "adjust their organization as to be in the best possible position to meet the contingency of my retirement" – which seemed to be advice to choose a new House leader who could eventually succeed him as national leader. This obscure counsel permitted the caucus to postpone any hard decisions, and they chose to keep Hanson as House leader until the session ended in mid-year.[84]

King handled the contradictory mandate of the conscription plebiscite on April 27 with consummate skill. The National Resources Mobilization Act would be amended to allow for overseas conscription, but none would in fact occur unless it later proved necessary. The Conservatives could fume that the government was doing neither one thing nor the other. Diefenbaker could lament: "What is the purpose of the repeal of this section unless there is to be action?" Yet the Conservatives could not vote against the bill without falling into self-contradiction: for it moved the country a step (if only a step) in the direction of overseas conscription.[85]

On the Hong Kong inquiry, the opposition was similarly outmanoeuvred, with disastrous results for party unity. While Arthur Meighen and George Drew urged the caucus to attack the government for covering up evidence of military incompetence through a secret inquiry, Hanson refused to lead the assault. In the atmosphere of wartime censorship, without evidence, without parliamentary leadership, the opposition's attack was limp. But it left relations between Hanson and Meighen shattered and Conservative tactics unclear. Hanson preferred the realistic effort to devise new policies that would prepare the party for a postwar electoral challenge, while avoiding excessive wartime criticism. Meighen persisted in his fanatic demand for confrontation and conscription. The *Globe and Mail* commented that "the Conservative group...in the House of Commons has sunk low."[86]

Neither leader wished to maintain his role, but neither knew what his next steps should be. To escape the stalemate, a small group of party activists led by J.M. Macdonnell, H.R. Milner, E.G. Phipps Baker, and Sidney Smith proposed a "round table on Canadian policy" – "an unoffical, unauthorized conference of laymen" that would discuss the party's future but exclude practising politicians. All of them were concerned to give the Conservative Party a new and progressive face that might check the growing appeal of the CCF. Hanson gave his support, and Meighen cautiously did so as well. Over the summer Rod Finlayson, a Winnipeg lawyer and former secretary to R.B. Bennett, took charge of planning the meeting, which would be held in Port Hope, Ontario, in early September. Finlayson and Macdonnell promoted the meeting in a series of interviews and articles during July and August, proposing a "New National Policy" that would combine the best features of free enterprise with full employment and guarantees of social security.[87] Their intuition about the party's future was congenial to John Diefenbaker.

On September 4, 1942, 159 delegates gathered in Port Hope to hear the same message from the chairman, H.R. Milner, and the keynote speaker, J.M. Macdonnell. Over four days they produced a series of resolutions affirming their progressive and internationalist beliefs, including support for a wide range of social benefits to be sustained by the free enterprise system. The only concession to Meighen was a muted demand for "immediate and complete conscription" for service anywhere in the world. "Here," wrote J.L. Granatstein, "was the Conservative answer to the socialism of the CCF. The 'Port Hopefuls' believed in private enterprise, in individual initiative, and in a minimum of state control. At the same time, however, they recognized that another great depression could not be permitted, and that if state intervention was the only way of preventing such crises, they favoured such intervention."[88]

Meighen privately described the conference's social welfare proposals as "flagrant and mischievous dishonesty" that would "cast away all the traditions of sanity and wisdom which have made us what we are."[89] But his active response was more complex. By this time he had decided to call a national leadership convention, and he set planning into motion. Milner was named chairman of the convention and Richard Bell, secretary. In early October the National Convention Committee announced that the meeting would take place in Winnipeg on December 9–11, 1942. The convention's resolutions and policy committee would be dominated by members present at Port Hope.[90]

Despite his qualms, Meighen recognized that the party would have to move left to counter the CCF and to undercut the Liberals. But he was determined to manage the selection of a new leader, rather than leaving it to the free play of party competition. John Diefenbaker and Howard Green seemed almost certain to be candidates from the parliamentary caucus; George Drew, Sidney Smith, and Murdoch MacPherson were frequently named as possibles; but none of them satisfied Arthur Meighen. A year before, in preparation for the planning meeting that led to his own selection, Meighen had canvassed the Liberal-Progressive premier of Manitoba, John Bracken, over his interest in the leadership. Bracken had declined. Now Meighen set out, through persistent lobbying among influential Conservatives, to draft Bracken. His objective seemed not so much to revolutionize party policy on Port Hope lines as to create a new national coalition that would rally broad postwar support among voters of all parties.[91] Bracken had the apparent attractions of a westerner, a non-partisan whose coalition label smudged distinctions while he offered safe, dull, conservative administration. Meighen was convinced Bracken could attract disgruntled Liberals to the party: "the one man whom the march of events and the juncture of fate point to."[92]

Bracken himself was endlessly hesitant. He refused to make any commitment before the convention, while Meighen's persistent lobby aroused "a swelling chorus of complaint" that the retiring leader and his friends meant to rig the choice of successor.[93] Diefenbaker was part of that chorus and he hoped to gain from it. But he, too, had difficulty making up his mind to run. His close supporters in Saskatchewan, among others, assumed that he would do so. Diefenbaker's Toronto Conservative friend, the lawyer David Walker, put a chill on the prospect in a letter on October 10:

It was very kind indeed of you to have your friend, Major Keown, the Conservative leader in Saskatchewan, call on me yesterday. He is a delightful personality and is a tremendous admirer of yours. In this matter, we had a great deal in common.

The Major asked me whether you had been considered as the leader of the Party to succeed Mr. Meighen. I informed him that I had had this matter in mind and had suggested you as a possible leading candidate to many of the people I met at Port Hope from east and west and since that time in political circles generally. He asked me to be frank with him in what reactions I had received and convey to you at once my impressions. Quite frankly, I was disappointed. Most people that knew you conceded that you were one of the most brilliant debaters in the House of Commons with one of the keenest minds and a tremendous fighter. Admitting all your abilities, the people I talked with, for one reason or another, including such silly reasons as your name and physique, refused to consider you seriously as their choice as leader of the Party. Every one of them conceded that you would be and should be a member of the Cabinet.

Since our friendship would not be worth-while unless we were frank with one another, I know that you will accept this letter in the spirit in which it is written.[94]

Walker's comments were countered in November by those of another Toronto supporter, the businessman George McGillivray.

I expect you are anxious to hear what I have picked up re the coming convention. In addition Dave Walker told me yesterday of his letter to you which, if I understand him properly, must have been, to say the least, upsetting.

First let me say this about Walker he did it thinking it a friendly act as you would desire to know the cons as well as the pros, and I think he can be depended upon to support you himself in any way he can...

I must say that my slant on it is entirely different from his. I think he is dominated to some extent by contact with Sydney [sic] Smith at Port Hope.

So far as I am concerned I have yet to meet anyone down here who is going to the convention with any preconceived views about how he is going to vote...

...The purpose of this letter isn't to build up your hopes. Both Dave Walker & I write what we think. He probably has far more extensive information than I but he is very much in the wrong, I think, if he indicates that the whole thing won't be anybody's baby at the convention.

I think the Conservatives here are making a serious error, following Port Hope, in indicating that their platform is to be "free enterprise" after the war unless they make it far clearer...All they seem to say is that it will be f.e. but not the same as...during the depression. This allows papers like the "Star" to say that we can call it what we will but the industrialist and capitalist will still be in the driver's seat and there will be little difference.

I wouldn't talk about f.e. so much. I'd talk of work for all and security for all & mention simply in passing that it was intended to get back to free enterprise as much as possible but always with the understanding that there would be f.e. so long only as it worked and that if it was necessary for government to step in and for gov't. to run things to prevent the breakdown that occurred previously then we're prepared to do it.[95]

The author added a postscript: "I've opened this up again to urge you to play up your name – Old Dutch stock like Theodore Roosevelt. Work the latter for all you're worth."

While Bracken temporized, four other western candidates finally came forward: Murdoch MacPherson, Howard Green, H.H. Stevens, and John Diefenbaker. A fifth, Sidney Smith, was rumoured to be waiting in the wings as an alternative to Bracken if he failed to show. The party seemed committed to a western, progressive conversion of some kind. Diefenbaker launched his candidacy formally on December 3 by declaring that he had decided to run "when he heard that the convention was likely to be a 'cut-and-dried' affair" – a coronation for John Bracken at the hands of Arthur Meighen and the party oligarchy. "It won't be as far as I am concerned. Delegates to this conven-tion are more than pawns."[96] Diefenbaker, along with the other internal candidates, had no pre-convention organization; like his recent correspondent, he trusted that the whole thing would be "anybody's baby at the convention."

Another Conservative friend, the serving military officer George Pearkes, offered Diefenbaker his advice shortly before the convention:

> As to what you shall say...it seems to me at the moment that the fight will narrow quickly to you and Bracken...Under the circumstances the point that should carry most weight I would think is an appeal to the delegates as men who have year in & out carried the party load. They know what loyalty to the party means & what it involves. It's like a lodge only better. You know when you meet some conservatives in the back room that you can talk freely & they take you into their confidence in the same way – no credentials asked. Any man who has worked for the party constantly for 20 yrs. can never let his party friends down and they know it. You can't serve the party master for 20 years and not be loyal to it whatever happens. But bring in a total outsider & what is the situation. It's true he's going to work with you to beat King – but that's all he's interested in – he's not one damn bit interested in the Conservative Party and the time will come when the Con. Party will find it out.
>
> ...
>
> There will be no one in the running with a better record for hard work and accomplishment than yours.
>
> They all dream of a great leader just as every girl dreams of a wonderful husband – one that will have all the parts.
>
> Well there's never been a great leader yet that in appearance had them all when he started – or actually had them either. He only got them with experience.[97]

On the evening of December 8 a party delegation met Bracken to present him with the convention's draft policy statement, a virtual repetition of the Port Hope declaration. Bracken accepted it, but still hesitated to enter a contested nomination battle in a party not his own. In the hope of carrying his followers with him, and demonstrating as well that he was not simply a candidate of the party establishment, Bracken set his price. He would enter the race if the party changed its name to Progressive Conservative before nominations were filed on December 10. The next day his letter setting out the condition was read to the convention; but instead of cheers – as Meighen expected – it was greeted with shouts of dismay. Bracken seemed to be seeking capitulation rather than sensible compromise. Milner promptly adjourned the meeting for the day.[98]

The next morning, debate on a resolution changing the party's name had to be postponed once again. When it was finally moved by Earl Lawson in the afternoon, it could not be seconded before opponents took to the microphones charging that a premature vote would prejudice the convention in favour of Bracken. Macdonnell saved the meeting from chaos by moving an amendment to postpone the question until after the leadership was decided.

Now Bracken would have to take his chances with the rest. The setback threw him into renewed indecision; with only a half-hour before the nomination deadline at 8 pm that evening, Meighen could not draw an answer from him. The other four candidates (and Sidney Smith as well, still a potential contestant if Bracken did not appear) waited in uncertainty at the auditorium along with the confused crowd. With only seconds remaining before the close, Bracken arrived in time to sign his nomination papers and make his pitch to the delegates.

In this bizarre atmosphere, the candidates' speeches were disappointing, relieved only by moments of surprise, venom, and low comedy. Bracken was uninspiring. Diefenbaker's nominator, David Walker, was shouted down when he insisted that the new leader "should be a Conservative; a Conservative, not an outsider. We don't want someone who is going to sell out our birthright for a mess of pottage." And when Howard Green began to speak, "suddenly, in the midst of a sentence he let go of the microphone, staggered backward, and fell in a faint, amid all the distinguished legs behind him."[99]

According to the same observer, Diefenbaker "was so stiff and starched in his manner I could scarcely recognize him." His words emerged in a "high, tense pitch."[100] But he had given the speech much thought and he read – unusually – from a prepared text. It was designed both to rally old Conservatives and to attract new ones. Diefenbaker began by contradicting his nominator: "All who have been nominated are worthy men, all of whom I would follow with loyalty and devotion, and if anything comes home to me on this occasion, it is this, what this Party needs more than leadership and policy is the loyalty to leadership, for however courageous and sincere that leadership may be, criticism will come, and we should here and now undertake that, whoever is chosen, we and each of us will not join in the symphony of Government Press abuse."

The Conservative Party, he admitted, was near extinction, a condition brought on by defeat, wartime self-restraint, and a tendency to hold on to outworn beliefs. Third parties had risen and fallen for two decades, but the Liberal Party had been the main beneficiary of their decline. Now the

Conservatives would have to enter the battle for their votes: "It is not too late to rehabilitate this Party. I am not fearful of the CCF if we stand for principle: if we have leadership that will fight instead of staying dormant. I have no fear of the CCF if we stand for something." What he stood for incorporated the progressive vision of Port Hope within some old-fashioned values: "We must fight for the preservation of Canada within the British Empire; with the public social minded we must fight for the security of the common man; fight for the return of our Democratic Institutions which are more in danger today than ever before; fight for a fair deal under a system of private initiative, whereby these that I have mentioned, the farmer, the laborer and the under privileged will be assured of the same security that can be provided under any socialistic form of Government, and if it cannot be done (and I do not believe that it cannot), then this Party deserves to perish."

Diefenbaker declared the party's search for a wartime coalition government at an end. "The time is now passed when we should come, with hat in hand, as a common mendicant, asking for alms at King's table...There will be no National Government under Mr. King." The Conservative Party had a record of patriotism, "of co-operation lustred by an attitude of country before Party, united in a common desire to win the war"; and yet Mackenzie King had called the Conservative Party a "mob." "That sneer represented an attitude of mind that demands action. In my vocabulary those words are 'fighting' words, though they were expurgated from Hansard...We have endeavoured to share in the Government – it has been refused; it has been spurned; it has been ridiculed. We have become sterile of ideas except for our demand for National Government. Why keep this up?"

The party should seek alliances neither on right or left, but instead should "restore itself from within." It should accept Edmund Burke's definition of conservatism as a "disposition to conserve and the ability to change." In the age of the common man, that meant fundamental change.

The Atlantic Charter promises improved labor standards, economic adjustments and social security. If the Empire fights for those principles, can the Conservative Party stand for or fight for less? Security must be our watch word. By security I mean – to every able bodied man a job, and to those who, because of age, physical or mental infirmity, cannot work, security without work. I mean security for employment; security in and while employed; security while not employed and of retirement, and of medical and hospital assistance, and of family in case of accident, ill health, invalidity and death...In short, by security I mean the guarantee of an opportunity for your sons and daughters to travel along the broadway of promise and hope instead of stumbling along the paths of hopelessness and despair...

...I believe that the principles of Port Hope will prove the hope of this Party. I believe that Canadian unity must be assured; that it must be built on the basis of a Canadianism that knows no racial origin; that out of the various races and creeds of this Dominion must evolve a united Canada.

Diefenbaker found his justification in the reforming spirit of Sir John A. Macdonald, "a most far-sighted man who was always ahead of his time," and in the party's record of pragmatic state intervention in the economy. But such intervention should avoid the arbitrary Liberal rule of wartime and the bureaucratic inclinations of the CCF. In a sweeping peroration, he quoted the Bible and Lord Macaulay, ending with Winston Churchill's appeal to beleaguered Britons to "stand by one another, true and faithful comrades, and do our duty, God helping us, to the end."[101]

Balloting took place the next day. Given the lack of committed delegates and a slate that was uncertain until the very moment of nominations, the outcome was unpredictable. Although Meighen had succeeded, in the end, in getting Bracken onto the ballot, the delegates had repeatedly shown their wish to be treated with respect rather than herded into his camp. Yet both deference and prudence suggested that Meighen's preference would carry weight. Wasn't Bracken, after all, the safest of these western progressives?

On the first ballot, 862 delegates cast their votes, and 432 votes were needed to win. Bracken just fell short, with 420; MacPherson was second with 222, Diefenbaker third with 120, Green next with 80, and Stevens last with 20. Stevens and Green withdrew before a second ballot, but MacPherson's supporters prevented his attempted withdrawal and Diefenbaker stayed in. On that ballot Bracken triumphed easily, with 538 votes; MacPherson trailed with 255 and Diefenbaker with 79. The losers moved to make the vote unanimous, and Bracken delivered a relaxed and effective acceptance speech. When the motion for a change in party name came forward, it was adopted without debate by enthusiastic voice vote. Bracken's and Diefenbaker's party had become the Progressive Conservative Party.[102]

Diefenbaker took this defeat with relative calm. He had not expected victory.[103] Walker's outburst had been unseemly, but Diefenbaker himself had behaved with dignity throughout. He left the convention with his reputation enhanced, both in the House and in the country. He had made new friends like the Toronto lawyer William Brunt and had widened his circle of political admirers. And the party had moved significantly in the direction he believed it should.[104] For Diefenbaker, MacPherson contributed the only sour note: "MacPherson and I had been friends for many years. But our personal relations were never to recover from my decision to stand as a candidate in 1942. My action was heresy, and a cardinal sin."[105]

Bracken met the parliamentary caucus in Winnipeg the day after his convention victory. The first issue was his entry into the House of Commons. Bracken was aware of the paradox that his nomination had been sponsored by the party's more reactionary wing, and he rejected the thought of plunging into divisive controversy in the party or the House. He told Mackenzie King that "he had never taken a party part in politics...he was just interested in the public service." He judged himself a poor debater. He knew from Meighen's experience that a by-election would be strenuous and risky. So, after taking advice from Meighen, Milner, and others, he decided not to seek early election to parliament. Instead, he would concentrate on touring and consulting.[106] This hardly seemed the fighting start that Diefenbaker had called for.

Since Hanson would not consider carrying on as House leader, the caucus would have to make a fresh choice. On December 19 Gordon Graydon, who had formally nominated Bracken, wrote to Conservative MPs on Bracken's behalf, inviting their suggestions. Diefenbaker understood that this was a form of election and that the contest was between himself and Graydon. But in January the prospect faded. "Even though Bracken did not want me as House Leader, I knew that I had enough support in caucus to make my selection a distinct possibility. The letter vote was taken in early January, 1943. About the middle of the month, Mr. Bracken visited Saskatoon to see his mother. He telephoned me to meet him. We chatted for two hours or so. Since nothing was said about the choice of a temporary Leader, I naturally concluded that someone else had been chosen. I learned later that Bracken had decided to ignore the results of the letter ballot and to put the issue of the House leadership directly before caucus when it met on 27 January, the day before the Opening of Parliament."[107]

Diefenbaker was involved in a complex civil fraud case in Saskatoon and found it difficult to attend the caucus meeting. He was only persuaded to do so by a series of solicitous telephone calls from Bracken. Although he was now less eager to win the House leadership, Diefenbaker believed that the chances of winning were good. He set out by train for the meeting.

We get snowed up in Northern Ontario. The train was to arrive here at 8 o'clock in the morning – didn't arrive until 8 o'clock at night. I arrive at the station and Mel Jack is there, secretary to Bracken. He says, "Come on over, they're choosing a leader." I said, "that was to be done this morning." All that day that group had worked to bring about the assurance that I would be defeated...I got up immediately and said, "I'm not standing." There were four or five names submitted. I was two short of a majority on the first vote. Graydon was next and...two dropped out. Then there was a second vote, again I said I'm not standing and I was still in much the same position, and it came down to the final between Graydon and myself. And I got up and I said, "Now I've told you I'm going west to take this case...I don't want this job. I'm very certain. There's my ballot marked for Graydon." He beat me by one vote.[108]

This was a puzzling incident, perhaps a more painful rebuff to Diefenbaker than the convention defeat, since it seemed to involve a concerted campaign against him in caucus, supported by the new leader. The memory of it rankled. Yet his own equivocation must have been a source of doubt and confusion to members during the balloting: in a sense he was both in and out of the contest. Those who took him at his word must have believed that he did not want the job. What he may really have wanted was an impossible show of unanimity in his favour.

JOHN DIEFENBAKER'S DAYS WERE SINGLE-MINDEDLY DOMINATED BY POLITICS. IN Ottawa he allowed no time for distractions: the House of Commons was his life. There he found fellowship, conflict, drama, and comic relief. His mother and father in Saskatoon watched his career with obsessive interest, reading Hansard and the press clippings for mention of his name, applauding, urging him on, and reporting the details of their own mundane lives in regular letters. John apparently wrote to them almost daily – although few of those letters survive. After 1943 William's letters to John became less frequent, but Mary maintained her own staccato correspondence. She complained more and more about the laziness of her husband, the inadequacy of the hired help, and the faults of "huns," "indians," Liberals, and the local Baptist congregation.[109]

Early in March 1944 Diefenbaker asked his parents for their advice about a prospective visit to Australia with a parliamentary delegation. His letter provoked two months of tense family debate, at first focused on the trip's safety and political implications. Father wrote to son on March 14:

A number of things come up...

...Will prominent persons be called upon to go? If not, why? Has Gordon Graydon been asked to be one of the number? Would he be glad to go and thus let one of the other members substitute for him while away? How much of your parliamentary attendance time would it require? Would your constituents favor your being away from parliament that long? Would the long and possibly tedious boat trip be of much health benefit? Would it be dangerous at this time in particular? If an election be set at such a time as to...preclude your active participation...how much of your chances to win...would be lost thereby?

Considering everything favorably, as I see it you would gain some prestige, you would see Australia...learn quite a bit about the country...be amongst others of your company, feted and dined and come home with a knowledge which would...come good in making public and parliamentary speeches thereafter.

...And what does Edna say?...

P.S. – Just as to what your mother thinks about your going, I don't know.[110]

That postscript warned of more to come. A few days later Mary Diefenbaker wrote: "Now about that trip you would like to take. I dont know what to say about it, its up to you. If King should go to the country you might be out of luck, and you could go to Australia some other time. you are still young. I dont feel like writing tonight will do better next time."[111]

The warnings of political danger – the hints, even, of a plot to get John out of the way so that he might miss a general election – covered a more personal affront. The trip would mean John's absence on his parents' fiftieth wedding anniversary on May 2. The swirl of parental doubt meant that he could not make up his mind about the journey. He suggested, in exchange for his absence, that they should later visit Ottawa; but Mary fussed about that. On April 19 she wrote:

We received your letter today, and see you are still very undecided about your trip. Well John I dont know what to say about it, you will have to decide for yourself. I dont want you to consider us at all we are all right. so if that is on your mind for get it. The only thing that troubled me was the danger of the trip, and you told me there was no danger, and strange to say you got me to believe it, and as far as going east I dont know what to say about that with the hot weather coming on, and Edna can tell you I cant get clothes here, and I wont go with my old clothes. I dont know how we could get ready in such a short time. and just forget about the 50th anniversary. let it ride the same as the other 49, for that does not worry me at all of course it would have been nice if the whole family could have been here we could have gone to the

Bessborough for dinner, but that cannot be, so let us forget it. If we were going East it would not be necessary for you to come back for us. surely we could make it alone. I dont want you to fly here. Had a letter from Elmer yesterday he was glad to see you and was quite worked up about your trip.[112]

In the end, a mother's disapproval won the day and Diefenbaker gave up the Australian trip. But neither he nor Edna went to Saskatoon for the anniversary. He trusted instead to a telephone call and a flood of roses. Mary wrote to John that evening to spill out her self-pity.

I was sorry I did not do better over the Phone. I took asparin all morning trying to keep cool, so as I could talk to you, but just before you called the Roses arrived and it knocked me out. Fifty Roses when all I wanted was sons. I never was so disappointed in all my life. Even after getting Edna's letter saying she wished you folks could be here but that Politicks seemed to have upset everything. I never thought that politics would keep you from coming home to our golden wedding. As you told me it was the one reason why you did not take (or want to take) the trip to Australia. I told you then to forget about it. But when you did'nt go, I did think you would be here today. but politics comes first. I did not know you loved them that much. Well John I have shed a lot of tears today, and I heard your Dad crying too. but he is not like me he dont say anything and I just rave. I had a letter from Elmer the other day. he said he did not know what you were going to do. but there would be a letter from you when he got back to Winnipeg. I think he would have tried to get a 48 [hour leave]. Well the Big day will soon be over and I am thankful for that I have not eaten a thing since morning I got some dinner for Will. but could not choke any thing down myself There are few live to see their fiftieth anniversary I am not saying this to make you feel bad. but I just cant understand it. Elmer phoned from Winnipeg said he could not get here...I got a new dress or will have it this week. Its very nice and cost money. Now John write and tell me why love.[113]

John wrote to Elmer a few days later to report that he was "equally disturbed" at missing the anniversary, and that "I had the same experience as you did...I wrote home today explaining the situation as much as I could, but apparently there is nothing that can be done now."[114]

Since September 1941, Elmer Diefenbaker had been a member of the Royal Canadian Air Force. After training in Trenton, Ontario, he was appointed as a flying officer in the administrative branch and posted to No. 2 Training

Command in Winnipeg as a lecturer and supervisor of air cadets. Soon after the anniversary débâcle, in June 1944, Elmer was involved in some kind of disciplinary affair leading to his suspension from duty. William wrote to John on July 14 to say that "we are wholly in the dark so far as word from him is concerned...I have so far not said a word about the affair, to any outsider, and think it more than wise to continue that attitude." John seemed to have intervened on Elmer's behalf; William noted that John "had been a real brother to Elmer" and would no doubt give him work if that were temporarily needed. For several months Elmer was retained in the RCAF without duties, until receiving an honourable discharge in February 1945.[115]

Elmer had already returned to the family home in Saskatoon when, on February 12, William Diefenbaker died at seventy-seven years of age.[116] More distressing still, for John, was Edna's condition.[117] In wartime letters to his mother and father, John periodically mentioned that Edna was unwell, but the nature of the complaint was unclear.[118] John was still unusually dependent on his mother, which meant constantly catering to her whims; on the one occasion in 1944 when he defied her, the emotional price had proven to be high. That was a continuing source of annoyance and frustration for Edna. So, apparently, was her new life in Ottawa.

Edna had no extensive public life of her own. She existed as John's satellite and devoted servant. She shared and nursed his grievances over lost battles and social slights.[119] John was both demanding and preoccupied, expecting Edna to devote herself to him but refusing to give much thought to her concerns, or to allow time for any joint recreations. Diefenbaker lived his political life at a high nervous pitch, which left him moody and unpredictable as a husband, prone to sudden bouts of rage and suspicion. He needed Edna to reassure and calm him, to feed him a proper bland diet for his ever-queasy stomach, even to advise him as he dressed.[120]

When Edna lobbied hard for the advancement of her "Donny Boy" – as she often did – some politicians and reporters drew back. She was too pushy. She also, inevitably, heard and absorbed the frequent criticism directed at her husband for his aggressive ways in the House.

In Prince Albert Edna had been the object of tongue-wagging about her romantic friendship with a handsome young widower who courted her on the dance floor and sometimes visited her at home during John's daytime absences.[121] She was naturally high-spirited and flirtatious, and found that her charms could lead to dalliance. In the greater anonymity of Ottawa, without the moorings of home and community, yet facing the same desperation in her life with John, she found similar diversion – and worried about John's jealousy and the potential scandal of discovery. Rodney Adamson, the gregarious Conservative MP from Port Credit, Ontario – who enjoyed his knowledge of Ottawa's political lowlife – was one of her confidants in that distress. He wrote in his diary in May 1942 after a lunch with Edna and John: "Talk to Edna afterwards about her lousy lover in the Maritimes tell her John would murder her if she was found out or it created a scandal."[122] Whether the initiative for this conversation came from Edna or Adamson is not clear, but Edna obviously revealed some intimacies. Adamson used crude language in the diary to describe her exuberant sexual appetites and John's indifference. A few days later Adamson noted cryptically: "Go up to House and talk to Edna again about her morals."[123] He was neither prudish nor judgmental; the words suggest no more than a mordant concern about her anxieties and her discretion. Almost two years later, in February 1944, Adamson wrote again in his diary that "Edna also has a boy friend Rennie in the Lord Elgin."[124]

Although contemporary convention meant that reporters did not write, or newspapers publish, accounts of politicians' private lives, Ottawa gossip soaked up stories of all kinds. Edna's indiscretions were probably known to others in and around the Conservative caucus and the press gallery. Titillating gossip might not matter – might even be a source of fascination – when it involved a private member of parliament, but for a potential leader it could be a hindrance. Was this, perhaps, an unspoken factor in the selection of a new House leader in January 1943? Ottawa in the 1940s reflected the country in its repressed and puritan spirit. It was a place where hypocrisy was king: while a man's infidelity could be accepted as evidence of his vigour and daring, a woman's was shocking and probably depraved. Edna knew the conventions and prejudices of the time, and accepted most of them. Her very audacity must have caused her anguish.

The summer of 1944 was particularly difficult for Edna. The allied invasion of Europe in June meant that a victorious ending of the war was expected within months – and that meant an intensified focus on domestic politics. The government was in the fourth year of its term, and an early election could be anticipated. When John and Edna came west to Prince Albert in mid-August, he planned to begin his active campaign for re-election in Lake Centre. To assist him, John invited Bill Brunt and his wife, Helen, to stay with them. Without domestic help to clean and reopen the house, Edna suggested either that the visit be postponed or that the Brunts stay in a local hotel. John insisted. Before their arrival, Edna's eighty-one-year-old mother began opening up the house, but soon injured her hand in the washing machine and found herself briefly confined to hospital. Edna's niece Sheila rushed to Prince Albert from Saskatoon to take charge of both the patient and the household preparations.

Within days Edna and John arrived; the Brunts followed immediately afterwards. For a hectic week the visitors were entertained, Maren Brower was cared for, and John pursued his constituency affairs with Brunt at his side. Towards the end of the visit, Edna and her family were crushed by news that the husband of another niece had been killed in action at Caen. And then, without a pause, the whole Diefenbaker family arrived from Saskatoon for one week in the house. Once again John had refused Edna's request to postpone the visit. By August 1944 Edna detested her imperious mother-in-law and found the cloying relationship of Mary and John intolerable; yet she kept a typically polite front as mother and son fawned on each other. But alone with Sheila, Edna broke down in tears of strain and frustration.[125]

Another incident, apparently that same summer, also tested the couple's fragile equilibrium. During her housecleaning in the basement, Edna discovered John's long-discarded military uniform, mildewed and moth-infested. Without reflection, she burned it. When she told John that evening, he responded with tears and fury: "And you did not even save my epaulets, you did not save my epaulets." Next day at the law office, Diefenbaker raged to his secretary. "He was absolutely furious...he stormed around all day, shouting: 'Edna burned my uniform. She burned it! I planned to be buried in it.'" By the end of the summer, Edna was speaking bluntly and harshly to close friends in Prince Albert about John's short temper and selfishness.[126]

While many women surmounted such troubles, Edna apparently could not. She was still John's conventional partner, determined to support and promote his career despite all her discontents. Before the summer of 1944 she was again depressed and confused, and accepted renewed sedation with tranquillizers. She began to lose her hair, one of the sources of her attractiveness, and took to wearing a turban to conceal her embarrassment.

In the spring of 1945 she suffered a breakdown and was sufficiently ill to be referred to a Toronto psychiatrist, Dr Goldwin Howland. Diefenbaker corresponded with Howland in 1945 and 1946 over the serious state of his wife's health, but only a few of Howland's letters can be found in the Diefenbaker papers.[127] He apparently diagnosed a psychiatric illness, probably mild depression and an obsessive neurosis.[128] Edna herself seemed to regard her condition as a nervous illness, perhaps the result of prolonged used of tranquillizers.[129] It could also have been a sign of the menopause – a passage of life that was scarcely to be thought about in the male society of the 1940s.

John, meanwhile, was inextricably wrapped up in his political life. In

April 1945 he travelled to the founding conference of the United Nations in San Francisco – not as a member of the Canadian delegation but as an unofficial observer who managed to wangle his way into the opening ceremony at the Opera House. On April 25 he sent Edna a postcard:

> My dear –
>
> Please keep this – because it will be stamped today. See the movies of the opening ceremony and you will – believe it or not see me on the outside side – 9 rows back from the front and in front of the speakers – 4 seats behind F.M. Smuts whose hand I shook. It's an interesting story how I got in – Gordon Graydon figured it out – Hope you are feeling better – write me or wire me...
>
> Love and the best[130]

After San Francisco, Diefenbaker returned to Canada in May to plunge into the election campaign, which had been called by Mackenzie King for June 11. Edna, although under Dr Howland's care, took some part in the campaign. On July 10, at Edna's request, he wrote to Diefenbaker to report that, after a relapse in June, she was in improved health. "I think we may expect from time to time, relapses, but she will finally get well." Howland made no mention of Edna's symptoms or of a diagnosis (both of which had presumably been discussed in earlier conversations or letters), but his letter takes for granted that he thought he was dealing with a mental rather than physical illness. The language is stilted. "I have handled the case with very careful attention, studying her every mental condition, studying all the underground condition of her mind, using every modern method of psychotherapeutic measures, using much the same methods you would use in your legal practice. I have had to judge her reactions to people and to those not living about her and I might say it is one of the hardest cases I have had, causing me great anxiety as to whether this was going to be a permanent case or not."[131]

Howland now expressed an unexplained confidence in Edna's recovery. But the balance of the letter suggested, not too subtly, that a major cause of her illness might be Diefenbaker's own attitudes and behaviour.

> I am not anxious about her recovery now, but am anxious how you will manage the case when you take over and it will depend on you more than anyone else whether she remains well or not. She is a very fine woman, indeed, and her ideals are the best and she is completely wrapped up in your interests but it would be better if she had more interests of her own. She dislikes housekeeping which is, unfortunately part of her life's work.

I have a feeling that between now and the time the House opens in Ottawa that perhaps it would be possible for you and your wife to take a holiday together for two or three weeks. I do not feel certain whether starting her directly at work at home is quite the wisest thing after such a serious illness. Perhaps you and she might decide to have a holiday and I almost think she would sooner go to Ottawa than back at home. She was tremendously interested in your saying you might start practice in partnership in Vancouver. She said "it is the wish of my life and perhaps my husband is becoming tired of sitting on the Opposition of the House."

This seemed to be a strong plea from Edna, conveyed through the medium of her psychiatrist, that John should abandon politics for the sake of a life more tolerable to her. In his conclusion Dr Howland emphasized Edna's respect for, and dependence upon – or fear of – her husband. "During her whole time here I do not think she has said a single thing against you, which is very unusual for a wife. But she is terribly afraid you will be disappointed when you see her, so, for Heaven's sake, when you do come be delighted with her condition. She does not think you realize how ill she has been. She certainly was in a poor condition when she arrived in Toronto."[132]

The advice about a change of career was delivered tentatively and casually, and was unlikely, by itself, to prompt John Diefenbaker to alter direction. At best, it might have been the starting point for more precise discussion and analysis of the couple's difficulties. Diefenbaker either missed, or chose to ignore, Howland's point, and there is no evidence that such discussion took place. Diefenbaker's political life did not change. Over the summer Edna remained in a state of distress, and in the autumn the couple decided on a more radical course of treatment. Then began a long nightmare.

Diefenbaker had known of the Homewood Sanitarium at Guelph, Ontario, since at least March 1934, when its superintendent had visited the Prince Albert penitentiary to examine Diefenbaker's client Steve Bohun before his execution.[133] Dr Howland had made use of a nursing director from Homewood to assist in his observation of Edna during the summer.[134] By 1945 the private psychiatric hospital, like others in North America, was treating mental disorders experimentally with doses of electric shock therapy. In late September, Diefenbaker took his wife to Homewood for further examination and possible treatment.[135]

Soon after her arrival in Guelph, Edna wrote John pleading for him to visit and, one way or another, to rescue her from incarceration.

Really John you must come to see the situation. Dr. Mackinnon has no interest in me whatever he wont see me. now John this is just a place for people who can afford to keep their relations out of mental hospitals.

They are practically all mental here Dear or have no home. They give shock for those who can afford it & can take it but apparently they dont want you cured here.

There is no routine at all. Oh God if I only could explain it to you Dear.

John you couldnt get well seeing what I see I thought it would only be nervous patients – but its every thing on my floor they are on their own & will be here for years. there isnt a hostess to arrange our day or walk with us. No body sleeps & every body is on pills.

You must come Ill never improve here talk about throwing your money away for no purpose you must get up at 7.30 & then stay alone as the living room is filled with people who seem to look normal but in reality they are not.

There is a sweet girl here who had too many drugs & spent 3 mos in a rest in Toronto & came to see if she could have shock but cant so is going home to-day she is the only person I can talk to normally. I can see why Dr. MacKinnon doesnt want you here for a month he is a liar & no heart. Thinks he is quite the big shot what all did you tell him he told me you had explained my case & wont let me give him my history told me frankly he didnt believe me now John you know I want my feelings back & I liked my life.

My hair has practically gone dead & is coming out completely apparently they have never had a case like this before.

If you dont come – Im going to leave Ill try home Ottawa or any place but there is nothing conducive to health here they are really tough John. How I wish I knew if it was drugs or break down no one here has had the head or vacancy I have had so I wonder if its too many drugs for years.

Howland knew his stuff when he said dont come here.

I could battle the hair get a wig if necessary Well John do something Im not committed and you know Im sane.

please please come otherwise Ill write mother & she will come I know. There must be some one who can tell why this stony feeling is here my skin is dead also my head & they must have run into like cases some where – Im not hysterical nor panicky Im reasoning it out & if you were here you would understand it it just means years if you leave me dear its just a money making place John.

You must investigate Your speech was fine dear Im hungry for news no one here talks my language Dear. I think an apt with a nurse would be better & not much more.

Miss Cooper told me drugs took her feelings & taste away altho she never lost her sense of touch in her skin & body she said her head was stony not as bad as mine but she only had them 3 mos it was sodium amital she took every 2 hrs for 2 months a Dr gave them to her to get settled enough to work.

Now you must do something John as I definitely realize this state will never change here even you will see there is a definite change for the worse here.

If mabel were only in Toronto & could come up she would see how this environment is so injurious to one – its fine for people who are definitely mental they rave on & enjoy the place but my place is in Ottawa with you my brain is so clear its just something has gone wrong with my nervous system its either drugs or the breakdown Id like so much to see another physycriast as he would know which is wrong with me if my feelings come back you would not waste your money as for drugs they are giving me new ones that make me sleep longer & I know they arc stronger Well that isnt a cure is it? They give me pheno Barb after meals & I throw it down the toilet as I have turned to stone so I dont need them at all.

Dr. MacKinnon isnt the man you think he is Dr Bough is human & believes me when I say my head has such queer sensations at times & then stony & tells me he thinks its drugs plus a depression due to my age – & he did say they were considering shock.

Please tell me you will come soon otherwise Ill go clean crazy & disgrace you Dear & so far Ive been normal through it all Ive been alone in my room now for hours & you never expected that & if you are upstairs you are confined to barred rooms & John you wouldnt let them do that when my mind is clear its all emotions & nerves & fear from my hair which is wrong & you know it.

Come come soon & try & find if I can have shock & get well.

All My Love
Edna[136]

But the dreadful experience continued for months. Diefenbaker did what he could to conceal Edna's whereabouts during the fall and winter of 1945–46, and few friends knew that she was at Homewood. David Walker and Dr Herbert Bruce were exceptions; Walker apparently accompanied John and Edna when she was admitted at the end of September and visited Edna from time to time.[137] He told Simma Holt that he thought there was no need for Edna's presence at Homewood, and recalled that Diefenbaker, too, wanted her home. But Diefenbaker apparently deferred to medical advice to keep her there. Finally, in March 1946, Edna received five applications of electric shock therapy. Soon afterwards, she was released from hospital and returned with John to Prince Albert. There is no available report on the result of her treatment, but as David Walker recalled, "something made her well again."[138]

The nightmarish episode left Edna embittered. She told her friend Estelle McGregor that "she had been through the most terrible treatment, that it was completely unnecessary, that she thought she had needed some rest and medical help, but not what she got." "It can never," she was reported to have said, "be the same again with John after what happened." But to reveal the matter would undermine John's political life, and she would not do that. Diefenbaker needed her loyalty – and in the absence of any conceivable alternatives, she needed him. The experience, however, left John with lingering anxieties about Edna's mental rather than her physical health – anxieties that reflected the prejudices of the time and his own ambitions as well as more unselfish worries about her condition. In polite society, diseases of the mind (like alcoholism, venereal disease, or bastardy) were a subject of shame, a realm of popular ignorance and intolerance. John Diefenbaker shared those prejudices without reflection. His Prince Albert medical friend and political associate Dr Glen Green recalled that Diefenbaker "had a fear of mental problems...he felt it was catching, as did most people of his vintage, and so the farther he was away from it, the happier he was."[139] Above all, his career, driven by a more and more palpable longing for glory, came first. If Edna's collapse somehow reflected her frustration with John's single-minded quest, then that devotion allowed him scant means of confronting the problem.[140]

William and Mary Diefenbaker's wedding, 1894. They are accompanied, on the left, by Mary's sister Sadie Bridgeman and William's brother Ulysses. (All photos reproduced courtesy of The Diefenbaker Centre unless otherwise indicated.)

Mary Diefenbaker appeared strong and confident at the age of twenty.

John, posing with Elmer at the age of six or seven, already had his characteristically penetrating stare.

*The Diefenbaker
family in 1902.*

*John at the age of twelve, bundled in a buffalo coat
in an oxcart with his Uncle Edward.*

The artist James Flux idealized Mary Diefenbaker and her two sons on the Saskatchewan homestead, as Mary dreamed of her Highland Scots ancestors resisting dispossession. The watercolour was painted in the 1950s.

Lieutenant John Diefenbaker was twenty-one in this studio portrait of 1916. He was about to be posted overseas.

Diefenbaker received his degree of Bachelor of Laws from the University of Saskatchewan in the spring of 1919.

Diefenbaker opened his law practice in the prairie village of Wakaw, Saskatchewan, in the summer of 1919.

In 1929 Diefenbaker, as a provincial candidate in Prince Albert, expected to become attorney general of Saskatchewan if he won his seat. He lost the contest, but the Conservatives formed the government and perished in the Depression. Back row: David Burgess and Dr J.T.M. Anderson; front row: Samuel Branion, Diefenbaker, and Dr Fred MacLean.

*Edna Mae Brower,
of Saskatoon,
in her late twenties.*

*Edna and John were married in June
1929 from the home of her brother in
Toronto. Her wedding dress was made
by Lucien Lelong in New York City.*

*In the wartime election of 1940,
Diefenbaker won Lake Centre for the
Tories, one of only two victories in
Saskatchewan.*

Now an MP, Diefenbaker was a sober and serious presence in this 1942 portrait.

CHAPTER 5

New Name, Old Party

1945-1951

IN DECEMBER 1942 THE CONSERVATIVE PARTY SHOOK ITSELF HALF-AWAKE BY choosing John Bracken as national leader. John Diefenbaker, despite his own double disappointment, was satisfied with the party's apparent change of direction, but regarded Bracken with a respect that fell short of enthusiasm.[1] On the single occasion when he invited the leader into his constituency in 1943, Bracken thoughtlessly touched an old nerve by telling the rural audience that farmers did not need lawyers to represent them in parliament.[2]

Meanwhile, the balance of war was shifting gradually in favour of the Allies, the Canadian Army in Britain was not in combat, and voluntary recruitment was holding up. Mackenzie King, in his diary, allowed himself a bit of comfort about the war effort and the weakness of his domestic opponents. He was pleased that Diefenbaker, "the most bitter in his attacks" in the House, had not been chosen parliamentary leader, and he smugly reviewed the list of his fallen Conservative challengers. "There never was a more complete confounding of the politics of one's enemies than is exhibited by this debacle of the old Tory party which has tried to cover up its disasters by giving itself a new name. In one round, while they have been talking of my not being a leader, I have succeeded, after defeating Bennett as the leader of the Conservative party, his successor Manion as the next leader, Manion's successor Meighen as the next leader, and now witnessing the fourth leader...without a seat in the House."[3]

The party did not threaten King and his Liberals. J.M. Macdonnell insisted that the Tory "Old Guard" would have to be ousted from control by the creation of a new organization and fundraising group to assist the leader. Others, too, agreed that these changes were essential. In early 1943 Bracken named the vigorous young organizer Richard Bell – who had already assumed the role in practice – as national director; Gordon Graydon became president of a revived Dominion Progressive Conservative Association, replacing the elderly

J.R. MacNicol; headquarters staff were hired; a monthly tabloid, *Public Opinion*, was planned to begin publication in August; and a network of supposedly non-partisan "Bracken clubs" was promoted across the country.[4] But these acts of national organization remained hostage to the uncertainties of war, the tactics of the other parties, the whims of the powerful Ontario Conservative Party, and the political talents of the new leader. Within months the effort to reform the party and to place it solidly at the centre of the political spectrum had failed.

Meanwhile, the Ontario Tories were on the rise under George Drew's leadership. When the fading Ontario Liberal government went to the polls in August 1943, it collapsed before its two rivals. Drew's highly organized Conservatives won thirty-eight seats, and the CCF was close behind with thirty-four. The Liberals ran third with fifteen seats. The victory gave an immediate boost to federal Conservative morale, but that was soon dispelled when it became clear to Bell that Drew's organization was seeking to take control of the national party. An initial proposal to displace the national executive in favour of a Toronto committee chaired by the businessman Henry Borden was rejected by Bracken.[5] But Bell was convinced that Drew and his corporate associates had longer-term mischief in mind. In a 1944 memorandum on party organization he wrote: "Some of the Drew people are in too much of a hurry to advance the cause of their own leader in federal affairs and have not hesitated to say so at the same time either directly or inferentially damning the present federal leadership. In the opinion of a considerable number of the federal members, the basic trouble is the desire of the Ontario Party to have control of the representation in the House of Commons from Ontario after the next election as a means of controlling a future convention of the Party and determining the future leadership of the party."[6]

The immediate concern of Conservative business leaders was to counter what they saw as the dangerous socialist threat now posed by the CCF. For them, that meant a frantic assertion of free enterprise propaganda and a renewed effort to commit the federal Conservative Party safely to a right-wing agenda.

Mackenzie King and the Liberal Party were equally rattled by the socialist challenge. Their response was to move left with the tide of popular opinion, to reassert their claim to the broad middle ground tentatively sought by the Progressive Conservatives at Port Hope and Winnipeg. Cabinet and party, under King's astute guidance, made their preparations during the fall of 1943 and announced their program in the speech from the throne that began the 1944 session of parliament in January.[7]

That message established the foundations of national policy for the post-war period. The government committed itself to "a national minimum of social security and human welfare" that would include full employment, price stabilization, family allowances, health insurance, and contributory old age pensions. It promised to introduce the family allowance scheme during the 1944 session. For the prime minister, the postwar program would fulfil the vision laid out twenty-five years before in his book *Industry and Humanity*.[8] Its more immediate sources were the Beveridge Report in the United Kingdom and the Marsh Report in Canada, which had given form to the widespread sentiment that the suffering of the 1930s must never be repeated. Diefenbaker called the program "the most tantalizing bill of fare ever offered to the Canadian people."[9]

Family allowances were shrewdly designed as the government's first venture into postwar welfare. They would mean monthly, direct payments to every child-rearing family in the country; they would catapult the Liberal Party to the left of the political spectrum and undercut the CCF; and they would divide the Tories. Without waiting for his MPs, Bracken pronounced the plan a "political bribe" to be opposed, and he probably had a majority with him when debate on the measure began in caucus. Diefenbaker recalled that "I was the only Member in our caucus, to begin with, not prepared to oppose it. It was demanded by some that I either oppose the measure or leave the Party...After long and stormy arguments over two or three days, all but one Conservative Member supported the bill."[10] In fact, Diefenbaker had a persistent ally in Howard Green throughout the discussion in caucus, while many others were open to persuasion because they recognized the measure's popularity. Rodney Adamson noted the outcome on July 26, 1944: "Long caucus about family allowances. I take stand against them...Bracken is anti also but bows to Howard Green, Diefenbaker, the Western and Maritime Members. Perhaps this is good strategy. I say I will not vote for measure and will stay away."[11]

Diefenbaker and the progressive wing had won the preliminary battle, but the party nevertheless lost the war. When House debate opened on the bill, Diefenbaker led off for the Conservatives with a resounding statement of agreement in principle, aimed both at the public and at his own party.

With the objective provided for in this bill there can be no disagreement; for if I understand it aright it means that...an endeavour will be made to achieve equal opportunity, particularly for those in the lower income brackets, and to give to many who to-day are denied freedom from fear and freedom from want the hope of something better in the future than this world and this country have seen before...

Changes are taking place and tremendous changes are about to take place. We in the parliaments of the empire to-day must recognize that. The state must guarantee and underwrite equal access to security, to education, to nutrition and to health for all. That assurance is inexorable through the awakening of the spiritual being of man everywhere and the recognition of all men of their responsibilities for the welfare of all other men, not only within their own state but beyond its confines. Too often some of us are afraid to approach new horizons because there has been no experience to guide us.[12]

Diefenbaker found his inspiration in the "reforming zeal" of R.B. Bennett – whose New Deal legislation, he reminded the House, had been dispatched to the courts by his successor, Mackenzie King, and declared largely unconstitutional. So he took the caucus's agreed line that King should now refer the family allowance bill to the Supreme Court for a constitutional opinion. Failing that, the Conservatives would support the measure. Adamson described Diefenbaker's address as "his finest speech in the House...it is obvious that he has taken wind out of King's election sail" by the promise of Conservative approval.[13]

But Gordon Graydon and Herbert Bruce left a contrasting impression of covert opposition and grudging, tactical acceptance. Bruce made his leader's claim more specific: the bill was "a bribe of the most brazen character, made chiefly to one province and paid for by the taxes of the rest"; and privately he pointed out that the beneficiaries would be French Canadian "families who have been unwilling to defend their country." The premier of Ontario, George Drew, made that divisive charge public by challenging the right of Quebec "to dominate the destiny of a divided Canada."[14]

Mackenzie King was amused by these voices of a departed age and by the silence of most Conservative members; the most generous thing he could say about Diefenbaker's legal doubts was that "the raising of a constitutional issue amounts simply to throwing up a sort of smoke-screen."[15] That was a fair reading of the Conservative position. The bill passed second reading by 139 to zero.

Bracken's failure to enter the House of Commons, or to inspire voters on his national travels, left the caucus more and more dissatisfied. While fundraising was markedly more successful after the Winnipeg convention, it remained the jealous preserve of a small group of Toronto and Montreal businessmen, "a few rich men," in J.M. Macdonnell's dismissive phrase.[16] The Toronto contingent had given their initial confidence to Bracken, but they were all admirers and confidants of George Drew. Bracken's selection, in their eyes, was a dubious experiment indulged in out of deference to Arthur Meighen. The whole progressive tilt of Port Hope and Winnipeg was also, for them, a matter of expediency. If Bracken could not quickly transmute it into votes, they were prepared to abandon him and reassert their rigidly free enterprise and Anglo-Canadian instincts. After Drew's provincial victory he seemed to them, more obviously, the leader-in-waiting – a position confirmed by the overwhelming election of the CCF to power in Saskatchewan in June 1944. In Bracken's – and Diefenbaker's – own territory, the Progressive Conservatives lost all their deposits. The electorate was undoubtedly moving left, but it seemed unimpressed by a Conservative Party uncertain or opportunist about its principles.

The opposition was shackled in its wartime role, since that called for constant affirmation of its loyalty to the cause. Diefenbaker told parliament that the House could not fulfil its duties if it acted as "a cockpit of contending factions, each desirous of preparing for the hustings." Instead, he saw parliament's primary wartime function as propagandist: "to strengthen the resolution of the people to carry on to the end; to energize our people against the apathy that too often follows military successes." But he added another that was covertly partisan: "to assure our men and women of the forces that other men, with the necessary equipment, will be available as reinforcements and to see that our manpower is fully mobilized and put to the greatest possible use."[17]

On that issue of manpower and reinforcements the Tories appealed to their English-speaking constituency with the claim that they were more loyal, more patriotic, than the government. But it was a chancy thing. The language of conscription and "race" was dangerous – and Mackenzie King was a master of the patriotic game. What was more, the rural Conservative electorate was probably as sensitive about compulsory service as were French-speaking voters. The farms needed labour. As long as voluntary recruitment for overseas held up, the Conservative Party had to focus its criticisms on labour allocation and the call-up for home service: Why was it not fairly and evenly applied across the country? Why did so many conscripts evade service? Why was enforcement so lax?

Beneath this litany of hints there was a hidden ethnic line. What John Diefenbaker called "the inequality of call-up and the inequality of service...ordained by this government" meant that the King government favoured French Canadians, and did so for political gain.[18] This kind of complaint was relatively harmless to the government, yet it was meant to sustain an undercurrent of suspicion outside Quebec – for exploitation if and when battlefront losses began to mount.

Until the Normandy invasion, few Conservatives chose openly to revive the call for overseas conscription. But in the summer of 1944, with casualties mounting in Italy and in France, the patriotic issue was not to be resisted. In mid-June the new national chairman of the party, C.P. McTague, called for the dispatch of home service conscripts as overseas reinforcements. The decision, he insisted, was a matter of national honour; the troops had never been need-ed for home defence but were needed overseas. Bracken endorsed the demand.[19] This opening emboldened what Adamson called "the Globe group" (those Conservative MPs like Herbert Bruce and Earl Rowe who were close to the publisher of the *Globe and Mail*, George McCullagh, and to Drew) to press in caucus for a House motion in favour of overseas conscription. But the MPs baulked. "Caucus," wrote Adamson, "is 100% against taking this suicidal step. Really a great show and a sock in the eye for the Toronto crowd."[20] Instead, the party produced a thoroughly confusing budget amendment that criticized the home defence army and called for its use on the farms, in industry, or overseas – or all three. Diefenbaker's long and almost wholly irrelevant speech on the amendment prompted the impish Liberal backbencher Jean François Pouliot to respond: "The hon. member for Lake Centre (Mr. Diefenbaker) appeared to be more illogical than ever. He said he supports the amendment; he spoke against it and apparently he will vote for it. I cannot understand him. If he made a speech of that kind in Saskatchewan, his own province, then I am not surprised that not only has his party been wiped out but all remembrance of it has been wiped out in the last election."[21] Given the variety of shadings on the amendment, Pouliot wondered whether Diefenbaker, or Green, or Rowe, or Bracken, or McTague spoke for the Conservative Party. "They meet each day in caucus," he taunted, "Why do they not take advantage of it to tune their violins and come into the house with a united front? They go to the right; they go to the left; they look to the right and they jump to the left. That has been the Tory policy since the beginning of this session, in fact since the begin-ning of the war."[22]

The real conscription crisis erupted in October 1944, when the minister of national defence, Colonel J.L. Ralston, returned from Europe to insist, on military advice, that 15,000 home defence troops should be called overseas before the end of the year. King and a majority of his government disagreed, but the cabinet was harshly divided and near breakup. After two weeks of hes-itation, King summarily fired Ralston and appointed General A.G.L. McNaughton as minister on a pledge that he would find the necessary reinforcements from the home army through voluntary transfers. But that desperate effort failed, and on November 23 the prime minister forestalled another cabinet collapse by reversing direction and committing 16,000 conscripts to overseas duty. By doing so he saved the unity of his cabinet (only C.G. Power resigned in protest) and his caucus.[23]

Throughout November, as the recruiting and cabinet crises intensified, the Conservative Party and the English language press mounted a noisy and often vicious campaign for full overseas conscription. The demons of national hatred, so far contained, were loosed again. After November 23 there were anti-conscription riots in Quebec. Power lamented that "I envisaged the prospect of one-third of our population uncooperative, with a deep sense of injury, and the prey to the worst elements amongst them, and worst of all, hating all other Canadians."[24] In English-speaking Canada sentiment seemed to be overwhelmingly in support of conscription, either partial or complete, and the Conservatives sought to ride the wave. The opposition amendment to the government's motion of confidence asked that all NRMA conscripts (there were more than 100,000) should be "enrolled to serve in any theatre of war," including the Pacific, where conscription had never featured in the government's calculations. Without any explicit mention of the French-English divide, Diefenbaker played on the familiar theme that "partial conscription" meant unequal sacrifice that would "endanger the last vestige of unity in this country." Although it was evident that the Liberal majority would sustain the government in its policy of desperate gradualism, Diefenbaker insisted that "there are hon. members all over the house who will say privately that they believe in everything in the amendment. There is no politics in it."[25]

There was politics in it. The Conservative Party had again abandoned Quebec to the Liberals by exploiting English-speaking Protestant prejudices. On the surface the debate was less damaging than in 1917, but that could be put down to the government's caution (or cynical realism) more than to the opposition's reaction. The Conservatives carried their condemnations into General McNaughton's by-election campaign in the Ontario riding of Grey North, where a colourless candidate defeated the minister of defence in early February 1945.[26] Bracken campaigned actively, and the victory briefly enhanced his reputation. But the issue was a fading one, as allied victories promised an early end to the war in Europe. That came on May 8.

By this time it seemed clear to Mackenzie King and his party that the election could be fought on postwar issues. On April 12, after consultation with his cabinet, King announced that the general election would take place on June 11, 1945. After a brief interlude in San Francisco to bask in the glory of the founding conference of the United Nations, he returned to Canada in mid-May to open the Liberal campaign. For him this would be an election of "sharpened barbs carefully concealed by platitudes," emphasizing his own long experience of government and the opposition's inadequacy.[27] The Liberals offered Canadians the attractive prospect of welfare, full employment, national unity, and international cooperation; the Conservatives, they claimed, offered racial division and Tory reaction. On the left, the CCF preached a more progressive message of reform and government activism, warning against a return of destitution under Conservative rule. Mackenzie King's response to the CCF was to appeal for votes that would count towards a majority, to ensure "strong and stable government in Canada in these very critical years."[28]

Conservative national advertising stressed the earnest character of John Bracken, "this Lincolnesque man – who has never known defeat at the polls."[29] Despite the formal platform of the party, which still reflected the progressive tone of the Port Hope conference, Bracken chose initially to conduct a negative campaign against the King government's hesitations on the conscription issue. King's policy, he charged, was "one of irresolute and feeble compromise" intended to satisfy a disloyal minority.[30] The Conservatives, by contrast, would commit all conscripts to fight in the Japanese war. The party, which managed to nominate only thirty-one candidates in Quebec, had clearly abandoned all hope there, but it squandered support in English-speaking Canada with such bravado. There was no international pressure on Canada to shift its conscript forces to the Pacific, and no obvious target for Canadian military operations. As Canadians turned away from the tensions of war with relief, the Conservative campaign made no sense.

According to his habit, Diefenbaker conducted a highly personal campaign in his constituency of Lake Centre. He defied his party on troops for the Japanese war.[31] He campaigned for the construction of a South Saskatchewan River dam, a perennial enticement offered to voters by Jimmy Gardiner at election times and lost in the mists thereafter. John's brother, Elmer, was the reputed author of one of the Lake Centre slogans in that campaign: "It'll be a dam site sooner if John is elected."[32] Despite the reassurances of his organizer that "you have nothing to worry about," Diefenbaker could foresee the real possibility of defeat, and he campaigned at a frantic pace.[33]

In Ontario the federal campaign was accompanied by a provincial election, and on June 4 the Conservative government of George Drew won a powerful majority. While that gave the national Conservatives a brief tonic, its real effects on the national campaign were obscure. Mackenzie King rationalized the Liberal defeat as a victory for majority government, a check on CCF hopes, and a spur to Quebeckers to reject the dangerous federal Tories in that province. While he expected to lose seats to the Conservatives in their Ontario heartland, he predicted a solid Liberal majority in the country.[34] In retrospect, Diefenbaker judged that "Drew, in beating back the CCF threat in Ontario, had exhausted the party's resources at a time when they were most needed federally."[35] National opinion polls gave the Liberal Party a comfortable lead of 39 percent, to 29 percent for the Conservatives, 17 percent for the CCF, and 5 percent for the nationalist Bloc Populaire. Wide regional variations meant that the figures would not necessarily translate into House of Commons seats.[36]

The election result was a disappointment to both Liberals and Conservatives. The government's majority was pared to the margin, with 125 seats, while the Conservatives elected 67, the CCF 28, Social Credit 13, and independents 11. In Quebec, King won 53 out of 65 ridings, but in Ontario his seats fell from 55 to 34, and in the West from 44 to 19. In Ontario the Conservatives were the beneficiaries, with a total of 48 seats – or more than two-thirds of their total membership in the House. In the west, the CCF were the victors – especially in Saskatchewan, where Jimmy Gardiner and John Diefenbaker were isolated survivors in a sea of eighteen socialists. The prime minister lost his seat in Prince Albert, and was elected in a summer by-election for the Ontario constituency of Glengarry.[37]

Bracken won his own contest in Neepawa, Manitoba, but the great hope that he could deliver the west to the Conservatives was unfulfilled. After 1945 the Conservative caucus was more, not less, dominated by its Ontario contingent, which now included twelve members from Toronto alone. They showed slight desire to give Bracken another chance. Diefenbaker wrote that "Bracken was now labelled a loser. The Liberal argument that Mr. Bracken did not have the knowledge of national affairs so necessary for one occupying the position of Leader was widely disseminated through the press, and was even widely accepted among Conservative party supporters."[38]

For three years more, Bracken led the party in the House conscientiously but without inspiration, a drab leader with no clear sense of purpose, increasingly dispirited by the party's drift. Drew's Ontario supporters were now aggressively pursuing the succession on his behalf, and, without any broader constituency, Bracken lacked authority to put them down. His resistance was gradually worn away.

Meanwhile, the country entered an era of postwar readjustment and economic growth under Mackenzie King, while Canada established its reputation abroad under the internationalist leadership of Louis St Laurent and his activist aides at External Affairs. The King government, with the support of its enlarged and highly competent wartime civil service, began its planning for peacetime in the midst of war. Its chief objects were to avoid a postwar depression, to provide citizens with national minimum standards of welfare, to preserve tolerable relations between French- and English-speaking Canadians, and to take Canada's place as a fully independent middle power on the international stage.

The Liberal cabinet was subtly transforming itself from a party government into something more all-embracing and permanent – an administration built on wide national consensus that included the open or tacit support of business and the senior civil service. In the public mind, the prospect of any alternative to a Liberal government grew dim. Certainly, in that atmosphere of postwar complacency at home and new strains abroad, Bracken's Progressive Conservatives offered no real challenge. If they had a continuing role, it seemed limited to vigilant criticism in the House, meant to keep the governors honest.

Diefenbaker was not an opponent of Bracken's continuing leadership, but neither was he a fervent advocate. He believed, with undoubted accuracy, that the Conservative Party had been governed too long for its own good as a private club. Like Bracken, he was not a natural ally of the Toronto power-brokers, and he had come to Ottawa with his suspicions of the party's reactionary core well entrenched. More than that, by habit and instinct he was not a team player. He followed his own course in the House, sometimes in conflict with the caucus. His new colleague Donald Fleming – a peppery Toronto lawyer and former city councillor – soon noticed that Diefenbaker played shamelessly to the press gallery and could not be relied upon for regular and slogging work in committee. He had a reputation in caucus as "a prima donna and a loner" who resented being upstaged, bore mysterious grudges, and had frequent temper tantrums.[39] He seemed to trust only those few acolytes who gave him complete and uncritical support. His manner provoked doubt or resentment among other members of caucus, who suspected his radical instincts and pressing ambition, were jealous of his flair for the limelight, or thought him untrustworthy and unpredictable. He sensed and perhaps exaggerated these doubts, but would not change his ways. He knew that he would have to make his way to the leadership he coveted by finding support beyond the traditional centres of power in the party.

Thus Diefenbaker understood and shared Bracken's wish to create a new party around the old. But he saw also, after 1945, that Bracken himself had failed. Diefenbaker could not participate in Toronto's covert efforts to displace Bracken, because he knew that George Drew was the favoured successor. But equally, he saw in the succession his own chances too. He knew that Bracken would not last, and he believed that, when the time came, a convention would not necessarily deliver a foregone verdict as it had in 1942. The need to cut into the Liberal consensus by appealing to progressive sentiment in the west and elsewhere would remain, unless, by some miracle, the party could make a breakthrough in Quebec in alliance with the Union Nationale. But that would be a project for the right wing, not for Diefenbaker. By 1946 John Diefenbaker was unchallenged in caucus as the spokesman for progressive causes. With broader contacts, a stronger national reputation, and better organization than in 1942, he thought he might carry off the succession. And if not? Well, most of the time he knew he was in this game for life. He nurtured, and was sustained by, his old sense of destiny.

The lacklustre Conservative caucus was strengthened in 1945 by the addition of some promising new members, including Donald Fleming, the reformist Toronto businessman J.M. Macdonnell, the bright young British Columbia veteran E. Davie Fulton, the veteran officers George Pearkes and Cecil Merritt, and the Calgary oilman A.L. Smith. Fulton and Pearkes were already admirers of Diefenbaker, and he returned their faith with advice and guidance about the ways of the House.[40]

Diefenbaker was in sympathy with the broad lines of government policy, but he prodded at its weak spots as he sensed them: the maintenance of wartime regulation and secrecy, the inflated central bureaucracy, excessive government spending, and a worrying indifference to the rights of citizens. The issues he chose for emphasis broadened his own reputation as a champion of decency and individual rights as much as they gave benefit to his party.

With the end of the war, the Grand Alliance of Britain, the United States, and the Soviet Union had rapidly fallen apart in mutual distrust. One element in that collapse involved the defection of the cipher clerk Igor Gouzenko from the Soviet Embassy in Ottawa in September 1945, carrying with him information of extensive Soviet spy networks in Canada, the United States, and the United Kingdom. The King government handled this unwelcome intelligence like news of some loathsome infection in the family. It sought urgent advice from London and Washington, took unusual steps to prevent any publicity, and prepared for the possibility of quarantined treatment by passing a secret order-in-council under its wartime powers. For five months nothing was publicly known of the affair, and the order-in-council lay dormant. The prime minister cherished hopes that it might fade away entirely, thus avoiding any offence to Soviet feelings. In February 1946, however, news of the defection was leaked to the press in Washington, apparently by frustrated British and American security chiefs who wished to alarm their political bosses about the Soviet challenge.[41]

Mackenzie King was forced reluctantly to act. A royal commission consisting of two Supreme Court justices, Robert Taschereau and R.L. Kellock, began secret inquiries into Soviet spying under the 1945 order-in-council. On February 15, 1946, fourteen Canadians were detained for secret interrogation, without access to counsel, in a search for evidence that might justify the laying of criminal charges. Prime Minister King confided his political disquiet about these unusual measures to his diary: "I can see where a great cry will be raised, having had a Commission sit in secret, and men and women arrested and detained under an order in council passed really under War Measures powers. I will be held up to the world as the very opposite of a democrat. It is part of the inevitable."[42] King's fatalism about "the inevitable" reflected a faith even stronger than Diefenbaker's that his life was under direct management from on high. He saw himself now as God's chief servant in maintaining freedom against the Soviet hordes.

In March 1946 the commission published three interim reports, leading to arrests and charges under the criminal code and the Official Secrets Act. When the House of Commons reconvened that month, the Gouzenko affair was on everyone's mind. As King had expected, the case invited Diefenbaker's indignation, and it formed the theme when he spoke in the throne speech debate on March 21.[43] He saw in the case not just the germ of international communism, but a separate disease infecting the Canadian government.

Diefenbaker began with a note of sarcasm that brought interruptions from the Liberal benches: "I have no apologies to offer for the position I intend to take. I have no apology to make for not having received support from the communist party." The Liberal Party, on the other hand, had received and accepted such support in the 1945 election. An imprudent Liberal remarked that "We are here, though...We are on this side," to which Diefenbaker responded: "Oh yes. There is the policy; the end justifies the means."

But this was only mischievous scene-setting. The main charge was that the use of emergency powers to detain and interrogate citizens was a violation of the historic rights of the subject, a violation that reflected the government's habitual wartime disregard for liberty. It demonstrated the need for a Canadian declaration of rights.

> I say, Mr. Speaker – and it is not doctrinaire or a technicality – to say that these orders in council sweep aside Magna Charta, habeas corpus and the bill of rights. Some say the people of Canada are not interested in that. Sir, I do not believe the minds of liberty-loving Canadians, however much they

hate communism, have become so apathetic in six years of domination by a state in a period when the political doctrines of regimentation... have been in effect. I believe the time has come for a declaration of liberties to be made by this parliament. Magna Charta is part of our birthright. Habeas corpus, the bill of rights, the petition of right, all are part of our tradition. The United States has its own bill of rights, and I think out of the events of the last few years a responsibility falls upon parliament to assure that Canadians, as well as others in the empire and the people of the United States, should have established by their legislature a bill of rights under which freedom of religion, of speech, of association and of speech [sic], freedom from capricious arrest and freedom under the rule of the law, should be made part and parcel of the law of the country.[44]

The occasion was telling, and the government was ill at ease in its actions. It could only plead that the overriding needs of security, or reason of state, justified its deeds. A few days later Mackenzie King told the House with "immense relief" that the secret order had been revoked.[45] Of the eighteen persons eventually tried in Canada, only eight had convictions sustained. In the short run, public opinion supported the government's actions. But John Diefenbaker – with only a few other members – had found a symbolic issue of conscience and an illustration of the corruptions of power now infecting the King government. The issue was genuine. It was a subject that suited his individualism, his sense of tradition, his sympathy for the voiceless, and his rhetorical genius.

In April and May 1946 he returned to it, in debate on the Canadian Citizenship Act, when Diefenbaker made clear the American inspiration for his views on citizenship and nationality. He noted that the provision of formal Canadian citizenship was supported by the official opposition, but embellished that support with arguments notably his own. The bill, he said, "achieves a life-long dream of mine" that Canadians should enjoy "a new vista of their responsibilities and privileges as citizens." He hoped that the bill would help "to encourage and develop in this country mutual trust and mutual tolerance...for Canada's destiny and Canada's future can and will never be achieved on the basis of racial prejudice."[46]

His objective, beyond the legislation, was to see the creation of "an unhyphenated nation...the prophetic dreams of nationhood, the vision of Macdonald and Cartier, remain as yet to be completed...Canada must develop, now that we achieve this citizenship, unity out of diversity – a diversity based on non-homogeneous peoples of many religions, peoples of

clashing economic differences based on distance, and jurisdictional differences as between federal and provincial authorities. The great challenge to
our generation is to fuse these clashing differences." This was the American
myth of the melting pot. He quoted his own words of 1944 in praise of the
American example. "As I have said before, no one thinks of Mr. Roosevelt as
a Dutch-American. No one thinks of General Eisenhower as a German-
American. No one thinks of Mayor LaGuardia of New York as an Italian-
American. They are great Americans."[47]

For Diefenbaker, the citizenship bill inevitably raised two other issues:
the need to eliminate records of ethnic origin from the Canadian census, and
the need for a Canadian bill of rights as a declaration of traditional British
rights in Canada. The logical links might seem tangled, but for Diefenbaker
belief in common citizenship, common rights, and national unity was one
whole, born of his prairie experience both personal and political. The identification of ethnic origins in the census offended him as a reflection of prejudices he had felt in his own life. A bill of rights would alert Canadians to the
dangers of political intrusions on their liberties like those so recently demonstrated – intrusions that might often have a racial or a religious basis. Later in
the debate he attacked the government's efforts to deport Canadians of
Japanese origin under a 1945 order-in-council.[48]

Diefenbaker's amendment, to provide for a declaration of rights on the
certificates of citizenship issued to new Canadians, was rejected by the
government. But Paul Martin, in his reply on behalf of the cabinet, showed
his prudent respect for the case made by the member for Lake Centre.[49] He
reminded Diefenbaker that Canada had adopted the British, not the
American, system of government. Canada had no organic law, no revolutionary constitution to which a bill of rights could be attached. Instead the country was, in Tennyson's words,

> A land of settled government,
> A land of just and old renown,
> Where freedom slowly broadens down
> From precedent to precedent.[50]

If parliament desired such a change, it should be accomplished "on the basis
of a bill by itself, when all aspects could be considered and all the implications
noted, a bill which would be the result of mature and careful judgment,"
rather than "a subsection of a section which prescribes conditions for the issue
of certificates."[51] Martin was a match for Diefenbaker in parliamentary

give-and-take, if not quite in populist instinct. Both the *Globe and Mail* and the Winnipeg *Free Press* took up Diefenbaker's claims that Canadian rights were being steadily whittled away, and many members of the House showed interest in the idea of a Canadian bill of rights. A *Globe* editorial noted that "too few members of the House of Commons have interested themselves in the liberties of their constituents. There has, however, been one outstanding exception among them. He is Mr. John Diefenbaker, the Progressive Conservative member for Lake Centre. Mr. Diefenbaker has not only been a tenacious but a brilliant and rugged guardian of all civil liberties."[52]

More than any other MP, Diefenbaker had become a public tribune, focusing and echoing complaints about the government's disregard for rights. Members of the King cabinet – whether out of troubled conscience or political alertness – were themselves sensitive to the issue. In Quebec, the Union Nationale government of Premier Maurice Duplessis was engaged in an aggressive battle to suppress the Jehovah's Witnesses, using its own Padlock Law and the Criminal Code in its efforts to uphold the Catholic faith. The Witnesses responded with a national campaign for toleration, and by June 1947 they had accumulated half a million signatures on their petition to parliament for a Canadian bill of rights.[53] In Saskatchewan the new CCF government had sponsored passage of a provincial bill of rights, the first to be enacted in Canada.

At the United Nations, wartime atrocities had prompted discussion of an international declaration of rights. In May 1947 the King government, responding to the mood of the times and to Diefenbaker's nudging, proposed a parliamentary motion to establish a joint committee on human rights and fundamental freedoms. The government thus hoped to put itself on the side of the angels, taking its distance both from Quebec's intolerance and from its own wartime record. But as Ian Mackenzie said in support of the motion, that did not necessarily mean support for a Canadian bill of rights. "It is well," he concluded, "that Canada should play her part in drafting and proclaiming to the world an international bill of rights as a guide and a direction post for the freedom-loving peoples of the world. It is less evident that Canada, free Canada, heir to the common law, should tamper with her heritage of liberty by seeking to inscribe in statutes the freedom that is inherently ours."[54]

Diefenbaker did not want to tamper. He wanted to repair a damaged heritage – and more than incidentally, to undermine the Liberal government that had initiated or tolerated recent infringements on Canadian liberties. He laid out the case with care and eloquence in a speech that became the touchstone for all his later approaches to a bill of rights.[55] He favoured an international declaration of rights; but that, he insisted, "will not be sufficient to establish and assure rights in our country." To do so would require a specific, Canadian declaration of rights, adopted "either by way of constitutional amendment or by statute."

Diefenbaker recognized a paradox at the heart of the parliamentary tradition. Canada had inherited the English charters of freedom, but from the Star Chamber to the Gouzenko case those charters had been violated. He could even concede, as he had in his support for wartime emergency powers, that there were occasions when basic rights must be curtailed. But that should be done deliberately, by parliament, not the executive. And citizens should always have access to the courts to prevent abuse.

From the beginning of his campaign, Diefenbaker thus had two objectives: to renew ideals in a solemn declaration and to guarantee the right of appeal against the arbitrary acts of government. His list of abuses was long, and it applied both to federal and to provincial governments. A province had interfered with freedom of religion on the ground that it was a provincial right, yet those affected had no means of protecting that "charter right" by appeal to the Supreme Court of Canada. The federal government had sought to deport Canadian citizens and had limited economic freedom, detained and questioned persons in secret without access to counsel, and made administrative rulings that could not be challenged in the courts.

Diefenbaker saw remedies both legal and political. At the legal level, he wanted assurance that no laws or orders could apply without the right of appeal. At the political level, "what is needed are civil liberties by declaration of parliament which will guard the individual against the state. It might be argued that another government, another parliament, can revoke a bill of rights passed by parliament. True; but has not history shown that when laws are put upon the statute books, having the support of a vast majority of the people, they stay there?" He offered his own draft declaration of rights for study by the committee.

In addition, Diefenbaker made several specific proposals. The War Measures Act, standing on the statute books since 1914, "constitutes an invitation to any government in the future...to declare an emergency to the detriment of the rights of our people." It was necessary in wartime, "but in the days of peace, with the challenge that the state is making to the rights of the individual...the act should be repealed." The presumptions of guilt contained in the Official Secrets Act "which deny an innocent person his full rights of defence" should be removed. The Public Inquiries Act should be amended to deny commissions the power to examine witnesses in secret. Parliament should declare that judges should not sit on commissions of inquiry "dealing with matters in any way of a political nature," as had occurred in the Hong Kong inquiry of 1942 and the Gouzenko inquiry of 1946. As a public broadcaster, the CBC should no longer possess the power to regulate its own competitors.

The member recognized that his speech left some loose ends. In particular, he had not dealt with the issue of constitutional entrenchment or the possible application of a federal statute to the acts of provincial governments. These were confusing matters, since the BNA Act made no clear or complete allocation of power over rights and freedoms. But he noted that the 1938 Supreme Court judgment in the Alberta Press Case suggested that "every freedom is guaranteed to every Canadian and that when the British North America Act was passed it was never intended that any provincial authority should be allowed to derogate from those freedoms which are the inherent right and heritage of every Canadian and British subject." A declaratory bill passed by the federal parliament, at the least, would strengthen the hand of the minister of justice in disallowing provincial laws that limited individual freedom.

In his peroration, Diefenbaker linked his concerns with his own personal history, noting that "I speak with feeling on the subject."

> I want to see a bill of rights declare the principles of liberty for all racial origins who come here and have come here because of their passion for liberty and their belief in tolerance. My right hon. friend mentioned that my mother's grandparents came to Red river with the Selkirk settlers. They came for the same reason that those who came later did so, because of intolerance and the denial of the right of the individual to have recourse to the courts of Scotland. They came to this country, as thousands since have come, because they believed that here they would find justice, righteousness and tolerance without regard to race and creed...Though we may speak different languages, all of us have the same heartfelt concept of liberty. With the trend that is taking place, having regard to the unanimity there is in this country, surely we in this parliament will join together...in a great crusade to assure, not only freedom today to every individual under the law, but freedom to those who will come after us.[56]

For this western outsider, the issue shrewdly combined principle, personal grievance, and political advantage. The element of advantage could conveniently, perhaps even unconsciously, be cloaked in righteous garb.

Praise for the speech was widespread. A Canadian Press dispatch, taking too easily for granted that the government now intended to sponsor a bill of rights, said that "the clear-thinking, brilliant-debating, realistic" member from Lake Centre was "father of the idea." "It was a great speech. When the history of the Canadian constitution is written and the passage of the Bill of Rights becomes recognized for the great milestone of freedom that it will constitute, Diefenbaker's address undoubtedly will be re-read as one of the great speeches by which the cause of human liberty has been advanced in the Canadian Parliament."[57] Elmer wrote to his brother that "the newspaper accounts are more than laudatory...You have carved yourself a niche in history. It stands out as a milestone in Canadian history and is the Magna Carta of Canada."[58]

But once in committee, Diefenbaker's initiative languished. The government had diverted the pressure and had no intention of bringing forward a bill. Diefenbaker wrote to Glen How, the lawyer for the Jehovah's Witnesses who had organized the mass petition, that "the Government is trying to ditch the whole question of civil rights but I am glad that we got as far as we did." To another correspondent he wrote: "As far as the Bill of Rights is concerned there is no possibility of it being enacted so long as the present Government is in power."[59] As he had foreseen, the committee recommended against either a constitutional amendment or a parliamentary statute.[60] Diefenbaker continued to advocate a bill over the next decade, while a growing body of academics, legal scholars, and trade unionists echoed his concerns.[61] In 1950 a Senate committee considered the issue again, noting that an entrenched bill of rights would require prior agreement with the provinces on an amending process and that parliament should avoid any unilateral effort to invade provincial jurisdiction. Instead, the committee recommended a Declaration of Human Rights applying only to federal legislation.[62] No action followed.

DESPITE THE EVIDENCE THAT WARTIME RECOVERY AND THE POSTWAR BOOM HAD been stimulated by government policy, John Diefenbaker remained a fiscal conservative unaffected by any scent of Keynesian economics. With the return of peace, he favoured tax cuts and strict reductions in the national budget. The issue seemed straightforward and politically attractive, and he pressed it hard. "I believe this," he told the House in July 1946, "that a Trojan horse has found its way into the camp of the people of Canada, it consists of a desire to overexpend and a refusal to control, regardless of the demands in all parts of this country for curtailment. Over and over again the attitude has been, spend, spend, spend!...The government has the billion dollar mentality."[63] As illustration of "the philosophy of this government," Diefenbaker recalled a remark of the minister of reconstruction, C.D. Howe, in 1945: "I dare say my hon. friend could cut a million dollars from this amount; but a million dollars from the war appropriation bill would not be a very important matter." Diefenbaker gloated: "That is the philosophy; that is the psychology."[64] Thus was born a recurring Conservative taunt, later simplified to the question "What's a million?" – a taunt aimed more and more specifically at Howe, whose autocratic style laid him open to such barbs. Diefenbaker genuinely admired Howe's magnificent efforts as "the genius of Canada's war production," but found him an irresistible target because of his impatience with opponents in the House. For Diefenbaker, Howe was a useful symbol of Liberal excess and Liberal hubris.[65] In fact, Howe was sceptical of central planning and quickly restored management of the postwar economy to the hands of private enterprise. In fixing on an issue of style, Diefenbaker preferred to miss the substance, with which he had no argument.

For Jimmy Gardiner, the perennial Liberal minister of agriculture and western party boss, Diefenbaker was a troublesome gadfly. His presence in the House offered daily proof that Gardiner's skill in limiting the Saskatchewan opposition was imperfect. And Diefenbaker was not even the main challenger in the province. Liberal weakness on the prairies had been driven home by the party's crushing defeat at the hands of the CCF in the provincial election of June 1944. In 1945, when Gardiner was in charge of national organization for the party, the Liberals suffered another huge setback in Saskatchewan. They lost ten seats while the CCF gained thirteen.[66] In Lake Centre, the Conservative tribune held on against the tide, increasing his majority from 280 in 1940 to 1009 in 1945.[67]

Gardiner was determined to erase those political embarrassments, and he focused part of his efforts on the redistribution of parliamentary seats and the redefinition of constituency boundaries. When the redistribution bill of 1947 emerged from cabinet and committee, Diefenbaker's Lake Centre seat, among several Tory ridings, was somewhat mangled.[68] Diefenbaker complained that "to Lake Centre has been added a voting strength of 4,900, of whom only 286 were Progressive Conservatives in the last elections." In particular, he noted that sixteen townships containing a substantial CCF majority had been sliced from the minister of agriculture's constituency and added to Lake Centre.[69]

Diefenbaker rallied the Conservative caucus and the party leader to his defence, but in fact his case was disingenuous. Diefenbaker himself had been a member of the Saskatchewan subcommittee that had approved the boundaries. As its chairman, the Liberal MP Walter Tucker, told the House, the subcommittee had conceded most of Diefenbaker's requests and he had signed a unanimous report. Diefenbaker, he said, had been exclusively preoccupied with his own riding, and the subcommittee "did, I am a little ashamed to say, more or less gerrymander things in favor of the hon. member for Lake Centre. But we did that knowing he was the only Conservative member in Saskatchewan, and he kept saying that he could not get elected unless we did something."[70]

Diefenbaker blustered at these revelations. He insisted that the boundaries remained gerrymandered against him, and referred contemptuously to Tucker as "the Minister of Agriculture's waterboy in Saskatchewan" who "repeatedly found himself in a position in which he had to do what he did not desire to do, but was ordered to do it by his dictator in the province."[71]

The CCF member of the subcommittee commented drolly that the Liberals, with only two seats to save in the province, had chosen sensibly to protect the minister at the expense of the Conservative next door – just as the Conservatives would have done if they had been in power. But he agreed with Tucker that the subcommittee's emendations had partly restored the balance.[72] Diefenbaker emerged from the debate looking less than candid. Later in the day he went to Tucker's office – at Edna's insistence and in her company – to apologize for his personal comments.[73] In public, however, he held to his story of a blatant gerrymander. Gardiner, wrote Diefenbaker in his memoirs, "had done everything that the mind of a machine politician could envisage, short of destroying my constituency altogether."[74] The episode deepened doubts in the Conservative caucus about the trustworthiness of the member for Lake Centre.

By 1948 there were no big issues in Canadian politics. In foreign policy, as the dangers of the Cold War deepened, there was virtual consensus that the country had no choice but to shelter under American protection while playing helpful mediator at the United Nations when it could. Domestically, after an exchange crisis in 1947, there was spreading prosperity and a diffuse spirit of faith in an unlimited future. The country was in the hands of a safe and unadventurous team. John Diefenbaker continued to build his singular reputation as a free-swinging critic, populist free enterpriser, and defender of human rights, travelling the country on an endless circuit of speechmaking. But his party was in the doldrums. There seemed no central issue around which to shape a challenge to Liberal dominance.

Early in the year, the elderly and failing Mackenzie King announced his intention to retire, and in August the Liberal Party chose his preferred successor, Louis St Laurent, as its new leader. Just weeks before that convention, John Bracken was persuaded to resign his leadership, and a Conservative convention was called for October. Those who successfully belled the cat (including Ray Milner and J.M. Macdonnell, now the national president of the party) did so only after they had been assured that George Drew would seek the national leadership. After a third provincial victory in Ontario in June, his record of success in the heartland dazzled the federal party managers. They dreamed even of a breakthrough to French-speaking voters, since Drew had won six French language ridings in eastern Ontario.[75]

In June 1948 Diefenbaker went south to Philadelphia to observe the Republican Party's nominating convention, and then to Prince Albert to keep his hand in at the law office. He had no warning of Bracken's imminent resignation, writing sceptically to David Walker on July 13 of a Winnipeg editor's claim that efforts were under way to replace Bracken with "an Ontario man." Diefenbaker invited news: "If you hear anything at any time that might be of interest won't you sit down and drop me a line as I find myself entirely cut off from everything of a political nature so long as I am in Prince Albert."[76]

Four days later Bracken's resignation was announced, and by the end of July the national executive had settled on a convention in Ottawa in two months' time. Diefenbaker had already made his decision to run and he threw himself at once into a busy summer campaign. In what was still a well-contained party affair, however, he felt no need to make a public declaration of his candidacy for several weeks. David Walker took charge of the national campaign, Bill Brunt sought Ontario delegates, and Jack Anderson managed the campaign in Saskatchewan. Diefenbaker himself conducted a large, scatter-shot correspondence while dashing to speaking engagements in six provinces.

Initially he wrote to his friend Mickey O'Brien, an advertising executive in Vancouver, to suggest a spontaneous campaign of letters to the press in his favour. That evolved, under Walker's guidance, into an independent advertisement for Diefenbaker. He told Walker that "I will know nothing about that officially but would like to look it over, as I told you, before it goes out."[77] The ad appeared in Saskatoon and Winnipeg with local signatures in late August, and Diefenbaker commented: "The effect of the grass roots movement has been tremendous. All of Winnipeg was talking about it when it came out...I went down to the Star Phoenix today and there too one after the other of the press men spoke of it as being one of the most spontaneous movements ever started. If other cities and towns will follow that lead it will mean a great deal."[78]

In August and September Diefenbaker spoke or met delegates in Saskatoon, Winnipeg, Vancouver, Toronto, Edmonton, Calgary, Halifax, Saint

John, and Montreal. He was confident about solid delegate support in Saskatchewan and Manitoba, with some in British Columbia, and wrote that "the situation in Ontario is unbelievably good and I haven't changed my view about getting 40% of that province."[79] But those prospects were offset in Alberta, Quebec, and New Brunswick, where delegates were unreceptive.[80] And he was worried by the number of delegates-at-large to be chosen by provincial party organizations. "These need not be Conservatives nor reside in the constituency for which they are allotted. I do not have to go any further than that to indicate how this may work out."[81]

Like Diefenbaker, George Drew held back from any formal announcement of his candidacy while his organizers rounded up commitments from delegates, the two shadow campaigns feeding rumours of uncertainty, dispute, or weakness in each others' camps. Both sides speculated about overweening ambition in the other candidate. One of Drew's men in Calgary wrote that "we all have our weaknesses and Diefenbaker's is too much personal ambition. In my opinion, he would be much wiser, and in the end much stronger, if he did not contest the leadership."[82] Walker commented that Drew "has dreamed of being the Prime Minister of Canada for thirty years and he is waiting for public demand to increase. He does not wish to appear to be preaching for a call. People feel he is so ambitious that even at the last moment an enthusiastic demonstration would swing him into the arena."[83] These were still times of sham gentility, when an early declaration of intent looked unseemly.

The autumn of 1948 was a time of anxiety and fear of war in Europe and North America, as the democracies of the west confronted an abrasive Soviet Union. For several months the Soviets had blockaded rail and highway traffic from the western zones of occupation in Germany to West Berlin, while Britain and the United States mounted a vast airlift to supply the residents with food and fuel. In Washington, planning was under way for a North Atlantic treaty of mutual guarantee, which would offer its European members the assurance of American military support in the event of war. The spy scare of 1946 was still a fresh memory. A wave of anticommunist sentiment, sometimes amounting to panic, had swept the United States and Canada since the spring. In this atmosphere, politicians could not avoid declaring their loyalties. The easy temptation was to demonize the entire political left, to link democratic socialism and trade unionism with communism and subversion, even to call for a ban on the Communist Party.

Diefenbaker's senses were acutely tuned to the moods of the moment and he was bound to enter the anticommunist debate. In his preconvention speeches he made the subject his central theme. Diefenbaker shared the dominant anticommunist prejudices, but gave them his own populist twist. In a speech to Toronto Rotarians on September 10 he called for a campaign to educate Canadians against the enemies of free enterprise. On one side these were the communists, socialists, and central planners "promising as they do freedom from work, taxes and responsibility." Their dreams, he said, were both empty and incompatible with individual liberty. He commended labour leaders for purging the unions of communists, and suggested vaguely that "real teeth should be put in the law, in place of the false teeth which permit Communists to operate almost with impunity." But there were enemies on the other side, too. Diefenbaker warned against the sins of big companies, "the unfair business practices of the few," which "if not eliminated, will destroy free business enterprise for the many."[84] He knew that the Rotarian audience of small businessmen and professionals matched his most likely supporters at the coming party convention.

The Liberal Toronto *Star* – hardly a neutral observer – entered the Conservative fray by suggesting that "the big money boys" had arranged for John Bracken's retirement in order to promote George Drew, "a leader they can depend upon," to the leadership.[85] The *Globe and Mail* responded angrily on September 14 that the *Star*'s "anti-Drew complex" had now spread to the entire Liberal press in Canada. It was suggesting not only that Drew was the candidate of the "financial moguls," but also that he was disliked in the Maritimes, Quebec, and the West. On the contrary, the *Globe* insisted that "there are several obvious and excellent reasons why Mr. Drew should be considered a suitable man for the national leadership. He is the only Progressive Conservative Premier now in office. He has won three general elections in Ontario, the most populous province. He has given Ontario sound and progressive administration."[86] The *Star*'s caustic reply was that the federal party leadership was "what he has been after all along, and nobody who has watched him flitting hither and thither for years, making speeches on national and international issues to the neglect of Ontario issues, can have thought anything else."[87]

Diefenbaker was the first to declare his candidacy on September 17. "It is because," he said, "I believe I have something to contribute to Canada in a Crusade to mobilize Canadians everywhere for Canada."[88] He announced a seven-point program of internationalism, "an end to the pampering of those who indulge in Communist subversive activities," the restoration of parliamentary authority, the protection of provincial legislative powers, the promotion of free enterprise, the preservation of liberty under a national bill of rights, and generally fair and just treatment for all Canadians.

He was asked whether he would defeat George Drew. "'Of course I will,' he replied, and then with a smile, he added: 'I mean that seriously, although I would not have said it two weeks ago.'"[89] Diefenbaker relished the game. His Commons secretary R.J. Gratrix noted earlier, "I have never seen the Chief more optimistic and enthusiastic." To his mother, Diefenbaker wrote: "I cannot hope to win but it's a good fight. I had a press conference today and told them I would defeat Drew. That's cheek in his view."[90]

In Toronto, Diefenbaker's campaign chairman, David Walker, predicted "a sweeping victory at Ottawa" on the basis of two special advantages: Diefenbaker was a House of Commons man who had mass appeal. The contrast with Drew was unmistakable, though unspoken.

His forte is the House of Commons. Being in the House of Commons and having proved himself a great leader, why shouldn't he be officially confirmed in his position and given the leadership we have been looking for since Bennett dropped out in 1937?

The Conservative party has made one mistake after another in our choice of leaders. Now we have a man in the House who has earned his spurs, and we must not lose this final opportunity...

Out West...they fear if Diefenbaker doesn't get the leadership, the Conservative party will be considered as a central-Canadian bloc...

The genuine wave of enthusiasm which has swept Canada seems to me to be a grass-roots movement...Diefenbaker has gained the confidence and affection of the man on the street, the man on the back concessions, and labor considers him their friend.[91]

Walker showed the talents of a natural pitchman. Delegates from the west, he said, would favour Diefenbaker by a majority. In Quebec, he had been "literally inundated with offers of help and promises of support at the convention from French-speaking delegates." The Maritimes were "very enthusiastic," and in Ontario Diefenbaker would have "a good majority" of the constituency delegates. Walker was uncertain about the Ontario delegates-at-large, to be appointed by the party organization.[92]

Three days after Diefenbaker's declaration, George Drew announced his candidacy, and a few days later Donald Fleming did so too. The press assumed that Drew would carry the convention with the overwhelming support of Ontario and Quebec delegates, but Fleming's entry brought speculation about his ability, as the only bilingual candidate, to cut into Drew's Quebec support.[93]

While the *Globe and Mail* led the press campaign for Drew, the Toronto *Star* reminded its readers in two editorials on the eve of the leadership convention that the Ontario premier had condemned family allowances in 1944 as a bribe to Quebeckers who would not fight in the war.[94] On its front pages, the *Star* gave Diefenbaker flattering treatment. "Diefenbaker, 2-1 Said the Choice of Average Man," reported Robert Taylor, citing the evidence of a man-in-the-street poll conducted in "politics-wise Ottawa" by "an ardent supporter of Mr. Diefenbaker." The article did not add, as it might have, that the pollster was one of the Diefenbaker organizers whose names had been omitted from the delegates-at-large list.[95] From the parliamentary press gallery, the *Star* reported that gallery members predicted (27–4) that Drew would defeat Diefenbaker for the leadership, but favored Diefenbaker (18–9) when asked, "Who would be best for the party?"[96]

The candidate himself received similar unsolicited signals that his leadership would find popular support beyond the party. From Victoria, the crusading feminist Nellie McClung wrote: "If the friendly good wishes of a hard shell Mackenzie King Liberal can bring any help to you – you certainly have mine – I have admired your courage, and clear thinking, for a long time and hope you will be the new leader. You are young, modest, straightforward, and have an open mind. So we hope you'll win. My kindest wishes to Mrs. Diefenbaker."[97] From Kingston, the historian A.R.M. Lower wrote:

> Just a line to say that I hope you come out on top in the Conserv. leadership. Altho' I am not of your political faith, I don't think we differ much on essentials.
>
> If we must have Tories, they will be relatively immunized under your leadership. But beware of Toronto, my dear sir.[98]

On September 30 the convention opened at the Ottawa Coliseum, the drab hockey rink where the Liberal Party had met to choose a leader in the previous month. The Liberal meeting, said J.B. McGeachy of the *Globe and Mail*, had been a polite one guided by a "sanctified hierarchy." But this occasion was raucous, "immeasurably less polite, less formal and more like the convulsion of nature which a political meeting under a democracy ought to resemble." There was talk of a party machine, he wrote, but no one could say who ran it, and the delegates were "a fractious and rebellious lot." George Drew, looking "rather like a swan in a duck pond (as he must inevitably do at all political meetings, not to his own great advantage)," was acting affable but "decidedly restrained." His publicity seemed to consist entirely of reprinted press articles.

171

The Diefenbaker campaign – the word is quite in order here – has a much less improvised air. There are Diefenbaker headquarters right off the foyer of the Chateau Laurier – an enormous, rather cheerless room in which comely young women hand out Diefenbaker leaflets. These certainly do present the Saskatchewan crusader as the able and attractive figure he is, and they leave nothing out. One of them deals neatly with the silly suggestion that his name is a handicap. "His unusual name," it says, "like that of Eisenhower and Roosevelt, is an asset." This leaflet names nineteen points for Mr. Diefenbaker, rather reminding one of Clemenceau's remark, when he heard of Woodrow Wilson's fourteen, that the Almighty had been content with ten. But the Diefenbaker drive is a real grass roots movement, and the consensus is that he will make an excellent run.[99]

Frank Swanson of the Ottawa *Citizen* also noticed the double contrast: between staid Liberals and lively Tories, and between the Diefenbaker and the Drew campaigns. "At the Liberal meeting, there was no open solicitation for votes on the scale being used by the Conservatives. It looked more like a U.S. national political convention today with leadership buttons and ribbons on nearly every lapel, campaign signs around the outside of the Coliseum and a constant undercurrent of back-room leadership chatter in evidence every-where."[100] The Diefenbaker organizers had made "the smartest move of the convention" the previous evening at the Château Laurier by holding "an impromptu campaign meeting in one of the large convention halls. It attracted a capacity audience, many members of which were wearing Drew and Fleming buttons." Swanson reported the claim of Diefenbaker supporters that votes were moving to him as a result, and concluded that the race had tightened.

While the press saw inspired planning in the Diefenbaker campaign, Walker insisted just the opposite. A campaign had indeed been organized, he said, but when Diefenbaker arrived, "he cancelled the events which included a reception for 2,000 persons, use of a sound truck to promote his candidacy and slogans and banners. Mr. Diefenbaker said he would not stand for that. He said that if people wanted to vote for him they would have to do so on his own personal ability. He said he wouldn't buy his votes." The Bay Street lawyer told reporters that one of the slogans prepared for display would read "Dief: The Man from Main Street – Not Bay Street"; but Diefenbaker had vetoed it. He preferred supporters "because they liked and admired him and not because of sectional or other reasons."[101]

The convention opened with a tub-thumping keynote speech from the Ottawa *Journal*'s Grattan O'Leary, pouring his Irish scorn on the bloodless party of Mackenzie King. John Bracken followed with his valediction, calling on Conservatives to avoid the extremes of communism on the left and an exclusive commitment to business on the right. Instead, he urged, "this party can follow the straight path to reasoned progress and become what it has never fully succeeded in becoming in this century – the crusading party of the common man in every walk of life."[102] That sounded more like support for John Diefenbaker than for George Drew; but Bracken, by now, was discarded and uninfluential.

Nominations and speeches by the candidates were scheduled for the second night of the convention, after a full day of lobbying for votes. When Drew – apparently uninvited – entered a caucus meeting of Quebec delegates during the day, the rumour was spread by "the Diefenbaker forces" that he had been booed; but Drew's spokesmen were quick to advertise their denials, and by evening the incident seemed to result in a hardening of Drew's wide support among Quebec delegates.[103]

Old murmurings about Diefenbaker's name and ancestry made the rounds among convention delegates, and on nomination day the Ottawa *Citizen* devoted an editorial to the subject. "It is an unhappy commentary...on the outlook of Canadians generally," said the *Citizen*, "that as an aspirant for his party's leadership Mr. John Diefenbaker has felt impelled to deny that he is of German origin. As it happens, Mr. Diefenbaker is of Dutch descent, and a fourth generation Canadian at that."[104]

Each of the three candidates took care to have one English-speaking and one French-speaking nominator; Diefenbaker's seconder, Roger Roberge, drew attention in his speech to the candidate's reputation as a "great champion of minority rights" who would protect Quebec's language and religion despite his inability to speak French. Diefenbaker himself, in a twenty-minute speech, appeared typically "lean and earnest...occasionally wagging an admonitory finger."[105] He called for "a crusade to arouse our people to an eagerness to become the servants of Canada"; condemned "the pagan and diabolical advance of Communism" without favouring a ban on the Communist Party;[106] and in one breathless sentence told the convention what kind of party he thought the people of Canada desired:

> Canadians are asking for a party that will honestly try to end class warfare and hatred; that will regulate injustice and exploitation in enterprise while retaining an expanding free initiative; that will accept social security as a means not an end and will now launch a social security contributory plan while continuing to provide adequately for the aged and afflicted; that will

arouse the creative and productive capacity of Canada by lifting the horizons of opportunity; that will push outward the frontiers of enterprise; that will assure the many young men and women in this country (who look with suspicion on us) that only under responsible free initiative is there opportunity to rise to the top however humble one's origins; that will protect our people against unfairness.[107]

Diefenbaker's speech seemed slightly strained, perhaps the result of campaigning so hard against the odds. By contrast, Drew conveyed "an impression of smoothness and power with still some to spare."[108]

The last-minute contest for delegates spurred Diefenbaker's hopes, but the result was crushing. Drew swept to victory on the first ballot, with 827 of 1242 votes, while Diefenbaker managed only 311, centred in the west and Ontario. Donald Fleming followed at a distance with 104.[109] Dick Sanburn commented in the Ottawa *Citizen* that the convention had bowed "to unseen but crushing pressure from above, and the Man from Main Street who was going to vote for Diefenbaker switched his ballot to Drew." Delegates played safe in the end; but Sanburn was convinced that the most popular candidate had lost. "No man, probably ever before in Canadian political history, had such a wealth of spontaneous loyalty and fierce support as John Diefenbaker. You could see it, you could hear it, and almost feel it among the hundreds of delegates. And non-delegates all across the nation were talking the same way."[110] Sanburn added that, "warranted or not," many Conservatives believed that Drew was the man "with Montreal and Toronto financial interests behind him." "One western Conservative told this writer that it would be a long, colossal task for Mr. Drew to break down that suspicion, whether it was true or not. And he feared the taunts and jibes the Liberals will fling."[111] The party, he concluded, had regained its pre-Bracken reputation.

John Diefenbaker was wounded again. And he suffered what looked like personal insult when he visited Drew's suite in the Château Laurier that evening to offer congratulations. "I walked into that gathering," he recalled a quarter century later, "and it was as if an animal not customarily admitted to homes had suddenly entered the place."[112] He left Ottawa the next day for Prince Albert.

Messages of support in defeat began to pour in. Diefenbaker's friendly antagonist across the aisle of the House, Paul Martin, the minister of national health and welfare, wrote that he had deserved the leadership. "You, John, could have been the leader...You had a great body of supporters among the delegates but unfortunately there seemed to be adverse considerations which

I can only suspect. I do know that the newspaper men were fully behind you and they are real friends to have."[113] One of many delegates who campaigned for Diefenbaker, Bill Archer, wrote from Montreal:

> John, the leader is not always the best man, that is very important to note. The qualities desired in leadership are not necessarily those which make a man. You have such a depth of sincerity, such a brilliant mind, such an independence of spirit, that these very virtues are such as to take from you the other requisites of leadership...
>
> Out of all this John, I hope you will realize that there is so much to be done – and *so much that only you can do!* George can't win the next or any election without you by his side, fighting as valiantly, inwardly and outwardly, as though your positions were reversed...
>
> John, don't be despondent, be of good cheer, rest and relax for a while...remember there are many who labour without reward of any kind. It is more difficult, but then were you ever one to set aside a task because it was too difficult? Not from my knowledge of you![114]

Most poignant of all were two letters from Davie Fulton in Kamloops, one handwritten to "Johnny," the other formal and "more abstract." The handwritten note said:

> I should like briefly to try to say how my own personal feelings are.
>
> It's hard to express them adequately. My admiration & affection for you and for your conduct are quite unbounded. I *know* you have suffered a tremendous blow, and am heartsick – and believe me, I am hurt deeply for you. Under the circumstances, to write and ask you in a cool and dispassionate manner to continue your work just as though you hadn't suffered a deep personal injury is difficult and may seem a little unreal.
>
> But that is what I'm doing, because I believe it's the thing you should do. I also believe it's the thing that will make you happiest in the long run (I hope I don't transgress). I *know* it will be the salvation of the Party, and, I believe, of the country. It would be a shame if your contribution were lost now.
>
> I said before, however, you don't owe the Party a thing: the obligation is *all* the other way. That's why you can continue to do so much for it, and for the country. But you are, therefore, entitled to the most definite assurance that your position will be that of first lieutenant – any cabinet position you want, and that the new leader *wants* you and wants you to fill that position...I think

he is a sufficiently big man, & sufficiently realistic, to take that position himself & make the offer. The genuine co-operation of the two of you will carry us over every difficulty...

My regards to your wonderful wife & my friend Edna.

Love from Pat too!

How's about coming out for some shooting?[115]

The second letter insisted that "the vote does not reflect your Party's feelings toward you," and repeated Fulton's urgings that Diefenbaker should take his place beside George Drew in order to make possible a "march forward across the whole breadth of the Dominion with a united party and people behind him. Without this I fear there is again the danger of sectionalism...I know that the whole nation feels the same way and I am confident that I speak for all your friends, both in and out of the House of Commons."[116]

Diefenbaker's campaign manager in Manitoba, G.S. Thorvaldson, found solace in the thought that "the leadership contest was a grand fight...there is general agreement on this point – that the convention would have been as dull as ditch water if a few of us had not created a contest between Drew and Diefenbaker...It is, of course, easy for us to say now that we are complete amateurs in a show of this kind. On the other hand it is well to recollect that we had against us the whole power of the Ontario political machine as well as the power of the Duplessis machine."[117]

Diefenbaker nursed his wounds in private. He told Archer that he was not discouraged, and wrote to Arthur Lower that "things turned out much as I had expected but I have nothing to regret for having been a candidate for the leadership."[118] A letter to his old friend and constituency manager Jack Anderson hinted more openly at his resentments: "If the vote had taken place on the night of the speeches the vote that I received would have been very much larger than it was but during the night the pressure was applied and nothing could hold back the forces during the night. I reduced the number that I would have received 225 over night and the number I estimated on the day of the vote was 375. I wrote that number down so it is not after thought."[119]

Similar suggestions about Diefenbaker's "unexpectedly small" vote appeared in prairie newspapers, and on October 8 the *Globe and Mail* responded in an editorial titled "The One Sour Note." The *Globe* suggested that "in all probability he would have obtained more votes had it not been for the inept and discreditable tactics by which his campaign manager, Mr. David Walker, sought to further his cause."

While Mr. Diefenbaker at one point dissociated himself from the tactics, Mr. Walker persisted in them right down to the day of the vote. Workers acting under his generalship not only circulated rumours and innuendoes which could have caused deep personal acrimony, they adopted and gave currency to the malicious reports and disreputable slogans manufactured by hostile Liberal journalists in their campaign to discredit Mr. Drew. As events were to show, this was a great disservice to their candidate and to the party as a whole.

Delegates who came to the convention intent on getting the best possible leader for the party, according to their personal appraisal of the men, naturally viewed with suspicion the cloud of disparaging rumours circulated by Mr. Walker and his associates. They could not be expected to realize that it was generated, not by the candidate, but by partisans who were as politically ambitious as they were irresponsible and immature. But now that the facts have emerged, and responsibility for the only sour note clearly established, the men who produced it should be well marked and given a wide berth in future. They have nothing to contribute which is of value to the party.[120]

For John Diefenbaker those were fighting words. He replied on October 15 that he accepted his defeat "with equanimity and with malice to none," because his aim was to assure the unity of the party under its new leader. But he could not ignore the unfair references in the editorial to David Walker "and associates."

I know of nothing that Mr. Walker and "his associates" did that was not done in a spirit of fair and honorable competition and for that reason any suggestion that I at any time disassociated myself from him or them in what he or they did has no foundation.

...I am shocked that he should be singled out by you for exile from his party. Your proposal that the "associates" of Mr. Walker be purged from the party is startling for it places all who worked in my support under an unsupported suspicion of wrong-doing.

While fully realizing that unity above everything else is necessary if victory is to crown the magnificent work done by the convention any unjustified criticism of my friends and supporters at any time and in particular when such criticism endangers that unity will always bring me to their defence.[121]

W HEN THE HOUSE OF COMMONS RECONVENED IN JANUARY 1949 IT FACED BOTH A
new prime minister and a new leader of the opposition. The session would
probably be short, since Louis St Laurent was expected to go to the country
for a mandate by early summer. In the meantime there were first impressions
to be made and parliamentary housekeeping to complete. For the government, the most important measures were a budget, the resolution bringing
Newfoundland formally into the federal union, and ratification of the North
Atlantic Treaty. The prime minister was already a familiar and genial presence
in the House. George Drew was known only by his Ontario reputation as a
domineering premier, an aggressive debater, and a handsome patrician: "the
Big Chief" to friends, "Gorgeous George" to his mocking Liberal critics.[122]
Drew was determined to establish himself as a forceful leader, and he quickly
imposed unity on the previously fractious Conservative caucus. Grant Dexter
of the Winnipeg *Free Press* commented: "To one sitting in the press gallery, the
Conservative party often appears to be not unlike an orchestra with Mr. Drew
as the conductor. At one wave of his hand, the sixty-eight are silent. At another,
heckling and general uproar breaks out in such volume as to drown out an
opponent. Yet even in the midst of such a demonstration, if Mr. Drew desires
to hear what this opponent is saying, he merely raises his hand and the three
score and more adult men hush up as if their wind pipes had been slit."[123] His
maiden speech was an overbearing denunciation of government policy and
the new prime minister, which gave his parliamentary career a bad start. The
courtly Louis St Laurent did not seem to merit such treatment. Liberals took
it as a personal affront, and even Conservatives were embarrassed.[124]

Drew's domineering was not accompanied by any clarity in the party's
program. One of his first efforts – to link the Liberals with communist subversion and demand a ban on the Communist Party – was greeted with contempt from the government benches, and in March his own party conference
rejected the policy.[125] Diefenbaker was prominent among the opponents of
banning. Through the winter of 1949 "heckling and general uproar" were the
sum of Conservative policy, as the party confidently assumed that the Liberal
government was heading for defeat under its new leader.[126] Conservative gains
in two by-elections – one of them in Quebec – sustained that hope.[127]

In April, St Laurent dissolved parliament for a June election and set
out on a dignified progress by train across the country. The nation was prosperous as never before, and prosperity was the government's message.[128]
The prime minister spoke colourlessly of the government's record, but made
up for dullness with his patrician charm. "He has the attitude," wrote one
reporter, "that sane people obviously must vote Liberal and it's a waste of time

to keep on telling them so."[129] The public responded with faith and personal affection. In Quebec he was a favourite son; elsewhere he was a kindly uncle. Other members of cabinet gave support in St Laurent's benign campaign.

By contrast, Drew conducted a hectic individual crusade of abuse against ministers and civil servants. His most familiar complaint, that the engines on the North Star aircraft owned by Trans-Canada Airlines were too noisy, attracted more ridicule than respect. In Quebec, where he had hoped for strong support from Premier Duplessis, Drew was disappointed. St Laurent was too popular, and Drew's old record too familiar, for the canny premier to risk his own credit openly. The Union Nationale machine was active in the Conservative cause, but Duplessis himself kept silent. His party could deliver candidates – more than twice as many as the Conservatives had nominated in 1945 – but few votes.[130] In Ontario, on the other hand, the Toronto *Star* led a crude campaign to discredit Drew's tenuous Quebec ties. Two days before the vote, the *Star* asked under photos of Maurice Duplessis and Camilien Houde: "Shall These Two Men Become Canada's Real Rulers?" and proclaimed in a front-page banner: "Keep Canada British/Destroy Drew's Houde/God Save The King."[131]

Diefenbaker kept close to home in Lake Centre, where he had built his personal support well beyond that of the party. He was uncertain about CCF strength in the riding, which had grown by redistribution in 1947. That gave him the excuse (as though he needed it) to campaign hard in every village and township, venturing outside the constituency for only a few speeches elsewhere in the province. Under persistent pressure for support from other Tory candidates, he also made brief campaign visits to other provinces.[132] When advertising material arrived in Lake Centre from party headquarters ("We must have had almost a ton of it"), Diefenbaker judged it useless. Late one night he and Arthur Pearson loaded it into a boat at Regina Beach on Last Mountain Lake and, in irreverent defiance, dumped it in the waters.[133]

Diefenbaker couldn't resist a bit of modest red-baiting mischief when he suggested in a broadcast that "all the Communists in Lake Centre were going to vote for my CCF opponent." The CCF premier, Tommy Douglas, challenged him to name them. The candidate – who claimed to have Communist Party membership lists in his hands – responded that doing so would consume too much costly radio time. Instead, he offered to read "a list of the Communists who were not going to vote CCF" if Douglas would supply that. The contretemps died in a standoff, while the Communist Party asked members to spoil their ballots.[134]

The opposition's hopes were crushed on June 27, when Louis St Laurent was rewarded with overwhelming victory in 193 ridings. Conservative membership in the House fell from sixty-seven in 1945 to forty-one in 1949, while the CCF fell from twenty-eight to thirteen. In Quebec, Drew elected only two MPs. The Conservative Party lost votes in every province from Ontario west. In Saskatchewan, John Diefenbaker retained his lone Conservative seat with an increased majority of 3422: a rebuke, in his eyes, both to the Liberals who had gerrymandered his constituency and to the Tories who had chosen George Drew as party leader.[135] On that bittersweet night, John and Edna looked ahead to four more years of demoralized opposition in Ottawa.

———

FOR TWO YEARS AFTER HER HARROWING INTERLUDE AT HOMEWOOD SANITARIUM IN 1945–46, Edna spent longer periods at home in Prince Albert than in Ottawa. Although John assured friends that she was in good health, that seemed to be a cover for worry and uncertainty. Perhaps he felt more comfortable alone in Ottawa during parliamentary sessions as long as Edna was unwell – although his own remaining letters give little indication of his feelings about such personal matters.[136] Edna was undoubtedly troubled and unhappy in Prince Albert, despite the presence of her mother and friends like Lorne and Mabel Connell. Only a few undated letters from Edna to John remain from this period. In one, she confesses her loneliness and insecurity: "I wish I could fly down & see you I dont seem able to face that train trip alone so far."[137] In another, written in the spring of 1947, she expresses pleasure at a telephone conversation with him the previous day, reports on her illness, and pleads, "I love you John & want to be with you always."

> To-day my throat has been terrible & I get very discouraged when it is like this as Im desperately afraid it is some thing serious because if it was poisin it should be gone now.
>
> I felt pretty good all week but this day has surely taken the pep out of me. Just pray for me Dear I want to get well & be with you this is no life for either of us.[138]

Shortly afterwards she tells her husband:

> The papers & your letters have been grand its all there is to break a very monotonous life but that is not your fault. My throat has been very bad the last few days & I get very discouraged I wonder if I am right in my conclusion Im being patient & hoping the poisin is the cause & that it will eventually leave me...

Im lonesome for you & dont let myself think of how happy I was in Ottawa with you when I was well – if only this pain in my throat & head leaves Ill never ask for another thing.

I see how busy they are in Ottawa with gay parties & all & I dont envy them all I want is my health...

...Tomorrow is another day and Ill be like Scarlet & go on.[139]

Beside the dreams of Ottawa, small town Prince Albert paled. Edna appealed to John's own memory in a desperate call for rescue: "You hated PA & longed to get east so you can't wonder."[140]

One of John's responses was to suggest that they should look for a house larger than 22 Twentieth Street, and in the summer of 1947 he purchased 246 Nineteenth Street, a spacious dormer-windowed home on the ridge over-looking downtown Prince Albert. In October they moved, and Edna turned enthusiastically to the task of redecoration. A friend, Gertrude Cote, recalled an evening with Edna when, removing the last bits of storage from the base-ment of the old house, they discovered a dusty bottle of vintage wine. The two sat on the kitchen floor and drank themselves generously into a haze. "She told me afterwards," reported Mrs Cote, "even John chuckled about it."[141]

By 1948 Edna had regained her health and confidence, and she returned to Ottawa more regularly with John for sessions of the House. Their journal-ist friend Patrick Nicholson thought that "her husband gave her all the kind and loving care needed for recovery,"[142] including the welcome prospect of living away from the Château Laurier Hotel. For the winter session of 1948 the Diefenbakers took an apartment at 61 Cartier Avenue, behind the defence department's temporary wartime buildings.[143] Here at last was a second home, a place to cook, and, on weekends, to entertain friends for dinner. Tom Van Dusen, then a young reporter with the Ottawa *Journal*, remembered that "members of the Press Gallery were familiar visitors in their downtown apartment. At such dinners John Diefenbaker was an animated host who kept us all entertained with anecdotes and inspired by his grasp of the problems of the day... at a time when the Liberal Party seemed to have secured a perpetual lease on power."[144] Aside from a few political friends like the Fultons, the Brunts, and the Walkers, gallery reporters and their wives were the most com-mon visitors; with them the couple could indulge their irreverent wit and John's great talent for mimicry.[145] Edna was a vivacious hostess, "quite an extro-vert, a very talkative person," a companion who softened John's aloofness with her instinctive and embracing warmth.[146] Her meals were "delectable," and "drinks were in plentiful supply, including several brands of imported wine."[147]

By this time Edna was once more, as Diefenbaker told a broadcaster in 1948, "his right hand man," assisting in his parliamentary office, watching his interventions in the House from the gallery above, sitting on the platform and "looking most decorative" at his meetings.[148] She still longed for a different life, but did not expect it. Diefenbaker occasionally toyed with offers of a business appointment or a lucrative legal partnership in Toronto or Vancouver, but Edna knew he could not forsake his vocation. She was in it with him, for better or for worse.[149]

Edna's desire to be at his side reflected a certain sense of sexual jealousy – a jealousy that was probably mutual. John was aware of Edna's old flirtatiousness and desire for affection; Edna was aware of John's magnetic appeal to women, both as a man of arresting appearance and as a prominent politician who was often on his own. In 1947 she wanted to know whether Diefenbaker had been assigned a male secretary, John Gratrix, for his parliamentary office. That happened, and Gratrix accompanied Diefenbaker on his campaign for the party leadership in the summer of 1948 – no doubt a safer companion, in Edna's eyes, than another woman.[150] Following one further reference to his secretary, Edna added: "Be good dear & keep me from worrying as you know the things I fear"; and again: "I'm trying not to worry you & you know I'm ill & can't help but imagining things." She wanted to be in Ottawa "with you if you want me," "if only I thought I was well enough & looked presentable."[151] This marriage of twenty years had become, for them both, a necessary bondage, a common commitment to John's ambition that both appeased and fed their separate insecurities.

Reassuring appearances were kept up, but all was not well for long. In February 1950 Diefenbaker wrote to the Battle Creek Sanitarium, the fashionable rest-cure centre founded by Dr John Harvey Kellogg of breakfast cereal fame, apparently seeking treatment for his wife. The sanitarium promised a "cheerful, wholesome atmosphere" in "the congenial company of guests...from all parts of the world and all walks of life...Our physicians, dietitians and physical directors arrange a plan of health reconstruction including treatment, diet, exercise and rest according to each patient's individual requirements. There is also arranged for the pleasure of our guests a varied and enjoyable daily program of lectures, demonstrations, concerts, health question-box talks, and a variety of indoor and outdoor sports."[152]

This was nothing like Homewood, but neither was it home. It was a place of "health reconstruction" for wealthy neurasthenics – or as one writer has described it, "a temple of positive thinking, abstention and wise eating."[153] If John was planning a sojourn there for Edna, his judgment (and perhaps his medical advice) must have pointed, as in 1945, to depressive or psychosomatic ailments rather than physical ones.

For three months the record reveals nothing of Edna's life. Was she a patient at Battle Creek, more distant and secret even than Homewood had been? In April, in a letter to John, Mary Diefenbaker mentioned receiving a letter, a news clipping about the Royal Family, and a gift from "Ollie" – the nickname of Diefenbaker's youthful friend Olive Freeman, then a widow living in Toronto. "I knew where you would be last week end," Mary tells her son, "when she told me where she was." [154] Had the MP, so dependent on womanly support, sought out the comfort of his old Saskatoon acquaintance when Edna again needed hospital care? Diefenbaker's mother, who was privy to most of his secrets, wrote familiarly of a friendship he would not easily reveal to anyone else, least of all to his possessive wife. Edna's very clinging possessiveness might have been part of the problem, as he struggled to diagnose it and cultivated another attachment.

By early June, Edna was certainly in Ottawa again with John. Mary Diefenbaker offered hope that Edna "is feeling better." [155] The parliamentary session stretched out through the summer, and the couple were together only briefly during July and August in their Prince Albert house. Edna entertained and travelled with John to constituency meetings as though nothing had changed, but friends noticed that she tired easily and that there were signs of swelling in her face and neck. [156] By early September they had returned to Ottawa. Diefenbaker wrote to Herbert Bruce: "Both of us are in the best of health. In fact, as far as she is concerned, she has never been better throughout her entire life." [157] In retrospect, that reassurance looks more like gentle deception, or self-deception. The couple looked forward to visiting Washington, DC, at mid-month, where the first joint meetings of the Canadian and American Bar Associations were to take place. Superficially, the trip was a success: for John, as an annual chance to cultivate his widespread legal-political network; for Edna, as a happy autumnal jaunt to the eastern seaboard and beyond the limits of her Prince Albert–Ottawa life. [158]

But privately, Washington marked a point of anguish that called forth all of Edna's stoical reserves. There she sought a second medical opinion about her illness, which was confirmed during her brief return to Ottawa. She was suffering from acute and untreatable leukemia. She confided this to her friend Patricia Fulton, but perhaps not to her husband, who was about to depart on a major overseas journey to Australia and New Zealand as a delegate to the conference of the Commonwealth Parliamentary Association. [159] On November 11 Diefenbaker left Vancouver by plane, professing to believe that Edna was still in good health.[160] There were doubts, however, about his mother's condition, and he assured her from Auckland that he could return within two days "if you are not feeling too well."[161] (That could have been, too, his tacit signal that he worried about Edna and would return at short notice if necessary.) Before his departure, John and Edna exchanged fantasies about a rendezvous in Hawaii in December. But immediately on his arrival in New Zealand, John told his mother that he had arranged to return directly to Saskatoon before Christmas.[162] There was no plan for a Hawaiian vacation.

For four weeks Diefenbaker hobnobbed timorously with the mighty, taking care to instruct Elmer and Edna to supply the Saskatoon and Prince Albert newspapers with the details. He had two speeches to make, and it was all a little heady: "I am (as you will see) the only non Honorable in the group. I hope that I do all right. I will try...It is amazing all the peoples that are here – colors and races."[163] He reported smugly that the Quebec delegates (René Beaudouin, Adélard Raymond, and Daniel Johnson) were "ill-treated" and resultingly "annoyed," apparently because they missed out on some of his own privileged invitations.[164]

Despite rising at four in the morning to write one speech, Diefenbaker was mostly indulging himself: "I think this is going to be a real vacation...Too much playing around and eating. (I have gained...7 (Yes, seven) pounds! I will have to diet soon.)...I am so fat that I cannot even bend down."[165]

On December 22 he returned to Prince Albert to find Edna "most critically ill" in the advanced stages of acute lymphatic leukemia.[166] The doctors advised immediate entry into St Paul's Hospital in Saskatoon; instead, the family spent Christmas at Mary Diefenbaker's, and on Boxing Day John took Edna to hospital to begin a six-week vigil at her bedside. No one expected her to leave; since there was no acceptable treatment, the hospital could provide no more than palliative care. John booked an adjoining room, while Edna's mother, Maren, boarded close to the hospital.[167] This time John had no wish to conceal the seriousness of Edna's disease, and word of her illness spread quickly. Diefenbaker was missing from his seat on the front bench when the House reopened late in January.

Edna's friends rallied with an extraordinary and spontaneous flow of encouraging cards, letters, flowers, visits, and telephone messages. Members of the small parliamentary press gallery set up a message centre for Edna, and one reporter wrote to her: "As I walked into my place in the Gallery today I instinctively – or automatically – turned my head to see if you were in the public gallery behind us. And I know that others here also missed you. Please get well and come back to us. We are all rooting for you."[168] David Walker, like others, could not conceal the sadness in his praise:

> So Johnny will miss those de luxe home cooked meals for the time being.
> What a housekeeper you are! What a cook you turned out to be! Edna, my
> dear, I couldn't have believed you were such a mistress of the culinary art!
> To see is to believe! And after sampling your cooking at Ottawa, I wasn't too
> surprised at the delectable morsels produced at Prince Albert. What a won-
> derful time we all had last July, didn't we? How you shine in your own home!
> What a grand crowd of friends you have in P.A.! How well-liked you are by
> them! *And why shouldn't you be?* For you in your heart are *kindly disposed* to
> nearly everyone. Yes, Edna, you are doing a good job out there. You are a
> great wife for John.[169]

Both of them knew that this was a letter of affectionate farewell.

When Paul Martin, the minister of health and welfare, learned of Edna's illness, he inquired of medical friends about treatments for leukemia and arranged to import supplies of an experimental drug from New York for use by Edna's doctors. The treatment was unsuccessful, but Diefenbaker was everlastingly grateful for this act of kindness. "Diefenbaker's gratitude rather embarrassed me," Martin wrote. "I had done very little, but he seemed to handle me a little more gently thereafter."[170]

While Diefenbaker was in New Zealand, a Canadian troop train carrying soldiers on their way to the Korean War had collided head on with a CN passenger train at Canoe River, British Columbia. Several wooden railway cars had telescoped between newer steel cars, and twenty-one passengers, most of them troops, had been killed. The railway soon pointed to human error as the cause, and attention centred on a young telegrapher, Jack Atherton. In early January, 1951, he was formally charged with manslaughter in the death of an engine fireman, on the allegation that he had omitted two words from the dispatcher's order to the troop train, thus misdirecting it into the path of the passenger train.

Atherton had grown up in the village of Zealandia in Lake Centre riding. With charges pending, his father turned for support to his member of parliament, the renowned criminal defender John Diefenbaker. Diefenbaker was inclined to accept Alfred Atherton's claim that his son had sent the dispatch correctly, but he would not take the case. Edna was too ill to leave; parliament had the next call on his time; and he was not a member of the British Columbia bar where the case would be tried.

Atherton knew Edna's reputation as a persuasive influence on her husband, and in desperation he talked his way to her room in St Paul's Hospital at the end of December. She sympathized, was convinced, and promised to intercede. When she told John, he protested that he would have to pass the BC bar exams and pay his bar admission fee. Edna pleaded that the telegrapher was an innocent victim and a scapegoat. She asked John to take the case for her sake, and he could not resist this last claim of sentiment. He made a promise to Edna, met with Jack Atherton, and agreed to act in his defence.[171]

In early February 1951 Edna Diefenbaker died, with John at her bedside. The outpouring of tribute was unique. Arthur Laing, Howard Green, and Jimmy Gardiner broke precedent in the House of Commons with eulogies to an MP's wife; press gallery reporters and columnists spilled out affection for this "unelected member of parliament," this "gay and lovable personality"; the Prince Albert *Daily Herald* spoke of her "quick instinct" for friendship towards "those who were in desperate need of its qualities."

> In the press gallery, and in the ranks of those who work on the fringe of parliament rather than as members, there are many who remember the friendship of Mrs. Diefenbaker as the force which brought meaning back to the lives that were becoming badly mangled – had gone badly astray.
>
> For the bruised spirit, there is no healing agent so wonderful as understanding which grows naturally out of an undemanding impulse to friendship...
>
> There are other things to be remembered, too. She was, of course, a partner in and contributor to all those attributes of greatness that have found expression in her husband's career – helped shape them and give them effect in senses that can be recalled by every Ottawa observer.
>
> Still, those were not things apart. They came, too, out of the same inner loveliness, recognized by all who knew her best, which gave Mrs. Diefenbaker the greatness that was her own.[172]

The First Baptist Church in Saskatoon overflowed with mourners for Edna's funeral service, which was conducted by three ministers from Saskatoon, Prince Albert, and Calgary. The congregation included several railway porters, friends of Edna in the companionship of long Canadian rail journeys east and west. When she was buried in the Diefenbaker family plot at Woodlawn Cemetery in northwest Saskatoon, an engine and caboose waited on the line beside the graveyard, the crew standing, heads bared, for the burial service. They too knew Edna and the Brower family from years of travel.

Perhaps they had heard as well of her dying intercession in the Atherton case. This was a rare kind of recognition typical of pioneering Saskatchewan.[173]

John Diefenbaker was stricken and unbalanced in his grief. At First Baptist Church he insisted that Edna's coffin should lie open in the entrance-way. When he entered the church with Edna's brother and sister-in-law, Jack and Susan Brower, he approached the body and "ran his fingers through her hair as she lay in the coffin," lamenting that it had been parted on the wrong side and that he had been abandoned.[174]

John had promised Edna that he would eventually rest with her at Woodlawn, so her coffin was lowered four feet deeper than normal to allow space for a second coffin to lie above.[175] The deep grave was filled with earth and mounded with flowers that froze in the February snows.

CHAPTER 6

The Big Fish

1951-1956

J OHN DIEFENBAKER DID NOT RETURN TO THE HOUSE OF COMMONS UNTIL April 1951, when he made a brief appearance for the budget debate. During March he paid the British Columbia bar admission fee of $1500 and took his provincial bar exam in Vancouver – which proved to be a pro-forma, two-question oral. Diefenbaker then appeared for Jack Atherton at his preliminary hearing for manslaughter in Prince George, BC, and early in May he returned for the trial. For him the case was emblematic. The defence of a common man, possibly victimized by authority, was something uniquely suited to his instincts. For the prosecution he faced the deputy attorney general of the province, an ex-colonel in whom the defence attorney sensed hints of a haughty military manner. Here was something to be exploited.

Diefenbaker was by now well briefed in the intricacies of railway telegraphy and was assisted at the defence table by his partner Roy Hall. In the courtroom he had a watcher, the son of his House colleague George Pearkes, playing the role so often filled by Edna: listening and reporting on lay reactions to the evidence as a way into the minds of jurors.[1]

Despite his preparation for the case, Diefenbaker was still distracted and suffering deeply. Hall recalled that "he was in a state of shock at the preliminary hearing," and at the trial "he seemed at times to be in a trance...he was acting from instinct rather than through normal concentration."[2] Nevertheless, his old courtroom guile remained. He had decided to call no evidence or witnesses. He knew that there had been a heavy snowfall the night before the crash, which might have left traces of snow on the telegraph wires. He claimed to have found one precedent for a broken telegraphic transmission, when a seagull had dropped a fish on snow-covered lines and interrupted a message. "This example was not well authenticated," he wrote, "but it was all I had... I hammered home my one example of the bird and the fish."[3]

Diefenbaker's other, more telling approach was calculatedly subversive. The charge concerned the death of a railwayman, not any of the soldiers. But he was determined to plant a germ of doubt about the railway company's indifference and irresponsibility towards its passengers in the accident. So when a CNR official took the stand to testify on technical matters, Diefenbaker asked: "I suppose the reason you put these soldiers in wooden cars with steel cars on either end was so that no matter what they might subsequently find in Korea, they'd always be able to say, 'Well, we had worse than that in Canada.'" Crown counsel objected; the judge said it was a statement rather than a question; and Diefenbaker responded with sarcasm: "My Lord, it was made clear by the elevation of my voice at the end of the sentence that there was a great big question mark on it. This man is an intelligent man. Right up at the top of the hierarchy. It's a long question, but it won't be difficult for him. He'll be able to break it down."[4]

The judge debated whether the comment was admissible, until the impatient crown attorney fell into Diefenbaker's trap: "I want to make it clear," he told the court, "that in this case we're not concerned about the death of a few privates going to Korea." As Diefenbaker could see, what he meant was that the specific charge related to a railwayman rather than to the soldiers. But his words conveyed an attitude, and Diefenbaker would not spare him. There were murmurs on the jury benches. "Oh," said Diefenbaker, "you're not concerned about the killing of a few privates? Oh, Colonel!"

According to the mischievous account in his memoirs, for the rest of the trial Diefenbaker feigned deafness. "It did not matter what question the Colonel asked, whether favourable to me or to him, I would say, 'I didn't quite hear you, Colonel.' Every time I said 'Colonel,' the reaction of the jury was not such as would have been judged entirely warm towards the Crown or its case. The jury acquitted after a very short consideration of the case."[5] Diefenbaker had won a popular victory, redeemed his promise to Edna, and endeared himself for life to Jack Atherton and his fellow railway workers. The case was celebrated in the press and became one of his major political assets.

T HE LIBERAL GOVERNMENT RETURNED IN 1949 TO ITS CENTRALIST, NATION-BUILDING mission with a fresh assurance edging towards arrogance, confident that the Canadian public would grant it an indefinite mandate. A chastened George Drew faced the inevitable press speculation about his retirement, and still deeper reservations in the caucus; but he proved his mettle by leading the party steadily and courageously in the new House, and quickly put the leadership issue to rest.[6] By the end of May 1950 the opposition had been cheered by three by-election victories in Ontario, restoring J.M. Macdonnell to the front bench and bringing in George Hees and Ellen Fairclough. A year later there were four more Conservative gains, and in 1952, another four. Hees was a handsome businessman, athlete, and veteran with a brash and exuberant manner; Fairclough was a former Hamilton city councillor. Tory morale was recovering for the next electoral assault, but Liberal self-confidence was barely dented.

The year 1950 saw the outbreak of the Korean War, the beginning of rearmament, and a vastly increased defence budget. The cabinet's annual measures extending transitional emergency powers year by year since 1945 had now brought it to a new period of wartime crisis justifying further emergency legislation. With the creation of the Department of Defence Production in 1951, those powers centred more and more distinctly in the hands of one minister, Clarence Decatur Howe. Howe relished his power, was impatient of criticism in the House, and could easily be roused to fury by the taunts of George Drew, Donald Fleming, Howard Green, or John Diefenbaker. He gradually gave his opponents a dictionary of pithy lines to quote against him. "If we wanted to get away with it," he replied on one occasion to Howard Green, "who would stop us?"[7] Even the charming Louis St Laurent, in his complacency, could turn short tempered when faced with these troublesome critics across the centre aisle.[8] In the end they could not defeat the government's measures, but they made mighty nuisances of themselves in debates that the Liberals seemed to regard as time-consuming distractions.

Through this parliament, Diefenbaker retained chairmanship of the Conservative caucus justice committee, but his leadership was erratic. The indefatigable Donald Fleming filled in for him during these lapses. When revisions to the Combines Investigation Act were introduced in 1952, Fleming noted that "I carried the lead at all stages. Diefenbaker took no part in the proceedings at any stage."[9]

He was in limbo. His role in opposition now stretched over twelve years, two failed leadership contests, and two general election defeats for the party. The Conservatives were little stronger in the House than they had been when he entered the chamber in 1940. George Drew was secure in the leadership, at least until another electoral disaster. Diefenbaker was not close to Drew, although he believed he had his respect, and he remained distant from many of his caucus colleagues. Several younger MPs threatened his predominant place as a parliamentary critic. His Liberal opponents treated him with undoubted caution, but seemed less fearful of him than in the early years. He was unusually thin-skinned for a politician: "morbidly sensitive," in the journalist Blair Fraser's phrase. And his wife was gone.[10]

Diefenbaker's sense of destiny wavered. He toyed with the prospect of abandoning politics and returning to legal practice in Ontario.[11] Yet he was conspicuous, a favourite of the press, and the party's most sought-after public speaker. He craved the limelight and took on more speaking engagements away from Ottawa. He was especially buoyed by the adulation of the minority communities whose rights and interests he promoted – Jehovah's Witnesses, Ukrainians, Jews, Indians, all those English-speaking Canadians who felt themselves to be outside the old British Canadian mainstream. For them he held a beacon that justified his quest.[12]

Above all he revelled in the contest of politics. If he was briefly indecisive about a future in opposition, he would surely rise to a challenge. The 1952 redistribution of parliamentary seats gave him that challenge.[13] Saskatchewan's dwindling population (it had lost 64,000 residents in the decade since 1941) meant that the province would lose seats. The Liberal government proposed to amend the Constitution to limit the extent of that loss, but in the end the province would have one less member than in the existing House. Redistribution was still conducted by self-interested wrangling in parliamentary committees with Liberal majorities, with the boundaries finally confirmed in a Redistribution Act. For the prairies, the job was again managed by the unrelenting partisan Jimmy Gardiner.

The result was that Lake Centre constituency, in the middle of the province, was shorn of ninety townships possessing an overall Diefenbaker majority. The remnant was merged with Moose Jaw and parts of Regina to produce a constituency with strong Liberal and CCF voting strength. "The riding," Hees protested to the House, "has been literally mutilated...For all practical purposes one can say that it has been obliterated."[14] The mutilation was deliberate and defiant. The Liberal majority sought to rid the House of an annoying antagonist.

For many Saskatchewan voters that was too much. Diefenbaker's supporters urged him to fight on wherever he had the best prospect of election, and a plan soon emerged to fashion a non-partisan nomination for him in Prince Albert. Diefenbaker's own story is that the project was inspired and proposed by two Prince Albert political opponents, Fred Hadley (a Liberal) and Tommy Martin (a Social Crediter), during a fishing trip with him to Lac La Ronge in July 1952 – to which Diefenbaker's response was "Oh, the idea is ridiculous."[15] The truth seems to be that the idea originated among Conservatives, who tacitly approved a non-partisan front as a means of strengthening Diefenbaker's chances. His political friend George Whitter, a former Conservative candidate in Prince Albert, recalled that he first proposed to Diefenbaker that he should run in his home town. The MP took some time to respond, but Whitter remembered that during a fishing trip to Lake Waskesiu "after quite a talk you gave me the go-ahead to start the ball rolling. This was to try and repeat Lake Centre, by getting people of all political beliefs to pull together."[16] Whitter then arranged a private meeting of Prince Albert Tories, "to set the stage and then disappear to the back ground ranks. We wanted new blood, new faces and above all people from other parties who were friends of yours. I was delegated to see Fred Hadley as he was a known Liberal and Kiwanian."[17]

From this point the cover story was played out, Diefenbaker acting the innocent. Hadley invited him north for another fishing trip, and one evening while the party listened on radio to Adlai Stevenson's acceptance of the Democratic nomination for president, Hadley asked: "Why don't you run in Prince Albert?" Diefenbaker feigned surprise, "spent the next couple of days fishing, and very little more was said about my contesting Prince Albert." For the record, Diefenbaker insisted that he had agreed only to think about the request after his return to Ottawa. But his brother, Elmer, who was present, wrote triumphantly to their mother on a postcard from Lac La Ronge: "We're just going back to Waskesiu & John has enjoyed himself as much as I. This is a great spot & we got the big fish. Fred Hadley has a fine cabin here."[18]

Diefenbaker showed his usual caution in an uncertain situation. He allowed preparations to go ahead in Prince Albert, but consulted supporters in his old constituency about the chances there. He agreed with Bill Brunt that Elmer should tour Qu'Appelle riding to survey prospects in that district. The outlook seemed best in Prince Albert, but nothing was guaranteed.[19]

While Diefenbaker claimed ignorance, Hadley and his mostly non-Conservative associates worked diligently to prepare the way for "the big fish" in Prince Albert. The regular Conservative organization faded out of sight as Whitter had proposed, an all-party executive appeared, and "Diefenbaker Clubs" sprang up throughout Prince Albert constituency during the autumn. The MP returned home at Christmas, and again at Easter, to face what he called "one of the most extraordinary examples of citizenship in action that I have ever known." But he had still not made up his mind and he worried over his dilemma without resolution until the end of April 1953. In February, one of the organizers in Prince Albert wrote to Diefenbaker projecting a local majority and urging "that you should declare yourself anytime now – to be fair to us – and to the other constituencies which you are considering."[20] Diefenbaker spun it out for another three months. Finally, after addressing an enthusiastic mass meeting at the Orpheum Theatre in Prince Albert on

April 23, he let himself be convinced, accepting nomination at an overflow convention in May.[21] The forces of destiny – with suitably discreet nudges – were at work again. Local enthusiasm for him was genuine, and once the issue was settled he responded with fresh zest for the battle. But in private he was typically pessimistic. He wrote to Olive Palmer: "I am a long faced, dour, melancholy person every time I think of getting into the P.A. fight, but being in I must get out and work. There is quite a lot of encouraging support but it wouldn't bring a win at this time. I have to take 3,000 votes from each of the other parties. What a menacing picture. However, a faint heart never won an election either."[22]

In December 1952 Conservative MPs believed they had been handed a winning election issue with publication of the Currie Report on irregularities in domestic military spending. The report confirmed more than one hundred improprieties, the result of inept administration and minor fraud, which had gone uncorrected despite repeated internal complaints since 1949. For the press and the opposition, the most colourful claim of fraud was that "horses were hired by army personnel and placed on the payroll." The assertion stuck in the public mind, despite the prime minister's subsequent denials and the investigator's equivocal insistence that horses were indeed being paid "under the names of non-existent labourers."[23]

Whether horses or wraiths, the government was embarrassed. When the House resumed after Christmas, the prime minister proposed the creation of a select committee to examine military spending since 1950 – a diversion, Diefenbaker claimed in response to the motion, intended to produce a whitewash. Donald Fleming, Douglas Harkness, J.R. Macdonnell, and Davie Fulton added their protests, but the government's majority held. Fleming observed caustically that the Conservatives needed someone on the select committee "who was tough, a fighter, a lawyer with experience in cross-examination, a sense of tactics, and a knowledge of the rules. The need was tailored precisely to the specifications of John Diefenbaker, but John was not responsive where a tedious committee job was involved." Fleming took the place that Diefenbaker declined, and as expected, the Liberal majority produced an innocuous report in May under Conservative protest.[24] The issue died without arousing more than mild public amusement and a faint echo in the next election campaign.

For the Conservatives, the other contentious issue of 1953 was the government's annual proposal to extend special emergency powers for one further year – a measure that delegated wide discretionary authority to the government. The Conservatives' front-bench team of Drew, Green,

Diefenbaker, Fulton, and Fleming hammered away on the perennial complaint that the Liberal Party preferred rule by decree to normal parliamentary government. The Liberal majority seemed unaffected. The session ended early to allow a substantial delegation of MPs to attend the coronation of Queen Elizabeth, and in mid-June parliament was dissolved for a summer election.

The government felt confident enough to campaign without any visible program. Drew responded with a sixteen-point manifesto, but emphasized that, if victorious, he would reduce taxes immediately by $500 million. In the existing atmosphere of prosperity and political apathy, that was rash. The Liberal Party suggested that the Conservative leader was irresponsible, and demanded to know what helpful programs – such as the universal old age pension adopted in 1950 with all-party agreement – he would eliminate to achieve his goal. Drew and all his candidates remained on the defensive for the rest of the campaign. The government, after all, was Liberal, practical, benign, and all-wise. It was foolish to imagine that any ragtag bunch of inexperienced critics, however scrappy, could improve on that blessed regime and its smoothly integrated public bureaucracy. Conservative candidates in 1953 were up against the divine order of things.[25]

Diefenbaker declined his invitation to the coronation in order to begin the Prince Albert campaign. "Experience," he wrote, "should have taught me that the only thing a Conservative candidate could expect there approached extinction."[26] But he had a new all-party team of enthusiasts headed by Fred Hadley, and he threw himself frantically into the summer campaign. He began by instructing the Conservative national office that all advertising in Saskatchewan would require his personal approval. In Saskatchewan this would be his, rather than the Conservative Party's, election campaign.[27]

Diefenbaker's drivers took him over dusty roads to every point in the constituency, to Weirdale, Snowden, Big River, Torch River, Nipawin, Shellbrook, Codette, and Canwood, returning late at night to Prince Albert while Diefenbaker slept in the back seat. At Canwood, Diefenbaker's companion and driver George Whitter recalled that the candidate promised "to kiss a couple of old ladies...if you won the election." At Big River there was a restless meeting dominated by "a huge drunk lumber jack," but by the end of the evening "he was with us instead of against us." Finally, there was a meeting in Nipawin and another drive home. "It was fair night in P.A. and we must have passed hundreds of cars in the dust coming back...You were exhausted and sound asleep, but just as always when we hit the steel planks on the P.A. bridge you woke up."[28]

Four times in July Diefenbaker campaigned nationally for the Conservative Party, in Ontario, British Columbia, New Brunswick, and Nova Scotia, flying overnight and catching his rest where he could between banquets and fairground meetings. But when he returned to Prince Albert he professed no connection to the party. Among his colleagues in the House, only Davie Fulton spoke in the constituency, drawing large French-speaking crowds in Albertville and Devil's Lake in enthusiastic support for Diefenbaker.[29]

The candidate for Prince Albert was by now an accomplished stump orator who played the crowd with ease, his voice resonating tremulously as he mocked his opponents, jowls shaking, eyes piercing, an outstretched arm delivering lightning bolts, his denunciations ending with jaws fixed in right-eous self-satisfaction. He covered the essential Conservative themes of Liberal arrogance, extravagance, and indifference to parliament. But above all he offered himself as the tribune of his people. The crowds listened in awe and admiration to this Saskatchewan prophet who stood beyond party. For them it seemed a matter of indifference whether the Conservatives formed a government, but he had to be in parliament.

Diefenbaker had campaigned at a merciless pace, and on voting day his organization toiled from dawn to deliver his voters to the polls. When the counting ended, he had won Prince Albert with a majority of three thousand and one. "This was a stunning home-town victory," wrote Dick Spencer, "for the man who had, until this night, been rejected by the very people whose love and loyalty he wanted most."[30] But nationally – as everyone expected – the Liberals retained an overwhelming majority against marginal opposition gains. Thirty-three of the Progressive Conservatives' fifty-one seats were in Ontario, with only six in the prairies and four in Quebec. Diefenbaker was once more the sole Conservative MP from Saskatchewan. On August 11 the Calgary *Herald* reflected editorially: "The Conservative Party may now realize, at long last, that it made a grievous error at the Ottawa convention in 1948. It chose the wrong man for its leader!"[31]

DIEFENBAKER HAD RENEWED HIS YOUTHFUL FRIENDSHIP WITH OLIVE FREEMAN Palmer, now widowed and a senior civil servant with the Ontario Ministry of Education in Toronto. After Edna's death, John's weekend trips to Toronto grew frequent, although he kept his meetings with Olive discreetly quiet. Even his close friend and adviser Bill Brunt took months to discover the identity of Diefenbaker's Toronto friend. But David and Bunty Walker were in on the secret, conspiring in good humour with John and Olive to contain knowledge of the courtship. In 1952 the couple became engaged. Olive slipped naturally into the role of counsellor, comforter, and family correspondent, with frequent chatty letters to John's mother and brother. In December 1953 John and Olive were quietly married in a Baptist church ceremony in Toronto.[32]

Olive Diefenbaker, like Edna, was a supporter and protector of her husband – although in very different ways. Where Edna had softened his stiffness and self-importance, and eased his relations with clients, voters, the press, and politicians, Olive sustained him with her complete loyalty, dignity, strong will, and sense of propriety. Edna had encouraged John's mischievous and irreverent side, as did some of his secretaries, but Olive did not. She was "a stern Baptist" and a teetotaller who took herself seriously and lacked her husband's impish sense of fun. She was not, like Edna, simply resigned to John's ambition. She joined him late in his career, helped to revive it, and dedicated herself to its fulfilment. She reinforced his grievances, his suspicions, and his sense of destiny. She was a formidable aide to her husband for the rest of her life. John was devoted to her – perhaps even intimidated by her – and as sensitive to her pride as to his own.[33]

John's mother was now over eighty and demanding more attention from her two sons than ever. Olive understood the family balance and gave Mary her constant, flattering attention. John's visits to Saskatoon continued, often with the supporting presence of his wife.

John's brother, Elmer, had returned to the family home from Prince Albert in the late 1940s, drifted through a variety of travelling sales ventures that never amounted to much (including an agency for "lovelight perfume lamps"), and came to rest as an organizer for the Saskatchewan Retail Merchants' Association. In the Diefenbaker family there was room for only one vocation. On his travels throughout the province, Elmer soaked up political gossip and transmitted every scrap of trivia, prejudice, lore, and misinformation to his brother in a never-ending flow of meandering reportage. John encouraged the correspondence, and Elmer gradually assumed the role of disciple and devoted assistant. The traveller's job seemed more and more a front for his amateur intelligence service.

Diefenbaker remained senior partner in his Prince Albert law firm through the mid-1950s, sharing in the company's profits but contributing only intermittently to the firm's work. The other partners, Jack Cuelenaere, Roy Hall, and Clyne Harradence, were initially prepared to put up with the imbalance because the Diefenbaker name drew business through the door. But Diefenbaker's absence in Ottawa, and his congenital disorganization, meant that files often went astray. The papers that he moved back and forth between Prince Albert and Ottawa, recalled Harradence, "weren't packed, they were just dumped" in boxes. "Armfuls of correspondence, some of the legal files that he had been working on...we never saw again." Diefenbaker wrote to Hall in 1953 to complain over the office's neglect of one estate that "I am getting in wrong over this...This is a large estate and will do me irreparable harm unless it is looked after. I cannot understand what has happened about it." On another occasion Diefenbaker lost a bank draft. Secretaries were periodically directed to clean out and sort the disordered drawers in Diefenbaker's office desk of clippings, correspondence, bus tickets, stamps, and refuse, but chaos soon returned. The staff knew that when Diefenbaker swept up the morning's incoming mail, it might disappear forever. Hall remarked to Harradence in the early 1950s: "Could you ever imagine this man being prime minister of the country? He can't even run a four-man law office."

In the words of his secretary Bunny Pound, Diefenbaker would regularly fail to bill the "funny little people with hats in their hands" who came to seek his advice. Eventually Cuelenaere took over the work of collections. Diefenbaker used the law firm as his constituency office, and he expected the partners to perform routine personal chores for him. In the spring of 1954 he instructed Harradence to have the Diefenbaker garage cleaned out and the garden prepared and planted with "an assortment of vegetables – carrots, peas, beans, etc., and tomato plants when the season is ready...Olive wanted to do this but she won't be back in time so it will be quite a surprise if you can arrange to have it done."

By 1955 relations among the partners were strained. Diefenbaker's name attracted fewer clients, yet he seemed determined to involve himself marginally in as many files as possible in order to maintain his claim on the profits. Although Harradence appeared on the firm's letterhead, he could not clarify his status as a partner or his share of the profits with Diefenbaker, and eventually left the firm in frustration. In 1957 Cuelenaere – who had carried the burden of the company's business for more than a decade – also chose to leave the firm after an unresolved dispute over the distribution of profits.[34] One pillar of Diefenbaker's career appeared to be crumbling.

A few months earlier, Diefenbaker had taken on another high-profile murder defence – "almost without a fee," he wrote to the accused's father, "because I feel that a grave injustice was being done."[35] Donald Keith Cathro had previously been convicted of murder, along with three companions, in the killing of a convenience store proprietor during a robbery in Vancouver. Cathro's conviction was sustained on appeal, but the Supreme Court of Canada ordered a retrial on a legal technicality. Diefenbaker was engaged as defence counsel for the new trial in the Supreme Court of British Columbia, where he appeared in January 1956 before Mr Justice J.V. Clyne and a jury.

The evidence suggested that Cathro and a second assailant, Chow Bew, had shared in strangling the victim, Ah Wing, in the course of robbing his store. But Diefenbaker asked the jury to convict his client of robbery rather than murder. The judge recalled Diefenbaker's summation:

> With little or no evidence to support his case, he tried to persuade the jury that Cathro had come to rob but not to participate in any act of violence. He pictured a scene in which Cathro, seeing Chow Bew attacking Ah Wing, rushed between them to separate them and to save Ah Wing from injury. In the ensuing struggle Ah Wing was supposed to fall, causing Cathro to fall on top of him with Cathro's knee striking and breaking Ah Wing's voice box, resulting in his death. Diefenbaker produced a very tense moment in court when he said, "And now, gentlemen of the jury, I shall show you how it happened." With his gown flying in the air the future prime minister of Canada rushed across the court and threw himself on the floor in front of the jury box and almost under the counsel's table.
>
> The assize room in the old court house was a large room, and it was crowded during this trial. The judge's bench stood quite high above the counsel's table and the rest of the courtroom, so that, in fact, Diefenbaker had practically disappeared from my sight. There was dead silence in the room. I, of course, could not allow this sort of nonsense in my courtroom, so I said, "Mr. Diefenbaker, if you will come out from underneath the table I will be able to follow your argument more clearly." The courtroom burst into laughter and Diefenbaker concluded his address somewhat sheepishly.[36]

Clyne noticed that, although the accused was twenty-six years old, Diefenbaker appealed to the jury's sympathy by referring to him throughout as "this boy." In his charge to the jury, the judge emphasized the lack of evidence supporting Diefenbaker's theory. He told them that, in law, the charge of murder could not be reduced to one of robbery as Diefenbaker had proposed. He concluded that Cathro had intended to commit robbery and, in doing so, had inflicted grievous bodily harm that "was likely to cause death." The jury returned a verdict of guilty. Clyne sentenced Cathro to death, with a recommendation for clemency since he may not have intended to kill and had no previous record. The sentence was eventually commuted. Clyne wrote that Diefenbaker "was very eloquent before juries and could present a persuasive argument, but in my opinion he was not a very good lawyer."[37]

GeORGE DREW'S SECOND GENERAL ELECTION DEFEAT AS LEADER OF THE PARTY WAS followed inevitably by speculation in the press about his retirement.[38] Drew hoped to remain, and his supporters knew that he would need renewed endorsement to maintain his authority in the caucus. Planning began for a national meeting of the Progressive Conservative Association in the autumn of 1953 to give him that support. Suspicions of disloyalty centred on John Diefenbaker; Drew's advocates (and Diefenbaker's opponents) were determined to turn the issue into one of loyalty. "To deserve loyalty on the part of others," Fleming later wrote, "a leader must have proven himself loyal as a follower...I hoped that my loyalty would never become suspect as Diefenbaker's was in these grim circumstances."[39]

Diefenbaker knew the dangers of disloyalty and was careful to offer Drew no overt challenge, so Drew's immediate problem was to stifle the rumblings rather than to put down revolt. The party meeting was orchestrated to that end. Diefenbaker's Saskatchewan associate – and once-competitor – Murdoch McPherson was recruited as keynote speaker, opening the meeting with an appeal for renewed confidence in the leader. The loyalists were cued to rise in ovation for Drew, and did so enthusiastically. "Even those opposed to George's continuance were too embarrassed to remain in their seats under the direct observation of those of us who were standing and applauding. The whole audience was on its feet, none daring to appear not to applaud. This was accepted by the press and by the meeting itself as a rousing and unanimous endorsement of George Drew's leadership. Our strategy had succeeded beyond our hopes. To all outward appearances George was securely confirmed in the leadership: at least the known opposition to him had been driven underground for the time being."[40]

Diefenbaker's position of isolation within the caucus was reinforced. While he believed that Drew's "palace guard" intended to freeze him out of any preferment, he professed satisfaction that Drew sometimes invited him to lead in debate for the party, to attend conferences, or to take speaking engagements on the leader's behalf.[41] Drew certainly made no effort to bring Diefenbaker into his inner circle; he was never a member of what became known as the "Five O'Clock Club" of Drew's intimates, who met regularly in the leader's office for drinks and gossip.[42] But Diefenbaker's aloofness in caucus was above all a matter of his own style and his own suspicions. Behind the facade of civility he disliked and resented Drew, and remained ill at ease among his colleagues. As Dalton Camp, the party's new director of publicity, recalled: "He rarely attended caucus, was not usually available to the Whip's Office when it was attempting to organize the schedule of opposition

speakers, and beyond the call of the duty roster for attendance in the House."
The party's office staff dealt with him cautiously, using Davie Fulton as intermediary when they wished to make contact. For Camp, Diefenbaker was an
enigma: a popular public figure always distant from his own associates.[43]
Diefenbaker remained lonely and insecure. He did not trust people, and was
rarely confident that they trusted him.

The Progressive Conservative Party, which remained the formal vehicle
of Diefenbaker's ambition despite his distance from its centre, was in flux. The
national president, George Nowlan, was replaced after 1953 by another young
MP, the flamboyant and equally ambitious George Hees. Fearing that Hees
would install his own national director after the retirement of Richard Bell,
Drew's inner circle persuaded Earl Rowe's son William to take that job. The
younger Rowe set about to modernize the national office by developing its
advertising, publicity, and research activities, but the organization depended,
inevitably, on the leader's inspiration and popular appeal. Although Drew had
the superficial confidence of his party, there was widespread feeling that he
could never win a national election. His platform manner and appearance –
double-breasted, upright, stiff – had stereotyped him indelibly and unfairly as
a patrician snob. The Ontario provincial party of his successor, Leslie Frost,
kept aloof from the national party, and elsewhere Drew was regarded indifferently by local Conservatives. The new and promising provincial leaders of
the party – Hugh John Flemming in New Brunswick, Robert Stanfield in Nova
Scotia, Duff Roblin in Manitoba – were never close to him. In British
Columbia, Drew was in open conflict with the provincial leader, Dean
Finlayson, by 1955. Whatever others might do to revive the party's national
fortunes seemed blocked by the limitations of the leader and his image.[44]

Meanwhile, the Liberal government of Louis St Laurent was beginning
to stumble. By 1955 St Laurent himself was tiring of the political game and
deferring regularly to the domineering ways of his "minister of everything,"
C.D. Howe. The Liberal journalist Bruce Hutchison commented on "the tired
look of the government and its leader." "The Old Man," he wrote in April, "is
really through and the sooner a new one is found...the better. The boys in
Ottawa may not realize it, but St. Laurent has just quietly faded out of the
picture in the last six months."[45] In June 1955, when Howe introduced a bill
to extend his special powers without time limit under the Defence Production
Act, the Tories seized the moment to filibuster and arouse popular complaint.
After extended, acrimonious debate, the prime minister finally took advantage of Howe's absence from Ottawa in July to amend the bill and impose a
time limit. This was a signal victory for the Conservatives and a tangible boost

to party morale in the House. But Hutchison observed that "the fact undoubtedly is that the country has lost all interest in national politics at the moment, being sated with prosperity. No government can easily defeat itself, however it tries, under these conditions."[46] He missed the slowly percolating undercurrents of popular discontent.[47]

So did Howe, who was now promoting the rapid construction of a natural gas pipeline from Alberta to the east after years of delay. For the minister, this would be his last great national project, matching the Canadian Pacific Railway in its nation-building potential, bringing cheap prairie energy to the industries and homes of central Canada. The great industrial expansion of the early 1950s had created an urgent energy shortage in southern Ontario; for Howe, the challenge required a dramatic response. The government's settled policy was that the line should be built entirely within Canada, sweeping north of Lake Superior through the hard rock of the Canadian Shield. Howe agreed with the American owners, Trans-Canada Pipe Lines Limited, that the government should finance construction on the prairies with a loan of $80 million and that a crown corporation should build the northern Ontario section of the line. The company, in addition, would be permitted to export surplus gas to the US market on a Manitoba branch line. The cabinet had previously delayed Howe's efforts to get the project under way. Now, under his intense pressure, it agreed that the enabling legislation should be introduced under closure in May 1956 to permit construction to begin by July 1. The use of closure to limit debate was unusual; its introduction before any discussion was unprecedented. Howe was determined to defy the opposition and revenge his parliamentary humiliation of the previous year – all in the service of his national vision.[48]

The Conservative caucus – heartened by its success in the last session and sensing public suspicion of both government aid to an American corporation and Howe's contempt for parliament – determined to resist his effort to stifle parliamentary debate on the bill. This time the Tories had the support of the CCF caucus as well, and Davie Fulton coordinated parliamentary tactics with Stanley Knowles to assure maximum damage to the government's tight timetable and good reputation.[49] The result, over five weeks of turbulence in the House of Commons, was a stunning embarrassment to the ministry. The prime minister, dejected, disspirited, and silent, seemed to have lost control of his government. The pipeline legislation was finally passed under closure a few days beyond the cabinet's self-imposed deadline on June 7, but only after an unprecedented series of upsets and noisy disruptions in the Commons. Howe had his bill, but he and his colleagues had been shamed by their display of impatience and ruthless indifference to democratic forms and the popular will.

The Conservative attack on Howe and the government was led with ingenious panache by George Drew, Davie Fulton, and Donald Fleming. It concentrated on procedural issues and came to focus on the role of the Speaker; the substance of the government's measure was scarcely discussed. On May 25 there was an extraordinary incident when Fleming was suspended from the day's sitting by formal vote for having attempted to speak to a point of privilege in face of the Speaker's denial. As Fleming walked down the central aisle of the chamber to withdraw through the main south door, the Conservative and CCF members were on their feet applauding the martyr; and when he reached Diefenbaker's desk, the Saskatchewan member cried out "Farewell, John Hampden!"[50] In Fleming's absence, Ellen Fairclough draped a Union Jack over his vacant desk. This was high political theatre, conducted with instinctive skill by an opposition confident that it had both propriety and public support on its side.[51]

Surprisingly, Diefenbaker played only a secondary role in the opposition's tenacious fight to protest and delay passage of the pipeline legislation. He was in the House for most of the extended debate, voted with his party, and spoke in debate on May 17. He was well informed about the history of Trans-Canada Pipe Lines and its extended negotiations with the federal government. He was contemptuous of the pipeline promoter, the Texan millionaire Clint Murchison; questioned the monopoly privileges of Trans-Canada; ridiculed the domineering manner of the minister, C.D. Howe, and the silence of the prime minister; condemned the improper use of closure before debate had begun; and asked that a parliamentary committee should examine all aspects of the pipeline issue. But the point of his speech remained strangely vague. Partly, that reflected Conservative difficulty in framing an alternative to the government's policy; partly, it indicated that Diefenbaker was uncertain about his own party's tactics.[52]

In caucus, Diefenbaker made clear that he did not favour a policy of obstruction or cooperation with the CCF. In his judgment, voters would not support a campaign of obstruction; and he found it difficult to ally himself with his chief political opponents in Saskatchewan. As a matter of habit and pride, he was reluctant to work closely with his own caucus. He shared the interests of prairie producers and voters whose natural gas would at last be available for sale in eastern and American markets. This was also Social Credit's justification for supporting the government. But Diefenbaker's political sense, in this case, was wrong. "Fortunately," said Fulton, "we were right and the press supported us one hundred percent."[53]

Three weeks of distracted conflict over the pipeline had upset the government's financial timetable, and in early June it found itself needing an urgent vote of interim funding. With a renewed filibuster, the opposition could have forced a dissolution of parliament and an early general election. But George Drew baulked, and supply was granted. Diefenbaker, who was absent from the House, protested privately that the opposition, this time, should have obstructed the vote. He was quick to learn the lesson of the pipeline and would never again underestimate the impact of an unrestrained parliamentary struggle. For three weeks, the House had been the centre of national attention, as it had not been for two decades.[54]

The parliamentary session straggled to its end in August. The Liberal government was shaken if still uncomprehending; the Conservative and CCF opposition were revived and newly confident. The Conservative front bench looked forward to renewing the battle when parliament reconvened in the autumn. Then came misfortune. Before the House adjourned, George Drew withdrew in strain and exhaustion, naming Earl Rowe as interim parliamentary leader. In the following weeks his health did not improve. His doctor and his wife urged him to resign; and others close to him, knowing that the party needed vigorous leadership at this crucial time before a general election, counselled withdrawal as well. In late September he offered his resignation, and the party was thrown unexpectedly into a leadership campaign.[55]

Diefenbaker's candidacy was taken for granted. He was the party's most celebrated front-bencher, and his ambition for the leadership was well known. He indicated to his friends at once that he intended to run. George Pearkes wrote from Victoria to say that "the Pearkes family is three hundred per cent behind you as the new leader of our Party and the next Prime Minister of Canada," promising that "this time we will make certain that you carry the convention. We must not let Bay Street get away with any fast work."[56] But "Bay Street" was one leap ahead of him. David Walker reported that the party's Ontario organizer, Harry Willis, had surveyed the province and found Diefenbaker to be the favourite, destined to "win the convention on the 1st ballot." Willis speculated that Fleming and Hees "will cut one another's throats," that Diefenbaker might achieve a unanimous convention, and that the National Executive might even give Diefenbaker the leadership without a convention. The acting leader and pillar of the old caucus establishment, Earl Rowe, was reported to be "*almost convinced* you are the man." Walker was awed by this sea change: "What can one believe?"[57]

Well, not quite everything. It was true that Leslie Frost and his chief organizer, Alex McKenzie, who had managed the Ontario delegation for Drew at the 1948 convention, had decided to ride the tide of Diefenbaker's popularity despite any lingering doubts about his character. It was true that they had persuaded George Hees to abandon his own campaign and throw his support to Diefenbaker.[58] But Earl Rowe – with his long experience of Diefenbaker in the House – remained unconvinced. As the tide mounted, he met in Ottawa with Léon Balcer, the party president, George Nowlan, J.M. Macdonnell, Grattan O'Leary, Richard Bell, and Donald Fleming to consider a "Stop Diefenbaker" campaign. Fleming agreed with the group that he would withdraw his candidacy if they could persuade Sidney Smith, by then president of the University of Toronto, to enter the race. If Smith would not run, Fleming believed he had their promise of support. Smith declined the approach, Fleming announced his candidacy, and the cabal dissolved without coming to Fleming's aid. Only Macdonnell, of this group, worked actively for him. "It became obvious," Fleming concluded, "that even those who were not ready to support Diefenbaker were reluctant to show their colours against him. This was based in some cases on the belief that he was bound to win, in others on fear of his reputed vindictiveness. I doubt if they gained anything from their abstention." Fleming lamented that Diefenbaker supporters attacked him as the candidate of "the establishment," while he could never find its members. His sole base of support was in Quebec.[59]

Despite his answer, Smith was approached several times in October and November to reconsider. Each time he refused. Rumours were widespread, and talk of the "Stop Diefenbaker" lobby fed the Diefenbaker organization with fuel for its unnecessary, but convenient, anti-establishment campaign. In mid-November Diefenbaker's friend Patrick Nicholson wrote of "the Tory party machine controlled by that nebulous group of back-stage string-pullers," "the Old Guard, desperate to retain its macabre throttle on the jugular vein of the Conservative party...now seeking madly for some other candidate, some other means, to prevent the democratisation of the party under Diefenbaker's enlightened leadership." But he recognized that "the machine, that hard core of MPs, Bay Street millionaires and other political string-pullers," were now hopelessly outnumbered.[60]

The machine, in fact – the new machine – was in Diefenbaker's hands, although he would not admit it. Once again David Walker and Bill Brunt were his closest advisers, but a national campaign had blossomed instantaneously – and as close to the party establishment as anyone could hope. Diefenbaker had not only Leslie Frost and the Ontario organization, but Robert Stanfield in Nova Scotia, Hugh John Flemming in New Brunswick, Duff Roblin in Manitoba, and Toronto advertising man Allister Grosart, who had been

George Drew's national organizer for the 1953 election campaign. In the House of Commons, to his surprise and pleasure, he had Gordon Churchill and a "large committee" of MPs representing 80 percent of the caucus. He had early campaign promises of $7500 to be raised in Ontario, Manitoba, and British Columbia, and the expectation of more. Approaches were even under way to assure the discreet support of Premier Maurice Duplessis in Quebec. Such impressive stirrings of national enthusiasm had been unknown in the Conservative Party for twenty-five years.[61]

The National Executive of the party called the leadership convention for early December in Ottawa. Once his campaign was rolling, Diefenbaker humbly announced his candidacy:

> In the last two weeks I have been deeply moved and encouraged by the messages that have come to me from many of my colleagues in the House of Commons, from a multitude of people in all walks of life, and from one end of Canada to the other, asking that I allow my name to be put in nomination.
>
> I need hardly say that the guiding purpose of my public life has been to serve Canada, to do what I can to restore the Conservative Party to a position where it will best serve all the people, and in so doing to make a prosperous, strong, and united Canada.
>
> To the many people who are asking what I plan to do, I give my answer in a few simple words: I have not sought for myself and I shall not seek the high honour of leadership. But if Canadians generally believe that I have a contribution to make, if it is their wish that I let my name stand at the leadership convention, I am willing.[62]

This time the campaign was meticulously, though simply, planned, despite the assurance of a Diefenbaker victory on the first ballot. The candidate had been disappointed too often to take such things for granted. Although Grosart was there to help, the planning committee noted that "no public relations man or press agent is required." Diefenbaker would make "a few speeches, say nine," across the country. Drew would be praised. Duplessis's support would be solicited. Committees in each province would canvass every delegate, pointing out to them "what the man in the street thinks." Protests would be made against vote rigging at the convention. A Diefenbaker hospitality suite would be booked at the Château Laurier, but with "no liquor to be supplied to delegates." As Diefenbaker's train crossed the nation on its way to Ottawa, reception committees would meet it at every stop. The influences from south of the border were unmistakable: this was to be Canada's first presidential leadership campaign.[63]

Diefenbaker's two challengers, Donald Fleming and Davie Fulton, could not match it. Fleming toured the country alone but concentrated his efforts in Quebec where, he believed, Diefenbaker's campaign under Pierre Sévigny was making no progress.[64] Fulton, an admirer and long-time supporter of Diefenbaker, was persuaded to run, as Diefenbaker had done in 1942, not to win but "to stake out a claim" for the future.[65]

There was only the appearance of a contest. On November 24 the Gallup Poll of Canada declared that Diefenbaker had the support of 55 percent of Conservative voters, ahead of Fleming with 14 percent, Hees with 5 percent, Smith with 4 percent, and Fulton with 2 percent.[66] That breakdown seemed roughly to reflect the reports of delegates' sentiments. But a week later, Gallup offered reassurance to the Liberal government with evidence that its popularity remained at 50 percent – actually three points higher than in August – while Conservative support was frozen at 31 percent.[67]

While Diefenbaker concentrated his energies on the leadership campaign, momentous events were taking place in the larger world. In October the Hungarian revolution raised temporary hopes that the Soviet bloc was in collapse, but in early November Soviet and Warsaw Pact forces brutally crushed the revolt as the West offered no more than rhetorical complaint and began to accept the flood of escaping Hungarian refugees. Simultaneously, Britain, France, and Israel conspired to attack Egypt in a mad effort to restore the recently nationalized Suez Canal to international ownership and to overthrow President Nasser. This plot brought down the ire of the United States, divided the Commonwealth, and faced Canada with the nightmare of a major Anglo-American dispute. Gallup reported that 43 percent of Canadians supported the Anglo-French invasion of Egypt, while 40 percent opposed it. The Canadian interest pointed to some great feat of compromise, and the ingenious secretary of state for external affairs, Mike Pearson, in intimate consultation with John Foster Dulles of the United States and Dag Hammarskjöld of the United Nations, produced a ceasefire, a withdrawal of forces, and the first of many UN peacekeeping operations to hold the fragile line between antagonists.[68]

At the end of November – just two weeks before the Conservative leadership convention – the House of Commons met in special session to debate the Suez and Hungarian crises. As opposition foreign affairs critic and potential leader of his party, John Diefenbaker shared the limelight with Louis St Laurent and Mike Pearson. The government sought formal support for its conciliatory role at the United Nations and its contribution to the peace-keeping force, which was now complicated by Nasser's objection to participation by the Queen's Own Rifles of Canada.[69] The Conservative Party, like the Canadian electorate, was torn between its loyalty to Britain and its support for the United Nations. It could hardly oppose the government's initiative at the United Nations, but neither could it safely condemn the British and French aggression. There was no unity in the caucus. Diefenbaker was forced to walk a narrow and weaving path, and chose to play the statesman in doing it. He emphasized the need to restore "the old alliance between Britain and the Commonwealth, France and the United States" in face of an aggressive Soviet Union and an expansionist Egypt – the two of them aiming, in his fancy, "to take over the Middle East and then, having done that, to take over Africa, to mobilize the people of the Moslem world...There is the blueprint." This was exaggeration of Churchillian proportion. He took credit for having proposed a UN force in the Middle East eight months earlier, when the government, he said, had denied its usefulness. He objected to the careless words of the prime minister, who had appeared to link Britain, France, and the USSR as common oppressors of the weak. And he criticized the government for having allowed "a thug," President Nasser, to dictate the personnel, location, and tenure of the UN force.[70]

Diefenbaker concluded by suggesting a new Quebec conference that would bring together the leaders of Britain, France, and the United States, "without malice, without vituperative statements and without words of grandiloquent content, and in that city lay the foundations for once more re-establishing in the free world a unity which, unless it is achieved and achieved immediately, may result in irreparable harm." That big idea, if it came to fruition, might just surpass Pearson's recent achievement at the United Nations – which Diefenbaker had managed neither to praise nor to condemn.[71]

The idea of a conference was a will-o'-the-wisp, but the speech hit the right political note. Fleming wrote that Diefenbaker "was able to appear as the shining light who avoided smaller issues and idealistically rallied support to the United Nations. His speech was described by the press as a tour de force." Fleming knew he was beaten.[72]

On December 10 the Conservative leadership convention assembled in Ottawa, meeting once more in the dreary ambience of the city's hockey rink – but enjoying relief and refreshment at the Château Laurier. More than thirteen hundred Tory delegates poured into Ottawa for the convention, most of them, according to Dalton Camp, "immediately apprehensive, secretly awed, and aware they are entering enemy territory."[73] Yet among the organizers, there was an insouciant spirit entirely new to the party. Eddie Goodman, who handled the Ontario campaign for Diefenbaker, noticed at once that the Diefenbaker hospitality suite, where liquor was banned on Diefenbaker's personal order, remained empty, while Fleming's and Fulton's rooms, catering copiously to drinking delegates, "were full to the brim."

> I knew something had to be done. The Diefenbakers' personal suite in the Chateau Laurier was next to the hospitality suite. I moved them to a corner suite beside my own bedroom and away from the din. I then called a meeting of the campaign committee, which only I attended, as no one else had been notified, and passed an amendment to the no-drinking rule. The result: a full hospitality suite. I did not fool Diefenbaker – one seldom did – but he bowed without comment to political necessity.[74]

The delegates gathered on the first afternoon to hear Grattan O'Leary's silver-tongued homage to George Drew, and Drew's own graceful retirement speech – written for him by Grattan O'Leary.[75] That evening they assembled again for Robert Stanfield's keynote address. This quiet man told the clan that Drew had left his party "united, strong and in good spirit. Whoever succeeds George Drew will do well to maintain and stimulate this unity, for without it we are unworthy and incapable of success." Stanfield appealed for national policies to assist the poorer regions, to overcome poverty, to aid the sick, "to uplift and elevate the state of mankind in this society." When finished, he slipped unobtrusively out of the Coliseum and returned by air to Halifax.[76]

Beyond the discreet and efficient management of the Diefenbaker campaign by Gordon Churchill, George Hees, and the agents of Leslie Frost's Ontario party, the most significant elements in his organization at the convention were young Conservatives, rallied by the students Ted Rogers, Hal Jackman, Tom Bell, Brian Mulroney, and other enthusiasts. They were nicknamed "Rogers' Raiders" and provided "a spirited presence and muscle that is unique to the convention," spurred by Diefenbaker's own suspicions of an old guard that might still deprive him of the prize.[77] Camp noticed that there was "a peculiar hostility" among the Diefenbaker forces, "an undercurrent of malice, a sense of an impending blood-letting, in which the victorious would all avenge the past."[78]

Diefenbaker himself revealed the primary source of that undercurrent on the day before the convention opened, when he encountered the co-chairman Richard Bell on the platform arranging with carpenters to raise the low podium. Bell told Diefenbaker: "John, these crazy people have put the platform podium away down there. It is no good for you or for me."

Diefenbaker responded: "Ho...You are building it for Fleming, eh? – up to your old tricks." Bell did not take this as a jest.[79]

There would be no drama in the convention's outcome; reporters and critics found its substitute in a conflict over the choice of Diefenbaker's nominator and seconder. Diefenbaker had selected an easterner, Hugh John Flemming of New Brunswick, to nominate him; and a westerner, his House colleague George Pearkes, to second the nomination. But Pierre Sévigny, Diefenbaker's new advocate in Quebec, had expected to be his seconder. When he discovered Diefenbaker's choice, he took his complaint to party president Léon Balcer and to Gordon Churchill – and Balcer took it to the press. Balcer, who had managed the appointment of most Quebec delegates to support Donald Fleming, claimed the authority of a party tradition that "dated back from the previous convention" calling for one English and one French nominator. A stream of supplicants offered their advice. George Hees, Duff Roblin, and Dalton Camp sympathized with Balcer and Sévigny, while Gordon Churchill regarded the issue as a crucial test of Diefenbaker's firm resolve. The English-speaking doubters saw the issue as symbolic and little related to delegate votes. Could Diefenbaker signal his sensitivity to Quebec? Flemming and Pearkes both offered to step down, but Diefenbaker was intransigent. There were few delegates to be swayed in Quebec; he probably had a majority without them; and Canada was one unhyphenated country. When Sévigny met him in his hotel suite, Diefenbaker exploded in rage "and started to harangue me in a loud almost screaming voice...he went on for what seemed to be a very long time. His face was pale, his head shaking, his dress was in complete disarray, and the strange pale blue eyes were literally blazing with anger. His flow of temper ended as quickly as it started." Diefenbaker stuck with Flemming and Pearkes. The affair left a residue of unease that close observers preferred, for the moment, not to analyse. At the very moment that power fell into his hands, Diefenbaker had begun to sow distrust and confusion around him.[80]

That evening in the Coliseum, the candidates were nominated. For this first television convention, the campaign committees produced copious placards, banners, badges, balloons, and noisy displays. The dominant Diefenbaker forces did their best to shield their opponents' signs from the television cameras – in Fleming's eyes, a "shabby, contemptible trick." Diefenbaker's old rival Murdoch MacPherson of Saskatchewan nominated Davie Fulton, emphasizing Fulton's youth and that of other eminent leaders past and present, in unspoken contrast to Diefenbaker, now sixty-one. James Maloney of Ontario nominated Donald Fleming and sharpened the warning: "I suggest to you with great respect that we should now choose a man who not only has great ability but who is old enough and yet not too old, one who is strong and healthy and who is of a disposition and temperament that he can stand up to the grave responsibilities and discharge the tasks that lie ahead." The words would change no votes, but they gave unsubtle testimony to the whispered doubts about Diefenbaker's health and mental balance.[81]

Fleming and Fulton each produced seconders from Quebec and made forgettable speeches. Diefenbaker, after stumbling awkwardly through an apology for his English-speaking nominators, and two excruciating sentences in French, made a better show – perhaps because he could sense that the audience was already with him. For the reporter J.B. McGeachy, "the Diefenbaker effort was emotion undiluted." Sévigny was overcome by this man transformed: "The voice was clear, the phrasing beautiful, and the thoughts strong and inspiring. The interruptions were numerous, the applause at times deafening. And as he proceeded, the magnetism of the man, the hypnotic qualities which were to entrance a whole nation came to the fore. He spoke with an obvious sincerity and an inspired fervour...the vast audience became subdued, silent and enthralled." Diefenbaker sang his old themes of equality, fairness, freedom, and Canadian revival – and pledged his devotion: "I have one love...Canada; one purpose...Canada's greatness; one aim...Canadian unity from the Atlantic to the Pacific." He urged the party to banish defeatism and, with him, "not to win the election after the next election or the next election after the next but...the next election." Such faith, such heart-on-the-sleeve pleading was unfamiliar to Canadians bred in the calm rationalism of postwar Liberalism. The audience roared.[82]

Despite Diefenbaker's explanation that his nominators represented Canada from east to west, many Quebec delegates remained offended by his rebuff. Before voting the next day, they met in insulted conclave. As balloting began, Sévigny and others worried about a violent display on the floor, but nothing occurred. The vote confirmed a decisive first ballot victory: 774 votes for Diefenbaker, 393 for Fleming, 117 for Fulton. Fleming and Fulton rushed to Diefenbaker's side, took him by the hands, and led him to the podium, where Fleming moved that the election be made unanimous. As the rafters rang, a body of Quebec delegates led by Léon Balcer rose in a spontaneous, and at first unnoticed, wave and left the auditorium. When silence came, the new leader thanked the audience, appealed for party unity from sea to sea, and prophesied that "I will make mistakes, but I hope it will be said of me...he wasn't always right, sometimes he was on the wrong side, but never on the side of wrong." The meaning was obscure, but the sentiment was conciliatory. He promised to work for victory "not for victory itself, but on behalf of the people of Canada," and recalled "in all humility" the words of R.B. Bennett at the leadership convention of 1927: "This will be my attitude, this will be the stand that I shall take, 'Whosoever of you will be the chiefest shall be servant of all.'" Olive too – sporting a giant turban out of the Arabian nights – joined her husband on the platform to beam serenely upon the audience and to promise she would improve her French. The triumph was undoubted, though for Diefenbaker it was tinged with embarrassment.[83]

CHAPTER 7

On the New Frontier

1957

THE VICTORY WAS SATISFYING, A BALM FOR PREVIOUS DEFEATS AND REBUFFS, A proof of his capacity to inspire and to persuade. John Diefenbaker had brought to his side many new enthusiasts who sensed in him a zeal, a determination for battle, and a sympathy for the complaints of the common man that had long been missing from the Conservative Party. His election to the leadership was proof that the party could lift itself beyond its old Ontario base. Although he had won with the support of the caucus and the Ontario party, that did not make him their prisoner. He would be no one's prisoner. In his eyes, they had at last recognized the talents they had long ignored. They had given him his due.

For eight years he had secretly nursed and brooded on a grievance he could not forget. Now, in victory, his thoughts returned to the evening of George Drew's triumph of 1948. Early in the morning of December 15 he summoned Dalton Camp to his hotel room. There, in the half-light of a winter dawn, the blinds still drawn, Diefenbaker sprawled on a bed in his dressing gown while Olive sat nearby.

> Then he began to talk about Drew; my senses were now alerted and I could hear Olive rustling in her chair. He was only interested in the unity of the party, he was saying, and bringing everyone together. It had not been that way with Drew, back in 1948, at the last convention.
>
> Nor was he blaming Mr. Drew, he said, his voice tinged with the memory of his private sorrow; perhaps Drew was not to blame. But after the balloting, at the 1948 convention, he had come to Drew's suite – right here in this hotel – and knocked upon his door to congratulate him personally and offer him his loyalty and co-operation.
>
> When he stepped into the room, the celebrations had stopped and everyone fell silent. Then he spoke to Drew and left, because he was not invited

to stay. And when the door had closed behind him, he heard the room erupt in laughter. Laughter, you see: they were laughing at him, mocking his gesture, his decent gesture to Drew.[1]

Camp was puzzled by this recollection, and took it to Drew when he saw him later that day.

When I repeated Diefenbaker's account of the night of the 1948 convention, Drew seemed genuinely shocked. To the contrary, he said, he had made every effort to be conciliatory and had invited Diefenbaker's company in the evening celebrations, but Diefenbaker had begged off. There certainly had been no scene in the suite as described by Diefenbaker.

Eight years ago it had happened, or not happened. I persuaded myself that perhaps both men were right. A deeply sensitive and defeated man, such as Diefenbaker, could easily be wounded by the mere sight of Drew's forces in jubilant celebration, and he could as easily have been slighted or ignored by them. Or perhaps Drew, who had changed a good deal during the eight years of his luckless leadership, from the crusading, conquering hero of the Ontario Tories to this presently spent and uncertain man preparing to leave Stornoway – perhaps, eight years ago, he might have affronted the man he had defeated, even without being aware he was doing so.

If none of this had happened, why would Diefenbaker have told me? If he did not believe it himself, why did he want me to believe it? I decided I did not know, but that sometime, later, I might find out.[2]

This was a strange, private beginning, made more confusing by events of the previous day. After Diefenbaker's victory, Donald Fleming had visited Diefenbaker's entertainment suite at the Château to offer congratulations and support to the new leader. "I was accorded a very warm welcome," Fleming recalled. "Dief hailed my visit as the proof of party unity behind his election. I recognized many of my friends in caucus in the excited throng. Thus the leader's crown passed to the brow of John Diefenbaker. He had achieved a high goal, one that he had long and ardently and openly pursued. Having succeeded, he turned on those who had denied it to him sooner."[3] Fleming could see no commitment to reconciliation, to "the necessary and urgent task of cementing unity within the party." Perhaps that would come; or perhaps, for Diefenbaker, reconciliation could only mean loyalty – complete loyalty – to him.

The convention reminded Diefenbaker that he had severe critics in the party. The acting leader, Earl Rowe, and the national president, Léon Balcer, who should both have maintained a scrupulous neutrality among the candidates, had publicly rebuked him. His age, his health, his temperament had been questioned from the platform. There had been a walkout. As the convention adjourned, William Rowe had submitted his resignation as national director of the party. If Diefenbaker's triumph was tarnished, wasn't that, in some measure, the fault of his foes? Who now deserved the benefit of the doubt?

"In victory: magnanimity." This maxim is a practical rule of prudence, a means of restoring trust. Within a political party, with other opponents to fight, it is a double necessity. It makes the real battle possible. Diefenbaker knew that, and he would strive for it as much as he could. But his wounds and his distrust were deep, the products of a lifetime as an outsider, and there would be turmoil as he struggled to overcome them.

Although he had gained the support of much of the parliamentary caucus under Gordon Churchill's leadership, he was conspicuously opposed by most of the front bench. Diefenbaker made peace with his two challengers, Fleming and Fulton, and assured them they had his trust. He knew them well enough to sense the genuineness of their loyalty. But he could not embrace his other opponents, Earl Rowe, Jim Macdonnell, Dick Bell, Léon Balcer, Roland Michener – and he showed his distaste.[4] The feelings of antipathy were mutual. On the night the convention ended, Richard Bell told his wife: "I'm through with politics. If we can do something as evil as that, I don't want anything further to do with it." George Drew expressed his private dismay: "The party's finished," he told Bell. "It won't be more than three months before Diefenbaker has lost control. He gets his eye on one thing, and he concentrates on it, and he gets it up and makes a speech on it. Then he goes away for two weeks to recover. The party needs people around to pick up the pieces afterwards."[5] The *Globe and Mail* reflected editorially on "a stubborn, unreasoning prejudice" against Diefenbaker among Quebec delegates to the convention, "accompanied at its lower levels, by accusations of quite incredible malevolence. All around Ottawa this week, anti-Diefenbaker yarns were circulating which would be funny if they were not so vicious."[6] Some of that talk originated with the party's Ontario fundraisers, who recognized that Diefenbaker would win the leadership. Dalton Camp quoted one of them: "'If Diefenbaker wants it, let the crazy son of a bitch have it.' It had become a philosophy for the reconciled – Diefenbaker could not be stopped. Though he would be difficult, if not impossible, as a leader, and a failure, after one election he would retire and the party could find a younger, abler man. Diefenbaker had been around a long time, so let him have it. The Grits would win the next election anyway."[7]

That was also the comforting assumption among Liberals. Their view of Diefenbaker, as the *Globe*'s George Bain noticed, had been transformed. Before the convention, Diefenbaker had been the Liberals' favourite Tory, the one robbed of the leadership in 1948 by the party machine, someone associated with liberal causes, a man of the people. Now he had become, according to Liberal sources, "indecisive, temperamental, a lone wolf too long accustomed to going his way to get the caucus to pull together and, therefore, not a good leader. Also, he passed his peak, lost much of his appeal to the electorate, and even became a less sought after orator. In fact, between September and December he became pretty much of a dead loss...the Conservatives made a terrible mistake. They aren't going to win the next election anyway, and for the long pull they want a younger man."[8] Dismissive Liberals said what jaundiced Conservatives thought. Could Diefenbaker prove them wrong?

The new leader had assets as well as liabilities. He had long courted the press and had strong friends in the press gallery: Arthur Blakely of the Montreal *Gazette*, Patrick Nicholson of Thomson Newspapers, Judith Robinson and Peter Dempson of the *Telegram*, Charles Lynch of Southam Press, and Richard Jackson of the Ottawa *Journal*, among others. For everyone in the gallery he was good copy. His popular appeal was proven and it went beyond party. He was the challenger of power, the crusader in good causes who had at last, by sheer determination, faced down and overcame the old guard. With his election as leader the ground had shaken inside the party; it was now his task to transmit those tremors outwards into the country. Sympathetic responses to the opposition campaign on the pipeline, the recovery of the Conservative Party in New Brunswick, Nova Scotia, and Manitoba, and the early signs of a general stirring against the boredom of prosperity and Liberal complacency suggested that the time was ripe.

Diefenbaker's very limitations as a party man might now be his political strengths. That seemed immediately obvious in Prince Albert, home of the Diefenbaker Clubs, where he and Olive returned to an all-party victory banquet on December 28. Eight hundred celebrants dined with the Diefenbakers in the Armouries under the chairmanship of Liberal mayor Dave Steuart, who offered the new leader a silver key to the city. Diefenbaker accepted the honour of this "family gathering" with pride still touched by disbelief. "As on the night of his first election victory in Prince Albert in 1953," wrote one observer, "eager, happy supporters approached him with affection, yet with a kind of deference and reserve. They did not grab him or slap him on the back. They shook his hand and tried to say something polite and timely. 'You'll be prime minister, John.' 'This is only the beginning.'"[9]

But inside the party, in December 1956, the results of his triumph were anything but clear. The new leader remained suspicious of staff in the party's national office, despite William Rowe's early departure as national director.[10] Diefenbaker muddled for weeks over a successor while Allister Grosart, Gordon Churchill, and Dalton Camp separately attempted to manage the party offices and protect their long-serving occupants. George Hees hovered in the background, also hoping for a leading organizational role. At the end of January 1957 Grosart, Churchill, and Camp signed a temporary agreement assigning duties among the triumvirate and giving Churchill effective dominance. Camp began planning for an election campaign but met frustration. "Churchill dithered. He could not be prodded from his House of Commons office. To Gordon a discussion of a problem was indistinguishable from a decision; memoranda became plans in progress; a private understanding was immediately assumed to be a wide consensus; he would not answer mail, all communication was verbal. Gordon spent his days confronting his problems and considering the possibilities; at the end of the day, nothing had been untouched and everything had come under the close scrutiny and the intense, frowning gaze. Yet nothing was decided, nothing achieved."[11]

After three weeks, Camp wrote to Churchill setting out his comprehensive thoughts on an election campaign, suggesting an urgent need for decisions on funding, advertising, platform, and timetable. Shortly afterwards, Diefenbaker announced that Churchill would take charge of Tory headquarters and organization, while George Hees would tour the country to prepare for the national campaign. The arrangement lasted a few days, until Churchill gave up his role without warning, apparently to be replaced by Allister Grosart. This prompted Camp's resignation as director of publicity. Diefenbaker, who had not spoken to Camp since the convention three months earlier, met him three days later, by accident, at the annual press gallery dinner, embraced him, and demanded: "What is this?...What is that letter all about?...I have not read it, you understand? I have not received it. It does not exist...Now, I want you with me. Do you understand? I want you with me, and that's all there is to it!" Out of the confusion, Grosart emerged as national campaign manager while Camp took charge of national advertising and campaign control in the Atlantic provinces.[12] This chaos, eventually given shape by nervous energy, a convincing cause, the leader's inspiration, and public sympathy, somehow produced a powerful national campaign.

Across the country, party nominations went forward for a spring election. Conservatives attended their constituency conventions in untypical numbers, with fresh convictions and new glimmerings of hope. From Ottawa,

Diefenbaker sought out a few leading candidates on his own – three of them unsuccessfully. Eugene Forsey, the feisty research director of the Canadian Labour Congress and connoisseur of the rules of parliament, who had fought the 1948 by-election for the CCF against George Drew, declined the leader's invitation on personal grounds. Charlotte Whitton, the equally feisty mayor of Ottawa, seemed to want into the race but could not decide on a suitable constituency; and when she engaged a city councillor in a mild fistfight she killed her chances.[13] Pierre Sévigny, the party's contact with Premier Duplessis, pleaded to Diefenbaker that he was already overworked and underappreciated as an organizer in Quebec, could not find a winning constituency, and "would much prefer to run in a by-election sometime after the June balloting."[14]

Before the vote there was one more session of parliament. It would be short, commencing in early January. The Liberal government remained confident despite its mauling over the pipeline. Louis St Laurent courteously informed the new leader of the opposition in February that he would dissolve the House in April for a general election on June 10. The government had a minimal program for the session: finance minister Walter Harris's budget, a modest scheme of hospital insurance, and legislation to create the Canada Council, which would be endowed with the windfall proceeds of $100 million from two large estates. The Harris budget was a cautious affair, predicting continued growth in the economy, holding the line on taxes, projecting a surplus of $152 million, and offering a modest increase of $6 a month (to $46) for old age pensioners.[15]

Confident and unflamboyant leadership, the assumption of federal predominance, a gradually emerging scheme of social welfare, a respected place in international councils: these were the marks of the postwar Liberal regime. They were familiar, generally satisfying, and unexciting. By 1957 they were tinged indelibly with complacency. The party had ceased to generate policy, and its electoral organization had withered. Members of the government – and many, even, among the observant public – judged that the Liberal Party, with its inheritance of Mackenzie King's genius for caution and sound administration, had found the keys to everlasting power. Comfortable administration seemed to have replaced politics. Few Liberals believed that Canadians would be so foolish as to turn them out. Yet the pipeline debate had left its residue of unease, not so much over policy as over the government's heavy-handedness. The regime's self-assurance was troubling, and the Conservative message that Liberal cabinets had usurped the House's powers – and thus, perhaps, the country's liberties – struck popular chords.

In 1957 John George Diefenbaker was the ideal person to exploit the country's unease, to revive the national political duel. After years of calm, the voters were ready for some turbulence, some stirring of the blood. Diefenbaker was soon being referred to familiarly as "Dief" and "Dief the Chief": the formerly private nicknames quickly took their place as icons beside the image of "Uncle Louis," which now seemed old-fashioned, quaint, decrepit, tired like the man. Besides affectionate informality, Diefenbaker's nicknames came to symbolize the evangelistic reformer thundering from the platform as from the pulpit, decrying the sin of pride, offering leadership on the way to the promised land. His excitement was electric. In the early winter of 1957 he criss-crossed the country testing and refining his message.

During this short session Diefenbaker spent less time than usual in the House. After a brief respite over New Year's at Lord Beaverbrook's home in the Bahamas, he was back in parliament to speak in the opening debate in January.[16] He moved a Conservative amendment on supply in February. He attacked the Liberal budget in March for its overtaxation, its lack of generosity to pensioners, and its failure to assist the poorer provinces. He embarrassed the government by supporting proposals in the preliminary report of the Gordon Commission on Canada's economic prospects to limit the effects of foreign investment. He lectured the cabinet on its indifference to farmers. Above all – with an election approaching – he gave Conservative MPs fresh energy and confidence, sustaining the initiative that had built up during the pipeline debate of the previous year.

Diefenbaker's performance in the House was practised and melodramatic. When parliament met in January, the country faced a national railway strike that gave the new leader his theme: the country was drifting under a government that was tired and smug. Patrick Nicholson described the scene.

> He had pushed aside his chair in his familiar gesture, clearing a little space of floor between desks and chairs. In this corral he paced like a caged lion while he denounced the government, now angry, now hectoring, now pleading and now questioning. With right hand on hip, in his familiar stance holding back the imagined counsel's gown, he asked innocently: "What does the government do?" Then the accusing forefinger shot out towards the Prime Minister, and he charged: "It continues its policy of being resolute in irresolution." When the Prime Minister smiled at his words, he snarled back: "The Prime Minister smiles regarding a problem that affects the hearts and purses of Canadians everywhere, that affects the economy of this country."

The assault continued for forty minutes, as "his scathing and sarcastic words rang nasally round the Commons Chamber like a trumpet call of a Guardian Angel," ending in a motion that accused the government of "indifference, inertia and lack of leadership...and disregard of the rights of Parliament." Members of the cabinet shifted uneasily, knowing there was truth in his words.[17]

THE MOST DISTURBING POLITICAL EVENT OF THE SESSION OCCURRED ON APRIL 4, 1957, when the Canadian ambassador to Egypt, E.H. Norman, jumped to his death from the roof of the embassy building in Cairo. Norman had entered the Canadian foreign service in 1940 with a distinguished academic record in Japanese studies from the University of British Columbia, Cambridge, and Columbia. His initial posting in Japan was followed during the Second World War by intelligence work in Ottawa; and in 1945 he was reposted to General MacArthur's headquarters in Tokyo to assist the occupation administration. In 1950 he was recalled to Ottawa for an intensive security review that resulted in his formal clearance. In 1951 and later, his name featured in testimony before the US Senate internal security subcommittee as a possible Soviet agent, and in mid-March 1957 Norman's purported record was raised again. The legal counsel to the subcommittee, Robert Morris, read into the record excerpts from an "executive agency security report" casting doubt on Norman's activities, and transcripts of the hearings were released to the press. By this time Norman occupied the sensitive role of Canadian ambassador to Egypt, where he had arrived just before the outbreak of the Suez war in 1956.

On March 14, 1957, in the House, the new leader of the opposition asked the secretary of state for external affairs, Lester Pearson, "whether, if it is found that there is no justification for these allegations, the strongest possible protest will be made to the United States against this attack which is detrimental not only to the Canadian diplomat but to Canadian international relations."[18] The minister replied that the subcommittee had improperly released its record without previously informing the Canadian government. The transcript, he said, "contains a great many innuendoes and insinuations that Mr. Norman was a Communist." These claims were previously known, and Norman had been cleared years before in "a special and exhaustive security check." Pearson praised Norman as "a devoted, efficient and loyal official... who is doing extremely important work at a very difficult post in a way which commanded my wholehearted admiration and deserves my full support." The subcommittee's "slanders and unsupported insinuations" should be regarded with contempt, and the Canadian government would be making strong protests to the United States for this treatment of a senior Canadian diplomat.[19] For the moment Pearson's statement and Diefenbaker's support seemed to end the incident. Two weeks later Pearson wrote to Diefenbaker: "Our Ambassador in Cairo, Herbert Norman, has written to me to say that the reaction in the House of Commons to the renewed allegations against him in the United States Senate Subcommittee has increased his pride in and devotion to our institutions and our sense of fair play. Mr. Norman asked if I would pass on to you the expression of his sincere appreciation for the thoughtful and considerate manner in which you introduced the subject in the House on March 15th. This I am very glad to do."[20]

When Norman fell to his death four days later after carefully preparing several suicide notes, Pearson told the House that Norman had been "deeply and understandably distressed by the resurrection...in Washington of certain old charges affecting his loyalty and which were disposed of years ago after a careful investigation...There will be much sorrow in America as in Canada at this terrible consequence of the Committee's recklessness." Diefenbaker added his own strong words. "I am shocked to learn of the death of Herbert Norman. Canada will be the poorer without the special knowledge of Asian affairs possessed by this devoted public servant. His tragic death seems to be attributable to the witch-hunting proclivities of certain congressional inquisitors in Washington who, lacking local targets, felt impelled to malign and condemn Canadian public servants as well. Desirable as it is to preserve our freedom against communism, this is but further evidence that trial by suspicion and conviction by innuendo have terrible results in the lives of those subjected to it."[21] From across the aisle, Pearson wrote a brief note of gratitude: "John – I have been deeply touched by your words – and I want to thank you very sincerely for them – as not only Norman's chief – but as his old and close friend. Mike Pearson."[22]

The Canadian and American press echoed the parliamentary condemnations. For the next few days Diefenbaker maintained his common front with the government, while rumours circulated in Washington that Pearson too was under suspicion by congressional investigators.[23] To one critic who warned Diefenbaker of the dangers of communist subversion he replied:

> The Secretary of State for External Affairs, on behalf of the Government, has made it perfectly clear on several occasions in recent years that a very thorough investigation of Mr. Norman under Canadian security procedures failed to show any justification for the charges which were levied against him by certain persons in the United States. If we are to indulge in the sort of

trial by slander and conviction by innuendo, which is one of the principal badges of communism where it is in power, I do not see how we can pretend to have a better system of government than that existing behind the Iron Curtain. My remarks in the House of Commons last week on Mr. Norman's death related wholly to our traditions of freedom and justice – traditions which do not exist under communism.[24]

A whirlwind of rumour, accusation, and denunciation followed Norman's death. In Canada, comment focused on the US Senate subcommittee's reckless disregard for the rights of a Canadian citizen in publicizing secret and unsubstantiated claims. But in Washington it emerged that the State Department had authorized release of the subcommmmittee's testimony. The issues – of suicide, secret intelligence, and the Cold War – were grist for the gossip mills and tempting subjects for political conflict. Yet Canadian politicians were restrained by decency in a personal tragedy, by solidarity with the government on subjects of national security, and by reluctance to strain relations with the United States. Diefenbaker shared these attitudes, and chose – like the minister – to focus his complaints on the irresponsibility of American congressional committees. On April 9 he asked Pearson whether Canada had lodged its protest "against the extra-judicial investigations of Canadians by congressional committees." The next day Pearson made a formal statement to the House in reply. He read the Canadian letter of protest and the American response, which noted the independence of Congress and insisted that "any derogatory information developed during the hearings of the Subcommittee was introduced into the record by the Subcommittee on its own responsibility."

In an effort, apparently, to limit the scope of Canadian criticism, Pearson then entered dangerous ground. He read the text of a new diplomatic note to Washington asking for assurances that "in the reciprocal exchange of security information" between the two countries, the US government would not pass such information to any body beyond executive control "without the express consent of the Canadian Government in each case." Without such assurances, Canada threatened to withhold future security information dealing with Canadian citizens.[25]

The opposition's initial response was to commend Pearson for the government's directness. But as the implications of his words took hold, two disturbing possibilities emerged. The new request to the US suggested that the original source of the "executive agency security report" read to the subcommittee might be the RCMP security service; and if so, that in turn suggested that the reports about Norman's early communist associations were believed to be accurate by the Canadian government. Pearson had previously suggested the opposite. For Diefenbaker, the potential issue was now political and demanded pursuit. Had Pearson misled the House? On April 12 Diefenbaker asked: "In order to clear up the matter once and for all, will the Minister say that the allegations and statements made before the Subcommittee of the United States Senate...specifically were untrue, unjustified and had no basis in fact?"[26]

Later in the day, Pearson responded with a further statement, in which he conceded for the first time that Norman was known to have had communist associations as a university student. Nevertheless, the minister insisted, the Canadian government's security review had found him "a loyal Canadian in whom we could trust, and the decision was made to retain him...His loyal and devoted and most valuable service over the years in positions of increasing importance have never given us any cause to regret that decision." But he did not answer Diefenbaker's question about the accuracy of the subcommittee's record on Norman.[27]

Diefenbaker replied that Pearson's statement was "equivocal," and added that if no Canadian security information had passed to the Senate subcommittee, the government's latest protest to the United States was meaningless. He asked: "Did any portion of the information transmitted by Canadian security bodies find improper use in the records of the United States Senate Committee?" In an extended and intricate round of debate, Pearson denied that any American security agency had misused Canadian intelligence, but was unclear about the source of the subcommittee's information on Norman. Diefenbaker complained that Pearson had "either spoken too much or too little." CCF and Social Credit spokesmen agreed, and the discussion ended in confusion.[28]

The episode exposed unexpected weaknesses in the political skills of Lester Pearson: he seemed to have walked into a morass, and in his distress to have dug himself in deeper. The House was left feeling that it had been deceived, that the government was floundering, that the truth remained hidden.

Was this an issue to be exploited in the forthcoming election? Diefenbaker was under conflicting pressures. He shared the government's commitment to the Cold War alliance with the United States, and accepted its corollaries of a common defence and pooled systems of intelligence gathering. He understood the need for ministerial discretion and silence in matters of security, and was sympathetic to the personal aspect of the case. He was a committed civil libertarian with a strong sense of fairness. On the other hand, he was attracted by hints of conspiracy, he could see Pearson's discomfort, he was genuinely offended by the Senate subcommittee's impudence – and he was now aware, through press reports and his own correspondence, of much more sweeping charges of subversion that vaguely included Pearson himself.[29]

The daily pressure for debate ended when the House was dissolved on April 12. Diefenbaker had a short time to reflect before the rough and tumble of the election campaign. One supporter wrote to him that reports of his assault on Pearson were "very disturbing...I feel more jolted by your attack than at any other single incident and am doubtful whether the P.C. party is putting expediency ahead of principle...To attempt to belittle Pearson for an apparent political advantage for election purposes is wrong from every point of view. It is bringing Cdn politics down to the U.S. level...In short it is the smear tactics of a U.S. Congressional Committee." Instead, he urged Diefenbaker to give Pearson proper credit for his protests, but to urge a more independent Canadian foreign policy.[30] There were other, similar letters. By early May his own staff cautioned Diefenbaker to put the issue aside on the ground that the subject was in bad taste, and that to pursue it would alienate many "lukewarm Liberals" who were ready to vote Conservative.[31] Diefenbaker did so, and the Norman case was virtually unmentioned during the next two months of campaigning. Mike Pearson, alone among Liberal ministers, seemed immune from criticism. But the incident marked the first occasion when Diefenbaker had reason to doubt Pearson's word, or to perceive his innocence in the parliamentary battle. The politician stored away his suspicions and insights in his capacious memory.[32]

DONALD CREIGHTON'S MAGNIFICENT TWO-VOLUME BIOGRAPHY OF THE COUNTRY'S first prime minister, Sir John A. Macdonald, was published in 1952 and 1955.[33] The biography, with its entrancing picture of a practical and sometimes roguish visionary, found an eager audience among English-speaking Canadians who craved knowledge of and pride in their own history. For the slowly reviving Conservative Party, Creighton's *Macdonald* was a timely gift. Members began to recall the party's historic beginnings in their rhetoric.

On the inspiration of Donald Fleming, Conservative motions in the parliamentary supply debates of 1956 and 1957 urged that "the welfare of the Canadian people requires the adoption of a national development policy which will develop our natural resources for the maximum benefit of all parts of Canada." The wording was meant to echo John A.'s National Policy, and to assert the party's forward-looking interest in economic growth.[34] But this was mere rhetoric: there was no program to match the aspiration. In November 1956, as the Conservative leadership convention approached, Diefenbaker's

Prince Albert friend Dr Glen Green asked his brother-in-law, Merril W. Menzies, a young economist who had recently completed his doctoral thesis on Canadian wheat policy, to write him with some thoughts on Conservative economic policy. When a bulky forty-three-page reply arrived, Green sent it on to Diefenbaker. Diefenbaker read it and indicated his interest to Green; and in January 1957 Menzies's wife June – also an economist – followed up with a letter of impassioned political analysis to the new leader. Two weeks later Merril Menzies himself wrote to Diefenbaker, offering six to eight months of service to Diefenbaker in an "intensive study of national economic policies and problems." The project would be jointly conducted by husband and wife, and Menzies emphasized that their approach "would be one of bringing economic analysis to bear on national problems, while leaving the political analysis to yourself." "This suggestion," Menzies noted, "may well be unique in Canadian politics, but if you think that it could make a valuable contribution to the development of a rounded and effective national policy it might be worth experimenting with it for a few months." Diefenbaker saw the opportunity. After cursory inquiries about Menzies and a personal meeting in Vancouver, he offered Menzies an appointment as his policy adviser during the election campaign. For eight weeks in April, May, and June, Menzies accompanied Diefenbaker on the campaign train, producing a stream of memos as background for Diefenbaker's election speeches. He became Diefenbaker's prolific idea man.[35] His wife disappeared into the background, though she presumably continued in informal collaboration with her husband on what they had initially seen as a joint venture.

Menzies had worked for the Liberal government, as an executive assistant to justice minister Stuart Garson, until after the 1953 general election. But he had left Garson out of frustration, convinced that the Liberal Party had slipped into a doctrinaire free market policy that left no positive role for the state in economic development. In the years since 1953, he had worked out what he saw as a coherent approach to Canadian economic growth which found its historic basis in Macdonald's National Policy. Menzies was convinced that development, if left to the market, would shatter the east-west links of the national economy and bring economic integration with the United States. After 1950 the Liberal Party had taken that path, and under the inspiration of C.D. Howe it would not deviate from it. Only a revived Conservative Party, in Menzies's view, could save the country from disintegration. But under George Drew the party had remained frozen in reaction, blindly committed to "free enterprise," and lacking any understanding of the historic role of the national government. Menzies told Diefenbaker: "I have been acutely conscious of the

emphasis you have been putting on the need to formulate a national development policy...The fact that you as a politician have discerned the necessity of
such a policy is greatly encouraging to me after many years of frustration."[36]

Menzies's call for a program of development inspired by Macdonald's
continental policy, aimed particularly at growth in the Atlantic provinces, the
west, and the north, and infused with passionate conviction was brilliantly
attuned to John Diefenbaker's mood and intuitions in 1957. Menzies's
approach justified and gave coherence to Diefenbaker's long-nurtured sense
of political grievance by transcending his personal resentments: what he had
felt, Menzies seemed to tell him, was not merely personal frustration, but the
nation's forgotten destiny. Diefenbaker had been right to think that both the
Liberal and the Conservative parties had neglected, misconceived, and
betrayed the country's interests. He was right to think that under his leadership the nation could rediscover itself. He was an outsider because those at
the centre had lacked vision. Now he could give the nation back its purpose
and its soul.

Merril Menzies was a scrupulous analyst with a sense of the complexity
of the Canadian economy and a scepticism about slogans and stereotypes. But
he was moved by an overriding belief in a distinct Canadian existence that
might be lost. That conviction reflected the views of other thoughtful
Canadians in the 1950s, including many Liberals like the mildly nationalist
royal commissioner Walter Gordon and the Montreal *Star*'s editor, George
Ferguson. Menzies alone managed to shape his thoughts into a political and
economic framework of justification for the leadership of John Diefenbaker;
and once in Diefenbaker's company, he fed Diefenbaker the phrases and
slogans the party leader needed to convey that passionate vision to the country.
As never before, Diefenbaker was inspired – and Menzies was his muse.
Diefenbaker himself had no talent for coherent economic and social analysis.
His political discontents had previously been expressed in sharp but disconnected criticisms of his opponents. Now Menzies – another westerner who
viewed the country from outside the Ontario-Quebec heartland – transformed
those criticisms, like magic, into a positive vision. As the letters and memos
flowed from Menzies in the spring of 1957, the leader took his pencil to them,
underlining, making marginal summaries, reshaping Menzies's thoughts to
his own electoral needs.[37]

"From Confederation until the early 1930's," Menzies wrote, "there was
a powerful unifying force in the nation – what Bruce Hutchison is fond of
calling the national myth. This unifying force was the challenge and the
development of the West. It engendered a powerful but not xenophobic

nationalism and was made possible and given shape and direction by Macdonald's National Policy." That policy had effectively ended in 1930.

> *Since then we have had no national policy* – and we have had no transcending sense of national purpose, no national myth, no unifying force.
>
> Practically throughout the entire course of this period, bankrupt of any sense of national purpose, there has been a Liberal administration in Ottawa. This has been particularly unfortunate since that party has *never understood* the significance of national policy and the imperative need for a transcending sense of national purpose.
>
> They have been vaguely aware of the vacuum and have attempted to fill it by policies designed to mitigate regional disparities in income and welfare. This was a necessary task but as one actor remarked of another: "He's a fine chap. There is absolutely nothing wrong with him – except that he has no character!"
>
> Liberal policy has no character, no vision, no purpose – with appalling consequences to our parliamentary system and national unity. Regionalism in many vital respects is growing not diminishing (B.C. for example). The national government is tolerated because its policy is to keep everyone comfortable (more or less) and to "keep the boom going" – but it is not respected. It is undermining parliamentary government and national unity by failing to provide a transcending unifying force – the essential myth – by its deliberate determination to avoid a national policy, by its acceptance of a policy of drift which can have only one conclusion...
>
> Time is running out and only the Conservative party can stem this complacent drift...The present drift can only be stemmed by a new unifying force, a new national policy, a new national myth.
>
> That is why I have proposed a new national policy – the NEW FRONTIER POLICY; a new national strategy – that of "Defense in Depth"; a new national myth – the "North" in place of the "West" which "died" a quarter of a century ago.[38]

Menzies insisted that a Conservative "New Frontier Policy" would be distinct from the passive, piecemeal, pork-barrel approach of the Liberal Party. "The difference between the Liberals and Conservatives is fundamental – it is one of principles – and it is vital for our future that the nation become alive to that difference." The best way to assure that was "to enunciate a new and striking policy which sums up that difference, and then to dramatize that *Policy* by a few audaciously far-sighted proposals."

In his paper for Glen Green, Menzies had linked a series of programs in a national scheme: an export policy that would assure Canadian use of the country's energy resources; a national electricity grid; power development on the Columbia and Fraser rivers in British Columbia, the Hamilton River in Labrador, and the Bay of Fundy; and construction of the South Saskatchewan dam. Now he focused on the romantic idea of the North with an "audacious proposal." There should be a new province between the 60th and 65th parallels, including the southern Yukon, the southern Mackenzie Valley, and Great Slave Lake. There, he foresaw that mining and hydroelectric power would provide "the dynamic impulse" – to be followed by agriculture, forestry, the fishery, and a local consumer market. The new province would be Diefenbaker's new West; its creation and settlement, Menzies hinted, would make Diefenbaker the new nation-builder, the new Macdonald. The proposal was accompanied by a series of detailed suggestions for railway, highway, waterway, hydro power, and public service projects to be planned and financed for the north by the federal government.[39]

The idea of a new province was too audacious for Diefenbaker, but the inspirational language and many of the projects were not. He incorporated them in his election speeches. He listened more and more to Menzies and was flattered by his adviser's encouragement. On Menzies's urging, he disregarded most of the party's formal efforts to produce policy statements and an electoral program, picking up only those that repeated or reinforced his own and Menzies's thoughts.[40] By mid-April Diefenbaker could already sense that what he said had resonance in the country. Others in the party sensed it too, and they threw themselves energetically into the campaign behind him. What John Diefenbaker said was Conservative policy – and nothing else mattered.

WHEN PARLIAMENT DISSOLVED, THE CONSERVATIVE PARTY WAS READY TO LAUNCH its election campaign under the new leader. Diefenbaker's parliamentary office was in the efficient hands of Derek Bedson, the former private secretary to George Drew. The party's research staff under Donald Eldon was working in tandem with Merril Menzies to provide a series of policy statements consistent with Diefenbaker's views. Allister Grosart was coordinating the national campaign, and fundraising was progressing well. In the key province of Ontario, Diefenbaker had confided local organization to Premier Leslie Frost and his provincial party.[41] Dalton Camp's advertising firm, Locke, Johnson, had produced a campaign slogan that summed up the party's miraculously transformed character: "It's time for a Diefenbaker government."[42] The opening rally of the national campaign would take place at Massey Hall in Toronto on April 25, 1957.

Despite these encouraging signs, Diefenbaker doubted his own performance. "I think I will be through the session without too much trouble – altho' I don't think I have done at all well and am just getting full control now," he wrote to his brother on April 11. "It's a very onerous and trying position as L.O. – no one can really know unless he has the job."[43] His congenital difficulty in organizing his time, his thoughts, and his files had worsened with his new responsibilities. "Tomorrow I shall start on working on my speeches for Newfoundland," he told Elmer. But three days later he wrote that "I have absolutely nothing ready for Newfoundland at all and will have to put the speech together after I get there." On top of that, he could not complete his income tax return because he had lost his previous statement, "and I think the best thing to do would be to call on the authorities...and have them help me make it out." He sent Elmer a memorandum for safekeeping until he could meet officials in Saskatoon to settle the affair.[44]

As leader of the party, Diefenbaker could devote little time to his own constituency or to family matters. For help and reassurance in both, he depended on Elmer. John's mother was now bedridden, and after two months of anxiety about nursing assistance at home she was moved to the University Hospital in May.[45] At a distance from Prince Albert, Diefenbaker worried, too, that he might lose his own seat. "I wonder how things are going in Prince Albert," he wrote to Elmer in February, "for the Grits are out to beat me at all costs...Gee it would be my end if I got defeated personally and I would be *out* for sure."[46] "I hope that the PA situation is in fair shape, although I am worried," he repeated a few days later. "What they are doing there I do not know but will call Roy Hall in a few minutes."[47] In late March he reported that "the National Organization in Ottawa seems to be operating very well now under Al Grosart but I am naturally concerned about Prince Albert. I think one of these weeks when you are free I wish you would spend some time up there and make a survey of the situation and let me know what you think of things...I could arrange for an advance of $500 and your expenses."[48] When Mary Diefenbaker's illness kept Elmer at home, John lamented: "I wish you could have gone to Prince Albert as I certainly will need help there."[49] For his only intensive campaign visit to the constituency from April 18 to 24, Diefenbaker hoped "that you will be able to attend all these meetings – you know so much about sound electioneering and get votes which no one else can succeed in getting."[50]

The Liberal Party, which had run third to Diefenbaker in Prince Albert in 1953, was determined to recover the seat in 1957. The party appointed a full-time local campaign manager and in early April it held an overflow nomination meeting in the Arcade Hall, preceded by a noisy motor cavalcade. Dr Russ Partridge, a local dentist and former provincial party president, was acclaimed as the Liberal candidate. Diefenbaker's organizers were briefly worried. They revived the Diefenbaker Clubs of 1953 and renewed their efforts to recruit Liberals and CCFers to the cause.[51] For seven days in April John and Olive travelled the riding, attending meetings in Shellbrook, Smeaton, Nipawin, Canwood, Debden, Macdowall, and Choiceland, before flying back to Toronto for the opening of the national campaign. From then on, Prince Albert was out of his hands as he toured the country from east to west and back again.

When the leader flew into Toronto, his schedule was already looking frenetic. "This Pace Can Kill," the *Globe and Mail* commented editorially. Diefenbaker's leadership was "fresh and vigorous," but the editors doubted it could long remain that way at the existing pace. His campaign managers, they advised, should slow him down for his own sake.[52] They didn't quite understand their man: Diefenbaker was reporting excellent health and an increase in weight.

He reached the platform at Massey Hall that night before a "wildly enthusiastic" audience and stood arm-in-arm with his Ontario candidates before his introduction by Frost as "a great Canadian, a man of the people, and the next Prime Minister of Canada."[53] This was the first of many appearances by the premier in the campaign. He made clear throughout that he was committed to Diefenbaker as someone who could deal fairly with the provinces in tax-sharing, and his Ontario organization provided muscle, both financial and human, to the nationwide campaign.[54]

Diefenbaker had arrived in Toronto with three draft speeches, prepared for him by Merril Menzies, Rod Finlayson, and Allister Grosart, "so that you could choose between them, or make use of parts of all of them."[55] As they had expected, the address that emerged on stage was his own, its unity emotional rather than logical. His aides knew that once Diefenbaker launched himself before an audience they could have no control over what he said, so their practical advice was limited to a few essentials. "Stress leadership, vision and a positive approach to problems," Menzies suggested, "rather than being driven by the Liberal campaign to fighting on ground of their choosing – chiefly on negative issues and on criticism." This was safe, since Diefenbaker had already made that choice of emphasis. His speeches were upbeat and evangelical, looking ahead to an era of bliss. But there was always some balancing reference to Liberal darkness, the loss of national purpose, the extinction of parliamentary government, if Canada could not recover "all the wisdom, all the faith and all the vision" of John A. Macdonald. Diefenbaker did not quite tell his audience he was John A. incarnate, but he insisted on a place in the apostolic succession. And in that succession, his contact was direct. No one stood between the Old Chieftain and the new Chief: an intervening half-century of Conservative leaders had vaporized.

> I am of those who believe that this Party has a sacred trust, a trust in accordance with the traditions of Macdonald. It has an appointment with destiny, to plan and to build for a greater Canada. It has a sacred trust handed down to us in the tradition of Macdonald to bring about that Canada which is founded on a spirit of brotherhood, vision and faith – one Canada, with equality of opportunity for every citizen and equality for every province from the Atlantic to the Pacific.[56]

The new leader promised to place before the country, "not a policy of criticism alone, but one based on the needs of the present, the building of one Canada." In that Canada, the provinces and Ottawa would share revenues in "a healthy division and balance...in a spirit of unity and amity, with mutual tolerance and respect." All would benefit equally from a great new initiative.

> We intend to launch a National Policy of development in the Northern areas which may be called the New Frontier Policy. Macdonald was concerned with the opening of the West. We are concerned with developments in the Provinces with provincial cooperation, and in our Northern Frontier in particular. The North, with all its vast resources of hidden wealth – the wonder and the challenge of the North must become our national consciousness. All that is needed, as I see it today, is an imaginative policy that will open its doors to Canadian initiative and enterprise. We believe in a positive National Policy of development, in contrast with the negative and haphazard one of today. We believe that the welfare of Canada demands the adoption of such a policy, which will develop our Natural Resources for the maximum benefit of all parts of Canada.

What is more, a new government would preserve and increase Canadian ownership of industry and resources, reduce taxes to eliminate surplus budgets, begin a vast and humane immigration program, provide farmers with fair prices, assist small business, end government monopolies in air transport and television broadcasting, restore parliamentary freedom, increase old age pensions, and resist communism at home and abroad. The party would take the country "back to the vision and the idealism of Canada's first Nation Builder...My purpose and my aim with my colleagues on this platform will be to bring to Canada and to Canadians a faith in their fellow Canadians, faith in the future in the destiny of this country."

The message was positive, generous, utopian, a dreamscape for a people who "ask for a lift in heart." Diefenbaker gave it to them. If there was contradiction, obscurity, imprecision, and wild hyperbole, so be it. What Diefenbaker offered first was faith. The rest could be left for another day, for without faith there would be no victory. The audience responded to his extraordinary gleaming eyes, his undulating voice and shaking jowls, his dashes of self-mockery and sarcasm, his assertion of that enticing northern vision. After Massey Hall, heartbeats quickened. Something was in the air that the Liberals could not manage. With variations of anecdote and local colour, the Massey Hall speech became the model for the entire campaign.[57]

From Toronto, Diefenbaker began a six-week odyssey, travelling twenty thousand miles by special railway car, air, and auto to every province.[58] On the train, he was accompanied by Olive and a personal staff of six: George Hogan as train manager, Derek Bedson as private secretary, Merril Menzies as research assistant, Fred Davis as personal photographer, and two secretaries.[59] A small group of reporters, usually only five or six, accompanied the tour, to be joined by local and regional correspondents at every stop. By later standards, the entourage and camp followers were a distinctly modest company.

As the campaign progressed, their mood changed from uncertainty to slightly disbelieving hope. The country was responding.[60] Friendly headlines in the *Globe and Mail* traced the leader's progress across the country: "Ontario Enthusiasm Moving East" (April 29), "Ontario Premier's Aid Could Help Turn Tide" (May 4), "Crowd of 1500 at Guelph Welcomes PC Chieftain" (May 14), "Diefenbaker Finds Trend Toward PCs" (May 16), "Liberals Are Worried PC Party Tells West Audiences" (May 20), "Diefenbaker Hailed by 3800 in Victoria" (May 22), "Diefenbaker Receives His Greatest Acclaim in Vancouver Overflow" (May 24), "Liberals in Panic: Groundswell for PCs Noted by Diefenbaker" (May 30), "PC Leader's Campaign Likened to a Crusade" (June 1).

Diefenbaker's choice was a whistle-stop campaign that made room for endless brief stops, handshaking, and repetitive speeches. In mid-May the *Globe* still complained that his pace was too hectic and fatiguing, his message too ill-focused. "He is making dozens of minor addresses which draw purely local attention, when he ought to be making a handful of major ones which forcibly impress themselves – and himself – upon the situation."[61] The

American Embassy, reporting the campaign to Washington, made a similar judgment: "Indications at the present time are that the opposition parties, led by the Progressive Conservatives, have thus far failed to develop issues which might capture and fire the imagination of voters across Canada... Mr. Diefenbaker, while an earnest and capable orator and possessed of a zeal that can arouse audiences thus far seems to lack the political appeal necessary to draw a large enough following to defeat the Liberals."[62]

While Liberal candidates played on the party's authority and experience, Diefenbaker stressed his links with local communities and the common people, and his interest in their needs. He cared, he had roots, he was one of them. Wherever he could claim them, his ties were personal. In Toronto he recalled that he had first seen the City Hall as a child in 1900 when the Boer War veterans returned; in Greenwood he spoke of his happy school days; in Scarborough he remembered his early years; in Saskatoon and Prince Albert he had come home.[63] Olive – despite a painful and recurrent slipped disk – was always with him on the platform, smiling regally and passing him reassuring notes and reminders.[64] By now she was his closest and most trusted counsellor, a calm presence as he raced across the country. The frenetic schedule let up only on Sundays; John Meisel calculated that Diefenbaker campaigned actively for thirty-nine days (as compared with Louis St Laurent's twenty-eight) and made personal appeals in 130 constituencies (as opposed to fewer than 120 for St Laurent).[65]

What the *Globe and Mail* missed in its editorial comments on his lack of focus was the way Diefenbaker "forcibly impressed" himself on his audiences. His impact was made not by extended discussion of complex issues, but by his urgency and zeal, his appeals to national greatness and common sacrifice, his promise of deliverance. As Meisel noted, his imagery "was highly evocative to anyone reared in the Christian faith...The voter needed only to vote for the Diefenbaker party and he would at once become allied to those who were creating a dazzlingly bright and promising future. Each voter could, so Mr. Diefenbaker seemed to say, participate in an effort which would make his own dreams come true."[66] By contrast, Prime Minister St Laurent was the dignified corporate chairman dryly reporting another successful year. "He seemed," commented the Winnipeg *Free Press*, "hardly to recognize the existence of a dissident group of shareholders demanding a change in the management."[67]

John Diefenbaker tapped the country's discontents. The mood and the momentum of the campaign were increasingly with him and his party. His audiences grew larger, his appeals more confident, his jokes and anecdotes more relaxed and perfectly timed. Flattering pictures from his tour photographer blanketed the national press. Louis St Laurent, on his side, grew more irritable and aggressive. While the Conservative campaign had a vital centre and a target of attack, the Liberal campaign seemed listless, inflexible, and insensitive. As the mood turned against them, Liberal candidates squabbled publicly and made headlines by offending their audiences. The most vivid incident occurred at the prime minister's rally in Maple Leaf Gardens, when a protesting youth was pushed roughly from the platform.[68] The party's insistent criticism of the Conservative slogan "It's time for a Diefenbaker government" played into the opposition's hands. For the Conservatives, every mention of it was free publicity; and it suggested that Liberals too could vote for Diefenbaker without becoming Tories. In 1957 Diefenbaker could not be discredited – even when, at the last moment, he falsely accused the prime minister of impropriety in seeking Liberal votes from members of the armed forces. In the circumstances, this seemed no more than normal electoral exaggeration.[69]

The leader of the opposition kept up his breathless pace of whistle-stopping and overnight flights into early June, speaking half a dozen times or more each day. Diefenbaker had exhausted the handful of national reporters who kept with him through the campaign and showed signs of strain himself. The *Globe*'s Clark Davey recalled: "At the end of the day he was wiped out...We did not know how he did it. Near the end, he was in Edmonton and he made a speech that was absolutely incomprehensible. It was gibberish." The crowds didn't care; they just cheered.[70]

Diefenbaker knew that the tide was with him, but a lifetime of political defeat had taught him caution. A Conservative majority would require gains of more than eighty-two seats – and no one was predicting that. The country had forgotten about political landslides. Gallup showed growing Conservative support, but a comfortable Liberal lead in popularity. Members of the press travelling with the Conservative leader – a few of whom were unblushing enthusiasts – talked of thirty or thirty-five gains. When Peter Dempson asked Diefenbaker on June 1 for his prediction, Diefenbaker was confident enough to respond, off the record, that he expected to win ninety-seven seats – but that was still thirty-six short of a majority. "I couldn't believe he was serious," wrote Dempson. "I decided it must have been wishful thinking on his part."[71]

In retrospect, critics suggested that Diefenbaker had ignored or abandoned any appeal to Quebec in 1957. The basis for this claim was two strategy documents written by Gordon Churchill after the 1953 election, pointing out that disproportionate campaign spending in Quebec in 1953 (and earlier) had failed to produce results. To form a government, Churchill concluded, the party should distribute its electoral funds equitably across the country, with special attention to reinforcing strength in Ontario, the west, and the Atlantic provinces.[72]

When Churchill's first paper was publicized by the Toronto *Telegram*'s Judith Robinson in 1954, the *Financial Post* accused him of saying that "time spent wooing support in Quebec is wasted." Members of the caucus were displeased, and Churchill "subsided into a discreet silence." Diefenbaker alone, among his colleagues, told Churchill that "those articles of Judith Robinson's were good. You were right." In January 1956, when Léon Balcer became president of the party and publicly forecast twenty-five Quebec seats for the party in 1957, Churchill fumed.

> I was annoyed but kept silent. Once again, I thought, we will place the main emphasis on Quebec; once again funds will flow to that province; once again the other areas of Canada will be taken for granted or be neglected. How long and how often would the Conservative Party, in good faith of course, and with the best of motives, immolate itself in a vain attempt to achieve the impossible? To me it was the negation of practical politics. A party exists and struggles in the hope that it will eventually form the government. Its major effort must be in those areas in which it has strength, with the hope that the less favorable areas will not be entirely unproductive.[73]

Churchill proceeded to write his second paper, "Conservative Strategy for the Next Election," but revealed it to no one until he had committed himself to Diefenbaker's leadership. He showed it to the candidate shortly before the convention, and Diefenbaker took note. "The success of the Conservatives in the general election of 1957," Churchill later wrote, "was not the direct result of my strategy paper of 1956. No such claim has ever been advanced. I had simply set down on paper for the first time a realistic view of politics. By great good fortune an equitable distribution of funds was made in 1957; no area was deprived of attention, the leader had no illusions as to where support could be expected. Quebec was not neglected. The final results, again by good fortune, corresponded with my forecast."[74]

This was astute politics. In 1957 the party allocated national campaign funds to provincial organizations in strict proportion to the number of seats, at $3000 per constituency. Quebec, like the rest, received its share, but other regions benefited from a fair distribution as compared with 1953.[75]

Diefenbaker visited the province three times during the campaign, struggled through one campaign speech in his execrable French, and questioned why his bilingual colleague Donald Fleming could manage only three major speeches in Quebec.[76] But in a notable display of prudence, the Quebec campaign was left primarily to Léon Balcer, Pierre Sévigny, Paul Lafontaine, William Hamilton, and the low-key efforts of Maurice Duplessis and the Union Nationale machine. The party's Quebec forces were divided uneasily between Balcer, with his Duplessiste links, and an ineffective "Comité des Bleus" inspired by Paul Lafontaine, which boasted among its members "the sons of three former ministers in the federal cabinet(s)" of Borden, Meighen, and Bennett.[77] The Comité looked backward rather than forward.

As the campaign closed, the *Globe and Mail* rose above its doubts and pitched enthusiastically for change. "Mr. Diefenbaker is fully competent to become Prime Minister...This is the man, this is the party, Canadians should vote for on Monday," the editors wrote on June 8.[78] On election day the paper spoke to Canadians in Diefenbaker's own terms:

> They can improve their nation, they can improve their own status in it, by getting out and electing a Conservative government headed by Mr. John Diefenbaker.
>
> Mr. Diefenbaker has conducted a most courageous and convincing campaign. He has persuaded countless thousands of Canadians that with him as their leader they can enjoy greater freedom, greater progress, and greater security in both.[79]

But doubt remained widespread that the Tories could win. On June 8 *Maclean's* magazine went to press assuming a Liberal victory. Reporters for three Conservative-inclined newspapers, political scientist Murray Beck observed, "perceived many of the signs of political upheaval, but...generally interpreted them to mean no more than insubstantial losses for the Liberals."[80] The last Gallup Poll before the election gave the Liberals 48 percent of the vote and the Conservatives 34 percent, without any breakdown of seats.[81] The American ambassador, Livingston Merchant, cabled Washington that the Liberals would probably win a clear majority with slight losses, commenting that the campaign was "thus far marked by absence of clear national issues and apathy among voters in many sections of Canada. Several Cabinet Ministers including Pearson experiencing tough fight but favored [to] be re-elected."[82]

Diefenbaker's own travelling campaign manager, George Hogan, wrote out his predictions on the last weekend before the poll and handed them to the leader in an envelope. "Not less than 75; not more than 111," he guessed.

Lib	150
Tory	82
CCF	20
Socred	7
Others	6
	265

Hogan saw the campaign as a preliminary: "We have destroyed the outer defences of Liberal power, and now, for the first time in a quarter of a century, are in a position to attack the fortress itself." All credit for this achievement, he believed, lay with John Diefenbaker: "not only because of an oratorical marathon that has aroused the nation, but for a political shrewdness that has squeezed the last ounce of advantage from our party's limited opportunities and limited resources."[83]

The campaign's Ontario manager, Eddie Goodman, was slightly more hopeful. He told Diefenbaker that the party would win between ninety and a hundred seats and would deprive the Liberals of a majority. "If we could win a few in Quebec," he added, "we could beat them." Diefenbaker, he recalled, "pierced me with his magnetic gaze and said slowly and deliberately, 'No, I am going to win. I am going to get the largest block of seats in the House. I feel it every place I go, and while I know that other leaders have believed this in the past, I am sure that the support I am getting from people who are not Conservatives will project itself into seats.'"[84]

"It has been a tremendous fight and I am still in wonderful shape physically – truly amazing," John wrote to Elmer on June 4.[85] He was at his peak as the marathon ended with a mass meeting in Hamilton on June 7. On Saturday, June 8, John and Olive flew overnight from Toronto to Saskatoon (their third overnight flight during the long campaign), arriving for the early morning drive to Prince Albert, where they would await returns at home. But even now – recalling old failures and humiliations – the leader worried over his own seat, so for him the campaign was incomplete. He gave last minute instructions to Elmer:

> Naturally my worry is P.A. You can vote at the advance poll in Saskatoon as you will be absent as a traveller – and then be in P.A. on Election day.
>
> (1) I'll arrive in Saskatoon on Saturday morning flight June 8th at 6.30 am (Tell *Svoboda* so he can arrange Radio or T.V.).

(2) Then to PA for Sat and Sunday after seeing Mother if it can be arranged as we leave Saskatoon by car at *8 am*...

(3) Be sure that all the *polls* are carefully scrutineered and if a school for scrutineers could be held to go over their rights and duties it would help an awful lot. (Ask Art Pearson re this)

(4) Art phoned that they would have a reception on Sat. (that's fine) – do they want me to make a rapid run through the Constituency – if so it should be put over Radio showing time when I will be at each place. (This is just a suggestion – It might be better for me to be on Central Avenue on Saturday afternoon.)

(5) Every vote will count so be sure that cars will be picking up all those people on North side of River before 7.15 am – so that Clyne H. and his friends won't beat us to the draw. I have told Art P about this. Tell him to excuse repetition...

...I am feeling fine.

Give Miss Pound and all in the Committee Room my best.

John[86]

Despite the candidate's anxieties, the local campaign seemed well in hand. The city was saturated in politics, perhaps slightly bored, and ready for a decision. After some routine mainstreeting on Saturday in company with a retinue of political friends, Diefenbaker, looking "drawn and tired," set out for a final meeting in Nipawin. There he predicted victory in public for the first time: "On Monday," he told his friendly audience, "I'll be prime minister."[87]

LIKE HIS CAMPAIGN WORKERS, DIEFENBAKER WAS UP EARLY ON ELECTION DAY. THE weather was wet and cool. John and Olive voted early at a poll three blocks from the house, and then the local boy mainstreeted down the hill from home for most of the morning. "He walked the length of the main part of Central Avenue and back, shaking hands and greeting old friends, tossing off a quip to one, an inquiry to another, and of course never at a loss for a name."[88] In the afternoon he slept, to be awakened only with the early returns from the Atlantic provinces.

In the company of Allister Grosart, Elmer, Olive, and the Connells, Diefenbaker received the early results at home on CBC radio in a mood of growing exultation. Twenty-one seats in the Atlantic provinces – a gain of fifteen; nine in Quebec – a gain of five; sixty-one in Ontario – a stunning gain of twenty-eight. By the time the count reached the Ontario-Manitoba border, eight ministers – including the giant C.D. Howe – had lost their seats and an unbelievable Conservative victory looked likely. At home in Prince Albert, Diefenbaker took his lead in the first poll reporting and never looked back. By the end of the count he had a 6500-vote advantage over the second-place CCF candidate. The Chief and his entourage trooped downtown to the campaign committee rooms in the Lincoln Hotel as first reports from western Canada began to cascade in. There, too, the Liberals trailed, but prairie and British Columbia victories were shared three ways among Conservatives, CCFers, and Social Crediters. The Liberals stalled at 105, and the Conservatives moved ahead, though still short of an overall majority. As local and national results were chalked up on tarpaper panels in the Lincoln Hotel basement, the room vibrated with whoops and cheers.[89] In the back rooms the whiskey bottles were broken out.

But John Diefenbaker was not present for most of this local drama. In 1957 Prince Albert had no direct link to network television, so the leader had agreed to fly to Regina to appear on CBC television. From the Lincoln Hotel, Diefenbaker was driven to Prince Albert airport for the ninety-minute flight to the south. In the Canadian Pacific aircraft he sat with a few journalists, receiving the latest returns from the pilot's radio and quietly studying the draft text of his prepared remarks.[90] These had been typed on two pages of Diefenbaker letterhead, subsequently torn in half to produce four sheets, and embellished in his own sweeping handwriting. There were originally two variations of the speech, a winner and a loser, but by flight time Diefenbaker had discarded the loser's paragraph and stroked out the alternative second-paragraph heading, "If Conservatives Win." That great "if" had dissolved in certainty, and Diefenbaker would later deny that he had ever prepared a substitute.[91] (The opening and closing paragraphs fitted either victory or loss.) Sometime that evening he added another few handwritten sentences, both impulsive and humble, to his winner's declaration.

In Regina, confident now that he had won a plurality of seats, Diefenbaker was led to a barren TV studio for the victory address to the nation. This was his public dedication. He faced the camera directly.

My fellow Canadians:

This is a moment not for elation but dedication. The complete results are not yet known but I feel that at this time I must express my deep gratitude and appreciation to all of those whose votes today were cast on behalf of the Party which I have the honour to lead. In joining with me and the Conservative party in our crusade for a new awakening of the spirit of parliamentary democracy, they have shown beyond doubt that ours is a cause in which millions of Canadians fervently believe without regard to party. I acknowledge with warmest thanks the hours of hard work, the good wishes and the devotion of so many of my fellow Canadians to the Conservative Party and myself.

This is a great day for our Party and I believe for Canadian democracy. As for our responsibilities to our fellow citizens we shall accept them I can assure you with the greatest humility. This is not the time to attempt to restate the issues of the campaign. We believe that the stand we have taken on many issues was the only one possible in the light of the facts. We are naturally deeply gratified that we have been endorsed by the people of Canada, but we are not unmindful of the great responsibility which has been placed upon us.

Diefenbaker turned his text slowly to the handwritten page.

I shall honor the trust you the Canadian people have given me.

I shall keep the faith – and maintain the spiritual things without which political parties as with individuals cannot lead a full life. I ask your prayers. With God's help I shall do my best. "He who would be chiefest among you shall be servant of all."

He paused to gaze deeply into the camera's eye, and continued with the last page of typescript.

I now give you my pledge that we shall stand by the principles which we have enunciated during this election campaign. Our task is not finished. In many respects it has only just begun. I am sure that you will agree with me that conservatism has risen once again to the challenge of a great moment in our nation's history. In answering that challenge we have done our best to express in word and action what we believe to be the will of millions of Canadians from the Atlantic to the Pacific.[92]

Prince Albert was exultant. In the leader's absence, his committee rooms had overflowed. A local radio station urged citizens to drive to the airport for "the new prime minister's" return at midnight. Dick Spencer described the scene:

A dizzying feeling of victory was sweeping the downtown as Central Avenue and the business core filled up with cars and horn-honking drivers. A steady stream of cars moved north over the railway bridge and turned east along the river road to the airport half a mile out of town. Local police constables were despatched by Chief Reg Brooman to help with parking at the airport. A sound car from the committee rooms, driven by Ed Jackson, swept ahead. "John'll wanna make a speech," Jackson explained.

An estimated fifteen hundred to three thousand people watched the plane land and taxi to a stop...Flash bulbs popped and a huge cheer went up as John Diefenbaker stepped out of the plane onto the ramp that had been wheeled out. He was dressed in a light grey raincoat. He doffed and waved his grey homburg and beamed a huge smile of victory. He feigned disbelief at the size of the crowd, raised his arms, shook his head and pressed into a sea of noisy well-wishers.[93]

Diefenbaker vainly shouted some words from his television address to the cheering crowd, then "tumbled into the lead car for a tumultuous cavalcade back into town" and was swallowed up in the Lincoln Hotel mob. A speech was impossible as well-wishers engulfed him, and he was soon rescued through a back door for the short drive home.[94]

On Tuesday morning Louis St Laurent telephoned. For the prime minister's first call, Diefenbaker was absent in town, relaxing for a haircut at McKim's two-chair barber shop, behind the cigar store and newsstand.[95] Eventually St Laurent reached Diefenbaker at home, offering his congratulations and indicating that he expected, after a cabinet meeting, to give his resignation to Governor General Vincent Massey. Overnight the results had stabilized, and there was no doubt about winners and losers. The Conservatives had won 112 seats, the Liberals 105, the CCF 25, Social Credit 19, and independents 4. M.J. Coldwell and Solon Low, the two minor party leaders, had indicated their readiness to cooperate with a new government. St Laurent seemed eager to go.

While the congratulations poured in, Diefenbaker drove to Saskatoon to visit his mother at the University Hospital. This was his private dedication. Mary Diefenbaker, his lifelong goad, admonished John once more. "Do not forget the poor and afflicted," he recalled her saying. "Do the best you can as long as you can." Diefenbaker's memory of the occasion was equivocal and perhaps resentful. "And that was the last time," he wrote, "that she, with her Highland ancestry and their refusal to exult, ever said anything about the fact that I had become Prime Minister of my country."[96]

The next day he flew off to Lac La Ronge on a fishing expedition with Fred Hadley, Tommy Martin, Harry Houghton, Duff Roblin, brother Elmer, and three reporters. Dressed casually in plaid shirt and Cowichan sweater, he perhaps caught three pickerel but was photographed with the whole team's catch of eight. None of Diefenbaker's fish, reported Peter Dempson, was large.

> As he was leaving the boat at the end of the day, one of his friends jokingly said as he was exhibiting his catch:
> "Not much of a fish you caught there, eh?"
> "No," replied Diefenbaker, a grin spreading across his face, "I caught the big one yesterday."[97]

Diefenbaker was in an expansive mood. "It was the happiest time in his life," Clark Davey remembered. "He was full of stories and anecdotes and boasted that Donald Fleming and Alvin Hamilton could have any portfolios they wanted."[98] After two days on the northern waters, the prime minister–elect was ready for Ottawa.

CHAPTER 8

Rt Hon.
John George Diefenbaker

1957-1958

THE CANADIAN GOVERNMENT'S OFFICIAL AIRCRAFT HAD BEEN BOOKED BY two Liberal ministers, Ralph Campney and James Sinclair, for their last privileged flight to Ottawa, so John and Olive Diefenbaker took the regular overnight TCA flight from Saskatoon to Ottawa on June 13–14. The lapse in protocol was unsettling, and when Air Canada lost one of his suitcases at Prince Albert airport, Diefenbaker was furious. Clark Davey was still with him and witnessed the incident. "He had a temper tantrum and jumped up and down like a little kid... 'Don't they know who I am?' he shouted. 'I'm the new prime minister.' I was on the phone talking to the rewrite man at the *Globe* and I repeated what Dief had said. The lead for the story was changed to 'An angry John Diefenbaker flew out of his hometown tonight.' When we arrived in Toronto, someone handed Diefenbaker a copy of the morning *Globe*. And Christ, Dief went berserk at me."[1]

In the early morning at Ottawa airport the Diefenbakers were greeted by several hundred cheering supporters, still high on the party's unexpected success. The victor stopped briefly at the Château Laurier, before meeting Prime Minister St Laurent at 10 am.[2]

The Liberal cabinet had met the previous day to discuss its fate. While they recognized that the decision rested with the prime minister, several ministers argued that he was responsible to parliament, not the electorate, and thus should not resign "until he had tested in Parliament whether or not it was the people's wish that the government should remain in office."[3] But a majority considered that hanging on would be "virtual political suicide...This seemed evident when one reflected on the fact that by far the bulk of Liberal membership had been elected in the province of Quebec and in Newfoundland."[4] Louis St Laurent indicated his intention to offer the government's resignation, but said he would not do so until the military vote had been counted over the weekend. The cabinet also deferred decisions, which had earlier been postponed until after an expected Liberal victory, on the integration of Canadian and American air defences, US Air Force overflights of Canada carrying atomic weapons, and amphibious American military exercises in Labrador.[5] These were sensitive matters better tossed to the Conservatives. Next day, in a brief and final session, the St Laurent cabinet made one last decision in search of political credit. Large pay raises were approved for civil servants, the military, and the RCMP – which added $110 million to annual federal spending and erased two-thirds of the surplus projected in the Harris budget.[6]

St Laurent told Diefenbaker at their meeting that he accepted the election result and would resign unless the military vote significantly altered the balance of seats. That would leave the prime minister–designate with, at most, a week to select his cabinet and begin its work, since he would have to leave for a meeting of Commonwealth prime ministers in London on June 23. The military vote changed only one seat, so on Monday, June 17, 1957, Louis St Laurent offered his resignation to Governor General Vincent Massey. At 8:25 in the evening John Diefenbaker, wearing an impeccable double-breasted grey suit and black homburg, arrived by taxi at Rideau Hall and was formally invited by the governor general to form a new government.[7] The cabinet would take office four days later. When Diefenbaker reached his House of Commons office early next morning, a telegram from Elmer awaited him. "Congratulations on the occasion of a dream at the tender age of six at last coming true stop you will serve Canada with distinction I trust for many years stop love to Olive and best wishes to the first lady of the nation who has done so much to make the victory possible."[8]

There is no evidence that Diefenbaker gave any thought to the makeup of a Conservative cabinet before election day. Afterwards, he faced what Gordon Churchill called "a hurried-up job."[9] The prime minister–designate was on the telephone consulting close friends about his cabinet after June 11, and on June 18 Bill Brunt took charge of Diefenbaker's schedule as he began to meet prospective ministers in Ottawa.[10] His approach was both orthodox and coy. He planned no major change in the organization of ministries or the balance of representation in cabinet, although he wished to push the boundaries slightly to include a woman and a minister of non-British, non-French origin. As he met members and juggled his lists, Diefenbaker invited his visitors to express their preferences, but did not tell them his own. The exception was Davie Fulton, whom Diefenbaker invited to take the Speakership of the House of Commons. But Fulton refused to do so because that would finish his career in partisan politics.[11] He was young and he still had his eye on the leadership. Although there were more than sixty new members in the Progressive Conservative caucus, Diefenbaker limited his choices to previously sitting MPs. That preference reflected his respect for parliamentary experience – and his caution about the unknown. His new members had not yet gathered in caucus, and most were no more than names to the leader.

Drawing on his list of re-elected members, Diefenbaker had slight room for manoeuvre. Only one member, Earl Rowe, had any previous cabinet experience, in the last days of the Bennett government in 1935; but Rowe was no friend, and Diefenbaker was determined to pass him by. J.M. Macdonnell, the long-time Conservative finance critic, expected that ministry, but Diefenbaker suspected him of abiding antipathy and would not trust him. Ellen Fairclough was the obvious token woman; and Michael Starr, the member from Oshawa whose ancestry was Ukrainian, was the leading candidate among the "new Canadians." The first team was certain to be drawn from the remaining crew of front-bench critics, Fleming, Fulton, Churchill, Green, Hees, Pearkes, Nowlan, Harkness, Hamilton, MacLean, and Balcer. Diefenbaker ignored all special pleadings for places in cabinet – except, in the end, those of Olive and Bill Brunt, who asked him to be kind to J.M. Macdonnell. Diefenbaker reluctantly slipped him in at the last moment as a minister without portfolio. When rumours circulated in Toronto and Montreal that George Hees would get Trade and Commerce, protests from "certain people" resulted in a shift to Transport.[12]

But that was not yet known. The ministers-designate were summoned to Rideau Hall for the government's swearing in at 11 am on Friday, June 21, most of them still uncertain what their jobs would be. As they entered they were given a mimeographed list of the ministry, discovered their roles, and were led into the governor general's library for the administration of oaths. The ceremony was discreetly private – without press, without families – followed by handshaking and mutual well-wishing, and an equally private official photo session on the patio. The new ministers stood stiffly around Vincent Massey for their group picture, mouths tight in nervous half-smiles as they considered their sudden change of fortune.

Prime Minister John George Diefenbaker had appointed sixteen ministers to fill twenty-four cabinet posts. He held three of them himself, as prime minister, president of the Privy Council, and secretary of state for external affairs. Howard Green would be minister of public works, acting minister of health and welfare, and acting minister of defence production. Davie Fulton was minister of justice and acting minister of citizenship and immigration. Douglas Harkness was minister of northern affairs and natural resources as well as acting minister of agriculture. And Léon Balcer – the lone French-speaking MP in this first draft – was solicitor general and acting minister of mines and technical surveys. Familiars filled out the picture: Fleming in Finance, Hees in Transport, Pearkes in Defence, Churchill in Trade and Commerce, Nowlan in National Revenue, MacLean in Fisheries, Starr in Labour, Fairclough as secretary of state, William Hamilton as postmaster general, and Macdonnell and Browne as ministers without portfolio. This was an incomplete beginning, sufficient in Diefenbaker's eyes for the ministry to begin its work before he rushed off to the Commonwealth meetings in London. A second draft would have to be called when he returned in July. In the event, the last appointments to cabinet were completed only five days before parliament met in mid-October.[13] The ministry looked respectable, though not spectacular: a workmanlike and modest start.

For the new Conservative prime minister, the letter of congratulation he received that day from his former leader, George Drew, was particularly generous and reassuring:

My dear John, –

This is a great day for you, for our party and for Canada. I know also what this day will mean to Olive who has been such a magnificent teammate throughout the whole campaign and to your dear mother who has had the unique happiness of seeing her son become Prime Minister of Canada. You are indeed fortunate that she has been spared to feel a mother's pride in this splendid achievement.

You go forward supported by a mounting flood of good-will such as has sustained few Prime Ministers in the past. You have won that good-will not only by the effectiveness of your own efforts during the election but also by the gracious manner in which you accepted victory on June 10th.

May I also congratulate you on the skill with which you have handled the difficult and complex problems with which you were confronted in forming a government. You have laid a firm foundation for the steady growth and expansion of our party.

God bless you in your great undertaking. May the days and years ahead bring health, happiness and success to Olive and yourself.[14]

The clerk of the Privy Council and secretary to the cabinet, Robert Bryce, guided Diefenbaker adeptly as he prepared for his first cabinet meeting. Bryce, although still in his forties, was one of the bureaucracy's old hands. He was an economist who had spent sixteen years in the Department of Finance before becoming clerk in 1954. In the days before the swearing in, Bryce had pre-pared an agenda of mostly routine items and had instructed the prime minister on the essentials of cabinet protocol. Diefenbaker summoned his ministers to their initial meeting at 3:30 that afternoon in the Privy Council chamber of the East Block, but no one at Rideau Hall had thought to tell them where theyshould go to find their departmental offices.[15] By various means they found them and met their senior civil service advisers. And at mid-afternoon they assembled in the old council chamber.

The meeting lasted for an hour. Diefenbaker opened by laying down his rules. There was to be strict secrecy about cabinet discussion, and no comment to reporters as ministers left cabinet meetings. Cabinet would normally meet, as Liberal cabinets had done, every Thursday morning, but there would be additional meetings as necessary. Diefenbaker said that Louis St Laurent had told him – apparently to Diefenbaker's surprise – that it was the British practice that cabinet minutes from the previous administration were not available to a new one, although the cabinet secretary might use his judgment in briefing ministers about previous decisions "to ensure orderly continuity of govern-ment business." Diefenbaker added that he "had told Mr. St. Laurent he was prepared to follow this principle if it were followed in the United Kingdom. During his forthcoming trip to the United Kingdom he proposed to ascertain for himself just what the British practice was and if, as he assumed, it was in accordance with the account given by Mr. St. Laurent, he thought it should be the agreed practice in Canada." Members agreed.[16]

Beyond routine housekeeping measures, this first cabinet made two sub-stantial decisions. It approved the prime minister's recommendation that George Drew should be named as Canada's high commissioner to the United Kingdom; and it approved immediate construction of a road from Cassiar to Stewart, in northwest British Columbia, the estimated cost of $12 million to be shared equally with the province. The highway had been mentioned in Merril Menzies's proposals for northern development, and the decision to support work in the summer of 1957 suggested that the new government was quick off the mark in carrying out its promises. The Conservatives gained credit for the decision, although the Liberal government had agreed to the same terms earlier in the year but had not yet signed a formal agreement.[17]

The next morning cabinet met again to complete its preliminaries. Various acting ministers were named, and staff appointments for the prime minister, leader of the opposition, and ministers were approved. Diefenbaker outlined a code of conduct for ministers that required them to resign from business directorships and legal partnerships, or from offices in companies doing business with the government. He asked that ministers who received long-service military pensions "should examine their own positions," and he raised the question whether ministers should hold company stocks or act as executors of estates – but left those issues aside "for the moment." Ministers accepted the prime minister's direction to give up all company directorships.[18]

Cabinet next considered documents from the defence and external affairs departments recommending the extension for one year of the "Canada–United States Agreement on Overflights," originally approved by the St Laurent government for a five-month period ending July 1, which gave the United States Air Force interim authority to carry MB–1 air-to-air atomic weapons in interceptor aircraft flying over Canada. The agreement provided that aircraft armed with these weapons would enter Canadian airspace only "when it has been definitely established that a probably hostile aircraft has entered the air defence system," that they would be permitted to operate from Canadian bases, and that US and Canadian forces would be trained and prepared for salvage operations in case of accidents. The Americans assured Canada in general terms that they had "taken the utmost precautions" in designing the weapons to assure "a minimum possibility of public hazard when employment of the MB–1 is necessary." The recommendations for extending the interim agreement came from both departments before the Conservative ministry took office, and they were accepted on faith by the new government after brief discussion.[19] Thus the Diefenbaker cabinet began, in apparent innocence, a long and eventually turbulent flight with its partner in continental air defence against potential attack from the Soviet Union.

Before departing early from the meeting, Diefenbaker spoke briefly about his plans for the conference of Commonwealth prime ministers. He confessed that he had no precise thoughts, but wished to assure the non-white peoples of the Commonwealth "reasonable advancement and equal opportunities." He hoped to maintain Louis St Laurent's close understanding with Prime Minister Nehru of India. He intended to support "staunchly" the idea of the Commonwealth and to urge the strengthening of trade and economic ties among its members. He would not, he said, make direct reference to the extent of Canadian trade with the United States, which some of his ministers considered to be too great, but might propose a Commonwealth trade and economic conference aimed partly at altering that balance. Ministers seemed to agree that "serious study...without delay" would be useful, but they reached no consensus on Canadian trade policy or a trade conference. Policy on this issue – such as it was – would remain in Diefenbaker's hands.[20]

Before his departure the prime minister was briefed by Donald Fleming and Gordon Churchill on the advice of senior officials in the Departments of Finance, Trade and Commerce, and External Affairs about trade and economic matters. They had pointed out the difficulties facing any trade initiatives in the Commonwealth; Fleming told cabinet that "all the officials with whom the matter had been discussed...cautioned against expecting too much on the trade side." But he concluded that their advice was "not entirely negative." His own judgment was that every means of improving Commonwealth trade should be explored. Ministers recognized that Europe was moving steadily into the Common Market and the European Free Trade Area, and that a proposal for a Commonwealth trade meeting might serve as a counterbalance or a delaying tactic: "If it were agreed to hold discussions in Ottawa in September, the British might not move so fast on the FTA front."[21]

On Sunday the prime minister of two days left for London accompanied by his wife, Olive, George Pearkes, Robert Bryce, and Jules Léger, then undersecretary of state for external affairs – and the conference briefing books already prepared for Louis St Laurent.

JOHN DIEFENBAKER ASSUMED OFFICE JUST THREE MONTHS SHORT OF HIS SIXTY-second birthday. He was in sprightly good health and overflowing with the nervous energy stimulated by a winning election campaign. But his hearing was failing, which encouraged his tendency to engage in monologue rather than conversation. At cabinet, he began by sitting at the end of the big oval table, but soon moved to the middle of one side to hear his ministers more easily.[22] His distrust of colleagues, which had always been close to the surface in the opposition years, now seemed subdued by his convention and electoral victories and the remarkable rapport he had achieved with voters. While his closest associates in cabinet were men he had trusted, he included others – Douglas Harkness, George Nowlan, Ellen Fairclough, Léon Balcer, J.M. Macdonnell – in a deliberate effort to overcome old suspicions. On their side, memories of the tantrums, the moodiness, the aloofness of the man from Prince Albert were suspended as the party savoured its victory and gave credit to the one who had, above all, achieved it.

The prime ministership was the first executive office that John Diefenbaker had ever held. "There is great scepticism as to his ability to put together a truly effective Cabinet and administer it with skill," reported the American ambassador after his initial soundings on June 18.[23] Diefenbaker had run a small law office marked by informality and disorganization; he had been a token vice president of the Canadian Bar Association and an officer of the Commonwealth Parliamentary Association, a Kiwanian, and a mason.

But he had never directed and managed anything on a national scale except the 1957 campaign – which had been, to a remarkable extent, an emanation of his personality, shaped in combat from the platform. He knew that elections were chaotic dramatic performances rather than orderly processes, and the 1957 campaign gave him fresh confidence that he could dominate the big stage. But that was different from leading a government. In his new role he would have to call upon untested powers and reserves. For his closest advice, he had leant upon a few friends whose political experience was narrower than his own: a few electoral managers in Saskatchewan, a few disciples in Toronto, some legal associates in Vancouver, Winnipeg, and Montreal, and a handful of friendly reporters and editors. Now he would need more help than that.

His cabinet ministers were untested too. They began their work with a sense of justification. They had fought the campaign to defeat an overbearing and complacent government, and the public had supported their cause. They shared with the leader some impressions about what the government should do: respect voters of all backgrounds and regions, respect the provinces, respect parliament, encourage development, and lower taxes. But they had had scant opportunity to think through the implications of those generous sentiments. In the previous two years they had proved themselves relentless parliamentary critics of a failing ministry, but none of them had sat at a cabinet table or managed a government department. They seemed genuinely humbled by their accession to power and they dedicated themselves earnestly to their tasks. The new government's tone was soon set by the overawed seriousness and rectitude of John Diefenbaker, Howard Green, and Donald Fleming – just slightly offset by the considerably more rakish charm of George Hees.

The prime minister was supported by a small political staff, initially of eight persons, transferred from the opposition leader's office under the direction of an efficient private secretary, Derek Bedson.[24] Robert Bryce remained as clerk of the Privy Council and cabinet secretary, his task being to advise the prime minister on policy and to manage the flow of government business. Bryce's experience and wisdom were indispensable to Diefenbaker from the first moment, and the prime minister recognized at once that he needed him. Bryce was a solid rock round which the tempests often raged. By mid-summer 1957 he was joined by another career civil servant, Basil Robinson, as the prime minister's foreign policy adviser and liaison with the Department of External Affairs. He had been a foreign service officer for twelve years, with postings in London and Paris as well as Ottawa.[25] Both Bryce and Robinson were examples to the prime minister that the senior civil service was something more than a local branch of the Liberal Party, as he had darkly suspected from the opposition front bench.[26]

THE COMMONWEALTH CONFERENCE WAS JOHN DIEFENBAKER'S FIRST APPEARANCE on the international stage as prime minister, and he relished it with the enthusiasm of a schoolboy. "Naturally," he remembered, "I would be greatly impressed by that meeting because the impossible had happened and there had been a change of government in Canada."[27] Three events especially affected him: his speech to the Canadian Club of London, his encounters with Winston Churchill, and his private conversation with the queen after a state dinner at Windsor Castle.

On Dominion Day he took Mike Pearson's place as guest speaker to the Canadian Club of London, where he showed impish pleasure in telling his audience a story.

> I said, "This reminds me of the fact that three weeks ago in Trail, B.C., I was speaking there in the rink, and the loudspeaker system was apparently not working very effectively, for I got a notice, a placard that said, 'Get closer to mike'; and Pearson had been following me or preceding me in this part of the campaign. Very obviously there'd been some arrangement made by the Liberal party that he should and I said, 'He was here last night and that's as close to him as I ever hope to be'; but I didn't realize then that I would be taking his place."[28]

Twice Diefenbaker met his political idol Winston Churchill: first, by invitation at the Churchills' home in Hyde Park Gate; then again, at a dinner hosted by Prime Minister Macmillan at 10 Downing Street. Churchill was eighty-two, now contentedly weary in retirement but still consuming large quantities of champagne and brandy. When Diefenbaker refused to join Churchill in a snifter of brandy, the old man expressed astonishment that Diefenbaker could be a teetotaller – to which Diefenbaker replied that he was a teetotaller but not a prohibitionist. Olive added defensively: "That's not quite so. He takes a glass of sherry now and then."

Churchill intended to flatter. Lady Churchill told Olive that when Sir Winston heard the Canadian election results "he was so excited he danced." And when Olive remarked that everyone seemed interested in the outcome, Churchill shook his jowls: "Interested?...Why shouldn't they be? It's the most important event since the end of the war."[29]

At Windsor Castle, Queen Elizabeth invited Diefenbaker to see the room used as an office by Elizabeth I.

> We went down quite a long corridor into this room and it's just as it was left by Elizabeth I. It's a circular room as I recall it, possibly oval and there's a fireplace on the north side, and that was the fireplace that the Chancellor, Walsingham, stood by as he got Queen Elizabeth I to sign the death warrant of Mary Queen of Scots; and the Queen described this place and she said, "I often come here"; and I said, "I hope that your reign will be as glorious as hers was," and she said, "That's what I'm trying to do. I hope it will be."[30]

Diefenbaker was impressed by the queen's "phenomenal...comprehensive and extensive" knowledge of politics and world affairs. And he was charmed by her display of interest in him.[31]

The conference of Commonwealth prime ministers, which lasted over twelve meetings and eight sitting days from June 26 to July 5, was an occasion for Diefenbaker to meet his fellow leaders and to observe the multiracial gathering at work. Perhaps because it was his first meeting, Diefenbaker recalled it as "the most impressive...of the Commonwealth conferences that I attended. There was a greater spirit of give and take, frank discussions, strong opinions expressed." But the conference faced no urgent problems. After the recriminations arising from the Suez war, it was a time for reconciliation.

On a wide range of international issues, the Canadian prime minister offered orthodox comments. He took the NATO line that the only realistic policy towards the Soviet Union was to build an effective common defence. Like his Liberal predecessors, he intended to maintain close cooperation with other members of the Commonwealth. He would sustain Canadian support for the United Nations Emergency Force in the Middle East. He probed for Southeast Asian reactions if mainland China were to be admitted to the United Nations. On disarmament, he raised the possibility of a Canadian offer of "open skies" aerial inspection of the Arctic – a subject of earlier Canadian consultation with the United States. On all these themes he stuck closely to his Liberal briefing papers.

Despite telling cabinet a few days earlier that he would not do so, Diefenbaker referred to the problems of heavy American investment in Canada and welcomed investment from other countries as long as it was not excessively "speculative." He urged Britain to assure the conference that if the United Kingdom entered the European Free Trade Area, free entry of Commonwealth agricultural products to Britain would be maintained. In response, the British chancellor, Peter Thorneycroft, said it was Britain's "firm intention" to maintain existing Commonwealth agricultural preferences.[32]

Canada's only novel contribution was Diefenbaker's announcement that he intended to call a Commonwealth trade conference in Ottawa, to be preceded by a meeting of Commonwealth finance ministers in Canada later in 1957. Here Diefenbaker was harking back to Bennett's Ottawa conference of 1932. The initiative was greeted sceptically as "Diefenbaker's scheme" by the *Economist* and the Manchester *Guardian*, and probably more doubtfully by the British government itself, which called for a round of preliminary meetings of officials to smoke out Canada's meaning – or perhaps to scuttle the whole vague project. Britain's attention, it seemed clear, was already turning to Europe, but Harold Macmillan still hoped to deflect Canada's new enthusiasm for Commonwealth trade as politely as he could. In the face of scepticism about a trade conference from Australia, New Zealand, and South Africa, Macmillan played the diplomat's role of peacemaker and gained the conference's support for a preliminary conference. Diefenbaker was grateful. He took this euphemistic response as evidence that "there was quite a favourable reaction" and pressed on with his plans. Favourable press reaction in London was limited to the *Daily Telegraph* and the *Daily Express*, which Diefenbaker, in his days of euphoria, read with rose-coloured glasses. In Canada the press response was widely favourable, although the Toronto *Telegram* admitted that the prime minister "has not indicated what he intends."[33]

Diefenbaker seemed to make that partly clear to a press conference on July 6 following his return to Ottawa. What he did – perhaps inadvertently – was to add a second proposal to the agenda, something that would dramatize his previous call for a Commonwealth trade conference. Under the headline "Canadian Trade Offer to Britain/ Mr. Diefenbaker's $625M. Plan for Imports," *The Times* of London reported:

> Mr. Diefenbaker, the Canadian Prime Minister, told a Press conference... that Canada had as a planned objective the diversion of 15 per cent of her present imports from the United States to imports from the United Kingdom. Such a diversion would make a substantial difference to trade with the Mother Country without actually hurting trade with the United States.
>
> He thought Britain could meet Canadian requirements in this field because, with the development of atomic energy for peaceful purposes, Britain's industrial output would be bound to improve, particularly her exporting capacity. Whether she was interested in the Canadian market, however, was another matter...

As to the possibility of a Commonwealth trade conference, he was a little vague. The Commonwealth Finance Ministers would be coming to Ottawa on September 17 following the Washington meeting of the International Monetary Fund and the World Bank, and they would examine the situation whereby such a Commonwealth meeting could be convened.[34]

Richard Jackson of the Ottawa *Journal* wrote similarly on July 8, under the headline "Aims to Divert 15% of Canadian Buying to Britain," that the prime minister had said: "Diversion of 15% of Canadian buying to the British market would make 'a substantial improvement' in trade with the United Kingdom without damaging business relations with the U.S."[35] Jackson did not call the proposed diversion a "plan" and left open the possibility that Diefenbaker was doing no more than offering an example, but the headline left less room for doubt. When the prime minister reported to cabinet on the Commonwealth conference later in the day, he did not draw special attention to the issue of trade diversion.

Canadian and American editorial reactions focused on the 15 percent figure. Canadian comment noted sympathetically that the government was serious about facing the billion dollar trade deficit with the United States, while American responses suggested the need to take a fresh look at the size of the American trade surplus. The Conservative Winnipeg *Tribune* insisted that "Prime Minister Diefenbaker was not picking figures from the air when he remarked that he would like to see about 15 percent of Canada's imports from the United States transferred to British suppliers." It quoted a 1950 statement by the Canadian businessman James S. Duncan that a shift of 15 percent of imports from the United States to the United Kingdom would almost double British exports to Canada. But the editorial added: "So far, details of how a switch...could be effected have not been made public."[36]

As his words reverberated, Diefenbaker took a short holiday in Saskatchewan. When he returned to Ottawa late in July, he told a reporter that his "objective" of a 15 percent transfer of Canadian purchases was "reasonable, equitable and obtainable."[37] Whatever he had intended by his original comment, the figure had hardened with exposure, and he was not retreating from it.

While the Canadian cabinet formally ignored the prime minister's remarks, the British cabinet took notice. On July 9 Macmillan told his colleagues that Diefenbaker "had emerged as a man of considerable strength of character and purpose." Ministers agreed that the Canadian proposal to increase trade should not be neglected, and that Britain's proposals for a European free trade area would have to be reassessed "to take full account of the initiative by the Government of Canada."[38] Two weeks later the president of the board of trade proposed a positive but prudent response to the "offer by the Prime Minister of Canada to divert $625 millions of Canadian imports from the US to the UK." He noted that the proportion of total British trade with Canada receiving preferential treatment had fallen since the 1930s and that there might be something to gain in a new trade agreement between the two countries. Both sides, however, would have to make clear what benefits were being offered. If Canada proved "unexpectedly generous...it might even be possible to contemplate the creation of a free trade area embracing the two countries." Ministers thought it unlikely that Canada would be willing to face the industrial competition of free trade, but agreed that the issue should be further studied. Canada's initiative would be welcomed in the House of Commons in the next few days.[39]

The British cabinet remained sceptical of the proposal for a Commonwealth trade conference, which was now tangled in the talk of trade diversion. But ministers were wary about discouraging a wider trade conference, particularly if nothing were to come of the Anglo-Canadian initiative. "The new Canadian government were well disposed to the UK," read the cabinet minutes, "and if we failed to respond to their constructive proposals they might encounter serious political difficulties." Given Britain's sensitive negotiations in Europe, this was also no time to offend a Commonwealth partner unnecessarily. The high commissioner in Ottawa was told to give no indication to the Canadian government that Britain had reservations about a full Commonwealth trade conference. The line to be taken at the meeting of finance ministers in September was that Britain should "take the lead in endorsing it" if other countries showed any support; and if not, Britain should try to save Canada's face by proposing continuing talks among officials.[40]

By the end of August the British cabinet was carefully calculating its response to the 15 percent initiative. A Canadian memorandum made clear that Canada did not intend any major discrimination against American trade, which was ruled out by the General Agreement on Tariffs and Trade. So the chancellor, Peter Thorneycroft, reflected on the implications of a British free trade offer.

> One way in which such a diversion of trade could be brought about, without involving Canada in a breach of her international obligations, would be for her to enter into a free trade area with the UK. It was true that, in the short term, such a development would yield greater advantages to the UK than to Canada and for that reason it was unlikely that the Canadians would look

favourably on such a suggestion. But, even so, it would be good tactics to put it forward, as a safeguard against any criticism that we had failed to respond to the Canadian initiative. If the Canadians rejected the proposal, we might suggest that in return for the removal of the UK's quantitative restrictions on Canadian imports, Canada should undertake both to reduce her tariffs as far as possible in our favour and to reinforce the sterling area reserves, preferably by agreeing to hold part of her reserves in sterling. In present circumstances the Canadian reaction to this proposal might also be adverse...Failing any agreement...we should have to fall back on relatively minor measures designed to improve the flow of Anglo-Canadian trade. These, while useful, would have little marked effect.[41]

The cabinet agreed to negotiate with Canada on these lines and went on to discuss tactics. Ministers recognized that if Canadian officials learned of the British position before their ministers did, the plan "would be subjected to destructive criticism." Officials would immediately see the disadvantages for Canada and smother it in private, without even the political benefits of a well-publicized failure. It was better suited for discussion between ministers "on a broad political plane rather than for discussions between officials." Since there would be little time for ministers to meet bilaterally at the trade talks in September, cabinet agreed that the minister of agriculture, Derick Heathcoat Amory, should broach the plan to Diefenbaker during a visit to Ottawa early in the coming month.[42] A few days later George Drew, who had now taken up his post in London, reported that British ministers were keenly interested in increasing trade with Canada in the light of Diefenbaker's suggestion.[43]

Amory presented the British scheme to Diefenbaker and Fleming on September 9, but Fleming did not report the delicate issue to cabinet until eleven days later. Amory, he told cabinet,

had been authorized to put forward a proposal that Canada and the U.K. enter a free trade area. The U.K. would reduce as soon as possible its present quotas on Canadian products and manufactured goods but beyond that had nothing to offer. In exchange, British manufacturers would have free entry into the Canadian market. The suggestion had been thoroughly examined and before Mr. Heathcoat Amory returned to London he had been informed that it was too radical and one-sided to be acceptable...

During the discussion, the very slight advantages and the positive disadvantages to Canada in a free trade area with the U.K. were mentioned. Canada simply could not be led into a position which had the appearance of subservience to the U.K. No doubt, however, the U.K. government was under heavy pressure to show the British public that they regarded the 15 per cent diversion suggestion seriously and had, therefore, made the proposal they had.[44]

For Diefenbaker and Fleming, the British offer had not merited consideration by the Canadian cabinet. It was rejected outright following a meeting with senior officials. The prime minister's unthinking overture had brought an unexpected and embarrassing response – "a bombshell," in Fleming's words. The Canadians hoped to dispose of it quickly, silently, and, if possible, unexploded.[45]

The British felt no similar compunction. For one thing, the cabinet in London was told that two Canadian ministers disagreed with the decision to reject and there was perhaps a slight chance it was not final. But above all, UK ministers

> emphasised that the Government should not allow themselves to be placed in a position in which they were unable to reply to public criticism in this country, based on the mistaken belief that they had failed to respond constructively to the offer by the Canadian Prime Minister to divert a substantial proportion of Canadian imports from the US to the UK. There might be some advantage, therefore, in allowing the proposed Anglo-Canadian Free Trade Area to be further explored in the discussions with Canadian Ministers, if a suitable opportunity arose. We should also seek to ensure that this proposal received sufficient publicity to illustrate our readiness, in principle, to engage in a continuous and long-term effort to foster Anglo-Canadian trade.[46]

On the opening day of the Commonwealth finance ministers' meeting at Mont Tremblant, the London *Daily Express* exploited a carefully timed leak and gave the free trade proposal the publicity the British cabinet sought. When Peter Thorneycroft and Donald Fleming met the press together the next day, Thorneycroft confirmed that the idea had been proposed by Britain. Fleming brooded unhappily beside him. Now the scheme was certainly dead.[47]

Perfidious Albion had outwitted John Diefenbaker. He knew he had stumbled into something awkward, but seemed unaware of what had happened. While others were embarrassed by Canadian ineptitude and annoyed by the signs of British cynicism, Diefenbaker was easily flattered by the attentions of Harold Macmillan. As Macmillan's ministers prepared the unwelcome offer, he wrote privately to Diefenbaker that he shared the Canadian desire for expanded trade "in full" and that the Canadian initiative "has caught the imagination of people here."[48] At the same time, he recommended to the queen – and quickly saw to completion – Diefenbaker's appointment to the United Kingdom Privy Council. From September 23, Diefenbaker could style himself "Right Honourable."[49] By the end of September, with Diefenbaker placated, Britain could turn its attentions once more to its plans for entry into the European Free Trade Area.

For a short time the prime minister lamely kept up the pretense of major trade diversion to the United Kingdom. At cabinet in early October, ministers opposed any open rejection of the British offer and suggested that a joint Canada–UK trade communiqué should mention "the government's declared objective to shift 15 per cent of Canada's imports from the United States to the United Kingdom."[50] When Gordon Churchill led a delegation to Britain in November, Diefenbaker said to a reporter that he still believed in shifting 15 percent of Canada's imports. "I would never have enunciated such a principle last July if I had not thought it possible."[51] A few months later, as imports from the United States continued to grow faster than those from the United Kingdom, he told an interviewer that the figure had never been an expression of government policy: "At no time did we say that we were going to divert 15 percent. I said, as an example, that if 15 percent were diverted the result would be to bring about a reasonable deficit in our trade with the U.S. and, at the same time, assure us markets that are virtually non-existent today."[52]

Trade diversion was off the table; it had been a three-month wonder benefiting no one. But the Canadian government still wished to demonstrate its interest in Commonwealth trade by promoting a major Commonwealth conference on the subject. That was the sole purpose of the meeting of Commonwealth finance ministers at Mont Tremblant. The British, who were anxious not to offend further, were warm supporters of the Canadian proposal, and it sailed through with unanimous agreement. The Commonwealth Trade and Economic Conference would be held in Canada in 1958. Donald Fleming and John Diefenbaker were pleased to have fulfilled an election promise and took credit for that. But they remained frustrated by the press's concentration on the fiasco of trade diversion and the British offer.[53]

THE PRIME MINISTER'S ABSENCE FOR TWO WEEKS AS THE NEW GOVERNMENT BEGAN its work meant that there were many loose ends to be picked up on his return. Under the chairmanship of Howard Green as acting prime minister, cabinet held six meetings while Diefenbaker was in London. The first few sessions were long, and after one week in office Green told cabinet that several ministers had complained that "meetings had been so frequent and lengthy that little time was left for individual ministers to attend to their own departmental business." Members agreed with him that, for the interim, pending the prime minister's adoption of regular procedures, no items except urgent ones should be placed on the agenda without one day's notice and submission of an explanatory memorandum.[54] That seemed to make little difference. The intense schedule was maintained on Diefenbaker's return, and in the remaining twenty-six days of July cabinet met eleven more times. Indeed, except for gaps during short summer holidays and election campaigns, Diefenbaker kept his ministers at this exhausting pace for his entire term of office. In less than six years the cabinet met eight hundred and twenty-six times, or, on average – year in and out – almost three days each week.[55]

Diefenbaker's first display of mistrust towards ministers came on July 11. He was "deeply disturbed" that there had been leaks of information after recent meetings. In particular, the press had learned prematurely of George Drew's appointment and of the prime minister's proposal to visit President Eisenhower. Diefenbaker warned that he would ask for the resignations of ministers who did not respect cabinet secrecy.[56] In October he told cabinet he was "very disturbed" by accurate press reports about proposed increases in old age security. "Nothing," the minutes said, "would be more upsetting for him than to have to ask a Minister to resign."[57]

Cabinet secrecy was a matter, primarily, of partisan prudence, a means of depriving opponents of information that might give them political advantage. There was another level of security policy involving the shielding of Canadian "secrets" from the agents of foreign powers – which meant, during this era of the Cold War, chiefly spies serving the Soviet intelligence services. Soon after his return from London, Diefenbaker was provided by Bryce with detailed briefing papers on that aspect of government security.[58] One part of the policy dealt with the classification and secure handling of documents; Bryce gave the prime minister a booklet outlining "all the minutiae of physical security" that had been approved by the previous government's Security Panel and commented that these procedures offered no serious problems. On the other hand, the policy on "the loyalty and reliability of people" raised "one of the more difficult and unpleasant problems of our times." This policy was contained in "Cabinet Directive No. 29," approved by the Liberal cabinet in December 1955. Bryce outlined its features in his own memo and enclosed a full copy of the directive for the prime minister. The document noted that security was "a part of good administration," normally to be dealt with at the departmental level. Good administration, it suggested, might be threatened "either by persons who are disloyal or by persons who are unreliable because of defects in their character." Disloyalty was defined essentially as membership or belief in the Communist Party.

> It remains an essential of Canadian security policy that a person who is a member of a communist party, which is substantially subservient to the dictates of a foreign power, or a person who by his words or actions consistently shows himself to believe in Soviet communism, or in any other ideology which advocates the overthrow of government by force, should not when known be permitted to enter the public service. Such persons discovered within the public service must not be allowed access to classified information. It is a matter for consideration in such cases as to whether it is desirable to remove such persons from the public service.[59]

"Unreliability" was defined more vaguely, but seemed to be a euphemism for homosexuality: "Persons who are unreliable from a security standpoint, not because they are disloyal, but because of defects in their character which may lead to indiscretion or dishonesty, or may make them likely subjects of blackmail, must not be employed in any position where they may have access to classified information. Such defects of character may also make them unsuitable for employment on grounds other than security."[60]

The policy provided that government departments should carry out security reviews of all persons having access to classified documents and making use of information supplied to them by the security agencies. After careful examination, departments were instructed to resolve any remaining doubts about loyalty or reliability "in favour of the state," not the individual. Quarterly reports were to be filed with the Security Panel listing the numbers of persons dismissed, permitted to resign, transferred to other posts, denied access to classified information, and denied employment.[61] The policy was applied widely, to the military services, "mass communications," and the defence industries as well as the public service.

Bryce pointed out to Diefenbaker that "perhaps the most distinctive feature of security policy in Canada" was that a person denied access to classified materials or dismissed from employment "is not normally told that action has been based on security grounds; and as a result there is no appeal or official review system of the kind used in the U.K. and the U.S." While a review system had been studied, the Security Panel had recently decided that it would involve too many "practical disadvantages" and should not be put into effect.

Bryce recognized that the right of appeal, and the right to know the reasons for an employment decision, arose from "principles of natural justice." But he cited three grounds for ignoring such principles: an appeal process would usually mean "some public knowledge" of cases, possibly embarrassing to the individuals concerned; it might compromise the sources of information relied on by the security services; and it would tend to limit the discretion of officials ruling in individual cases. These were remarkably self-serving justifications for a confidential vetting system that deprived its subjects of elementary justice. Bryce took comfort from his view that the RCMP security service was a reliable source of information, and that departmental security reviews were conducted with "maturity and prudence" under the oversight of the Security Panel.[62]

John Diefenbaker, whose public reputation was built on his defence of civil liberties, read and marked the Bryce memorandum. He underlined key sections of Bryce's summary of the rule relating to the employment of members of, or sympathizers with, the Communist Party – and wrote in the margin "Norman." This seemed to be an implied criticism of Pearson's support for the beleaguered diplomat rather than a comment on the rule itself. Beside Bryce's report that the Security Panel had recommended against an appeal system, Diefenbaker placed a question mark. And beside Bryce's claim that an appeal system "ideally" would give the appellant access to the information on which the decision was based and thus might reveal intelligence sources, the prime minister wrote "?Why?" Such signs of scepticism were fully consistent with Diefenbaker's long-standing belief in the right of appeal against administrative acts. But he did not pursue his doubts; the existing policy was maintained without reference to cabinet. For Diefenbaker, it seemed, the communist challenge to the state overrode the normal claims of civil liberty, just as the threat of a wartime enemy had done for him in 1940. This time, the power of decision was in his own hands, and he chose caution. On the subject of Herbert Norman, Diefenbaker now possessed one further bit of evidence in the wording of the security policy – but it related to Pearson's potential political embarrassment rather than to Norman's rights as a public servant.[63]

For Diefenbaker, filling out his cabinet was a more pressing preoccupation during the summer of 1957. In early August he named Douglas Harkness as minister of agriculture and Paul Comtois as minister of mines and technical surveys; two weeks later Waldo Monteith became minister of national health and welfare, and Alvin Hamilton minister of northern affairs and natural resources.[64] Harkness was a decorated veteran from Calgary and a member of the House since 1945; Comtois was an undistinguished agronomist;

Monteith was a chartered accountant from Perth, Ontario; and Hamilton was one of Diefenbaker's successors as party leader in Saskatchewan.

There was speculation in the country about who Diefenbaker might eventually appoint to External Affairs; some writers proposed innocently that Pearson should be called back to the ministry by his political opponents.[65] That must have struck the prime minister as vaguely sinister: the department, after all, was the home of the "Pearsonalities" and needed special watching. One of Diefenbaker's friends in the consular service, Leo Dolan, wrote to him confidentially that autumn that External Affairs was distributing press excerpts critical of Diefenbaker and favourable to Pearson: "I still would watch the 'Pearson cult' in External...Since when should your department publicize the prospective leader of your opposition?"[66]

Diefenbaker enjoyed the element of uncertainty created by his temporary stewardship of the department and sought in these early days to impose his permanent control over it. His plans for the office were uncertain, and one of his own stories suggests a casual outcome. Early in September he realized that he would be expected, as minister, to attend the annual session of the United Nations General Assembly. That would mean another extended absence from Ottawa, leaving Howard Green as acting prime minister during the crucial early months while the government's program was being developed. Diefenbaker decided not to risk that, but instead to appoint a minister who could go at once to New York for the General Assembly. When the prime minister spoke at Dartmouth College in early September, Sidney Smith, the president of the University of Toronto and sometime would-be candidate for the Conservative leadership, was in the audience. Diefenbaker asked him to take the job, and within a few days Smith had been plucked from academe to become secretary of state for external affairs.[67]

The appointment did not begin well. At the press conference following Smith's accesion, the prime minister promptly rebuked him for supporting Liberal policy on Suez and insisted this was not government policy.[68] The press greeted the nomination of a distinguished public figure with praise, but Smith's lack of political experience and Diefenbaker's own attraction to the international stage meant that the minister remained in the prime minister's shadow for the eighteen months before his sudden death in March 1959.[69]

―――――――

THE PRIME MINISTER'S FIRST FORAY INTO THE UNITED STATES OCCURRED ON September 7, 1957, when he received an honorary degree from Dartmouth College and chose the occasion to talk about the "neighbourly problems" of the Anglo-Canadian-American community – the old North Atlantic Triangle in which Diefenbaker saw Canada's place. He had a message of both friendship and candour. The natural friendship of the two countries, he said, had grown out of their shared heritage of freedom, and was now deepened by their common defence of democracy against "the Red Menace." In face of that menace, "unity is the only certain hope for the survival of freedom everywhere in the world." The parallel interests of the two countries meant that they could trust one another and speak frankly about their differences. In that spirit, he wished to "deal with one or two economic matters that are causing unrest within my country."

Canada, he noted, was a major trading nation, yet 60 percent of its exports and 73 percent of its imports were accounted for in cross-border trade with the United States. Canadian exports to the United States were primarily raw or partially manufactured materials, because US tariffs blocked sales of most manufactured goods. This concentration of trade, and its nature, had "inherent dangers for Canada. It makes the Canadian economy altogether too vulnerable to sudden changes in trading policy at Washington." Canada also suffered a continuing and increasing deficit in commodity trade with the United States, amounting to $1.3 billion in 1956. Canadian grain exports were declining in the world because of unfair American surplus disposal programs. As a result, Canada had an unsold wheat surplus in 1957 of 700 million bushels. The overriding challenge of military and economic aggression by the Soviet Union, he argued, demanded economic as well as military cooperation in the west. He hoped that the joint US–Canadian cabinet committee on trade and economic questions – due to meet in Washington in October – would resolve the issue of surplus agricultural disposals.

His second concern echoed that of the Gordon Commission on Canada's economic prospects. There was, he said, "an intangible sense of disquiet in Canada over the political implications of large-scale and continuing external ownership and control of Canadian industries." More than 60 percent of Canadian manufacturing, mining, and oil production was owned in the United States, and most American-owned firms did not offer stock to Canadians. Yet Canadians expected American companies to serve Canadian interests and not to undermine Canadian independence.

Diefenbaker offered no clear cures for Canada's "intangible sense of disquiet" beyond calling for a spirit of cooperation in economic affairs similar to that in defence. His appeal to the American audience came back again and again to the need for a common defence against communism, the preservation of a "steadfast and undiminished unity...in our great quest to maintain freedom."[70] Be reasonable with us, he insisted, because we face a common enemy. That was both an appeal to America's higher self-interest and an indication of the limits within which Diefenbaker's foreign policy would function. Because he believed in the Red Menace, he believed also in the need for American protection from it. Canada could not afford to unsettle the great neighbour too much. Diefenbaker might show more public irritation at the strains of the relationship than his Liberal predecessors had, but he too accepted its benevolence and its necessity, and sought its benefits. The new government's attitude to the United States revealed, in Basil Robinson's words, "a suitable blend of goodwill and vigilance."[71]

Advances in military technology and the Cold War had transformed American and Canadian military planning. The North American continent, once safely insulated from direct attack by wide reaches of ocean, was now accessible by long-range bomber, and potentially by intercontinental missile. As the postwar conflict between the Soviet Union and the United States grew more and more tense, the military consulted their polar maps and discovered the vast expanses of northern Canada lying mute between the two great powers. The flashpoints of war might be in Europe, where the forces of East and West confronted each other on the ground. But if war should occur, American cities and industries would, for the first time, be natural targets. Canadian skies offered the shortest routes for Soviet bombers travelling from Russia to the continental United States. As early as 1946 defence planners had begun to consider joint air defence systems on Canadian territory meant to protect American territory. After 1950 preparations intensified, and three successive radar detection networks were approved and constructed, each further north than the last: the Pinetree Network, just beyond the Canadian-American border (completed in 1954); the Mid-Canada Line (completed in 1957); and the Distant Early Warning Line, along the Canadian Arctic coast (completed in 1957). These systems were built on American initiative, which the Canadian government reluctantly seconded. Ottawa skirmished endlessly with Washington over issues of cost, jurisdiction, and sovereign control of the facilities – sometimes in public, more often in private.[72] By the mid-1950s, circumstance fed a widespread public sense that Canadian independence was being reduced as the friendly neighbour leaned intrusively into Canadian territory.

Air defence required interception as well as detection. As the radar networks went up and the possibilities of nuclear war grew more real, the issue of where air battles might be fought came into focus. The American interest dictated that Soviet bombers carrying nuclear weapons should be destroyed as far beyond US air space as possible. Acting on recommendations of the

Permanent Joint Board on Defence, the St Laurent cabinet had granted rights of interception over Canada to the United States Air Force, and in one of its first acts the Diefenbaker government had extended the agreement covering the use of American air-to-air nuclear weapons over Canada.

The United States Air Force sought more: not only joint air defence planning but a fully unified operational command. In the face of hesitation by the Canadian chiefs of staff, a joint military study group on the subject was created, and it recommended a joint command in December 1956. After a short period of negotiation, the American and Canadian military chiefs agreed on all terms. On the expected date of Canadian cabinet approval on March 15, 1957, however, the draft proposal was withdrawn. Canada informed the United States that "it would not now be possible to give formal approval to the paper as it was possible this matter might leak to the press, and as Canada–United States relations could become an issue, it was considered advisable not to have the paper approved until such time as it was not a political issue."[73] Agreement, that is, would await the Canadian election.

Two days after the election, the Canadian chiefs of staff proposed to the departing Liberal government that the "almost completed international agreement" should be approved "subject to confirmation by the incoming government." The price of inaction, they suggested, might be a delay of several months under a new government, "quite a serious deterioration in Canada–US military relations," perhaps some adverse publicity, and the creation of doubts "as to whether international agreements with Canada had continued validity."[74] St Laurent nevertheless told his cabinet the next day that the decision should be left to the new government.[75]

Because Diefenbaker and his minister of defence, George Pearkes, left Ottawa for the Commonwealth conference just after they took office, the recommendation for integrated air defence operations did not reach them until mid-July. Pearkes and Diefenbaker both accepted Canada's place in the Western alliance in principle, and had no desire to challenge the relationship either in North America or Europe. They were easily convinced by the chief of defence staff, General Charles Foulkes, that delay was undesirable and that approval meant implementing a decision already made by the previous government. "Unfortunately I am afraid," Foulkes told a House of Commons committee in 1963, "we stampeded the incoming government with the NORAD agreement."[76] That was not a judgment admitted by Diefenbaker and Pearkes, but they obviously gave themselves little time to study or reflect on Foulkes's advice. Pearkes received the documents from his chiefs of staff on July 22 and forwarded them to the prime minister with his recommendation the next day.[77] Diefenbaker decided that approval did not require a cabinet decision, and four days later the prime minister indicated his government's support to the American secretary of state, John Foster Dulles, during his brief visit to Ottawa. On July 31 Pearkes brought to cabinet his recommendation that Air Marshal C.R. Slemon should be appointed deputy commander-in-chief of the new Canada–United States Air Defence Command. The prime minister explained briefly: "An integrated Canadian-United States Air Defence Command was to be created with its operational centre at Colorado Springs. The appointment of a Canadian as Deputy Commander-in-Chief would give Canada a proper measure of responsibility in any decisions that might have to be taken to defend North America against an attack. In a recent conversation with the U.S. Secretary of State, he had emphasized the importance which Canada attached to a voice in any decisions resulting from information obtained from the Distant Early Warning Line."[78]

No background memorandum was given to cabinet, although one had been prepared, and there was no discussion of the prime minister's announcement. Air Marshal Slemon's appointment was approved, and the next day the two governments announced the creation of "a system of integrated operational control of...air defence forces...under an integrated command responsible to the Chiefs of Staff of both countries," with headquarters in Colorado Springs. Joint plans would be developed "for immediate use in case of emergency." The press statement noted that "this bilateral arrangement extends the mutual security objectives of the North Atlantic Treaty Organization to the air defences of the Canada–United States Region."[79] The prime minister may not have been stampeded, but he knew little about the implications of his decision. His own attempts to understand and defend what he had done came only gradually in the months that followed, as the integrated command took shape and questions about it arose in parliament and the press.

THE PREVIOUS GOVERNMENT HAD INVITED QUEEN ELIZABETH TO OPEN THE NEXT session of parliament on October 14, 1957. John Diefenbaker told his first cabinet meeting that this would be a historic event, the first time a monarch had opened the Canadian parliament. The change of government meant that the timing of the visit might be awkward, since the new cabinet was impatient to proceed even earlier with its legislative business. But the dates – which also included a royal visit to the United States – were fixed and nothing could be done to alter them. Cabinet confirmed the timetable and set to work planning its legislative agenda with that in mind. Ministers recognized the great political bonus to be gained from a royal launching of the Conservative program.[80]

The cabinet's plans for the parliamentary session were ambitious. Ministers were eager to introduce as much attractive legislation as quickly as possible, to prepare the ground for another – and decisive – general election. Then they could settle in for the long haul and the more complex issues of trade, defence, and national development. As summer and autumn passed, cabinet approved further salary increases for civil servants, farm price supports, emergency financing for Nova Scotia collieries, increases in low-cost housing loans, federal aid for New Brunswick power development and Yukon highways, and restrictions on agricultural imports to protect domestic producers: a cornucopia of special benefits reaching into all regions of the country. The flow of announcements made clear that this was a government that cared for its electors – and its potential electors. Much more was promised once the new session had begun.

THE ASSUMPTION OF POWER AND THE TRIUMPHANT VISIT TO LONDON WERE HEADY events, and Diefenbaker wanted to let people know about the enchantments of office. He reported breathlessly to Elmer and his mother on the Commonwealth conference and his return to Ottawa. "The first thing I must do on landing is to review the guard of honor etc. You will be seeing all this on T.V." And days later, "Olive and I got back yesterday noon and moved in to the PM's Home last evening. It's a fairy place."[81] He corresponded and talked widely with friends in the press, and on the evening of his return from London John and Olive turned up at Patrick Nicholson's home. John wanted especially to see the two Nicholson daughters before they went to bed. Settled side-by-side on a sofa, he reminded them of fairy stories told by their father and recalled his visit to "a famous old castle" called Windsor where he dined on gold plates with a queen, a tall prince, and "a real fairy princess of great beauty called Margaret."[82]

Diefenbaker kept up the pace of the election campaign, accepting invitations through the summer to open fairs and kick ceremonial footballs, delighting now to be honoured as prime minister. In Saskatoon, "we went to the Fairgrounds with a *police* escort! What do you know about that!"[83] For the autumn, a frenetic schedule took shape. In September there was an address to the Canadian Bar Association, the Dartmouth College affair, quick trips to Quebec City and Charlottetown, and a speech at the United Nations; in October, a McGill degree, the queen's opening of parliament, and a visit to Washington; in November, a dominion-provincial conference; and in December, a meeting of the NATO Council in Paris – not to mention the continuing marathon of cabinet meetings and lightning trips across the country. The public responded to this human dynamo, turning out in large numbers at his appearances with displays of affection and curiosity. On his sixty-second birthday in September, fellow passengers on an overnight TCA flight from Charlottetown to Ottawa serenaded him boisterously with verses of "Happy birthday, dear John."[84]

Diefenbaker was up by dawn on most mornings, jotting notes to his family and anticipating the day to come. He worried about Olive, who had suffered a painful neck injury when she fell during the flight to England, but he shared her pleasure in her first grandson, born to her daughter, Carolyn, just before the election. Uncle Ed was a puzzle: Diefenbaker wrote to him after the victory, sent him a scarf for his birthday, and asked him to write recollections of the family's pioneering life; but for months there was no reply. John was offended. Mother was a more serious problem: her doctor reported that she was suffering "spells" in her hospital bed, shouting and accusing the nurses of stealing her belongings, expressing resentment and hostility to everyone, confusing time and place. Diefenbaker wrote and visited frequently, but had trouble deciding what might interest her.[85] Family history, the queen, and his own recreations were the staples.

> Last evening I went to Hamilton...I was met there by a reporter from the "Spectator" who advised me that he had found a Diefenbaker wagon that grandfather had made and that arrangements were being made to purchase it for the Museum. I only wish we could find out what happened to the wagon he sent to Father in 1909...
>
> Day by day the arrangements are being made for the visit of the Queen...The security forces are visiting our residence today to make a full examination in order to protect the Queen during her visit. The house will be searched from top to bottom the morning of the day that she will be there, and again late in the afternoon, and during the day of course guards will be on duty. The Americans can't understand why I haven't got anybody guarding me! This morning one of them told me it was very dangerous for me to be around.
>
> Monday I am going to have some fun. I expect to go to Toronto and intended to have no one know about it, to attend the Ringling Brothers circus, but I see it is in the paper today.[86]

In all this rush there was no time to think. "Another heavy day," Diefenbaker wrote on September 19. "Cabinet all morning; Defence Committee until now (4 pm) – then on to Smith's Falls to open a Trade Fair.

267

Olive is so busy too she can't turn around. Weather is hot today but I have a cold that is holding on."[87] As he departed two days later to address the UN General Assembly he told Elmer: "Just leaving for New York and no speech even started...Herewith is a set of stamps for your collection – a *first* issue."

The queen's visit to open parliament was the grand ceremonial occasion for John Diefenbaker and his new government, and a subject of preoccupation as the day approached. "I am so far behind in a lot of my work," he told his mother at the end of September, "that I don't know when I will ever catch up but there are some things that have to be done in the next ten days as the Queen will arrive in thirteen days."[88] Diefenbaker fussed over family plans. "I do hope Elmer can come. The arrangements for the dinner at our home will give him an opportunity to be seated at a table at which there will only be 16 besides the Queen and Prince Philip and her Lady-in-Waiting and his Aide. It should be a wonderful experience."[89]

Elmer arrived in Ottawa on October 13 for the next day's opening of parliament, joining the Brunts as a guest at 24 Sussex Drive. For the occasion, Diefenbaker had rewarded his most loyal aides, Bill Brunt and Arthur Pearson, with appointments to the Senate. Elmer – whose travels usually took him to fly-specked prairie hotels – was blissful.

> I spent my first night at No 24 Sussex Street last night. It is a fairy castle, surrounded by beautiful grounds and overlooking the beautiful Ottawa River. Just now I am looking through windows on all sides. I was conducted through the entire place last night and that experience in time and things to be seen was unlike [sic] going through a museum.
>
> There is a large staff of servants, who wait on you hand and knee – so that is something different for me.
>
> ...
>
> Just now the P.M. with morning coat, top hat, etc., was picked up by the new Buick, Mounted police on guard with the salute and the P.M. will have his cabinet meeting with the Queen present. The valet brought him into the Sitting room & announced, "Gentlemen, the Prime Minister."[90]

The ceremonial meeting of the Canadian Privy Council would be followed by the opening of parliament. Although Diefenbaker opposed the entry of television cameras into the House of Commons on principle, he had suggested to cabinet that the first visit of a reigning monarch might offer a suitable exception to the rule. Ministers agreed, on condition that the CBC would offer "an appropriate commentary on the meaning and significance of the events"; so the lights and cameras were rolled into the Senate chamber for an unprecedented show of Canadian pomp and Conservative advertising.[91] In the prime minister's eyes, this was a kind of restoration: of respect for parliament, the monarchy, and the British connection, a restoration of all those traditions he believed the Liberal Party had let slide towards oblivion.

Elmer became the family scribe for the occasion, and two days later he recorded it all. "I have seen everything," he wrote. "Every body has been wonderful and I seem to know everyone."

> The opening of parliament was a brilliant affair and we were seated in the Governor General's box, where you could see everything...
>
> The Queen was beautiful, radiant, and indeed she had a regal appearance. It was a great sight to see her and Prince Philip seated in the Senate Chamber...
>
> The big event was the Prime Minister's dinner last night. It was considered a great affair. The beauty of the whole set-up was indeed beyond words.
>
> It was a tremendous job and it took six hours to set the table. I was shown the 14 pheasants beautiful, fat and plump, before they were roasted...The Queen was most beautiful. She laughed gaily, totally informal and relaxed and the Prince a real man just laughs whole heart'ly. He has a wealth of knowledge and I would say, would stack up on any quiz show. He is just interested in everything.
>
> ...
>
> Everyone remarks that John and Olive have done a most outstanding job in the carrying out of the plans of the Royal Visit. They made no errors and could not have done any better.[92]

It was, as Elmer wrote, a grand day. Thanks to the CBC, the whole country watched as the morning-coated prime minister met the young queen alighting from the royal landau at the steps of parliament. Together they passed under the Peace Tower into the Centre Block while the carillon rang out above and the crowds clapped. The crimson Senate chamber shone with the colours of judicial robes, dress uniforms, and evening dresses as the queen entered to take her seat on the dais with the prince at her side. John Diefenbaker sat to her right. Members of the Commons were summoned according to the ancient ritual and crowded into the entranceway facing the royal couple. The newly elected Speaker of the House, Roland Michener, claimed the "undoubted rights and privileges" of the House of Commons from the queen, and she, through the Speaker of the Senate, granted them. Then she read the speech prepared by her Canadian government.

The speech carried forward the government's summer promises of largesse. Old age, blind, disabled, and veterans' pensions would be raised; funding for provincial old age assistance would be increased; agricultural floor prices would be introduced; cash would be advanced for farm-stored grain; supplementary and married women's unemployment insurance benefits would be extended; hydroelectric power and water storage projects would be assisted on the Saint John, South Saskatchewan, and Columbia rivers; a new national development policy would promote resource exploitation; an aggressive trade policy would open up markets for Canadian products abroad.[93] The outlook seemed benign and the government's intentions generous. This was a pre-election agenda.[94]

From Ottawa, Queen Elizabeth flew off to Washington with the Canadian prime minister, for the first time as a state visitor there in her role as queen of Canada. This constitutional sleight-of-hand must have meant little to the Americans, who wanted only to see the British monarch, but it was a triumph in Diefenbaker's eyes. In Washington the prime minister met with President Eisenhower, Secretary of State Dulles, and Vice President Nixon, and established that "there was no limit to Mr. Eisenhower's congeniality and friendliness." He raised with the president the issues of American agricultural surplus disposal policies and Canadian criticism of the government's entry into the integrated air defence system. Eisenhower assured him of the American wish to cooperate and to avoid conflict with Canada, and Diefenbaker left feeling confident that "Canada's position was more clearly understood and...our interests would be better protected."[95]

At home in parliament, the government proceeded quickly with its legislative program.[96] Louis St Laurent had announced his intention to retire as Liberal leader in September, but would carry on in the House until his successor was chosen in January. Both St Laurent and M.J. Coldwell, the CCF leader, promised cooperation in achieving the ministry's electoral promises. With the Tories in the ascendant, there was nothing to be gained in fractiousness – and everything to be gained in avoiding a government defeat in the House. St Laurent put his party's interest in the language of the public good: "In the final analysis our view is that the will of the majority in parliament and, even more, of the majority in the country, should prevail."[97] There was little doubt now about who enjoyed the benefit of that majority will.

There was no danger of defeat in the House, but the government did not have a totally free ride. Liberals repeatedly chided the government with talk of increased unemployment and recollections that "Tory times are hard times." There were, indeed, worrying signs of an economic downturn that sent the cabinet scurrying for policies to stimulate jobs – including winter works, more funds for public housing, and tax cuts for individuals and businesses. In November the first hints of confusion over the integration of Canadian and American air defences began to emerge as the opposition pressed for details of the deal. Diefenbaker wrote to his mother that "the Liberals keep kicking me around…I need not tell you that when I was a boy and saw my way to this position, I didn't know how much work there was (and worry)." Diefenbaker was still unable to organize his time efficiently. "This weekend," he reported, "the P.M. of England (Macmillan) and the Foreign Minister will be here. That means an almost all night session on Friday night for me."[98] In late November he lamented: "Today I should be getting ready for the Dominion Provincial Conference on Monday. I am really not ready for it at all and will have to put in many many hours of work. Unfortunately, I promised to go to Toronto to a Shrine meeting tonight and I am trying to get out of that because it is just impossible."[99]

Still, the pleasures outweighed the pains. Diefenbaker enjoyed his celebrity, his hectic and unending travel, his sense of hobnobbing with the great and titled, his opportunities to embellish the family legend.

> Last evening Olive and I entertained the Governor General and he was accompanied by Brigadier MacLean who is an outstanding Clansman and maintains the Highland tradition in every way and came in Kilts.
>
> I told him that I was going to Paris to the meeting of the fifteen heads of State in the middle of December and on my stop-over in England I would like to go up to Northern Scotland to Kildonan and go over the place where your grandparents came from. He immediately entered enthusiastically into the plan and is going to arrange to go with me, and I will spend a day or so in Sutherlandshire, Inverness and Argyle, and when I see you at Christmas time I hope to have lots of information for you.[100]

As he descended into Paris for the NATO heads of government meeting he told his mother:

> This Conference will be the most important since the war for the Free world and I hope that I shall be able to do something. Certainly I will never attend a world Conference again that will be more important to peace and the future…
>
> Yes and one year ago today at this very hour I became Conservative leader!![101]

271

On December 21 John and Olive returned to Canada, to spend Christmas Day in Saskatoon. This was the prime minister's celebration, hosted and catered in his private railway car resting by the CN station – on the very site, Diefenbaker recalled, where he had engaged Wilfrid Laurier in conversation almost fifty years before. Diefenbaker's mother came by ambulance from the University Hospital to join John, Olive, and Elmer for the day. Immediately afterwards, the couple departed with the Grosarts for a holiday at Lord Beaverbrook's house in Nassau, Bahamas, and for sea fishing on the Beaver's chartered cruiser.[102] By early January they were back in Ottawa.

DESPITE ITS OCCASIONAL MISSTEPS, THE DIEFENBAKER GOVERNMENT WAS ENJOYING a long honeymoon in office. The press was refreshed to see new faces, intrigued by the prime minister's energy, and gentle in its early judgments. The public, quickly accustomed to what it had done on June 10, decided that it liked the idea of dishing the Grits and turned its enthusiasms to the Tories. The Gallup Poll over the summer and into the autumn showed growing Conservative support across the country. Thoughts of a second and decisive round were bound to arise, and there were strong temptations among ministers to enter a new campaign while opinion was at full tide in their favour.[103] It seemed likely, though, that the opposition would not oblige them by combining to defeat the minority government in a House of Commons vote. Ministers knew that the Liberals, CCF, and Social Credit were tired, demoralized, and debt-ridden: they would hang on in the new parliament as long as they could. But how soon, in that case, could a new government legitimately ask the governor general for a fresh dissolution of parliament without a defeat in the House? The issue had been disputed thirty years before, when Lord Byng's refusal of a dissolution to Mackenzie King just eight months after an election threw the country into constitutional turmoil. At the centre of that conflict was Eugene Forsey (then a young lecturer at McGill University), who took the governor general's side in the dispute with King and his defenders. Although King's election victory in 1926 meant that Forsey lost the battle, his honour seemed secure and his reputation blossomed with publication of his *Royal Power of Dissolution of Parliament in the British Commonwealth*. He was still, as we have seen, an antagonist of the Liberal Party in the 1950s. Diefenbaker considered him his doughty ally.

But Forsey was above all a parliamentary constitutionalist, and Conservative talk of an early election reminded him of King and 1926. Early in August he wrote to the Ottawa *Journal* to raise the alarm. Howard Green had said that only the queen's visit prevented an election in the autumn, and that there would be an election before the summer of 1958. Forsey objected. Parliament was elected "to transact public business, and ought not to be dissolved except for grave and substantial reasons of public policy." A fall election without a session of parliament would be "a gross violation of the Constitution." A snap election after a short fall session would be just slightly less unconstitutional, unless there had been obstruction or a government defeat. And a fresh election by July 1958 could only be justified if the government were defeated, or repeatedly sustained by the Speaker's casting vote or by narrow margins of one, two, or three votes, or if there had been "prolonged obstruction" of House business. If the government's program were approved by parliament, he asked, "what right has any Government to put the country to the tumult and expense of a second election within a year merely because some of the support comes from people with a different political label?" The *Journal* printed the letter, but omitted its stinging conclusion:

> To announce, eight or ten months in advance, that whatever Parliament does, it will be dissolved next spring seems to me to be a very odd way of showing respect for Parliament. Elections are serious matters. They disrupt business. They interrupt the orderly conduct of foreign policy. They cost money, millions to the public treasury, millions more to the parties and the candidates. A second election within a year can be justified only on grounds of public necessity. A clear majority for the Government over all other parties is a convenience for the Government. It is not, in itself, a public necessity. It becomes so only if the conduct of the opposition parties makes it so. Mr. Green, and you, may feel confident that this will happen. If it does, the remedy is ready to the Government's hand. But until it does, a party committed to restoring and maintaining the rights of Parliament should allow Parliament to do the public business it was elected to do.[104]

Forsey copied the letter to J.M. Macdonnell, and at the end of October, hearing "persistent talk" of an election, he sent it also to the prime minister with a covering letter. Forsey commented to Diefenbaker that, with parliament now in session, the only new element was Conservative irritation at Liberal attacks. But that was "no reason for dissolving a newly elected Parliament."

> I can hardly believe that the Government contemplates asking for a dissolution in the near future except for some such grave reasons of public policy as I outlined in my letter to the *Journal*; and I should hate to see

Conservative Ministers preaching the King doctrine that a Government is entitled to a dissolution any time it feels so inclined. I am afraid the Liberals would make devastating use of the Conservative arguments in 1926, and the Conservative Party would to a large extent lose what I think was its main advantage in the last election: a public conviction that it was acting from *principle.* The Government's course since it took office has strengthened that conviction. I think it would be a tragedy for the party and for the country if anything were done to weaken it.[105]

Ten days later Diefenbaker wrote to reassure Forsey:

I am glad that you wrote to let me have your comments on a possible early dissolution of the present Parliament. I fully agree with you concerning the weighty reasons which should govern any request for dissolution of a newly elected Parliament and I should like to assure you that these reasons will be in my mind should the occasion here arise to consider requesting such a dissolution. It is the purpose of the new Government to make its decisions on those parliamentary and democratic principles in which we both believe so profoundly.[106]

Forsey had given Diefenbaker's political conscience an uncomfortable nudge. The temptation to dissolve early remained strong; but with Forsey on the watch, Diefenbaker would have to take care about his justifications.

In mid-January the Liberal Party held its leadership convention, which, as expected, brought Mike Pearson into the succession in easy competition against Paul Martin. Pearson had the advantage, for a defeated party, of an engaging personality and a non-partisan record. His distinguished career as secretary of state for external affairs had just been capped by receipt of the 1957 Nobel Prize for Peace for his inspiration in creating the United Nations Emergency Force. Diefenbaker begrudged that award, but felt confident he was a match for Pearson in the House of Commons. On the weekend of the Liberal convention the prime minister was immobilized in bed with a strained back, so he was free to watch – and joke about – the proceedings. "I saw one of the banners that the Young Liberals carried which was entitled 'Diefenbaker Raw Deal.' Even so, advertising wherever it comes from is always acceptable so long as one doesn't have to pay for it."[107]

Diefenbaker was now living day by day awaiting the opportunity to dissolve the House. He wanted an election in the first few months of 1958, but directed all his sensitive antennae to detecting the right occasion for the choice. Despite Forsey's warning about constitutional proprieties, the leader's calculations were absorbingly political. "The session is rapidly coming to an end," he wrote to his mother on January 31. "The legislative programme for the session has all but been completed and about all that remains is the passing of the Estimates. Everybody seems to expect an election. There is a general demand that it should take place soon. What decision I will come to will have to be determined within the next short while."[108] By this time he was at the point of decision and already on the road as though the campaign had begun. The week before, he and Olive had been in Winnipeg for a large public reception – "we shook hands with 3500 people (and my hand is very swollen)" – and a Ukrainian dinner for six hundred.[109] Then he was in Halifax for a few hours to receive an honorary degree from St Mary's University. The next day he was back in Ottawa for a ceremonial presentation in front of the Parliament Buildings of a sleigh built by his grandfather, an appropriate symbol both of his own national roots and the rigours of a winter election.[110]

The prime minister had been handed his pretext for an election on January 20, 1958, when Pearson took his seat as leader of the opposition. The subject of debate was a vote of interim supply, and a Liberal motion of non-confidence was expected. In the minority House, it was always possible that the two smaller parties might vote with the official opposition to defeat the government and force an election, even though the Liberals might not intend it. A motion that assured CCF support for the government, however, would not risk that. In the aftermath of his convention victory, Pearson received conflicting advice about how to make his debut. Should he enter the House swinging – and risk defeating the government – or should he hedge his criticisms in some way that would assure a government majority? The over-ingenious Jack Pickersgill provided him with the answer, and Pearson went into the House without telling his own caucus what he would do.[111]

After a standard assault on the government for a failing economic record, Pearson told the House that an election would "prolong and perhaps intensify the uncertainty and the fear for the future which now exists." Canada's trade was stagnating, export markets had been threatened, the budget was in deficit, Canadians were worried and confused. Before an incredulous audience, which included many in his own caucus, Pearson called for a government that would "implement Liberal policies," and invited the Conservative cabinet to resign.[112]

That would bring the Liberal Party – defeated, discredited, and failing in the opinion polls – back to power without an election. Was there a more perfect demonstration of Liberal arrogance? Pearson slouched to his seat in uncertainty over what he had done. "Mike, it is sad to see you come to this," Donald Fleming called out. Diefenbaker could scarcely believe his good fortune. He turned across the aisle to Howard Green and laughed: "This is it."[113]

And then, clutching a mass of loose foolscap sheets in his left hand, rallying all his fury and his sarcasm for one mighty explosion of rhetoric, he rose to reply. He spoke for more than two hours, with a break for the dinner recess. His wattles shook, his eyes glared, his index finger stabbed the air before him. Liberals heckled and Diefenbaker bulldozed them. Conservative back-benchers cheered him on. "Pearson," recalled Fleming, "looked at first merry, then serious, then uncomfortable, then disturbed, and finally sick. His followers knew all too well that he was destroyed."[114]

Diefenbaker contrasted Pearson's boldness at the leadership convention with his new cowardice: "On Thursday there was shrieking defiance; on the following Monday there is shrinking indecision...The only reason that this motion is worded as it is is that my hon. friends opposite quake when they think of what will happen if an election comes...I do not want to speak of this motion in crushing terms, but there is no other expression that can be applied to it than this. It is the resignation from responsibility of a great party."[115]

The prime minister had prepared himself for an attack on the Conservative economic record. Now he was angered by the realization that the Liberal Party had made itself look ridiculous, but would not hand him a voting defeat that would justify dissolution. He was determined to humiliate the opposition, to destroy any lingering atmosphere of civility in the House, to create his own justification for an election – and probably to win it decisively in this single performance as well. He was thinking and feeling on his feet as the speech took its destructive shape.

Sometime before this fateful day, Diefenbaker's friend Patrick Nicholson had come to him with what he called a "hidden report" prepared in February and March 1957 as one of an annual series of confidential documents for ministers on the economic outlook.[116] Nicholson had obtained it through some direct inquiries after Paul Martin had casually told him the previous summer that the Liberal government "had been warned of trouble ahead."[117] Yet now the Liberal Party was blaming the Tories for that trouble. Nicholson smelled Liberal deceit; and once he had the report, he was convinced. It was signed by the associate deputy minister of trade and commerce, Mitchell W. Sharp. As Nicholson pointed out, the report noted symptoms of economic slowdown "that typically are found in the later stages of a cyclical expansion." Costs were rising, export sales were falling, housing construction was declining, investment and consumer spending were likely to be down, unemployment was growing at more than the usual seasonal rates. "This," said the report, "is a disquieting pattern."[118] Nicholson was alarmed.

> I saw at once that this report was political dynamite. I had been looking for something which would substantiate my suspicion that, in charging that the Conservative government had caused the rise in unemployment, the Liberals were once again trying to rewrite history in total disregard of the facts and to their advantage. But instead, I had laid my hands on something of more far-ranging sensation. True, it proved my suspicion to be well-founded. But it went much further. It discredited the former Liberal government for failing to prepare against a recession of whose imminence it had been warned, and which in fact had begun to reveal itself... five months before the Liberal non-precautionary budget and eight months before the general election which had evicted the Liberal government.[119]

Nicholson decided not to use the document himself because it was restricted, but to deliver it to his political friend the prime minister. He explained to Diefenbaker that it would rebut the claim that "Tory times are hard times." Besides, he joked, if Diefenbaker made use of it, Nicholson might escape the charge of revealing official secrets. The prime minister was fascinated as he skimmed through the report, "taking in each page in about four seconds." He thanked Nicholson for his help, and smiled inscrutably.[120]

On January 20 Diefenbaker carried the "hidden report" into the House, and once Mike Pearson had made his mistake, the prime minister knew that its revelation would mark the dramatic climax of his denunciation. He showed no hesitation about using a confidential document offering advice to a previous government. The weapon was too tempting to neglect; the very daring of his act would deepen the shock of his words. "I intend to establish as clearly as the printed word will make possible," he hinted, "that...my hon. friends concealed from the Canadian people the facts."

> Across the way, Mr. Speaker, sit the purveyors of gloom who would endeavour, for political purposes, to panic the Canadian people at this time...You (Mr. Pearson), secured the advice of the economists in your own departments and were advised as to what the situation was in March 1957. This record [the "Canadian Economic Outlook"] was given to each and every one of you... They had a warning...Did they tell us that? No. Mr. Speaker, why did they not reveal this? Why did they not act when the House was sitting in January, February, March and April? They had the information...You

concealed the facts, that is what you did. What plans did you make? Where was that shelf of works that was going to be made available whenever conditions should deteriorate?...When we came into power and looked for the so-called shelf there was not one solitary suggestion of a program available to meet the situation.[121]

Diefenbaker slashed away. For Donald Fleming, "It was his finest hour...It simply overwhelmed Pearson and crushed him."[122] For Paul Martin, this was "one of the greatest devastating speeches" in Canadian history.[123] But for the eloquent CCF member Colin Cameron:

> It was a rather tragic scene we witnessed...I give the Prime Minister full marks for a magnificent hatchet job...And yet I wonder if that is the role which the Prime Minister of Canada should play. I wonder if he should have rushed with such relish into the abattoir...When I saw him bring whole batteries of rhetoric, whole arsenals of guided missiles of vitriol and invective in order to shoot one forlorn sitting duck – a sitting duck, indeed, already crippled with a self-inflicted wound – I wondered if the Prime Minister really believes in the humane slaughter of animals.[124]

After the speech, Pearson crept out of the House in dismay, while Diefenbaker basked excitedly in the cheers of his followers.[125]

An election now seemed inevitable. The prime minister played the line for another ten days. On Saturday morning, February 1, his cabinet approved Diefenbaker's proposal to seek a dissolution of parliament. The main headline in the *Globe and Mail* that morning had already announced it.[126] The prime minister flew to Quebec City to meet Governor General Massey, returned with his approval, and late in the afternoon rose in the House to announce that parliament had been dissolved for an election on March 31 because the government needed a majority to protect itself from Liberal obstruction.[127] The unspoken reason was that Diefenbaker, his cabinet, and his caucus expected to crush the opposition. Forsey learned for a second time that calculations of crude political advantage, not constitutional propriety, ruled Canadian electoral politics. In this belief, Mackenzie King and John Diefenbaker were perfect soulmates.

CHAPTER 9

Visions, Dreams, and Fallen Arrows

1958-1959

FROM THE OUTSET, JOHN DIEFENBAKER'S 1958 CAMPAIGN WAS EXTRAORDI-nary. Allister Grosart planned a whistle-stopping cavalcade by rail across the nation, passing at least twice through each region.[1] It began on February 12 in Winnipeg. Long before the speeches started, Winnipeg Auditorium was jammed with noisy enthusiasts. When the doors to the hall were closed, crowds outside surged and broke them down. The prime minister, surrounded by colleagues, candidates, and camp-followers, was mobbed as he struggled to the podium. That night, and in the weeks to come, the leader's words found resonance in his listeners' hopes and dreams. Diefenbaker's audiences became his worshippers as his passionate phrases floated over them. Merril Menzies's themes of 1957 had been sharpened and simplified. Diefenbaker promised not material prosperity alone, but a vision of northern development that would make the community morally and politically whole. "I saw the opportunity," he later wrote, "of giving leadership in the building of a great nation in which the population of Canada would more than double by the century's end."[2] The country's new riches would be drawn, overwhelmingly, from the vast and unknown northlands of the Shield, the Yukon, and the Northwest Territories. For Diefenbaker, the north was as unpopulated by Native peoples as it had been for the English monarchs who first claimed it. In that assumption, he reflected the common understanding. But he saw a place for Native Canadians, as individuals, within the nation. They were among the neglected and excluded with whom Diefenbaker identified himself.

To reach the territories, Diefenbaker promised funding for a program of "roads to resources" that would open the empty lands first to mapping, surveying, and prospecting – and then to exploitation and settlement. Canada's destiny, he insisted, lay over this northern horizon, and it was a destiny to be shared by all the nation's southern citizens. Diefenbaker was one of them, an "average Canadian." He served them, he dedicated himself to them, and in 1958 they followed him as a man of his word. In a great peroration he swept back the curtain of the tabernacle. "This is the vision, One Canada. One Canada, where Canadians will have preserved to them the control of their own economic and political destiny. Sir John A. Macdonald saw Canada from east to west: he opened the west. I see a new Canada – a Canada of the North... This is the vision!"[3]

Pierre Sévigny was there to hear "this magnificent flurry of eloquence." Diefenbaker, he understood, had succeeded in "grasping the people" to him. "When he had finished that speech, as he was walking to the door, I saw people kneel and kiss his coat. Not one, but many. People were in tears. People were delirious. And this happened many a time after."[4] Eddie Goodman saw the same thing happen elsewhere. "Wherever we went in Ontario during the 1958 election, we were greeted by thousands who literally just wanted to touch the hem of Diefenbaker's garment. In Leamington, a lovely small town in south-western Ontario, more than four thousand people lined up to shake his hand. By the end of the night his hand was so tender that he could not touch it... I have never seen such adulation before or since in political gatherings in this country."[5]

While Diefenbaker led the crusade, his ministers and candidates shared the aura. William Hamilton described Sévigny's introduction of the prime minister in Montreal's Craig Street armoury: "'Levez-vous, levez-vous, saluez votre chef! Rise, rise, salute your chief!' And that whole place, thousands upon thousands of people, jammed into that auditorium, just tore the roof off in a frenzy."[6] For Michael Starr,

> That was the most fantastic election. We ministers were crossing paths back and forth like it was never done before. I spoke at five meetings in Saskat-chewan, starting at ten o'clock at Cutworth. I said, "Who in the world is going to be there at ten o'clock?" The place was jammed, 550 people. It was fantastic.
>
> I went into little places. Smoky Lake, Alberta, where nobody ever saw a minister. Canora, Saskatchewan. Every meeting was jammed; outside there were speakers for those who couldn't get in. It was just fantastic, the most extraordinary experience that I have ever had.
>
> ...
>
> I got the biggest thrill in some of these small places out west. The halls would be filled with people, and sitting there in the front would be the first Ukrainian immigrants with shawls and hands gnarled from work. I would speak for about twenty minutes in English and then I would switch to

Ukrainian and the tears would start to run down their faces. A man came to me one day and he said, "Now I can die, I have met a minister of Ukrainian extraction."

This really swept the West. I don't care who says what won the election: it was the emotional aspect that caught on. Diefenbaker used to come to meetings in that election and the people would mob him, virtually mob him, and he would have to back up. They would be swarming at him just to touch his hand.[7]

In his account of the Diefenbaker years, Peter Newman titled the chapter on this campaign "The Charismatic Rampage of 1958." The prime minister's audiences, he said, "came away lost in a cause they did not fully comprehend."[8] The campaign could hardly be described except in the language of religious revival. Many were swept along; others joined in to be on the winning side. Gordon Churchill wrote to Diefenbaker that "there is no doubt something amazing is happening...The people are out to finish the job they began last summer."[9] The prime minister moved back and forth across the country preaching conversion and commitment. Opposition leaders knew that their prospects were hopeless and struggled lamely to keep up a facade of confidence in the face of small and silent audiences. Too often their words revealed their desperation. Mike Pearson chose the path of humility, admitting Liberal failures and setting his "quiet reasoned approach" against his opponent's "agitated eloquence." That only seemed to make his partisans cringe.[10] When he called Diefenbaker's "roads to resources" a scheme of construction "from igloo to igloo," Diefenbaker pounced on him again for his Liberal condescension.[11] While campaign contributions rolled into Conservative accounts, the opposition parties remained destitute. Grosart had a national campaign fund of $2.5 million to dispense (more than twice that of 1957), and distributed $6000 each to constituency organizations in every province.[12]

"The vision" first proclaimed in Winnipeg quickly became "the Vision," something almost tangible that Diefenbaker called forth each night. "Join with me," he implored his audiences, "catch the Vision." "Everywhere I go I see that uplift in people's eyes that comes from raising their sights to see the Vision of Canada in days ahead." The campaign had become a mission of healing. "Instead of the hopelessness and fear the Liberals generate," the Chief explained, "we have given faith; instead of desperation we offer inspiration."[13] A simple campaign poster contained black footprints and the slogan "Follow John!"[14] And the electorate responded, in the cities, in the small towns, in the prairies – even in Quebec, where Maurice Duplessis threw the Union Nationale machine into the campaign to keep up with his own voters. "We had a stopover at Three Rivers last night," Diefenbaker wrote to Duff Roblin on February 23, "where some 3200 sat down to dinner. It is almost unbelievable, the feeling that exists in Quebec among our followers. I don't forget there has been optimism expressed in the past as to the outcome, but this time the leaders, without exception, tell me that they have never seen anything like this in fifty years."[15] Two weeks later Diefenbaker's secretary, Marion Wagner, wrote to Derek Bedson from the prime minister's train that he had been mobbed during a short stopover in Montreal: "They were almost hysterical and just wouldn't let him put a foot off the train...Actually it was a bit frightening."[16] Everywhere, as the winter campaign concluded, Diefenbaker's ministers predicted massive majorities.

After his third trip of the campaign into the province of Quebec, Diefenbaker flew back to Prince Albert on election eve "in buoyant spirits." Olive was with him, stoically disguising the back pain that had dogged her throughout the winter. The prime minister followed his morning round of mainstreeting on election day, rested in the afternoon, and began to receive reports of "a smashing victory," as the *Globe* reported, "while he relaxed in a hotel room bed in his underwear."[17]

The victory was unprecedented. Diefenbaker and the Tories had won 208 seats (with majorities of seats and votes in every province except Newfoundland), the Liberals only 48, the CCF 8, and Social Credit none. In Quebec, Conservatives took 50 percent of the popular vote and fifty of seventy-five seats; in Saskatchewan, 51 percent of the vote and sixteen of seventeen seats. The country had bonded with its new Chief. When Diefenbaker spoke to the nation on television that night, he told his audience that "the Conservative Party has become a truly national party composed of all the people of Canada of all races united in the concept of one Canada...This is a victory...not for any one person of the party but rather a victory for the kind of Canadianism in which we all believe." He compared his circumstances – puzzlingly – to those of Abraham Lincoln at his first inaugural, and called, in Lincoln's words, for "intelligence, patriotism, Christianity and a firm reliance on Him who has never yet forsaken this favoured land." With the prayers of Canadians to aid him, he hoped for "that wisdom that comes from Divine guidance."[18]

On election night, Pearson cabled Diefenbaker offering his congratulations and wishes for "health and strength" in face of the heavy duties of office. Next morning the prime minister acknowledged "your warm and generous telegram" in more than routine terms. "Olive and I were deeply moved by your kind personal reference...May I extend to Marian and yourself our best wishes for the years ahead and my own assurance that I shall ever hope to maintain that friendly personal relationship which has always existed between us and which transcends whatever differences there may be between the public roles we are individually called upon to fill."[19]

The same day an avid election watcher in Washington, Vice President Richard Nixon, wrote to Diefenbaker:

> I want to take this opportunity to congratulate you on your overwhelming victory at the polls yesterday.
>
> I, personally, could not have been more pleased that you have now earned a majority mandate from the Canadian people. Now that the election is over, I assume I can make that statement without being charged with attempting to interfere in Canadian political affairs!
>
> As I told you when you were in Washington, I followed your first campaign with great interest. There is no question but that history will record that you are one of the truly great political campaigners of our time. The fact that within the space of just a few months you were able to do what you did against what appeared to be insurmountable odds, is an achievement which has seldom been equalled in history.[20]

Diefenbaker was flattered and returned the compliment. "I need not say," he replied, "how much your reference to me as a campaigner means to me, coming from one whose record merits the accolade of the greatest campaigner of our time."[21]

THE DIEFENBAKERS FLEW OFF IN EARLY APRIL FOR A SHORT HOLIDAY AT THE MID Ocean Club in Bermuda, where Olive could rest her back and John could reflect on his great triumph. The victory – and the widespread praise that followed it – had confirmed his sense of destiny. "It was an interesting study," he wrote to a university president, "to watch Canadians in all political faiths during the campaign respond to the challenge of a greater Canada which in reality is but an extension northwards of Sir John A. Macdonald's national policy."[22] Yet he was also unnerved by the overwhelming display of confidence and expectation implied in the election result. To Elmer, he wrote: "When I think of the tremendous problems facing me in the days ahead I am frightened but – never dismayed. The rest will make it possible to face up to them."[23] In principle, he recognized the dangers of his good fortune. "One thing which must be guarded against is complacency and its twin arrogance, which are often the aftermath of great political victory. As for me I intend to maintain as close a relationship with the people as is possible and to ask various outstanding Canadians to give me the benefit of their views from time to time."[24] He wrote to ask his Conservative colleagues in the new House of Commons "that you let me have your opinions on urgent national problems as soon as you can conveniently do so but not later than two weeks from now."[25]

With the first Conservative majority in Quebec since 1887, the prime minister was widely expected to broaden his cabinet representation from that province. This would be a necessary step towards consolidating support in Quebec and assuring "as close a relationship with the people as is possible" among French-speaking voters. But Diefenbaker fumbled. Among the new Quebec members there were several with impressive records.[26] Diefenbaker asked his cabinet about potential Quebec ministers from the new crop of members, and in mid-April William Hamilton offered two suggestions, both negative: avoid naming Pierre Sévigny, on the grounds that both English- and French-speaking supporters would resent him as "personally self-seeking and not too competent, with a social-climbing wife who has done nothing whatsoever to make people like either of them better"; and delay any offer to Charles-Edouard Campeau, an accomplished former director of planning for Montreal, until he had gained some "feeling of this government's attitude" on patronage questions. After that, Hamilton thought Campeau might be suitable for public works.[27] Diefenbaker had little basis for judging his Quebec members and hesitated for four more weeks. In mid-May he appointed Raymond O'Hurley, an English-speaking former timber-grader, as minister of defence production, and Henri Courtemanche, deputy Speaker during the short parliament of 1957–58, as secretary of state. Neither could handle his role, and neither added political credit to the government. As in 1957, none of the new Quebec members was brought into cabinet. Meanwhile, Léon Balcer's rage grew in the obscurity of the solicitor general's office, and Paul Comtois read newspapers beneath the cabinet table to avoid discussion in a language he could not grasp.[28] Without any trusted advisers from Quebec, Diefenbaker relied upon his correspondence secretary Claude Gauthier, his English-speaking cronies, and a few French-speaking correspondents for his limited knowledge of the province. He seemed unaware that his response to Quebec's support might be inadequate, yet in that initial misstep he probably lost the chance for another parliamentary majority. He could never make up for it.[29]

The prime minister and his ministers recognized that a large caucus would be difficult to manage: "You simply couldn't give all that number of private members adequate attention, couldn't give them sufficient responsibility," recalled Howard Green.[30] Soon after the election Diefenbaker told cabinet "that, in order to engage the interests of the large group of new government supporters in the House, thought should be given to the setting up of committees early in the session to investigate a number of problems." He asked ministers for suggestions, and when the House reconvened in May, the government announced its intention to create two new standing committees on estimates and on veterans affairs as well as a select committee on broadcasting.[31]

Despite his initial good intentions, ministers and members saw Diefenbaker's attitude to caucus change. He attended less often and he neglected to consult any longer about the details of legislation. According to Richard Bell, "caucuses became John Diefenbaker telling of his readings from Mackenzie King. At every caucus, we were regaled with something from Mackenzie King, who had become, for some reason or other that nobody could quite understand, John's great hero."[32] This was, for Diefenbaker, a chance to display an old admiration and to identify himself with another master of the trade.

For the short run, the government had overwhelming public support. Its popularity in the polls continued to grow for six months in the afterglow of the election. But for the longer run, confidence would have to be maintained by new policies, clearly and simply defended. The easy reforms – adjustments to Liberal welfare programs, regional aid, and agricultural support – had occurred during the short parliament. Now the Tories would have to give content to the "Vision" and show that their plans for the country made sense. The prime minister's congenital caution, disorganization, and shallow intellectual focus weighed against that likelihood, and no previous experience had prepared him for this success. Once confirmed in his majority, Diefenbaker gradually fell victim to his pride, which had always coexisted tenuously alongside his insecurity. The great victory fed and infected it. Two ministers noted the effects: Douglas Harkness believed that the victory "persuaded him that he was in an unassailable position. He was able to persuade himself that his views were always correct and that he could carry the Canadian people with him." Donald Fleming observed that "1958 undoubtedly confirmed Dief's opinion that we all owed our advancement to him." Diefenbaker, he wrote, "could not bear the thought of losing ground," and acted henceforth as though he was running a perpetual election campaign.[33] His worth, his self-confidence, and his government's justification all depended on the sustaining force of concentrated public adulation. He alone had created that adulation, and he alone could maintain it through his gifts of communion with the people. If it failed, that could only be because he had failed – or because he had been betrayed and conspired against. He had always resisted any admission of personal failure. Victory made him more isolated, more vulnerable, less able to share leadership with his cabinet team, and more dependent on what he could read in the winds of public taste. Within months of March 31 there were worrying hints of troubles to come.

THE FIRST OF THESE HINTS HAD A SURPRISING SOURCE. THE NATIONAL GALLERY OF Canada, whose collections had begun in 1880, had been buying European as well as Canadian art since 1907. In recent postwar years its director, Alan Jarvis, had vigorously pursued additions to the European collection with the blessing of the Liberal government. In February 1958 the gallery's trustees sought cabinet's permission to purchase the Breughel painting *Landscape with Christ Appearing to the Apostles at the Sea of Tiberias* at a price of $350,000, from funds previously appropriated. None of the Diefenbaker cabinet had perceptible reputations as patrons of the arts, and the party had criticized the previous government for its extravagant spending. With an election on their minds, they preferred to defer a decision on the gallery's recommendation.[34] On May 2 Davie Fulton, as the acting minister responsible for the gallery, brought a new recommendation to cabinet, asking approval to purchase both the Breughel and a Lorenzo Monaco at a total price of about $450,000. After some critical comment about the price of the Breughel, the purchase was authorized.[35] Five days later Fulton reported that funds had not, after all, been appropriated for the Breughel, and would have to be authorized in a supplementary estimate if the purchase were to proceed. Cabinet supported the minister's decision to suspend negotiations for the painting.[36] Three weeks later, after Ellen Fairclough had become the minister, Fulton told cabinet that agents for the gallery had already purchased both paintings before cabinet's decision to halt the purchase, and that lawsuits might result from the cabinet's reversal. He said that Jarvis's statements on the issue "appeared to be inconsistent," that Jarvis "was not too knowlegeable with respect to matters of finance and administration," and that he should return to Canada at once to clean up the "mess." Cabinet agreed.[37] After several more discussions in which blame for the affair was focused on Jarvis, cabinet confirmed its refusal to provide funds for the purchases despite the likelihood of lawsuits. Jarvis resigned as director of the gallery, and – despite the government's claims of financial prudence – appearances suggested that the ministry had been inept, philistine, and indifferent to its own and the gallery's reputations for integrity.[38]

THE NEW PARLIAMENT OPENED ON MAY 12, 1958. THE PREVIOUS SPEAKER OF THE House, Roland Michener – who had gained respect and been re-elected as an MP – was generally expected to be named Speaker once more. But the prime minister, believing that Michener had deferred too much to the opposition, asked cabinet to consider the implications carefully. Would Michener's re-election promote the notion of a permanent speakership – which Diefenbaker had favoured in opposition – and offend Quebec? Ministers thought not, and Michener was acclaimed with warm support from Liberal and CCF members. As the twenty-fifth parliament progressed, Diefenbaker's patience with Michener's conduct of the House quickly faded. Several times the sparks flew between them, and Diefenbaker privately berated his ministers for imposing Michener on him.[39]

The new House was dominated on both sides of the aisle by government members, while the opposition occupied little more than a fringe immediately to the Speaker's left. Opposite the prime minister sat Mike Pearson, Paul Martin, Jack Pickersgill, and Lionel Chevrier, the lonely survivors of Liberal governments past. The new House leader of the CCF, Hazen Argue, and his tiny band of seven sat beside them, closest to the Speaker.

Given the visionary tone of the Conservative campaign and the scale of the triumph, the speech from the throne seemed remarkably prosaic. The cabinet's preoccupation with unemployment was reflected in plans for expanded public works grants, extended aid for house building, and a six-week extension of unemployment insurance benefits for seasonally unemployed workers. At the same time, the speech warned of the need for public spending restraint to contain inflation. A new regulatory agency would be created for radio and television. Legislation for a bill of rights would be introduced during the session. The parliamentary committee system would be expanded, and a system of simultaneous translation would be installed in the House of Commons. The government's proposed Commonwealth Trade and Economic Conference would take place in Montreal in September. This was no proclamation of a new age, but rather a signal of the government's essential caution.[40]

Fleming's first budget reached the House, after long gestation, on June 17. It too was a product of caution. Fleming had guided its preparation with obsessive care and concern for secrecy. "The papers which I was obliged to take home at nights," he wrote, "I actually took into the bed with me." The budget speech, delivered to an evening session in a crowded House, was the longest, most detailed, and most piously solemn in Canadian history. "I spoke for over two hours," Fleming recalled, "and finished as strongly as I began. I did not take even one sip of water throughout." Faced with the unexpected pressures of an economic slowdown and the previous year's tax reductions and increases in spending, the minister announced a small deficit of $39 million for 1957–58 and an anticipated deficit of $648 million for 1958–59 – the largest ever predicted. Fleming was unhappy with that prospect, offered only limited tax reductions, and admitted that the economic situation restricted the government's options. But he ended with the confident claim that "we have not veered and shall not veer from our unshaken belief in the shining future of Canada."[41] The budget was mildly expansionary and seemed carefully balanced for the circumstances.

Fleming retained the limelight in the following month, when the government made a massive intervention in the bond market with a conversion loan to refinance the outstanding issues of wartime Victory Bonds, totalling $6.4 billion – or almost two-thirds of the national debt, all due to mature before 1967. Soon after the budget speech, the governor of the Bank of Canada, James Coyne, proposed to Fleming that the whole of this Victory Bond debt should be managed by a single longer-term conversion, at attractive interest rates, to be launched almost at once through a highly publicized promotion campaign. The minister and his deputy accepted the scheme, and Fleming took it to the prime minister for his approval before submission to cabinet. Diefenbaker agreed and set a date for cabinet discussion, while Fleming proceeded with arrangements, conducted in utmost secrecy, to launch the conversion. At cabinet on July 11 Fleming introduced his plan, but was confronted by "several western ministers" who objected to the prospect of higher interest rates and certain cash adjustments. Fleming recalled: "The opposition was so outspoken that Dief began to wilt and weaken. Instead of lending the plan his support he withdrew to the neutral sidelines. I was appalled at the situation, because with Diefenbaker's full approval we had commenced calling in the organizers to meet in Ottawa. I was irretrievably committed to the plan, as Diefenbaker had committed himself, but I could not withdraw my support as he appeared about to do."[42]

Diefenbaker played briefly for time. Howard Green and Davie Fulton were instructed to meet with Coyne and representatives of the financial community, and to report their judgments to cabinet the next morning. Fleming prepared to resign if his commitment was not sustained, but to his relief, Green and Fulton gave their support and cabinet approved the conversion loan. It was launched with Fleming's announcement in the House on July 14, with a two-month period for conversion. That evening Fleming and Diefenbaker promoted the loan in a national television broadcast, Diefenbaker in English, Fleming in French. No word of Diefenbaker's hesitation and the cabinet's division emerged, but for Fleming the affair "inevitably shook my confidence in the reliability of Diefenbaker's promises of support. I never fully accepted them after that."[43]

But Fleming did not fully reveal the source of his disquiet. The evening of the loan announcement, Diefenbaker and Gordon Churchill met with Fleming to tell him – according to Churchill's account – "that now he had got what he wanted, he would have to be more careful in saying 'no' to some of the other worthwhile projects coming before cabinet." Churchill believed that Fleming would now have to accept the western ministers' package of financial assistance to prairie farmers.[44]

By September 15 about 90 percent of Victory Bonds had been converted. Fleming described the campaign as "not only the largest financial operation in Canada's history, but the greatest success."[45] The market was more equivocal, and holders of the new bonds began to sell at discounted prices. For a short time the Bank of Canada bought bonds to support the price, but abandoned this policy in October rather than create an expanding flow of new money. In the following year the bank began to explain its new monetary restraint by referring to an excessive growth of the money supply in 1958. As high rates of unemployment continued into the 1960s, the bank's restraint became an increasing irritant for Diefenbaker and his government. What had initially seemed a bold and successful financial operation became, before long, an unanticipated source of difficulty for the cabinet. The loan decision, and Diefenbaker's hesitation, reflected a still-implicit conflict between the restrictive approach of James Coyne and the bank, at that time supported by his minister Donald Fleming, and the expansionist instincts of the prime minister. By 1961 Fleming had shifted sides, and the irritant had festered into an infection requiring surgery. In retrospect, Merril Menzies believed that "Mr Diefenbaker knew perfectly well that he had been sold a terrible bill of goods, very much against the interests of Canada." As a matter of convenient housekeeping, the cabinet had accepted the conversion loan, with its restrictive consequences, at a moment when that was bound to discourage economic recovery. "This," said Menzies, "demonstrates something that I've often felt about Mr Diefenbaker – that when his experience and technical knowledge in the sometimes complex and very disputatious field of economics weren't quite adequate to analyse a problem or a policy, his instinctive feel about it was often right on. When he listened to his instincts, he was right. But when he listened to his advisers during this critical period of 1958 and 1959, he was almost entirely wrong."[46]

Meanwhile, Fleming faced, and acceded reluctantly to, the pressures for fresh assistance to prairie farmers. A series of transportation and grain-growing subsidies were proposed to cabinet, with Diefenbaker's adamant support, by early August. Fleming warned cabinet of the increasing deficit, hinted at the need for an increase in taxes, and again considered resignation. But before the end of August he had accepted the cabinet's approval of two measures of supplementary spending totalling $115 million, to provide for acreage subsidies and for foreign loans for the purchase of Canadian wheat and flour. Fleming rationalized his loyalty by noting that his big project, the Commonwealth Trade and Economic Conference, was about to open in Montreal.[47]

The conference was the culmination of Diefenbaker's 1957 campaign to promote the Commonwealth. Its preparation rested with Fleming, Churchill, and Macdonnell, and civil servants from several departments. The massive meeting, with more than 160 delegates from fifteen independent or "emerging" nations, lasted for two weeks in early September. As chairman of the conference, Fleming defined its purposes as the expansion of trade, the development of resources, and the strengthening of economic, cultural, and spiritual ties among the Commonwealth's member nations. With so broad and unspecific a mandate, it was above all an exercise in mutual education, good fellowship, and managed propaganda. Any possible subjects of disagreement, such as the convertibility of sterling or Diefenbaker's proposal for a Commonwealth bank, were excised from the agenda during the early planning stages. "There was no bargaining at the conference," Fleming wrote, "indeed not even a semblance of it." At the end, the conference produced a 9000-word report announcing a major Commonwealth scholarship program financed largely by the United Kingdom and Canada, improved international telephone services, and a new Commonwealth economic council to meet annually. Coincidentally, Britain announced the removal of some import restrictions on agricultural products. All delegations left Montreal in good spirits, lauding the conference as a beacon for mankind and patting each other, and themselves, comfortably on the backs for their cooperative efforts.[48]

DESPITE HIS BUSY SCHEDULE OF CABINET MEETINGS, ALMOST DAILY APPEARANCES IN the House for Question Period, and ceremonials for visiting VIPs – during early summer there were visits by Prince Bernhard of the Netherlands, President Heuss of Germany, Prime Minister Nkrumah of Ghana, Prime Minister Macmillan, and President Eisenhower – the prime minister could not resist taking up a steady flow of invitations for speeches and honorary degrees. He was working long hours, eating well, and putting on weight. "What a life it is to be Prime Minister!" he told his mother jokingly in May after "a hot and heavy couple of days in the House – trading punches with Mr. Pearson and enjoying myself in doing it." In June there were speeches to the Zionist Assembly and the International Conference of Baptist Youth in Toronto; honorary degree ceremonies at Wesleyan University in Connecticut and Bishop's University in Lennoxville, Quebec; the Macmillan visit; and a day of celebrations on June 21 to mark the first anniversary of Conservative power. "I hope," he wrote about the Baptist meeting in Maple Leaf Gardens, "in this case I will have a speech ready and not be in the position I usually am in being unprepared in every regard until the last moment." The week following that address he spoke in Manitoba, Saskatchewan, Quebec, and Ontario and reported to his mother that "it has been a long and trying week and I am glad there are no more ahead." Ten days later, after three days with the Eisenhowers and some late nights of anxiety over British and American military intervention in the Middle East, Diefenbaker wrote that "Olive and I are not taking any more social engagements than are absolutely necessary. I don't think I could do my job as Prime Minister if I were to accept five percent of the social engagements."[49] But honorary degrees were another matter: the offers were piling up, and in September and October he accepted four more, at the University of British Columbia, Toronto, the University of New Brunswick, and Laval.[50] Speeches, too, remained irresistible and unprepared. October 2: "I haven't got any kind of a speech that is good, but I will have to make the best of it." October 18: "Last evening I spoke at a dinner here to the Press Gallery – and as usual didn't have a speech ready, so had to rush one into existence at the last moment." October 22: "Altogether I am piled up with work. We will be returning tonight and I have to get ready for tomorrow when I speak to the Women's Canadian Club here."[51] Very occasionally, the burden of an unprepared speech was too much for him: "I was supposed to speak to the University Professors meeting here this noon hour but decided a few minutes ago not to go."[52]

In 1958 the prime minister pursued his interest – partly stimulated by citizens eager to offer homage – in promoting the record of his Bannerman ancestors. "Tomorrow," he wrote to his mother in September, "I will be in the Scotch settlement district of Simcoe County and will have pictures taken of your grandparents' (the Bannermans) graves, both of whom lived to be very old...I will have a restoration job done on the stones."[53]

Faced with his killing schedule, Diefenbaker welcomed the prospect of occasional retreat to a country home at Harrington Lake. The house, lake, and surrounding forests – about fifteen miles from Ottawa in Gatineau Park

– had been purchased in 1951 by the Federal District Commission. After a few years of summer rentals that failed to cover the costs of maintenance, the house had been offered by the commission in 1957 as an official residence or government guest house. Bryce conducted informal soundings among his senior colleagues in Finance and External Affairs, and eventually guided the proposal for a prime ministerial country residence through cabinet.[54] On the assurance that the costs of reconditioning and refurnishing would be minimal, Diefenbaker had accepted the idea – though with a briefly lingering sense of guilt at the thought of such luxury enjoyed at public expense. "I suppose there will be some criticisms but as it is not being used to any extent and was to be the Prime Minister's summer home I cannot see how there can be any objection...The only reason it was not used by Mr. St. Laurent was that he preferred to be close to his home in Quebec City."[55]

Olive and John spent their first weekend at Harrington Lake in mid-May, "the most restful day and a half that I have spent in over a year and a half." The fishing made it perfect for Diefenbaker. "I went fishing and caught four speckled trout," he told his mother. "I have never tasted anything better than those trout. They weighed from 1 1/4 to well over 2 lbs. and you may be sure I will be out fishing a great deal during the summer." Harrington, he decided, was "a wonderful place," despite the black fly bites "which I didn't feel because I was so interested in the fish!"[56] He was there again for weekends in July and August, and for more interludes of fishing through the rest of his term. Sometimes that meant only an hour or two at "the country place," to cast his line in the silence.

THE PRIME MINISTER'S DECISION TO JOIN THE UNITED STATES IN AN INTEGRATED North American air defence system, taken hurriedly in the summer of 1957 without cabinet discussion, became the first major source of controversy for the new government. During the autumn of 1957 questions in the press and from the leader of the opposition alerted Diefenbaker to the political implications of the oral agreement. During his visit to Washington in October he sought and obtained President Eisenhower's confirmation that the use of NORAD forces would require prior consultation with both governments. Soon afterwards, he directed George Pearkes to discuss a joint statement with the United States that would confirm such political control.[57]

In November 1957 Diefenbaker made a statement to the House on Canadian-American defence cooperation. It revealed little beyond claiming that the NORAD agreement had been made within NATO and that it simply fulfilled arrangements made by the previous Liberal government.[58] He did nothing to explain its nature beyond describing NORAD as a "comprehensive air defence system...against the manned bomber."[59] Critics remained ignorant about the chain of command, the extent of civil control, the Canadian units assigned to the joint command, and the potential loss of Canadian sovereignty involved. Privately, Diefenbaker suspected that Pearson's questions on the subject had been based on leaks from the Department of External Affairs – and his suspicion remained, despite the doubts of his advisers Robert Bryce and Basil Robinson, and the absence of any evidence to sustain it.[60]

At the NATO heads of governmment meeting in December, Diefenbaker – to the surprise of his aides – described NORAD as "an integral part of our NATO military structure" that would report to the NATO Council "in a manner similar to that followed by other NATO military commands." A few days later he seemed to tell the House of Commons that NORAD would simply inform NATO routinely of its activities. "Diefenbaker was not above being deliberately ambiguous," wrote Robinson, "and it seems quite likely that he was aiming to work both sides of the equation, using fuzzy language as a bridge between opposing aims."[61] A link with NATO might reassure Canadians that the government was not dealing bilaterally with the Americans; but the vagueness of his claim would not discomfort Washington, which opposed any intrusion of multilateral military planning into North America.

The scholar Jon McLin noted later that Diefenbaker's November statement "was an early example of a Diefenbaker trait which was to show itself on later occasions: he found it easier and/or more congenial to attack the former government...than to explain what his own government was doing."[62] Comments by George Pearkes and Sidney Smith compounded the initial confusion and suggested, accurately, that there was little coordination between their departments on the subject. In January 1958 Pearkes promised an opportunity for debate once a detailed exchange of notes had occurred between the two governments; but when Smith tabled the exchange in May he denied debate on the ground that NORAD was no more than "an amplification of and extension under" the NATO treaty.[63] The next day, in response to widespread criticism, Diefenbaker reversed the government's position and offered debate on a resolution of support for the agreement.

The government's initial reluctance slighted parliament in a way inconsistent with Diefenbaker's previous claims. The approach seemed to arise from the prime minister's own uncertainty about the undertaking and from his confusion about its meaning – a confusion he could never escape. The debate on NORAD, when it finally came in June 1958, only deepened the muddle.

The agreement itself offered this rationale for integrated air defences:

> The advent of nuclear weapons, the great improvements in the means of effecting their delivery, and the requirements of the air defence control systems demand rapid decisions to keep pace with the speed and tempo of technological development. To counter the threat and to achieve maximum effectiveness of the air defence system, defensive operations must commence as early as possible and enemy forces must be kept constantly engaged. Arrangements for the coordination of national plans requiring consultation between national commanders before implementation had become inadequate in the face of a possible sudden attack with little or no warning. It was essential, therefore, to have in existence in peacetime an organization, including the weapons, facilities and command structure which could operate at the outset of hostilities in accordance with a single air defence plan approved in advance by the national authorities.[64]

The governments agreed that the integration of forces "increases the importance of the fullest possible consultation between the two governments on all matters affecting the joint defence of North America, and that defence co-operation between them can be worked out on a mutually satisfactory basis only if such consultation is regularly and consistently undertaken." Air defence plans were to be jointly approved in advance; the NORAD command would be responsible to both the Canadian and the American chiefs of staff, and through them to the two governments. Planning was intended to allow for "rapid implementation in an emergency," which might include "temporary reinforcement from one area to another, including the crossing of the international boundary, to meet operational requirements."[65]

When he moved acceptance of the agreement, Diefenbaker insisted that he wished to avoid controversy. His party had supported Liberal defence policy in opposition, and he expected the Liberal opposition to do the same. But he cloaked his words in obscurity. He insisted that NORAD was an outgrowth of the NATO chain of command involving no loss of sovereignty – and in the same breath recalled that no one had complained of a loss of sovereignty when Canadian forces were placed under NATO's authority in Europe. "Survival," he said, "knows none of the fineries of a nationalism that used to exist."[66] The country, it seemed, had both given up and not given up sovereign authority.

Canadian air officers, Diefenbaker explained, would act in NORAD under Canadian rules of engagement adopted by the previous government in

1951. If Canada and the United States were attacked, the prime minister assured the House that there would be "close and frequent consultation" at the political level. "That is taking place, and I will go no further than to say that the present provision for consultation makes consultation almost instantaneous." Henceforth it would occur both in peacetime and in wartime. He recognized that "the time available for consultation in an emergency may be very short." That put a premium on earlier discussion between the two nations about the circumstances "which could conceivably lead to this country being committed to war." But here his language once more grew tangled: consultation was meant "to ensure the maintenance and preservation of our joint co-operation to the end that we shall, as a result of the achievement of this agreement – again, as I said a moment ago, without the loss of the sovereignty in our country – be joined together for our preservation and the maintenance of those things which are our common heritage in this country."[67] If the agreement seemed relatively straightforward, Diefenbaker's defence of it was not. The *Globe and Mail* described it as "an ambiguously worded excursion into the maze."[68]

Pearson followed Diefenbaker in debate. He agreed that continental defence should not be a subject of dispute, nor should Canada regret a loss of sovereignty that was intended to pool Canada's strength with that of her friends. For the Liberal Party, the issues were "the doubts, ambiguities, confusions and contradictions in regard to the meaning of what has been done." The government's handling of the affair had been "a comedy of confusion and contradiction" from the beginning.[69]

Pearson charged that the arrangement had emerged backwards. It should have been discussed in the cabinet defence committee and cabinet, negotiated with the United States and signed, discussed and approved by the House of Commons, and only then put into operation. Instead, it was "brought hastily into existence" without cabinet discussion, and announced without the completion of any agreement. If, as the prime minister claimed, NORAD had simply taken over Canada's previously existing role in North American defence, then "there was no justification for the kind of haste, the kind of sloppy procedures" that had occurred. He denied that the Liberal government had been on the point of agreement when it lost power. Although there had been military discussions, no consideration had ever taken place in the defence committee or in cabinet. The issue was deferred before the election because it could not have been examined responsibly by ministers during a campaign. Pearson – as the only minister aside from the defence minister who had seen any of the documents – realized that it needed extreme care.

"Indeed, there had been developments in the field of air defence, arising out of ballistic missiles, which counselled caution and counselled the most careful kind of consideration. I suggest to my right hon. friend that this agreement did not get that kind of consideration."[70] He pointed out, correctly, that NORAD "has no organic connection with NATO at all." Its commanders were not appointed by and did not report to NATO, and the secretary general of NATO, Paul-Henri Spaak, had himself denied the connection.

Pearson could find no answer in the prime minister's statement to questions about the authority of NORAD and its relation to the two governments. Who would be consulted in emergencies? Who would control Canadian squadrons? Could information from NORAD launch US Strategic Air Command bombers towards Russia's borders? The leader of the opposition focused widespread press and public concern about the agreement, and about Diefenbaker's competence in entering into it. His questions remained unanswered.

When debate ended, the Liberal opposition joined the government in support of the resolution, and the issue died. Its legacy was dual. On the one hand, Diefenbaker's handling of the affair had permitted gratuitous conflict between two ministries and unease in parliament. And when the criticism he faced had bruised him unexpectedly, his response had been to blame his opponents rather than to clarify the new relationship. On the other hand, Canada had made its commitment to partnership in North American air defence "in a big way," with military, political, and economic consequences that no one could yet foresee.[71] Nine Canadian fighter squadrons were assigned to the NORAD command. In July the prime minister announced the creation of a joint Canada–US cabinet committee on defence policy to carry forward consultation at the political level.[72]

DURING THE SHORT TERM OF HIS FIRST PARLIAMENT, DIEFENBAKER HAD FOUND little time for concentration on foreign policy. Yet his interest in an international role was intense. He believed in the value of personal diplomacy, and looked forward to new occasions for travel and meetings with other leaders. In June and July 1958 Diefenbaker welcomed the British prime minister, Harold Macmillan, and the American president, Dwight Eisenhower, to Ottawa and reinforced his friendly relations with both leaders. Once he had his parliamentary majority, Diefenbaker also decided on a round-the-world tour to Europe and the Asian Commonwealth, modelled closely on that of Louis St Laurent in 1955. Diefenbaker would be joined by Olive; his brother, Elmer; his new private secretary, Gowan Guest; his foreign policy adviser, Basil

Robinson; his Ottawa doctor and fellow Conservative MP, P.B. Rynard; and his press officer, James Nelson.[73]

Summer and fall 1958 was a time of international tension. The United States, Britain, and the Soviet Union continued their nuclear weapons testing in the atmosphere and their development of long- and medium-range missiles. In September the Soviet Union renewed its intermittent pressure to end four-power occupation of Berlin and to absorb the divided city wholly into the German Democratic Republic. In the West, Berlin was seen as the most likely flashpoint for war. In July a military coup in Iraq and Syrian-sponsored challenges to Lebanon and Jordan had brought intervention by American forces in Lebanon and British forces in Jordan in support of their beleaguered governments. Those interventions had prompted the expected Soviet bluster, as well as complaints from France that its traditional role in the Mideast had been ignored. The possibility of a great-power summit to discuss nuclear tests, arms inspection, and other points of tension was being promoted by both the British and the Soviet leaders. The new French prime minister, Charles de Gaulle, had written to Macmillan and Eisenhower expressing unsettling thoughts about a NATO triumvirate of the United States, the United Kingdom, and France which would diminish the influence of other members of the alliance. In a period of continuing Cold War, the international balance seemed particularly uncertain as new weapons proliferated, regimes changed, and leaders tested one another's intentions.

Diefenbaker hoped to learn more about the state of the world in consultations with Harold Macmillan, Charles de Gaulle, and Konrad Adenauer, as well as to establish his own presence in the wider world. In London, the prime minister wished to cement his personal links with Macmillan, to promote Commonwealth trade, and to reassure himself about the protection of Canadian interests as the United Kingdom moved closer to Europe. In Paris, he sought to discourage de Gaulle's NATO initiative, with the support, especially, of Britain and Germany. In Asia, Diefenbaker looked for personal education – about Commonwealth aid and trade, the new military regime in Pakistan, Indo-Pakistani relations, and Asian attitudes to Communist China. Everywhere, he wanted to gather fresh impressions and make new friendships.

Robinson wrote to External Affairs several weeks before departure that "the atmosphere in the prime minister's office was like that of a family preparing for a tourist excursion around the world." Believing that "there was still an ad hoc character to much of his participation in the process of reaching decisions" about foreign policy, Robinson worried that Diefenbaker would pay insufficient attention to his briefing papers – which, according to External's habit, were voluminous.[74] He also had warnings for Canadian diplomats on Diefenbaker's path: "The Prime Minister is an early riser and is generally in particularly good form early in the morning. That is the time when we...try to get decisions from him and this becomes less easy as the day wears on...It is a cast-iron rule that he likes to go to bed as early as possible and from all points of view this is desirable since if he tires he tends to be difficult." Olive, he reported, was "quite militant about rest and relaxation time for him." Since Diefenbaker was "a little bit harder of hearing than he will admit," he preferred meeting in small groups, and speaking to the person sitting on his right side.[75]

Diefenbaker departed from Ottawa airport on October 28 with ceremonial good wishes from members of his cabinet and the diplomatic corps. In New York he spoke to the Pilgrims Society and met with the secretary general of the United Nations, Dag Hammarskjöld. Afterwards, Diefenbaker told Robinson that he was particularly concerned to see the summary of his conversation with Hammarskjöld before its dispatch to the Department of External Affairs; he did not want anything "political" to be reported. During the flight to London, Robinson was told that the prime minister was "agitated" on the subject. Robinson knew that Diefenbaker's mistrust of the department was again the issue.

> I went to the back of the plane, where the prime minister and Mrs Diefenbaker were sitting, and told him I had heard of his concern and assured him that reports on his meetings would not be sent to Ottawa without his approval...This immediately caused him to throw aside some papers, fix me with a very severe eye, and say: "I'll tell you frankly. What I am worried about is that Pearson is going to find out what is in these reports 24 hours after they reach Ottawa." I said that I simply did not believe this sort of thing was going on, but he went on at length in the same vein. When we got to London, the telegram was dispatched in slightly revised form to Ottawa and New York.[76]

Robinson also wrote privately to the new undersecretary, Norman Robertson, to say that "the immediate problem is that in view of the Prime Minister's instructions, it will be difficult if not impossible to keep the Department informed on what the Prime Minister actually says in his conversations...In the longer run, the problem is, of course, worrying since it illustrates the depth of the suspicion with which the Department is regarded." But Diefenbaker seemed to forget the incident; Robinson's fears were groundless.[77] The prime minister seemed simply to be reminding Robinson, in his particular way, about who was in charge. He might have been less polite if he had known what Robinson was reporting privately.

Diefenbaker began his seven-week odyssey in London on October 30. He was welcomed attentively by Harold Macmillan, who had been briefed for the visit by the British high commissioner in Ottawa. Diefenbaker, the high commissioner reported,

> is inclined to view affairs in personal terms and he is susceptible to personal influences...there is little in the way of articulate political design in Mr. Diefenbaker's attitude to the tour. His mind does not work that way. He tends to grope his way towards the understanding and handling of problems by drawing on personal experiences and impressions taken from all kinds of sources and he is not approaching this tour with any preconceived and detailed plans.
>
> In essence he looks on the trip as a goodwill mission and he has no desire to get seriously involved in policy discussions. This is confirmed by the composition of his party: he is not taking a single senior adviser.[78]

The high commissioner said that Diefenbaker admired and respected Macmillan, who thus had "the best possible opportunity for influencing him in the right direction." This meant encouraging Canada to take a larger role in Commonwealth affairs, warning Diefenbaker about Prime Minister Nehru's "lack of realism" about the Soviet Union and "intractability" in dealing with Pakistan, and curbing Diefenbaker's tendency to criticize American policy when in Asia. In general, the high commissioner wrote as an imperial father still seeking to guide his wayward colonial son. "Mr. Diefenbaker's propensity to rush without consultation into dramatic public statements on delicate issues of policy has shown no signs of abating. It would be helpful if it could be brought home tactfully to Mr. Diefenbaker what embarrassment can be caused in this way. There is special danger that he may be led into ill-considered off-the-cuff statements at press conferences."[79]

Macmillan had his own reasons for cultivating the Canadian. He knew that Diefenbaker's rhetoric about the Commonwealth had strong popular appeal in the United Kingdom and he wanted Diefenbaker's goodwill as he sought to turn British policy away from the Commonwealth towards Europe. Thus he praised and supported Diefenbaker's enthusiasm for Commonwealth trade because he thought it had little substance, and he reassured the Canadian prime minister that their economic policies coincided, which they did not. For two years Macmillan succeeded in this game of artful flattery.

Before his departure from Ottawa, the prime minister posed for a Karsh portrait, deeply sober, manicured, and impeccably dressed, the image of states-manlike seriousness of purpose. The official photograph greeted his arrival in London in poster display on the front page of the mass circulation *London Illustrated News*. Diefenbaker had aroused curiosity during his debut at the Commonwealth conference of 1957; now, after his great 1958 triumph, he was a fabulous creature in Britain. In six days he would make the most of it. The visit began with a daytime reception at Canada House, a private dinner with Prime Minister Macmillan, and an evening reception at 10 Downing Street. Next morning there was a long discussion with Macmillan, and courtesy visits to the Archbishop of Canterbury and the Queen Mother. Then the party departed for the weekend in Scotland, where Diefenbaker and company were guided by Roy Thomson to Kildonan in search of his Bannerman roots. They located a house where – Diefenbaker told his mother – a grandfather may have spent his childhood, but the identification was uncertain.[80]

Back in London on November 3, Diefenbaker had longer discussions with Macmillan, attended a Lord Mayor's lunch at the Mansion House, and dined in the evening at the Upper Brook Street home of his high commis-sioner, George Drew. Next day – despite flu and a high temperature – Diefenbaker and Olive lunched with the queen and attended an afternoon reception, before the prime minister addressed a massive evening meeting of the Commonwealth and Empire Industries Association at Royal Albert Hall. As usual, his speech was shaped out of drafts from half a dozen sources, pulled together in a nervous, last-minute rush at the prime minister's bedside.[81]

The result was a triumph, aimed at his chosen audience of old imperialists and Commonwealth boosters. Lord Beaverbrook's *Daily Express* trumpeted Diefenbaker's "stirring message of faith" with a banner front-page headline and seven photographs of the prime minister. "A vast audience jam-packing London's Albert Hall, say 6,000 – 3,000 more failed to get tickets – were warmed in heart and in turn warmed the heart when Mr. John Diefenbaker, Canada's Prime Minister, gave fire to his faith in the British Commonwealth last night."[82] Diefenbaker called on his audience to "banish doubts," to "go forward with new enthusiasm," and to await the Commonwealth's "greater appointment with destiny than in all her glorious history" as its trade barriers fell still further. Commonwealth trade, he insisted, was a great weapon in the battle against communism. And he spoke his own catechism.

Over the centuries,the genius for government of Englishmen created an Empire which in this century and generation, by the exercise of wisdom and humanity, has become the most improbable, and yet most noble, association of all – a partnership of free peoples, in unity but not in political uniformity. Its ark of the covenant is the preservation of freedom...

If causes for this miracle of statesmanship are sought, what better place to look than London. Here stands the Mother of Parliaments, the creator and guardian of a political tradition based on government by consent, government by debate, government under the rule of law founded on the human person. The source of its strength is found in the symbol of Westminster Abbey standing through the centuries beside the Parliament of Westminster. The spiritual values symbolized by the Abbey have shaped and humanized British political tradition and, wherever freedom lives, in the new and living Commonwealth, free men have cause to look to Westminster in thankfulness for the past and hope for the future.[83]

Macmillan followed Diefenbaker to the rostrum to praise him for "a great speech from a great man" and to bask in the applause. He, too, looked forward to an election. When Macmillan claimed that Britain and Canada had always promoted free trade in the world, a voice cried out, "You believe in free trade with Europe. You are a hypocrite." Macmillan responded, to laughter: "I thought there was a truce." He turned to wish Diefenbaker well on his journey: "You will take with you your message and your faith. You will leave behind you the inspiration of your own enthusiasm and the memory of your buoyant personality."[84]

The visit established an affectionate rapport between the two leaders that seemed genuine on both sides. Macmillan noted after their first meeting that Diefenbaker was "in a very happy and relaxed mood."[85] He trusted Diefenbaker to challenge de Gaulle's proposal for three-power hegemony in NATO, and to probe de Gaulle's meaning, without conveying any rebuff that might damage Britain's interest in European trade. And he was fascinated to hear that Eisenhower had been angered by the suggestion that Canada might vote for the admission of Communist China to the United Nations. Diefenbaker told Macmillan that he had no intention of doing so, at least for another year. As the leaders parted, they exchanged gifts emphasizing their common Scots heritage: from Macmillan to Diefenbaker, a Macmillan family history; from Diefenbaker to Macmillan, Donald Creighton's two-volume life of John A. Macdonald.[86] As Diefenbaker moved around the world, the two exchanged frequent, careful comments on Diefenbaker's meetings with other leaders.

In Europe, Diefenbaker proved himself in his meetings with de Gaulle and Adenauer. Even his sceptical foreign affairs adviser Basil Robinson admitted it.[87] He matched them in dialectical skill, they were impressed, and their respect for him was evident. With each of them, Diefenbaker broadened his own insights about the world and gained confidence in his own abilities – as he had with Macmillan in London. He was at his best in their company. In Paris, Diefenbaker also had useful meetings with the secretary general of NATO, Paul-Henri Spaak, and the commander of NATO forces, General Lauris Norstad. Norstad briefed Diefenbaker at length on NATO military strategy, which then emphasized the introduction of tactical nuclear weapons in the first line of European defence – to which Canada had agreed in the NATO Council meeting of December 1957.[88]

Robinson described Diefenbaker's meeting with Prime Minister de Gaulle as "an absorbing exchange." De Gaulle sat opposite Diefenbaker "like a giant eagle, blinking his enigmatic eyes slowly and turning his head from side to side as if surveying some great global battlefield." When Diefenbaker asked whether the prime minister's recent letters to Eisenhower and Macmillan were meant to stimulate consultation in the alliance (which was acceptable to Canada) or to create an inner triumvirate (which was not), de Gaulle responded with sweeping comments on the new world balance. Now that NATO had checked any possible military threat from the Soviet Union, and the possibilities for negotiation had improved, de Gaulle believed that Anglo-American dominance of Western policy-making was no longer appropriate. He pointed out that the United States and Britain had landed troops in the Middle East during the summer without any consultation, despite France's large interests in the region. His letters were intended to raise the issue of consultation rather than to dictate any plan. Diefenbaker supported de Gaulle's concern for better consultation and expressed his reassurance about the general's intentions. He asked for, and received, de Gaulle's word that the issue would not be raised at the coming NATO council meeting, and gained de Gaulle's permission to report this guarantee to Chancellor Adenauer and the Italian prime minister, Amintore Fanfani. On European trade and the Common Market, Diefenbaker made clear his hope that the market would be open to Canada's agricultural trade. The meeting was followed by "a superb lunch in the best of humour," in which de Gaulle showed "a mischievous benevolence" towards the Canadian prime minister.[89]

After the meeting, Robinson telephoned Downing Street on Diefenbaker's behalf to report the prime minister's impressions, particularly that de Gaulle had no plan for a NATO triumvirate and that he could see no bargaining link between de Gaulle's views on NATO and his approach to Britain's talks on European free trade. Macmillan found this bit of intelligence significant.[90]

From Paris the Diefenbaker party travelled by air to the RCAF fighter base at Grostenquin for a ceremonial visit that included a "simulated scramble" of aircrews and a mass takeoff of F–86 Sabre jets, visits to the base high school, hospital, recreation centre, and hockey rink, and a formal dinner and dance in the officers' mess. Here the Diefenbakers were joined for the day by Olive's daughter, Carolyn, and her husband, Don Weir, who were living at the nearby Canadian airbase at Metz, where Don was teaching high school.[91]

The European trip concluded with two days in Bonn and one day in Rome, where the prime minister continued his political discussions with Adenauer and Fanfani, and the Diefenbakers had a short audience with Pope John XXIII. In Bonn, Diefenbaker was particularly impressed by Adenauer's staunch anti-communism, his commitment to the NATO alliance and the American presence in Europe, and his belief in German reconciliation with France. Diefenbaker agreed that American "leadership and co-operation" were essential for European freedom, and was delighted by Adenauer's quip: "Adenauer, Eisenhower, and Diefenbaker – what a threesome!"[92] No more shame about the German name.

Adenauer and de Gaulle had met for the first time only a few weeks before, and Diefenbaker felt the vibrations of that encounter: "It was one of the experiences of my life to have been present so soon after the historic meeting of de Gaulle and Adenauer and to hear from each of them, in the absence of and without the knowledge of the other, the same magnificent message, a message of peace."[93]

The Diefenbakers were enchanted by their audience with the newly elected Pope John XXIII. The conversation went so well that the prime minister joked, "How does it feel to be Pope anyhow?" And the pontiff laughingly answered, "Well, here I am near the end of the road and on top of the heap."[94] Diefenbaker could delightedly share that sentiment.

From Rome, the party flew southeast to Karachi by way of Tehran, and the beginning of four weeks in Asia. In the Asian Commonwealth countries of Pakistan, India, Ceylon, and Malaya, Diefenbaker was on less certain ground than in Europe. Beyond a few stereotypes about the value of the Commonwealth, the dangers of communism, and a romantic perception derived from Kipling, he knew little of this side of the world. He was about to be showered with new – and sometimes disconcerting – impressions.[95]

Pakistan had been under military rule since mid-October, where the presidency had been seized by General Mohammed Ayub Khan just before Diefenbaker's arrival; earlier, there had been doubts about coming to Karachi at all. As the military dictator's first foreign visitor, Diefenbaker was able to offer key early judgments about the new president. He arrived in Karachi understandably "edgy and apprehensive."[96] But Diefenbaker was impressed by Ayub Khan, who struck him as an honourable soldier (he was a Sandhurst graduate with a distinctly British military manner) and a populist who "loved the common people."[97] "He is firmly in the saddle," Diefenbaker wrote to Macmillan on November 15; "his mission was and is to keep Pakistan [from] falling into Communist hands because of divisions being created through political manoeuvring and competition. Martial law has been displaced in large measure. The President is highly regarded by the people as a whole as a Saviour of the nation. His expressed desire is to restore order and thereafter, to bring about the elective process in due course."[98] Macmillan replied, "I am sure that your visit will have done a great deal of good in confirming General Ayub in his pro-Western policies. Let us hope that he has the ability and strength to carry them out."[99] Both Western leaders were henceforth Ayub Khan's firm supporters. From Karachi the prime minister visited Lahore, Peshawar, the Khyber Pass, and the joint Canadian-Pakistani hydroelectric project at Warsak, which had given Canadians, he later wrote, "a personal sense of identity with Pakistani efforts to build the economic and industrial strength of the country."[100] But Diefenbaker was disappointed by Pakistan's limited awareness of Canadian aid and by its distinctly muted interest in the Commonwealth – which offered Pakistan no support in its conflict with India over Kashmir. Diefenbaker had no intention of fishing in those waters.[101]

Diefenbaker's doctor had advised him to avoid fresh milk and water in Pakistan, and to be careful about eating local foods. The result, according to Robinson, was that the prime minister "merely toyed with the food served at the inevitable banquets," grew weak and gaunt, and had to cancel one afternoon's engagements. He revived, however, to receive an honorary degree at the University of Punjab in Lahore, "an occasion to which he rose with eloquence." At another reception that day, Elmer made the homely comparison to one of his hosts that Pakistani military hospitality was "just like the Shriners back home." By the end of the visit Robinson noted that the prime minister "was jaunty again, the chuckle had returned, and those piercing eyes were alight with enjoyment and anticipation."[102]

In India, Diefenbaker faced a week of incessant activity: several conversations with Prime Minister Nehru, banquets, receptions, speeches to parliament and the University of Delhi (and another honorary degree), even a daylong, exciting, but happily fruitless tiger hunt with the Maharajah of Kotah. Diefenbaker saw Pandit Nehru as "a transplanted Englishman" and admirer of things British, despite his life of resistance to British rule. He was impressed by Nehru's wide interests and his political realism. Nehru favoured recognition of Communist China, as Diefenbaker already knew, but he was surprisingly relaxed about Chinese pressures on Formosa and the offshore islands, and felt that China offered no immediate challenge to American policy in Southeast Asia. Diefenbaker responded to Nehru's criticisms of American attitudes by asserting that he had no complaint about American policies towards Canada. "He had," wrote Robinson, "...been critical in the past, but his experience since coming into office had been that the Americans were going out of their way to remove causes of unnecessary friction."[103]

In Ceylon the Diefenbakers were greeted warmly by the populace and somewhat less warmly by the neutralist prime minister, Solomon Bandaranaike. Diefenbaker dismissed Bandaranaike's views with sarcasm in the memoirs: "A semi-intellectual leftist, he believed that Ceylon would achieve its greatest destiny if it sat in the neutralist camp and did not become too closely allied with Britain and the Commonwealth. So far as the policies of the USSR were concerned, he considered it the course of reason to adopt an attitude of benevolence in all his judgments."[104] Diefenbaker was disconcerted by Bandaranaike's curt dismissal of Commonwealth trade and aid, and his apparent indifference to communist economic strategy. Both the governor general and the Canadian high commissioner told Diefenbaker that the West's views were not making an impact in Ceylon. The prime minister responded for the defence,

> in his only major speech in Ceylon, by underlining the purity of Canada's motives in contributing through the Colombo Plan. It sounded a little off-key, but it was his way of warning his audience of parliamentarians against the insidious purposes of communists, both foreign and Ceylonese, in their midst. For good measure he added a warm testimonial to the United States, just as he had done in New Delhi. The effect of this on the audience was one of puzzlement, but Diefenbaker was quite unrepentant. Whenever on this journey he sensed a coolness towards the United States, he felt it his duty to speak in support of Canada's neighbour and ally, if only as an act of solidarity with his esteemed friend, the president. Three years later he might not have offered quite as solid support to Eisenhower's successor.[105]

In Kandy, "that oasis among oases, that other Eden, demi-paradise" (as he described it), Diefenbaker rode an elephant and Olive's name was given to a new variety of rose.[106]

By comparison with Bandaranaike, Diefenbaker found his next host,

Prime Minister Tunku Abdul Rahman of Malaya, both warm and politically sympathetic.[107] The Tunku was staunchly anti-communist, at war with communist rebels in his own land, and an outspoken supporter of American policy towards China. He warned Diefenbaker that Canadian recognition of the People's Republic would be taken in Asia as support for Chinese expansionism. On the same day, Diefenbaker told a press conference that Canada had made no decision on the subject: "We do not intend to take any course which will weaken the opposition to Communism anywhere or be so interpreted as constituting on the part of Canada a weakening in our stand."[108] Privately, he realized that non-recognition imposed an unhelpful isolation on China. But faced with constantly conflicting arguments and the opposition of the Eisenhower administration, Diefenbaker preferred to leave the issue in permanent limbo. The views of Ayub Khan and Tunku Abdul Rahman had reinforced his indecision.

In Singapore – still a British colony – Diefenbaker sought advice from the British governor and commissioner general for Southeast Asia about whether Canada should cut its aid to neutralist Ceylon and increase aid to pro-Western Malaya. The British responded that the best policy, despite neutralist success in playing off East and West in appeals for competitive gifts, was to persevere in giving specialist aid that might strengthen "integrity and independence." The British commissioner reported to London that – in spite of their hectic twenty-four-hour schedule in Singapore – the Diefenbakers "were in surprisingly good form, she especially, relaxed and interested, and appeared much less fatigued by their tour than might have been expected."[109]

In a brief two-hour stop in Djakarta, Diefenbaker met the Indonesian prime minister and again emphasized his concern that Asian governments should not let local communists subvert democratic institutions. He favoured a liberal policy on foreign investment and told his host that Canada had found that American capital was "not as avaricious as it was made out to be in other parts of the world."[110]

In Australia and New Zealand the Canadian prime minister felt himself once more on solid ground among old friends in the British family. Diefenbaker reported his European and Asian conversations in detail to his Australian and New Zealand colleagues, enjoyed warm hospitality from Robert Menzies in Australia, and made familiar speeches to friendly audiences about Commonwealth brotherhood. The British high commissioner in New Zealand wrote that "the feeling in Government circles here is that he made the right noises about the Commonwealth but did so in a rather diffuse and woolly manner. The speeches at the Government Lunch in fact were protracted and a common comment after them was that in long-windedness 'Walter [Nash] has at last met his match.'" Diefenbaker offended the Indian high commissioner by claiming that Canada had no ulterior purpose in its Colombo Plan assistance to India, but "that its main purpose was to combat communism."[111] Aside from that unthinking slip, the official side of the journey passed easily and the party went off to the resort of Wairakei for four days' holiday. The next day Diefenbaker received word that his mother was ill, and arrangements were quickly made to return to Canada the same day.[112]

For the prime minister, the tiring journey had been an unqualified success. Diefenbaker told a Canadian television audience on December 21 that he was "more convinced than ever of the importance of these personal meetings with national leaders...The normal diplomatic channels are still of the utmost importance, but there are times when direct communication between those in high authority, often by long distance telephone, becomes desirable and indeed essential."[113]

In Diefenbaker's absence his government, working under Howard Green as acting prime minister, had kept a low profile. "Ottawa," Patrick Nicholson wrote to the prime minister in early December, "is a very quiet place, uneventful almost to the point of causing alarm." But Diefenbaker, ever alert to the political winds, had heard of fresh conflicts among his ministers. Nicholson reassured him: "I think you have been receiving unduly alarmist reports about your Cabinet's solidarity."[114]

The new government had easily dominated its first two sessions of parliament, but few observers expected that to continue in 1959. George Bain commented in the *Globe and Mail* that the government could no longer coast on the prime minister's "heady phrases...of oratorical vision," or blame the old Liberal regime for the country's economic ills. Now it would have to produce its own remedies. He predicted difficulties in three areas: fiscal and monetary policy, defence, and agriculture. Defence policy had been "in an apparent muddle for months. The controversy and uncertainty over the Arrow jet fighter is the most dramatic example of the problem, but more generally it is becoming clearly evident that the whole defence establishment needs overhauling."[115]

The Diefenbaker government inherited the dilemma of the Avro Arrow from its Liberal predecessor. The A.V. Roe Company of Malton, Ontario, had begun designing the supersonic CF–105 Arrow interceptor in 1953, when the government committed itself to development planning. The confident prospect was that a successful prototype would lead to a large RCAF order for the fighter plane by the late 1950s, to replace the subsonic CF–100, another product of A.V. Roe. Over the next three years, design and development went forward on the tailless, delta-winged airframe at A.V. Roe, on the engine at Orenda Engines – an A.V. Roe affiliate also located in Malton, on the ASTRA radar fire control system at the RCA company in the United States and at Westinghouse in Hamilton, and on the Sparrow II missile at Canadair Limited in Montreal.[116]

By 1955, complications in designing the fire control system and reductions in RCAF requirements from twenty squadrons to nine squadrons raised doubts about the project among Liberal ministers. "I can say," C.D. Howe told the House of Commons in June 1955, "that now we have started on a program of development that gives me the shudders."[117] Nevertheless, active development and tooling up went forward on the assumption that the aircraft would go into production, and there were no realistic assessments of development or production costs until 1957. With an election approaching in the spring of 1957, the Liberal cabinet postponed any decision on the future of the project, just as it had postponed consideration of NORAD.[118]

The new government approached defence spending in a spirit of cost-cutting, and in September 1957 it agreed, on the recommendation of the minister of national defence, to eliminate production of the final Mark VI version of the CF–100, for a saving of an estimated $66 million.[119] The decision brought an immediate – and harsh – political response from A.V. Roe and Orenda, who threatened to lay off almost three thousand workers before July 1958. The minister of labour, Michael Starr, suggested to cabinet that Avro "was adopting a vindicative [sic] attitude and that in their lay-offs they were going far beyond what was necessary." Ministers noted that the three Conservative MPs for the Malton area "had been elected on a programme that there would be no lay-offs," and estimated that 10,000 votes might be lost if the decision were sustained. Urgent talks were arranged with the companies for the same evening.[120]

The cabinet record shows that – with another election approaching – ministers were preoccupied with the political rather than the military effects of the decision. This put the two companies in a strong bargaining position, which they exploited skilfully. They told Pearkes and his colleagues Fleming, O'Hurley, and Hees that 3200 layoffs were in prospect, 1200 of them directly resulting from the CF–100 cancellations. There would also be large layoffs among the subcontractors. Avro and Orenda also awaited a more crucial cabinet decision on the future of the Avro Arrow, and warned that both companies would close if the project were cancelled, throwing 15,000 employees onto the street. Pearkes told them that a decision on the Arrow would come within a week, and with that assurance they agreed to withhold layoffs until then. When cabinet met the next day, members noted that "these layoffs would be the first major increase in unemployment directly attributed to action of the government and efforts should be made to lessen the effects which could influence the government's chances of re-election."[121]

By the end of the month, after further talks with the companies, Pearkes brought a compromise package to cabinet. It would reduce layoffs to a politically manageable 1450 persons, some by attrition, while adding millions to federal spending. Pearkes proposed that the government should buy an additional twenty CF–100 Mark Vs, costing $10 million, to be given away to NATO allies as mutual aid, and that development of the Avro Arrow and its components should be continued for a further twelve months, at an added cost of $173 million in 1958–59. This would involve the completion of thirty-seven pre-production aircraft, some of which could go into service if production followed. Cabinet agreed.[122]

For their part, Orenda and A.V. Roe made some adjustments in production and staffing, but gained contracts for twenty CF–100s and the assurance of another twelve months' development of the Arrow. For its part, cabinet "went a long way towards solving the problem" of layoffs at Malton, but took "a tremendous gamble" with the Arrow. No test flights had yet taken place. The minutes noted ominously that "$400 million would have been spent before it was known if the aircraft could be put into use in the R.C.A.F. However, there was no time to study and weigh the programme in its entirety." More generally, ministers understood that the politics of such support for the re-election of three MPs required a parallel show of generosity elsewhere.[123] This was expensive damage control. Above all, it indicated to A.V. Roe that the Diefenbaker government was politically sensitive and that it capitulated easily under pressure.

If the manufacturers were reassured by the Diefenbaker cabinet's acts of appeasement, the minister of defence had few illusions. When he wrote to Diefenbaker in January 1958 to recommend an early election, he anticipated hard decisions on air defence in the coming months. "I am having a study made of the nature of the threat. Present indications are that it is quite possible we may have to make radical changes. For instance, it is not at all clear that we need to proceed with the construction of the CF–105. If next summer we have to cancel development of this aircraft, the aircraft industry at the Avro plant will be seriously dislocated with possible large-scale layoffs of personnel. This would of course affect our Members who represent constituencies in that area."[124]

By mid-summer, following studies by the defence chiefs, discussions with the American military, and review in the cabinet defence committee, Pearkes was ready to recommend those radical changes. In the meantime the first test flights had occurred, with spectacular success, and the defence department had sought American orders for the aircraft. Pearkes met his American counterpart in Washington in August and learned that the United States would not consider a Canadian aircraft purchase. Instead, Defense Secretary Neil McElroy outlined new air defence plans involving Canadian participation and urged them on Pearkes.[125] The Canadian minister accepted them, and on August 22, 1958, he brought his proposals to cabinet. They preoccupied ministers in six meetings extending over a full month.[126] When the marathon was finished, they had accepted American Bomarc missiles (probably to be armed with nuclear warheads) as a partial replacement for the Avro Arrow, cancelled development of the ASTRA fire control system and the Sparrow II missile designed for use in the Arrow, and postponed a decision to sustain or cancel production of the Arrow and its Iroquois engine for a further six months, until March 31, 1959. In the meantime, the development programs at A.V. Roe and Orenda Engines would proceed. This unstable and confusing compromise reflected a divided military leadership, a divided cabinet, a determined industrial lobby, and Diefenbaker's attempt to bring them all together by delay.

There were now at least five compelling influences on the decision: escalating costs that seemed beyond the capacity of the Canadian government; doubts about the technical nature of the potential Soviet threat, whether bomber or missile; a military preference for tactical atomic weapons for defence as well as attack; an interest – both economic and political – in maintaining a large and sophisticated Canadian aircraft industry; and an overriding American influence on the shape of Canadian defence policy. The government responded by simultaneously inching sideways and forwards. In the process, the prime minister preferred not to sort out too clearly what policies his government was actually pursuing.

Pearkes offered cabinet a straightforward analysis of air defence policy for the 1960s, evidently based on his Washington briefings.

The assessment of the threat to North America had changed. In the 1960s, the main threat would probably be from ballistic missiles with the manned bomber decreasing in importance after 1962–63. However, a combination of the two might be the threat until Soviet manned bombers were depleted. The rapid strides in technology were such that to provide a suitable manned

310

fighter to cope with heavy jet bombers was extremely expensive. Further-more, ground-to-air missiles had now reached the point where they were at least as effective as a manned fighter, and cheaper. The original require-ments in 1953 for between 500 and 600 aircraft of the CF–105 fighter had been drastically reduced. Subsequently, thought had been given to reducing it still further now that the BOMARC missile would probably be introduced into the Canadian air defence system. Finally, the cost of the CF–105 programme as a whole was now of such a magnitude that the Chiefs of Staff felt that, to meet the modest requirement of manned aircraft presently considered advisable, it would be more economical to procure a fully devel-oped interceptor of comparable performance in the U.S.[127]

Pearkes recommended to cabinet the defence committee's proposals for two Canadian Bomarc missile bases, additional heavy radar installations, and negotiations with the United States on cost-sharing for these projects. Since the defence committee and the military chiefs of staff were divided on the future of the Arrow, Pearkes made his own recommendation that devel-opment of the CF–105 should be cancelled at once. He proposed further studies on the purchase of an alternative American fighter plane and on two additional Bomarc bases, but without any commitment to buy aircraft for at least one year.[128]

The United States Air Force had already incorporated Bomarc missiles into its defence plans, and the two bases now proposed for Canada simply involved moving elements of the network northwards into Ontario and Quebec. Pearkes explained to cabinet: "There were considerable advantages in adopting BOMARC. It was cheaper than the CF–105, in terms of men and money, and just as effective. The missile could be fitted with an atomic war-head and the U.S. would probably supply heads on the same basis ("key-to-the-cupboard"), as they made atomic weapons available to the U.K."[129] He estimated the full costs of substituting Bomarcs for Arrow interceptors, without any American cost-sharing, at $520 million, or less than half the production costs of one hundred Arrows.[130] During the first days of cabinet discussion, the US Defense Department eased the minister's efforts of persuasion by indicating its interest in cost- and production-sharing for both Bomarcs and radar instal-lations. It emphasized that its chief concern was to complete the heavy radar system. Since the cabinet's agonies arose over the future of the Arrow, with all its political complications, the addition of two Bomarc bases and more radars seemed a deceptively simple affair. On September 8 cabinet authorized Pearkes to begin negotiations with the United States on those projects. At

Diefenbaker's urging, a decision on the Arrow was postponed for two weeks "pending further examination of various alternatives."[131] That adoption of the Bomarc was understood by members of the cabinet as a signal of the Arrow's eventual demise seems likely; the choice was undoubtedly a gesture of cooperation with the Americans. Given the cabinet's immediate focus, the accompanying implication that the weapon might be armed with atomic warheads was noted without apparent concern.

Pearkes told cabinet that he had previously supported completion of the Arrow, but that its high costs, coupled with the declining threat from bombers, had led him to change his mind. His recommendation "meant that the government would have a year to decide whether it should re-equip air defence fighter forces wholly with the BOMARC, or an alternative aircraft, or a combination of both. Within that time there should be a better understanding of Soviet intentions as to whether they were likely to introduce more or better bombers, or go completely into missiles." Other ministers warned that "the most serious aspect of the proposal" would be the loss of more than 25,000 jobs. On the other hand, maintenance of the Arrow program would add $400 million a year to the defence budget, increase both taxes and the deficit, undermine the government's credit, and stimulate inflation. The dilemma was profound: military and financial considerations pointed to cancellation, but abandoning a Canadian aircraft to purchase an American replacement "would be a serious political mistake."[132]

Before the cabinet's second discussion of the subject, Diefenbaker, Pearkes, and Fleming met with F.T. Smye, the vice president of Avro Aircraft, and John Tory, a director of A.V. Roe. They recommended maintenance of the Arrow and Iroquois programs, but cancellation of the missile and fire control systems in favour of American alternatives. They pointed out that Avro had opposed the original RCAF recommendation of those systems. Production of one hundred CF–105s over the next four years would give the company "a reasonable opportunity" to find other business, but cancellation would mean the loss of 25,000 highly skilled jobs and dispersal of many employees to the United States, "never to return."[133]

Following this meeting, Diefenbaker admitted his "perplexities" about the Arrow to Robert Bryce and asked for his advice. The cabinet secretary gave the prime minister a forthright memorandum on September 5, recommending policies that extended the logic of Canadian-American defence integration implied in the minister's proposals. He suggested immediate cancellation of the Arrow program, adoption of the two Bomarc batteries and relocation of others into Canada, purchase of "40 or 50" American F–106 aircraft, formal negotiations with the United States to accept nuclear warheads for Canadian Bomarcs and interceptors on the British two-key model, and agreement with the United States on an "integrated defence production program" for aircraft and missiles. Bryce explained that his views had changed because the military threat was shifting from bombers to long-range missiles, and because the costs of the Arrow could no longer be justified. He concluded with a subtle political point linking the Arrow's cancellation to the acceptance of nuclear warheads. "I think it would help in putting across this difficult decision to the public and perhaps help somewhat in deterring the Russians if we could announce at the same time our decision to make arrangements to use nuclear defensive weapons in Canada, though not to produce them."[134]

At the next discussion in cabinet, the prime minister noted that ministers were "relatively well agreed on the purely defence aspects"; the problem remaining was "the effect on employment and the general economic situation." Fleming led the argument for immediate cancellation. Given the escalating costs and the absence of a compelling military need, he could see no middle course between cancellation and production. Going into production would distort the government's budget priorities and undermine its plans for general development. Others responded that cancellation now might be "the one psychological factor" that would tip the economy into a serious recession, whereas a reprieve of a few months might give the companies time to prepare replacement projects, and take the economy into better days when it could absorb large layoffs.[135] Despite the judgment of the minister of finance, the elements of a compromise seemed to be emerging. Next day the prime minister called for delay of "a week or two" to find it.[136]

Two weeks later, on September 21, Diefenbaker told cabinet that he had met with Crawford Gordon, president of A.V. Roe, who had made no new proposals; Pearkes and Fleming reported that Gordon's estimates of savings involved in cancelling the fire control and missile systems were imprecise and exaggerated.[137] Cabinet remained irreconcilably divided on the "central question" of cancellation: it would have major economic and psychological effects, but production contrary to military advice might open the government to charges "of wasting many hundreds of millions of dollars for what were political or economic reasons. That might seriously shake the confidence in the government of the man in the street."[138]

The prime minister proposed a precise compromise: the development stage of the Arrow and Iroquois should be maintained until the end of March 1959, at a cost of about $86 million (already covered in current estimates), but production should not begin. In the meantime, reviews should determine whether to continue or suspend the project, and whether to proceed with alternative missile or aircraft purchases. Cabinet approved his suggestions, confirmed the decisions to build two Bomarc bases and new radar installations, and wrapped up its prolonged deliberations the next day by agreeing to cancel the fire control and missile systems at once. The minister of defence suggested that the latter decision foreshadowed the probable termination of the Arrow in six months, but that door remained open.[139]

It was obvious to members of the cabinet that their temporizing decision was made on economic and political – not military – grounds. The prospect of massive and concentrated autumn layoffs was too much to face, but so was the prospect of an open-ended drain on the budget, stretching through the whole parliamentary term. Diefenbaker gave them – and A.V. Roe – six months to think about a final choice. Ever after, he claimed that the September decision warned A.V. Roe bluntly of a stay of execution, with six months to compose its affairs.[140] But A.V. Roe could as easily believe that this second reprieve marked the way in which the Diefenbaker government made its hard decisions – by gradual capitulation under political pressure. Six months would bring them closer to production. Would the government then dare to destroy this beautiful technical marvel?

On September 23 Diefenbaker announced the changes of policy in a low-key press statement that gave priority to the decisions on the Bomarc, additions to the Pinetree radar system, and a new computer guidance system (SAGE or semi-automatic ground environment) for Canadian NORAD forces. When he turned to the future of the Arrow, he seemed to be giving gentle but unmistakable notice of termination.

> In view of the introduction of missiles into the Canadian air defence system and the reduction in the expected need for manned, supersonic, interceptor aircraft, the government has decided that it would not be advisable at this time to put the CF–105 into production. The government believes, however, that to discontinue abruptly the development of this aircraft and its engine, with its consequent effects upon the industry, would not be prudent with the international outlook as uncertain and tense as it is. As a measure of insurance with present tensions as they are, therefore, the government has decided that the development programme for the Arrow aircraft and Iroquois engine should be continued until next March, when the situation will be reviewed again in the light of all the existing circumstances at that time.
>
> Although both the Arrow aircraft and the Iroquois engine appear now to

be likely to be better than any alternatives expected to be ready by 1961, it is questionable whether in any event their margin of superiority is worth the very high cost of producing them by reason of the relatively small numbers likely to be required...

...

It now seems evident that in the larger weapon systems now required for air forces, Canadian work in the design, development and production of defence equipment will have to be closely integrated with the major programmes of the United States. The U.S. government recognizes this and they are now prepared to work out production sharing arrangements with us. To accomplish effective integration of defence production resources of Canada and the United States will require time and continuing efforts of co-operation.[141]

Diefenbaker paid tribute to the "excellent scientific and technical teams...created for these projects" (with some fuzziness about whether he was referring to the cancelled ASTRA and Sparrow systems, or the still-surviving Arrow and Iroquois), but added that "it will be recognized, I believe, that as the age of missiles appears certain to lead to a major reduction in the need for fighter aircraft, Canada cannot expect to support a large industry developing and producing aircraft solely for diminishing Canadian defence require-ments." To do so would be "not only wasteful but unjustifiable."[142] For Diefenbaker this was a generous, six-month golden handshake for A.V. Roe, offered as he turned southwards into the American embrace. With his friend Dwight Eisenhower in the White House and the frightening prospect of nuclear war always in the background, Diefenbaker accepted that shift to the south as both comforting and inevitable.

Although the short-term outcome turned on economic factors, the prime minister apparently did not seek the advice of his economic adviser, Merril Menzies, until the cabinet decision had been made. On September 23 Menzies responded to "our brief discussion" by noting that the decision "eases the problem of adjustment within the industry for the time being." He assumed, however, that production would not follow, and that "it will be necessary for the Government to take action to mitigate the serious structur-al disruption of the Canadian aircraft industry which must ensue." He proposed that cabinet should commit from $10 million to $20 million (10 percent of the savings arising from the current decision) to an urgent study of how best to shift "the human and material resources presently engaged...into new fields of productive research and development." Such an announcement would assure that "the needs of a vital Canadian industry, as well as the employment of some of the most highly skilled and specialized Canadians will not be forgotten."[143] Diefenbaker ignored the suggestion.

Despite their interest in the decision, members of the Conservative caucus and the press gallery learned nothing of cabinet discussions until the prime minister's announcement on September 23. The press was universally surprised by what it saw as the government's toughness, and almost universally supportive. "The plain truth is," wrote Blair Fraser in *Maclean's*, "nobody thought the government would have the courage to make such a painful decision. The fact that the decision was right didn't carry enough weight. It meant an early end to more than twenty thousand jobs, most of them in the very heartland of the Conservative Party. It went against the emotional urges of all Canadian air force men, and of most air-force veterans. It disappointed a big Canadian industry with many big Conservative shareholders. In short, it was political poison, of a kind to scare any politician out of a year's growth."[144] The *Globe and Mail* welcomed the decision as "not only wise and courageous, but one which will save the taxpayers a good deal of money." It added, however, that the Arrow development team must be kept together, and foresaw that the economies might make production of the aircraft possible.[145] "No one can say positively whether or not the cabinet decisions...were the right ones," the Saskatoon *Star-Phoenix* commented in an echo of the cabinet's own uncertainty. "But it can be said emphatically that the government acted forthrightly and courageously."[146]

A.V. Roe put on a bold face. Crawford Gordon told Avro employees that he expected a decision in six months to go into production after all.[147] Preproduction building of the test models, and flight testing, went forward at a hectic pace. In late October he explained to the company's annual meeting his reasons for confidence. Manned interceptors, he said, remained essential to North American defence; pilotless anti-aircraft missiles like the Bomarc complemented but could not replace them. The Arrow remained the obvious, custom-designed aircraft for the RCAF, and the cost savings in fire control and armaments meant that the purchase price would now be "compatible with the Canadian economy." Gordon conceded that he had no assurance from the government about the forthcoming decision; his confidence rested solely on the strength of his arguments. He closed with some political warnings. The aircraft industry was now "a spearhead of advancing technology and...a major factor in national development and international prestige." Avro and Orenda had put Canada into the first rank, with 4000 "highly skilled engineers and technicians" whose dispersal would destroy the country's potential. Above all, he predicted a loss of national independence. "Complete reliance on other countries for even the crucial weapons with which to defend ourselves would be a long step backward from the position of independence which this country has been laboriously building over the years. Our right to an independent and authoritative voice in world affairs would, in my opinion, be greatly diminished."[148]

Beyond these public statements, there was no direct communication between the prime minister and the company during the autumn. While Diefenbaker made his world tour, A.V. Roe and its supporters mounted an intensive public lobbying campaign in the Toronto region. Letters of support for the company flowed steadily to the prime minister's office and to the press, and inspired feature articles on the Arrow proliferated.[149] When the cabinet next discussed the issue following Diefenbaker's return, the prime minister expressed his extreme displeasure. "If the government decided to continue development it would be accused of giving in to a powerful lobby. Pressure was coming from other sources in Ontario too. Even if he thought the decision reached last September was wrong, he was determined, because of what had happened since, to adhere firmly to it."[150] Pearkes told cabinet that the United States had reiterated, at recent meetings of the Canada–US joint ministerial committee on defence in Paris, that it had no interest in purchasing the Arrow. He took for granted that the program would be cancelled. Cabinet agreed that it would decide on the future of the Arrow before the opening of parliament in January, but the conclusion already seemed clear. No provision for building the plane was included in the draft estimates for 1959.

Still the prime minister hesitated. The decision was postponed through six more meetings of cabinet from December 31 to February 14 as ministers canvassed the prospects for softening the blows on Avro and providing alternate means of air defence. No minister openly opposed a decision to cancel, yet discussion flowed endlessly and repetitively like the tides. Finally, when Avro threatened layoffs unless there were an immediate increase in its approved spending limits, cabinet agreed to make a formal decision on February 17.[151]

That day Diefenbaker told cabinet an announcement cancelling the Arrow was being prepared and that "it included a section on arrangements with the United States for production sharing and a section on the acquisition by Canada of nuclear weapons for defence." J.M. Macdonnell and Donald Fleming reported that Premier Frost had challenged a decision to halt the Arrow in "strong terms" and "pungent language." But nothing would alter the prime minister's determination; every further delay would add to the unnecessary cost. The announcement would be made in the House on Friday, February 20, and communicated to the companies at the same time.[152]

Diefenbaker told the House of Commons on February 20 that the government had examined "the probable nature of the threats to North America in future years, the alternative means of defence against such threats, and the estimated costs thereof."[153] It had decided on immediate cancellation of the Arrow and Iroquois programs because the threat of attack by bomber was diminishing, and because alternative means of meeting that threat had developed earlier than expected. Defence would focus increasingly on intercontinental missiles rather than long-range bombers. The United States had drawn the same conclusions and had cancelled aircraft projects similar to the Arrow.

For the moment the government had made no decision about a replacement for the Arrow, and had no other work for the Avro and Orenda factories. But it would meet "all outstanding commitments...equitably." Diefenbaker expressed regret for the decision, but insisted that "there is no other feasible or justifiable course open to us. We must not abdicate our responsibility to assure that the huge sums which it is our duty to ask parliament to provide for defence are being expended in the most effective way to achieve that purpose."

Diefenbaker said that the previously announced Bomarc bases, SAGE electronics, and additional radar stations would be financed jointly by the United States and Canada, with the United States meeting two-thirds of costs; that construction would be done by Canadian firms; and that production of the technical equipment would be "reasonably and fairly" shared between the two countries. Because "the irresistible dictates of geography" had made defence a joint enterprise, Canada would contribute fully "in terms both of quantity and quality in deterring and resisting aggression."

Acceptance of the Bomarc meant that "careful thought is being given to the principles that in our opinion are applicable to the acquisition and control of nuclear weapons."

> The full potential of these defensive weapons is achieved only when they are armed with nuclear warheads. The government is, therefore, examining with the United States government questions connected with the acquisition of nuclear warheads for Bomarc and other defensive weapons for use by the Canadian forces in Canada, and the storage of warheads in Canada. Problems connected with the arming of the Canadian brigade in Europe with short range nuclear weapons for NATO's defence tasks are also being studied.
>
> We are confident that we shall be able to reach formal agreement with the United States on appropriate means to serve the common objective. It

will of course be some time before these weapons will be available for use by Canadian forces.

Diefenbaker coupled this commitment with his government's opposition to the independent production or control of nuclear weapons, continuing disarmament negotiations, and the solidarity of NATO policy. Canada accepted reluctantly "the need in present circumstances for nuclear weapons of a defensive character," but the ownership and custody of nuclear weapons in Canada would remain with the United States. Their use from Canadian soil, however, would only result from joint decisions under agreements approved in advance by both governments. The government had made grave choices after "much soul-searching," and the prime minister expected that the House would place them "above partisan political considerations."[154]

The statement was subtly framed so that the discussion of nuclear weapons overbalanced the cancellation of the Arrow and reduced it to secondary importance. Given the sobering state of the world and the weight of the cabinet's dilemmas, who would dare to challenge its anguished choices? Mere contracts, mere employment, mere national technology were trivia beside the apocalyptic spectre of atomic warfare. That trivializing contrast lay behind all discussion of nuclear weapons; it was a tempting device for suppressing practical debate. Diefenbaker sensed its usefulness as surely as did the US Department of Defense when it offered the Bomarcs to Canada on enticing terms. He fell into its trap. He had disposed of the Canadian aircraft in a Faustian pact.

Three ministers passed him notes of congratulation in the House. "You have left unsaid nothing that should or could have been said. Magnificent," wrote Davie Fulton. "A tour de force," wrote J.M. Macdonnell. "That put everything in its right perspective. A great speech," wrote George Hees.[155]

The message from A.V. Roe was less reassuring. Late in the afternoon Diefenbaker received an "extra rush" telegram from Crawford Gordon.

As a result of telegrams of termination of the Arrow and Iroquois programs have found it necessary to suspend all operations at Malton with exception of essential plant protection our officers meeting with officials of the department of defence production Monday to discuss termination procedures earnestly request meeting with yourself and ministers of defense and defense production at your earliest convenience to discuss future government wishes in connection with employment of Malton facilities technical personnel and labour force urgent reply.[156]

Avro and Orenda had closed the factories and dismissed their employees within moments of the announcement. The prime minister was shocked. "A more callous act would be hard to imagine. Yet I was the one who was excoriated and condemned. Every effort was made to place the responsibility on me."[157] Next morning his friend Oakley Dalgleish placed the *Globe and Mail*'s leading editorial, "The Beginning – and the End," on the front page. He offered more disquiet. "The important thing, the only important thing," Dalgleish wrote, "is the future of the engineering, technical and research establishment that brought the Arrow into being."

> The Prime Minister's judgment on the Arrow and its future must as we have said, be accepted. The fact remains, however, that the Government has no program or policy by which to put anything in its place. It is on this fact, we believe, that the Government's decision – and the consequences thereof – must ultimately be judged...
>
> The Prime Minister now tells us there is nothing to put in the place of the Arrow. We will share only in the development of the Bomarc program, and the nature of that sharing is disagreeably clear. We Canadians will be allowed to dig the hole; the Americans will put up the building. That simply is not good enough.
>
> And here is the irony of it. Most Canadians will recall that in the early postwar years we were not permitted to share defence production with the United States; the reason the United States gave being that we lacked the necessary "know-how." So, at great trouble and cost, we acquired the "know-how." Still, there was no sharing. And now, what? Now, the brilliant array of engineering and technical talent which built up this great Canadian industry will be dissipated. Now, these highly-trained men and women – the one national asset – will probably go. Where? To the United States.[158]

This was the reaction of a political friend. That evening there was another, from Leslie Frost. He had learned of the decision when he was passed a note in the Ontario legislature reporting a news announcement of the cancellation. He wired Diefenbaker:

> Strongly urge finding substitute work and programmes not necessarily governmental taking place of Arrow as I discussed previously with Fleming. People of course concerned with Arrow decision as it effects Canadian independence but fundamentally the public alarm is caused by mass unemploy-

ment and the plight of a large number of municipalities which will create an acute problem if reasonable alternatives not found...While the Arrow decision is important the primary problem is what is to be done as a result. On this depends public reaction. All expect collaboration of industry and government...All Ontario government services are available...in finding a reasonable solution.[159]

For Washington, Bomarc–SAGE, the radars, and the nuclear commitment were the significant elements in Diefenbaker's announcement. But at home in February 1959 they had no substance. What mattered to Avro, to Toronto, to Ontario was the sudden and brutal loss of thousands of jobs. Crawford Gordon, in his desperation, knew how to dramatize that loss. He used the loudspeakers on the production floor and sent his displaced workers home to their families. Diefenbaker, the politician, for once in his life had neglected the local effects of his acts. He was outsmarted and embarrassed. Dalgleish and Frost expressed the resulting doubts and anxieties of Diefenbaker's own cabinet and caucus. They still supported him. But faced with the substance and manner of the decision to scrap the Arrow, they began, nervously, to reassess their commitment. The Chief knew it, and put up his guard.

February 23, 1959, was the fiftieth anniversary of the flight of the *Silver Dart* at Baddeck, Nova Scotia – the first powered flight in the British Empire.[160] Cabinet's prime business when it met that morning was to prepare its defences for an emergency debate on the end of the Arrow. Members noted that "the two principal points of criticism...were, first, that no efforts had been made to provide alternative employment for the Avro workers and, second, that Canada would be still further dominated by the United States." Three lines of defence were discussed: Avro had been "well aware" of the likelihood of cancellation, but had made no alternative plans; the decision rested on "the best military advice available"; and substitution of the Bomarc for the Arrow would involve large savings. But ministers implicitly conceded failure on the issue of American domination.

As regards the point that cancellation would mean that Canada would be still further "under the wing of the U.S.," it should be remembered that maintaining freedom from U.S. control was a continuous struggle. It might appear that the present decision was a retrograde step. But there would be other opportunities to assert Canadian sovereignty and independence. For example, it might be necessary in the near future to introduce legislation to ensure the independence of Canadian companies.

> It would be unwise to blame the U.S. for the outcome of the Arrow contract.[161]

Instead, the relationship would be given a positive spin. This outcome was not an example of domination but of integration, and out of it would come the growing benefits of a Canadian share in American defence production contracts.[162]

Paul Hellyer, who led the opposition's attack on the government, took the expected line that the decision was sudden, harsh, and destructive of an advanced Canadian industry. He urged Diefenbaker to take "some immediate, positive, forward-looking action...to stop the exodus of Canada's future from this country, and to bring about that vision of national development which he has placed before us."[163] Mike Pearson added that "it has been our major indictment of the government since the day this session began that it was guilty of fumbling, confusion and delay in its policies, and guilty of failure to plan ahead. There could surely not be any better example of this than the situation which now confronts us."[164] But Pearson did not directly challenge the government's decision – except to ask why it had been so long delayed. On the central issue of a joint defence policy with the United States, he gave his support for hard bargaining to assure that Canada would receive more than the "tag ends of orders and nothing else."[165] Pearson's most emphatic disagreement with the prime minister came over the control of nuclear weapons. He agreed that Canada should possess "the most modern and effective weapons." He agreed that Canada should not manufacture nuclear weapons, but should obtain them from the United States if they were necessary for defensive purposes. But in that case "they should be under Canadian control, and...arrangements to this end should at least be attempted with the United States authorities."[166] The opposition's attack was remarkably mild – and even supportive in its defence of the Canadian against the American interest in the affair.

The prime minister's response began in amused ridicule of his opponents for their own inconsistencies. But he was soon attacking the Liberal Party for wanting his government to "squander nearly $800 million of the taxpayers money" merely because a project was already under way. "I realize," he insisted, "that defence production is an important weapon in the battle against unemployment. However, I say with all the seriousness that I can put at my command, that the production of obsolete weapons as a make-work program is an unjustifiable expenditure of public funds." He cited similar decisions to abandon advanced fighter planes in the United States and the United Kingdom. He too believed that the government should seek a "fair and just distribution" of defence contracts with the United States, but warned against demanding too much of the nation "on whose shoulders rests in large measure the maintenance of freedom not only of our country but generally throughout the free world today."

Then Diefenbaker turned to the accusation that seemed to trouble him most: that Avro had been taken by surprise. He pointed to editorial after editorial during the previous autumn that took the September decision as notice of cancellation; and he accused the company of mounting an intensive lobbying campaign to save the Arrow, a campaign that had cruelly deceived its own workers about what was coming. He poured it on. The company had been constantly advised, consulted, and warned by ministers and officials, but had made no practical suggestions for alternative projects. Finally, he denounced the company for abruptly dismissing its employees. Avro knew what the decision would be; and it also knew that there was $50 million in the estimates to meet the company's readjustment costs. That day, in fact, the company was calling back 2500 of its staff. "I say that its attitude in letting out thousands of workers, technical workers and employees, on Friday, was so cavalier, so unreasonable, that the only conclusion any fair-minded person can come to is that it was done for the purpose of embarrassing the government."[167]

This was a spirited defence, made in the prime minister's familiar manner: by attack. Diefenbaker had done something to lessen the political damage of the dismissals, and felt satisfied that he could turn away from the decision and move on. In the weeks that followed, the government negotiated termination contracts with the company, and eventually decided that the seven existing CF–105s should be blowtorched to scrap.[168]

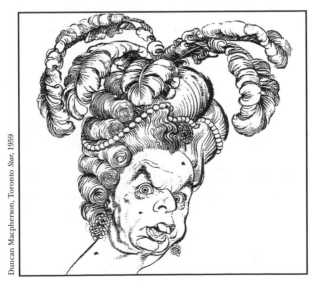

Duncan Macpherson, Toronto *Star*, 1959

"Then let them eat cake!"

THE LESSON THAT EMERGES IS NOT THAT THE DIEFENBAKER GOVERNMENT MADE AN autonomous decision to stop production of the Arrow. It is that both development and cancellation took place under the friendly guidance of the US Department of Defense and the US Air Force, within their changing calculations of the Soviet threat and the American interest. American guidance came at three levels – technical, military, and political – through consultation among associates who shared common purposes. Usually the Canadians accepted American proposals without dispute. Development proceeded without question until April 1958, when the Americans suggested that Canada should accept the Bomarc–SAGE missile and ground control systems on Canadian territory as the latest elements in defence of US Strategic Air Command bases. The Canadian desire to be a good and self-respecting partner dictated acceptance, sharing in costs, and Canadian local control. For Canada this added burden meant that the costs of the Arrow would be too high for political acceptance – unless the production run could be substantially extended through sales to the US Air Force. But when George Pearkes went to Washington in August with that request, he came home instead with no sales and Bomarc–SAGE tucked under his arm. From that time on, Pearkes favoured cancellation of the Arrow on the grounds of cost and revised American estimates of the Soviet threat.

There is no evidence that Diefenbaker challenged the judgments Pearkes brought back from Washington. He accepted Bomarc–SAGE without question. He accepted as a matter of solidarity that Canada should join the United States in arming its defensive weapons with nuclear warheads. He shared the financial anxieties of his puritanical finance minister. And he took for granted that an American aircraft would have to be acquired, in time, to take the place of the Arrow in the common defence system. Only within this general scheme could it be argued that the Arrow was uneconomic. But Diefenbaker, as the fervent advocate of Canadian independence, had no interest in clarifying the full circumstances, or in admitting that the decision was encouraged, welcomed, and effectively dictated by the Pentagon. Perhaps he did not fully understand what had happened; perhaps it was better for him not to try.

Seen in this light, scrapping the Arrow was the easy decision for Diefenbaker, not the difficult one. The economic dislocation was unfortunate, and the prime minister's repeated postponements showed both his human and political sensitivity to that prospect. But putting the Arrow into production and service after August 1958 would have meant an early decision to defy American defence plans, although it seems conceivable that the Eisenhower administration might have shown its reluctant understanding. He had no wish to do so. In February 1959 Diefenbaker preferred to cut costs and take applause from Washington rather than Toronto, where he believed himself invulnerable. The Arrow's sacrifice, he hoped, would put Canada in a strong position to bargain for a real share in American defence contracting – and the criticism he faced gave him useful support in that bargaining. The defence production sharing agreements were the eventual result. Diefenbaker's reputation for courage and fighting spirit was enhanced, because he had faced down an industrial giant. But otherwise the outcome was discouraging. Avro Canada never recovered, and thousands of scientific and technical staff moved south to the United States. Canadian pride in the country's achievements and potential was undermined. And the cabinet revealed a kind of political ineptitude that few observers had expected. It was deficient in analytical power, and in the most elementary talents of manoeuvre and compromise. "This action," reflected Leslie Frost, "was the beginning of the decline of the Diefenbaker government. The method adopted completely lost the confidence of business and industry. In a space of some ten months, the overwhelming vote of confidence of March 1958 was completely lost."[169] The accusations of fumbling and confusion had begun to stick. The weaknesses of the ministry were those of the prime minister himself.

CHAPTER 10

"History Is a
Hanging Judge"

1959-1961

OR DIEFENBAKER THE ARROW DECISION WAS NOT A PARTICULARLY TROU-
bling one. He had a united cabinet and caucus, and faced an opposition reluctant to criticize the government's logic. The press, too,
was broadly sympathetic and took the prime minister's cue in calling
for real American concessions on the sharing of defence contracts.
Diefenbaker was in good spirits, still exhilarated by his mastery of
parliament and his command of the headlines. A week after the Arrow cancellation he wrote to his brother: "This has been a pretty terrible week. From last
Friday when the announcement was made until today everything that could be
said in the way of criticism has been said, but I think there has been a change
for the better in the last few days. I have always found that strong criticism of a
proper course disappears when the facts catch up with the fiction."[1]

Shortly before the decision he had attended the annual dinner of the press
gallery, where "everybody had a lot of fun at my expense. That is in the order of
things." He could afford the good humour, in his satisfaction with power and
the assurance of a place in the pantheon. He urged his mother and Uncle Ed
to give him their memories of the family because "all this will be needed in the
years ahead when my biography is written."[2] While rummaging through old files
he had discovered a relic that might have more current and light-hearted use.

> I found a notice of arrest that was served on me in 1928 by the police when
> we were travelling in Northern California, for having committed the alleged
> offence of cutting in. You will remember that I was to be locked up until the
> date of trial but was finally released and had to pay a heavy fine.
>
> The University of California wants to give me an Honorary Degree and
> if at any time I am able to accept I intend to produce the certificate of arrest
> so that they will appreciate the kind of treatment that was handed out to me,
> now thirty-one years ago.[3]

And those honorary degrees kept piling up. In the spring there were more, from Mount Allison, Western, Montréal, the Royal Military College ("the first Honorary Degree they have ever presented"), Michigan, and Princeton. Diefenbaker was losing count. "I keep you advised as to how many LL.D's and DCL's &c.," he told his mother in April, "and with the others in the next few weeks it will bring the number up to around twenty-two."[4] On his way to Lansing, Michigan, in early June he counted twenty; but after Princeton a week later, he again counted twenty.[5]

Diefenbaker maintained a punishing schedule of cabinet meetings, attendance in the House, speeches, continual travels, chats with cronies, and unscripted interviews with visitors to the prime minister's office. Entire school classes or individual students on their first, wide-eyed tours of the Parliament Buildings sometimes ended up in the prime minister's office to hear riveting monologues from the Chief after chance encounters with him in the corridors. Such diversions kept his timetable in chaos and his staff in knots. But they knew nothing could be done to change him: He loved his audiences too much for that. They fed him and buoyed his spirits.

The cabinet's marathon sessions continued. The economy and unemploy-ment were constant preoccupations, turning to obsessions at budget time. Before presentation of the 1959 budget in early April, six meetings of cabinet lasting a total of twelve hours were devoted to detailed dissection of Donald Fleming's proposals, which called for tax increases of $350 million to cut the current year's deficit by half in 1959–60 and a continuing tight rein on new expenditures. The minister of finance faced "a welter" of contradictory counterproposals in an exercise he found "almost degrading." He blamed this on Diefenbaker's "lack of experience and a certain timidity" in a field outside his competence: "He had no thought that a budget should be an entity and that the Minister of Finance needs some freedom in constructing it." But Fleming was tenacious in defence of his conservative position, and finally the cabinet came round to it. When Fleming presented it to the House on the evening of April 9, it was greeted with general praise by commentators as a moderate and judicious contribution to economic recovery. The Liberal and CCF responses – criticizing high taxes, spending, and deficits in the light of Conservative election promises – seemed harmless enough in the circumstances. Diefenbaker might have saved hours of his ministers' time by guiding them quickly into support for Fleming's proposals, but he seemed incapable of doing that.[6]

Given Diefenbaker's 1958 majority and his mastery of the House of Commons, the accusation of critics that he ran a "one-man government" was bound to arise. Blair Fraser of *Maclean's* devoted a column to the subject in March 1959 and carefully qualified his judgment. He had no doubt that Diefenbaker was "a towering figure" who dominated his cabinet, but that did not mean imposing his will on them. Rather – as the cabinet record confirms – he gave them unlimited opportunity to express their opinions, provoking their frequent annoyance at his delays. He dominated by monopolizing ministers' time in endless meetings – often on Saturdays and Sundays – and by hectoring them about attendance. He seemed to need consensus.[7] The astute political insider Roy Faibish commented about the work of cabinet committees he attended:

> If there wasn't a consensus and he didn't think the person holding out was a fool, to the exasperation of those of us who knew we were on the right course and wanted to get on with it, he would roll it over, bring it up another time, try to bring him around, almost like a lawyer trying to bring a jury around so you've got all the twelve heads nodding. In the end he usually decided, but he took so long that he was accused, properly, of procrastination.
>
> Parallel with the accusation that he was a one-man government was the charge that he was indecisive. He wasn't indecisive. He took a long time making up his mind because he had difficulty being arbitrary.[8]

Someone else might call that indecision. The hesitation reflected Diefenbaker's effort to avoid personal blame for political errors. "If something went wrong," George Hees recalled, "he didn't want to be the person that had made the wrong decision. If a thing went right he took the credit for it, but he never took the blame if it went wrong." So he set his ministers off arguing to eventual consensus – or to exhaustion.[9] Diefenbaker would range slowly down the cabinet agenda, seeking opinions around the table, jotting notes on responses, rarely offering his own views, and postponing any outcome in the absence of consensus.[10] His desire to escape blame was more than a political instinct: It was something more personal, even anti-political, an absence in his political makeup. Eventually that absence crippled him. For now, it was a source only of murmurings in cabinet and among idle back-benchers.

The prime minister was not an active policy-maker. He came to power with a few general objectives, no timetable, and no strategy. Above all, his instincts were tuned to his daily portion of adulation – and to the next general election. He did not normally intrude on the legislative programs of his ministers, or on the administration of their departments. His interest, in cabinet, was to weigh the political consequences of measures – and if they seemed risky, to move with the utmost caution. Otherwise, he was happy to give ministers their heads.[11]

Diefenbaker had no patience with discussion of long-term policy in cabinet: immediate issues and immediate public attitudes were his concern. "Occasionally we did make an attempt," Davie Fulton recalled, "but...the prime minister would be quite insistent...you were engaged in things that were going to erupt. So we would sort of let things go...finally we just simply accepted what the prime minister seemed to want." If ministers persisted, Diefenbaker implied that they had hidden motives. "Your motive might be your own cause, or to undermine him; that began to be apparent in cabinet. There was tension in cabinet, and disappointment in cabinet, and frustration in cabinet."[12]

The secretary of cabinet, Robert Bryce, managed the agenda and the staff budget. Diefenbaker depended on that one, firm source of order in an office that was otherwise disjointed and undisciplined. Although Bryce was the permanent civil servant responsible for the work of the Privy Council Office, there was not yet any clearly organized prime minister's office. It was emerging gradually, through effusion from the Privy Council Office. Diefenbaker had insisted on a small staff, with a budget no larger than that of the St Laurent office (about $50,000, not including his own salary). After Derek Bedson left to join Duff Roblin in the summer of 1958, Allister Grosart complained to Diefenbaker that the office had no focal point. But the prime minister would not make up his mind on a successor. Finally, as "about the sixteenth choice," Grosart suggested hiring a young Conservative lawyer from Vancouver, Gowan Guest. Although Grosart told Guest that Diefenbaker had no idea what Guest would do – and Diefenbaker confirmed it in his own telephone conversations – Guest agreed to join the office as the prime minister's private secretary in August. He set out for Ottawa in his Ford convertible, on the prime minister's helpful advice to "go across Montana." When he arrived in Ottawa and inquired further about his duties, Diefenbaker told him: "I expect you to figure that out." He told Guest that he had no idea what anyone in the office did, aside from his personal secretaries. So Guest tried to take charge of "the process affecting Diefenbaker": his correspondence, his visitors, his briefing materials. Guest had some success in clarifying the duties of the office staff, but none in imposing order on Diefenbaker himself. He soon learned that the Chief's habit was to let things flow around him as he responded to crises and immediate enticements. Anyone within range, at any time, might be called upon for "stuff" for speeches; anyone was a suitable audience for the prime minister's latest belly laugh. "Stuff" did not mean a draft speech. It meant "sound cadences, ideas, bits and pieces," usually gathered from several sources and assembled in an untidy bundle. Diefenbaker told Guest that the content of his speeches was unimportant.[13]

Almost a year after joining the prime minister, Guest confronted Diefenbaker with a three-page memo on office organization, neatly assessing "The Problem," "The History," "The Solution," and "The Personnel." "The basic problem," he wrote, "is lack of executive direction." Guest proposed either that the whole operation should be reabsorbed by the Privy Council Office or that a "responsible head" should be named to run the prime minister's office. He favoured the latter, and suggested his own interim appointment as "Executive Assistant to the Prime Minister...personally accountable...for any and every failure in the office, and for the overall provision of any and every service required by the Prime Minister." The effort failed: Guest got the title, but not the responsibility. Diefenbaker would not delegate his authority to a chief of staff.[14]

By the autumn of 1960 Guest had lost his early enthusiasm for the job and returned to his law firm in Vancouver. Despite the confusion generated by the Chief, Guest left him with genuine affection. He told Diefenbaker that he was thankful "for a friendship, an experience and an opportunity the like of which no other young Canadian has ever been privileged to have."[15] Meanwhile Merril Menzies, the brilliant idea man of 1957 and 1958 who had languished for more than a year as a casual adviser in the prime minister's office, resigned in frustration to take a civil service appointment. He had vainly sought to convince Diefenbaker of the need for long-term economic planning from a Conservative perspective. The Chief could not see the point.[16]

D IEFENBAKER CONTINUED TO CULTIVATE HIS FRIENDSHIPS WITH THE PRESS, BUT relations changed – at first subtly, then more crudely. In 1957 and 1958 those ties had paid political dividends, and he expected the advantages to continue. He offered privileged access, scoops, enticing hints, and trial balloons to Peter Dempson of the *Telegram*, Richard Jackson of the Ottawa *Journal*, Patrick Nicholson of Thomson Newspapers, James Oastler of the Montreal *Star*, Charles Lynch of Southam, and more favourites.[17] To others he gave occasional benefits, such as places on the prime ministerial aircraft. In return, he wanted respect and loyalty. First came respect, for him and for the office of prime minister. He was no longer "John." In the press scrum that Diefenbaker attracted in the corridors of the East Block, reporters yelled questions at him and thrust microphones into his face. If they called him "John," they could expect an invitation into his office and a personal rebuke. "What happened?" reporters asked Jean Leblanc of Canadian Press on one of these occasions. "He gave me hell for calling him John. He said he's prime minister and he should be called prime minister."[18]

Then came the expectation of loyalty. Diefenbaker saw it as the decent balancing of favours. When Charles King of Southam Press accompanied him to Vancouver in September 1958 for an honorary degree ceremony at the University of British Columbia and then on to a fishing expedition in the Yukon, the prime minister took for granted a friendly report. Instead, King wrote that the other degree recipients, Mike Pearson and M.J. Coldwell, had received louder applause than Diefenbaker (to his "consternation"), and that the excursion to the Yukon had cost $10,000 in public funds for one small trout. When Diefenbaker read the stories on the return trip, he exploded at King's discourtesy.[19] If old buddies turned objective or critical, Diefenbaker saw them as traitors. The Montreal *Star*'s James Oastler told Peter Newman:

> After John became prime minister, he expected that his past friendship with reporters would prevent them from criticizing his performance. He felt...that you're either wholeheartedly for him, or you're against him. He refuses to understand that good newspapermen – even those who were his cronies – can't let personal feelings interfere with their objectivity. Because he can't comprehend the motives of correspondents who write critically about his administration, he interprets their comments as personal insults. At the same time, the reporters who had been his friends also feel betrayed, because he no longer shares his confidences with them. Of course he can't. No prime minister can. The office necessarily formalizes human relationships.[20]

But Diefenbaker did, for a time, make mischievous use of his closest confidants, Richard Jackson and Peter Dempson, to test the winds on appointments and policies – forgetting his hints and claiming innocence when public reactions to their speculations were hostile.[21] As the government faced more and more contentious problems, the relationship soured. Journalists sensed the prime minister's devices and began, in Nicholson's words, "to seek out rather than to shun opportunities to criticize Diefenbaker's administration and to present him in an unfavourable light."[22] One after another, Diefenbaker came to distrust his old intimates in the gallery and to cast them among his permanent foes. In his greatest furies of betrayal, there would be angry calls to friendly publishers or editors to register the latest black marks against their hacks. Occasionally that led to firings or reassignments.[23]

In Toronto, Diefenbaker counted on the editorial support of both the *Telegram* and the *Globe and Mail*. The editor of the *Globe*, Oakley Dalgleish, provided Diefenbaker with good offices in his dealings with the premier, Leslie Frost, and influential advocacy in the business community. The *Telegram* offered more populist access to urban voters, and Diefenbaker made sure that his links with the publisher, John Bassett, flourished. As so often with Diefenbaker's close political friendships, this one had a personal side as well. Bassett and Diefenbaker carried on regular correspondence and visited one another along with their wives. "I became devoted to him and I felt he had the same feelings for me and looked on me almost as a son," Bassett recalled.[24] The prime minister valued Bassett's advice on policy, which was appealingly laced with flattery. After Diefenbaker's first attendance at the NATO Council in December 1957, Bassett told him that he was "a man touched with true greatness and of international stature."[25] After the 1958 election Bassett wrote, "You have revolutionized Canadian politics in the best sense, and...through your personality you have put public affairs back in the public realm."[26] In March 1959 he praised Diefenbaker's kindness and humanity.

> I was more touched than I can tell you that you would come to the airport to meet me and then again later in the day you were not too busy to carry on a long telephone conversation with a worried painter who was afraid that he was going to lose his job. I was once more impressed by your very deep and real concern for other people. I think it is this faculty, which you are also able to impart to others, that you really do care about them that lies at the base of your great political success. How unusual it is to see one who is unchanged by such a triumph as has been yours, and because you are unchanged I am sure your triumph is but the beginning.[27]

Bassett's "ardent support" was reflected in the *Telegram* by steady editorial praise and endlessly favourable reporting and photographic coverage of the prime minister.[28] In 1960 Diefenbaker responded by inviting Bassett to become Canadian ambassador to the United States. Bassett gracefully declined after an evening in New York with Lord Beaverbrook, who advised him that "the idea is preposterous." "You would be exchanging a seat of power," Beaverbrook thundered, "for the life of a messenger boy...A flunkey! If you want to go into politics yourself, actively, there is only one way. You must be an elected representative. You must stand for Parliament, if that is what you want. If you accept this job you will do yourself and your friend and sponsor an equally bad turn. Diefenbaker will be criticised for conferring a political favour. You will be a political liability...It would do you ill and do him ill."[29] Bassett took Beaverbrook's advice and became a candidate in 1962.

The press could be cosseted and openly criticized, if it could not be controlled. Dealing with the CBC was more perplexing. As the Conservative Party had promised, legislation created the Board of Broadcast Governors in 1958, removing the CBC's general regulatory role. Under the BBG, commercial television stations unaffiliated with the CBC – including Bassett's CFTO – were soon licensed as its competitors.[30] The managerial adjustment resulting from the CBC's rapid growth and changing status had proven difficult, and in December 1958 a bitter producers' strike began in Montreal over union recognition. The conflict dragged on for three months, through picket-line violence, a strikers' "march on Ottawa," disputes between Minister of Revenue George Nowlan and Léon Balcer over the strike's legality, accusations from the striking French-speaking producers of an English-speaking conspiracy against them, and various failures of mediation that led, eventually, to recognition of the union and a settlement in March. In the midst of battle the new president of the CBC, Alphonse Ouimet, collapsed with a heart attack. Nowlan (who reported to parliament for the CBC) learned quickly from the complex affair and adjusted his approaches, but Diefenbaker and other English-speaking ministers remained baffled and insensitive. The conflict hardened the nationalist views of Quebec producers like René Lévesque, and heightened the growing alienation of the two language communities. For Diefenbaker it was nothing more than an unfortunate labour-management dispute.[31]

Meanwhile, political commentary on CBC radio and television remained a nuisance to the government and annoyingly beyond its reach, since all parties accepted the formal independence of CBC programming. For Diefenbaker's taste, and that of many Conservative MPs, CBC political broadcasts too often purveyed Liberal or socialist propaganda that undermined support for the government. The prime minister did not hide his distaste from colleagues and reporters, but could not give direction to CBC management without being accused of impropriety or censorship. By April 1959 ministers were expressing their concern in cabinet that too much CBC commentary was "unjustifiably and unnecessarily critical of the government."[32] Friendly journalists like Patrick Nicholson reflected the prime minister's judgments in their columns, and there is no doubt that the acting CBC president, Ernest Bushnell, was aware of displeasure in the prime minister's circle. One Sunday in March while John Bassett was lunching with the Diefenbakers at 24 Sussex Drive, for example, they listened to what Bassett called a "vitriolic attack" on the prime minister by the reporter Michael Barkway on CBC radio. Bassett telephoned Bushnell in Diefenbaker's presence to tell him that Barkway's comments had been "vicious...unbalanced and indefensible," while Diefenbaker sat enjoying the tirade. "Imagine that," Bassett remembered the Chief's comment. "Wouldn't it be wonderful to talk to those fellows like that, Olive?"[33]

A major source of Conservative annoyance was the early morning program, "Preview Commentary." In mid-June Bushnell ordered the program cancelled, leaving the impression with the Toronto producers that the decision had been made under pressure from the government. The word in the CBC was that "heads would roll" unless the program disappeared. The supervisor of talks and public affairs, Frank Peers, and thirty-four national producers thereupon resigned. The Commons was in uproar. Nowlan insisted, as he always had done, that "I have made no representations to the CBC, directly or indirectly, at any time or at any place, with respect to any program of the Canadian Broadcasting Corporation."[34] Within days the CBC board of governors overruled Bushnell and ordered reinstatement of the program. Most of the producers returned. A subsequent parliamentary inquiry was unable to find any proof of political interference, although Nowlan freely admitted that he had let Bushnell know that he thought the CBC "was very loosely run" and should avoid controversy. Evidence was given that Bushnell had spoken to Ouimet of "this megalomaniac Diefenbaker." Although Nowlan and Diefenbaker were more careful after this episode to avoid any hint of direct interference, other ministers wished differently. For journalists, the lesson of the affair seemed to be that reporting about this government demanded constant vigilance. The gap was widening inexorably.[35]

THE CRISIS THAT PROMPTED MICHAEL BARKWAY'S CONDEMNATION OF THE Diefenbaker government in March 1959 was provincial in origin, another glancing blow that helped to wear away the sheen of the 1958 victory. In January the International Woodworkers of America had struck the Grand Falls, Newfoundland, mill of the Anglo-Newfoundland Development Corporation in the first serious bid to improve working conditions for the province's loggers. The company employed scab labour to keep the logging camps operating, the strikers set up roadblocks, and the company called for RCMP escorts for their trucks. (The RCMP served under contract as the provincial police force.) But the blockade succeeded, and the mill's lumber supplies ran down. The company faced defeat. It was supported by a sycophantic local press and some of the province's religious leaders, who warned against surrender to a foreign union aiming to dominate the province. Within a few weeks, writes Joey Smallwood's biographer Harold Horwood, "an atmosphere of hysteria began to build, a kind of public madness that had not been seen in Newfoundland since the days of the religious riots more than half a century earlier."[36]

Premier Smallwood played no role in the dispute until February 12, when he broadcast his denunciation of the union as outsiders spreading "their black poison of class hatred and bitter bigoted prejudice" in his "decent Christian province." He promised the companies that he would certify a new union and break the strike. The legislature quickly did what he asked. When the Newfoundland Federation of Labour rejected the new union as a fake, the premier broadened his attack against the entire labour movement. Early in March the legislature acted again, decertifying the IWA locals and giving the provincial government power to dissolve any union whose officers had – in Smallwood's words – been "convicted of such heinous crimes as white slavery, dope peddling, manslaughter, embezzlement, such heinous crimes as these." In fact, none had been.

While unions across the continent raised strike funds to support the Newfoundland IWA, the strikers blocked logging roads around Badger, near Grand Falls. Smallwood ordered the RCMP and the Newfoundland Constabulary into Badger in force, and on March 10 strikers and police engaged in violent combat on the roads. In the chaos many loggers were beaten; one Newfoundland policeman was injured and subsequently died. At the same time the provincial attorney general appealed to the minister of justice, Davie Fulton, for an additional fifty RCMP constables under the terms of the province's contract for services. The RCMP commissioner, L.H. Nicholson, insisted that the reinforcements were needed for relief of his overextended units, not strike-breaking. Fulton agreed with him, but would not comply without clearing the decision with cabinet. On March 10 and 11, while reinforcements waited at airports in Moncton and Sydney, Fulton asked cabinet to support their dispatch to Newfoundland. But Diefenbaker recalled the unfortunate, anti-labour role of the police in Winnipeg and Regina in 1919 and 1935 and refused to agree. Donald Fleming, George Nowlan, and Newfoundland minister W.J. Browne joined Fulton in arguing for compliance with the contract, and Diefenbaker called for a cabinet committee to examine the matter overnight. The committee, consisting of Fulton, Nowlan, and Browne, recommended support for the request. Still Diefenbaker resisted: Smallwood, he suspected, was trying to draw him into a strike-breaking role. Against Fulton's urgent appeals, the prime minister was intransigent. If he was proven wrong, Fleming recalled him saying, "he would take the responsibility personally and resign." Finally Fulton, and then other ministers, bent to his will under this threat.[37]

Fulton considered resignation, but after gaining the assurance of Nicholson that the existing detachments were not in jeopardy, he refused to order any reinforcement. The RCMP commissioner resigned on the ground that the contract with Newfoundland had not been fulfilled. Fulton tried unsuccessfully to persuade him that he should not resign because the agreement left the decision to the minister. In the House he justified the refusal by arguing that it had been necessary to maintain the RCMP's integrity as a national police force. But he was chastened and politically weakened by the affair.[38]

Diefenbaker told the House of Commons, in effect, that Smallwood had precipitated the violence and that the federal cabinet had concluded "it would be provocative and likely to cause further outbreaks of violence" to send in more police.[39] The suspicion lingered – in the minds of ministers, among others – that by refusing reinforcements Diefenbaker had put politics above the government's formal obligations.[40]

The defeated strikers reluctantly joined the province's union, and the company signed a contract at the wage level suggested two months earlier by a conciliation board. Smallwood railed on against international labour and the Diefenbaker government, and in August he won an election by fighting those absent foes. Diefenbaker, in his memoirs, righteously rejected the criticism that he had "courted the support of organized labour" during the strike, insisting that his government had acted only in the public interest and despite the political cost. "Would Canada," he asked, "have been well served had every working man and woman come to regard the Royal Canadian Mounted Police as a strike-breaking force?" That was a defensible political position, except for the awkwardness over the policing contract – which he ignored. Inside cabinet he had won, not by persuasion, but with a vague threat of resignation that left several ministers uneasy. Curiously, Diefenbaker believed he had suffered the unfair judgment of fate in the affair, but he claimed to accept it. "History," he quoted Lord Acton, "is a hanging judge." Perhaps; but it was not the loggers' strike alone that put him into the dock.[41]

Under the terms of Newfoundland's 1949 union with Canada, a royal commission was to offer advice within eight years on the province's continuing need for federal financial assistance. Accordingly, the McNair Commission had reported in August 1958 with a proposal that federal funding should rise to $8 million annually by 1961–62 and remain at that level thereafter. The Smallwood government had requested $17 million annually. Fleming brought the Department of Finance's variation on McNair to cabinet in early March: it called for unconditional payments of $8 million per year for five years after

1961–62, ending in 1966–67. Instead, cabinet agreed to terminate federal support in 1961–62, and to consider Newfoundland's needs beyond that as part of its general fiscal arrangements with the other provinces.[42]

The decision was made before Ottawa's involvement in the loggers' strike, but Diefenbaker announced it afterwards, on March 25. The statement, which had been drafted for him by Fleming, contained one harsh and ungenerous sentence: "The proposed payments will be unconditional and will be in final and irrevocable settlement of the provisions of Article 29 and the contractual obligations of the union consummated in 1949." Henceforth, it seemed, federal grants would be a matter for Ottawa's discretion. At the last moment W.J. Browne appealed to the Chief for delay and reconsideration; but the press release was already in the hands of reporters in the gallery. Here was new ammunition for Smallwood's bitter campaign against the Diefenbaker government. Smallwood – who matched his Ottawa rival in ego and melodramatic genius – draped Newfoundland's public buildings in black bunting for the tenth anniversary of confederation with Canada on April 1. Within weeks, he could claim, Ottawa had again reneged on its contracts. The debate raged intemperately over the summer as the legislation passed the House.[43]

IN THE EARLY AFTERNOON OF MARCH 17, 1959, DIEFENBAKER WAS CALLED FROM HIS seat in the House of Commons by Basil Robinson to hear that his secretary of state for external affairs, Sidney Smith, had died suddenly of a heart attack. Diefenbaker was "stunned and profoundly upset." After brief consultations, he returned to the chamber, told his seat-mate Donald Fleming, crossed the aisle to speak to Mike Pearson, and conveyed the disturbing news to the House. For a few moments MPs stood in silence, before the prime minister moved adjournment for the day. Diefenbaker remained troubled that he had not noticed the strain under which Smith had been working, but perhaps he could not be blamed for that. Smith had found the adjustment difficult. On the other hand, he was expansive, genial, loyal, and uncomplaining, and would never have let Diefenbaker worry about his personal concerns. By 1959 he had found his feet in the House and seemed comfortable in his secondary role behind the prime minister. Diefenbaker was pleased with the choice, and happy that a steady and routine relationship had been established. Its abrupt ending was shocking.[44]

The House adjourned again on March 19 for a state funeral at Chalmers United Church. For almost three months afterwards, Diefenbaker held the portfolio as he had in 1957. "I don't know where or to whom to turn for a

Foreign Minister," he wrote to Elmer.[45] There was widespread press speculation – mischievously fed by the prime minister himself – about a successor. The leading candidates seemed to be Fulton, Hees, and Nowlan, until Diefenbaker floated the name of Donald Fleming to his willing dupes Peter Dempson of the *Telegram* and Richard Jackson of the Ottawa *Journal.* They obliged him with their front-page musings. Simultaneously Diefenbaker encouraged Fleming by telling him, "In all the communications I have received on the appointment to External Affairs you are away in the lead." But when Dempson and Jackson visited Diefenbaker in mid-May, he teased them again. "Before either of us could say anything, the Prime Minister pointed to a stack of letters on his desk, said: 'Forget about Fleming. I'd like to let you read these, but I can't. Anyway, they've given me my answer.'"

For two weeks Fleming had been preparing himself for the call. Now Diefenbaker invited him in to tell him that "we can't afford to appoint you to External Affairs. You are indispensable in Finance." Diefenbaker chose Dempson to receive the scoop.

> On the following Friday, I was again in Diefenbaker's office. Jackson hadn't been able to accompany me because of illness. It was early June. I told him I was anxious to get a good story for our Saturday editions, and wondered if he could now reveal the name of his new External Affairs minister.
>
> "Oh, I can't do that," he snapped. "Everyone in the Press Gallery would be mad at me." He paused, obviously enjoying keeping me guessing. "Who do you think it is?"
>
> I replied that by process of elimination, I had reached the conclusion that it had to be Howard Green. But I wasn't convinced he was the man.
>
> Diefenbaker studied me for a few moments, not saying anything, a perplexed look on his face. Finally he got out of his chair and walked to one of the windows overlooking the lush lawns in front of the Parliament Buildings. He stood silent, his hands on his hips. After what seemed like an interminable time, he beckoned me to his side.
>
> "Those lawns," he said wryly, pointing out the window. "They sure are nice and *green,* aren't they?" He was smiling. That was all he said.

The *Telegram* broke the story, and a few days later it was confirmed. Green was the complete loyalist, Diefenbaker's supporter since 1942. Besides, as Diefenbaker confided to Robinson, "the 'ambitious ones' would be disappointed."[46]

Howard Green was a colourless man of utter probity. He had been an industrious House leader and chairman of caucus, but had little international experience. He had not left North America for forty years, and his views on foreign policy seemed limited to a traditionalist belief in the British connection and a distaste for the United States. At External Affairs he was remembered for his cold denunciation of Canada's creative diplomacy in the Suez affair. Robinson noticed that even Diefenbaker seemed nervous: "On the day before Green's appointment, Diefenbaker told me that the new minister would need all the department's help, and that, bearing in mind some of the things he had said in the past on foreign policy, he 'would have to change some of his ideas.'"[47] A curious beginning.

The prime minister postponed any further cabinet changes until the adjournment of the House in August, when he brought in two new ministers. Green gave up Public Works to the Chief's old friend David Walker, and Pierre Sévigny became associate minister of national defence. To make room for Walker as a Toronto minister, the gentle J.M. Macdonnell offered his resignation. This was a loss, not so much to the cabinet's inner strength (where his talents had been neglected) as to its fraying links with the Toronto business and financial establishment. The belligerent partisan David Walker could not make up for that.

Diefenbaker's other major appointment of 1959 was universally acclaimed. Soon after taking office, he had persuaded Vincent Massey to extend his term as governor general; but Massey expected to retire in the summer of 1959. Diefenbaker began his soundings for a successor by reflecting that he might find him among retired businessmen or Commonwealth prime ministers. The name of Robert Menzies was mentioned by the press, but Diefenbaker was too unsettled by Menzies's brusque intelligence to consider him. Olive's favourite was James Duncan, the former president of Massey Harris, but Diefenbaker told her: "You can't have Harris after Massey!" In response to "persistent stories," John Bassett wrote to the prime minister to warn him against appointing George Drew, who was "doing a fine job in London" and was "eminently suited for that post." Drew's weakness as a politician, Bassett thought, had been that he could not identify himself with ordinary people the way Diefenbaker did. "Thousands of Canadians," Bassett wrote, "would feel that in some way you have failed them, if you made such an appointment." Instead Bassett made his own suggestion. "As you probably know, The Telegram has publicly suggested Georges Vanier, first because I know him personally from many years of association to be a wonderful man with a charming wife eminently fitted by background for such a post, with no political affiliations whatsoever, and secondly, because I can not help but think in terms of politics, I think such an appointment made by you would have tremendous significance in building up a national Canadian concept."

Vanier had a distinguished military and diplomatic record, beginning in the First World War as a founding officer of the Royal Twenty-second Regiment – the "Van Doos" – and ending as Canadian ambassador to France from 1945 to 1953. Diefenbaker responded with enthusiasm and asked Bassett to raise the matter with Vanier. He did so during a visit to Montreal, and informed Diefenbaker that Vanier would accept the honour with pleasure. In July 1959 the prime minister conveyed the invitation formally to Vanier, and in September the new governor general was installed in a colourful, televised ceremony in the Senate chamber. Diefenbaker and Vanier spoke eloquently in both languages of the centuries of shared heritage among French- and English-speaking Canadians. The government's popularity in Quebec soared briefly by 10 percent. Throughout his term, Vanier and his wife, Pauline, graced Ottawa with their words and presence, sustaining some of the country's dignity as the political conflict grew increasingly rough.[48]

There were weeks of ceremonial for the Diefenbakers and other ministers in June and July 1959, when Queen Elizabeth and Prince Philip spent more than a month in Canada and the United States. The centrepiece of the royal visit was the formal opening of the St Lawrence Seaway at St Lambert, Quebec, on June 26, conducted jointly by the queen and President Eisenhower, and followed by passage of the royal yacht *Britannia* through flotillas of warships and pleasure craft up river from St Lambert to Beauharnois. The Diefenbakers also met the royal couple on their arrival in Canada at St John's, Newfoundland, on June 18, welcomed them in Ottawa in early July, joined them on the *Britannia* for two days' journey through the lakes from Windsor to Chicago, and met them again in Halifax on August 1 in the company of the whole federal cabinet as they prepared to depart for England. For Diefenbaker and his artlessly royalist ministers – and for the crowds who greeted the visitors – this was a beguiling summer festival for the Canadian monarchy.[49]

Diefenbaker broke his travels briefly in mid-June for a day's fishing at Harrington Lake. But the House was in session until late July, and he was approaching exhaustion. On June 18 he wrote: "This has been a heavy week. Tomorrow will be a trying day in the House and I am really looking forward to a weekend of rest." On June 20: "2 years is a long time, and while I have enjoyed every minute of it – being Prime Minister is a hard and trying job." On July 2: "I am really tired out after one week of various functions." On July 7: "Olive and I returned from Chicago at 4 o'clock this morning and I am tired out." On July 9: "The Session should be over in two weeks – and then I shall try to have a 10 day holiday. I need one for I haven't had even a few days." On July 18: "I have two major speeches to make on Monday in Quebec and have not any new material, and for that matter no ideas. Three or four have given me their suggestions and when I throw the omelet together tomorrow morning I will have to unscramble it and come up with something." Finally the session ended and there was relief by July 24: "The last four days have been the laziest that I have had for a long, long time...I have been able to have a bit of rest although spending a few hours a day in the office." But Olive was under medical care, suffering severe back and leg pains and swollen legs, and having difficulty walking – apparently a result of the injury suffered during her flight to England in 1957.[50]

Over the summer and autumn of 1959, Diefenbaker, assisted by friends, supporters, and history buffs, diligently added to the materials of his legend. "I wish you could see the collection that I am getting of Sir John A. Macdonald's mementos," he wrote to his mother. "They are coming in from everywhere and I will have a tremendously interesting collection." A few weeks later he visited the "Scottish Settlement" of West Gwillimbury, northwest of Toronto, where he located the graves of his Bannerman great-grandparents in the Presbyterian Auld Kirk Cemetery. The Dominion Archives soon provided him with records of the Bannermans' arrival at Red River in 1813, a fifty-acre land grant from Colonel Talbot near London, Ontario, and George Bannerman's oath of allegiance to the crown, sworn in 1818. In October he told his mother that a Conservative group planned to buy his birthplace in Newstad, Ontario, for $10,000, to restore it as a national monument. A bronze plaque, he expected, would announce that "here, to William Thomas and Mary Florence Diefenbaker...was born a son on September 18, 1895." Copies of the Diefenbaker homestead documents were being sought by his staff; and Uncle Ed had sent his revised memoir of those days on the land, which "brought back to mind many things which had been completely forgotten."

And still the personal honours flowed in: 1959 and 1960 brought three more honorary degrees, from Windsor, Wayne State, and DePauw; the Freedom of the City of London ("the highest honour that can be given to anyone in England...it is an honour that does not come to very many," he told Mary); and induction as Chief Many Spotted Horses of the Blood Indians.[51]

JOHN DIEFENBAKER'S REPUTATION WAS MADE AS THE CHAMPION OF CIVIL LIBERTIES. His most prominent commitment, on achieving office, was to adopt a Canadian bill of rights. During the minority parliament of 1957–58 that goal was deferred in favour of more immediate political measures. But once the majority was achieved, it headed the government's agenda. Diefenbaker's old ally in the cause, Arthur Lower of Queen's University, wrote to him soon after the government was formed to offer encouragement.

> I trust that during your term of office, you will do your best to bring forward such matters as guarantees for civil liberties, in order to familiarize the Canadian people with them and to educate them. I do not really think that a Bill of Rights would be practical politics just yet, but it well may be that certain minor matters can be attended to and that educative debates can be arranged. I would urge you to look into this whole nasty business of R.C.M.P. file-compiling. I suspect they have a file on you: I know they have one on me. Why? There is not a single incident in my whole public career which is not open to the light of day, and I am sure you can say the same. Why, then, this endless compiling of files? Already these have gone so far that people are afraid...This is the negation of self-government. If you do nothing more than relieve to some degree the spirit of fear imposed by our over-zealous police-men, you will have deserved well of your country.[52]

In April 1958 the prime minister promised the Canadian Congress of Labour that his government would introduce a bill to assure that rights would be "defined and guaranteed in precise and practical terms to all men by the law of the land."[53] One of the inevitable issues of dispute was the extent of parliament's power under the federal Constitution to enact such legislation, and in the summer Diefenbaker received inconclusive advice on the question from the constitutional lawyer Bora Laskin. Laskin, however, was inclined to believe that the federal parliament could protect the traditional political free-doms on the ground that they were "in no sense local values but, indeed, underlie the very structure of our constitutional system." In this case, parlia-ment could forbid discrimination as part of the criminal law.[54]

Under Fulton's supervision, officials in the Department of Justice took the initiative to prepare draft legislation. Cabinet discussed referring the bill to the Supreme Court for an advisory opinion on its constitutionality, but the prime minister was reluctant to do that. Instead, cabinet decided to give it a political test. On September 5, 1958 – as the session was about to end – Diefenbaker introduced Bill C–60, "An Act for the Recognition and Protection of Human Rights and Fundamental Freedoms," with no intention that it should be adopted in its original form. The bill would be floated to stimulate debate, die on the order paper, and be reintroduced, perhaps after amend-ment, in a subsequent session. The bill, Diefenbaker told parliament, "will not do everything," but it was intended to "curb the human tendencies of national governments to take shortcuts in ruling the people."[55] His emphasis was clearly on the bill's educative effects as a declaration of existing rights and as a restraint on Ottawa's powers alone. It would be adopted as a simple statute, would offer guidance to lawmakers as they drafted future federal laws, would contain exemptions for periods of emergency, and would contain no sanctions. These features were consistent with the prime minister's enduring attitudes. They avoided the strains of a long search for federal-provincial agreement on a constitutional amendment, as well as the intellectual conundrums of a profound debate on political values. The bill was a politician's tentative step out onto a high wire – but a step that no other federal politician had dared to take. By its nature it was unsatisfactory to parliamentary traditionalists, to advocates of an entrenched bill in the American style, to French-speaking Canadians uneasy about possible infringements on Quebec's claims, and to social democrats seeking greater protections for economic and social rights.[56]

The *Globe and Mail* welcomed the government's tentative approach: "The issues involved are both vitally important and highly complex, and it is desirable that Parliament and the public should be given ample time to consider them."[57] The challenge was instantly taken up at the annual meeting of the Canadian Bar Association, where delegates, attacking on all fronts, called the bill "downright dangerous," "window dressing," "a political show," a useless piece of paper unless it were entrenched in the Constitution.[58] Others – notably the prime minister's political associate Eddie Goodman – gave it warm support.[59]

Intense public discussion continued through the autumn and winter. In December the prime minister was disappointed by the comments – this time public – of Bora Laskin. With the draft bill before him, Laskin had sharpened his judgments: he was an opponent of the Diefenbaker compromise, and he was in full cry. He shared the government's belief that there were certain essential assumptions governing conduct in the Canadian democracy, but he found the bill "disappointing in its approach, unnecessarily limited in its application and ineffective in its substance." It was "merely a timid and tepid affirmation of a political and social tradition," had no application to the provinces, and even within the federal realm was so narrowly drawn that its "grandiloquence of expression" would lack any effect in concrete cases. It was not enough, he insisted, simply to see the bill as "a beacon of direction to legislators, to courts and to all public administrators." Since the Canadian courts had begun to find implicit guarantees of rights in the British North America Act, he speculated that "we would be as well off without a Bill of Rights as to have one so limited in its reach, so limited in its effect as Bill C–60."

Laskin found the bill's "declaratory approach" suitable for the Universal Declaration of Human Rights, which applied to a world of nations at various stages of political evolution. But "surely it is hardly satisfying to a community like Canada to be fed on the same bubbly mixture...when we have inherited a mature tradition of political civil liberty and have carried it into even broader fields?" He rejected the government's judgment that a constitutionally entrenched charter of rights was unachievable. Conceding the difficulty of agreement with the provinces, he saw no reason why Ottawa should not ask Westminster to amend the BNA Act to restrain federal legislative powers. And if, as he thought, there were genuine legal doubts about the reach of a federal bill, cabinet could also ask the Supreme Court for an advisory opinion on whether such an amendment might actually apply to the provinces as well. He could not conceive, for example, how freedom of speech, religion, and association could be bisected into federal and provincial segments. "Shall we talk, for example, of freedom of speech in a federally-controlled bank or railway or uranium mine, and of provincial freedom of speech on provincial highways and in retail stores or factories?"

This was root and branch criticism, scarcely softened by Laskin's concluding comment that the country should be grateful that the government had promoted discussion of "an issue of transcendental importance." Eddie Goodman agreed with Diefenbaker that the speech "does not give enough appreciation of the courage that the introduction of the Bill required and of the benefits that are to be derived from it."[60] Over the following two years there was continual legal criticism, but as Edward McWhinney noted: "No significant lowest common denominator of agreement was evident among the professional legal commentators' detailed criticisms of the draft Bill...Under the circumstances there were those who, recognizing the immense practical and political difficulties and the inevitability of angry criticism...would counsel Prime Minister Diefenbaker to follow the course of discretion and shelve his draft Bill, once the first public disenchantment with the Bill became apparent."[61]

But that was not his way. Diefenbaker was slow to move on contentious issues, but once committed he was aroused to combat rather than to reflection by public criticism. On an issue so central to his reputation and identity he could not give up the cause. He let the debate wash on, inconclusively, for almost two years, determined in the end to have his bill. In September 1959 he told the Canadian bar meeting that he would proceed by simple act of parliament because the provinces would not "abdicate their constitutional rights" in a constitutional amendment. The *Globe and Mail* commented that Diefenbaker was missing a chance to confront and settle the whole issue of constitutional amendment, but he had no intention of losing his bill in that morass.[62]

In December 1959 another civil libertarian whom Diefenbaker respected, F.R. Scott of McGill University, privately expressed doubts similar to Laskin's and carefully outlined two means of entrenching the bill in the Constitution. The first echoed Laskin's suggestion that Ottawa alone could request the United Kingdom parliament to add the bill to the BNA Act as a limitation on federal powers, thus binding future parliaments. The second recommended an additional amendment to the BNA Act, proposed in the same way, "declaring that any province whose legislature adopts the Bill of Rights shall be thereafter bound by it to the same extent and degree as is the Parliament of Canada. Thus the provinces can come in one by one, as fast as they like." Until the blessed day when Canada could finally bring the Constitution home, such amendments at Westminster would "at least indicate that we are more serious as a nation about the protection of basic rights than is suggested by the present Bill C–60."[63]

These comments, like Laskin's, were insulting to Diefenbaker. Despite their ingenuity, he did not plan to pay them any heed. He would not complicate the debate by any effort to amend the Constitution. Neither the provinces nor Westminster would share credit for his achievement. The prime minister replied dryly to Scott, "I will refer to the several points raised by you when the Bill is before Parliament."[64]

Diefenbaker introduced the bill to the House for the second time on Dominion Day, July 1, 1960, intending this time that it would receive rapid passage into law. The measure, he said, was "the first step on the part of Canada to carry out the acceptance...of the international declaration of human rights or...the principles that actuated those who produced that noble document." It would guarantee to all Canadians the rights and benefits of citizenship – to the extent that they fell under federal jurisdiction. That was a limitation, he admitted, "but in reply I say it will at least represent the essence of the conscience of the people of Canada." He suggested that the bill "embodies a pledge for all Canadians": "I am a Canadian, a free Canadian, free to speak without fear, free to worship God in my own way, free to stand for what I think right, free to oppose what I believe wrong, free to choose those who shall govern my country. This heritage of freedom I pledge to uphold for myself and all mankind."[65]

The government gave the bill priority in debate for the week that followed. Whatever criticisms the opposition made of the measure's weaknesses, they could not risk opposing it in principle, and on July 7 it received unanimous approval on second reading. Diefenbaker concluded debate with a display of the anguished personal feelings that had moved him in his cause.

> I can speak on the subject of mixed racial origin, Mr. Speaker. Had my name been that of my mother it would have been Campbell Bannerman...I know something of what it has meant in the past for some to regard those with names of other than British and French origin as not being that kind of Canadian that those of British or French origin could claim to be.[66]

He still felt the ancient pain of "second-class citizenship" and was determined to inoculate all Canadians against it. On July 1 he noted proudly that legislation had been adopted during the session to give the vote to "the first citizens of Canada," treaty Indians and Eskimos.[67]

The bill now passed to committee for several weeks of hearings that included familiar testimony from supporters and critics, including Professors Lower and Scott. After the defeat of a score of Liberal amendments and the addition of a flowery preamble, the Canadian Bill of Rights was adopted on third reading by another unanimous vote of the House. On August 10, 1960, it was proclaimed into law.[68]

During its first year, the Bill of Rights was invoked in about a dozen court cases and sustained in only one tax dispute. It caused "a ripple on the Canadian legal and legislative scene, but certainly not a splash," in the view of one reporter. It was ten years before the Supreme Court applied the non-discrimination principles of the bill to erase some sections of the Indian Act. As an educational and propagandist device, by contrast, it was an instant prize for the Conservative Party. The government printed 20,000 copies of the bill on ornamented parchment, in seven colours, embellished with the prime minister's flowing signature and his pledge as a "free Canadian." They were offered for sale at one dollar each, and became familiar decorations in police courts and classrooms across the land.[69] John Diefenbaker considered the bill to be his greatest achievement, and wrote sixteen years later in his memoirs:

> Those law professors and politicians who condemned it had closed their eyes to what was happening. All the laws of this Dominion were made to conform to it. It became the standard and the pattern for those Canadian provinces that wished to enact their own provincial Bills of Rights. No less important were the individual acts of fine citizenship which the Canadian Bill of Rights inspired. For example, I was most impressed when my long-time friend and colleague, the Honourable David Walker, in consequence of his commitment

to the concept of non-discrimination, initiated, as President of the prestigious Lawyers' Club in Toronto, the sweeping aside of any barriers preventing Jewish membership.[70]

That was a legacy of decency for a conservative country still shackled by its historic fears and prejudices.

The widely distributed parchment copies of the bill contained only part one of the legislation, which outlined the traditional liberties and legal rights "declared to exist" in Canada. But that list included an escape clause, allowing parliament to limit or deny those same claims by indicating in any bill that it intended to legislate "notwithstanding the Canadian Bill of Rights." (This would become the model for a similar escape clause in the Trudeau Charter of Rights of 1982.) Even more startling was the final section of the act, which provided that any actions taken in a state of emergency under the War Measures Act would not constitute violations of the Bill of Rights.[71]

Critics pointed out that the prime minister himself, in the early postwar years, had favoured repeal of the War Measures Act because it permitted arbitrary cabinet rule. Diefenbaker's response recalled his complaisant wartime attitude to the authority of the state. The power to rule by decree was necessary because Canada was living in "trying and dangerous times" under the threat of nuclear war. Therefore, emergency rule was legitimate as long as the proclamation of an emergency was subject to review by parliament. The Bill of Rights amended the War Measures Act to provide for such review. Diefenbaker's parliamentarism thus allowed him a certain sophistry in his commitment to civil liberty: rights were only what parliament declared them to be. This attitude was perhaps a key to his reluctance to entrench these rights in the Constitution. He genuinely rejected the belief that they should exist beyond parliament's power. But that reasoning justified the same invasions of rights he had complained about in wartime, as the use of the War Measures Act demonstrated in October 1970. Diefenbaker could never untangle the logical dilemma, except by claiming that parliament had been mistaken to approve emergency powers in 1970. "The important thing was," he argued weakly in the memoirs, "that in principle it preserved the rights of Parliament and was a defence against the government's using the War Measures Act under circumstances where it really was not justified."[72] In 1970 such principle buttered no parsnips.

For Diefenbaker there was another, still lower, level of sophistry and hypocrisy in his approach to civil rights. Under the rationale of the Soviet threat and a common allied approach to intelligence methods, the entire subject of security vetting of civil servants was managed beyond the sight of parliament or the cabinet. Diefenbaker had approved, with some doubts, the policies supervised by the Security Panel when he came into office, and he received regular reports of the panel's activities from its chairman, Robert Bryce.[73] At the very time that he was enshrining his declaration of rights in law, his own government was acting, with his knowledge, to deprive Canadian civil servants of employment through Star Chamber proceedings on grounds of "defects" or "weaknesses" of character. (The phrases were vague, but referred chiefly to homosexuality.) Diefenbaker's doubts led initially to a request to the Security Panel for a reconsideration of security procedures involving "weaknesses of character" in June 1958. The result was not an easing of policy, as he had perhaps intended, but an alarmist report to the panel in October 1959. Homosexuals were declared to be unreliable and "unsuitable for employment from the point of view of good personnel management, quite apart from the security considerations."[74]

This report produced irreconcilable divisions among members of the Security Panel and no recommendation to cabinet to alter the existing, illiberal policies. On the basis of the report, the RCMP security service began general investigations into homosexuals in federal employment during 1959. It reported 363 "confirmed, alleged, and suspected homosexuals" in thirty-three departments and agencies. It identified 153 of these persons as "confirmed" cases; and of these, 116 were no longer in government service, through firing, resignation, retirement, or death.

The RCMP's evidence-gathering was notoriously sloppy, but departments seemed to act with alacrity under the existing guidelines when they received security reports. The security service also investigated more than three hundred private citizens identified as homosexual in 1959 in order to gather "the most complete picture possible." The RCMP expressed some concern that departments were firing suspects before investigations were complete. During the next decade the numbers of persons on RCMP suspect lists for homosexuality, both inside the civil service and among the general population, grew steadily.[75]

Bryce made a general report on the Security Panel's discussion of homosexual cases in a memorandum to Diefenbaker and Fulton in January 1961. He reflected the views of the more liberal members of the panel, including his own and Norman Robertson's, in suggesting that inquiries should henceforth be limited to employees susceptible to blackmail by foreign intelligence services. In those cases, Bryce proposed that the Security Panel should review files before any departmental actions took place. These recommendations –

which were clearly aimed at narrowing both the range and the damaging personal results of RCMP snooping – still allowed for dismissals, transfers, and induced resignations without due process under the existing cabinet directive. In addition, Bryce recommended a program of psychological research designed to work out "tests to identify persons with homosexual tendencies" as a screening device for federal employment. His recommendations received the approval of Diefenbaker and Fulton in 1961.

A year later Bryce received an extensive and decidedly loony preliminary research report proposing a larger project aimed at identifying homosexuals on the basis of eye movements and pupil dilation when reacting to nude pictures. The Security Panel approved that project, with funding, in February 1963, as one of the last acts of the Diefenbaker government.[76]

Paradoxically, as the scholars Robinson and Kimmel point out, at the same meeting, and on the basis of American experience, the panel also supported a more permissive and liberal approach, handled on a case-by-case basis, to the removal of homosexuals from posts requiring security clearance. That led the new Liberal government, in December 1963, to adopt a revised Cabinet Directive on Security. But sweeping RCMP investigations continued without any clear cabinet mandate.[77]

This odious security policy resulted in the arbitrary disruption of scores of careers and lives, including those of senior civil servants personally known to Diefenbaker and whose cases he reviewed. It was carried out in the hysterical Cold War atmosphere of the late 1950s and 1960s with the tacit approval of the official opposition, as Liberals and Conservatives traded places in power.[78] For John Diefenbaker, the record must be judged against his unusual claims of virtue as a civil libertarian. On grounds of "national security" that the prime minister preferred not to question too closely, he countenanced secret investigations and rulings, without any legal protections, directed at citizens whose careers were in his care. This was not, on his part, a policy of active persecution; it was a policy of omission. Diefenbaker preferred to accept the advice of his permanent advisers, and to leave in place a system which, in principle, he rejected. Arthur Lower's complaints about RCMP security files only hinted at the possibilities of abuse. The reality was worse.

In the same period Diefenbaker dealt with one security case in a more direct way. In December 1960 Davie Fulton received a report from the RCMP commissioner indicating that Pierre Sévigny, the associate minister of defence, had been intimately involved with a Montreal woman, Gerda Munsinger, who might pose a security risk. Fulton recalled:

I went at once to see the prime minister, and told him that I wanted to discuss it with him. What should we do? I expected to have some sort of an investigation; but...he said, in my presence, "My God! This is terrible!" and he reached for the phone and called Sévigny, and said, "Get over here right away!" And without any chance to discuss with me as to how we might handle this...he had him over here and presented him with the facts and said, "What in the hell did you do?"

Sévigny admitted it: he said, "Yes, I did. But don't worry; I never gave a state secret away. I would never give a state secret away. I would resign at once if I had ever done it."

Diefenbaker accepted his word, and I think I did too...What was I to do? I didn't know how I could report this to the commissioner, so I'm afraid that I...left the commissioner up in the air...I found out later that he was very dissatisfied, and thought that the minister had taken no action on the matter at all, when in effect the prime minister had settled it. That was...typical of Dief...that he would do it that way instead of the normal way.[79]

The prime minister recorded his own memory of the incident in April 1966.

My first knowledge of the Munsinger affair was when Mr. Fulton called me and said he wished to take a matter up with me...I said that I was available immediately if he would come to my office, which he did.

He gave me a general outline of what had been brought to his attention by the Commissioner of the R.C.M.P., and informed me that in the course of investigating Mrs. Munsinger it was established by tapped telephone operations that Mr. Sévigny was seeing her from time to time and that on one occasion he went to her flat in Montreal around midnight and did not leave until early morning.

Mr. Fulton placed before me only one document, and as I recall it was two pages in length setting out the facts. She had had a suspected background of relations with Russians shortly after the war, and furthermore her suite was in a building in which the Russians had a trade office...

After some discussion I immediately called Mr. Sévigny and informed him that while I was no judge of morals, this type of conduct caused me great concern; that he was consorting with a woman of loose character and that all relations with her must cease at once. I pointed out her alleged past in Europe and Mr. Sévigny took the strongest objection to any suggestion that he in any way would do anything of a disloyal nature.

He finally said that there would be no more meetings with her. I again stated to him I would not accept any evasive explanations... *"This must end between you and this woman forthwith, period."* He then replied that Mrs. Munsinger intended to return to Germany.

I saw Mr. Sévigny again a day or two later and asked him, "Has this ended?" and he replied, "Yes," and said, "She will be leaving Canada shortly."

Some days later I asked Mr. Sévigny for unequivocal assurance that his relations with Mrs. Munsinger, whether social or otherwise, had ended and he said they had, and added that she had left Canada.[80]

Diefenbaker continued the story in another memo written two days later.

When it was decided she would leave the country it is alleged that Mr. Sévigny required $500.00 which was supplied by Bill O'Bront. [sic]

Before leaving the country she went to Morgan's store where she purchased clothing, etc., and issued a cheque which was refused by the bank because of insufficient funds on deposit. She was immediately arrested. This was on the Friday before she finally left Canada. She was freed on bail and $50.00 with the understanding that she would leave for Germany on Sunday. Transactions by O'Bront were carried out by Leo Robidoux, chauffeur to O'Bront, who allegedly paid the $50.00 fine that was imposed on her for fraud and it was he who picked up her ticket, gave her pocket money and drove her to Dorval Airport.[81]

Fulton offered Diefenbaker further information, presumably from the RCMP, and expressed some anxieties about loose ends in a handwritten note soon after Munsinger's departure:

The person whom we were discussing recently has now left on her trip to Europe.

An interesting feature of her trip is that she received a message to call at a certain place in Munich where she will be given $500. There were no conditions or instructions given in the message: presumably if any are to be given they will be given when the money is delivered.

A feature of this case is that the legal opinion is that a person who has been given the status of landed immigrant and acquired Canadian domicile, cannot be prevented from returning to Canada under the Act as it stands, even though landing was obtained by suppressing relevant information about criminal record, etc.

351

All that can be done now would be to await her return to Canada, then prosecute her for an offence committed after she had acquired domicile – then, if a conviction is obtained, she may be liable to be deported. You will appreciate the implications – what she might say – if we were to start prosecuting her for any of her questionable activities in Canada.

In short, I am afraid the problem and the potential danger is still on the doorstep if she returns.[82]

On December 21, 1960, Diefenbaker saw Sévigny again, and left him in suspense about his future in the cabinet.

Colonel Sévigny came in to advise that he was going away on vacation and I told him that circumstances were such that his business demands may necessitate his resigning from the Cabinet although not from the House.

He seemed greatly concerned about this but I told him I didn't see any way out and that the person in question, while now in West Germany, could not be denied returning to Canada.

I said I would discuss it finally with him early in the New Year.[83]

Diefenbaker received no evidence that Sévigny had breached security. The "person in question" had conveniently departed, so Sévigny remained in cabinet. The brief episode had occurred entirely in private, and it seemed best to keep things quiet. Diefenbaker knew that, as long as Sévigny stayed, he had enhanced command of the minister's loyalty. And he could take satisfaction in his own compassion. In 1966 he wrote:

I had not then nor have I now any doubt about Mr. S. being a loyal Canadian. His war record – his heroism on the battlefield even after he was grievously wounded – these attest to his devotion to Canada. He was unwise and very indiscreet in his association with this woman – but he was no traitor nor the making of one, so being satisfied that Canada's interests had not been jeopardized I refused to destroy this gallant French Canadian and to embarrass his family and friends when there was no reason to do so. And I am as satisfied now as I was then that I took the right course.[84]

Diefenbaker gave Sévigny the benefit of the doubt – something he had not done in those cases not of imprudence or disloyalty but of "weaknesses of character," brought to him earlier that year from the Security Panel. For the time being, the associate minister's indiscretions had damaged no one except

Mrs Munsinger; and she had departed for Munich with the promise of a $500 bonus.

———

IN THE MONTHS AFTER HOWARD GREEN'S APPOINTMENT AS MINISTER OF EXTERNAL affairs, international tensions were easing. Just as Green became foreign minister, the stern anti-communist voice of John Foster Dulles was silenced by his death from cancer. He was replaced as secretary of state by the more soft-spoken Christian Herter. Nikita Khrushchev's jovial tour of the United States in September 1959 was followed by an invitation to President Eisenhower to visit the USSR. A moratorium on atmospheric nuclear tests continued, while the United States, Britain, and the USSR pursued negotiations on a test ban treaty. Plans progressed for a great-power summit meeting in the spring of 1960, now actively supported in Washington. As tensions softened, Green threw himself energetically into the international disarmament campaign, with the enthusiastic support of the opinion polls. Canada joined a new ten-nation disarmament committee and played a leading role in a United Nations program to monitor radioactive fallout from nuclear weapons tests. Green, who admitted he was still learning on the job, showed rosy confidence in the prospects for peace, general disarmament, and Canadian prominence in the world.[85]

Diefenbaker told the House of Commons in January that his government's policy, in the evolving situation, was both to promote disarmament and to maintain the country's defences. Negotiations would continue with the United States, so that "the necessary weapons can be made available for Canadian defence units if and when they are required." The prime minister added that "Canada retains its full freedom of choice and decision" in approving the use of nuclear weapons by Canadian forces.[86] That was premature speculation, true only in the sense that there was not yet any agreement to acquire the weapons. The Bomarc missile, meanwhile, continued its spectacular series of test failures at Cape Canaveral, Florida, while George Pearkes insisted that it would nevertheless become "a vital element in the air defence system."[87] The Toronto *Star* cartoonist Duncan Macpherson pictured a feathery and prancing Pearkes as a "white-crested Bomarc booster."[88]

By late spring the atmosphere had darkened. Disarmament talks stalled, and east-west relations were disrupted by Soviet destruction of an American U–2 spy plane on an illicit photographic mission over Siberia. In mid-May the Paris summit meeting collapsed in black comedy and embarrassment over the incident.

As these discouragements played out, Diefenbaker was on another stage, attending his second meeting of Commonwealth prime ministers. This time the Commonwealth faced the troubling issue of South African apartheid. Harold Macmillan had delayed a prime ministers' conference until after his election victory in September 1959 ("You've never had it so good!" was the winning Conservative theme), but had now invited members to meet in London in May 1960. The prime minister of Ghana, Kwame Nkrumah, indicated that the issue of South African racial policy should be discussed at the meeting. In November, however, Macmillan circulated a message to all members from the prime minister of South Africa, Hendrik Verwoerd, objecting that "there can be no interference at such discussions or conferences in the domestic affairs of member countries...we would regard as interference any criticism or discussion, formal or informal, of the policy or action of a member related to its domestic affairs." Macmillan replied that "the convention of non-interference has always been fully understood and accepted among us all."[89]

The harshness of South African policy, and the frequency of violence resulting from it, now made that convention of self-restraint and mutual self-interest unrealistic. In January 1960 the Canadian Labour Congress presented a brief to the Diefenbaker government indicating its support for the exclusion of South Africa from the Commonwealth. Diefenbaker replied, with surprising vehemence, "I would not bring before the prime ministers' conference, or indeed support, any action that would exclude the Union of South Africa from the councils of the commonwealth of nations."[90] A few days later he clarified his position to the House:

> Certainly, in so far as I am personally concerned, I have at all times strongly pressed for the need of action being taken to the end that discrimination based on colour, creed or other reasons should be abandoned everywhere in the world.
>
> However, I do underline the fact that the representation of the C.L.C. was for action leading to the expulsion of South Africa from the commonwealth, and I made it clear that I would not take any part in bringing in a motion for action in that regard...It is clear that in the statement made by the Prime Minister of the United Kingdom no approbation was given to such a course as that suggested in the brief presented.[91]

Meanwhile, Macmillan was touring the African countries of the Commonwealth seeking to contain the incipient conflict. In South Africa, in mid-February, he called for recognition of the "winds of change" sweeping the continent: an appeal that seemed to be aimed directly at the South African government. Diefenbaker worried that "his own tactical freedom at the conference might be pre-empted" by Macmillan, and speculated that "Macmillan would not have spoken as he did if he had not been tipped off about South Africa's intention to leave the Commonwealth."[92]

Public appeals to Diefenbaker to take a harder stand in opposition to South African policy mounted to a crescendo by the end of March, after the police had killed sixty-seven blacks during disorders at Sharpeville. Diefenbaker also heard from Robert Menzies that Tunku Abdul Rahman of Malaya "felt compelled" to raise the issue in London because apartheid was a "denial of...respect for rights of the individual...which British institutions of government...inherited by commonwealth countries are intended to guarantee." Diefenbaker could instinctively sympathize with the Tunku's reasoning: Menzies reported that the Malayan leader was "constantly relating his thoughts on South Africa to deep racial, linguistic, cultural and religious differences which he is trying to bridge in creating [a] new Malayan nation with British institutions of government."[93] The UK government, on the other hand, made clear its desire to maintain a policy of non-intervention in order to protect the delicate relations of its African colonial territories with South Africa,[94] Under these pressures, Diefenbaker responded in two ways: by sharpening his public criticisms and by indicating privately that he expected "informal discussions" of apartheid at the Commonwealth conference, despite the convention of non-interference.[95]

Diefenbaker's shifting position reflected conflicts within his own administration.[96] Howard Green, his department, and the cabinet urged a course of extreme moderation on the prime minister at the conference, but Robert Bryce, who would be Diefenbaker's chief adviser in London, was more radical. Basil Robinson summarized Bryce's position as it had taken form by early April:

1. that the future usefulness and reputation of the Commonwealth as such in world affairs depended on a common acceptance of certain basic social and political standards which South Africa did not accept;
2. that Canada should consider initiating South Africa's withdrawal from the Commonwealth so that its non-white members could hold up their heads; and
3. that though there would be a strain on relations with the United Kingdom and Australia, Diefenbaker could be sure of a place in history if he had the courage to put a stop to our present hesitations.[97]

On April 11 the prime minister went into the House uncertain of his line on South Africa, bearing conflicting texts for a statement from Bryce and from

Robinson. He cobbled it together as he spoke, suggesting vaguely that there might be a major debate on South Africa after the Easter recess, and even more vaguely that the time was coming for a declaration of Commonwealth principles. Afterwards he departed for Easter in Saskatoon, "carrying with him speech drafts and briefing notes for the visit of President de Gaulle and for his own impending visit to Mexico, both of which would take place in the following week."[98]

Returning to the subject after this hectic interval, Diefenbaker told cabinet that he was annoyed by Macmillan's confusing comments on South Africa. The UK parliament had passed a unanimous resolution, in Macmillan's absence, condemning the policies of the South African government. Now Macmillan told Diefenbaker that he was inclined to present the parliamentary resolution to the Commonwealth conference, but to say that "it was not necessarily the view of the government of the United Kingdom." Diefenbaker speculated to cabinet that South Africa would make trouble at the conference.

> In the face of what had been said about South Africa, Louw (the foreign minister) could quite conceivably move for the free admission of all peoples within the Commonwealth to other Commonwealth countries. If this issue was brought out so starkly the white nations would be acutely embarrassed; it would mean the beginning of the break-up of the Commonwealth. Was Canada willing to open its doors wide to coloured immigrants?

"Altogether," Diefenbaker judged, "the situation could only be described as a mess."[99]

On April 27 Diefenbaker spoke in a House debate on South Africa with comments again patched together from "a mess of press clippings, diplomatic reports, and fragments of once pristine prose."[100] Several days earlier the situation had grown more critical when Prime Minister Verwoerd was wounded in an assassination attempt, "suffering himself," as Diefenbaker's notes said, "from the fearful tragedy that has engulfed that country."[101] Once again the prime minister condemned apartheid, but he left less certain the issue of South Africa's continuing membership in the Commonwealth.

> In the few moments remaining I am going to deal with some of the suggestions, "Throw them out of the commonwealth." I reiterate the views I have expressed before that there is no merit in such action. Such a course may have some superficial attractions but what of its objections? It would respond to natural feelings of distaste for racial policy; it may commend itself for its

purgatory effect. What would it solve? Would it bring relief to the 10 million blacks in that country? Would it share the views on discrimination? You are going to throw the 10 million blacks out. The whites who do not hold the same views as the government of the day you are going to throw out into outer darkness. That is what some say.

There is no machinery provided in the commonwealth to do so, as there are no qualifications as to beliefs required for membership in the commonwealth. One of the greatest hopes I have for an ultimate settlement is that South Africa has not withdrawn itself from the commonwealth and the fact that it will be represented in London at the prime ministers' conference assures that the channels of informal communication have not been closed.[102]

At the end of the month Diefenbaker flew to London for the conference with Bryce, Robinson, and Fulton. His intention, he told Robinson, was "to test the South African reaction, to feel them out." If they responded favourably, he would be able to justify his caution; if they did not, he could report at home that all reasonable efforts at persuasion had failed.[103]

In London the press emphasized the dangers of an irreconcilable split among the prime ministers, pitting Nkrumah and Tunku Abdul Rahman against Diefenbaker and Menzies on the South African question.[104] The reality was more subtle. Under Macmillan's sensitive guidance, the meeting steered through the shoals to a unanimous communiqué containing two paragraphs on South Africa. Diefenbaker "played a quiet role" that encouraged informal discussion and gave South Africa generous opportunity to show signs of flexibility in its racial policies. But South Africa offered no concessions. The communiqué asserted that "the Commonwealth itself is a multi-racial association" that sought "to ensure good relations between all member States and peoples." More crucially, the meeting found an appropriate means both to delay, and allow for, a collective judgment on South Africa's future relations with the Commonwealth:

> The meeting noted a statement by the South African Minister of External Affairs that the Union Government intended to hold a referendum on the subject of South Africa becoming a republic. The Meeting affirmed the view that the choice between a monarchy and a republic was entirely the responsibility of the country concerned. In the event of South Africa deciding to become a republic and if the desire was subsequently expressed to remain a member of the Commonwealth, the Meeting suggested that the South

African Government should then ask for the consent of the other Commonwealth Governments, either at a Meeting of Commonwealth Prime Ministers or, if this were not practicable, by correspondence.[105]

Following the referendum, the initiative would lie with South Africa to seek renewal of its membership if it wished to do so. But since Commonwealth conferences worked by consensus rather than formal voting, the meaning of "consent" to such a request remained intentionally vague. On his own copy of the communiqué, Diefenbaker scribbled in the margin: "Implies unanimity." Diefenbaker told parliament on his return that "these significant words ... require no interpretation," and proceeded to give it: "This established clearly that membership in the commonwealth is not a formality. These words...make clear that the prime ministers were not prepared to give an advance assurance that South Africa might remain a member of the commonwealth in the event that a decision was made to adopt the status of a republic."[106]

The next steps were South Africa's. Diefenbaker was satisfied with the delay. He had shifted prudently with the circumstances, and foresaw that a choice was coming. But he was not yet ready to go as far as Robert Bryce, who had supplied him with draft remarks for the House which he did not use. They indicated Bryce's own convictions and his understanding of the prime minister's mind, and they were prescient.

> I think I can claim without immodesty to have been the strongest and most consistent advocate of racial and personal equality.
>
> In keeping with that belief I shall be introducing within a few days a Bill of Rights which is intended to express in legislation the fundamental principle upon which in my opinion our own social relationship is based and upon which alone the Commonwealth can survive.
>
> Surely if there is one common principle, above all others, which unites us within the Commonwealth, with all its races, religions, colours and creeds, it is our belief in racial and personal equality...
>
> One thing I wish to make emphatically clear. We did not temporize on this vitally important subject. We shall not temporize. By persuasion, by argument in personal contact, we shall seek to gain acceptance throughout the whole Commonwealth of the supreme principle of our society that every man is equal before God and that appropriate laws should state that belief.[107]

That would mean a Commonwealth without South Africa. Diefenbaker might reach that point, but his first object was to preserve the Commonwealth association as a whole and to avoid any open confrontation between white and non-white leaders on the South African issue. A confrontation would, in effect, mean a shift to decisions by majority vote, and the prospect prompted Diefenbaker to repeat to cabinet his fear about migration policy in another form. "If Commonwealth Conferences should once adopt the majority vote as a means of reaching its [sic] decisions, the non-white majority at the next conference would probably support free migration of peoples. Such an immigration policy was clearly unacceptable to the Canadian people."[108] Privately, Diefenbaker had turned the issue into something more complex than South Africa's continuing membership in the Commonwealth. How could the subject be dealt with in a way that would not divide the Commonwealth along racial lines and open the white countries to justified accusations of racism and hypocrisy?

South Africa scheduled its constitutional referendum for October 1960. In early August, Verwoerd announced that if the vote favoured a republic, his government would request continuing membership in the Commonwealth. Macmillan wrote to Diefenbaker and other leaders predicting that "very difficult issues may arise for us all." He suggested "that it would be in the general Commonwealth interest if we could all say as little as possible at this stage." In a covering note to Diefenbaker, he asked for advice on how to respond to a republican vote in October. "It will need," he warned, "very careful handling."[109]

The whites-only referendum, as anticipated, delivered a narrow verdict in favour of republican status. Diefenbaker worried that, because "public opinion in Canada was so strong...he could not possibly afford to adopt at the next meeting an attitude as tolerant of South Africa as he had before and during the last meeting."[110] That view disturbed the UK high commissioner to Canada, Joe Garner, and Macmillan, who noted on a letter from Diefenbaker in mid-November: "John Diefenbaker is going to be troublesome about South Africa. He is taking a 'holier than thou' attitude, which may cause us infinite trouble. For if the 'Whites' take an anti–South African line, how can we expect the Browns and the Blacks to be more tolerant?"[111]

Macmillan cabled Diefenbaker at length, appealing to him not to commit himself against South African membership before the next Commonwealth conference, which had been arranged for March 1961. Diefenbaker was annoyed by a sense that Macmillan was ignoring Canadian advice on the issue in favour of Menzies, and that he was badgering Canada. But Diefenbaker's indecision was as marked as that of Macmillan. He "fretted about how to play his cards, his political instincts telling him to keep his own counsel until the moment for decision was at hand."[112] And he was getting no help from External Affairs. A long memo from Howard Green in late December offered no clear recommendations, while another one in mid-January tried to square the circle. It could find no principle for barring South Africa from membership which did not raise problems of consistency for other members. Instead, the department suggested that the conference might renew South Africa's membership while issuing some kind of comment on racial policies. The statement "would be neither a clarion call for the ending of racial discrimination nor a heated denunciation of South Africa." It would take "a firm stand" on race relations, but "without splitting the members into white and non-white camps." Altogether, "It would deplore the present unwillingness of South Africa to move toward a moderation of its racial policies; emphasize the strength of opposition in the Commonwealth to racial discrimination; deprecate a radical solution such as the exclusion of South Africa in a Commonwealth accustomed to mutual tolerance and understanding; but make it clear that tolerance alone cannot be stretched indefinitely to bridge a wide gap in fundamental principles." That seemed like an elaborate recipe for continuing indecision. Diefenbaker marked his copy of those words with a question mark – a sign of indecision squared.[113]

According to Robinson, the paper took into account Diefenbaker's growing instinct for further postponement, but "he was clearly drifting in response to the pressures of the moment."[114] He had received a paper from Professor Donald Creighton arguing for exclusion, and both the Toronto *Telegram* and the *Globe and Mail* called for an initiative from Diefenbaker, "the author of a new Bill of Rights and a life-long advocate of constitutional and individual liberty." The new members of the Commonwealth, according to the *Telegram*, expected Canada "to speak out and to save the Commonwealth in its new form as a multi-racial family of nations."[115] Robert Bryce, who had consulted widely with Commonwealth colleagues since the 1960 conference, added his discreet voice for exclusion in a handwritten note to Diefenbaker. "The main reason for excluding South Africa is to *strengthen* the Commonwealth. Keeping S.A. in will really weaken it – and more and more people will simply pay lip-service to it. The chief value of the Commonwealth in the next decade, as you have said publicly I think, is to be a bridge between the rich white peoples and the poor coloured peoples. Endorsing S.A. now will seriously harm its value for this purpose. R.B.B."[116]

When Diefenbaker sought the advice of cabinet on February 11, he found them hopelessly confused and divided. A stream of advice from George

Drew in London suggested the attractions of postponement. By the end of the month Diefenbaker still had no fixed position and no public commitments. He flew to London in early March in the same state of indecision as in 1960, fearful of failure, hoping for postponement, and with no desire to take to the barricades.[117] In his first press conference on arrival at London airport, he baffled reporters with his polished Diefenbakerisms.

> The question of continued membership within the Commonwealth is one...for discussion and consideration by this Conference among other things and I am sure that each will give to the consideration of this trying problem that same spirit that in the past has characterized the members of this Commonwealth and that in the passing years has brought about changes, based on experience, not always immediately accepted but ultimately achieved through the process of consideration, discussion and the realization of the need that the Commonwealth shall be maintained in strength and in power for peace everywhere in the world.[118]

For ever and ever, amen.

The conference began on March 8, 1961, with three days of general discussion on international policy, as delegations probed and manoeuvred cautiously on the South African question. Diefenbaker had with him Davie Fulton and Noel Dorion from cabinet; George Drew; and Robert Bryce, Basil Robinson, and Geoffrey Murray from External Affairs. During the preliminaries – and despite his own preferences – Bryce was delegated to search informally for some means of avoiding a direct rejection of South Africa's request for renewed membership.[119] On March 9 he presented Diefenbaker with his proposal, suggesting that the prime minister should discuss it with Macmillan during the weekend at Chequers.

> The alternative course...appears to be to couple together consent to South Africa remaining a member with some announcement, which should be made at the same time as the news about South Africa comes out, that the Prime Ministers decided to proceed at their next meeting to consideration of a statement of principles to which members of the Commonwealth might be expected to subscribe. It could be said, though perhaps not in the agreed statement, that the action in regard to South Africa made necessary a declaration of principles to ensure that the views of the members of the Commonwealth were not misinterpreted as an implication of their granting consent to the continued membership of South Africa.[120]

Bryce urged Diefenbaker to discuss the proposal with no one until he knew Macmillan's views. Only if Macmillan thought the approach feasible should he mention it to other prime ministers, since "any overtures along these lines on Canada's part are almost certain to leak out because Canada's attitude on this question is the biggest news of the whole Conference."[121]

The next day, Bryce wrote privately to Diefenbaker to advise against the proposal he had made in his formal memorandum.

> I hope you will excuse my writing to you this personal note. I may not have a chance to speak to you before you go to Chequers.
>
> I am impelled to urge you to consider again carefully the main decision on South Africa before committing yourself finally to "consent plus a declaration." As you know I have felt all along that it would be in the best interests of the Commonwealth and Canada to refuse consent. I want to repeat the arguments.
>
> What does concern me at this time is the damage this decision may do to your own reputation both at home in Canada and in other countries. If you consent, I believe people will think and say that you have not lived up to the high ideals which you have stated so eloquently and so often. No words will be able to make up for the lack of action.
>
> On the other hand if you are known to have taken the lead in refusing consent you will be hailed, here in London, at home in Canada, and throughout much of the world as a man who has courage as well as convictions. It will be unpleasant for a few days here, but I think you would be happier in the end.
>
> I have refrained from putting forward the point in meetings with Mr Drew and the Ministers, as it is such a personal matter, but I wanted you to be aware of my thoughts on it.[122]

Diefenbaker carried this troubling appeal to conscience and political interest with him to Chequers, along with more baggage. Earlier in the day he had met with a South African United Front delegation led by Oliver Tambo of the African National Congress, who also urged rejection of South African membership. That meeting was known to the press – which probably narrowed Diefenbaker's moral options.[123] He could still not find a satisfactory position.

Diefenbaker spent a weekend of nervous consultation on the "consent plus" option, including a long telephone conversation with Howard Green, who told him that the cabinet favoured an "uncompromising denunciation of apartheid" and was concerned for Diefenbaker's reputation, but opposed a

Commonwealth declaration of principles. That wasn't much help. On Sunday, March 12, the Canadian delegation thrashed about in its efforts to draft the prime minister's statement for next day's Commonwealth meeting. Diefenbaker took with him to the meeting a heavily rewritten text which declared apartheid "repugnant to most of the world," insisted that "the positive act of consent which South Africa is asking us to take at this meeting" could not be a formality, and ended by proposing to defer any decision on South African membership until after agreement on a declaration of Commonwealth principles at a future meeting. Diefenbaker told his Canadian colleagues that this approach would probably result in a South African withdrawal – which seemed the least divisive possibility. Diefenbaker had thus reversed the proposed order of events from "consent plus a declaration" to "a declaration plus consent," requiring South Africa to endorse a statement on racial equality before it was considered for readmission. But other prime ministers could not understand his appeal for delay. At the end of the day it was clear that the "consent plus" option, as well as Diefenbaker's scheme for delay, were dead, but the substance of his position remained. Macmillan told the meeting that it could not avoid a declaration of principles. The issue had narrowed to its content, and the possibility of South African agreement to the wording.[124]

That afternoon Davie Fulton reported to a press briefing that Diefenbaker had told the conference "it is time for the Commonwealth to draw up a declaration of the principles for which it stands," and admitted to a questioner that other prime ministers had agreed with him. There was a "considerable body of support," but he could say no more because "we are in the midst of a pretty tense and important discussion and ways are being sought of finding an acceptable solution to this problem."[125] Robinson could see that Diefenbaker, "while not seeming or aspiring to form a coalition with his non-white colleagues, had drawn apart from Macmillan, Menzies, and Holyoake of New Zealand and, of course, Verwoerd."[126]

Macmillan opened the second day of discussion on South Africa by offering a draft statement on racial policy for the final communiqué. After Verwoerd and Menzies objected that the language intruded into domestic affairs, Diefenbaker responded that the issue was an international one. The Commonwealth, he believed, could unite only on the principle of non-discrimination. If South Africa wished to maintain its membership after becoming a republic, it would have to acknowledge that its racial policy was inconsistent with the Commonwealth's principles. That required a statement of principles in the communiqué. The effect would be to force a choice on

South Africa rather than on the other members. South Africa could either acknowledge the divisions its request had caused and withdraw its application as premature, pending completion of its constitutional changes and "clarification" of its policies, or it could remain a member by recognizing "the same principle of non-discrimination on grounds of race and colour as is recognized in the United Nations Charter."[127]

When Macmillan produced a revised draft statement at the afternoon session, Verwoerd complained once more that it prescribed too much. The Canadian prime minister read to him the final paragraph about South African policy.

> They considered that this policy was inconsistent with the basic ideals on which the unity and influence of the Commonwealth rest, and with the Charter of the United Nations. They affirmed their belief that, for all Commonwealth Governments, it should be an objective of policy to build in their countries a structure of society which offers equality of opportunity for all, irrespective of race, colour or creed.

Diefenbaker asked Verwoerd two questions. Would he accept this paragraph in the communiqué? Verwoerd said "No." After Macmillan suggested adding that "this could be the view of others but not Mr. Verwoerd's," Diefenbaker asked whether Verwoerd "would allow this paragraph to be included in final Communique." Verwoerd replied "Definitely not!"[128] Instead, he defended South Africa's policies as "separate development," and asked that the paragraph "should be erased completely." "This," Diefenbaker recorded, "means we accept application." He handed a note to Fulton: "Do you perceive any hope of agreement?" to which Fulton replied: "Not yet. Some are moving towards delay, but not yet enough."[129]

That evening Robinson wrote that "everyone is looking for a formula to prevent extreme action" – which he later interpreted to mean "that the mood did not favour an active measure to *expel* South Africa."[130] Under Nehru's guidance, the non-white members had insisted firmly but decorously on a decision, while Macmillan managed the debate with supreme skill in his search for a means of keeping South Africa in.[131] Diefenbaker stood in the middle, but in the end found himself in principled agreement with his non-white colleagues as they pressed Verwoerd backwards towards the door. Renewal of South African membership on the Commonwealth's terms had been ruled out by Verwoerd's intransigence; postponement remained unacceptable to the non-white members; and no one wanted a bitter decision to expel. That left the initiative – for retreat – to Verwoerd. "South Africa," thought Robinson, "is being confronted with a take-it-or-leave-it proposition."[132]

The next day Macmillan made one more effort at compromise. Verwoerd, he said, would accept the previous draft communiqué if he could add a substantial paragraph in defence of South African policy. Eventually a new draft was circulated in which Verwoerd "deplored the accusations of racial discrimination levelled against South Africa by member countries which he considered to be themselves guilty of such practices," while other members simply "adhered to the views they had expressed."[133] This was too much. Diefenbaker, Nehru, Nkrumah, and Nigerian Prime Minister Abubakar Tafawa Balewa objected, and any hope of agreement collapsed. Verwoerd requested a recess, met alone with Macmillan, and returned to say that South Africa was withdrawing its application to remain in the Commonwealth.[134] According to Diefenbaker's notes, the South African prime minister departed in full defiance, defending his country's "national pride and self-respect...shocked by hostility at this meeting," and predicting imminent disintegration of the Commonwealth.[135]

Once the South African issue was resolved, the other members abandoned the task of drafting a declaration of Commonwealth principles; but Diefenbaker told reporters that non-discrimination was an "unwritten principle" of the association. That was "in keeping with the course of my life."[136] On March 17, after an overnight flight across the Atlantic, Diefenbaker came to the House of Commons at 11 am. He offered a sober and untriumphant account of the conference, noting that "we tried to do whatever was humanly possible to avoid a break without making a sacrifice of basic principles." Diefenbaker saw dignity and restraint all round. "Those who belonged to non-white races showed an attitude of endeavouring to bring about some compromise"; Dr Verwoerd did not reciprocate, "but I do not want hon. members to conclude that he was lacking in forbearance. He is a wonderful personality; he is a kindly burgher. In the face of strong and sometimes provocative criticism he maintained throughout an impressive courtesy and calm."

> Was the result unavoidable? I think it was. Over the years I have contended that in a multi-racial association it had become clear beyond doubt that if the commonwealth is to be a force for good, as it should be, there must be a measure of general agreement that discrimination in respect of race and colour shall not take place. I do not think we can compromise that principle if we believe that the commonwealth has a mission for all mankind. It would lose its power to meet challenges and opportunities in the future. I

am more convinced than ever as to the power of this institution touching every part of the world...

There will be some who will say, and they will speak with great energy, that we should have pressed for the expulsion of South Africa. I remind those that speak in that vein that Ghana, Nigeria, India, Pakistan, Malaya and Ceylon did not follow that course. I think the fact that this break had to come and that South Africa should have withdrawn its application was the best course that could be followed.[137]

For his contribution to this prudent and principled result, explained without flamboyance, Diefenbaker received general praise. Unexpectedly, the occasion marked a high point of his prime ministership. Both in the United Kingdom and in Canada, press reports tended to exaggerate his active role in the affair. What was notable was not that he had assumed a role of leadership, but that Diefenbaker, alone among the representatives of the old Commonwealth, had sided with the new, non-white members on a matter of principle. That had prevented a division along racial lines that might have been destructive. But in the end it was Verwoerd who had taken the decision and relieved other members of their embarrassment. Diefenbaker's initial idealism about the Commonwealth had now been tempered by hard political experience, while Macmillan's early and interested regard for the Canadian as a useful partner had distinctly cooled.

CHAPTER 11

"Hazard ...
Our Constant Companion"

1960-1961

W HEN THE 1960 SESSION OF PARLIAMENT OPENED ON JANUARY 14, THE Diefenbaker government had lost its novelty, the Liberal front bench had grown in confidence, and the rebirth of the political left was advancing with labour and popular endorsements of a "New Party" to take the place of the CCF. The Conservative Party's fragile dependence on Quebec's Union Nationale government was shaken by the death of Premier Duplessis in September 1959, briefly infused with energy by the succession as premier of Diefenbaker's friend Paul Sauvé, and shaken anew by Sauvé's sudden death in early January. Diefenbaker told his mother: "Tomorrow I am going to St. Eustache, just out from Montreal, to attend the funeral of Premier Sauvé. He was only 52 years of age and had a brilliant future ahead of him, and many have expressed their views in the past few months that he would succeed me as leader of the Conservative party and probably PM."[1] Diefenbaker's vision of Quebec politics began at the top and never penetrated far below, where an awakening was beginning after a sleep of decades. Although Sauvé sensed the change, his Union Nationale – so long in alliance with traditionalist and reactionary forces – was an unlikely means of leading or containing it.

The speech from the throne of January 1960 announced a modest legislative program for the session. In his response, Mike Pearson called the government's plans "unimpressive and superficial," failing to confront the problems of unemployment, defence, agriculture, and public finance. *Saturday Night* pronounced Pearson's speech "a logical, carefully documented indictment of the administration" which had kept "the jaded members of the press gallery" in their seats. The columnist Austin Cross, once Diefenbaker's admirer, termed Pearson's opening "a good speech, a brilliant speech, a humorous speech." But the prime minister used a smart trick to gain the advantage: He kept the major revelations of policy for his own speech, which followed

Pearson's. Diefenbaker announced a royal commission on government organization, an effort to amend the Constitution without recourse to Westminster,
a proposal to reform the parliamentary committee system, and continuing
negotiations with the United States on double key control from both capitals
of nuclear warheads on Canadian weapons. Then he turned on the Liberal
Party for its unpardonable arrogance. The CCF member for Port Arthur,
Douglas Fisher, lamented that "the government and the Prime Minister have
their second wind now, but it is still the old wind we hear soughing; attack,
attack, attack interminably."[2]

In January 1960 Diefenbaker unexpectedly announced the resignation
of his secretary of state, Henri Courtemanche, and his appointment to the
Senate for what the prime minister discreetly called reasons of health. Later,
in 1961, Courtemanche was disbarred for accepting $60,000 in kickbacks from
federal grants to the Jean Talon Hospital in Montreal, and resigned his Senate
seat on the Chief's demand.[3] Diefenbaker was not faring well with his Quebec
ministers: O'Hurley was stumbling in Defence Production; Comtois was little
more than comatose; Sévigny was an object of suspicion after December 1960;
and Balcer's talents remained untested. André Laurendeau commented in *Le
Devoir* in September that "French-Canadians have never, since R.B. Bennett,
felt themselves so distant from the country's business as they are under Mr.
Diefenbaker."[4] But there were weaknesses elsewhere as well. George Pearkes
had become a Blimpish target as he fumbled over the Bomarc missile and the
confusing imperatives of American defence policy; Gordon Churchill was performing indifferently in Trade and Commerce and ineptly as House leader;
Alf Brooks, the minister of veterans affairs, was, like Pearkes, an aging veteran of two wars who was ready to accept retirement to the Senate.[5]

After three years in office, the cabinet had produced only a handful of
demonstrably capable ministers: Green, Fleming, Fulton, Hees, Harkness,
Alvin Hamilton, Nowlan, and Starr. It would need rearrangement and bol-
stering before another election. By mid-summer Diefenbaker had decided to
provide Pearkes with a parachute into the lieutenant governor's mansion in
British Columbia, and Brooks a seat in the Senate. Those departures would
require a general shuffle. Diefenbaker began his consultations in August, and
fussed over a decision for more than three months. His parliamentary strategist Gordon Churchill encouraged the hesitation by telling him that "if an election is likely next year, it would be advisable to make as few cabinet changes as
possible." He offered a barrage of reasons. Ministers were now experienced
in their jobs; thrown into new portfolios they would be unsure of themselves
and subject to "a lack of co-operation" from their senior civil servants. The

existing cabinet could be presented to the public as a team. And the key prairie ministers, Harkness, Hamilton, and Churchill, would be especially vital in their present posts to hold the rural vote. Churchill therefore recommended only two major changes: Fulton should move to Defence, where he would be "fully competent to stand the strain of a difficult position"; and the recently defeated Conservative premier of New Brunswick, Hugh John Flemming, should come in to the newly created Department of Forestry.[6]

Diefenbaker also made a casual canvass of old cronies; on August 27 he noted the suggestions of the reporter Jim Oastler and the Manitoba senator Solly Thorvaldson.[7] Several times he produced tentative lists for himself, before finally announcing his changes on October 11. They were substantial: six shifts of ministry and four new members of cabinet. Douglas Harkness became minister of defence; Alvin Hamilton, minister of agriculture; Gordon Churchill, minister of veterans affairs but still leader of the House; George Hees, minister of trade and commerce; Léon Balcer, minister of transport; and W.J. Browne, solicitor general. As expected, Hugh John Flemming joined the cabinet as minister of forestry; the old Union Nationale insider Noël Dorion came in as secretary of state; Walter Dinsdale of Manitoba was appointed to Northern Affairs; and Ernest Halpenny of southwestern Ontario became a minister without portfolio. Diefenbaker considered George Nowlan for Transport, but kept him in National Revenue where he could remain a key adviser on unemployment and maintain responsibility for the CBC. With Balcer promoted and Dorion in, Quebec prospects suddenly looked better. But representation from French-speaking Canada remained remarkably thin, given the party's tenuous hold on fifty Quebec seats.[8]

Almost three years in cabinet had not taught the prime minister anything about organizing government business, and the haphazard schedules and endless meetings had increasingly frustrated his ministers. In February 1960 Diefenbaker told cabinet – as it already knew – that "the increasing frequency of Cabinet meetings was causing concern." He proposed a new system of cabinet committees that would take on "preliminary review of policy questions" and thus "reduce the work of the Cabinet as a whole." Some ministers responded that a regular schedule of meetings would offer relief, since that would allow them "to make other appointments on a firmer basis." They awaited Diefenbaker's proposals.[9] Within days Robert Bryce pointed out to the prime minister that there were already seven principal committees of cabinet: "It is not a complete list but gives you an idea of the number that are available and could be more effectively used if you wished to do so in order to lighten the load on Ministers generally." Bryce added that ministers should be encouraged to consult with one another before bringing issues to cabinet, and that major policies should be discussed with the prime minister "in order to acquaint him with the issues involved before the matter comes to Cabinet."[10] This seemed fairly basic good sense, but the advice had little effect on cabinet proceedings. Three new committees were created, but only one of them ever met. By early July there had been eighty meetings of cabinet since the new year. Coupled with the backlog of government business in the House of Commons and a growing list of unfilled senior civil service appointments, the cabinet's disorganization seemed to signal a progressive loss of direction and control.[11]

BY EARLY 1960 THE SOVIET UNION CLAIMED A SUBSTANTIAL FORCE OF INTERCONTINental ballistic missiles. When the Paris summit meeting collapsed in May with the Soviet leader's blustering departure, Western leaders were plunged into gloom. Khrushchev, it seemed, was both unpredictable and subject to close control by his military advisers. Renewed Soviet pressure on Berlin – the Western island in the communist sea – seemed likely. Khrushchev had vowed in Paris to deal no more with Eisenhower, whose term was in its last year. That meant at least eight months of uncertainty and danger in East-West relations. In June the Soviet Union walked out of the disarmament conference, and Harold Macmillan told his diary that the Paris summit had wrecked his own work of years, brought "an ignominious end" to Eisenhower's presidency, set back Khrushchev's "more conciliatory and sensible ideas," and brought the world "a step nearer to ultimate disaster."[12]

In this atmosphere of increased international anxiety, John Diefenbaker's instinct was to draw closer to his American and British allies. "This is not the time," he told a television audience on May 19, "to enter into criticisms or recriminations of our friends."[13] The Washington correspondent of the CBC, James M. Minifie, had stimulated wide debate in the country with the publication of his book *Peacemaker or Powder Monkey: Canada's Role in a Revolutionary World*, in which he urged Canadian withdrawal from NATO and NORAD in favour of diplomatic neutrality; but that was not something that Diefenbaker, Green, and their associates could contemplate. The government's renewed commitment to NATO and NORAD was echoed by the Liberal Party. In early June Diefenbaker travelled to Washington to reinforce that commitment and to urge closer consultation among NATO members in times of crisis. At Washington National Airport he told his hosts, "We must maintain our unity and strengthen it, and while striving for peace must maintain our defences against the propaganda of delusive ideas and the dangers of accurate missiles."[14] During Eisenhower's White House dinner that evening, Diefenbaker noted genially that Canada's creation had been hastened by the American Civil War, and that "during the war we sprang to the aid of both sides – we fought in the armies of the North and the South, and when the war was over we exulted with the North and shed tears for the South, and have been glorifying Lincoln and the Union ever since...These United States have reached a primacy of power with an awesome accountability to history and in that decisive role which calls for wisdom and patient courage and unity Canadians will be your friends."[15]

In his private discussions with the president, Diefenbaker sought reassurance that the Bomarc program, whose current funding had recently been denied by Congress, would be maintained. He offered hesitant and tentative support for a joint air defence exercise, "Sky Shield," for which joint planning had been under way for months. And he pursued discussion on an aircraft swap arrangement that would see Canada purchase sixty-six F–101 fighter interceptors while the United States purchased thirty-seven Canadair CL–44 transport planes. The subject of nuclear warheads for the Canadian Bomarcs was discussed, apparently without contention or agreement. In his own notes for the meeting, Diefenbaker prepared to press for "fair, full and equal participation" in defence planning because "with USA interdependence with Canada usually means that one is stronger than the other." Whether he actually spoke from the notes is uncertain.[16]

The meeting had been amicable and "neighbourly," as Diefenbaker told parliament. In cabinet, the prime minister reported that Eisenhower "was anxious to remove causes for differences" between the United States and Canada. The president had described the most recent American test firing of an intercontinental missile, which had travelled 9000 miles and "landed within a few hundred yards of the target." Eisenhower reassured Diefenbaker that "the U.S.S.R. has not a large number of missiles." Despite some doubts about whether the proposed air defence exercise "Sky Shield" would appear provocative to the Soviet Union in the aftermath of the failed summit, on June 15 the cabinet approved the joint operation, to be conducted sometime during September. The closeness of the American relationship was clearly comforting to the Canadian cabinet.[17]

During the summer Nikita Khrushchev rattled his (perhaps nonexistent) rockets against the Western alliance in support of the new Castro regime in Cuba. In July the Soviet Union shot down an American RB–47 reconnaissance plane in international airspace. Soon the Soviet leader was also railing against the United Nations and its secretary general, Dag

Hammarskjöld, for the Security Council's intervention in the Congo, where Canada was already contributing technical and supply units to a hastily assembled UN force in conditions of chaos.

After the aborted summit, Western governments had turned to the United Nations as their diplomatic focus, and a parade of government leaders was now expected to attend the General Assembly in late September. Khrushchev made clear his intention to participate, and was one of the first to arrive in New York. On September 15 Harold Macmillan – who had not yet decided whether to attend – wrote to his Canadian colleague urging him to throw himself into the grand debate.

> I do not know whether you are contemplating going to the Assembly yourself. There are arguments for and against. Mr. Khrushchev will no doubt make a slashing attack on America and the West. What one doesn't know is whether this is all he has in mind or whether he is prepared for something more constructive. In any case there is a good deal to be said for re-stating the Western case and at the same time trying to test out on the spot whether there is any prospect of restarting the kind of movement which I began in my visit to Moscow eighteen months ago. If there is any hope of this kind of progress, I am sure it would be helpful that some of the Commonwealth Heads of Government should be there to help promote a common purpose...The note, I feel, should be the rebuttal of the crude attacks of communism on the one hand, but on the other the development, in a calm and unprejudiced spirit, of sound and sensible approaches to the solution of some of the world problems with particular reference to disarmament. This might make an impact upon world opinion and especially the uncommitted countries. I would be interested to know what are your plans. If I were to go I do not think it would be in the first few days. The chance of doing anything serious would be better after Mr. Khrushchev's speech and when people might be looking for some positive action. By that time we shall also know more what is really in Khrushchev's mind.
>
> I should be extremely grateful to know your thoughts about all this. Your presence at the General Assembly would of course add enormously to our debating strength.[18]

This was an encouraging boost to Diefenbaker's ego: Macmillan seemed to place him in the big leagues. He brandished no rockets, but he could toss some cutting phrases. The prime minister sensed the opportunity. Two days later he replied:

Following receipt of your communication I discussed the matter with my colleagues and they are in general agreement that anything in the nature of a boycott by the Western Heads of Government would not be beneficial, while at the same time recognizing that attendance at the Assembly by any of them would be a propaganda victory for Mr. Khrushchev. I am informed that President Eisenhower will speak next Thursday and that Mr. Khrushchev will make his presentation on Friday. Canada's representative is to speak on the following Monday. I have refused to be committed on whether or not I will be attending the meeting and will follow that course during the coming week. After Khrushchev has spoken a decision will then be made as to whether I will speak for Canada on the Monday following in place of Mr. Green.[19]

Both Macmillan and Diefenbaker decided to attend before Khrushchev made his speech on September 23. Hammarskjöld and Eisenhower had opened the Assembly with conciliatory addresses intended to pacify Cold War conflicts, but Khrushchev preferred belligerence. In a three-hour performance he attacked Western colonialism and American military imperialism, defended his country's action in shooting down the U–2 and the RB–47, denounced the UN secretary general and proposed a three-person executive to replace him, and supported the removal of UN headquarters from New York to Geneva or Vienna.[20]

Diefenbaker would be the first Western leader to speak after Khrushchev's address, and he saw his response as the occasion to make his mark on the international stage. Against the advice of his officials, who preferred a constructive and moderate speech in the Pearson tradition, Diefenbaker wanted fireworks. "He simply insisted," wrote Basil Robinson, "on our helping him to find dramatic language in which to attack Khrushchev, with particular reference to Soviet domination of Ukraine and the Baltic states."[21] By the time the prime minister decided to take Howard Green's place on the podium, the Canadian speech was in its sixth departmental draft – and still in positive form. Diefenbaker now called for drastic surgery to the text. On September 24 Robinson worked on revisions all day before flying to New York in late afternoon with the prime minister, two External Affairs aides, and two secretaries. Following an evening meeting with Diefenbaker, the team of five worked through the night on a "framework" text. After two hours' sleep Robinson was back with the prime minister at 9:30 on Sunday morning:

by which time he was all over the floor of the bedroom with bits of paper. He gave me bits of the speech to polish and then later when Howard Green came with some sensible ideas, called me back for a further session. Ross Campbell and I worked from 2 p.m., stringing it together, re-writing some passages, and it was finally approved at 8:30 or 9. Putting it to bed took till 11...

On this day there was a low point around noon when it really looked as if P.M. was losing control but he came back very strong with Howard Green's help and a timely phone call from Grattan O'Leary with an eloquent concluding section. P.M. was very anxious for comment on speech as a whole. I said it was on the rough side and that he would please the U.S. but forfeit the role of peacemaker to the U.K. He took out the word "arrogant" at one point but showed no special worry at being deprived of peacemaking role.[22]

Next morning Diefenbaker delivered his speech, in the absence of Nikita Khrushchev, to a mostly appreciative audience. The Soviet delegate left in mid-speech. Diefenbaker began optimistically.

To some observers the Assembly in the past week gave the appearance of being a circus and a drama of personalities. Whatever their views, this fact stands out, that this is the most important and most representative gathering of the world and national leaders in all history. This meeting symbolizes the bringing-together of the cultures and philosophies of all races. It is our responsibility to ensure that out of this meeting shall come a testament to the capacity of rational men to achieve rational relations, to bring about the attainment of peace and to practise brotherhood and the raising of standards everywhere in the world...As one coming from Canada, I say that the United Nations constitutes the greatest hope for the middle and small powers, for the new and weaker states, indeed, for all the nations of mankind of every social and political system.[23]

But he quickly went on the attack:

In the last few days the Assembly has heard from the leaders of its two most powerful members. I had great hopes when I learned that Mr. Khrushchev was going to attend. I came here prepared to accept, to adopt and to agree with any good suggestion he might offer, for I am of those who believe that his suggestions must not be rejected out of hand. I have been disappointed. Mr. Khrushchev, in a gigantic propaganda drama of destructive misrepresentation, launched a major offensive in the cold war. He gave lip-service to the United Nations which, in my opinion, would be destroyed by his proposal for a triumvirate. That speech could not have been intended to bring the world closer to peace; yet, to bring the world closer to peace is the major reason for our being here.

We do not always agree with the United States, but our very existence – with one-tenth of the population of the United States and possessing the resources that we do – is an effective answer to the propaganda that the United States has aggressive designs. I say that to begin with President Eisenhower made a restrained, a wise and a conciliatory speech. He presented a constructive programme. He looked forward to a world community of peace. He opened the door to international conciliation and world fellowship. I am sorry to say that Mr. Khrushchev tried to shut that door...

I turn now to a subject dealt with at great length by the Chairman of the Council of Ministers of the USSR, the subject of colonialism. He asked for and advocated a declaration at this session for "the complete and final elimination of colonial regimes"...He has spoken of colonial bondage, of exploitation and of foreign yokes. Those views, uttered by the master of the major colonial power in the world today followed the admission of fourteen new members to the United Nations – all of them former colonies. It seems that he forgot what had occurred on the opening day...

Indeed in this Assembly the membership is composed in a very considerable measure of the graduates of empires, mandates and trusteeships of the United Kingdom, the Commonwealth and other nations. I pause to ask this question: How many human beings have been liberated by the USSR? Do we forget how one of the postwar colonies of the USSR sought to liberate itself four years ago, and with what results?

How, he asked, could the Assembly reconcile "the tragedy of the Hungarian uprising" with Khrushchev's claim that the USSR believed in colonial liberation?

What of Lithuania, Estonia, Latvia? What of the freedom-loving Ukrainians and many other Eastern European peoples which I shall not name for fear of omitting some of them?...

There can be no double standard in international affairs. I ask the Chairman of the Council of Ministers of the USSR to give those nations under his domination the right of free elections – to give them the opportunity to determine the kind of government they want under genuinely free conditions.

Diefenbaker chastised the USSR for its recent threats and propaganda attacks. "What good can there come from threats to rain rockets or nuclear bombs on other countries, large or small, to despatch so-called volunteers into situations already dangerously inflamed, to encourage political leaders to follow the line of extremism? Mankind, the peoples of all the nations, are fearful and anxious, and these fears and anxieties aggravate the tensions."

Finally, the prime minister turned to what remained of his earlier – and constructive – draft text. He called for an immediate return to negotiations aimed at "full disarmament, to be assured by effective control and inspection"; an end to nuclear testing; the banning of nuclear, chemical, and biological weapons; and the prohibition of weapons in outer space or on satellites in orbit. He urged enlarged economic and technical assistance to the less-developed world. He renewed his former appeals for a system of emergency distribution of food surpluses through a UN "food bank." He called for general acceptance of the compulsory jurisdiction of the International Court of Justice as a means of resolving disputes between nations. And he ended with Grattan O'Leary's flourish.

> We are not here in this Assembly to win wars of propaganda. We are here to win victories for peace...We are not mustered here under the direction and domination of any nation. We are mustered not for any race or creed or ideology. We are here for the hosts of humanity everywhere in the world. Peoples and nations are waiting upon us. Man's hopes call upon us to say what we can do. My hope is that we shall not leave this place without having done something for mankind, so that we shall be able to say to the peoples of the world that death's pale flag shall not again be raised in war, that fear shall be lifted from the hearts and souls of men. For this could be our last chance to achieve those objectives.

Moscow radio quickly denounced Diefenbaker's "malicious and slandering remarks." But the US ambassador to the United Nations called it "truly magnificent," and other voices in Washington joined the chorus of praise. From the US capital, Canadian ambassador Arnold Heeney wrote to Diefenbaker to tell him of its salutary effect there. Heeney, at Diefenbaker's request, had recently told the Americans that there was "widespread 'anti-American' sentiment" in Canada. That, he said, had caused them "serious concern and some bewilderment," because they felt "they have made considerable effort to meet Canadian complaints and difficulties." But Diefenbaker's warm endorsement of American leadership had been reassuring. Messages of congratulation poured in to the Canadian delegation, and the prime minister preened. In Canada there was general enthusiasm for the speech from all parties, most daily newspapers, and the ethnic press.[24]

Diefenbaker returned to Ottawa, but came back to New York two days later to hear Macmillan's speech and to meet Eisenhower, Macmillan, and a few Commonwealth leaders. Both Eisenhower and Macmillan warmly approved Diefenbaker's effort, and the whole episode gave Diefenbaker a burst of exhilaration. "For the moment," wrote Robinson, "it made him feel stronger, better informed, better equipped to deal with parliament, his cabinet colleagues, the press, the public at large, foreign diplomats, and those all-knowing officials who, he suspected, were still comparing him, in their lofty way, with Pearson."[25]

On September 29 Macmillan delivered a judicious and moderate address to the General Assembly, which was interrupted in midstream when Khrushchev removed his shoe and banged it on his desk in protest. Macmillan looked up from his text and calmly responded: "Mr. President, perhaps we could have a translation, I could not quite follow." Just afterwards, in a corridor outside the Assembly, Khrushchev and Diefenbaker seemed about to confront each other when Diefenbaker looked away – and lost a chance he at once regretted. Robinson judged that he must have feared "a rebuff or...a Khrushchev victory in repartee. Another example of his shyness and insecurity."[26]

Macmillan's advisers told Robinson that night "that Diefenbaker's hard line with the Soviet Union had made it easier for Macmillan to try to adopt a statesmanlike pose and thus preserve for himself some chance of exerting a mediatory influence on Moscow."[27] Knowingly or not, Diefenbaker had played the role Macmillan devised for him. But Macmillan's stage management had no useful effect. The Soviet Union had given up on negotiation with the West. Khrushchev was waiting for the change of American leadership that would follow the election contest between Richard Nixon and John F. Kennedy. That campaign – in full flight after the first televised election debate – focused not only on the personal battle but on American preparedness for the next phase of the Cold War. Kennedy's talk of a "missile gap" foreshadowed a new round of inflamed rhetoric and military assertiveness to match the poses of the Soviet leader; and by early November Kennedy was confirmed as the president-elect.

Diefenbaker was nervous about the change of regime. He admired Dwight Eisenhower as a war hero, a fatherly presence, and a personal friend. Eisenhower had always been scrupulous in his consideration for the sensitive Canadian, soothing potential conflict between the two nations and generously sharing his perceptions of the world. His departure created fresh uncertainties. Diefenbaker would have been comfortable with Richard Nixon: they were well acquainted, they were both outsiders suspicious of established power, they admired each other's political talents, and they had a common attitude to the world struggle. At home, Nixon offered no challenge to the prime minister's popularity. Kennedy, in contrast, was vigorous, handsome, a wealthy son of the eastern establishment – and his appeal had already generated enthusiasm in Canada which detracted from Diefenbaker's own popularity. Kennedy, indeed, offered a focus for those young, urban, educated voters who were losing faith in the prairie evangelist. Diefenbaker noticed – or anticipated – a change in the tone of the relationship from the beginning: for two weeks in November, Kennedy had not bothered to reply to the prime minister's message of electoral congratulations. More significantly, Diefenbaker sensed an aspect of Kennedy's character with unusual shrewdness. When Robinson met with Diefenbaker on the morning after the election, the prime minister called Kennedy "courageously rash" and said that the world had come closer to war. Kennedy, he thought, "had pushed himself to the top against all odds, had spoken of bringing world leadership back to Washington, and had given every indication of intending to pursue an active policy which the Prime Minister feared might prove dangerous."[28]

In January 1961 Diefenbaker received an unexpected telephone call from Eisenhower suggesting he should come to Washington to sign the Columbia River Treaty, which had been under intense negotiation between the two governments. The ceremony would be the last official act of the Eisenhower administration. For Diefenbaker, it was a final sign of his friend's grace and America's friendship – both of which Diefenbaker praised in his remarks at the White House lunch after the signing ceremony.[29] On his return to Ottawa, the prime minister wrote a short memo for his files reflecting Ike's flattery.

> During my conversations with President Eisenhower I told him I had just started a letter to him in longhand when I received the telephone message with the request I come to Washington. He told me there will be communications sent to all world leaders but that there would be five or six letters he would write in longhand. They would be to:
> The Queen,
> Nehru
> President of Mexico
> Adenauer,
> and myself.[30]

In fact, the president's departing letter arrived typewritten, but it was nonetheless effusive. "As the moment approaches for me to relinquish the duties of my present office, my thoughts turn to the friendly association I have been privileged to have with you over these many months. Nothing has been closer to my heart than the hope that the two of us might, through our joint efforts, bring our two peoples to closer mutual understanding and friendship. I assure you that whatever failures can be charged to me in this regard were of the head, not the heart."[31]

Vice President Nixon also sent a departing note of thanks for the prime minister's friendship, which "went beyond the ordinary requirements of protocol." He wished Diefenbaker well "as you continue to give inspiring leadership to the cause of peace and freedom in the world."[32]

Diefenbaker was already drawing contrasts between the old regime and the new. After his one-day visit to Washington, he recorded a comment about his talks with Ambassador Heeney.

> I discussed with him Dean Rusk and the conversation that he had with the new Secretary of State to be, who had expressed himself as one who wondered whether the special relationship between Ottawa and Washington could be continued without arousing suspicion or resentment on the part of the other close allies of the United States.
>
> I took the view that this was an evidence of superciliousness or condescension towards Canada. He stated that it was not. He felt that the reason for the question was to ascertain what could be done to strengthen the relationship between our countries.[33]

The prime minister, Robinson told his diary, was "apprehensive, and seems to be almost relishing the more pessimistic omens."[34] When Kennedy delivered his state of the union address at the end of January, Diefenbaker noticed that the president had made no reference to Canada and "allowed himself an unseemly mutter that Prime Minister Nehru had been singled out for special tribute in the company of Churchill and de Gaulle."[35]

Diefenbaker had not expected to visit the new president in the first few months of 1961. But when he heard that Harold Macmillan would be in Washington in April, he told parliament that he would be glad to see Macmillan in Ottawa and that he would like to go to Washington before the Commonwealth conference in March. A report from Heeney that Robert Menzies would be there on February 22 confirmed Diefenbaker's desire to be received before that date. Heeney was instructed to arrange it, and within a few days a visit was negotiated for February 20.[36]

At his news conference on February 8, Kennedy announced that he would be meeting briefly with his "old friend" the prime minister, but he called him "Diefenbawker."[37] The prime minister acknowledged the invitation in the House of Commons, noting that "the president said this morning that it was a good thing internationally for old friends to get together." But he was furious about Kennedy's slip, and asked cabinet to consider an official protest. He was dissuaded, but the old slight rankled.[38]

Dean Rusk's briefing paper on the visit prepared for President Kennedy began pointedly with an instruction that the prime minister's name should be pronounced "Deefen-BAKER." Rusk reflected that the United States faced "an evolving Canadian attitude of introspection and nationalism...a Canadian inferiority complex which is reflected in a sensitivity to any real or fancied slight to Canadian sovereignty. Thus the essential element in problems involving Canada tends to be psychological." Despite its self-assertiveness, however, he believed that Canada would support the United States in vital matters of international policy. But Canadian support could not be taken for granted, and some Canadian initiatives would be "most annoying, but...not fundamentally damaging." Most Canadians, he thought, were "favorably disposed toward the United States and believe that each country inescapably needs the other."

He pointed out that the Diefenbaker government faced "serious political and economic difficulties" and trailed the Liberal Party by five points in the polls. "The Conservative Party is now motivated largely by a desire to bolster its waning popularity," he reported, warning that the prime minister "will be strongly interested in anything which can add to his prestige. He may even suggest to you that anti-Americanism is so prevalent in Canada as to force him to employ nationalistic measures." The paper warned of a series of potential points of conflict. Since the abandonment of the Arrow, the government had failed to work out its defence policy; the cabinet was split on the subject of nuclear weapons; the defence budget was stagnant; and it was possible that "a drift toward a kind of unconscious neutralism could develop with a concomitant loosening of defense ties with the United States." The United States would have to "promote among Canadians a better understanding and an acceptance of the concept of full military interdependence."

The briefing paper described Diefenbaker as "vigorous, self-confident, and a shrewd politician," who was "not believed to have any basic prejudice against the United States." He was tempted to assert Canadian independence, "but...only when it has been possible without overwhelmingly serious consequences to U.S.–Canadian relations." Howard Green, on the other hand, was "less flexible and harder to deal with than the Prime Minister...leader of the more nationalistic element in the government...almost pacifist." "He has exhibited...a naive and almost parochial approach to some international problems which was first attributed to his inexperience but which is now believed to be part of his basic personality." Diefenbaker and his colleagues could be influenced by flattery: they were "favorably impressed when given friendly and intimate treatment by U.S. Government officials."[39]

Diefenbaker's briefings lacked any similar ventures into psychological analysis, but prepared him to discuss, among other things, the Canadian economy, the adverse trade balance with the United States, the state of negotiations over nuclear weapons, defence production sharing, Canada's trade with Cuba, and UN disarmament talks.[40] Above all, the meeting would be a test of the two leaders' reactions to each other. Diefenbaker was the nervous partner in that encounter, and Kennedy the brash and confident newcomer revelling in his power.

On February 20 Diefenbaker and his party flew south to spend three hours at the White House, involving a brisk meeting with the president and a working lunch. Diefenbaker told the president that he faced pressures to increase Canadian protection against American imports and investment; that his government favoured trade with China and Cuba, except in strategic goods; and that he hoped there would be no interference under American foreign assets regulations with Imperial Oil's sale of bunker fuel for ships carrying Canadian wheat to China. The president was sympathetic to this request, and the issue was later resolved. Diefenbaker told Kennedy that his cabinet had not yet made decisions on the acceptance of nuclear warheads or on American storage of nuclear weapons at its military bases in Canada. Those decisions, he said, would be influenced by American support for defence production sharing and by UN disarmament discussions. But Canada did wish to be ready for action, and would not limit itself to mere "birdwatching." The two leaders agreed that negotiations for agreements on joint control under the British "double key" model should proceed. For Kennedy, this was confirmation of a Canadian commitment; for Diefenbaker, it was an assertion of equality and a promise of time. Diefenbaker told Robinson the next day that there would be no agreement "while disarmament was being pressed forward but all the preliminaries would be completed so that there would be no hold-up should the need arise."[41]

During their break for lunch, Kennedy sparred facetiously with Diefenbaker, pointing out a stuffed sailfish he had caught on his honeymoon. "Have you ever caught anything better?" he challenged. Diefenbaker boasted that only a month before, in Jamaica, he had landed a 140-pound marlin in a tiring, three-hour engagement. Kennedy mocked him: "You didn't catch it!" When Diefenbaker examined the paintings in the Oval Office, he noticed several of American naval victories in the War of 1812, but none of British triumphs. Kennedy knew of no such victories. Diefenbaker told him of the capture of the American ship *Chesapeake* by the British frigate *Shannon*, and its internment in Halifax. "If I had that picture," Kennedy said, "I would put it up." The prime minister undertook to find one, and later directed the national librarian, Kaye Lamb, to search the galleries and print shops for the evidence. Eventually a print of bloody slaughter was located in New York and delivered to the prime minister.[42] As the visit ended, Kennedy took Diefenbaker on a jaunt for the photographers in the White House garden.

Diefenbaker was pleased by this first encounter. On the drive to the airport he told Heeney that Kennedy had "great capacity, a far-sighted judgment on international affairs, and an attractive human quality in private exchanges." By late afternoon the prime minister was back in Ottawa reporting on the meeting to the House of Commons. The meeting, he said, "was a revealing and exhilarating experience. The President...has the kind of personality that leaves upon one the impression of a person dedicated to peace, to the raising of economic standards not only in his own country but in all countries, and to the achievement in his day of disarmament among all the nations of the world." Diefenbaker's fears had been calmed. The prime minister told the House that Kennedy had accepted his invitation to visit Ottawa later in the spring, and the date was soon confirmed for mid-May.[43]

Kennedy responded differently to the meeting. The president told his resident historian, Arthur Schlesinger, that Diefenbaker was insincere and untrustworthy; to his brother Robert, he said, "I don't want to see that boring son of a bitch again." A friend of Kennedy's remarked to Knowlton Nash: "You could kick him. You could rob him. But you must never bore him."[44]

At Diefenbaker's urging, Macmillan came to Ottawa after his first visit to Kennedy in April and reported enthusiastically on his impressions. Kennedy was "more sensitive, more politically minded," more flexible than Eisenhower. Britain would do nothing to complicate his life during the early months of his term. Macmillan's enthusiasm triggered Diefenbaker's envy, and he responded peevishly. "Macmillan scarcely concealed his irritation at P.M.'s negative position," Robinson noted.[45]

A week later, on April 17, the disastrous Bay of Pigs invasion was launched and quickly collapsed in the absence of US air support or a local uprising. Diefenbaker's readiness to find fault with Kennedy was aroused, but the issues, as Robinson recalled, tore at his divided instincts: "outright suspicion of the (communist) regime in Cuba, the feeling that 'a stand' should be taken against it, on the one hand; and on the other, an acute concern that Canadian support for a risky American-sponsored enterprise should not be taken for granted." Diefenbaker asked for a draft statement for use in the House, and found the department's text "wishy-washy, soft, conciliatory." He told Robinson that the department's policy of appeasement "would simply postpone the destruction of the world." Robinson, exasperated by yet another display of the prime minister's perversity, replied that "he would surely not wish us to advance it." The statement that emerged on April 19 was harsher than the department had advised, and was read in Washington as Canadian support for American policy. When the prime minister heard that, he protested and asked for a further draft that would make clear the limits of Canadian support. But Green and Diefenbaker disagreed over the text, and the clarification never appeared.[46]

As Kennedy's visit approached, Diefenbaker involved himself in every detail of the complex arrangements. At the National Gallery, a nude sculpture was tastefully draped for Jackie Kennedy's tour. That was a simple matter, but "waves of indignation and anger" swept over Diefenbaker as he observed plans for the intrusions of American secret service agents guarding the president, even into the House of Commons, where Kennedy would address a joint session of parliament. "They want to put men with guns up all over the place!" Diefenbaker told his secretary, Bunny Pound. "They're not going to shove me around!" Robinson judged that these reactions affected Diefenbaker's concentration on the substance of his briefings and his general attitude to the visit. "And who," the normally sceptical foreign service officer wrote, "could blame him?"[47]

Diefenbaker's briefings involved preparations to discuss Soviet-American conflict over Berlin and Laos, the aftermath of the Cuban crisis, NATO, Britain and the Common Market, foreign aid, nuclear testing and disarmament, and the long-emerging triangular deal for Canadian interceptor aircraft and US mutual aid purchases of aircraft in Canada. Before he departed overseas for conferences on May 9, Green emphasized to Diefenbaker that there should be no custody and control agreement for accepting nuclear weapons in Canada as long as disarmament discussions were proceeding. That position now reflected angry conflict between the Department of Defence under Douglas Harkness – who wanted quick agreement on warheads – and External Affairs under Howard Green and the undersecretary, Norman Robertson. As a result, no negotiation had followed the Washington meeting in February.[48]

The Americans, in full awareness of this difference, applied their wiles in the diplomatic campaign. They would try to bypass Howard Green. On May 11 the American ambassador, Livingston Merchant, met privately with Diefenbaker to make specific proposals for the three-way swap agreement, which would involve delivery of sixty-six F–101Bs to Canada, Canadian assumption of control over sixteen Pinetree radar stations, and a $200 million US mutual aid order for F–104Gs for European NATO forces with Canadair Limited. The bite was in the tail: the F101s would come armed with nuclear weapons, and that would open the door to a wider agreement.

Diefenbaker told Merchant that he understood American wishes, but had "genuine concern" about Canadian opinion, on two grounds. First, there were strong divisions among the public – and not all the opponents were "communists and bums." Second, the Department of External Affairs was "riddled with wishful thinkers who believed the Soviets would be propitiated and disarmament prospects improved if only Canada did nothing to provoke the Soviet Union such as accepting nuclear armaments." Diefenbaker said that this was a "ridiculous" view, and that cabinet would have to reach a decision quickly. He would take it up shortly with his ministers, and, in the interim, he told Merchant not to raise the question with External Affairs. Merchant reported to Washington, "I am certain we have a strong ally in Prime Minister as well as in Harkness."[49]

Diefenbaker did not take the issue to cabinet, but discussed it twice with Robert Bryce and decided that a swap deal could not include nuclear warheads. He was not prepared to override Green in his absence, or to confront the public opponents of nuclear warheads.[50]

Meanwhile, Howard Green provoked a diplomatic flurry by remarking to reporters on his overseas flight that Canada would be ready to mediate the dispute between the United States and Cuba. The State Department expressed its concern to Arnold Heeney, and on the eve of Kennedy's departure for Ottawa Dean Rusk sent an "eyes only" message to the president about the increasingly awkward Canadian minister. Rusk suggested that Kennedy should "have frank talk with prime minister...about neutralist tendencies Canadian policy especially as presented by...Green." He cited three recent examples. First, at the NATO ministers' meeting just concluded, Green had favoured the reduction of tensions between the "two nuclear giants." He had thus "seemed to join the long parade of those who have wished to provide a bridge, meaning continuous concessions on our part to an insatiable power determined to pursue its world revolution by every available means." Second, Green's offer of Cuban mediation had distorted a general problem into a "bilateral

US–Cuban affair." When Rusk raised the issue with Green in Geneva, "he replied lamely that what he intended to say was that if he were asked to mediate he would be glad to do so." Third, Green had refused to participate in caucus discussions among the United States, the United Kingdom, and France over Laos in Geneva on the ground that Canada was a neutral member of the International Control Commission. All this worried Rusk.

> I would not suggest that president personify discussion by involving Green by name but rather press prime minister on general attitude Canada on questions directly affecting free world. Green is obviously bemused by great peace-making role which Canada (obviously usefully) plays in such situations as Suez, Congo and other affairs...Be it said, Green's point of view seems to be supported by considerable amount of Canadian public opinion. Suggest Merchant brief president this situation prior conversation [with] prime minister.[51]

The auguries looked troublesome on both sides as Kennedy left Washington for Ottawa on the afternoon of May 16. Kennedy was, as usual, well fortified with chemical injections to control his multiple physical ailments. Before returning home, he would have to call for more painkillers.[52]

On his arrival at Uplands airport, Kennedy made two gaffes, at least one of them deliberate. Despite fresh briefing, he persisted in mispronouncing the prime minister's name; and he commented lightly that he dared to venture into the French language after hearing the prime minister's efforts in his introduction. The crowd laughed; Diefenbaker was not amused.

On the long drive into the city, Ottawa's celebrated visitors were greeted by more than fifty thousand well-wishers. Soon afterwards, in a tree-planting ceremony at Rideau Hall, Kennedy lifted a silver shovel of dirt, felt a twinge of pain, and put his right hand briefly to his forehead in reaction. No one noticed, but over the next two days his discomfort worsened. Once on the plane for the return trip to Washington, he was in agony. He needed his crutches to allow him to disembark from Air Force One at Andrews Air Force Base.[53] But before that he bore the entire schedule of state dinners and receptions, a wreath laying, an address to the two houses of parliament, and meetings with the prime minister and cabinet. From the outside, all looked well, and the occasion was pronounced a success. The crowds were keen to see the Kennedys, and the president's address to parliament had enough supple phrases to make it graceful and memorable. It was above all a call to Canadians to maintain the country's role in freedom's cause "in these days when hazard is our constant companion." His trip, he said, was "more than a consultation, more than a good will visit. It is an act of faith, faith in your country and your leaders, faith in the capacity of two great neighbours to meet their common problems, and faith in the cause of freedom in which we are so intimately associated." There was just one slip in the speech to annoy John Diefenbaker: Kennedy invited Canada publicly to join with the United States in the Organization of American States, an invitation Diefenbaker had pointedly rejected in private talks earlier in the day.[54]

Kennedy and Diefenbaker met for two and a half hours on the morning of May 17 in the presence of their aides. Diefenbaker began by showing off his prize marlin and his print of the British naval victory in the War of 1812 – both of them freshly mounted on his wall with this occasion in mind. Diefenbaker directed Kennedy to a rocking chair beside his desk, which had also been borrowed for the occasion. When the formal conversations began, both leaders seemed well briefed and in good spirits, although Kennedy appeared tired. The president touched briefly on the Bay of Pigs, where he had allowed Cuban volunteers to invade without adequate or overt American assistance. Cuba, he believed, remained a serious problem for the United States as a Soviet ally and a centre for Latin American subversion. He hoped Canada would become more active in the hemisphere as a partner of the United States, but free of America's record of domination. Diefenbaker assured the president that Green's remarks about mediation in Cuba had been misreported; there would be no question of that. Kennedy reassured Diefenbaker that the United States had no intention of invading Cuba unless there were serious provocation or unless the USSR "cut us seriously" in Berlin. If there were a crisis, he said, the United States would "talk with Canada before doing anything."

Diefenbaker raised the subject of the Organization of American States by suggesting that Canada could be more influential outside than in, and stuck to his position despite Kennedy's urging that the country should join. He seemed more favourable to the president's suggestion that Canada should at least attend the next meeting of the inter-American economic and social council in Uruguay in July.

Kennedy pointed to increasing conflict in Vietnam and Laos, where he felt the international control commissions were failing. He gave notice that American military assistance to Laos might increase, and asked for a contribution of Canadian aid. Diefenbaker did not respond. On foreign aid in general, Kennedy appealed to Diefenbaker to increase Canada's contributions to 1 percent of GNP per year, which would amount to a five-fold growth from $69 million to $360 million annually. Diefenbaker countered that he faced serious domestic problems and could not alter the aid budget.

Kennedy indicated that he favoured British entry into the European Common Market for its contribution to European stability, and asked for Diefenbaker's comments. The Canadian prime minister made clear that Canada feared the loss of its agricultural markets. "The subject was not pursued," Robinson reported, "but one could sense Diefenbaker's displeasure at having it confirmed that the president was so firmly in support of British entry."

Diefenbaker raised the issue of nuclear weapons by warning that there were powerful interests in Canada, including university professors, clergy, and the Voice of Women, who opposed the acceptance of warheads for the Bomarcs. For the moment it would be impossible to sign an agreement, but by the autumn he hoped that he might influence opinion in a national speaking tour and bring about a change. He "was stung," Robinson recalled, by Kennedy's suggestion that a refusal to take nuclear weapons would put Canada in a neutralist position – something that Diefenbaker found unpalatable. On the proposed triangular weapons swap, Diefenbaker refused to accept the condition that the F–101s should come already armed. Kennedy responded that, in order to justify so large a contract to produce American F–104s in Canada, he would have to demonstrate a net improvement in continental air defence. Diefenbaker reiterated his judgment: Despite his own preference to accept nuclear warheads, he could not yet risk the challenge to public opinion. Accepting warheads for the F–101s would weaken his position. He suggested that the weapons should be stored in the United States, for transfer to Canada if necessary. At breakfast the next morning Kennedy came back to the issue of weapons, but Diefenbaker was unmoved. The issue was left unresolved.[55]

After Kennedy and his party left the prime minister's office on May 17, a member of Diefenbaker's staff found a single piece of paper they had left behind. It was a brief memorandum to the president, by his adviser Walt W. Rostow, of talking points headed "What we want from the Ottawa trip." There were four points, the first three beginning with the words "To push the Canadians...To push them...To push them...": towards an increased role in Latin America, towards membership in the Organization of American States, and towards a 1 percent foreign aid budget. The fourth point urged Canadian help in the international control commission for Indochina to achieve better monitoring of the Laotian-Vietnamese borders. All these points had been raised amicably in discussion.[56]

The memo was turned over to the prime minister. When he showed it to his foreign affairs adviser, Robinson urged Diefenbaker to return it with an explanation to the US Embassy. This would have been diplomatically proper.

But two days later, "in a post-mortem on the visit, the prime minister brought the paper out, remarking on its repeated use of the word 'push.' To him this personified the attitude of the Americans: they thought nothing of pushing Canada around. He seemed to be regarding the paper as a sort of trophy, and it was impossible to tell whether he would hold on to it for future display or return it as I had recommended."[57] The prime minister ordered the paper stored in his confidential filing cabinet, referred to as "the vault."

Meanwhile Livingston Merchant, who knew nothing of the misplaced memo, summarized the American embassy's impressions of the visit to Ottawa in a dispatch to Washington. He thought that the Canadians had been rapped helpfully on the knuckles, but could not predict the result.

> Embassy regards visit as entirely on plus side. President's forthrightness startled but did not offend Canadians who have been given much to think about, have had some of their complacency and smugness salubriously shaken, and will be examining their consciences as well as their pocketbooks. Whether this reaction will be translated into concrete action in increased aid, step-up in defense, end of irresolution on nuclear weapons, or greater involvement in hemisphere affairs is by no means certain and will become apparent only with time. At the least we should see a greater Canadian restraint in offering gratuitous advice unaccompanied by acceptance of responsibility.[58]

The day before, Diefenbaker offered his own, entirely favourable reactions in a letter to his brother. "The President and I had a private breakfast this morning and covered a number of important matters. We get along very well together. The opinion I formed of him when I first met him – a brilliant intellect and a wide knowledge of world events – was not only borne out but intensified as a result of our discussions in the last two days."[59] Diefenbaker wanted to get along with the president. But those troubling disagreements over weapons – made intractable by the state of Canadian opinion and the unresolved disputes within his own cabinet and his own mind – remained to be resolved. There was, as well, the insulting document now hidden away in his vault. And there were the tormenting memories of slights and joking taunts to remind him that Kennedy looked down on him, and probably laughed at him. That "callow young man" lacked Eisenhower's diplomatic graces. The prime minister would have been more disturbed to read Merchant's account of Canadian "complacency and smugness salubriously shaken" by the president's visit to Ottawa.[60]

JOHN DIEFENBAKER WAS NOW SIXTY-FIVE YEARS OF AGE. WITHOUT CHILDREN – APART from his step-daughter Carolyn – his family could only diminish. In July 1960 his uncle, Edward Diefenbaker, died in Regina. With Elmer's assistance, Gowan Guest made arrangements for the funeral in Saskatoon, and Diefenbaker flew west briefly by commercial airline to attend the ceremony. The will divided the small estate among John, Elmer, and Mary Diefenbaker, but John turned over his inheritance to Elmer. "It was nice of him to give me such a considerable share," John told Elmer, "but because of what you have done for him since he made the will in 1949 demands that I follow the course of doing what he would have done if he had made another will."[61] Burial took place in the family plot in Saskatoon, which prompted John's reflections. "There is room in that plot for five. This will make four and no doubt you will choose to be buried there too when your time comes. Olive and I have to decide on another plot. There has been some suggestion that it should be in Ottawa for I must say that I would not think it should be in Prince Albert. This, of course, can be decided after we talk things over."[62]

A month later, Elmer told John that an old campaign associate had died, and John responded: "Those that were with me in my first election in 1925 are now pretty well gone."[63] Meanwhile his mother remained in University Hospital in Saskatoon, where she had been bedridden under the care of Dr David Baltzan since the summer of 1957. Mary Diefenbaker was eighty-eight and suffered frequent spells of dementia. Diefenbaker had provided regular payments for her expenses, kept in touch with Dr Baltzan about her fluctuating condition, wrote and telephoned almost daily, and visited her on his frequent trips to Saskatoon. By Christmas of 1960 she was failing, and Baltzan told Diefenbaker that in these last stages he would seek his patient's comfort but would not prolong life to the point of torture. Baltzan commented that Diefenbaker had taken this advice in a mood that was "calm, composed and prepared."[64] Two months later, while Diefenbaker spent the day in Washington, Mary died. The two sons arranged the funeral at First Baptist Church in Saskatoon, attended by John, Olive, Elmer, the Brunts, the lieutenant governor, Chief Justice Emmett Hall, Mayor Sidney Buckwold of Saskatoon, Mayor John Cuelenaere of Prince Albert, and four hundred others, and buried their mother in the family plot. The Regina *Leader Post* commented that Mary Diefenbaker had been "a great Canadian mother": "This is an ideal story of mother-son relations, those primary relations that can mean everything to both and equip a man for the battle of life as no other relationship can." Patrick Nicholson commented in *The Scotsman* that the Diefenbaker home had been "a matriarchal oasis of intellectual activity amid the brawn opening up the prairies."[65]

Six weeks later, in a letter advising his brother of various matters relating to her will, John proposed that they should "make some arrangements to fix up the shack on the homestead so that it will be preserved." He continued: "If you are out that way you might make some enquiries as to how much it would cost to clean it up in general, put in windows and generally restore it. Of course I wouldn't want it used to store wheat for that would mean that the place would go back to rack and ruin again. I am surprised that it has stood up so well in the fifty-one years since we left."[66] That relic, they both knew, would be not so much a memorial to his homesteading parents as to their eldest son. He was the Abe Lincoln of the family.

JOHN DIEFENBAKER HAD COME TO POWER WITHOUT ANY COHERENT ECONOMIC strategy. He had taken for granted, like many Canadians, that the period of postwar expansion would continue indefinitely. Government's role was, through budgetary and monetary policy, to make adjustments at the margin to control or stimulate growth within reasonable limits, and to maintain full employment. In his years in opposition, Diefenbaker had lectured on the dangers of inflation and the need for lower taxes. Before achieving power, he had begun to echo the mildly nationalist views of Walter Gordon's royal commission about the effects of too much American capital investment in Canada. In 1957 and 1958 he had spoken grandly of Canada's expanding horizons of growth. But these were all rhetorical positions, adopted for political reasons. They did not reflect a considered understanding of the economy, and they were not necessarily consistent. "The Vision" of national development was a magical charm that never became a plan. What it amounted to after 1958 was a series of discrete aid and investment projects responding to regional demands for roads, railways, dams, power plants, and resource projects, put together under the energetic inspiration of Alvin Hamilton.

In Diefenbaker's eyes, fairness and social conscience required a more active concern for the poor, the unemployed, the ill, the elderly, and the farmers than the Liberal government had shown in its last, complacent years. But once those adjustments had been made, he did not expect that the economy would be a major preoccupation. When the economic slowdown came soon after his government took office, he was alarmed because it was unexpected, because he could not comprehend it – and because it recalled R.B. Bennett's failure to overcome the great depression of the 1930s. Unemployment rose to almost 8 percent by the summer of 1958, and Liberals were quick to proclaim that "Tory times are hard times." For the rest of his term, unemployment haunted and distracted the Diefenbaker cabinet, threatening it with the fate of Bennett in 1935 and another generation of Conservative exclusion from power. There was some recovery in 1959, but by 1960, despite the government's various injections of winter works, housing grants, and regional aid, the unemployment rate rose once more to 8 percent. The Liberal front bench, led by Mike Pearson, Lionel Chevrier, Paul Martin, and Jack Pickersgill, hammered away at the cabinet's ineptitude and apparent unconcern. The government's uncertain statistics added to the atmosphere of confusion. In February 1960 there were 500,000 persons registered in search of work, but Michael Starr admitted in debate that there were almost 800,000 drawing unemployment insurance. From the government's own back bench, the unpredictable New Brunswick MP Charles Van Horne attacked his party's record and warned that "we will all be kicked out at the next election if the government doesn't smarten up." For several days in early March, during discussion of the labour department estimates, there was disorder, sometimes beyond the Speaker's control, in the House. Liberals and CCFers prolonged debate while government back-benchers heckled and shouted them down.[67] The government was embarrassed both by the economic facts and by the opposition's unending protests.

Diefenbaker struggled for some means of escape. In a meeting of ministers on February 9, he sought opinions about when – or whether – there should be a budget, perhaps contemplating the option of dissolution and an election as a means of diverting attention away from the economy for a few months. That would put him onto ground where he was confident of his talents. But dissolution after only two years, with an overwhelming majority, would have been unprecedented and controversial. George Hees made the most emphatic statement in favour of a budget, which Diefenbaker summarized in his notes: "People expect their government to give accounting. Voter isn't concerned with Budget deficit. If we don't have a budget we are hiding. Must be open and above board."[68] The prime minister accepted both parts of that advice: There would be a budget in March, and he would not be worried by the size of the deficit. On March 3 he told a television audience that no one would suffer from unemployment while he was prime minister.[69]

"This," reflected the minister of finance, "was obviously promising far too much." Donald Fleming was struggling to produce a balanced budget in the face of incessant demands for increased spending from his own colleagues – and especially from the prime minister. With cabinet's agreement on an early budget, Fleming won at least a temporary victory against the Chief's schemes for renewed assistance to western farmers, and applied his strong arm against all other proposals for new spending. The estimates predicted an increase of only 1 percent in government spending for 1960–61. When he introduced the budget on March 31, Fleming reported an annual inflation rate of 1 percent, declining interest rates, high levels of domestic saving and investment, and reasonable but not excessive inflows of foreign capital. His proudest moment came when he forecast a slight budget surplus of $12 million for the coming year, and took his seat "to the sweet music of thunderous applause."[70] The press took the budget to mean that Fleming had won a precarious victory in the cabinet battle over spending, but showed little confidence that it reflected any longer-term purpose. One exception was Charles Lynch, who judged that Fleming had "brought the impression of firm, long-term planning into the record of a government that at times has seemed to be planning as it went along." With a further year of sustained growth, he foresaw the prospect of pre-election tax cuts in 1961 or 1962, and "an end to the old cry that Tory times are hard times."[71]

Within two months, Diefenbaker and Douglas Harkness, who was still minister of agriculture, were undermining the balanced budget with appeals to cabinet for acreage payments for unsold wheat, increased farm loans, and funding for the purchase of Canadian grain for foreign aid. Donald Fleming fought a delaying battle through six cabinet meetings, and denied Diefenbaker's efforts to gain these benefits before the Saskatchewan provincial election in early June 1960. The provincial Conservative Party, under its new leader Martin Pedersen, had promised provincial acreage payments and hinted at matching federal support of one dollar per acre. In his campaign for a fifth consecutive majority, Tommy Douglas sought a mandate to introduce universal medical care. The CCF was re-elected with an increased majority, and the Conservative Party elected no one.[72] With Gallup Poll support for the federal party in Saskatchewan below 40 percent, the prime minister rallied his forces in caucus, and on August 2 cabinet approved acreage payments to western farmers totalling $42 million. Fleming lectured ministers that the balanced budget was shattered, but his colleagues rebuked him for his lack of political sense. Diefenbaker, with "a knowing grin," told him: "There is no chance of balancing the budget. There never was."[73]

During the summer, facing renewed signs of economic decline, cabinet also authorized increases in funding for job training and winter housing construction. The prime minister summoned officials from Labour, Finance, and Trade and Commerce to Harrington Lake to advise him on the economic outlook and employment policy without the presence of their ministers. "No doubt a prime minister can do such things if he chooses," Fleming reflected caustically, "if he is unwise enough to sidestep his ministerial colleagues." When Diefenbaker proposed a cabinet committee that did not include the minister of finance to recommend new measures of economic stimulus, Fleming wrote to the prime minister declining any further responsibility for fiscal policy and threatening resignation. Diefenbaker quickly telephoned to insist, "I regard you with feelings bordering on idolatry. I'm sorry this has happened...I promise you this will never happen again." Fleming stayed on in an uneasy standoff – still, he believed, the cabinet's stern and necessary voice of financial prudence.[74]

Following three by-election defeats and one victory in October, Diefenbaker called the House of Commons back in November 1960 for an unusual autumn session to meet the unemployment crisis.[75] The session lasted more than ten months. The government introduced a range of measures of vocational training, public works, university capital grants, and export financing, capping it all with a supplementary budget just before Christmas. In it, a chastened Donald Fleming sought to explain the economic downturn – which he blamed on American and European decline and a fall in world resource prices – and the prospect of a substantial budget deficit. He offered a series of business tax incentives and predicted a new target deficit of $286 million. Privately, Fleming had opposed a new budget because "tactically it gave the appearance of emergency to the government's program. I thought that Diefenbaker was unnecessarily and prematurely over-reacting to a downturn in the economy. Perhaps this led us to shoot our bolt too soon." But once committed, he was as smugly satisfied with his performance as ever.[76] The Liberal opposition attacked the budget broadside, while the CCF criticized its failure to bring down interest rates, expand the money supply, or reduce the foreign exchange premium on the Canadian dollar. In January the government majority carried the budget resolution with ease, but the mood of political anxiety, disenchantment, and a cabinet at odds with itself lingered. None of the government's measures seemed likely to have much impact on the unemployment figures.

For months observers in the press and parliament had pointed to signs of strain between the governor of the Bank of Canada, James Coyne, and the ministry. Coyne had been appointed in January 1955 to a seven-year term, which would expire at the end of 1961. He held office "on good behaviour," and could only be removed for cause by an act of parliament. He was highly articulate, persuasive, and confident – even cocky – in manner. Fleming soon became aware, as minister of finance, that Coyne did not enjoy easy relations with the chartered banks. The bank's restrictive credit policies were a common subject of public complaint during the 1957 and 1958 election campaigns. Diefenbaker was henceforth convinced that Coyne was one of the enemy within. Coyne's dedication to tight money and a low inflation rate, he believed, was not only cruelly indifferent to human needs but subversive of Conservative policy.[77] Fleming shared Diefenbaker's anxiety about Coyne's abrasive and independent ways, but lacked the prime minister's distrust, and was determined to seek his cooperation. Fleming, like Diefenbaker, was concerned about high interest rates. After the confusions of the 1958 conversion loan, he first drew Diefenbaker's attention to the bank's high interest rate policy in August 1959 when he expressed his "deep concern" that it had reached an all-time record of 5.98 percent. Fleming promised that he would "review the situation intensively" with the bank.[78] Within days the prime minister had received complaints from a Vancouver broker, Norman Whittall, that the bank was destructively deflating the economy and disorganizing the money markets. "The time has come," Whittall demanded, "for you to decide whether the cabinet or the Bank of Canada is to control Canada's financial policy."[79] Gowan Guest passed on the correspondence to Fleming with the comment, "Mr. Diefenbaker indicated an increasing concern about the current monetary situation, and an increasing awareness of comments of this kind."[80]

Diefenbaker also sought the advice of Leslie Frost, who was closely in touch with the Toronto financial community. Frost responded "with no holds barred." He expressed his "alarm and dissatisfaction," noting that there was "an increasing lack of confidence in the Governor of the Bank of Canada and the policies followed by that institution." The bank's policy in the market was not one of leadership but of drift, "something after the fashion of a ship without a rudder."

> My investigations have led me to the belief that there is a widespread lack of confidence in the capacity of the Bank of Canada, including its Governor, to handle the present situation...My dealings over many long years with the banks and financial institutions have shown that they are like all human beings – they require strong and positive leadership. Confidence in the financial structure is a nebulous thing easily undermined and in many ways hard to restore.
>
> ...Should the whole economy of this country be dependent upon the unrestricted and uncontrolled decision of one man?[81]

Fleming arranged for the governor to meet with Frost, but Coyne apparently refused to discuss his policies with the premier. Fleming concluded that "the result was so bad that it would have been better if the meeting had never been held." The minister then arranged a meeting between Coyne and a group of ministers, where he judged that "Coyne handled himself well." But soon afterward Alvin Hamilton and George Hees, among others, urged Fleming "to remove the restraining hand of Coyne from the economy" in order to encourage expansion. Fleming pointed out that the government could not fire the governor: "I urged patience on my colleagues and others, and did my utmost to live with a situation which appeared to have become insoluble. I endeavoured to maintain as personally friendly relations with Coyne as his stiff, blunt, unaccommodating nature would permit."[82]

From the autumn of 1959, Coyne began to accept public speaking engagements across the country, initially at the suggestion of members of his board, to explain the bank's position in the "tight money" controversy. "It was clear to me," he recalled, "that both my Board of Directors and the Minister of Finance were solidly in favor of the kind of monetary policy which the Bank of Canada was carrying out under my management." Coyne could cite speeches of the prime minister and the minister of finance on "expansion without inflation" in support of that view. Fleming would not admit as much – or turned the claim around: The first of Coyne's speeches, he wrote, were "interpreted as being in accord with my declared aim to balance the budget."[83]

The latent conflict took on a sharper edge just before the budget of 1960, when Coyne suggested in his annual report that Canada was expanding too fast and living beyond its means, thus weakening its ability to meet the next recession. Gordon Churchill responded in the House in defence of high spending and a deficit trade balance. The Alberta back-bencher Eldon Woolliams brought cheers from the Conservative ranks by asserting that "we would rather listen to the optimism of the Minister of Trade and Commerce than to the statements made by Mr. Coyne that we have to tighten our belts and things are not so good in Canada."[84] Robert Duffy commented in the *Globe*: "In the lineup as it now appears, we have Jeremiah on the one side (let us not say left or right) in the person of Governor James E. Coyne...Opposing him is Pollyanna, the Minister of Trade and Commerce. Somewhere between them is the juggler, Finance Minister Fleming, and in the background, Prime Minister Diefenbaker, mystified. Mr. Fleming stands as close to Mr. Coyne as Mr. Diefenbaker is to Churchill."[85] For over a year, Fleming kept his silence, even when twenty-nine university economists publicly denounced Coyne in December 1960. "I was unable to discern," he later wrote, "whether the signatories were stressing the adverse balance-of-payments situation or the question of money supply." At the same time, Fleming incorporated several of

Coyne's proposals for limiting foreign investment in his supplementary budget.[86]

Coyne's visibility and independence were becoming an embarrassment. On December 1 the party's dean of the House, Earl Rowe, offered his comments in a letter to Fleming.

> It appears to me that Mr. Coyne is talking too much. He speaks as one independent of either Party. His remarks are hurting our Party, our Government and our economy.
>
> He repeatedly analyzes the situation, offering little solution and leaves the problem emphasized on our doorstep. I do not think this was ever intended to be his function.

Rowe sent a copy of the letter to Diefenbaker, with a handwritten addition in the margins. "Better destroy this when read, but Don was 100% in agreement – I suggested to him verbally if he couldn't stop Coyne talking & couldn't fire him he better plan for a Royal Com. on Financial Institutions – during which he couldn't talk."[87]

Fleming put the idea of a royal commission informally to the cabinet almost immediately, and discussed its composition with the prime minister. In February he made a formal proposal, which met the usual "welter of opinions" in cabinet and was not approved until just before his budget speech in June 1961. The commission was not appointed until October 1961 – which meant that however desirable it might be on other grounds, it did not serve Rowe's purpose of silencing James Coyne.[88]

The speeches continued, with the approval and sometimes the unanimous, restrospective consent of the bank's board of directors.[89] Coyne's increasing emphasis on the dangers of a large payments deficit and a growing foreign debt gave his speeches a notably nationalist flavour. In Calgary in October 1960 he declared:

> We are now at one more of the critical crossroads in our history, perhaps the most critical of all, when economic developments and preoccupation with economic doctrines of an earlier day are pushing us down the road that leads to loss of any effective power to be masters in our own household and ultimate absorption in and by another. The fact that the modern word for "absorption" is "integration" or even "economic integration" does not alter the essential nature of the result.

The country was spending more than it produced, while its own productive capacity was underemployed. Increased employment, he suggested, would only serve a national purpose if it were directed above all to the replacement of imports by home production. That could happen only slowly, through changes in the structure of the economy. "Easy credit, more debt and printing press money" were tempting but false means of escaping high unemployment. They were, on the contrary, expressions of the "soft-living, restricted working, borrow-from-the-other-fellow kind of philosophy which if allowed free rein will undermine our economic stability and progress and our national independence."

Unemployment should not be met by "inflationary finance," but by a cautious pay-as-you-go policy based on Canadian savings. Coyne offered few specifics, but hinted at an activist national policy of diversification, Canadianization, and improved education that might involve measures of investment and import control.[90] These were stirring and controversial words that strayed across the line of neutrality into political debate. Fleming pleaded that he had no responsibility, under the Bank of Canada Act, for the governor's words and policies.

By 1961 Fleming was alarmed at Coyne's celebrity and at the governor's ability to confuse the public and embarrass the government. He hesitated to ask Coyne to cease his speech-making, fearing that Coyne would take this request as interference with the bank's independence. He knew that the cabinet opposed Coyne's reappointment to a second term, but worried that such an announcement "would leave us with a hostile governor on our hands, and perhaps a bewildered and critical public, for nearly a year." A request for Coyne's resignation, he thought, "might precipitate a battle royal." Only parliament could dismiss him. Fleming felt trapped.[91]

On February 20 some directors of the bank criticized the governor at a board meeting for engaging in public controversy. Coyne responded tartly that his own speeches were non-partisan and that controversy had arisen only because he had been attacked by members of the opposition; meanwhile the minister had neither supported nor disavowed his views. Coyne accepted no further public engagements after that meeting, but he did fulfil two previous commitments in the weeks that followed.[92]

After Coyne's next address – to the Economic Club of New York in March 1961 – the Chicago *Daily News* called him "Canada's most controversial figure...on the verge of achieving international status as a row-provoker."[93] Fleming told the House of Commons: "I take no responsibility whatever for the contents of that speech or for any views expressed in it. The governor of the bank did not consult me before he made it. He did not undertake to speak for the government, and anything contained in that speech is his responsibility." Fleming's tone had hardened. He was no longer defending Coyne's "right as a citizen to make speeches," as he had done in February. When Paul Martin asked what the government proposed to do "in respect to those matters in that speech which are not in accord with government policy," the minister hinted at something more. "We shall continue to regard ourselves as servants responsible to parliament. We shall not seek to override the enactments of parliament. It will remain for parliament to decide in those circumstances what is the proper course to be taken."[94]

Coyne had written to Fleming in February expressing worry over the scale of capital inflow from the United States and the balance of payments, and suggesting tax and spending increases and temporary tariff surcharges. Fleming requested a meeting, which occurred on March 18 after the last of the governor's scheduled speeches. Remarkably, this was the first time that the two had discussed Coyne's speeches, although there had been twelve of them, begun sixteen months earlier. The encounter involved an exchange of accusations. Coyne asserted that the public had come to expect too much of monetary policy because the government had failed to explain its economic policies. Fleming replied that the governor's proposals would not solve the country's problems, but worsen them. His speeches should be limited to explaining how the Bank of Canada operated.

> I told him plainly that his public utterances had caused acute embarrassment to the government and to myself and had inevitably created the impression of a conflict of opinion between the government and the governor. I added that I personally had submitted to much criticism occasioned by his speeches, but had felt compelled to refrain from public comment on them. I told him very frankly that in recent weeks I had been asked whether he was attempting to undermine the government. I had been placed in the equivocal position of having to defend publicly the governor's right to make his speeches while in fact deploring his actions and strongly disagreeing with his proposals. I said flatly that the appearance that he was openly challenging the government was impairing public confidence in the Bank as an institution, and I regarded this as very serious.[95]

Coyne denied that he sought to undermine the government; rather, he was trying to "save the country from economic ruin." Fleming thought him "unblushingly unrepentant...too preoccupied with the question of the balance of payments and...very hostile toward the United States." The meeting ended in a standoff.[96]

Because Coyne had told him that he was not "getting his ideas through," Fleming invited him to meet with senior members of the finance department, the cabinet secretary, and several ministers. Here – after Fleming had repeated his claim of embarrassment and washed his hands of responsibility before the assembled company – Coyne reviewed his arguments in what Fleming called "a high-handed manner." A rude and angry argument broke out between Coyne and assistant deputy minister Simon Reisman. After the meeting ended, the senior assistant deputy minister, Wynne Plumptre, told the minister: "He's a very poor governor." The veil of dutiful respect fell from Fleming's eyes.[97]

On March 23, 1961, Fleming made a scrupulously detailed report on these meetings to cabinet, "including a sentence-by-sentence account of my discussions with Coyne." Fleming no longer defended him, and ministers now seriously considered how to dispose of this troublesome priest. While the minister of finance was "working on an economic program for the budget to cope with the deterioration in the national economy," the governor "was preaching contrary and totally unacceptable fiscal policies."[98] Fleming did not concede that Coyne had actually stopped preaching by that time.

Fleming knew that a Senate committee, controlled by a Liberal majority, intended to call Coyne as a witness, but that would not occur until late in April. Should the government, in the meantime, refer his annual report to the House committee on banking and commerce? Fleming thought "that would create unnecessary controversy." Cabinet opted for what it hoped would be a quiet solution. The minister of finance was directed to tell Coyne that his appointment would not be renewed in December; that he could take immediate retirement leave or full retirement; and that he would receive his full pension whenever he chose to go. But there was a caveat. Fleming had learned just before the meeting that the governor's pension, payable from December 31, 1961, would be $25,000, or 50 percent of his salary – and that struck the frugal minister as "extraordinarily large." Cabinet asked him to examine "the authority for so large a pension being paid after only seven years' service as governor."[99]

After almost four years of putting up with the fractious governor, Fleming and Diefenbaker had belatedly decided to confront him. Now they allowed their pentup frustration to cloud their political judgment. When Fleming sought information from his senior advisers about Coyne's pension, he learned that the directors of the bank had amended the by-laws in February 1960 to revise the bank's pension plan, and to raise the pensions of the governor and deputy governor to half their annual salaries; for Coyne, this provided about $6000 annually more than the general plan. The by-laws had been properly amended by unanimous vote, but the governor had neglected to publish the new pension by-law in the *Canada Gazette* as the act required. Fleming's own representative on the board had not reported the change to him. Fleming found this information "devastating." He reported at once to Diefenbaker, and on March 30 to cabinet. "My instructions to talk to Coyne and to propose his immediate retirement on full pension," he wrote, "were straightway withdrawn. What I had unearthed appalled me, shocked cabinet and enraged the Prime Minister."[100]

Cabinet discussion that day was raucous – and, as usual, indecisive. Everyone seemed to agree that the pension decision, and Coyne's acceptance of it without disclosure, had been "reprehensible." Coyne would have to depart at once. Ministers were inclined to reverse the increase in the pension, but Fleming persuaded them that legislation to do so would result in the resignation of the entire board. The meeting concluded without a decision on how to proceed.[101]

Fleming understood that legislation to dismiss Coyne would be politically dangerous. The same day he wrote to Diefenbaker: "I am concerned that if we introduce legislation in the House to amend the Bank of Canada Act we will be opening up a can of worms. The Grits would love a chance to debate at length relations between the Government and the Bank and the question of responsibility for monetary policy."[102] For four weeks over the Easter recess, Fleming and Diefenbaker avoided the issue in cabinet. On April 28 the minister raised it once more, without resolution. On May 1 there was another long discussion, in which the issue of cancelling the pension increase re-emerged. The minister warned that altering the by-law would threaten all the bank's pensions. He called instead for an early decision to terminate Coyne's tenure based on "his policy differences with the government, rather than on the by-law...I urged my colleagues not to take any action which would regain any sympathy for Coyne. Specifically I warned them not to make a martyr of him."[103] But just what Coyne's "policy differences" were, Fleming did not make clear.

Throughout May the minister juggled budget preparations with consideration of a Bank of Canada Act amendment to dismiss the governor. Fleming finally forced cabinet's hand on May 27 with the suggestion that the bank's quarterly board meeting in mid-June would be the appropriate time for the board to receive Coyne's resignation and consider a successor. Cabinet agreed that Fleming should meet Coyne to ask for his resignation, but it made no decision about the governor's pension.[104]

The next day Fleming met Coyne in the minister's office. "I told him that on the instructions of cabinet I was asking for his resignation prior to the board meeting on June 12. I stressed his provocative speeches, the public controversy they had engendered involving the government, the irreconcilability of his ideas with the fiscal plans of the government, and the consternation of cabinet on learning of the unusual pension provisions made for his benefit and of his failure to disclose these to the government." Coyne said that the board had acted on legal advice in amending the pension by-laws. He stood by the assertions in his speeches, but he regretted any possible embarrassment to the government. He asked whether his successor had been chosen, whether Fleming had discussed the appointment with the board committee charged with recommending an appointment, and whether he would receive his $25,000 pension.

Fleming replied that there was no successor and that he had not discussed the matter with the board committee. To the third question, he responded with a pedant's precision. "I felt bound to reply that the validity of the by-law was not beyond question, the government had been shocked on learning of it and had not yet reached a decision as to its position in regard to it. Perhaps events might have turned out differently had I been authorized to answer his third question affirmatively also, but cabinet was far from being in a mood to concede the pension." [105] The meeting was calm, and Coyne departed after telling Fleming that he would think over the request to resign. Fleming did not see Coyne again for two years, when "he walked past me without any glint of recognition" in the Royal York Hotel. [106]

But he did hear from him. Two members of the board of the bank met with Fleming on June 2 and again the next day, seeking reconsideration of the cabinet decision. Fleming told them it was final. On June 8 Fleming reported to cabinet. He expected that Coyne would seek a vote of confidence from his board and fail to get it, and that he would probably resign while fully defending his actions. The minister told cabinet that "it was imperative" that he should announce Coyne's successor in his budget speech on June 20. He recommended Louis Rasminsky, a deputy governor of the bank, and sought permission to offer him the job. Cabinet concluded that this would be premature. They preferred at least to await the board meeting on Monday, June 12. [107]

By that morning Fleming had received four letters from Coyne, all dated June 9. His sources had reported that nine of the eleven directors of the bank had met informally on the weekend and agreed that if Coyne did not offer his resignation they would adopt a resolution requesting it. Coyne had asked for a meeting with them, but had failed to show. The nine directors, Fleming was told, were unanimous in their support for Rasminsky as the successor. [108]

Coyne's first letter dealt with the issue of reappointment and the request for his resignation. It challenged the cabinet's procedure on the ground that, since the act required the board to recommend the appointment to cabinet, the first step should have been to discuss the subject with the board or its appointment committee before reaching a decision. On the request for his immediate resignation, Coyne professed his wish to assist a successor to take office "in the most efficient and co-operative way," and saw no reason why a successor should not overlap with him during his last months in office. He insisted that there would be no question of any differences with govern ment policy: "The Bank has in fact always co-operated fully with respect to Government policies and measures." He rejected any suggestion of impropriety in accepting the board's decision to increase his pension, and laid out the legal position in a separate letter. Finally, he said that "it would be wrong for me by precipitate action" to resign before the board had considered his position on June 12.[109]

Coyne's second letter expressed his view, which he thought Fleming must already know, that the relationship of bank to government should be clarified in law to give "overriding responsibility for monetary policy" to the govern-ment. That had always been the case in fact, he said, but Fleming had confused it by publicly denying responsibility.

> You must have had in mind a very narrow definition of the term "monetary policy" because most people would say that the term monetary policy includ-ed many fields of Government action other than the particular field in which the Bank of Canada operates. In any event monetary policy must be affected in its operations and the central bank must be affected in its views on mon-etary policy by many actions of the Government, including the size of the Budget deficit or surplus and the borrowing requirements of the Government...the extent and volume of lending by the Government or by Government agencies...and the extent of regulation by Parliament or by the Government over activities of various categories of lenders, borrowers, banks, investment institutions, etc.

Many people had told him, Coyne continued, that the doctrine that the government bore no responsibility for monetary policy was "bewildering and confusing." He felt that Fleming's statements might have created the impres-sion that the bank was "a free-wheeling agency so independent that it can carry on monetary policy contrary to the wishes of the Government," a freedom Coyne had never accepted. If there were "sufficiently serious" differences between the governor and the cabinet on policy matters, "it would, in my view, be the duty of the Governor to resign." The letter closed with a specific recommendation to amend the act by adding a provision from the Bank of England Act giving members of the government power to issue directions to the bank "as they think necessary in the public interest."[110]

Ministers nervously awaited the board meeting in Quebec City. At 2 pm a member of the board telephoned Fleming to say that "Coyne was in a truculent mood...but that if he were permitted to complete his term he would confine himself largely to administrative duties, making no more speeches; otherwise he would resist the request for his resignation." Coyne wished to meet with Fleming to state his position, and asked the board to take no action. Here was an invitation to a settlement, but Fleming rejected it. "I said very simply that cabinet had made a decision and I had no authority to alter it...Perhaps I should have temporized, though I am certain that cabinet would not have modified its decision already unanimously taken."[111]

Coyne chose resistance. The board of the bank reconvened the next morning, prepared to adopt a resolution calling on the governor to resign at once. Instead, Coyne asked it to deal with other business while he left the meeting. After two hours he returned to inform the board that he had made a statement to the press and would not resign. The board then adopted the resolution calling for the governor's resignation, "after prolonged consideration and with regret," by a vote of nine to one. Coyne, in the chair, did not vote. The meeting was immediately adjourned as the conflict went public.[112]

The governor's press statement offered defiance to the government.

On Tuesday, May 30 the Minister of Finance on behalf of the Government requested that I resign at once as Governor of the Bank of Canada without waiting for the end of my present seven-year term of office which expires December 31 this year. To aid me in my consideration of this matter he said the Cabinet were upset by the fact that the Bank's Board of Directors had taken action in February 1960 to improve the conditions of the pension which according to the rules of the Bank's Pension Fund had always been provided immediately on the termination of service of a Governor or Deputy Governor. He said the Government were considering what action to take in the matter of the pension, had not yet come to a decision, and wanted my resignation before they came to a decision.

Mr. Fleming also said the Cabinet were of the view that I had failed to discharge the responsibilities of my office in allowing the Board of Directors to take the action they did take unanimously and after thorough consideration in amending the pension fund rules, an action which the Department of Justice had said was entirely within the powers of the Board.

This slander upon my own integrity I cannot ignore or accept. It appears to be another element in a general campaign of injury and defamation directed against crown corporations, their chief executive officers and other public servants. I cannot and will not resign quietly under such circumstances.

For the sake of future Governors of the Bank, and in the interest of propriety and decency in the processes of Government and in the conduct of public affairs, I feel myself under an obligation to ensure that this matter is brought into the open in order that it may receive full consideration and discussion.

I may add that at no time has the Government expressed disagreement with the operations of the Bank of Canada under my management...There has likewise never been any occasion on which the Bank of Canada has failed to cooperate, so far as it was concerned in the matter, in support of Government policy. In financial matters we have always loyally played our part in carrying out positive Government policies.

...

The Minister of Finance has suggested to me that another reason the Government wanted me out of the way was that they were preparing certain programmes which were apparently thought to be of such character that I would oppose them.

This mysterious and alarming suggestion has not been clarified. Clearly I would be betraying the duties of my office to resign under such circumstances. It is for the Government to disclose to the public what it is they are planning to do. I have never opposed Government policy, and do not wish to do so. It is conceivable that at some stage and in some circumstances it would be the duty of the Governor of the Bank to resign on an important question of principle or policy, or on the other hand to make a strong public stand against some Government proposal. The Governor should not, however, resign merely because he is asked to do so. I continue to hope, in the present circumstances, that the processes of thoughtful consideration and discussion will enable the Bank to continue as in the past to take appropriate action within its own field of activity in support of the financial requirements and economic policy of the Government of the day.[113]

Coyne immediately flew back to Ottawa, convened a press conference, and distributed copies of his four letters of June 9 to the minister.

The government had lost control of events. Faced with a direct challenge to its authority and reputation, Diefenbaker and Fleming were both incapable of manoeuvre – even for their own political advantage. They could only engage the enemy head on. The next morning Fleming made what he called "a brief and dignified statement...packed with essential facts" in the House of Commons.[114] He called Coyne's statement "defiant and provocative," and condemned his record as governor.

> During Mr. Coyne's period in office, there has been a steady and deplorable deterioration in the relations of the Bank of Canada with the public. The Governor by a course of ill-considered action and a series of public declarations of policy on public issues quite outside the realm of central banking and by his rigid and doctrinaire expression of views, often and openly incompatible with government policy, has embroiled the Bank in continuous controversy with strong political overtones. Mr. Coyne's rigid attitude on the maintenance of high interest rates is one example. The Government's policy is expansionist aimed at the creation of more trade, more production and more jobs. The policies advocated by Mr. Coyne are restrictionist – restrictive of trade, restrictive of production and restrictive of jobs. The Government has exercised patience in the hope of avoiding further controversy, pending the expiry of his term of office on December 31st next, but its hopes have been frustrated by Mr. Coyne, and it can no longer postpone decisive action.
>
> Matters of high importance are awaiting decision and co-operative action by both the Bank and the Government. The need of teamwork between them and leadership by them has never been greater. It has become impossible to expect this kind of co-operation as long as the present Governor remains in office...

Fleming said that he had told Coyne that the main reason for requesting his resignation was "that the Government was convinced that Mr. Coyne's continuation in office...would stand in the way of the implementation of a comprehensive, sound and responsible economic programme designed to raise the levels of employment and production in Canada." In addition, he had told Coyne that "the Governor was lacking in a sense of responsibility in keeping with his high office, in accepting an additional benefit worth $13,000 per annum for life without ensuring that the matter was brought to the attention of the Government."

Fleming concluded by telling the House "that the Government will shortly invite Parliament to take appropriate legislative action to meet the needs of the situation." Coyne would be dismissed by act of parliament.[115]

This was the essential statement of the case for dismissal: Coyne's public statements had been "ill-considered" and had engaged the bank in public controversy; he had advocated views in conflict with the government's current policies; he could not be expected to support government policy in future; and he had not informed the minister of his pension increase. On Pearson's motion, the House went into an emergency debate on the subject. At its conclusion, Fleming derided the opposition parties for taking the part of the governor, who could hardly be a martyr on a pension of $25,000 per year at the age of fifty.[116]

Editorial comment was widely sympathetic to Coyne for wishing to defend his integrity, critical of him for defying the government's request to resign, and contemptuous of Fleming for his inconsistency. The Montreal *Star*, while recognizing the need for a swift resolution of the affair, condemned the minister:

> If Mr. Fleming has had his troubles, he has been asking for them for a long time. It is quite true, as he told Parliament yesterday, that he and other ministers have openly disagreed with Mr. Coyne on such subjects as foreign investment. He must indeed have found Mr. Coyne's speeches an embarrassment. But where Mr. Fleming was wrong, and where he remained obstinately wrong, was his refusal to accept responsibility for the country's monetary policy. This, he repeatedly said, lay solely within the jurisdiction of the Bank of Canada – a point of view rejected by his predecessors in office who knew that effective management of currency and credit could only be achieved by the Government and the Bank working together...
>
> Mr. Coyne has said that he got no directives on this point from the Government...Without directives Mr. Coyne naturally pursued those monetary policies which seemed to him sound. Not everyone agreed with him. Many were bitterly opposed to them. Mr. Fleming remained superbly aloof...
>
> This is much more important than any petty argument over a pension plan, or indeed any matter arising from the wide-ranging, controversial speeches of Mr. Coyne.[117]

In the Montreal *Gazette*, financial editor John Meyer lamented that a government had demanded a central bank governor's resignation "in such loud and insistent tone...It is a complete negation of all that a central bank stands for in matters of monetary integrity. A more sophisticated cabinet would have recognized this."[118]

On June 20 – which was also budget day – cabinet agreed to a simple, one-sentence bill that read: "The office of Governor of the Bank of Canada shall be deemed to have become vacant immediately upon the coming into force of this act." The dismissal bill was introduced on June 23 and adopted after four days of debate in the House on July 7. Apparently without prior thought, Fleming refused the opposition's request that the bill should be referred to the House committee on banking and commerce, where Coyne might be called as a witness.[119] But cabinet considered the issue again on June 30, and agreed that Coyne should not, in Fleming's words, be given "a forum to propagate his groundless political attacks against the government and play his publicity game."[120] That decision gave Coyne another issue. He was being impeached and tried by parliament without the opportunity for a formal hearing.

The Liberal opposition took full advantage of the government's disarray. Pearson excoriated the ministry for its failures of economic policy and its inability to manage relations with the governor. Yet he disagreed with many of Coyne's prescriptions, conceded that Coyne's usefulness had been destroyed, and recognized that his resignation was now necessary. Paul Martin and Jack Pickersgill went further in their invective, and were matched in return by Marcel Lambert, Dick Bell, and David Walker on the Conservative side. Members of the government suspected, and charged, that Coyne's continuing flow of statements and documents was being produced in collusion with the Liberal Party – in particular, through the intermediacy of Coyne's friend Jack Pickersgill. Pickersgill made an ambiguous denial, which added another theme to the tangled public discussion: Was Coyne in league with the opposition? The claim fitted Diefenbaker's endemic suspicion that his opponents and challengers were united in a single camp. Coyne seemed to be his own man, but in this confrontation he was open to tactical suggestion and aid from the official opposition. In particular, once he was denied a hearing in the House, the opposition arranged for one in the Senate, where there was still a Liberal majority.[121]

The governor of the bank was now engaged in guerrilla warfare against the government, his weapons a daily stream of statements and confidential documents responding to the minister's arguments.[122] In defending his charge that Coyne's policies had been incompatible with government policy, Fleming had retreated to the claim that once, in 1957, there had been a disagreement over the bank's rules on the liquidity ratios of the commercial banks. Coyne revealed that the banks had agreed with him and not with the minister – and that Fleming himself had subsequently changed his mind. Coyne defended his fresh breaches of confidence on the ground that he had been denied the means of making his case before a parliamentary committee. While members of the opposition could not endorse the governor's open conflict with the government, they seized – appropriately – on his right to a fair hearing before dismissal. That was the prime minister's Achilles heel.

John Diefenbaker had remained undecided about participating in the debate until third reading of the dismissal bill on July 5, apparently content to see his bulldog colleague carry the fight. Fleming was, after all, the minister responsible for the affair, so it was prudent to let him take the political wounds. He was a doughty fighter who could be relied upon, and he had a better understanding of the technical issues than the prime minister. But Pearson successfully shifted the ground that day.

> In the first place the governor of the bank has said he has never refused to co-operate with the government…If the governor says he has co-operated, and the minister says he has not co-operated, surely the only issue is that in a dispute of that kind, before the governor resigns – and if his usefulness is destroyed by the government, naturally he has to resign – he is entitled to his day in court. That is the issue. By "court" I mean an appearance before a committee of the House of Commons which is being asked by legislation to throw him out of his job. Could there be any more simple and elementary issue than that?[123]

Frank Howard of the CCF made the same point in less temperate language. He accused the minister of making statements of fact, "or what he claims are facts…interlaced…with some fiction, some imagination and hallucination," and then, when those facts were questioned, of insisting on his parliamentary right to have them accepted as true. "But Mr. Coyne does not have an opportunity to present his point of view to the people who are being asked to fire him, and to be examined on that point of view, as has the Minister of Finance."[124]

When the bill went to third reading the same day, Pearson intensified the attack:

> The issue is one of simply the fundamental right of justice and fair play, the right of a Canadian to be heard before condemnation and to be heard before the body which is condemning them. It is a right enshrined in that clause of the bill of rights which says that no Canadian act of parliament – and we are dealing with a Canadian act of parliament – no Canadian order

or rule or regulation or law, shall be construed or applied so as to deprive a person of the right to a fair hearing in accordance with the principles of fundamental justice for the determination of his rights and obligations. By a "hearing" surely is not meant...the right, in default of a hearing before a court or tribunal, to write letters. So I ask the government this question: How dare it violate this right...a government which so often boasts about its devotion to this same bill of rights.[125]

For Paul Martin and H.W. Herridge, Coyne was being accused and deprived of his rights by bill of attainder, the ancient means of trial in parliament for high crimes. Yet parliamentary practice was meant to assure that the accused could "defend themselves by counsel and witnesses before both houses."[126]

Diefenbaker, challenged by these claims that his own Bill of Rights had been ignored, rose angrily in self-defence. He was surprised, he said, to find "those who ridiculed, those who condemned" the bill were now its proponents. He recalled an obscure charge he had made against J.W. Pickersgill during the 1953 election campaign, which aroused Pickersgill's fury and a cry of "McCarthyism" against the prime minister.[127]

Briefly Diefenbaker turned his attack on other Liberal ministers "who in 1945 and 1946 and 1947 destroyed the rights of individuals in this country by order in council," and then he turned back to Pickersgill. One of Coyne's recent letters, Diefenbaker said, had referred to someone "in whom he places reliance." He glared at Pickersgill. "I look at that individual now and wonder whether I behold in fact the person who dictated certain portions of those letters." Diefenbaker timed the accusation just as the Speaker called for the day's adjournment; but after an appeal to the House, Pickersgill denied the prime minister's charge. As the Speaker rose to adjourn, Paul Hellyer had the last word: "The Prime Minister plunged to new depths this afternoon."[128]

Coyne responded the next day with a renewed call to be heard by a parliamentary committee, where he could present and be questioned about his complete record as governor. One paragraph of his statement referred to the prime minister:

Mr. Diefenbaker's contribution to this debate was to charge that my letters and statements were "dictated" by Mr. J.W. Pickersgill, M.P. Mr. Diefenbaker has been the evil genius behind this whole matter. It was his unbridled malice and vindictiveness which seized on the Bank of Canada's pension fund provisions with respect to the Governor and Deputy Governor as a clever stick with which to beat me, and intimidate me. If he had succeeded in getting me to resign meekly under such a threat, he would then have launched a smear campaign against me, which would have been represented as all the more damning because I had meekly resigned and admitted my error and guilt. Mr. Diefenbaker boasted about this in advance to some close friends. One of these was not so close as he thought.[129]

When debate resumed the next day, Diefenbaker returned to the attack in calmer but still deadly tones. He would not respond to "bitter personal attacks far beyond the realm of criticism ordinarily accepted and necessary for our parliamentary system. I have never answered personal attacks." And yet, "the last two epistles sent out from the ivory tower, irresponsible and intemperate, sent out on the letterheads and in envelopes belonging to the Bank of Canada and delivered by a personal messenger of the bank, make one wonder."

"Shame," cried some members.

"Sir," the prime minister continued, "these letters reveal an attitude which, if accepted by the government, would result in two sovereignties in Canada, the government of Canada and the governor of the Bank of Canada; but not in that order. They would set up a rival government."[130] This somewhat enlarged the case against Mr Coyne.

Diefenbaker turned to a 1953 speech by Jack Pickersgill, a "delightful dissertation" on the relations of public servants to politicians (followed by thanks from a certain J.E. Coyne) in which Pickersgill had declared that "one way to put it is that civil servants, like children, should be seen and not heard." But now, the prime minister insisted, "the government is challenged, and the sovereignty of parliament is challenged." He found defence in statements about the bank from 1934 and 1936 by Mackenzie King and his minister of finance, and he threw back at Mike Pearson his own words that the governor's usefulness had been destroyed.

Had Mr Coyne's rights been infringed? Was the government neglecting the guarantees in its own bill of rights? That was "utter hypocrisy." Parliament was sovereign; parliament was the source of rights. The opposition's claims were simply the result of misunderstanding the distinction between parliament and the courts. The courts determined the rights and obligations of individuals under the law, but parliament made the law and it could change that law. "There is no inviolable right," he declared, "to continue to the end of any term in any position that comes under parliament."

Any rights in the case of the governor of the Bank of Canada exist by virtue of an act of parliament...there is nothing in the bill of rights to suggest that there is any limitation on the power of parliament to change or repeal a law enacted by parliament. The tenure of office of the governor has been created by that act, and I underline and emphasize this fact.

...If there is any right, which there is not, I would refer the matter to the committee.[131]

Diefenbaker denied that Coyne's integrity could have been impugned by criticizing the increase in his pension. "The governor," he suggested, "had the right of veto in that matter. Is it impugning a man's integrity to say that he sat, knew, listened and took? Where is the impugning of integrity there?...The number of letters I am receiving on this question indicates that the people are beginning to think that these vast, swollen pensions deserve to be looked into." Coyne had hidden his pension from the government. But an ex–prime minister, Louis St Laurent, had a pension of less than $3000 a year.

How many people in public life receive a pension of that size? I have been in public life longer than Mr. Coyne. When I retire, no matter how many years from now it may be, I will be in the same position as Mr. St. Laurent.

Mr. Pearson: Oh, that is the reason...

Mr. Diefenbaker: That is true. I am glad the hon. member mentioned that, because he has given years of devoted service and I am prepared to admit it. I ask him not to answer this question. Does the hon. member think $25,000 a year is a fair pension?[132]

Diefenbaker's advocate Judith Robinson wrote in the Toronto *Telegram* that "being called an evil genius and vindictive and a menace by a disturbed public servant" brought out the best in John Diefenbaker: "It broadens his sympathy and makes him less prone to count petty scores with enjoyment."[133] But that was not a universal opinion. No members of the government other than the prime minister and the minister of finance took part in debate on third reading, and most members of the House seemed dismayed by the proceedings. The Coyne affair was a stinking, soiled rag to be held at arm's length until it could be safely dropped. The CCF member for Port Arthur, Douglas Fisher, closed the debate with some philosophic reflections about what had been going on. The prime minister, he conceded, had "made the kind of speech that impresses people and moves them along a certain line with him, persuading his listeners that somehow this parliament had a case and that somehow the governor of the Bank of Canada had got in the way and was impeding the whole role of the elected representatives as reflected in this parliament." But Fisher wondered. "There is a great deal of misunderstanding or, if you wish, nonsense talked about the responsibility of parliament and the supremacy of parliament. What is supreme in this particular parliament or in any Canadian parliament? Is it the Prime Minister? It seems to be that this is what it is." Fisher suggested a general election, in which Canadians could decide once and for all whether they "want to go on with a government that is so incompetent and so much given to procrastination." The day would come. For the moment, the government applied its majority to pass the bill by a vote of 129 to 37.[134]

Now the legislation passed to the Senate, where the Liberal majority had promised that Coyne would be given his chance to testify before the banking and finance committee. On Monday morning, July 10, James Coyne was called to the committee, where he testified for three full days in a crowded committee room reeking of cigars and perspiration. "Sitting through the emotional events on Parliament Hill," reported Walter Gray in the *Globe and Mail* on July 13, "was as trying as five consecutive Joan Crawford movies."[135] From the Parliament Buildings, after his final words, Coyne strode down Wellington Street and into the Bank of Canada, where four hundred employees presented him with a commemorative gold medal, inscribed "for his courage and integrity in defending the position of Governor of the Bank of Canada, June and July, 1961."[136]

Diefenbaker remained uncertain about the outcome. When two Conservative members of the Senate committee called him that afternoon to suggest that the dismissal bill should be dropped if Coyne would resign, the prime minister rejected the idea. "That cannot be accepted," he noted, "because then, if the matter were dropped, he would withdraw his resignation and we would be left high and dry."[137]

Next morning the committee voted on party lines, by sixteen votes to six, to report that the bill "should not be further proceeded with, and the committee feels that the Governor of the Bank of Canada did not misconduct himself in office." The Senate accepted the report, and the bill was dead. On the afternoon of July 14 James Coyne issued one final press statement to announce that he had resigned his office.

> This decision by the Senate, this verdict both by the Committee and by the full Senate, I regard as a vindication of my own conduct, of my personal honour and of the integrity of the position of Governor of the Bank of Canada

as established by Act of Parliament. It is my earnest hope that the result of these proceedings will constitute a precedent which will deter any Government in future from adopting methods designed to remove any person from high offices established by Parliament to be held during good behaviour such as the methods which have been attempted in the present case.[138]

At 6:21 pm Coyne, with his wife at his side, left the Bank of Canada by the front door through a crowd of bank employees. He kept his pension.

Cabinet had no difficulty in agreeing that Coyne's successor should be Louis Rasminsky, but for several days it also insisted that three other officials of the bank, including deputy governor Robert Beattie, should be dismissed for supporting Coyne. Rasminsky refused to accept such a dictation of terms, and ministers withdrew the demand rather than lose him. Rasminsky took office at Coyne's $50,000 salary, on agreement that the contentious pension by-law would not apply to him. On July 31 he issued a statement outlining his understanding of the governor's relationship to the government. While the bank required a "degree of independence and responsibility" to regulate credit and currency, he recognized that if there should be persistent conflict between the central bank and the government over monetary policy, the ministry should be able to instruct the bank about the policy it wished to be applied. If the governor could not conscientiously carry out such instructions, "his duty would be to resign and to make way for someone who took a different view."[139]

That was satisfaction for the cabinet, at a price. The government had suffered profound and self-inflicted wounds. The Toronto *Star* called for the minister of finance's resignation, and Ottawa gossip reached the newspapers that the prime minister hoped to counter criticism by moving Donald Fleming out of Finance.[140]

ON JULY 13 AN EXHAUSTED PARLIAMENT TOOK RECESS FOR THE SUMMER, MUCH OF its legislative business incomplete. Diefenbaker was glad to escape Ottawa briefly for a visit to Uranium City, Yellowknife, Fort Simpson, Whitehorse, and the new Inuvik townsite on the Arctic coast. He had with him his new executive assistant, John Fisher, the celebrated broadcaster who was known for his enthusiasms as "Mr Canada." He had joined the prime minister's office in April. Fisher brought fresh energy and his gift for words to Diefenbaker's aid. "He has been most helpful and prepared draft speeches for me," Diefenbaker wrote, although "I never follow too closely...But they are helpful. They constitute a kind of insurance."[141]

The Conservative Party had been trailing the Liberals in the opinion polls since the fall of 1960, but the minor parties were also showing gains. The public indicated increasing difficulty in distinguishing between the two major parties. On May 29 four by-elections in Prince Edward Island, New Brunswick, Ontario, and British Columbia, in seats won by the Conservatives in 1958, returned three Tories and one Liberal. Conservatives were encouraged, especially in Esquimalt-Saanich, where Social Credit and the New Party had split the vote four ways and given them a narrow victory in George Pearkes's old riding.[142] As Conservative fortunes declined, the prospect of a splintered vote looked increasingly attractive as a means of holding power against the Liberal opposition.

The Liberal Party had given itself new, if confused, vigour in a study conference in September 1960 and a three-day policy rally in January 1961. Resolutions at the rally gave the party a marked interventionist tone and a somewhat less certain nationalist impulse, which Pearson described as moving the party not right, not left, but forward. Ramsay Cook, writing in the *Canadian Forum*, saw little more than opportunism at work: "Clearly the new Pearson is but the old King – with a dash of Walter Gordon."[143] Meanwhile, preparations went forward for the founding convention of the New Democratic Party, which took place in Ottawa at the end of July. The firebrand premier of Saskatchewan, Tommy Douglas, was elected leader of the party, and a moderately progressive, expansionist, and nationalist program was adopted, including a commitment to the recognition of "two nations...two national cultures" as "the basis of Canadian life." In his speech to the convention, Douglas accepted Diefenbaker's recent challenge that the next election would be fought on the issue of free enterprise versus socialism. That, he suggested, was appropriate for a government engaged in sabotaging the CBC and reducing the role of the public sector in favour of private business.[144]

In Quebec, where the victory of Jean Lesage's Liberals in the 1960 provincial election had marked the symbolic beginning of the Quiet Revolution, a heady blossoming and transformation of the community was under way. The new Quebec state was engaged in a long-delayed process of secularization and modernization which threatened the shallow roots of Conservative support in the province. The old Union Nationale was shattered, divided, and unlikely to deliver much to the federal party in 1962 or 1963. Without links of his own in the province, Diefenbaker seemed oblivious of what was happening.

The long mid-term parliament had not been totally discouraging for the government. Diefenbaker took satisfaction in the massive wheat sale to China

that was confirmed by Alvin Hamilton in March; a measure launching preparations for the country's centennial celebrations in 1967; and Davie Fulton's
capital punishment bill, which created two categories of murder and limited
the death penalty to a narrow range of offences. Thus the prime minister
relieved his troubled conscience over Canadian executions, and removed from
cabinet most of the detailed reviews of murder convictions that it had faced
since 1957. Fleming's June budget had been expansionist, including an
income tax reduction, a promise to use the exchange fund to reduce the premium on the Canadian dollar and increase export sales, and a large anticipated deficit for 1961–62 of more than $800 million. The government
continued to juggle – and defer – a range of contentious issues through an
unusual number of royal commissions in progress, reporting, or anticipated.[145]

In March the federal government made new proposals to the provinces
for tax-sharing and equalization, suggestions that would end the fifteen-year
postwar experiment in centralized tax collection and free the provinces to
impose their own taxes at their own levels. Six of the provinces, including
Ontario and Quebec, complained at the terms, but Diefenbaker described the
scheme as a return to the true principles of confederation, and introduced
legislation to bring it into effect after the summer recess. Davie Fulton
appeared to be making progress, as well, in his search for agreement with the
provinces on a formula for amending the Constitution and bringing it home
from Westminster. By December, however, he faced declared opposition to his
formula from Quebec and Saskatchewan, and cabinet uncertainty about
whether to proceed.

Cold War tension had grown over the summer, after John Kennedy's
face-to-face encounter with Nikita Khrushchev in Vienna in May, a growing
exodus of East Germans to the West through Berlin, and the Soviet Union's
renewed threats to end four-power occupation of the city. The construction
of the Berlin wall in August eased the immediate pressures, but the Kennedy
administration had meanwhile undertaken large increases in its defence budget and military force commitments to Europe to demonstrate its resolve.
Diefenbaker told cabinet late in July that there was an imminent risk of war,
and ministers agreed that Canada must demonstrate its solidarity as a member of the Western alliance. In August, cabinet engaged in long discussions
over the military budget, Canadian forces in Europe, and the warheads issue.
Budgetary limits on defence spending were lifted in the absence of the minister of finance; military manpower ceilings were raised from 120,000 to
135,000; and 3000 additional troops were assigned to Canada's NATO forces,
resulting in increased spending of over $250 million per year. Fleming's

subsequent protests that the rate of inflation, interest rates, and the external value of the dollar would all rise were unavailing. On nuclear weapons – with a Canadian draft agreement ready for their consideration – ministers continued to baulk. Ground-to-air missiles designed for nuclear warheads were scheduled for delivery within a few months to domestic forces and to Canadian contingents in Europe, but the divided cabinet maintained the cautious line that the acceptance of warheads might appear provocative in a time of crisis. In September, after both great powers had resumed nuclear testing, Kennedy gave Canada a pretext for delay by announcing that the United States should, at least temporarily, refrain from providing nuclear weapons to any nations that did not already possess them. Privately, Diefenbaker was torn between his unambiguous commitment to the alliance and his compulsive desire to appease popular sentiment. In mid-September he told Elmer: "The world situation is terrible and people not knowing the situation are loud in their opposition to Canada having any nuclear defence. It is an ostrich-like philosophy which, while adhered to by many sensible people, is most beneficial to the Communists and of course receives their support." The prime minister remained, uneasily, among the ostriches.[146]

When the House of Commons resumed sittings in September, members knew that a general election was approaching, and they rushed to complete debate on the estimates. For ten days the government had no legislation to present, and when the House prorogued on September 28 only a few measures had been adopted. The historian John Saywell commented on the long session of 1961 that "organization and procedure deteriorated. Legislation was introduced, disappeared, and reappeared weeks or months later. There seemed to be an almost complete absence of communication between government and opposition, with both sides trying to catch the other off base."[147] One day in May the House engaged in extended discussion about whether it had any business before it, since Gordon Churchill had neglected to put anything on the order paper.[148] Regular attendance in the House fell off, even during major debates.

The government was distracted by its accumulating difficulties and the prospect of another election in the face of high unemployment and prairie drought. On July 30, when Diefenbaker asked his cabinet for advice about an election date, the replies were discouraging. George Hees wondered how the public would react to a dissolution when the government enjoyed so large a majority. Ellen Fairclough said, "Don't go now." Angus Maclean insisted that if unemployment weren't reduced, it "will destroy us." Waldo Monteith complained that Coyne "wasn't handled the right way." Noël Dorion asked:

"Why did you not give (Coyne) a chance to be heard?" Léon Balcer warned that Conservative members were not working in their constituencies. Only two ministers, Michael Starr and Gordon Churchill, recommended an election in 1961 – and, for both, the reasons were defensive. Starr believed that unemployment would be slightly lower in the autumn, and that "if we go now we can say measures are taking effect. If we don't we will have no answers to increased unemployment." In the meantime, the new socialist party "will make great inroads in Ont." Churchill agreed that there would be no fall in unemployment in the coming months, and that "nothing will be heard this winter but what socialist party will do." He conceded that "we are losing ground" in the House of Commons.[149] Facing that divided advice, Diefenbaker chose to wait until the spring of 1962.

When the lieutenant governor of Quebec died in October 1961, Diefenbaker seized the chance to lift the hapless Paul Comtois from cabinet and deposit him in Quebec City. That, in turn, necessitated some kind of cabinet shuffle – which might also provide him with a refreshed team for the forthcoming general election. As usual in such situations, the prime minister let rumour and the passage of time feed political speculation through a long autumn. The Toronto *Telegram* and the Ottawa *Citizen* suggested that Fleming would be leaving Finance because of his ineptitude in the Coyne affair, his string of budget deficits, and his abrasive relations with the press over British negotiations to enter the European Common Market.[150] Diefenbaker took no steps to deny the speculation, which stimulated Fleming's "smouldering resentment" against him. Diefenbaker never discussed the subject with Fleming. "Had he been a straightforward man," Fleming wrote, "I would have expected him to discuss the situation in a friendly and realistic manner with the person most concerned...But Diefenbaker was not a straightforward man."[151]

The prime minister had several other thoughts as well: elevating Noël Dorion to a senior portfolio and bringing in Jacques Flynn as concessions to Quebec; shifting Davie Fulton (another of the usual suspects) to a lesser portfolio; and granting the honorary title of privy councillor to the retired premier of Ontario, Leslie Frost. On December 19 Diefenbaker suggested to cabinet that there would be political benefit in Quebec if the changes – still unspecified – were to take place in Quebec City, where the governor general would be spending the holiday in residence at the Citadel. Ministers agreed, and the trek was announced to the press for December 28. That only heightened the gossip, still mostly centred on the fate of the minister of finance.[152]

On December 27 Diefenbaker summoned Fleming to his office for a chat, and when Fleming arrived at the East Block he was greeted by a crowd of reporters looking for drama. Fleming and Diefenbaker said nothing to the press after the meeting, but reports floated that the minister had faced down the prime minister and held on to his portfolio.[153] Fleming himself insisted in his memoirs that the meeting was cordial and that Diefenbaker rejected any thought of moving him out of Finance. The discussion had centred on whether there should be a budget before a spring election, and if so, what it should contain. Fleming said that there must be a budget, that it must not include further tax cuts, and that the deficit must be contained within reasonable limits. Diefenbaker, Fleming wrote, "listened intently, asked various questions, and did not commit himself."[154] But the minister left confident that he would remain in Finance.

Fleming had underestimated the prime minister's deviousness and sense of insecurity. Diefenbaker's handwritten jottings on the cabinet changes, dated the same day, identify Fleming twice as his proposed new president of the Privy Council, which would either have been an empty ministry without portfolio or, in Fleming's eyes when he reflected earlier about the job, a deputy prime ministership in charge of cabinet organization. That would allow George Nowlan to move to Finance, Davie Fulton to go to National Revenue, and either Noël Dorion or Jacques Flynn to take Justice.[155] The entire reconstruction of the cabinet depended on removing Fleming from Finance. Perhaps without realizing that, Fleming in fact forestalled Diefenbaker's plans simply by talking about his ideas for the next budget. The Chief – who lacked the executioner's nerve – could not bring himself to disappoint Fleming. And without that opening, the prime minister's whole scheme collapsed.[156]

Duncan Macpherson, Toronto *Star*, 1961

The Cabinet Maker

418

But the excursion to Quebec City was still on. Most of the cabinet departed from Ottawa by train that afternoon, accompanied by a gaggle of expectant journalists. On December 28 Governor General Vanier performed an anticlimactic ceremony, swearing in Dorion as president of the Privy Council (while he remained secretary of state) and Flynn as minister of mines and technical surveys. No ministers were shifted, demoted, or dismissed, and Quebec was once more insulted with minor pickings. At a press conference later in the day, Diefenbaker's best efforts could not disguise the embarrassment of the occasion. The train that evening carried a puzzled and disspirited cabinet back to Ottawa.

The editorials lambasted Diefenbaker for his missteps. Oakley Dalgleish's doubting *Globe* commented that "the Conservative Party cannot be anything but dismayed at this indication of division in the Cabinet"; the Ottawa *Citizen* suggested that "the Cabinet shuffle that never was amounts to the heaviest personal defeat Prime Minister Diefenbaker has suffered since he won the leadership of his Party just five years ago," and judged Fleming and Fulton to be "the architects of his defeat. They have told the Prime Minister what to do, and he has meekly bowed to their will." The Liberal Toronto *Star* commented that Fleming had put up with "weeks of shabby treatment" never once repudiated by the prime minister, but had triumphed when he stood firm: "Mr. Diefenbaker's efforts, like the theatrical excursion of his Cabinet to Quebec City, fizzled like a damp squib. As he has so often in the past, the Prime Minister back-pedalled in the face of strong resistance."[157]

When the House reassembled after the holiday, the most bitter attack on Diefenbaker was delivered by a Liberal MP from Quebec, Lucien Cardin. He focused not on Fleming and Fulton, but on the hollow propaganda of the Quebec visit.

It is unfortunate that apparently the Prime Minister does not want to give his Quebec ministers the authority and responsibility that were enjoyed and used so well under the successive Liberal administrations. It is extremely insulting to see how offhandedly the Prime Minister looks down on Quebecers as imbeciles, incapable of making any distinction between light and shadow, in such an essential and important field as the management of their own country.

The Prime Minister must greatly underestimate the intelligence, the temperament and the patient yet eager determination of French Canada to play fully and effectively the part to which it is entitled in the administration of the country, since he has chosen to come and laugh at us on our own doorstep at a time of social and political upheavals.

The prime minister, Cardin claimed, had made an "odious" visit to Quebec City, and his "demagogic and old-fashioned tactics" had undermined the real progress being made towards national unity. If members were scandalized to see a mere back-bencher speak of the prime minister "in somewhat less than flattering tones," well, the answer to that was that "the Prime Minister has been asking for it for a very long time."

> This is simply because he does not act like a real prime minister. He acts more like a silent movie hero who overacts his performance. The Prime Minister's attitude in this house lacks the dignity and the decorum so severely guarded by all previous incumbents of that high office, including all the Conservative prime ministers. I feel the time has come when the Prime Minister must be reminded that in our democratic form of government the Prime Minister is not above the truth. The office of prime minister is not above the law, nor is it above the rules of this house or above the standards of political decency, and it certainly is not above criticism.[158]

The scent of hatred was in the air.

CHAPTER 12

A Government
Disintegrates

1962-1963

W
HEN HAROLD MACMILLAN VISITED OTTAWA IN APRIL 1961 AFTER
his first meeting with President Kennedy, he left Diefenbaker
with a fresh anxiety. Macmillan reported that Kennedy would
welcome British association with the European Economic
Community, which then included the six nations of France,
West Germany, Belgium, the Netherlands, Luxembourg, and
Italy. Britain's efforts to organize the European Free Trade Area, or "outer
seven" – among itself and Norway, Sweden, Denmark, Austria, Switzerland,
and Portugal – had failed to produce substantial benefits, while the Common
Market of "the six," under French and German leadership, was beginning to
demonstrate its potential. The community, it appeared, would become a formidable economic and political force, inspired by the vision of Franco-German
reconciliation, the ancient memory of a single Europe, and the challenge of
resistance against the communist threat from eastern Europe. By the spring
of 1961 Macmillan had decided that Britain and the seven (or perhaps Britain
alone) should seek closer ties with the community; and now Kennedy had
urged him on.[1]

For both George Drew and John Diefenbaker, this was a shock that hinted
at British betrayal. Diefenbaker had invested his political capital in promoting
Canada's ties with Britain and the Commonwealth. A new British commitment
to Europe, he feared, would have both symbolic and practical effects, relegat-
ing the Commonwealth to the background and possibly threatening Canada's
preferential access to the United Kingdom market. Canada's delicate effort to
balance its economic dependence on the United States would be upset, and
Britain would be seen to rebuke the sentimental commitments of the Canadian Tory leader and his party. That signal of British indifference might be
particularly damaging during the coming general election campaign. From
June 1961 onwards the Diefenbaker government engaged in a frantic effort

to discover Britain's intentions, to protect what it saw as Canada's interests, to dissuade Britain from its goal, and then – uncertainly – to subvert the formal British application for admission to the community.

The confused nature of the Canadian campaign was a product of Diefenbaker's unreconciled emotions: his genuine affection for the United Kingdom, his sense of hurt and his desire to show it, his vague fear of economic injury, and his simultaneous unwillingness to accept criticism for his stance. It was also (and not by chance) an echo of Lord Beaverbrook's campaign in the pages of his *Daily Express* against British entry into Europe. Drew and Beaverbrook shared their views on the subject, and Drew provided Diefenbaker with frequent reports from the *Daily Express*. As the Beaver ranted in London, Diefenbaker seemed little more than his colonial sales agent, hawking the same old imperial dream from British North America. The Canadian government's campaign was controversial from the beginning, and especially upsetting to the old core of Conservative supporters because it publicly criticized Great Britain. It was disturbing also to others – including many businessmen and the Liberal opposition – who felt that obstruction would undermine rather than benefit Canada's political and commercial links with the United Kingdom.[2]

When Macmillan decided to send the secretary of state for commonwealth relations, Duncan Sandys, to meet Commonwealth heads of government individually to discuss Britain's interest in Europe, Diefenbaker protested that Sandys was the wrong person, that a meeting of Commonwealth prime ministers should be convened instead, and that France, in any case, would not agree to Britain's terms. "I told him that I had seen a report re France to the effect that France was continuing to insist that joining the Common Market must be on the basis of the full acceptance of the Rome Treaty, and that during the discussions that the United Kingdom Government had made it clear that it did not intend by joining to abrogate the trade and industrial products from Canada, nor Agricultural products from Canada, Australia and New Zealand."[3] Diefenbaker insisted that he did not object in principle to British entry, but press reports suggested that his purpose in calling for a full meeting of prime ministers was "to form a common front to protect Commonwealth trade interests in [the] British market." Failing that, a proposed conference of Commonwealth finance ministers in September 1961 seemed to be the first occasion for a collective response.[4]

In preparation for Sandys's visit to Ottawa, Macmillan assured Diefenbaker on July 3 that "the decision we have to take now is not whether to join the Common Market, but whether to open negotiations with a view to finding out what special arrangements would be obtainable. Previously we had hoped to avoid entering negotiations unless there was a high prospect of success. But since it is not possible to clarify the position in advance, we feel that the risk of a breakdown might have to be accepted." That seemed partly intended as reassurance to other Commonwealth countries that Britain would go into negotiations determined to protect their trading interests, and to accept rejection if it could not do so.[5] Macmillan explained that Sandys would discuss "how best to organise a system of close and continuous Commonwealth consultation to cover the period of preparations for negotiations, the negotiations themselves, and the eventual decision... whether or not to join the EEC."[6]

Diefenbaker and Drew were convinced that the Macmillan government had already made a decision in favour of entry, and that all this reassurance might be a trick. Open protest was thus a legitimate means of forcing a British retreat. But Norman Robertson and Robert Bryce were disturbed by the signs of public conflict, and argued for a return to quiet diplomacy. Bryce advised Diefenbaker that he should express Canada's apprehensions "without making any statement either to Sandys or in public that could be used to blame Canada for upsetting a move that is now the evident desire of the UK Parliament and public, as well as the UK government." Instead, he should argue privately that the United Kingdom had little bargaining strength against the six, and that if Commonwealth trade could not be protected, the association would be seriously damaged "at the very time that it appears likely to prove the most valuable in helping to bridge the widening gap between the white peoples and coloured peoples." The Commonwealth, then, was worth more to British power and prestige than membership in the community; the United Kingdom should recognize that and draw back.[7]

The prime minister let Howard Green, George Hees, Donald Fleming, and Alvin Hamilton take the lead in meetings with Duncan Sandys on July 14; but he met with Sandys as well, and added his own gruff message of opposition. He believed that the Commonwealth would be damaged: "that was my feeling and it might be emotional as I had a deep attachment to the Commonwealth." If the United Kingdom joined the market, Diefenbaker said, "Canada and Australia would be driven into closer relations with the United States." He suggested that the United States was trying to "push" the United Kingdom into the Common Market (a description of American methods that had particular meaning for Diefenbaker since he had acquired the Rostow memorandum in May), but Sandys denied it. The joint communiqué after the meetings reflected Canada's "grave concern" over the British initiative. The Canadian press responded coolly, in its turn, to Canada's obstructiveness.[8]

Following the Sandys mission, Macmillan told Diefenbaker in late July that his cabinet had decided to enter negotiations with the European Economic Community. He recognized that there were substantial Commonwealth trade interests at risk, but he reiterated that only negotiations could reveal what special arrangements could be secured. On the political side, he asserted Britain's belief that it could maintain its Commonwealth role more effectively from inside the community than from outside. He spoke of "consultation" and "close contact" with Commonwealth countries throughout the negotiations.[9] On August 3 the British parliament gave its support to a British application for entry.

Canada then took its campaign to the meeting of Commonwealth ministers of finance and trade in Accra, Ghana, in mid-September, where Duncan Sandys faced twelve countries opposing British entry to the community. The debate, occupying an entire day, was framed by an opening speech from George Hees and a closing speech by Donald Fleming. Hees argued that Britain would lose, not gain, economic benefits in Europe; that Canadian trade would face "an entirely new and seriously disturbing situation...extensive damage – and in some cases, irreparable damage"; and that Commonwealth ties of "tradition, trust and trade" would suffer. He urged Britain to maintain its Commonwealth trading arrangements unchanged. Fleming made "a pleading speech" dedicated, in his own words, to "the Commonwealth and its glorious contribution to freedom, peace, human government and the progress of mankind."[10] The conference communiqué expressed "grave apprehension" over the British initiative and doubted whether the interests of Commonwealth countries could be protected. The UK delegation, in response, promised "close consultation with all Commonwealth Governments at all stages in the negotiations."[11]

Christopher Young reported accurately in the Ottawa *Citizen* that Canada had led other nations in "ganging up" on Britain at Accra, and that they had offered Britain a choice between the European Economic Community and the Commonwealth. Having done that, Diefenbaker could not admit it. He told the House of Commons that Hees and Fleming had been misreported. A week later the *Financial Times* of London commented: "The extreme weakness of the New Zealand position is its strength, and the restraint with which its problems are put is far more likely to meet with a sympathetic response and understanding in London, and in the six, than the violence with which the Canadians plead their intrinsically far weaker case."[12]

That kind of comment was not helpful. Diefenbaker complained to Macmillan about unfair treatment from the British press, and henceforth, in his public comments, he was careful to emphasize Britain's right to choose and its promise of continuous consultation. "We are trying to strengthen Britain's bargaining position in order to assist the Commonwealth," Diefenbaker noted defensively.[13] But the peevish and resentful tone never disappeared.

Britain made its formal application for entry to the community in October 1961, but did not make the text of its presentation available to other Commonwealth governments. When the chief British negotiator, Edward Heath, made arrangements to brief Commonwealth diplomats in London in early November, Drew chose not to attend, in what seemed to be a show of Canadian displeasure. That was reported in the *Daily Express* as a "snub"; the *Observer* spoke of "an openly obstructive" Canadian attitude; and the *Guardian* reported that the Canadians were "simmering with indignation." The *Sunday Times* judged that Britain had little remaining patience with what it called "the Diefenbaker-Fleming administration." Canadian newspapers repeated the refrain.[14] All that flack prompted Diefenbaker to cable and telephone Drew instructing him to issue a statement at once "making it clear that no snub was intended"; and Drew immediately did so, declaring that the story was "absolutely false." Basil Robinson noted that "the incident was minor but, like the Accra affair, it illustrated the difficulty Diefenbaker had in coordinating the public statements of his senior colleagues on matters where his own feelings were mixed and his signal therefore muffled."[15]

As the United Kingdom pursued its negotiations over the next fifteen months, Diefenbaker kept a jaundiced eye on events, complaining frequently about the lack of consultation and taking pleasure in every sign of French intransigence. His cabinet reported increasing public distaste for Diefenbaker's running fight with the United Kingdom.[16] By the time that Macmillan agreed to a Commonwealth prime ministers' conference on the issue for September 1962, the British hoped for a quick and successful resolution; but Diefenbaker thought that unlikely. When Charles de Gaulle finally vetoed the British application in January 1963, Diefenbaker gloated. That was a mean ending to an episode that brought him political credit neither at home nor abroad. Macmillan, who saw "all our policies...in ruins" after the French veto, must have indulged himself in a bit of black humour when he asked Diefenbaker, on the same day, whether Canada would accept free trade with the United Kingdom.[17]

WHILE HE WAS PREMIER OF ONTARIO, LESLIE FROST PLAYED A DUAL ROLE IN HIS relations with John Diefenbaker, as a government leader in the industrial heartland and as a friendly mentor in matters financial and political. As premier he was not always successful, especially in his attempts to alter the fiscal balance between Ottawa and the provinces. As mentor he was a patient source of counsel, whatever his disappointments may have been in his role as premier. When Diefenbaker stumbled into his conflict with James Coyne in the summer of 1961, Frost was glad to see an old difficulty faced, but appalled by the mishandling of Coyne's departure. He offered Diefenbaker his advice on a successor; and once Coyne had gone, he moved quickly to repair the prime minister's frayed relations with Oakley Dalgleish of the *Globe and Mail.* This was necessary, Frost believed, as preparation for an election in 1962: "It is important from your standpoint, but also I think...from the country's standpoint. As a matter of fact, we cannot afford to have divisions among interests whose objectives are in common." Frost proposed that he and Diefenbaker should make a casual visit to Dalgleish at home, in order to "break the ice in a big way...His support in the business area is very important & the above 'gesture' would be overwhelming."[18] The meeting apparently took place, with amicable results that were evident in correspondence and *Globe* editorials for the next few months.

By that time Frost had decided to retire as premier. When he did so in November, he wrote to Diefenbaker to assure him that "my interest in the grand old party will remain as active as ever...To the Party I have devoted most of the active years of my life. This I propose to do in the future...I am interested in your success and the Party's success. It will be a pleasure always to give my aid and support."[19] A month earlier, Diefenbaker had offered Frost the Canadian ambassadorship in Washington, but Frost declined because he did not wish to leave Canada – and because he felt unable to adjust to the "social rigidities" of diplomatic life in Washington. He left open the possibility of a senatorship, although he preferred to see that reward go to "others who had given long and good service." Frost hoped instead that he could carry on with his role as facilitator and guide in relations with business and labour.[20]

Frost feared that Diefenbaker had lost direction and was heading for defeat in 1962. When the prime minister asked for his advice on policy in February, Frost responded at once in a series of letters suggesting an election manifesto drawing on ideas from persons inside and outside the party. In Ontario, he recalled, he "always bore in mind the fact that there are not enough Tories...to elect a Conservative government. They provide a great nucleus, but one has to go out into the highways and byways and get people, regardless of previous political affiliation and background. Many of my best supporters were people who had voted the other way a few years before." The other parties, he knew, had impressive "brain trusts" at work. What Diefenbaker needed was "a statement of policy, a manifesto if you will, which is confident, understanding, practical and appealing...Such a thing would be morale boosting and would give our people an objective around which they can rally." Frost appealed to the spirit of John A. Macdonald, in invocation of Diefenbaker's great 1958 campaign.

> There is a parallel today to John A's day. In 1877 certainly the winds of change were blowing much as today. The minds of people were perplexed. John A. sensed this and had a series of great picnics and made statements of policy from which evolved the national policy, a political philosophy which pretty much dominated the scene for nearly fifty years...My suggestion is that you prepare such a statement of policy and fit into the same the multitude of worthwhile things this government has done to carry out its purpose. The government in many ways has done a very remarkable job, but I am afraid the effect of these things is going to be lost unless they are part of a composite picture of policy.[21]

Specifically, Frost suggested tax reductions to spur economic growth, a confident acceptance of British entry into the European community, a generous immigration policy to bring to Canada "fine people from elsewhere, with all of their skills and creative capacity," and a general review of tax structure to reduce impediments to industry.

A week earlier, after a personal meeting with the prime minister, Oakley Dalgleish had written Diefenbaker with similar proposals to stimulate growth and to show "that your government understands the problems of business."[22] Diefenbaker told Frost that Dalgleish's letter was "cold," and Frost, always sensitive to the Chief's fear of criticism, reassured him. "Please remember it was really a memorandum. In my many associations with him he has criticized me on many occasions. Very often, unfortunately, I found he was right. When the chips were down, however, with due recognition to my frailties, he helped me and he was always prepared to assist me to put my story across, provided it was right. My job was to make sure that it was such and that I could sell it."[23]

This piece of counselling – both political and psychological – seemed to work. Diefenbaker met twice with Dalgleish, on one occasion for "about five hours," to discuss both his and Frost's proposals. He told Frost that "your ideas are excellent and the suggestions are of such a nature that I will gather together a number of the Ministers tomorrow to discuss the question at length."[24] The result was a request to both Frost and Dalgleish to give him ideas for an election manifesto. Frost responded at the end of March with a five-thousand-word paper prepared with the help of five long-time associates. "Back of this document," Frost wrote, "I have endeavoured to weave the conception which I followed during my years in office, going back to 1943, that in this country we should create an environment in which there could be expansion and development, and in which business could grow, flourish and provide employment. In my opinion, upon that depends everything."[25] Diefenbaker promised to study the paper in detail.[26]

Soon afterwards Dalgleish added his own comments, emphasizing that business had to be reassured that government understood its problems and would promote growth, and that Canada's friends abroad must be given similar reasons for confidence. There was more than implied criticism of Diefenbaker's record in this appeal: Dalgleish noted that investors looked on Canada with "both doubt and wonderment...I acknowledge that much of this has been created and sustained by the pessimistic talk of our own politicians, and others, about unemployment, etc., over the past two years. As you know I do not believe the pessimism is justified but at the present the proof that it is not must come from us."[27]

Frost's and Dalgleish's advice was intended to prop up a faltering regime, and above all to salvage some support for it in the business community. Parliament had reassembled in January to hear an uninspiring speech from the throne made up of odds and ends of unfulfilled election promises, plus another list of new spending promises; and the prime minister had delivered a defensive address which, in effect, accused the opposition of misgoverning the country since 1958.[28] What followed was a ragged and ill-attended session, as front- and back-benchers alike took to the hustings.

Almost two years had passed since the election of a reformist Liberal government under Jean Lesage in Quebec, and by now the Quiet Revolution was transforming the province. As the pressures for fairer treatment of the country's French-speaking minority mounted, the prime minister rejected suggestions for a royal commission on French-English relations. At the abortive cabinet meeting in Quebec City, Diefenbaker raised the subject of using French in cabinet meetings, but this was empty pretence, since Donald Fleming and Davie Fulton were probably the only two English-speaking ministers who could claim any facility in the language. At the same meeting Fleming proposed that federal government cheques should be bilingual. For six weeks the cabinet wavered inconclusively on the subject, until it agreed in February to the minister's proposal to introduce the reform as a simple administrative change, without legislation. His announcement to the House, on February 6, 1962, was an anticlimactic response to the awakening of French-speaking Canada.[29]

Diefenbaker expected an election within months, but he had not decided on a date, and found it painfully difficult to do so. The Gallup Poll, which he claimed to ignore, continued to show his party running behind the Liberals. His cabinet was tired, fretful, discouraged by its public failings, anxious about its division on issues yet to be settled, disenchanted with and yet intimidated by the leader who had brought them to power five years earlier. They knew now – all of them – that he had feet of clay. What held them together was not Diefenbaker's inspiration but the fear of defeat.

In the press gallery, an adviser told Diefenbaker in January 1962 that he faced "a dangerous degree of personal animosity among most of the members." He attributed this not to any failings of policy, but to resentment over a loss of "the close personal relationship they had with you some years ago" and sloppy disregard for the press in ministers' dealings with reporters before and after cabinet meetings. "The many complaints I hear," his correspondent wrote, "seem to be highly personal, giving the impression that some who recall earlier close relationships have become progressively surprised, hurt, annoyed and finally, vindictive." He suggested the institution of regular press conferences, which would give the prime minister a platform for his "established skill in reply and repartee" and restore a "more friendly reporting atmosphere." "Desirable questions" could be arranged, and undesirable ones would receive considered replies that might discourage reporters from "mak[ing] up their own answers as they are doing now."[30] Diefenbaker was not, by the winter of 1962, in a mood to make the disciplined effort that this would require, and he matched the press gallery's vindictiveness with his own.

According to Donald Fleming, the prime minister preferred to call a spring election without a budget. That would allow the cabinet to authorize patronage spending without any attempt to place it within a framework of fiscal policy – and would send the deficit skyrocketing for another year. Fleming argued with his usual passion for a budget, made his preparations, and at last got it in early April; but his appeals for spending restraint were unavailing. In late March and early April the ministry announced new federal loans for New Brunswick power projects, credits to China for additional grain purchases, new acreage payments for wheat farmers, extended freight rate reductions, more generous unemployment insurance payments, wider Maritime coal subsidies, and a frigate construction program for the Canadian navy. The throne speech had also promised increases in old age and disability pensions. The budget, on April 10, estimated a $745 million deficit despite what Fleming foresaw as a period of "rapid economic growth." The press represented this as a modest victory for Fleming against the "big spenders." Since the prime minister had ordered Fleming to deliver his speech in one hour, he was obliged to omit large parts of the text, to deliver the rest at breathless pace, and to ask the House for extra time. He finished at 9:50 in the evening – fifty minutes over the prime minister's allowance – leaving Mike Pearson just ten minutes to reply. That was all he received, since the House never returned to the budget debate. One week later, after revealing the cabinet's decision to build a causeway from the mainland to Prince Edward Island, Diefenbaker announced the dissolution of parliament for an election on June 18, 1962. The parliamentary reporter of the Montreal *Star* summed up the whole twenty-fourth parliament as "sometimes aimless, often ill-tempered, and always potentially explosive. Few will mourn its passing."[31]

THE CONSERVATIVE PARTY, WHICH HAD FLOATED THROUGH THE MIRACLE-WORKING campaign of 1958, had lost its enchantment with the leader. On Diefenbaker's suggestion, Allister Grosart called a meeting of key party organizers at the Queen Elizabeth Hotel in Montreal in the early winter of 1962 to discuss electoral prospects. He was shocked to hear from them that, in Dalton Camp's words, "the game was over...we'd probably lose the next election, or we'd take an awful pounding." Diefenbaker, they said, was a liability and should be kept off television. Other ministers should be out on the road to turn the focus away from the prime minister. The dissatisfactions spilled out all day as Grosart recorded their complaints and challenged their judgments. By evening he too was a casualty: the meeting marked "the absolute end of any confidence in Allister...they didn't believe in him and they didn't believe he was in touch with reality and they didn't think either that he would do anything about what they were telling him, or that he'd have any power or influence to do anything." The day ended in a drunken banquet at which Grosart, the wine expert, tossed the first empty bottle over his shoulder to shatter on the floor behind him, as everyone sought unhappy oblivion in alcohol.[32]

Diefenbaker preferred not to believe the pessimistic reports. He wrote to Elmer on March 23 that polls showing Conservative support at 21 percent in the west, Liberal support at 25 percent, and 39 percent of electors undecided were wrong. "Our members in the House are very enthusiastic and are anxious for an election and certainly would not be in that state of mind if the polls mean anything. They were so far astray in 1957 and 1958, and I haven't been advised of anything that would bear out the reports that are being given in this connection."[33] The people wanted an election, he believed. It would be "a tremendous battle," he told another correspondent, not because his government deserved criticism, but because the air was full of Liberal propaganda. "There will be no limit to opposition attacks, however unfair...it has become regular procedure."[34]

In response, Diefenbaker, on the encouragement of several supporters, was developing a campaign of attack that would cover both the Liberal Party and the New Democratic Party. The election, he said, would be a battle between free enterprise and socialism. Diefenbaker had tried out the theme in a March 1961 speech that prompted an angry response from his friendly nemesis Eugene Forsey of the Canadian Labour Congress. "Frankly," Forsey wrote, "that speech dismayed me...I don't think you are doing yourself or your government justice. You are making it appear that your main concern is a doctrinaire devotion to an abstract theory called 'free enterprise,' to which you are prepared to sacrifice almost anything; whereas it seems to me that, on the contrary, you have tackled unemployment and other problems without any such doctrinaire preconceptions, but in the traditional Conservative spirit: pragmatic, empirical, common sense, down to earth, looking for the best practical solution, whether it involves more government interference or less, more public enterprise or less."[35] Diefenbaker drafted a reply suggesting that Forsey must have momentarily lost his calm detachment out of commitment to "the socialist party." But he thought better and did not send it.

Nevertheless the theme still appealed to him. It would allow Diefenbaker to remind voters of his 1960 United Nations speech attacking Soviet communism and imperialism; it would identify the NDP as the party of regimentation; and by free association it would link a group of prominent new Liberal candidates and advisers with the wartime Liberal regime that had "paralysed Parliament and interfered with the rights of the provinces." It would even, at its nastiest, allow the prime minister to suggest cryptically that "softness on communism" was not something that Pearson should risk discussing. Diefenbaker tried out the broadened theme during the throne speech debate of January 1962, and he used it intermittently during the election campaign, when it ran as a discordant background melody.[36]

The officially advertised party program was more constructive. It was partly the product of Leslie Frost and Oakley Dalgleish's outline of incentives to business, and partly of a draft prepared in 1961 by an informal committee under Alvin Hamilton's direction. "To be believable," Hamilton told Diefenbaker, "it mentions what has been done on the first stage of the national development program. To appeal to the emotions, it speaks of the principles which guide the government. To build enthusiasm for the future, it outlines the eleven point program." The program promised a range of incentives and benefits, most of them previously announced, that marked a new scale of bidding for the popular vote out of public funds. It was matched by an equally bountiful Liberal platform. The bidding war would continue for the next twenty years.[37]

The prime minister's campaign, like his previous ones, saw him criss-cross the country by plane, train, and car, touching Newfoundland and British Columbia once, the Maritime provinces twice, the prairies three times, Quebec four times, and Ontario five times, usually arriving back in Ottawa overnight on Saturdays for a single day at home between weekly journeys. There were major rallies in London, Edmonton, Victoria, Vancouver, Quebec City, Montreal, Toronto, and Hamilton, and many visits to small town and rural constituencies where the party counted on fervent loyalty to the Chief.[38]

With none of Diefenbaker's magnetism on the platform, Pearson took the advice of his American pollster, Lou Harris, to emphasize the Liberal team. Still, the iron law of parliamentary campaigns thrust him willy-nilly into personal battle with the prime minister. Pearson opened his campaign in Charlottetown at the end of April by challenging Diefenbaker to a television debate on the Kennedy-Nixon model. Diefenbaker scoffed and turned him down. As he had told Eisenhower in September 1960, "Why advertise your political opposition?"

Diefenbaker was incensed that someone else was doing that. Early in May, President Kennedy hosted a White House dinner for Nobel Prize winners from the Western hemisphere, at which Pearson was one of the honoured guests. In Diefenbaker's eyes that was bad enough, but Kennedy compounded the crime in what was reported as a forty-minute private conversation with the Canadian opposition leader before the reception. Pearson told the press that they had discussed many subjects, including disarmament, NATO, and Britain's application to the Common Market. When the departing American ambassador to Canada, Livingston Merchant, arranged what he thought would be a fifteen-minute appointment with Diefenbaker at his Sussex Drive residence to offer his farewell on May 4, he walked unwittingly into a hurricane. The meeting resulted in a flurry of tough talk in Washington and the threat of a major diplomatic incident.[39]

Robinson warned Merchant before the interview that Diefenbaker "was in an extremely agitated frame of mind" over the political use Pearson had made of his meeting with Kennedy. Despite the warning, Merchant was unprepared for Diefenbaker's "disturbed and disturbing attitude." What he heard was a two-hour "tirade" in which "the exchanges, while personally friendly, became heated." Kennedy's personal meeting with Pearson, the prime minister said, was "an intervention by the President in the Canadian election." Pearson's associates would be bound to use the meeting as evidence of Kennedy's trust in Pearson: Walter Gordon had already done so the previous evening.

Diefenbaker added that he was "shocked" that Kennedy wished to get rid of Commonwealth preferences, and accused the Americans of thinking they "could achieve this by supporting Pearson who was prepared to accept without argument Britain's unconditional entrance into the European Common Market."

The Prime Minister then went on to say that Canada–United States relations would now be the dominant issue in the campaign. He said the campaigning would be more bitter than it was in 1911 and he referred to Champ Clark's statement during the course of that campaign which it took the Canadians until 1917 to recover from. (According to my recollection, Champ Clark who was the Speaker of the House of Representatives, said publicly something along the line that it was inevitable that the United States should annex Canada. The basic issue of that campaign was the question of a reciprocal trade agreement with the United States and the outcome of the campaign was won and lost on the slogan of the Conservatives, "No truck or trade with the Yankees.")

In his fury, Diefenbaker said he would have to confront the Liberal line head on – the claim that Pearson could better handle relations with Washington. "He thought he would probably be forced into this by the middle of or end of next week."

In countering the Liberal line, he said he would publicly produce a document which he has had locked up in his private safe since a few days after the President's visit to Ottawa last May. This document he says is the original of a memorandum on White House stationery, addressed to the President from Walt Rostow and initialled by the latter, which is headed "Objectives of the President's Visit to Ottawa." The Prime Minister says that the memorandum starts:

" 1. The Canadians must be pushed into joining the OAS.
" 2. The Canadians must be pushed into something else...
" 3. The Canadians must be pushed in another direction..."

Diefenbaker told him, falsely, "that this document came into his possession a few days after the president left, through External Affairs, under circumstances with which he was not familiar, but his understanding was that it had been given by someone to External Affairs." This authoritative evidence of the

American intention to push Canada, Diefenbaker told Merchant, "would be used by him to demonstrate that he, himself, was the only leader capable of preventing United States domination of Canada." The prime minister added that an investigation was under way to determine whether "some Liberal supporter of Pearson" in the Canadian Embassy in Washington had set up the interview with Kennedy. The incident, Diefenbaker said, would "blow our relations sky high."

Merchant reported that Diefenbaker was tired by an overnight flight from Newfoundland, where he had experienced "an exhausting and frustrating whistle-stop campaign," and that he was uneasy about his keynote address planned for that evening in London, Ontario. "He was excited to a degree disturbing in a leader of an important country, and closer to hysteria than I have seen him, except on one other possible occasion." Merchant felt that Olive was concerned about his state: She was "hovering over him when I arrived and obviously doing the same when I chatted with the two of them for about ten minutes before departure."

Merchant attempted a response, and reported that Diefenbaker was "willing to hear me out." He told the prime minister there was no reason to criticize Kennedy for taking the occasion to discuss international affairs with a prominent Canadian visitor. "It was childish to assume that this constituted any effort or intent to intervene in Canadian domestic politics." He offered his word that the US administration had no favourite party in Canada, and assured him of the president's great personal respect. But he implied that Diefenbaker was lying about how he had obtained the document, and delivered a stern diplomatic warning. "I urged him in strongest terms to discard any thought of revealing publicly the document which he said he had in his possession. I said that I had never seen or heard of it and that it was not conceivable to me that if such a memorandum were genuine, it could have been transmitted officially or unofficially to anyone in the Canadian Government." If the document was genuine, it was confidential advice to the president which "had no official status and was not intended for Canadian eyes. Moreover, I said that were he to reveal it publicly, there would be a serious backlash, if not in Canada, then certainly in the United States. People would ask how the Prime Minister had come into possession of such a privileged internal document addressed to the President of the United States, and why it had not been immediately returned, without comment or publicity."

Merchant felt he had made an impression on Diefenbaker, but could not be sure whether the prime minister would refrain from using the Rostow memorandum in the campaign. He had known Diefenbaker, at other times, to be agitated "only to find that two or three days later the storm had passed. On this occasion, however, his only assurance as I left, was that he would not raise this issue tonight, and in fact, he said half jokingly...that he would not bring it up until I had left Canada, since, as he said, it would be up to another American Ambassador to pick up the pieces and he didn't want to spoil my last few days in Ottawa."

The ambassador concluded: "We have a problem." At best, having blown his top, Diefenbaker would think again and act responsibly. "It is necessary, however," he advised, "that we take out any available insurance against the worst."

Merchant told George Ball that there was nothing to gain by interference in Canadian elections, or in the appearance of doing so. A successful intervention would label the winner as "a running dog of the United States" who would be "inhibited from acting along lines agreeable to us." After an unsuccessful intervention, "the winner would hate us." Since appearances had now given Pearson an advantage, he suggested some balancing gesture in Diefenbaker's favour, such as a quickly staged and informal meeting between Kennedy and Diefenbaker, arranged at the president's initiative.

As Merchant intended, this message was conveyed at once to the president. Kennedy's national security adviser, McGeorge Bundy, gave detailed instructions to Ball on a response, and Ball passed these on to Merchant on May 8, along with a copy of the original Rostow memorandum.[40] In a footnote for Merchant's information only, Ball said tartly that Kennedy had "no intention or desire" for an early meeting with Diefenbaker. The prime minister was on the campaign trail in Quebec, Ontario, Manitoba, and Alberta during the week, so Merchant asked to see him as soon as he returned to Ottawa on Saturday, May 12. Merchant hoped that "the cryptic nature of my message will exert restraint on him," although Diefenbaker had threatened "at some Quebec whistle-stop last night" to discuss the subject of a Canadian-made foreign policy later in the campaign.[41] While awaiting Diefenbaker's return, Merchant met with Robinson and conveyed Washington's concern about the general course of Canadian policy and the prime minister's "tirade." He told Robinson he had a message from Kennedy which, he hoped, "would have a restraining effect." Robinson, who was now due to be posted to the Canadian Embassy in Washington, left the meeting "overwhelmed by the size of the problem of explaining Canadian policy in Washington, especially on defence."[42]

Diefenbaker received Merchant at home on Saturday evening. The ambassador's instructions called for a coy diplomatic dance, which he performed. Afterwards, he reported the interview by telegram to Washington.

I opened by saying I had delayed my departure by reason my grave and growing concern over our talk on May 4. I said I had not reported to the President
his stated intent to reveal in present campaign his possession of confidential
document of the President presenting advice of member his personal staff.
I said I had only reported to the Department his belief Pearson intended
capitalize in campaign on private conversation with the President on Nobel
Prize occasion which I said had been informal twenty-minute chat in advance
of formal dinner. Then I said I had independently obtained copy Walt
Rostow's memo which I found unexceptionable and concerning four subjects which had been frequently discussed and regarding which I had
thought PM's personal attitude favorable. Verb "push" I said corresponded
to British "press" or Canadian phrase "seek to persuade."

PM did not interrupt as I went on to say that I had not reported his threat
to use existence or contents memo because consequences of his doing so
would be catastrophic. PM interjected "they would be so in Canada." I said
I was not talking of Canada but of reaction in the US. I said if he did this the
result in the US would be of incalculable harm with public opinion, in the
government and in his personal relations and that consequently I had delayed
my departure to urge once more that he abandon any such thought.[43]

Diefenbaker backed down. He told Merchant that "he had given [the]
matter further consideration and in light of what I had said to him on May 4
he had no present intention of using or in any way referring to [the] memo
in question. He said if he changed his mind he would personally telephone
me in Washington before doing so but he was now decided to discard any such
thought." According to Diefenbaker, only three other persons knew of the
memo – Green, Fleming, and Churchill, whom Merchant described to Ball as
"all...cool steady men."[44]

Merchant noted that Diefenbaker then set off on an "emotional sidetrack"
by insisting that the United States was "trying to push" Canada around, but
calmed down when the ambassador asked what evidence he could show for
such suspicions. He turned instead ("with Gusto") to the subject of his prairie
campaign tour, though bemoaning the time and travels still ahead. The ambassador concluded his report optimistically. "Notwithstanding fact PM nervous
and in my judgment on verge of exhaustion, I believe storm has passed and
that chances are now minimal that he will embark on all-out anti-American
line...At end conversation we both lowered our voices and with complimentary
close he bade me warm good night."

For the time being an understanding had been achieved, but the incident remains puzzling. If Diefenbaker, in a fit of anger and desperation, intended to use the Rostow memorandum, why did he warn Merchant beforehand? Was he hoping to be dissuaded from what would have been a dishonourable and self-destructive act? Did he expect that his threat would lead Kennedy to refrain from any further "intervention"? Why did he lie about the origin of the memorandum, in a way that could only be obvious to Livingston Merchant? Merchant later said that Kennedy had been "astounded and indignant" at this "species of blackmail," and that he was himself "baffled and finally appalled by Diefenbaker."[45]

Merchant's and Robinson's observations – that Diefenbaker was "disturbed," "overwrought," "extremely agitated," "excited to a disturbing degree," "closer to hysteria than I have seen him," "on the verge of exhaustion" – suggest a man on the edge. Perhaps his threat was not the act of a carefully calculating politician, but of an unsettled – and very fragile – spirit.

Despite his expressions of confidence, Diefenbaker was aware that his government and party were in trouble. The political atmosphere had changed since 1958, and the high expectations of that winter campaign could not be revived. Yet his own confidence and sense of stability rested on continuing signs of public support. The government had borne one critical blow after another since the cancellation of the Arrow in 1959. The prime minister's moodiness, disorganization, and indecisiveness had undermined the confidence of his own cabinet. Diefenbaker was also bewildered by the complex technical questions of economic, financial, and defence policy that now overwhelmed his ministry. He had managed – temporarily – to contain the nuclear weapons issue, but the others were more immediate.

In the days before his first interview with Merchant, the prime minister faced a perplexing monetary crisis, and on May 3 it became public. The Canadian dollar – alone among the major currencies and in defiance of the fixed exchange rate policy of the International Monetary Fund (IMF) – floated in value on the international markets. From a position in the late 1950s when it stood at a premium against the American dollar, it drifted gradually downwards to a rate of about 95 cents US by the winter of 1961–62. The persisting Canadian recession, five consecutive budget deficits, an increasing deficit on the current trade account, and, it seemed, general uncertainty about the policies of the Diefenbaker government had unsettled the exchange markets. Once the election was called on April 18, an unanticipated stampede in the sale of Canadian dollars began. In the month of April alone, the Bank of Canada's exchange fund sold $125 million of its foreign reserves to maintain the value of the Canadian dollar. That brought the decline in the exchange fund over seven months to about half a billion dollars, or one-quarter of Canada's total exchange reserves.

The government's chief financial advisers believed that Canada faced a continuing speculative run on the dollar and a potentially disastrous decline in its value. Diefenbaker was informed by Robert Bryce on April 29 that there was an exchange crisis, and senior officials met with Donald Fleming to discuss alternative responses. When they could not agree, Fleming recommended that the Canadian dollar should be pegged at 92.5 cents US. He gained Diefenbaker's reluctant support for an approach to the IMF to approve the decision, and subsequently arranged for a special meeting of the IMF board for the evening of May 2 in Washington. Early that morning Diefenbaker telephoned Fleming to say he had changed his mind, but Fleming and his officials insisted that the process was under way and could not be reversed. Diefenbaker told him: "It will cost us the election," and gave way. Cabinet, in the presence of eight ministers under Fleming's chairmanship, ratified the recommendation, and officials set off for Washington to present the proposal to the IMF board. Meanwhile, Fleming flew back to Toronto for his nomination meeting, where he made no mention of the devaluation. The decision was announced to the press at 11:15 that night.[46]

Diefenbaker suggested in his memoirs that the policy was mistaken; that Canada should have supported the floating value of the dollar through the election by selling reserves; and that it should have moved to a fixed exchange rate in an orderly way in the next budget. Instead, he claimed, it was forced to an emergency devaluation because the Kennedy administration "spooked" the New York money market "to get rid of my government." In this American conspiracy Diefenbaker saw the complicity of officials from the Department of Finance, "powerful interests" on Bay Street, the CBC, and the Liberal Party. The Liberals did, indeed, take advantage of the crisis – once devaluation had occurred – to ridicule the competence of the Diefenbaker government.[47] But there is no need for so elaborate an explanation of the affair. Diefenbaker admitted he had "no direct proof" for his claim, and there were enough objective reasons to explain the run. Once it had begun, pegging at a lower level, with IMF support, offered a reasonable means of stemming the tide.

Diefenbaker's conspiracy theory had apparently not taken form at the time of devaluation. If it had, he would certainly have added it to his catalogue of Kennedy's offences when he met Merchant on May 5. But the disturbing evidence of a government that had lost control – something that was bound to feature in the rest of the campaign – preoccupied and unsettled him, and he went into the meeting with Merchant carrying that burden of anxiety.

Harold Macmillan had also spent a day in Ottawa after his latest visit to Washington, asserting his commitment to the Common Market negotiations and emphasizing the president's eagerness to support those efforts.[48] If there were no great conspiracies confronting the prime minister, fortune, at least, was not working in his favour as it once had done.

The devaluation, which offered trade benefits for Canada, occurred in the worst possible political circumstances. A Winnipeg *Free Press* cartoonist lampooned Donald Fleming hoisting the remnants of a dollar to the mast. Jokes about the "Diefendollar" or "Diefenbuck" swept the country, and phony green bills with mutilated ends were soon circulating from St John's to Whitehorse. The easily caricatured administration seemed to have become its own caricature.

Diefenbaker was convinced that few of his ministers were pulling their weight in the campaign. Alvin Hamilton made an imprudent remark about a cabinet compromise on the dollar's value and suggested that he preferred a value of 90 cents US. Donald Fleming tried to explain the exchange crisis, but was too abstract. Ellen Fairclough had mysteriously avoided the press in a campaign visit to Vancouver, and in mid-campaign the prime minister complained that "19 Ministers have cancelled out the meetings arranged for them. I want the daily record of any Minister who did that."[49] In Quebec, a report to Diefenbaker early in the campaign suggested that the organization was "completely ineffectual" and doing nothing.[50] Apparently the leader would have to count on nothing more than his old magic on the platform.

In London, Ontario, the prime minister was joined on stage by Leslie Frost, his successor John Robarts, and most of the federal cabinet. Diefenbaker opened the campaign by defending the government's record and laying out a tedious "prosperity blueprint" – the Hamilton-Frost *mélange* of spending promises and business incentives, which did not add up to a coherent or inspiring program. The audience stewed in 90-degree heat and was not roused.[51] By mid-May Diefenbaker was complaining publicly about complacency among Conservative supporters. Later in the campaign, when he went on the attack, he could still bring his audiences alive with his furrowed brows, jokes, insinuations, and one-liners. Pearson's brains trust, he said, was "a cacophony of paragons, pseudo-economists, economic centralizers, and former bureaucrats." In the west he offered more promises of aid, and met his hecklers wittily – including a gaggle of Doukhobor women in Trail, British Columbia, who stripped naked before him – until the mass meeting in Vancouver on May 30.[52] That night he faced an arena audience of 7000 that was well sprinkled with protesters. Diefenbaker kept his temper in the face of constant interruptions, but could not silence them. Charles Lynch described the scene: "With the concessionaires taking a hands-off attitude, the prime minister was left to cope with the situation himself. Perspiring, running his hands through his flying hair, his eyes flashing, he talked of organized anarchy. He said he liked good fun too. He spoke of an Elizabethan sense of a grand design for Canada. He hammered on unity. All this was to no avail...John Fisher, bathed in perspiration, kept scribbling notes and passing them up to his chief...nothing seemed to work."[53]

Two days later, in Chelmsford, Ontario, the Diefenbakers faced "the ugliness and invective of a hysterical mob" as they made their way to their car with the local Conservative candidate. Diefenbaker used the demonstrations to suggest planned obstruction by the Liberals and the NDP: "They thought they silenced that speech, but they did far more for the Conservative party than all the speeches of the campaign." On June 7 Joey Smallwood handed Diefenbaker the evidence of collusion by forcing the St John's Rotary Club to cancel its invitation to Donald Fleming to address them on devaluation. An exhausted Diefenbaker found himself refreshed and aroused when cast in the martyr's role.[54]

When the Liberal Party advertised its claim that devaluation would bring higher prices for consumers, Diefenbaker issued a stern warning to the big companies: "I don't want any group or corporation in this country no matter how successful they may be, to take advantage of this situation. I serve notice here and now that if, in the next few days, this kind of thing is going on there will be action as effective as it is drastic." That left producers and retailers puzzled and fearful. Alvin Hamilton added his own threat that the government might undercut oil prices by building a national oil pipeline to Montreal.[55]

Despite outbursts of the old fire, Diefenbaker rarely created the excitement of 1958. But his challenger Mike Pearson aroused even less enthusiasm on the platform. By early June reporters were widely expecting a minority parliament. They watched rural Quebec with special fascination as the colourful leader of the Quebec Social Credit Party, Réal Caouette, brought out the crowds in the Quebec City, Saguenay, and Beauce regions with his rough-hewn words and promises of bliss. As the campaign ended, the prime minister appealed more and more to ethnic and anti-American sentiments. At the Ukrainian Hall in Montreal on June 11, he joked bitterly about the abuse of his name: Diefenbucks, Diefenbliss, Diefenbunkum; double, double, Diefentrouble/Diefenboil and Diefenbubble. "If I didn't have the name I have I don't know what the Liberal party would do...The playing with my name indicates what they think of those of non-French and non-English origin." He reminded his audiences that he was the leader who had dared to confront

Khrushchev at the United Nations, while Pearson was curiously soft on communism. In the prime minister's leaping rhetoric, Pearson had become simultaneously the candidate of big business, John Kennedy, and Nikita Khrushchev. Diefenbaker was the candidate of the people – except, it appeared, in rural Quebec, where Caouette matched his populism.[56]

In the last three weeks of the campaign, the Liberal lead in the Gallup Poll narrowed from 44–36 percent to 38–36 percent as voters drained away to the NDP and Social Credit. Diefenbaker and the Conservatives held their own. The *Globe* reported that "there is a vague, difficult to measure lack of confidence in Canada's political leadership of any stripe...The Conservative campaign has been essentially a one-man show with Mr. Diefenbaker the man. If they fail to win, he must take the blame; if they do win he can claim the victory, no matter how many seats they lose, for his own."[57]

Oakley Dalgleish offered the *Globe and Mail*'s measured support for the Diefenbaker government in a front-page editorial on June 5. The Liberals had offered "negative and destructive criticism," and had spent their time in opposition "fashioning new planks to fasten on the shaky structure of the Liberal Welfare State. Liberal irresponsibility has been amply demonstrated in this campaign. While the party spokesmen have gone about the country heaping criticism on the Government's budget deficits, alleging financial mismanagement, they have simultaneously promised, if returned to power, to launch vastly expensive new schemes for health and welfare and capital programs. The Liberals, in fact, have been consistent only in their inconsistency." "Our readers," the editorial continued, "will not need to be reminded of the occasions – far too numerous for our liking – when we have felt it necessary to criticize the Conservative Government in sharp terms." But those criticisms were usually directed not at its decisions, but at "its methods of implementing them." Sometimes the government had gone "too far, too fast," in redeeming its promises, but it had met those promises "more faithfully than any government since the turn of the century." Now Diefenbaker promised that the task of his government would be to create the business climate "to pay the bills and meet the challenge ahead," and he was bound to make "a sincere effort to translate these words into national policy." The editorial concluded: "On the record of the parties, without minimizing the mistakes of the past Conservative Administration, the Government, in our opinion, should be given a vote of confidence by the people of Canada."[58] That was no ringing endorsement, but it matched the sceptical mood of the country in the summer of 1962. The Montreal *Gazette* commented that the prime minister had "failed to make an effective appeal to Quebec, despite the fact that he has enlarged the flow of money to this province to a remarkable extent." In general, he had "left the impression of blurred aim and clumsy method."[59] The Edmonton *Journal*, which had supported Diefenbaker in 1958, switched its allegiance to the Liberals.

John and Olive were on their railway car in Prince Albert for election day on June 18 after a final rally in Hamilton and a weary appearance on national television over the weekend. The first news from the Atlantic provinces showed the Tories losing about a quarter of their seats to the Liberals; but as the polls closed and the count moved to Quebec and Ontario, the outlook darkened. In Quebec the Créditistes decimated the Conservatives in the countryside, taking twenty-six seats, to thirty-five for the Liberals (a gain of ten) and only fourteen for the Tories (a loss of thirty-six). In Ontario the Conservatives held their edge outside the cities, while the Liberals and the NDP made huge urban gains. The Conservatives were down to thirty-five, a loss of thirty-two seats. The government would be saved or overthrown in the west. Across the prairies, Diefenbaker's followers kept the faith: The Chief held forty-two of forty-eight ridings. In Saskatchewan the Conservatives actually increased their popular vote over 1958. Finally, maverick British Columbia split four ways to steal the majority away. Next morning Diefenbaker surveyed the wreckage: He held 116 seats to the Liberals' 100, Social Credit's thirty, and the NDP's nineteen. Five ministers – David Walker, William Hamilton, Noël Dorion, Jacques Flynn, and Bill Browne – had been defeated. The loss of ninety-two seats was devastating and incomprehensible. But the minority victory kept Diefenbaker clinging to power against an opposition whose unity was uncertain. Groping for words to a reporter, the prime minister took refuge in some typical advice of Sir John A. not to do anything quickly: "Precipitous action did not always result in wise decisions."[60]

Overnight, the Conservative Party had been transformed, in parliament, into a rural, English-speaking minority party. The Liberals and the NDP swept the cities, where they took over half the popular vote to the Tories' one-third. Even the ethnic vote was lost to the Liberals and the NDP; and young voters, similarly, turned away from the Conservatives. John Diefenbaker kept his strength among western farmers and the beneficiaries of his party's regional development grants. Those were narrow constituencies. The Liberals were disappointed that they had failed to overcome the government at a single blow, but the initiative had passed to them.

While Diefenbaker absorbed the electoral setback, he was faced with a second and more serious exchange crisis as he flew back to Ottawa. From the end of May the Bank of Canada's exchange fund had been forced to renew its massive selling of US dollars after a three-week respite. On election day alone, $41 million was sold into the exchange market, and in the next two days the bank's reserves fell by a further $110 million in the effort to maintain a 92.5 cent Canadian dollar. The speculators had descended in a horde, expecting a further devaluation as Canada exhausted its reserves. Fleming, with Diefenbaker's approval, was determined to maintain the dollar at its pegged rate, which required quick and massive support for the exchange fund from abroad. Louis Rasminsky and the senior officials of the Department of Finance rushed to design a program of borrowing and economic restraint that would meet the conditions of the International Monetary Fund and the foreign banks, and on June 20 the cabinet went into five days of continuous session to argue over its acceptance. Every hour was crucial, as reserves continued to decline by more than $40 million each day.[61]

Predictably, Diefenbaker appointed a committee of cabinet to meet with Bank of Canada and departmental officials, and wrangling continued into the evenings. The immediate need was to convince international lenders that the budget deficit would be reduced and the adverse trade balance improved. The prime minister judged such action to mean that "those in the bureaucratic and financial communities" had seized the opportunity of the crisis "to bring about a reversal of the declared fiscal policy of my government."[62] In the sense that "the declared fiscal policy of my government" was an unending series of budget deficits accumulated on political grounds, that was correct. As the reserves declined, the government had no reasonable options. Diefenbaker explained the reversal in his memoirs:

> Having failed to win a majority, we had now to stop the run on the dollar by other means. We were a minority government with a crisis on our hands. I had little choice but to accept the advice of the senior officials as to a program of emergency measures. Our exchange reserves had now fallen below the $1,000 million level, which these officials contended was the minimum we could safely hold. There was a danger that they could vanish entirely within a month or two, leaving us at the mercy of the market from day to day. The essence of the problem was to regain the confidence of foreign and Canadian investors in the Canadian dollar. The fact that they were wrong in feeling that we were not paying enough attention to "sound" financial policies was no longer the point. They were the ones whose opinion was important now.[63]

On Sunday morning, June 24, cabinet agreed to a package of emergency measures: temporary tariff surcharges ranging from 5 to 15 percent on about half of the country's imports; reduced exemptions from customs duties for Canadian tourists returning from the United States; a reduction of government spending amounting to $250 million annually; and Canadian borrowing of over a billion dollars (US) from the IMF, the American Export-Import Bank, the US Federal Reserve, and the Bank of England. That evening Diefenbaker issued a press statement announcing the austerity program before the opening of Monday's markets; and the next evening he made a national radio and television broadcast to explain his government's measures. Simultaneously the Bank of Canada set its rediscount rate at a record high of 6 percent. Diefenbaker insisted that the action was temporary, intended to "relieve the pressure on the Canadian dollar in the exchange field, to bring about greater stability in our international transactions and to strengthen our exchange reserves." He said that further, long-term measures would be introduced to improve the country's current accounts, and he called on Canadians to unite in common purpose to support his actions. Surprisingly, he did not recall parliament to discuss the crisis. "I think it well," he commented, "that Parliament should not meet until after a cooling-off period so that time will be given for political passions to subside and be followed by calm reason which, I have always found, is the basis of effective discussion and consideration." [64] The government, battered and bruised by election losses and the exchange crisis, needed time to regroup.

While the prime minister struggled in cabinet over the austerity program, Leslie Frost wrote to Diefenbaker to reassure him that "you are the only Conservative leader since John A.'s passing in 1891 who has managed to keep on top of the heap through three successive elections. I think this...adds to the measure of people's appraisal of your personality and ability to meet the challenge of these days and following." He added that the troubled financial and political situation was a "ready made situation for a leader who will grasp the nettle with both hands." That meant moving Donald Fleming out of the Department of Finance.

> Much as I like Donald, I do not think he can give the confident direction that is required. I think this job is for yourself...By actively assuming the leadership of the tops in industry, business and finance you can be unassailable and none of the competing parties could challenge you. If they do you would have built up a body of opinion which was lacking in this last election which would be enough to turn the scales. I am quite satisfied that our people are prepared to be told what they have to do. We have to work hard, tighten our belts and devote everything to development and expansion. [65]

This was encouragement to make the economic changes then being forced on cabinet, and to seek renewed alliance with the alienated business and financial communities. When Diefenbaker announced the government's emergency program, Frost wired two messages of congratulation. The second was a concise sermon: "Remember the positive side more exports hard work lower costs employment. Business incentives in other words an aggressive determined people aiming at a greater more prosperous country."[66]

Harold Macmillan also had words of comfort. On June 22 he wrote to say that he was working with the Bank of England to provide assistance in the emergency, and he added some armchair philosophy which pointed more to his own political difficulties than to Diefenbaker's. "You and I, who have been through the ups and downs of politics, know what a rough life it is. We here are having, as you have had, a strange movement away from the older Parties, which is perhaps a sign of the spiritual pressure upon young people today and the long drawn out contest between East and West. We older people know that it will last our life-time but the younger ones hope to see some sign of dawn. However, whatever the reason, it is rough going."[67]

A few days later Davie Fulton offered his advice from the inside. He thought the government's problem was one of both image and substance – and elaborated on the theme over seven pages. The government's image "generally was bad"; it was insufficient explanation to say, as Diefenbaker had complained during the campaign, "that Ministers did not get around the country enough or failed to make enough of the right kind of speeches. The trouble was that no coordinated presentation of the work of the Government as a whole was ever developed – or at any rate it was certainly not sufficiently developed, or developed in time." Before the next election, which he expected soon, Fulton insisted that "a strong picture should emerge of a Government which, even under the present difficult circumstances, accepts responsibility to govern and grapples on a planned basis with the problems now confronting us and introduces programs to meet both the short and the long-term needs of the country."[68] This was criticism that no minister had dared to offer before June 18.

Fulton accused the prime minister of making a false claim about the exchange crisis; what was worse, the claim was not believable. "The question is being raised: How could a situation of such proportions have arisen only in a few days? This in turn leads to the suggestion that the true facts are not being told." The government had to speak quickly and truthfully in a policy statement that would guide all ministers.

My suggestion is that the general effect of the statement would be to remove the impression that we are saying that the crisis developed only after the Election. We should, on the contrary, admit that the situation was serious prior to the Election (that is, during the campaign) and we should not minimize the fact that we took the action of pegging the dollar to meet a situation that was serious. We should not pretend otherwise. We should go on, however, to point out that the situation did not reach crisis proportions until just before actual voting day and in the four days immediately following.

...It seems to me to be...particularly essential to guard against the possibility of Ministers in their individual interpretations continuing to suggest that there was nothing to worry about until the Election was over – and then something suddenly developed. The public simply will not buy this and it would play into the hands of our opponents.

While his emphasis was on public relations, Fulton made clear that his worries related to deeper inadequacies in the government's performance. His letter came close to a declaration of non-confidence in Diefenbaker's leadership. Privately, Fulton had certainly lost that confidence.[69] Diefenbaker was shaken by Fulton's accusation that he had misled the public.[70]

The election results, the exchange crisis, severe press commentary, and Diefenbaker's correspondence all pointed to the need to give the cabinet a new face. Diefenbaker knew it, although he could not admit that he had actually done anything to justify the public's loss of faith. Partly, the problem was to replace five defeated ministers; partly, it was to shift the two ministers – Fulton and Fleming – who seemed to threaten his confidence most directly; partly, and most urgently, it was to recover some support in the business and financial community. The prime minister cast about desperately for advice, and in his conversations with Gordon Churchill he talked frequently of resignation.[71]

In that atmosphere Oakley Dalgleish offered his frank counsel, which he hoped would not seem "an impertinence." He recalled his previous support for Diefenbaker since 1956, and especially his suggestions after the 1958 victory that Diefenbaker should create an inner cabinet of half a dozen strong ministers and an advisory group of "proven and respected business and financial men to consult on...fundamental policies...I mention these conversations now, simply because they define the steps which I now urge on you. With the right group of consultants you can overcome the obvious deficiencies in the cabinet. Moreover, I am confident by this means you can take action on several fronts (which still needs to be taken) boldly and confidently, in the knowledge that the business community will co-operate and that the Liberals will have to go with you." Dalgleish told Diefenbaker that he wrote as a friend, not a partisan, "who shares your aspirations for this country." He pledged his own and the *Globe*'s aid in doing "anything and everything we can in the cause."[72]

The next day the prime minister's old confidant Bill Brunt, to whom Diefenbaker had just offered the speakership of the Senate, was killed in a car crash as he drove home to Hanover, Ontario. Brunt, like David Walker, had been his loyal supporter, electoral financier, and counsellor since 1942. Now Diefenbaker had lost one in defeat and another in death within three weeks.[73] The burdens grew heavier.

On July 12 the Diefenbakers attended Brunt's funeral in Hanover, in the course of which the prime minister talked at length with Leslie Frost. In his desperation, Diefenbaker proposed that Frost should join the cabinet as minister of finance – and once more, as in the previous autumn, Frost declined. His first response was lengthy and ambiguous, reasserting the view that his best service would be as an informal link to the business community and repeating most of Dalgleish's pro-business advice.[74] Diefenbaker noted on July 16 that "I phoned Frost and said I could not make anything out of his letter and would like to know what he meant." He meant no – but Frost suggested that Diefenbaker should let Dalgleish explain.[75] Diefenbaker persisted, in several telephone conversations with Frost and Dalgleish. Failing acceptance of the Finance portfolio, the fallback was a senatorship. Frost resisted all the prime minister's pleadings.[76]

Instead, he and Dalgleish proposed that Diefenbaker should invite Wallace McCutcheon of the Argus Corporation to join the cabinet. McCutcheon was unknown to Diefenbaker, and Frost recalled that the prime minister "was most diffident." Over several weeks, with no other prospects for strengthening the cabinet from Toronto, Frost and Dalgleish wore Diefenbaker down. McCutcheon was willing. He would resign his directorships and accept appointment to the Senate as a minister without portfolio. By early August Diefenbaker was reluctantly convinced, and at the same time smugly satisfied that he had mended his bridges to Bay Street.[77]

Meanwhile he was juggling other possible changes in cabinet with his usual uncertainty – a state worsened by exhaustion, the gloom of defeat, and personal grief. On July 13 Diefenbaker was stunned by the news that Macmillan had brusquely dismissed one-third of his cabinet, including the chancellor of the exchequer. This was ruthlessness beyond Diefenbaker's capacity and temperament. "I wish," he told Elmer the next day, "that I had enough members to make possible a general reconstruction, but that is impossible."[78]

The old cabinet met weekly for routine business while Diefenbaker shuffled his lists and hesitated. On the weekends he retreated with Olive to Harrington Lake, where she urged him to get away for a longer holiday. On July 21, as he stepped off the verandah onto wet grass, Diefenbaker turned his ankle in a gopher hole and heard "a sharp snap followed by severe pain and swelling." He had broken a bone, and was sent to bed by his doctors – who may have been prescribing for low spirits as much as for a broken ankle.[79] "Their advice was medically sound," Diefenbaker wrote in his memoirs, "but politically disastrous. An invalid's bedroom is neither an ideal place for Cabinet meetings nor a location suited to keeping track of the political manoeuvrings about one. But flat on my back I remained."[80] His secretary, Bunny Pound, suspected that he had chosen the accident: "Dief didn't want to go to the office...he wanted to be by himself for a while...so he fell in the gopher hole. This was sort of psychological. He didn't want to have any of this trouble. He just wanted to sit there in his bed, and grumble and growl and think about things...I think, possibly, he realized that he had bitten off more than he could chew. He had all of these talents, all this sort of semi-genius, but he had no control over it."[81] By mid-August, however, he was reassuring his brother that "I have been around the house now for several hours during the last few days and should be out of here soon." As he compared himself with "other members of the Cabinet whose health has been undermined by work," he reflected gratefully that "I have been so fortunate in not having been laid up at any time since becoming leader of the Party in 1956, excepting one mishap in January 1959 and the present one. I do not recall when I have been in better health."[82]

Diefenbaker had steeled himself to move Donald Fleming from Finance and Davie Fulton from Justice, and at the end of July he began meeting ministers to discuss the changes. Fleming recalled that when they met, Diefenbaker spoke with "disarming frankness...wistfully," as "a sorely troubled, almost beaten, man." Fleming recorded his words. "Don, you and I are in the doghouse. I think you should be relieved of the portfolio of Finance. You get the blame for everything, and it's hurting your future chances. I think you should have a portfolio that will give you a fair opportunity. I don't know how we will replace you in Finance. You know more about finance than anyone else in the House of Commons. In fact, you know more about finance than all the rest of the House of Commons put together."[83] The minister was struck by Diefenbaker's "unchallengeable sincerity," and concluded that "I must aim to be helpful, constructive and, above all, unselfish" as the prime minister struggled to keep the foundering ship afloat. He accepted Diefenbaker's wish that he should move to Justice, providing Fulton understood that the choice was the prime minister's.[84]

Negotiation with Davie Fulton was more troublesome. Diefenbaker began aggressively by claiming that "I found it difficult to speak fully with him because if the future was anything like the past it would find its way into the papers." He cited two incidents, most recently their December 1962 conversations over the previous cabinet changes. Fulton denied that he had passed reports of their private talks to reporters for personal advantage: "Mr. Diefenbaker, that's quite wrong, and if you persist in thinking that I am disloyal to you on a personal basis, there is only one course: you must ask for my resignation." Diefenbaker did not want that, and told Fulton he would be moving to National Revenue. Fulton replied that he could not accept such a demotion. On August 9, the day when Diefenbaker expected to announce his new cabinet, Fulton proposed Public Works as an alternative. After consulting his ministers informally, Diefenbaker agreed. But Fulton was alienated and already thinking about a move back to British Columbia to contest the provincial party leadership in the new year.[85]

Later in the day, Governor General Vanier met the cabinet at 24 Sussex Drive for a round of musical chairs. This cabinet shuffle was utterly unlike Macmillan's "night of long knives" less than a month before. No one was dismissed; three new ministers took their oaths; and six ministers shifted jobs. The only public surprise was the appointment of Wallace McCutcheon as a senator and minister without portfolio: "Kennedy's got McNamara," Diefenbaker boasted, "I've got McCutcheon." George Nowlan became minister of finance; Fleming, minister of justice; Fulton, minister of public works; and Ellen Fairclough left Immigration for the Post Office. Besides McCutcheon, the other additions were Richard Bell in Citizenship and Immigration, and Paul Martineau in Mines and Technical Surveys.[86] Green and Harkness, two equally loyal and upright ministers who were still at odds over nuclear weapons, were left where they were to carry on the combat. Diefenbaker, in his preoccupation, had not thought about that issue since the election. By some miracle of postponement it might simply evaporate. Pierre Sévigny wrote that the swearing-in "was not a very pleasant occasion. Though everything was done with admirable elegance and appropriate solemnity, we all knew that something was wrong, desperately wrong, and those who were present looked and must have felt uncomfortable."[87]

The cabinet changes couldn't bear much assessment. The press expressed general sympathy for Fleming, welcomed McCutcheon and Bell, noted Fulton's disappointment, and pointed to the cabinet's continuing weakness in Quebec. With the promotion of Nowlan and the accession of McCutcheon and Bell – none of whom had been Diefenbaker supporters in 1956 – the new cabinet seemed somewhat less a one-man show. Whether that meant anything would have to be tested.[88] Diefenbaker braced himself for the new parliament by rereading Donald Creighton's biography of John A. Macdonald and taking courage from "his victory over that 'malignant host' of enemies who tried to thwart his nation-building work."[89] The Chief could see his own malignant hosts gathering all around.

FOR TWELVE DAYS IN SEPTEMBER 1962 THE DIEFENBAKERS HAD A BRIEF OFFICIAL visit to London for another Commonwealth prime ministers' conference, with the usual hectic but pleasurable round of entertainment at 10 Downing Street and Buckingham Palace. For Diefenbaker the conference itself was less pleasant, since this was Macmillan's bow to Commonwealth consultation over Britain's application to enter the European community. As the delegation travelled to London, Basil Robinson found Diefenbaker "crotchety" and determined not to follow the advice of his cabinet and officials to play down his indignation. Macmillan led off discussion on September 10 and was followed by his chief negotiator, Edward Heath, whose long exposition, in Macmillan's judgment, left the prime ministers "exhausted – and I hope impressed." But for two days after that he faced "a broadside attack" led by Diefenbaker, whose speech, Macmillan felt, was "false and vicious." Diefenbaker repeated his demand for secure access to the British market for Canadian agricultural products, and predicted that President de Gaulle would not permit British entry to the market. Macmillan was furious and depressed by the antics of this "mountebank," this "very crooked man...so self-centred as to be a sort of caricature of Mr. Gladstone" who thought only of his own political advantage. But Macmillan realized that Diefenbaker was so deaf that he probably couldn't follow the speeches, and took satisfaction in presenting an innocuous conference communiqué for approval, knowing that Diefenbaker's deafness allowed him to "pass from one clause to another fairly rapidly." Robert Menzies, after initial protests, grew reasonable and "reverted to his favourite sport of teasing Diefenbaker." The communiqué translated all these goings-on into "the frank and friendly atmosphere which characterises Commonwealth meetings." The press – fed by the British delegation's hostile briefings – pointed to Diefenbaker as the dog-in-the-manger.[90]

THE PRIME MINISTER RETURNED TO OTTAWA ONLY A WEEK BEFORE THE OPENING OF parliament on September 27. Diefenbaker had recorded his intention to create an inner cabinet and a confidential economic advisory council "to be consulted on fundamental policies," as Oakley Dalgleish had suggested. During the early autumn, Wallace McCutcheon made some tentative contacts with prominent bankers and businessmen,[91] but as cabinet and House business flooded the agenda and Diefenbaker followed his erratic ways, the proposal drifted off into obscurity. The speech from the throne was a compendium of well-intentioned promises: a resolution to repatriate the Constitution from Britain; a federal-provincial conference on a distinctive flag and other national symbols; partial self-government for the Northwest Territories; an Indian claims commission; a national economic advisory board; increased farm credits; and initial planning for a national system of contributory old age pensions.[92] The government had reason for renewed hope in one respect: By mid-September the emergency economic program had successfully restored Canada's currency reserves and an attitude of confidence among the international financial community. Interest rates fell steadily during the autumn, and some of the import surcharges were removed as Diefenbaker had promised.[93]

Writing to Leslie Frost on October 7, the prime minister was confident: "The session," he reported, "has started out better than many had thought possible."[94] The reason was not that the government made any special impact (no legislation had been introduced), but rather that the opposition parties were careful to avoid any combined votes that might defeat it. As the session continued, the Liberal opposition gradually became more aggressive – and more frustrated by the absence of any cabinet policies to attack. Against the advice of George Nowlan, who urged the introduction of a new budget, cabinet agreed in October to seek interim supply covering most of the fiscal year, to avoid a major budget debate, and to reintroduce the budget resolutions from the previous April. The House filled its time with drawn-out and rancorous discussion of the estimates.[95]

Behind the scenes, shifting groups of ministers engaged in talk about how to deal with an inadequate prime minister. Diefenbaker had grown more irritable over the summer, more inclined to rage and complain at the slights of the press and the opposition. As he broadcast his complaints at every interview, his colleagues talked to one another with mounting concern.

They confided to friends who, in turn, spoke to other friends, and soon it was said that John Diefenbaker was sick, close to a nervous breakdown, under his doctor's care, and ready to resign at an early date. Members of his immediate entourage tried to encourage him. They asked the Leader to be less emotional, and begged him to use more discretion in his conversations with outsiders. Never one to accept advice too freely, the Tory Leader gave indications that he might mend his ways, but he kept on worrying and talking.[96]

"The cabinet was not at ease with itself or with its prime minister," Davie Fulton recalled. For perhaps one-third of its members, the problems of governing the country gave way to the problem of changing the leadership. "The uncertainty," Gordon Churchill remembered, "and the belief that Mr. Diefenbaker was not sure whether he wanted to remain leader were accompanied by all sorts of plans to relieve him of the leadership; and much energy was expended in the fall of 1962 trying to find ways of replacing him...A group of dissidents came to me asking me to urge Mr. Diefenbaker to resign, knowing full well that if I did so, Mr. Diefenbaker would almost certainly have stepped down. But I refused to do it, and some of them always held that against me thereafter."[97]

This was not organized revolt. It was frustrated and directionless complaint, stimulated by electoral failure, economic confusion, the prime minister's aging and loss of self-confidence. Very often, the vehemence of complaint was proportional to the intake of hard liquor. One group of ministers, including Nowlan, Halpenny, and McCutcheon, began to meet regularly in McCutcheon's office to drink and gossip at midday. They were joined by a varying band of drinkers and non-drinkers, freely exchanging forbidden thoughts about a replacement for the prime minister. One day when Churchill dropped by, McCutcheon asked whether he would be prepared to take over if Diefenbaker resigned. Churchill replied that he had told Diefenbaker the same day that if he departed, George Nowlan should take over. "That," said Churchill, "was indicative of the whole atmosphere of the time."[98]

N O SINGLE ISSUE OF POLICY DOMINATED THESE EARLY AND FORMLESS CONCLAVES. The government was in decay, and no one knew what to do about it. What brought the House and the country to attention – and the cabinet to its last paroxysm – was the Cuban missile crisis. At 10 am on October 22, 1962, Diefenbaker was informed that Livingston Merchant, the retired American ambassador to Canada, would arrive at 5 pm to brief him with an urgent message from President Kennedy. The White House had announced that Kennedy would speak to the nation on television at 7 pm.

The subject was Cuba. Since early September, reports and partisan warnings proliferated in the United States that the Soviet Union was sending offensive military weapons to the Castro regime. On September 13 Kennedy warned publicly that the United States "will do whatever must be done to protect its own security and that of its allies" if the Soviets established "an offensive military base of significant capacity" on the Caribbean island.[99] On October 15 the Canadian Embassy in Washington reported to Ottawa that the president was under intense pressure over his Cuban policy during the mid-term congressional election campaign. "The sense of national humiliation is so pervading," the embassy noted, "and the public feeling in favor of 'doing something about Cuba' is so strong that it is almost impossible to exaggerate the inflammatory character of the issue. The President and his colleagues are making a creditable attempt to maintain a public sense of perspective and restraint and it is very much in the Canadian interest that this attempt should not fail." The report urged Ottawa to support recent American measures affecting Soviet air and naval traffic to Cuba as a contribution to moderating the American debate. Ottawa responded positively.[100]

On the weekend of October 20–21, Robert Bryce and Norman Robertson learned from at least two sources that the White House had information that Soviet medium-range missile sites were under construction in Cuba and that a dangerous crisis was imminent. Bryce informed Diefenbaker as the information came in, but he knew nothing about what action the president contemplated.[101] Thus Diefenbaker had indirect warning that emergency planning was under way in Washington. Basil Robinson reflected on these events from the prime minister's perspective.

> He did not know the extent of the evidence or in what way the United States would react. But he had had more than twenty-four hours to get steamed up about what he was to be told and perhaps also what he would be asked to do. Despite what he had learned in advance, it would have been completely out of character if he had not been upset at being presented with the evidence of the Soviet missiles and the outline of the president's plans, at a stage when he could do little more than acknowledge their receipt. It was, after all, a very important development for the defence of North America, and it had been he who had entered (hastily, it will be recalled) into the NORAD agreement five years before. That agreement had underlined the importance which the two governments attached to the 'fullest possible consultation on all matters affecting the joint defence of North America.' The prime minister's resentment at the absence of genuine advance consultation should have come as no surprise.[102]

Kennedy informed Harold Macmillan of his plans by cable on Sunday evening, and dispatched emissaries on Monday to Ottawa, Paris, and Bonn to brief his other close allies. He apologized to Macmillan for deciding on action before consultation. The problem, he explained, was the need for security and speed. Macmillan appreciated Kennedy's position and, in a telephone conversation the next evening, pledged complete solidarity.[103]

At the White House the mood was "excited, almost chaotic" as Kennedy prepared his television address.[104] On Sunday afternoon US missile crews were placed on alert, mobile forces and aircraft were moved to Florida, and Strategic Air Command bombers went onto advanced airborne alert. Through the day on Monday, Kennedy carried on his regular public schedule while continuing his urgent private consultations and briefings.

During the day External Affairs prepared a background memorandum for the prime minister, summarizing its knowledge of events before Merchant's visit. "We are aware," it said, "through intelligence channels that as of October 16 the U.S.A. had satisfied itself through photographic and other intelligence media that offensive ballistic missiles with a range of between 1100 and 2200 miles were being installed in Cuba in sufficient number (an estimated 40) to directly threaten the security of U.S.A."[105] The department judged that – in the light of the president's previous public warnings – "the conclusion is unavoidable that the U.S.A. is about to embark on some counter action." This might involve a full blockade, or a "swift invasion and occupation," or bombing of the missile sites, an ultimatum to the USSR, and "full public disclosure...of the new Soviet capability in Cuba." Any of these actions was likely, the department thought, to lead at once to a Soviet countermove in Berlin – at the least a total blockade as in 1948–49. The situation "could clearly rapidly escalate into global war, and with the United Nations in session, it can confidently be assumed that some international endeavour will be made to avert war and bring about a negotiated settlement." The parallel was Suez in 1956, "when international action to contain and put an end to the fighting was instituted almost simultaneously with the national action taken by France and the United Kingdom to protect what they considered to be vital interests. The question arises as to whether there is again a role for Canada to play."

The department had a specific suggestion.

> The only action which could be taken in a United Nations context which might avert measures which could lead to conflict, would be a move in the Security Council to have a group of "neutral" nations – perhaps the 8 non-aligned members of the Eighteen Nations Disarmament Committee – conduct an on-site investigation in Cuba of the U.S.A. Government's charge that that country has permitted the installation on its territory of offensive nuclear

missiles. If vetoed in the Security Council or otherwise rejected by the Soviet Union and Cuba, the issue could be taken to the floor of the Assembly where an overwhelming vote in favour of such a proposal could be expected. Even if such a move failed to result in the admission of an investigation team to Cuba, it would at least have the virtue of confirming and exposing the aggressive designs which the U.S.A. maintains the Soviet Union has on North America. To be fully effective such a proposal would have to be discussed immediately with the U.S.A. Government before President Kennedy makes his announcement at 7 p.m. tonight as the possibility cannot be ruled out that his announcement may be of measures already ordered against Cuba.[106]

Diefenbaker drew double emphasis lines opposite this paragraph. The department had recommended an appeal to the president before his speech to "avert measures which could lead to conflict," and it did so in language that was bound to alert Diefenbaker's interest. Here, it implied, was Diefenbaker's Suez: his chance to match the achievement of Mike Pearson; his chance, perhaps, to win a Nobel Prize. In these delicate circumstances – facing a direct confrontation between the superpowers and in knowledge of the strained relations between Kennedy and Diefenbaker – the suggestion could be seen as either a counsel of prudence, or a careless appeal to a troubled prime minister's vanity. If Diefenbaker had followed the advice, there would at least have been private consultation with Washington before any public statement. A rebuff would presumably have involved no public embarrassment. The department would perhaps have been wiser not to give Diefenbaker ideas.

By some slipup, or calculation, Diefenbaker did not receive the memorandum until he returned home after his interview with Merchant, so there was no chance for any consultation by telephone with Kennedy before the president's broadcast.[107] At 5:15 pm Merchant arrived at the East Block with the American chargé d'affaires, Ivan White, and three intelligence officers.[108] Diefenbaker, Howard Green, and Douglas Harkness received them in the cabinet room. Merchant gave Diefenbaker a letter from Kennedy and a copy of the president's speech, both of them explaining that the United States possessed "clear evidence" that Soviet offensive nuclear weapons had been installed on Cuban soil, and announcing a naval and air blockade "whose object is to prevent the introduction into Cuba of further nuclear weapons, and to lead to the elimination of the missiles that are already in place." Kennedy added that he was requesting an urgent meeting of the UN Security Council, where the United States would present a resolution calling for the removal of "missile bases and other offensive weapons in Cuba under the supervision of United Nations observers." He hoped Canada would "work actively with us and speak forthrightly in support of the above program in the United Nations."[109] Merchant explained that the evidence had been gained by aerial surveillance, and he showed the Canadians large intelligence photographs of the missile sites.

Merchant felt that "the early minutes of our talk were a bit difficult." Diefenbaker was "somewhat brusque in manner," offended that he had not been consulted earlier, and "openly sceptical in attitude concerning the missile menace until the full intelligence briefing had been given him." Harkness received what he thought were "hazy" responses to his questions about the stages of alert of American forces, and expressed the view that a Soviet-American confrontation at sea would be more likely to cause general war than an American landing in Cuba. Diefenbaker requested a single brief change in Kennedy's text, which Merchant achieved. By the end, Merchant believed that Diefenbaker's "whole attitude swung around to sympathetic understanding and I had thought a willingness to give public support to the President." Merchant left the meeting to return to Washington, believing that Diefenbaker would not make any public statement until the next day.[110]

Diefenbaker returned home to watch the president's address, and only then did he read the memorandum from Howard Green intended for use before Kennedy's speech. Soon afterwards Pearson called Diefenbaker to ask for a statement in the House in response to the president's declaration. The prime minister could hardly refuse the request in such ominous circumstances. With his thoughts still jumbled, Diefenbaker jotted down a few phrases – "a sombre & challenging speech," "no time for panic," "time for quiet calmness and resolve and action in UN," "anything that looks like mobilization will be dangerous," and a reference to the key proposal from the Green memorandum: "Have a group of 'neutral' nations perhaps the 8 nonaligned members of the 18 nations disarmament committee conduct an on site inspection to ascertain if offensive nuclear weapons are installed." The prime minister was driven quickly back to Parliament Hill, reflecting grimly on a situation that could "rapidly escalate into global war."

With the notes in his hands, Diefenbaker told the House that he was responding to Pearson's request in order to appeal for unity and calm in a dangerous time. He did not challenge Kennedy's assertions, and insisted that "the existence of these bases or launching pads is not defensive but offensive." He did not criticize the United States for lack of consultation. But he challenged Soviet claims that their activities in Cuba were defensive, and he suggested inspection by an independent UN delegation to confirm the facts. If the suggestion had been made before the American ultimatum, no one could reasonably have seen it as a challenge to Kennedy's claims. But now the situation had subtly changed. The charges had been made, the ultimatum issued, and US naval forces were moving to the blockade lines. Before 7 pm only the Soviets had posed any threat to the peace; now, by their acts, the Americans did so too. As he concluded, Diefenbaker appealed for suggestions that might diminish "the obvious tensions that must grip men and women all over the world tonight...Our duty, as I see it, is not to fan the flames of fear but to do our part to bring about relief from the tensions, the great tensions, of the hour." Pearson agreed with the prime minister that the United Nations "should be used for the purpose of verifying what is going on."[111]

This was a reaction of solidarity tinged with scepticism and fear. It was not the declaration of unqualified support John Kennedy expected in so grave a crisis, but it was honestly ambiguous in the Canadian tradition, and it reflected the anguish in Canadian minds that evening. As two academic critics comment:

> To turn to the United Nations for assurance was not only consistent with Diefenbaker's own position before the crisis but also a typical Canadian response. Canada had consistently supported the UN, Canadian statesmen had played a major role in strengthening it, and the UN was the one area of world politics where the Canadians believed they could exert some influence. Canadian doubts, latent or implied, about the wisdom of American actions were a reflection of perceptions of the Cuban-American issue. Some Canadians, their suspicions raised by the original American denials of involvement in the Bay of Pigs operation, may have had doubts about US claims as to the existence of an offensive base. Many, including some Canadian officials, feared that the United States might once more be overreacting.[112]

A president with more understanding of Canada, less arrogance, and more respect for the Canadian prime minister might have ignored Diefenbaker's reserve. But Kennedy was already disenchanted with his neighbour and in no mood for indulgence as he turned to face down Nikita Khrushchev. Livingston Merchant's "surprise and disappointment" at Diefenbaker's response were echoed in the White House. At the Canadian Embassy in Washington – where reading and interpreting the US administration's perceptions of Canada was the reason for existence – the prime minister's remarks in the House "had pained and dismayed everyone."[113]

Almost at once the Canadian position grew more ambiguous. When Harkness returned to his office after Kennedy's address, the chief of the defence staff, Air Chief Marshal Frank Miller, informed him that American forces had gone on "DEF CON 3" alert. He requested permission to put Canadian forces – especially Canadian NORAD units – in the same state of readiness.[114] NORAD headquarters had mixed Canadian-American staffs, and the entire system was designed to operate in integration. Harkness agreed that he should do so, but after consulting the war book guidelines (which were being altered), he decided he should first consult the prime minister. Diefenbaker arranged to see him at once, and Harkness left his office confident that the decision would be no more than a formality.

Instead, Diefenbaker hesitated. He would not authorize an alert without a cabinet decision the next morning. Harkness returned to his office to discuss with Miller "what action we could take, without declaring a formal alert, which would put us in a position of maximum preparedness short of this." They agreed to order immediate "full manning of the three H.Q.'s... Intelligence and communication centres, warning orders to the Commands and manning of their communications." This amounted to virtually full, though informal, compliance with DEF CON 3. Diefenbaker was not informed.[115]

Next morning Harkness and his chiefs of staff reviewed the latest intelligence reports, "which were ominous." Russian freighters carrying missiles were still on course, apparently preparing to test the American blockade on the following day. Harkness directed the military to prepare all necessary orders for each stage of readiness to coincide with American actions, to take effect "as soon as I telephoned from cabinet that the alert had been authorized." At cabinet, he reviewed the intelligence reports and recommended an alert "if the situation deteriorated." All ministers, he judged, would have agreed, but "the Prime Minister argued against it on the ground that an alert would unduly alarm the people, that we should wait and see what happened, etc. He and I finally came to fairly hot words, but he refused to agree to the alert chiefly, I think, because of a pathological hatred of taking a hard decision." No conclusion was reached.[116]

The frustrated minister returned to his chiefs of staff and ordered all the actions they had discussed earlier that morning to be applied "in as quiet and unobtrusive a way as possible...These measures accomplished the majority of the purposes of an alert...but did not reassure the United States and our other allies, as the declaration of an alert would have done, that we were prepared to fight."[117] During the day Harkness continued to argue in favour of an alert, without informing Diefenbaker of his latest action. Diefenbaker would agree only to another special meeting of cabinet the next morning. That afternoon the prime minister had a heated telephone conversation with the president in which Kennedy objected to Diefenbaker's public call for UN inspection and urged him to order the appropriate military alert. Diefenbaker later recalled his complaint to the president: "When were we consulted?" and Kennedy's response: "You weren't." The conversation did not incline Diefenbaker to approve the alert.[118]

Cabinet on October 24, Harkness wrote, "proved to be a long and unpleasant meeting at which members...were asked for their individual opinions. Most favoured the alert. The meeting was about to end inconclusively when I made a final effort with a rather angry outburst that we were failing in our responsibilities to the nation and *must* act, which produced an outburst from the Prime Minister to the effect that he would not be forced into any such action." When Harkness returned to his office, Miller told him that the American Strategic Air Command and some naval forces had moved to DEF CON 2 ("immediate enemy attack expected"). Harkness went back to Diefenbaker, showed him the message, and insisted that Canada could delay no longer. The prime minister responded in agitation: "All right, go ahead" – and at last the formal alert was issued. In the end, Diefenbaker had acted with a wave of the hand, and without a cabinet decision.[119]

Meanwhile, the prime minister had made clear to the House, after discussions with Pearson, that his call for UN involvement had been intended to support, rather than undermine, President Kennedy's position.[120] But Canada's public stance remained confused after a CBC interview with Howard Green on October 24 in which he refused to offer endorsement of the American blockade and insisted that NORAD was not yet involved. The most he would say was that "the Americans have considered that the action has been necessary and they've taken it and I think that we must accept that fact."[121]

By Thursday morning Diefenbaker realized – as Bryce, External Affairs, and members of cabinet had advised him – that there was a need to clarify the government's stance for the sake of understanding in his caucus, among the Canadian public, and in Washington. Bryce and the department produced drafts for a new statement to the House, and that afternoon Diefenbaker reviewed Canada's actions in support of the United States and insisted that the crisis had been caused by the Soviet Union. Canada stood with its allies and was prepared for all contingencies. Canadian NORAD forces, he said, were at "the same level of readiness as the American forces under NORAD operational control."[122] Diefenbaker was now firmly on side. Two days later, as the confrontation played out, the Washington *Post* commented editorially that any differences between Canada and the United States over Cuba had been "swept aside by the Soviets' provocation...Whatever the outcome, it is deeply reassuring that no cool air is blowing from Canada."[123]

The crisis was not over. On Wednesday, Soviet ships had begun to turn back from the confrontation line, but there were provocative submarine movements in the western Atlantic, and construction work continued at the Cuban missile sites. President Kennedy's crisis team maintained its round-the-clock consultations as it made preparations for air strikes on the bases, while urgent communications were exchanged between the White House and the Kremlin. On Saturday, October 26, an American U–2 photographic spy plane was shot down over Cuba as Kennedy and Khrushchev engaged in negotiations on a secret deal to avoid nuclear war; and elsewhere the risks of unplanned military engagement mounted as American forces reached hair-trigger readiness. Cabinet ministers and senior officials in Washington, Ottawa, and other Western capitals prepared to move to their emergency headquarters and evacuate their families to the countryside. Diefenbaker told a staff member "we would all be obliterated in a few days."[124]

Diefenbaker was near distraction. He was receiving overnight briefings on the latest intelligence reports each morning at 6:30 am as he ate breakfast. Orme Dier, his new External Affairs liaison officer, recalled an incident in a letter to Basil Robinson.

> One episode that I will never forget occurred just before the crisis reached its climax. Bill Olivier and I were at the breakfast table at the appointed hour but the P.M. was not waiting for us. He surfaced about 20 minutes later, in his bathrobe as usual, complaining that worry had kept him awake most of the night. Indeed, he did look pretty beat. Just as I was placing our material before him, the butler appeared with the breakfast. I immediately retrieved the papers and stood aside while the repast was laid. As soon as the butler closed the door, the Chief stood up at his choleric best and almost literally laying his finger aside of my nose, gave me the best of his House of Commons dressing-down. Pacing up and down, he made it excruciatingly clear that I was a guest in his house, that he would not stand being humiliated before his staff, and that he did not need a civil servant to point out what was right or wrong. When I managed to make reference to security classifications, I was immediately shot down for impugning his awareness of such matters as well as for my rudeness and lack of respect. The tirade ended abruptly, breakfast and the documents were quickly ingested and the meeting ended in silence.

Later that day Diefenbaker explained that his outburst had been the result of lack of sleep. Dier took this as "an oblique apology," and "concluded that my boss was an extremely difficult but nevertheless human old curmudgeon."[125]

On Sunday morning, October 28, at 9 am Washington time, Radio Moscow broadcast Khrushchev's concession: Work at the sites would stop and the weapons would be dismantled and returned to the Soviet Union, in return for Kennedy's promise not to attack or invade Cuba. Kennedy responded at once to welcome "this statesmanlike decision," and both sides agreed on United Nations supervision of the dismantling operation. There was no announcement of the other American concession, which was carried out without fanfare in the following months: US Jupiter missiles located in Italy and Turkey, and targeted on the USSR, would also be removed.[126] The world relaxed.

Diefenbaker issued an unusual Sunday statement that morning.

Mankind will breathe more hopefully now that there is an early prospect that the threat to the Western Hemisphere from long-range Soviet missiles in Cuba will be removed.

This prospect has resulted from the high degree of unity, understanding and cooperation among the Western allies. In this the Canadian Government has played its full part. Indeed Canada was the first nation to stop over-flights of Soviet aircraft so as to prevent war material being carried to Cuba and as well to that end instituted a full search of all Cuban and Czech planes which are entitled under international agreement to use Canadian airport facilities.

The introduction of missiles into the Western Hemisphere has brought the world too close to disaster for anyone to indulge in either self congratulations or complacency at this time. I know there will be universal relief that in the last two days the outlook for the peaceful solution of the Cuban problem has greatly improved but there is a continuing need for negotiation on this and other potential sources of threats to world peace.

The United Nations deserves special mention for the worthy and constructive role it has played in this crisis.[127]

Diefenbaker rushed to the front of the parade – but only after his defence minister and his armed forces had acted surreptitiously to sustain the country's military commitments. The whole cabinet knew that the experience would have its costs. The prime minister's loyal lieutenant Gordon Churchill told Douglas Harkness after the October 24 cabinet meeting that "the country

461

just could not afford to have the Prime Minister in that position at a time of crisis – he refused to act when action was absolutely necessary."[128]

F OR DOUGLAS HARKNESS AND OTHER MINISTERS, THE IMMEDIATE RESULT OF THE Cuban affair was to reopen the subject of nuclear warheads for Canadian NORAD and NATO forces. The shock of the crisis, the sense that there was no time for consultation in an emergency, and new forebodings about the inability of the prime minister to make decisions under pressure pointed to the urgency of an agreement with the United States to supply the warheads. At the next cabinet meeting on October 30 Harkness raised the issue, and gained unanimous agreement that negotiations with the United States should recommence. Ministers agreed that Canada should accept warheads in Europe on the same terms as other NATO countries. In Canada, Harkness accepted a compromise: "We were to try to get an agreement under which the nuclear warheads, or essential parts of them, would be held in the United States, but could be put on the weapons in Canada in a matter of minutes or hours. This arrangement I did not think was likely to prove satisfactory, but it was a great relief to have the question settled as far as the European weapons were concerned and to have a basis to work from for the Canadian weapons." Negotiations were to be undertaken by Howard Green, Douglas Harkness, and a few officials, along with Gordon Churchill. Diefenbaker himself had added Churchill to the team, Harkness wrote, "evidently with the idea that he would hold the balance between Howard and myself and would prevent deadlocks occurring."[129]

In late November negotiations commenced in Ottawa. Agreement was quickly achieved over warheads for Canadian weapons in Europe, where the United States proposed its standard, two-key arrangement. Agreement on Canadian warheads was more difficult because of Green's insistence that Canada should be able to say that no nuclear weapons were stored on Canadian soil. The negotiators allowed for a maximum of two hours to arm the weapons in an emergency. But if warheads were to be stored across the border, large numbers of men and aircraft would be needed on standby to perform the task. The Americans produced several further proposals, none of which seemed practical, and by early December the meetings ceased. When Harkness sought Diefenbaker's approval for the European weapons agreement, the prime minister argued that he would accept only a complete package. In January US Secretary of Defense Robert McNamara told Harkness that the latest standby scheme was unworkable. The final American counterproposal, to store some parts of the warheads separately in Canada, was unacceptable to Green and Diefenbaker.[130]

Meanwhile, the Cuban crisis had precipitated open revolt in the Conservative Party. On November 8 George Hogan, who had served Diefenbaker through three election campaigns and was then the national vice president of the party, addressed a party group in Toronto and issued his text to the press, where it made headlines the next day.[131] Hogan sent a copy to the prime minister, noting that "it expresses a rather complete disagreement with our policy on Cuba and nuclear weapons." The policy, he said, "has done and is still doing more damage than any other single thing that has happened since we came into power. I gather from the press that the Cabinet is not solidly behind this policy. I profoundly hope so, because I believe we are in real trouble unless it is changed."[132]

In his speech, Hogan spoke of the party's long and instinctive commitment to Canadian independence from the United States, but rejected the view that "the Conservative Party, or any party, can build a constructive policy for Canada on a basis of anti-Americanism...There is a time to stand up to the Americans, and there is a time to stand by them; and I suggest that when the security of the North American Continent is menaced by the threat of nuclear attack, that is a time to stand by the Americans clearly, swiftly, and unequivocally." Canada was bound by geography, common tradition, and direct military alliance to joint defence of the continent. NORAD, he recalled, had been signed by the Conservative government.

In return for Canada's reasonable expectation to be consulted in advance about NORAD's activities, Hogan suggested four changes of policy to indicate solidarity with the United States. Canada should break diplomatic relations with Cuba, suspend trade, give the Canadian deputy commander of NORAD the authority to place Canadian air units on alert when necessary, and set a time limit on reaching agreement with the United States to accept nuclear weapons. On NORAD, he explained:

> The NORAD Agreement was founded on the assumption that the defence of one country was inseparable from the defence of the other. If enemy bombers or missiles ever start heading for our cities, questions of sovereignty and national control will swiftly become very academic. I believe we must either honour the NORAD Agreement or withdraw from it. To withdraw from it is unthinkable. But if we honour it we must do so in a way that will leave no doubt of our intention to be ready to respond swiftly and immediately to any hostile attack. Any other approach renders the whole concept useless.

On nuclear arms, Hogan endorsed the government's dedication to general nuclear disarmament. But Canada, he judged, was trying to influence attitudes from a position of weakness, "what in plain language amounts to a policy of unilateral disarmament." Tactical, defensive weapons were useful as part of the Western deterrent and were thus a stabilizing rather than a destabilizing influence. He suggested a last, "massive attempt" to achieve an agreement on nuclear disarmament. If that failed, Canadians should "consider ourselves free thereafter to acquire defensive nuclear weapons." This was a modest proposal, calling for less than the cabinet had already accepted. But it involved public disagreement with established policy, which remained obscure. Hogan believed that he spoke for the interests of the Conservative Party as well as the country: "Let us take a clear stand on behalf of our security, our principles, and our friends, and stick by it come what may." [133]

Diefenbaker read the morning papers and called Hogan at 8:30 am to tell him he had "done a complete job against the Federal Conservative Party." Later in the day the prime minister commented that Hogan spoke only for himself and not for the party. Others suggested Hogan's resignation. [134] But it was clear that he represented a powerful element of opinion in the party and the country in the aftermath of the missile crisis.

The prime minister performed a precarious juggling act as more and more balls were tossed into the air. The conflicts in his cabinet represented acrimonious divisions in the party, the House of Commons, and the country. For several weeks Diefenbaker toyed in cabinet with the prospect of an early election, to be fought on a pro-nuclear platform after acceptance of nuclear warheads. His colleagues, while favouring a nuclear agreement, opposed that kind of single-issue campaign. [135] In this atmosphere of disorientation, ministers prowled in and out of each other's offices searching for some means of dealing with Diefenbaker's foibles and the government's disarray. The Liberal opposition reflected the disturbed mood as it harried the government with growing impatience. The Social Credit Party, which held the balance in the House, seemed less and less reliable as it manoeuvred for advantage before the faltering government. In Washington it was obvious that the Kennedy administration, in the afterglow of its Cuban triumph, had no further patience with Diefenbaker.

The new American ambassador to Canada, the career diplomat W.W. Butterworth, arrived in Ottawa in early December and had his first interview with the prime minister on December 17. Neither Diefenbaker nor Butterworth mentioned the delicate issues of warheads, the missile crisis, or relations with Cuba. Each seemed to be taking careful measure of the other, and the conversation centred on Britain's negotiations for entry into the European Common Market. Butterworth reported to Washington that Diefenbaker, "although vigorous in speech and gesture...struck me as being unwell and exhibited evident signs of palsy or perhaps Parkinson's disease."[136]

President Kennedy and Prime Minister Macmillan had arranged to meet in the Bahamas just before Christmas to review the broad issues of East-West relations, the state of the alliance, and British weapons in the wake of the missile crisis. When Diefenbaker learned of the meeting, he invited Macmillan to Ottawa afterwards. Macmillan responded with an invitation to meet him in Nassau on December 21, following his meeting with Kennedy. Macmillan flattered Diefenbaker by proposing "a personal exchange of views on a number of international problems and in particular...the possibilities of negotiations with the Russians in the near future and of progress towards a general detente." Diefenbaker accepted the opportunity for discussion of the big issues with alacrity. Whether or not he expected any relief from his own nuclear problems at the meeting, there was always political advantage in being seen as a leading partner in the North Atlantic alliance. In fact, after Cuba, Macmillan too was feeling marginalized in an alliance dominated by Washington, and, like Diefenbaker, was seeking escape from his own political and military dilemmas. Kennedy was about to cancel development of the Skybolt missile project, and Macmillan sought recompense for the loss of a weapon for his V-bombers.[137]

The Canadian party flew to Nassau on December 21, where Diefenbaker joined Macmillan and Kennedy for lunch in what he described as "the ninth inning" of the Macmillan-Kennedy talks.[138] Photographs freeze a record of the false camaraderie of the occasion. Macmillan, at least, was satisfied that his negotiations had led to an American promise to provide Polaris missiles for a British fleet of nuclear submarines in exchange for the abandoned Skybolts, and in an unlikely bid for President de Gaulle's support, Kennedy had also proposed discussions on the creation of a multinational NATO nuclear force. Nothing in the lunchtime discussion touched directly on the sensitive Canadian issue of the warheads.[139]

During the next day and a half, Diefenbaker and Macmillan met several times. They engaged in the usual *tour d'horizon*, but Diefenbaker was especially interested in defence questions. Macmillan reviewed his negotiations with Kennedy over weapons, while Diefenbaker searched for parallels in the Canadian-American relationship. He could find only the most tenuous links in the leaders' hopes for further disarmament talks with the Soviets, the vague proposal for a multinational NATO nuclear force, and a general commitment to improved conventional forces.[140] Not surprisingly, Kennedy and Macmillan had shown no interest in Diefenbaker's problems during their own talks.

When Diefenbaker reported to parliament on the Nassau meetings on January 21, 1963, however, he had found what he claimed to be essential support for his attitude of indecision. "The agreement reached by Britain and the United States at Nassau," he told the House, "represents the first firm commitment to certain ideas concerning military policy in the western alliance which have been evolving for some time." The proposal for a joint NATO nuclear force, to include tactical forces in Europe, "has relevance for Canada and in the NATO Council is now the subject of intensive discussion in which Canada is fully participating." What was more, "Nassau raised the whole question of how political and military control will be exercised in future within the western alliance. The discussions of this subject are bound to continue for many months to come...and I would not expect any firm decisions in the near future. I can say this much – that the Nassau agreement aims at preserving an objective long sought by this Government – a limitation on the further enlargement of the nuclear family in the national sense." In Diefenbaker's interpretation, the message of Nassau was made-to-order. "The whole future direction and shape of the military forces of NATO are in the process of review. The enormous costs of modern weapons systems and the speed with which they become obsolescent dictate the utmost care in reaching final decisions. It would be premature at this stage to say anything further about Western defence policy until there is a clearer indication as to whether or not some form of NATO multilateral nuclear force can be worked out."[141]

But before that report to the House, the Canadian kaleidoscope had been severely shaken. The Diefenbakers remained in Nassau for the holiday, returning to Ottawa on January 2 after "a wonderful rest for Olive and me although she has suffered from the pain in her back more than usual."[142] In Nassau the prime minister addressed the local Kiwanis Club, but was disturbed that distorted press reports of his remarks might reach President Kennedy. He wrote a note to Basil Robinson in Washington to tell him that "at no time did I say, directly or indirectly, that the United States action violated NORAD. What I did say was that consultation had not taken place and there was no information until the late afternoon of the day that President Kennedy made his speech." If Canada, "having responsibility for joint air defence, had been consulted, we would have been in readiness to act forthwith." Robinson and his colleagues at the Canadian Embassy "did what little we could to spread the remedial balm."[143]

The day after Diefenbaker's return, the retiring NATO commander, General Lauris Norstad, arrived in Ottawa on a brief farewell visit. Diefenbaker cancelled a meeting with him, and Norstad was met at the airport by Pierre Sévigny, Air Chief Marshal Miller, and the press. Responding to a few questions, Norstad threw himself, by accident or design, into the Canadian controversy.

> Reporter: General, do you consider that Canada has committed itself to provide its Starfighter squadron in Europe with tactical nuclear weapons?
>
> Norstad: That is perhaps a question you should direct to the Minister rather than me, but my answer to that is "Yes." This has been a commitment that was made, the continuation of the commitment that existed before, and as the air division is re-equipped that air division will continue to be committed to NATO and will continue to play an extremely, increasingly important role.
>
> Reporter: In the field of tactical nuclear...?
>
> Norstad: That's right.
>
> Reporter: I'm sorry, sir – will play an extremely important role with or without nuclear weapons?
>
> Norstad: I would hope with both...We established a NATO requirement for a certain number of strike squadrons and Canada committed some of its forces to meet this NATO established requirement. And this we depend upon.

At this point Norstad asked Miller if he was saying anything more than had already been acknowledged in Ottawa, to which Miller replied: "I think you're quite right on that; quite right on that." The questioning continued.

> Reporter: Does it mean, sir, that if Canada does not accept nuclear weapons for these aeroplanes she is not actually fulfilling her NATO commitments?
>
> Norstad: I believe that's right. She would be meeting it in force but not under the terms of the requirements that have been established by NATO...We are depending upon Canada to produce some of the tactical atomic strike forces.
>
> Reporter: General, did you say that you believe that Canada has committed this Starfighter group to tactical weapons?

Norstad: No doubt – I know that they have committed the Starfighters, yes...

Reporter: Sir, do the Starfighters have any capability, in your view, with conventional weapons?

Norstad: They could have. But...we should have other conventional forces. We should not degrade their deterrent value by making them conventional.[144]

Sévigny was silent throughout the questioning, but eventually ended it. Norstad departed for Washington, leaving ministers scurrying for cover. Diefenbaker was infuriated but refused comment; others insisted Canada always fulfilled its commitments. The newspapers turned their questions back on the prime minister. Had Canada made a commitment to nuclear weapons or not? The headline of André Laurendeau's editorial in *Le Devoir* went further: "Do Canadians have a government?"[145]

Harkness urged Diefenbaker to resume negotiations to accept the warheads, but without success. Norstad's frankness prompted only stubborn denial. Diefenbaker "went on at length complaining about Norstad and arguing that the situation was now impossible." Harkness recalled:

> I pointed out the decision to secure the warheads had been made, that Norstad had said nothing we had not said ourselves, and that time had run out on us because our forces now had the weapons and thus no reasonable arguments for further delay could be put forward. He was completely evasive in regard to the whole matter and it became increasingly evident that he had changed his mind and was unwilling to proceed as agreed on about a month and a half earlier.[146]

Despite Harkness's advice that Green and Churchill favoured renewed negotiations, and that more than half the cabinet wanted an early decision, Diefenbaker kept the issue off the cabinet agenda. Harkness decided that he would resign from cabinet unless the question was settled "in a very short time."[147]

The Liberal Party's policy on nuclear weapons had been almost as confusing as the government's. Since January 1961 the party's official stance had opposed nuclear weapons for Canada's NORAD forces and accepted them for NATO units only if they were under collective NATO control. But Pearson's advisers, including the defence critic Paul Hellyer, pressed him to make an unequivocal declaration in favour of taking the warheads for the four weapons systems designed for them. On January 12, 1963, Pearson chose a speech in Scarborough, Ontario, to declare that he was "ashamed if we accept commitments and then refuse to discharge them." Canada should "end at once its evasion of responsibility, and...discharge the commitments it has already accepted for Canada," while also undertaking to renegotiate its way out of a nuclear role for the longer run. The declaration caused a substantial rift in his own party, but gave Pearson a new image of decisiveness that was bound to reflect badly on his rival. In Washington, the administration took note, and Basil Robinson reported a fresh sense that agreement could await another Canadian election, which would "result in a better prospect of a solution palatable to the United States."[148]

Harkness believed that Pearson's about-face relieved Diefenbaker of his most serious political problems. He could safely accept nuclear warheads without risking defeat in the House and a divisive election campaign. But when he met the prime minister to urge an immediate decision, the response was perverse. "To my complete surprise he took the position that we must now oppose the position taken by Pearson and delay any decision on acquiring the warheads. I told him that this was impossible – we would be completely illogical, would make ourselves look ridiculous and, from the political point of view, would lose the backing of many of our strongest supporters. I said that I could not support and argue in the House, or in an election campaign, any course of action differing from that decided on in November. We parted on strained terms."[149]

As the nuclear stormclouds gathered, the Progressive Conservative Party prepared for its annual meeting in Ottawa. Eddie Goodman, who was chairman of the resolutions committee, knew that the weapons issue was the only matter of controversy facing the meeting and that delegates would insist on debating a resolution favouring the acceptance of warheads. On January 15 his committee passed a "clear, but mild resolution" commending the government for its attitude on disarmament and urging it to accept nuclear weapons unless the great powers adopted a nuclear disarmament treaty before July 1963. In negotiation with Diefenbaker and Green, Goodman agreed to set that deadline back to December, but Diefenbaker subsequently ordered party headquarters not to print and distribute the resolution. Goodman and the national secretary, Flora MacDonald, went elsewhere for copies, and held a press conference to ensure that the resolution reached the public. Diefenbaker and Allister Grosart then altered the agenda of the meeting to place the prime minister's address just before Goodman's presentation of resolutions, and the Chief implored the meeting, with all his passion, "not to tie my hands in my quest for peace." Goodman admired the performance and commented to MacDonald: "At least we made the s.o.b. go all out to beat us."

The prime minister had one more device in his hands. When the applause died away and Goodman finally took the platform, he was faced with an amendment to the defence resolution providing that it should be "referred to the government for its consideration and decision" rather than approved. Goodman argued instead that Canada should "regain its self-respect by meeting its international obligations," but the meeting overwhelmingly adopted the amendment and saved the appearance of party-government unity. Diefenbaker had – momentarily – held off the storm.[150]

Harkness now believed that Diefenbaker intended "to back away from a nuclear position and the whole defence policy we had followed for the previous four to five years." He told four ministerial colleagues that he would resign unless the cabinet adopted a policy he could accept. At the annual meeting he faced awkward questions about Diefenbaker's leadership, but as a member of cabinet he felt bound not to comment. When Senator Thorvaldson, the retiring party president, praised Diefenbaker in his banquet speech and then told Harkness "in the most vehement terms" that "we must get rid of Diefenbaker or we had no chance, and...the cabinet must accomplish this," Harkness saw the irony. "This typified, I thought, the situation of a lot of Conservatives, then and later, who wanted to get rid of Diefenbaker, but wanted someone else to bell the cat."[151]

Cabinet had entered a period of terminal breakdown. On Sunday, January 20, as ministers met at Sussex Drive to prepare for the opening of the House, Harkness insisted that the drift would have to end. He called for agreement on "a defensible position," while Diefenbaker argued in favour of "no definite policy" until after an election. Ministers divided three ways: a few supporting Diefenbaker, more supporting Harkness, the rest remaining neutral and silent. Harkness eventually said that he would resign if Diefenbaker took the line of delay, but was persuaded to wait for two days, when the affair "was to be finally settled."[152]

The next day, after his House of Commons statement on the Nassau conference, Diefenbaker agreed to a general foreign policy debate later in the week, with a supply motion to follow in the days afterwards. At cabinet on January 22, Diefenbaker lectured on his difficulties and pleaded that Harkness's resignation would be "politically fatal." He promised to resign rather than allow that to happen, and proposed a cabinet committee consisting of Green and Harkness, under Fleming's chairmanship, to review the record on nuclear weapons and to find an acceptable solution. Without consultation, Fleming added Churchill to the team. Over two days the committee held ten meetings, reviewing all the relevant documents from cabinet, the cabinet defence committee, the NATO council, and the United States–Canada ministerial committee on defence. Faced with the voluminous record, Green conceded that commitments had been made and cabinet had repeatedly approved the adoption of nuclear weapons. Harkness, too, gave up some ground. Fleming produced a unanimous report calling for early completion of negotiations on Canada's nuclear role in NORAD "to secure the highest degree of availability to Canada," while allowing for clarification of Canada's NATO weapons at the ministerial meetings in May. That concession would avoid embarrassment to the prime minister for his previous references to NATO policy. Given the distance between Harkness and Green, this was a formidable achievement.[153]

When Fleming and Harkness presented the unanimous report to Diefenbaker on Wednesday evening, the Chief greeted them in a truculent mood. Fleming gave Diefenbaker a copy of the document and waited for his praise.

> Instead, after quickly glancing over it he angrily flung it down on the desk and said, "I won't have it." He repeated the words. There was nothing more for Doug and me to do than to say good night and leave. Outside he and I concluded it was all over...Our work had been rejected in the most offensive and peremptory manner. The last visible chance of rescuing the government on the issue of nuclear arms was gone, hopelessly squandered. I went home in despair. Dief had demonstrated that he was still capable of making decisions – wrong ones. But I had reckoned without his cunning.[154]

Harkness told colleagues once more that he would have to resign. Fleming urged him to await the prime minister's speech in the foreign affairs debate, while McCutcheon and Hees said they agreed entirely with him. "They urged me," Harkness wrote, "to stand firm against the Prime Minister and said that we should act on the offers to resign, which he had made many times during the crisis and throughout the period from the 1962 election on, unless he accepted the position set out in the memo."[155]

On Friday afternoon, January 25, Diefenbaker rose before a crowded House to respond to Pearson's indictment of his government's indecision. In familiar manner he ridiculed the inconsistencies in Pearson's own record while claiming logic in his own. His ministers listened as intently as others in search of that logic – and discovered only calculated obscurity. Canada had repudiated no undertakings, but it would not be pushed around by "anyone visiting our country." For Donald Fleming "this was without exception the most equivocal speech I had ever heard in the House of Commons. It surpassed Mackenzie King at his best. It confused even his own cabinet colleagues." The speech was the usual *mélange* of notes prepared by Robert Bryce and Diefenbaker himself. To his astonishment, Fleming saw in Diefenbaker's bundle of papers the special committee's memo, which Diefenbaker proceeded to weave, in disconnected bits, into his own text. Canada's NATO role would be determined in May; negotiations with the United States for North American weapons had been "going on quite forcibly for two months or more." "Every word of the memo now had full government authority back of it," Fleming concluded. "This was an enormous step forward, or so we thought." [156]

Harkness too was briefly encouraged. He decided the prime minister had come off the fence. When Diefenbaker left the House, Harkness followed him to the lobby, shook his hand, and offered thanks. Diefenbaker did not reply. Charles Lynch found Harkness in the lobby to tell him that the members of the press gallery were "completely confused." What did the speech mean? Harkness told him that the pro-nuclear message was contained in "four points near the end of the speech." Lynch was sceptical. [157]

The Saturday press took Lynch's line. Defence policy was "left hanging in mid-air," reported the *Globe and Mail*; "this is no policy at all," complained the Ottawa *Citizen*; others echoed their uncertainty. [158] Harkness was dismayed, and concluded that Diefenbaker had intended after all to maintain his ambiguity. He decided to issue a press release "to bring things to a head and thus decide the matter, and at the same time to make my own position clear to the country." Early on Monday morning he released a statement declaring that Diefenbaker had asserted "a definite policy for the acquisition of nuclear arms." Diefenbaker summoned Harkness to his office and exclaimed: "This is terrible – you've ruined everything – why did you do it?...You had no right to make such a statement – you have put me in an impossible situation." Harkness replied angrily that he was ready to resign at any time, and left when Diefenbaker refused any further argument. For two days Diefenbaker played a game of evasion in response to questions in the House; cabinet argued in circles; Harkness drafted his resignation; and delegations of ministers, led by Hees, Fulton, and McCutcheon, urged him to stay. On January 30, at a farewell party for the Fultons (who had now decided to leave Ottawa for British Columbia provincial politics), Hees, McCutcheon, Balcer, and other ministers pledged their word to Harkness that "we must get rid of Dief the next day." The atmosphere was "very peculiar." [159]

A shaky conspiracy was taking form. Diefenbaker was in a condition of "numb torpor." While Harkness and Fleming were still hoping to rouse him to a decision, perhaps half a dozen ministers had agreed he would have to go. Simultaneously, Oakley Dalgleish had reached the same conclusion, and was planning a *Globe and Mail* editorial making that demand. He was also in touch with Wallace McCutcheon, expecting to coordinate his public appeal with a cabinet revolt. McCutcheon, Nowlan, Fulton, Hees, and Fleming persuaded Dalgleish to hold his editorial for the following week, while cabinet made a final effort to resolve the crisis from within. McCutcheon, Nowlan, and Hees talked among themselves of Nowlan as interim prime minister while the party chose a new leader. Fleming thought of himself as the natural successor.[160]

The next blow came from Washington, where there had been outrage at Diefenbaker's January 25 House of Commons speech. Late in the afternoon of January 30 Basil Robinson was summoned to the State Department to receive a press release. It was "a frontal attack on the Canadian government for its nuclear policy."

The Department has received a number of inquiries concerning the disclosure during a recent debate in the Canadian House of Commons regarding negotiations over the past two or three months between the United States and Canadian Governments relating to nuclear weapons for Canadian armed forces.

In 1958 the Canadian Government decided to adopt the BOMARC-B weapons system. Accordingly two BOMARC-B squadrons were deployed to Canada where they would serve the double purpose of protecting Montreal and Toronto as well as the U.S. deterrent force. The BOMARC-B was not designed to carry any conventional warhead. The matter of making available a nuclear warhead for it and for other nuclear-capable weapons systems acquired by Canada has been the subject of inconclusive discussions between the two governments. The installation of the two BOMARC-B batteries in Canada without nuclear warheads was completed in 1962.

In addition to the BOMARC-B, a similar problem exists with respect to the modern supersonic jet interceptor with which the RCAF has been provided. Without nuclear air defense warheads, they operate at far less than their full potential effectiveness.

Shortly after the Cuban crisis in October 1962, the Canadian Government proposed confidential discussions concerning circumstances under which there might be provision of nuclear weapons for Canadian armed forces in Canada and Europe. These discussions have been exploratory in nature; the

Canadian Government has not as yet proposed any arrangement sufficiently practical to contribute effectively to North American defense.

The discussions between the two governments have also involved possible arrangements for the provision of nuclear weapons for Canadian NATO forces in Europe, similar to arrangements which the United States has made with many of our other NATO allies.

During the debate in the House of Commons various references were made to recent discussions at Nassau. The agreements made at Nassau have been fully published. They raise no question of the appropriateness of nuclear weapons for Canadian forces in fulfilling their NATO or NORAD obligations.

Reference was also made in the debate to the need of NATO for increased conventional forces. A flexible and balanced defense requires increased conventional forces, but conventional forces are not an alternative to effective NATO or NORAD defense arrangements using nuclear-capable weapons systems. NORAD is designed to defend the North American continent against air attack. The Soviet bomber fleet will remain at least throughout this decade a significant element in the Soviet strike force. An effective continental defense against this common threat is necessary.

The provision of nuclear weapons to Canadian forces would not involve an expansion of independent nuclear capability, or an increase in the "nuclear club." As in the case of other allies custody of U.S. nuclear weapons would remain with the U.S. Joint control fully consistent with national sovereignty can be worked out to cover the use of such weapons by Canadian forces.[161]

Duncan Macpherson, Toronto *Star*, 1963

Blast Off

At the State Department, Robinson was told that four years of discussions with Canada had "proved abortive and not for technical reasons." The recent Canadian proposals to store component parts in the United States amounted to "a contrived solution which might...create added confusion at a time of emergency and might mislead people as to the state of continental defence." The prime minister's disclosure of secret negotiations – which was made without notifying Washington – had caused "much concern," although this was not mentioned in the press release.[162]

Telephone lines between Ottawa and Washington crackled, and within hours the Canadian ambassador, Charles Ritchie, had been "recalled for consultation." Diefenbaker learned of the press release on a short trip to Toronto. As he returned to Ottawa late in the evening with Donald Fleming, he clutched the document in his hands, his eyes glowing fire: "We've got our issue now...We can call our general election now." Fleming replied: "No, John. You can't do that." Three times the brief dialogue was repeated.[163]

Cabinet met at 9:30 the next morning to face this latest and most serious storm. Ministers agreed unanimously on a strong protest, and under the leadership of Fleming, Hees, and Harkness, "beat off" Diefenbaker's proposal to dissolve the House that afternoon and enter an election campaign against the US administration. Instead, they bought a few hours' time: they would discuss dissolution after the day's debate in the House.[164]

When the House met, the prime minister condemned the American statement as an "unprecedented and...unwarranted intrusion in Canadian affairs." Canada, he said, would honour its obligations, but "it will not be pushed around or accept external domination or interference in the making of its decisions. Canada is determined to remain a firm ally, but that does not mean she should be a satellite." He added the stinging comment that Pearson's views bore "a striking resemblance" to those of the State Department. The three opposition leaders joined in rejection of the American statement, but insisted as well on clarification of the government's policy. Pearson pursued the line by moving adjournment of the House for an emergency debate, and after two appeals against the Speaker's rulings, the debate proceeded.[165]

Mike Pearson, Robert Thompson, and Tommy Douglas complained of the government's petty politics, tightrope walking, changes of direction, postponement and procrastination. Thompson's shift of tone was particularly threatening, since Social Credit votes had previously sustained the government's tenuous majority in the House. Only Harkness spoke for the cabinet, after Diefenbaker had agreed during the dinner recess that the minister could use his press release as a basis for his remarks. Harkness – ever hopeful – took this to mean that Diefenbaker "was prepared to accept my position on nuclear warheads."[166]

On Friday the pace of collapse quickened. In Washington Dean Rusk – responding to sharp criticism from the Washington *Post* and the New York *Times* – offered a limited apology for giving offence to Canada, but insisted that the administration was justified in "fairly setting out" the facts of the case. He would not say whether the State Department's press release had been approved by the president. Arthur Krock of the *Times* reported that the statement had been cleared by Kennedy's national security adviser, McGeorge Bundy.[167]

In Ottawa, cabinet met twice. Diefenbaker was not ready to declare himself in favour of nuclear arms, and repeated his call for a dissolution on the issue of American interference in Canadian affairs. Several ministers protested that the consequences for the economy and for Canada's defences would be dangerous. Diefenbaker insisted that he could win an anti-American campaign; "this, to him," Harkness judged, "was all that mattered." Debate churned on inconclusively, until Diefenbaker proposed another meeting for Saturday morning. Afterwards, discussion continued in ministers' offices. Now at least nine ministers talked of resignation if Diefenbaker launched an anti-American campaign. George Hees thought that a united front of critical ministers could persuade Diefenbaker to abandon the intention – or could force him out the next day if necessary.[168]

Diefenbaker frustrated that plan by dealing with a long list of appointments at the Saturday meeting. "It was," Harkness believed, "quite evidently a trick to prevent the discussion we had all come for...Finally he tried to get a snap decision on...dissolution on the American interference basis, without any discussion, by simply asking each member in turn to say whether he favoured dissolution or not – a straight yes or no without remark." Fleming, Hees, and Harkness protested and called for another meeting, but since the press gallery dinner was scheduled for that evening, members agreed to a Sunday morning, off-the-record meeting at 24 Sussex Drive. As they departed, ministers learned of the death that day of Chief Justice Patrick Kerwin of the Supreme Court of Canada.[169]

In the inevitable conversations after cabinet, this time at George Hees's room in the Château Laurier, Hees took on the task of opening the next cabinet meeting with the declaration that he would resign unless Diefenbaker did so.[170] By early evening, as the drinks began to flow in ministers' offices before the gallery dinner, Fulton, Starr, Bell, and Churchill were "kicking around" the notion that Diefenbaker "might accept the Chief Justiceship of the Supreme Court."[171]

The prime minister attended the gallery dinner in decidedly sombre spirit. The skits and songs were certain to be directed at his own dilemmas, and he was in no mood for them. With his imperfect hearing, he was especially offended by a parodic performance of "Jesus Loves Me": "The people love me/This I know/Allister Grosart tells me so." It included the lines: "Why they even say/I have Harkness's disease." This, Diefenbaker wrote, was slander: "That I was the victim of an advanced case of Parkinson's disease...They sang and acted out my physical and mental sufferings." Harkness, too, was an informal target during the evening, and early the next morning Diefenbaker received a telephone message that Charles Lynch had challenged Harkness to resign. If Harkness went, the Chief was told, three or four other ministers would follow, including Wallace McCutcheon. The informant would not say who the others were.[172]

As he prepared for the Sunday meeting of ministers, Diefenbaker also reflected that "my leadership had just endured a week-long editorial barrage from the pages of John Bassett's Toronto *Telegram*, and that this thundering might prelude some action by Hees or McCutcheon. At any rate, I was ready, or as ready as I could be in these circumstances."[173] The old warrior drew a certain stimulation from the prospect of battle – even against his own team.

At mid-morning all the ministers except Ellen Fairclough gathered in the blue dining room at 24 Sussex Drive. Diefenbaker sat at the centre on the window side of the long table, his back to the dramatic sweep of the Ottawa River and the Gatineau hills beyond. Howard Green sat to his right and Donald Fleming to his left. Diefenbaker began by calling for the dissolution of parliament that afternoon, in order to pre-empt an early defeat in the House. The election was bound to have "strong overtones of an anti–U.S. platform" because of the intolerable American intervention. He asked quietly for other views.

Hees was the first minister to speak. An election, he said, required a genuine national issue, one that divided the parties. Yet the issue of the American press release had united all parties – and Dean Rusk had already apologized. What the people wanted was a government that made its own decisions, but on defence policy they did not know what decisions the government had made. The public believed there were commitments to be carried out, that the planes and the Bomarcs should be armed with nuclear warheads. An election fought against the United States would mean a Conservative rout: Grosart, he said, had told him that the party would win only thirty-seven seats if it went to the country. Suddenly there were interruptions, some in support, some opposed. Hees did not reach the point of asking for the prime minister's resignation. The heat rose. Hees tried to continue and a voice cried: "Traitor!" The interjections grew louder.

Diefenbaker insisted: "I did not ask for this job; I don't want it, and if I'm not wanted, I'll go."

Harkness turned coldly on the prime minister. "You might as well know," he told him, "that the people of Canada have lost confidence in you, the party has lost confidence in you, and the Cabinet has lost confidence in you. It is time you went." Personally, Harkness said, he had no option but resignation.

Now there was pandemonium. Diefenbaker banged the table and rose to his feet. "Those who are with me stand up, those against me remain seated." Fleming and Bell asked what they were being asked to stand for, dissolution or confidence in Diefenbaker? The prime minister repeated his challenge. Some ministers stood, but moving left around the table, Fleming, Hees, Fulton, Harkness, Balcer, Flemming, Halpenny, Sévigny, Martineau, McCutcheon, and Bell remained seated. Eleven to nine against the prime minister – on an uncertain question. Diefenbaker sat, turned to Fleming, and whispered: "I'm going to tell them to make you prime minister." "You can't do that!" cried Fleming. Without a pause, Diefenbaker called out: "I propose that Donald Fleming be named prime minister. I will leave you to discuss the proposal. I will be in the library."

Some ministers thought Diefenbaker had said he was going to Government House to resign.[174] Two ministers told Patrick Nicholson later that the prime minister seemed at that moment like a "raging lunatic." Green and Churchill followed Diefenbaker to the door as Green cried: "Nest of traitors!" at those who remained. "I wouldn't follow Fleming anywhere," Churchill added. Mike Starr rose to follow them out. Alvin Hamilton joined him, yelling: "You treacherous bastards! No prime minister has ever had to deal with so many sons of bitches." More ministers straggled out as others sat stunned.

McCutcheon eventually suggested that all this was foolishness: "If everyone resigns, there won't even be a Cabinet left to fight an election." A delegation left the room to persuade the others to return. "Amid shouting of insults and disorder," everyone eventually came back except the prime minister.

Fleming now intervened in an effort "to restore the dignity of cabinet," urging them not to "make bad history." He acknowledged the prime minister's whispered words about the succession, insisted that he had no warning of the proposal, and said that he put party unity first. A sense of calm returned, and ministers began to talk of the conditions they would need to maintain their support for Diefenbaker. Bell tried out a draft resolution, which was generally agreed after a paragraph calling for immediate talks between Diefenbaker and

Kennedy on the nuclear issue had been eliminated. The rest of it read:

> The Cabinet expresses its loyalty to the Prime Minister and its willingness to continue to give him full support.
>
> Without in any way imposing any condition in respect of the foregoing resolution, Cabinet is of the opinion that immediate dissolution is most undesirable and that we should meet the House of Commons tomorrow and seek by every means to avoid defeat.

Harkness dissented, and said he would leave to write his letter of resignation. Green, in the chair, expressed the cabinet's thanks for Harkness's service in three ministries; and Harkness, grateful for this display of decency, shook hands around the table before departing.

Green, Churchill, Fleming, and Nowlan carried the message of reconciliation to Diefenbaker in the library, where he was quietly finishing a sandwich lunch in the company of Olive and his golden labrador retriever Happy. After brief reflection he returned and thanked the cabinet for its resolution of confidence. Diefenbaker suggested that some ministers should try to persuade Harkness to return, or at least to do no harm to the government in his letter of resignation. Hees and Fulton agreed to do so. At 2:30 pm the bizarre meeting ended.

Green and Churchill remained at Sussex Drive, and soon Diefenbaker called Fleming to return. He needed comfort. "We hashed and rehashed what had happened," Fleming recalled, "and I felt little was being accomplished." Olive served sandwiches, and about seven in the evening Fleming departed. Some time after that, when Nowlan and McCutcheon had joined the prime minister, Hees and Fulton returned to report they had persuaded Harkness to tone down his letter of resignation. Fulton then returned to the subject of the prime minister's resignation for the good of the party and the country. McCutcheon grunted his support. Diefenbaker asked who should succeed him. Hees and Nowlan were apparently mentioned, but when Fulton added that the new prime minister might appoint Diefenbaker to succeed Patrick Kerwin as chief justice of the Supreme Court, Diefenbaker invited the two ministers to leave the house at once. During the evening Harkness's letter arrived, with a note that it would be given to the press on Monday morning. He left cabinet declaring that "It has become quite obvious during the last few days that your views and mine as to the course we should pursue for the acquisition of nuclear weapons for our armed forces are not capable of reconciliation." Harkness alone had made his position clear.[175]

On Monday morning, February 4, cabinet met again to discuss the resignation and the coming confrontation in the House. Diefenbaker told Fleming: "You are going to be prime minister before this day is over...You and I are going over to see the Governor General this afternoon." Fleming doubted that Diefenbaker could dictate the succession, and later reflected: "Whether he meant this and whether he would have carried out his professed intention I do not know, nor will I ever know. He may have been in earnest, or he may have been testing out the strength of his position or my loyalty, or perhaps he was talking somewhat aimlessly."[176] Cabinet discussed its response to a Liberal Party promise of a royal commission on bilingualism and bi-culturalism, and agreed to propose a federal-provincial conference on the language question that afternoon. No one raised the subject of a replacement for the minister of defence. Diefenbaker also appointed his defeated friend David Walker to the Senate that day, and Walker joined him in Ottawa as the crisis deepened.[177]

When the House met, the balconies were crowded. Harkness made a statement on his resignation that concluded: "I resigned on a matter of principle. The point was finally reached when I considered that my honour and integrity required that I take this step." The prime minister's prolonged indecision and the cabinet's division were now matters of public record. The supply debate opened on a no-confidence motion by Pearson, worded deftly to attract the support of Social Credit and the NDP: "This government, because of lack of leadership, the breakdown of unity in the cabinet, and confusion and indecision in dealing with national and international problems, does not have the confidence of the Canadian people."[178] Who could deny it?

For the government, the crucial votes in the House now belonged to thirty members of the Social Credit Party under the leadership of Robert Thompson and Réal Caouette. For a few months after the 1962 election, Thompson had kept closely in touch with Conservative intermediaries, manoeuvring carefully to avoid the government's defeat and an early election. Now his members reported dissatisfaction with the government in their constituencies, and his contacts with the ministry had ceased. Thompson, fearful that his party would precipitate the government's defeat, wanted some significant concessions to offer his back-benchers. On February 1 he had sought out the journalist Patrick Nicholson to deliver a message to Senator McCutcheon. Social Credit would vote against the government on the supply motion unless it announced a timetable for action on four points: tabling the new spending estimates, introducing a new budget, carrying out some measures already approved by parliament, and clarifying the commitment on nuclear weapons.

McCutcheon thought the request reasonable, and promised a response by Monday morning. In the meantime, there were further discussions between Thompson, Nowlan, and Churchill similarly aimed at reconciliation.[179] Thompson also sent an emergency message to his Conservative friend in New Brunswick, Michael Wardell, whom Diefenbaker had recently appointed as chairman of a new federal agency, the Atlantic Development Board. Wardell was flown to Ottawa on Sunday afternoon from the RCAF base in Shearwater, Nova Scotia, in the company of the chief of the air staff. Thompson met him on arrival at Ottawa airport and briefed him during their drive to the Château Laurier, where Wardell telephoned Diefenbaker. As the prime minister absorbed the results of his chaotic cabinet meeting, Wardell gave him Thompson's conditions for support:

> T.'s terms: a simple statement by D. of his nuclear arms policy, or alternatively his acceptance of an inter-party committee on defence with the government retaining the sole responsibility for formulating policy. The statement was to be made in Parliament on Monday before the Liberal motion of no confidence, which would be on supply. The statement could embody three statements D. had already made which were "hidden in a mass of other words."[180]

Wardell added Thompson's other three points about the parliamentary timetable, "none of which," he thought, "could conceivably create an issue." In response, Diefenbaker "complained bitterly of T., said T. had lost no opportunity of publicly slighting him." Diefenbaker was exhausted, and promised to see Wardell in his office early on Monday morning. Wardell then consulted Hugh John Flemming, who told him it was essential "to reach an understanding with Green overnight," since Green was closest to Diefenbaker. "This advice," Wardell wrote, "was, I think, fatal." Wardell reached him, and Green said he had been with Diefenbaker during Wardell's earlier call and knew everything.

Next morning Green was with Diefenbaker when he met Wardell in the prime minister's East Block office – which was frenetic with ringing telephones, ministers and officials rushing in and out, and harassed secretaries. Wardell explained Thompson's terms again, said they were modest, and asked for a message which Thompson could give to his caucus that morning. Diefenbaker was hostile: "Thompson never loses a chance to humiliate me...Let Thompson know I will not be kicked around." But the prime minister left the issue for settlement with Green as he departed for the cabinet meeting, and Green offered no objection. Wardell told Thompson an agreement was possible.

At midday, Thompson gave Wardell a typed carbon copy of the Social Credit terms. He took them to Howard Green, who read them and said: "We shall have nothing to do with it. It is presumptuous and it is foolish of Thompson to make such suggestions." He predicted dissolution and an early election. There was no further communication from Diefenbaker on the terms. As Nicholson judged, "He did not deign to give that ultimatum the recognition of a reply: but he resolved to meet the undoubtedly serious threat by supplying the information in his own way and at his own time." [181]

Following Pearson's speech on his no-confidence motion, Thompson entered the debate just before the dinner adjournment. He quoted with approval that day's *Globe and Mail* editorial – which spoke of an early election as "a disaster" – and added that "We, in this party continue to stand on our previous policy...to go along with a reasonable discussion and debate on the supply motions that are yet to come and on the estimates which are yet to be brought forward." But when debate resumed at 8 pm, his tone had changed. "We have reached the point where we almost reluctantly, shall we say, believe it would be worse for the country not to go to the people to ascertain their will, than it would be to prolong the life of this Government which is not fulfilling its responsibilities as it should." He outlined the party's four conditions for support. "We did not intend to issue an ultimatum. In spite of our last minute appeal asking, begging, pleading that the government fill the vacuum that had been created because they have not done these things previously, we have no action." He moved an amendment to the Liberal motion framed around the Social Credit conditions:

> This Government has failed up to this time to give a clear statement of policy respecting Canada's national defence, and has failed to organize the business of the House so that the 1963–64 estimates and budget could be introduced, and has failed to outline a positive program of follow-up action respecting many things for which this Parliament and previous Parliaments have already given authority, and does not have the confidence of the Canadian people. [182]

Afterwards, he told Wardell that he had changed course because Diefenbaker had made no response to his approaches. [183]

Now there were wheels within wheels revolving. Nicholson, hearing a radio news flash reporting the Thompson amendment and predicting the government's defeat, drove back to Parliament Hill in a snowstorm, found Hees in the House, and arranged to meet him after the adjournment at 10 pm. He was determined to bring Thompson together again with a Conservative minister, and Thompson agreed to join them later. But Nicholson's own calculations had shifted. Once Hees had poured him a scotch-and-water from his "hospitable cupboard," Nicholson suggested that he could see "a broad highway leading to a continuation in office under a new leader and supported by thirty Social Credit votes...I don't know what he [Thompson] would say to you, because I haven't discussed it with him, but I've a good idea he might tell you that a new leader of your party might change a lot of pictures. I know his view is that this would scotch the need for an election now, and his party would support almost any new P.M. who would get on with urgent business." Hees was intrigued and agreed to meet Thompson, who was already on his way. But he wanted other ministers present, and quickly gathered Léon Balcer, Pierre Sévigny, and George Nowlan to his office by telephone. At about 10:30 pm Thompson joined the party – but took only ginger ale. He said there had been no response to his messages from Diefenbaker, and he was "through supporting this government of inaction."

One of the Quebeckers declared: "The anti-Dief boys in the Cabinet will force him out; wouldn't that satisfy the Socreds?" Thompson wondered why that hadn't happened. He would only accept deeds. The drinking party muddled on into the night towards a conclusion, consuming two bottles of scotch on the way. George Hees was assigned to bell the cat. He would meet Diefenbaker the next morning to demand his resignation, and later in the day the dissenting ministers would confront the prime minister together to ask for his resignation or deliver their own. Thompson told them that if Diefenbaker resigned before the vote, his motion would no longer apply. Social Credit would certainly give reasonable support to a new prime minister willing to meet the party's terms, but he would not accept Howard Green as prime minister. Well after one in the morning, Nicholson delivered Sévigny to his home.[184] The core of dissident ministers had abandoned their pledge of loyalty within thirty-six hours of giving it to the prime minister.

At 8 am on Tuesday, February 5, George Hees called at Sussex Drive to urge the prime minister once more to resign. He predicted the government's defeat in the House that day. No one, he said, would campaign with Diefenbaker if an election were called. But the government could be saved, with Social Credit support, if he resigned at once in favour of Donald Fleming. He mentioned once more, as an enticement, the vacant chief justiceship – on the very day of Patrick Kerwin's funeral. Diefenbaker consulted Olive, telephoned Gordon Churchill, and told Hees he could go to hell.[185] Later in the morning one group of ministers gathered at Hees's main-floor parliamentary office (while the press swirled in the hallways outside) to consider their next step after the failure of Hees's guerrilla attack. Unaccountably, they decided to wait twenty-four hours until after the parliamentary vote before challenging Diefenbaker again. They would ask for a meeting of ministers at 9 am, to precede the regular Wednesday caucus meeting at eleven. Meanwhile, Diefenbaker's loyalist ministers, Churchill, Hamilton, Starr, Dinsdale, and Monteith, were rallying Conservative back-benchers – who had so far been left out of everyone's calculations – to show their support for the Chief. A mid-morning radio report that George Nowlan had replaced Diefenbaker as prime minister was quickly denied, and the cheerleaders redoubled their appeals. As Diefenbaker made his way into the House at 2:30 pm he was greeted in the lobby by a cheering mass of faithful MPs.[186]

During a short question period, Paul Martin innocently asked Diefenbaker "if it was not communicated to the right honourable gentleman today that a number of his colleagues wished him to vacate the office of Prime Minister – and be replaced by one of his colleagues?"[187] The variation on that rumour was that Thompson had demanded Diefenbaker's resignation as his final condition for support – which was more or less true, although "demanded" was not quite the right word to describe what had emerged in the midnight hours. Wardell, who was in the Speaker's gallery with Olive, asked her whether the prime minister was aware that Thompson had not imposed that condition. She thought not, and asked Wardell to send a note down to Diefenbaker. He wrote: "Dear Prime Minister: I talked to Thompson this morning. He stated the same terms as yesterday: with a short concise statement on nuclear arms repeating your own previously expressed three points. He made no condition of your own resignation from office." The note was passed down by messenger. Diefenbaker read it, "looked up and nodded."

In this confusing atmosphere of speculation and intrigue, Diefenbaker took the floor. He attacked the Liberals, the military establishment, and the Americans, and eventually addressed himself to the Créditiste members who would decide the government's fate that evening: "If our hands are tied, they are tied not by the other two parties but by the official opposition. They bear the responsibility...We place before you our views on defence...We will bring in new estimates...within...one week...We will bring down a budget... by the end of February." On everything but the nuclear issue, Thompson's conditions had been fully granted. The Liberal opposition, Diefenbaker claimed, had simply treated the Social Credit Party as a joke. Pearson "loves thee, but he loved you not until yesterday." They should not join his league. Diefenbaker asked the House for its confidence. "The other day I saw the benefits of calling an election, thinking only of the political consequences in our favour. But I asked, 'What will its effects be on a rising economy in the years ahead and the months ahead, unless we get those things on the statute books that would continue the upsurge of the economy of Canada?'"[188]

But it was too late. Thompson awaited only the deed, and the deed had not been committed. His party would vote against the government. "What numbed or paralysed John Diefenbaker," Fleming wondered, "that he did not raise a finger to ward off defeat in the House when that could have been done?" He could not answer the question. When the House returned after dinner, the bells rang for the division on the Social Credit amendment, and 256 of the 265 members took their seats. Only two Conservatives were absent: Douglas Harkness, who was in his office, and Art Smith, who stood behind the curtains to watch the vote. When the roll was called, the Halifax Conservative Edmund Morris and the NDP member Harold Winch abstained, and two NDP members, H.W. Herridge and Colin Cameron, voted with the government. Otherwise, party lines held, and the government was defeated 142 to 111. The amended Liberal motion passed by the same count. The chamber erupted in singing, yelling, and paper-throwing while the prime minister made his barely audible announcement that he would go to the governor general the next day. The House adjourned into the teeming hallways. Upstairs, dissident ministers and their wives gathered at Pierre Sévigny's office while a Canadian Press reporter diligently recorded their names. Stories of the secret plans for Wednesday morning's cabinet coup, when the Chief would be unseated, flowed freely that night with the alcohol.[189]

Overnight, Hamilton, Green, and Churchill had arranged to reverse the order of the two meetings planned for the morning. The dissidents had already proven themselves disorganized, not to say feckless, and they had no effective means of preventing the further delay in confronting the prime minister. The caucus would take place at nine, the cabinet meeting at eleven. They would have to take their chances, first of all, in a meeting where western members loyal to John Diefenbaker held the majority. In a defensive campaign to sustain the prime minister that had been, on balance, as inept as the campaign against Diefenbaker, this was an astute move.

Both Oakley Dalgleish and John Bassett had been closely in touch and in loose collaboration with the cabinet dissidents over the previous two weeks. As the House vote approached on Tuesday evening, Dalgleish printed his postponed editorial, titled "Now Is the Time...," on the front page of Wednesday's *Globe*, calling for the prime minister's retirement so that "a strong man might succeed him" and avoid the government's defeat. But "now" was too late: minutes after the paper went on sale on the streets, the government fell. Dalgleish altered a few sentences to bring the editorial up to date for the final edition. It condemned the government's paralysis since the previous June, and lamented that the country had been thrown into "an election that could well be disastrous." The fault lay squarely with John Diefenbaker, who took no economic decisions after the 1962 emergency measures, who could not honour the country's military commitments to the United States, who obstructed Britain's efforts to enter the European Common Market, and who "continued to cling to the post of leader" after abdicating its responsibilities. His ministers – who could, Dalgleish claimed, have led the country sensibly – had been "frozen in enforced inactivity" by the prime minister. The editor offered Diefenbaker a dignified exit – or perhaps (still banking on what the dissidents said they would do that morning) simply the appearance of one:

> The man who could not lead the Government into action to cure Canada's economic difficulties is unfit to lead the Conservative Party into action in this election. For the sake of the party and the country, he should give up the leadership. In our view the country must always come first, but the welfare of the country is entwined with the welfare of the Conservative Party. In our system it is essential that we have two strong political parties. If Mr. Diefenbaker continues in the leadership he will do the party irreparable harm and perhaps destroy it as a national force.[190]

Bassett's editorial in the *Telegram* on Wednesday morning, titled "Diefenbaker Era Closes," could be read as though the palace revolt had already taken place. "At this moment both his party and the country see only the tragedy of this brilliant man with his myriad political talents, brought down by his inability to make and carry through hard decisions with purpose and determination...At sixty-seven, this man who flashed so brilliantly across Canada's political firmament less than six years ago, cannot expect again to lead his country. Possibly he will not even lead again his party." But Bassett sought to soothe his friend's departure with praise. The party and the country owed him "a tremendous debt of gratitude" for his restoration of the two-party system, the dignity of parliament and of the citizen, and the destruction of "narrow prejudice...When the passions of the last few days subside, when the public comes to realize the battering he withstood, the cheap jokes, the organized riots of the last election campaign, the cruel rumours about his health, the fury of some of those who could not believe he had deprived them of office – then the public will re-appraise his worth and his contribution to the land."[191] The two Toronto editorials were written for a single reader: If the prime minister wouldn't respond to the bad cop's insults, perhaps he would accept the good cop's blandishments.

When Diefenbaker walked into the caucus meeting in the Railway Committee Room at 9 am on February 6, he knew exactly what his opponents wanted. But he did not know what he wanted. Earlier, in his Commons office, he told Dalton Camp, Howard Green, and his secretary Marion Wagner: "That's it. Get the Governor. I'm going to advise him to send for Donald Fleming and they can have it. I don't want it, I'm finished, finished." Green protested: "Ah, come on now, John. We're not going to quit and you're not going to quit." Diefenbaker insisted: "No, I'm finished. Olive wants me to resign." Green told him he was going to contest the election and "have a lot of fun." Diefenbaker replied: "It may be a lot of fun for you, Howard, but it's not going to be any fun for me."[192] Diefenbaker and Green departed for the caucus meeting in this state of uncertainty. The prime minister remained in turmoil, unable to come to a decision on his own as long as his counsellors gave him contradictory advice. He did not know whether he would still be in power that evening. If the day ended in resignation, he did not know whether that would come as his own decision, or be forced on him by his ministers. The Chief needed others to make up his mind for him.

Hees, the chairman of caucus, seated at the centre of the table with Diefenbaker on his right, began the meeting by reading a long, prepared statement blaming the government's defeat on the prime minister and warning against an anti-American election campaign. After some time Diefenbaker interrupted: "What's going on here? Who is the leader of this party?" This, he said, was a meeting to hear the views of MPs, not of the chairman. He challenged Hees with more questions about the minister's recent actions. There was an eruption of shouting before Hees could continue. At some point (the accounts differ) Hees began to cry. When he ended, he announced his intention to resign. McCutcheon and Sévigny said they would join him. The shouting erupted again, as other ministers attempted unsuccessfully to make themselves heard. Diefenbaker rose again to speak, while his prairie claque cheered the room into silence. Perhaps half the cabinet had not joined the chorus. "If I'm not wanted I'll go," Diefenbaker yelled, and started towards the door. Some members cried "No! No!" while others rushed to surround him and prevent his departure. Diefenbaker dramatically retraced his steps and resumed his performance, talking of the big business plot against him as he stared down Senator McCutcheon. The Chief and his supporters were taking control of the meeting.

Alf Brooks, Grattan O'Leary, and Fisheries Minister Angus MacLean – sensing the palpable shift of mood in Diefenbaker's favour – spoke with the eloquence of passion for party unity, for a united cabinet, and for loyalty to the prime minister in an election campaign. There were cries that the dissidents should change their minds and shake hands with Diefenbaker. One after another ministers rose and declared their loyalty, some of them in shame, and finally George Hees gave in to the overpowering sense of the occasion. As Wallace McCutcheon tried to leave, "he was forcibly brought back to the front by several members, said he would stay in the cabinet and shook hands with Diefenbaker." Diefenbaker declared that he would stay if the caucus gave him unanimous approval, and asked all his supporters to stand. The room rose as a man. In this intimidating atmosphere, only Harkness and Sévigny dared to resist – and Harkness had to throw off Brooks and O'Leary as they tried to pull him to his feet. Diefenbaker, triumphant in what seemed to him unanimous endorsement and the conquest of his foes, announced that he would stay and lead the party. He leaned over to Hees, took his hand, and said, "George, we've got this election, and you and I are going to fight it together. I've got to have you beside me. I'll change the defence policy better to suit you fellows' views." Hees recalled: "I was so excited I jumped up on my feet, and I was crying; there were tears in my eyes. I figured here we were at last, in with a defence policy that meant something."

The meeting broke up in cheers and applause, as Diefenbaker and Hees launched themselves arm in arm from the room into the mob of reporters and cameramen at the door. "I still carry on," Diefenbaker exulted. "Tell them about it, George." Hees spilled over: "Best caucus we ever had; the show is on the road. We are going to knock hell out of the Grits."

His decision made, Diefenbaker walked back to his parliamentary office with Donald Fleming, who told him he would not contest the election. Diefenbaker said, "I've been thinking about the death of Chief Justice Kerwin and thought you would be a good person to be Chief Justice...Let's see what others think about it." But that, like so many other incautious or mischievous words of the prime minister, proved fantasy. An innocuous meeting of cabinet followed, and at one o'clock in the afternoon Diefenbaker visited Rideau Hall, emerging to announce that the House was dissolved and an election had been called for April 8.[193]

CHAPTER 13

A Leader at Bay

1963-1966

THE *TELEGRAM* WAS UNRELENTING. THE DAY AFTER DIEFENBAKER'S TRIUMPH in caucus, the lead editorial accused the prime minister of putting his own interest above that of the party: "John Diefenbaker yesterday decided that the sacrifice of his personal position as leader of the Progressive Conservative Party, and Prime Minister until April 8, was too great a price to pay to save his party, and perhaps his Government."

The political magic and force of personality that had once swayed thousands was strong enough to win support for his position from his party's caucus and his cabinet colleagues. But the Conservative Party, including many of the members who yesterday pledged their support mingling cheers with tears, will pay dearly for this decision.

The party, as a political entity, is split as never before. The members will pay their account on election day as many of them undoubtedly must realize even now. The Prime Minister will lead his party into his fourth campaign, and has the satisfaction of knowing that no cabinet colleague was strong enough to unseat him, and only one had the courage to leave him.

It is impossible to say what price will be paid for this leadership and this satisfaction of Mr. Diefenbaker, but it will be huge in terms of political currency.[1]

The prime minister, said the *Telegram*, had no reasonable policies for electors to judge: "no budget...no Government defense policy...no long range economic plans; no tax reforms; no...trade policies since Britain's failure to enter the Common Market...no comprehensive role for Canada in world affairs." He had just two lines of attack: "First, United States interference in Canadian political matters and, secondly, that the opposition parties obstructed the business of Parliament. *The Telegram* believes that Canadians will not accept either premise as a sound basis for returning the Government to office." The Chief's resignation would have been far better, offered now, "still in office, and thereby giving his party a fighting chance under new leadership, than later, shattered at the polls and reviled by the unforgiving and the unremembering."

Next day the *Globe and Mail* took different but equally deadly aim in its lead editorial, "A Matter of Morality." Its targets were George Nowlan, George Hees, and Wallace McCutcheon, the ministers who had come out of caucus denying any revolt in cabinet against the prime minister's leadership. They were lying.

> It is a matter of fact that some Ministers of the Crown who on Wednesday declared their allegiance to the great leader had, only two days before, their resignations ready in their pockets. It was to be the Prime Minister's resignation or theirs.
>
> Today the Prime Minister is still in office and the rebels, having deserted their cause, are still in the Cabinet. They have purchased their jobs, for a few weeks, doubtless to "preserve" the party.
>
> So now these men lead their tattered party into the election with lies on their lips and a dual standard of morality in their hearts. They have one set of morals for churchgoing and for the children's hour, and another for the smoke-filled rooms.
>
> Nor is this the full extent of their dishonor. They have abandoned the one among them who had the courage to resign, Defense Minister Douglas Harkness, and left at the caucus door all the support and admiration which they gave him in the hour of his decision. And they have attempted to place the blame for their own failings on others. They have said that all the reports of revolt in the Cabinet are mere press speculation, utter newspaper fiction.[2]

One day ministers spoke in confidence to the press; the next they accused it of falsehood in reporting their unattributed stories. "We want no more of these treacherous confidences," the editorial thundered. Ministers should be frank in admitting that the cabinet had been "in a turmoil, in a paralysis of indecision, for months. One of the basic problems of Mr. Diefenbaker's leadership has been his preoccupation with treason. He has been so busy seeking out conspiracies and suspecting everyone he has had little time for anything else." That was the reason for the prime minister's inability to govern, and for the *Globe*'s call for his resignation. Now that ministers had failed "to re-examine and re-assert their ideals," they stood before the electorate in the wreckage of their government. "The caucus settled nothing. The Prime Minister does not trust his Ministers; they do not trust him. There can be nothing among them now but more turmoil, backbiting and suspicion. Such is the sort of leadership they are asking the public to endorse." This was the bitter public testimony of former friends. The *Globe* was challenging the dissident ministers to come clean.

Wallace McCutcheon had privately established the conditions of his loyalty. After the caucus meeting, where he had opposed a campaign based on attacking the Americans, he wrote to Diefenbaker.

> You heard what I said this morning.
>
> I do not retract from that and I assumed when you shook my hand when I stood up at Caucus and announced that I was going to the country with you that you accepted my position.
>
> Lest there be any misunderstanding, I think I should now say that any statements which I regard as anti-American I will disassociate myself with publicly.
>
> I am prepared to defend your defence policy – with which you know I agree only as a matter of Cabinet solidarity.
>
> However, if the Secretary of State for External Affairs does not proceed expeditiously with the negotiations that you announced were under way then I will have to review my position.[3]

Eddie Goodman, too, had settled his conscience. On February 5, before the Commons vote, he had written to Diefenbaker tendering his resignation from the Ontario organization committee of the party. The job had taken a "crippling amount" of his time. "To these personal reasons for my desire to retire," he wrote, "there is now added the overriding and decisive consideration which is our strong disagreement on what is the proper defence policy for Canada. My views in this matter are clear to you as we have discussed them at length during the past few weeks."[4] He expected his friend George Hees to leave cabinet as he had boasted he would, and was astounded to hear radio reports of the caucus reconciliation. Goodman and Edward Dunlop (Hees's brother-in-law) flew at once to Ottawa and confronted the minister, who explained that he had been "swept away by the pleadings" of caucus and by Diefenbaker's fresh, though vague, commitments. "The truth of the matter," Goodman recalled, "was he's a warm emotional fellow, and with everybody, all his friends in the caucus and people whom he'd worked with for all these years, pleading with him not to destroy the party, he gave in, which is easily understandable." Goodman told him he "was an ass," and left Hees stewing.[5]

For two days, as he reflected on the challenges from Goodman, Dunlop, John Bassett, and the *Telegram* and *Globe* editorials, Hees attended cabinet meetings preparing for the election campaign. Pierre Sévigny, too, had agonized over the nuclear conflict and Diefenbaker's faltering leadership, but apparently expected to be promoted from associate minister to minister of defence after Harkness's resignation. Diefenbaker made no move during the week of crisis. On Friday evening, Sévigny and Hees decided to offer their belated resignations the next morning, and to persuade Léon Balcer to join them – still vainly hoping that a walkout would persuade Diefenbaker to retire. Balcer was summoned from Three Rivers for another late-night discussion at Hees's apartment, but he refused to resign. Early on Saturday morning, while the latest round of rumours busied the telephone lines to Sussex Drive, Hees and Sévigny arrived at the door carrying their letters of resignation. Diefenbaker was still upstairs in his dressing gown, so Burt Richardson led them to the library and chatted while the prime minister dressed.[6] Diefenbaker made his brief record of the interview a few days later.

> On Saturday my wife informed me about 9.15 a.m. as I was up in my room, that Hees and Sevigny had arrived. I said as they had not phoned this was rather surprising.
>
> I dressed and came down to the library and they were both standing and both smiling.
>
> Hees said: "I am here to reason."
>
> I said: "I am not going to listen."
>
> He laid his resignation on the little table.
>
> Sevigny said: "I too will have to resign," and then produced his.
>
> I said: "Won't you wait?" and they said "No," so I said: "That is the end," and they left me.[7]

Richardson thought that "the prime minister was thunderstruck. He took the resignations but he was practically speechless about this because it was so much of a surprise." The ministers still in Ottawa for the weekend were summoned to Sussex Drive for the latest emergency consultations. About a dozen turned up, and they in turn used the telephones to seek assurances of loyalty from those who were absent. By lunchtime it seemed clear there would be no more resignations, and Diefenbaker agreed that the vacant posts should be filled at once.[8]

"Olive has had a very hard and trying time," Diefenbaker wrote to his brother on February 8, "but there has never been anything but words of encouragement uttered by her."[9] He did not repeat to Elmer his earlier claim that she had counselled his resignation. Friends whose loyalties were personal and disinterested quickly rallied round. Helen Brunt telephoned and wrote:

> A phone call is so unsatisfactory. My purpose in calling as in this note is simply to say that I have the utmost faith in Our Prime Minister. I know he is doing what he believes best for Canada. And who are we to know better, who do not know anything of the matters at hand.
>
> Oh Olive I know the heartache when they hurt your man. It will heal but the scar is always there. And you know who your *real* friends are after it's over...
>
> ...I'm glad Bill isn't here. It would break his heart but then he would have been happy if he could have helped – whatever John did Bill went along with. They battled but if the P.M. was adamant Bill accepted it and that was the end.
>
> If I can be of any help any time, call me. I will do anything anytime.[10]

Diefenbaker seemed genuinely puzzled by the cabinet defections. "We will...face the sniping that goes on from those who left," he told Elmer. "I cannot understand Mr. Harkness. He agreed to the statement I made in the House of Commons on Defence, shook my hand after I delivered it, and then he went against me. Mr. Hees of course is another of those who through history reached out for the leadership too soon. He thought he was more powerful than he was. I did much for him but he continued to get himself into difficulties...It seems impossible to fathom the mentality of such as Harkness, Sevigny and Hees." But he was determined to fight on: "Elections are not won except in the last week. I am the underdog now and that means that the fight must be strongly waged."[11] The role was familiar and liberating. It meant "hard work on the part of your supporters. Hard work spells victory."[12] Diefenbaker thought he could see beyond the Bassetts, the Dalgleishs, the Goodmans, the Heeses and Sévignys – those of little faith and ulterior purpose – to the voters who admired and rallied to the underdog, to those ordinary Canadians who understood his quest as his betrayers could not.

Besides, there were others still loyally committed to the cause. In January, when Allister Grosart gave up the national directorship of the party, Diefenbaker announced the appointment of Dalton Camp to replace him, with the mutually agreed title of chairman of the national organization committee. He was prepared to act without salary as Diefenbaker's "personal representative to the organization at large," because "I have for you a personal affection and simple loyalty that has, since you assumed the leadership...no reservations or limitations short of my personal mental and physical limits." With an election bound to come soon, Camp reflected: "What is required, then, is fresh energy, enthusiasm and new direction to the organization. Enthusiasm must be rekindled, a tenacious will to win must become pervasive in the party. New techniques must be developed and applied and we obviously must [be] ready for battle. To all that, I offer to apply myself without stint or reservation and with optimism and confidence."[13] Camp, like Diefenbaker, enjoyed fighting the Grits. He reminded his leader that, since 1952, he had been involved in twenty-three federal and provincial election campaigns on behalf of the Tory party. Once the campaign had begun, he was rejoined in managing it by Allister Grosart.

On February 20 another prodigal returned. George Hogan – who had started the public phase of the party controversy over nuclear arms – wrote to Diefenbaker offering his full support in the election "both for the Party and for you personally." He had not changed his mind about accepting nuclear weapons, but conceded that "we are in an election campaign and the alternatives are either to reject the Party's whole programme because of one disagreement or to accept the whole programme in spite of one disagreement." Since all parties were internally divided on the nuclear issue, he said, "I can see no reason why the Conservative Party should be called upon to suffer for its nuclear differences while the other parties are allowed to profit from theirs. As I see it, the essential difference between the Conservatives and the Liberals on this question is that while our approach is to adopt no policy until May, theirs is to adopt two policies until April." He wished Diefenbaker success in the campaign.[14] The new premier of Ontario, John Robarts, pledged his organization's aid as well.

Despite this evidence of renewed support from members of the party in Toronto, Diefenbaker was determined to see his struggle from what was, for him, a traditional perspective. On the platform, he was fighting not only the Grits and the Kennedys but also his old antagonists "the Bay Street and St. James Street Tories" who had inspired "the desertions and insurrections" of the previous weeks.[15] When he addressed a large joint meeting of the Empire and Canadian Clubs and the Toronto Board of Trade in mid-February, he joked that "Daniel in the lion's den was an amateur performer compared to me."[16] And some of the enemy, he suspected, remained within. On February 11 he appointed Wallace McCutcheon to George Hees's vacant portfolio of Trade and Commerce in the hope that he "might help to still some of the storms surrounding us" – and because "our circumstances had not allowed me the luxury of firing him." But McCutcheon, he later wrote, "spent the entire election threatening to resign, with appropriate media fanfare, if I treated forthrightly the major issues of the campaign...I thought him the biggest political double-crosser I had ever known."[17]

While McCutcheon cautioned Diefenbaker against an anti-American campaign, *Newsweek* magazine provided the prime minister with a safe target of attack for its February 18 cover feature on "Canada's Diefenbaker: Decline and Fall." Diefenbaker's dark and scowling face, brows furrowed, lips pursed, jowls almost shaking, hair flying into the title line, dramatically lighted from below to emphasize every crease, landed on the newsstands in the first week of the Canadian campaign.[18] Inside, the story described the political crisis for American readers in terms familiar to Canadians, but included a few tendentious sentences describing that extraordinary face on the cover.

> Diefenbaker in full oratorical flight is a sight not soon to be forgotten: the India-rubber features twist and contort in grotesque and gargoyle-like grimaces; beneath the electric gray V of the hairline, the eyebrows beat up and down like bats' wings; the agate-blue eyes blaze forth cold fire. Elderly female Tory supporters find Diefenbaker's face rugged, kind, pleasant, and even soothing; his enemies insist that it is sufficient grounds for barring Tory rallies to children under sixteen.[19]

Dalton Camp seized the initiative by photocopying the *Newsweek* feature and sending it immediately to all Conservative constituency presidents. "Although the target of this derogatory tirade, the Prime Minister, has made no comment," Camp wrote, "I believe the members of this organization will condemn it in the strongest terms. The article not only attacks the person of the Prime Minister, but the office as well, and is obviously calculated to overtly inflame public opinion. It is difficult to recall any American publication making a more abusive and inflammatory attack on the head of any state, friendly or otherwise."[20] The prime minister saw conspiracy at work. He told his audiences, and repeated the charge in his memoirs: "Who, among those who voted in 1963, will ever forget the Kennedy-conceived message conveyed to the Canadian electors by the cover and contents of the 18 February issue of *Newsweek*: its editor was President's Kennedy's close friend."[21] Ben Bradlee, it was true, was one of the president's intimates, and Diefenbaker was not in Kennedy's good books. But the notion that the cover article was "Kennedy-inspired" was no more than a hunch, an expression of Diefenbaker's heightened sense that his enemies were uniting and closing in. If damage really was intended, Washington must have been disappointed. The mischievous cover picture probably assisted more than it harmed the Diefenbaker campaign. Diefenbaker's response of theatrical indignation was both calculated and genuine, the reaction of a professional performer with a thin skin. His audiences could sense, and sympathize with, his anguish while they also relished the performance.

Publicly, the policy of the Kennedy administration was to remain strictly neutral after the flareup of January 30. It would not comment on the Canadian election. Privately, there was outspoken distaste for Diefenbaker in the White House and the State Department, which was echoed in dispatches to Washington from the American Embassy in Ottawa. In a long telegram on February 3 commenting on the consequences of the State Department press release, Walton Butterworth offered a withering assessment of the Canadian cabinet and its policies, and an encouraging prospect of better times ahead. Butterworth was in no mood for tempered judgment. For six years, he reported, the United States had tolerated Canadian "foot dragging" in continental defence and "pretentious posturing" in other areas of foreign policy, until "our sudden dose of cold water" produced an "immediate cry of shock and outrage." But the "traditional psychopathic accusations of unwarranted US interference in domestic Canadian affairs" were rapidly subsiding as Canadians began to face the "hard realities, as set forth in the Departmental release."

> Preponderance of evidence available – news media, editorial comment, private citizens expressions of views – indicate shift of public attention from US statement to clear recognition Diefenbaker indecisiveness, with frequent and widespread reaffirmation of identity of US and Canadian interests and explicit acknowledgment that Canada has somehow gone astray. Department will recall this was basic aim of exercise...i.e. to bring Canadian thinking back to state of relevance to hard realities of world situation. Defense policy, particularly nuclear weapons issue, was key element this psychological problem, and its resolution will have profound bearing on Canadian attitude toward other less important foreign policy questions.
>
> For past four or five years we have – doubtless correctly – tolerated essentially neurotic Canadian view of world and of Canadian role. We have done so in hope Canadians themselves would make gradual natural adjustment to more realistic understanding...
>
> Inconclusive outcome last June's general elections...fumbling and indecision during Cuban crisis, continued...evasiveness on vital defense matters suggested reappraisal necessary...
>
> In effect we have now forced issue and outcome depends on basic common

sense of Canadian electorate. Our faith in their good judgment is based on our reading that public has been way ahead of political leadership of all parties...In short we think Canadian public is with us, even though some liberal politicians have been afraid we have handed Diefenbaker an issue he can use against them and US. We think Canadians will no longer accept irresponsible nonsense which political leaders all parties, but particularly progressive-conservatives under Diefenbaker, have got away with for several years.

If our appraisal is sound and if trend continues, we face transitional period uncertainty, probably until general elections return a new government with an absolute majority and thus a clear mandate...World has changed and Canadian people know it. Polls show strong Canadian majority support for acquisition nuclear warheads and for close cooperation with us. Cuban crisis last October evoked widespread evidence public unhappiness with Foreign Minister Green's moralizing and Diefenbaker's flexible inaction...

We should not be unduly disturbed at steam of resentment which first blew off upon publication of Department's release. Diefenbaker's reaction was expected. He is undependable, unscrupulous political animal at bay and we are ones who boxed him in...Let us also face fact that we are forcing Pearson to go faster and further than he desires in the direction we favor...We have reached point where our relations must be based on something more solid than accommodation to neurotic Canadian view of us and world...

As this appraisal indicates, we see grounds for optimism that over the long run this exercise will prove to have been highly beneficial and will substantially advance our interests. We have introduced element of realism which no government, whether progressive-conservative or liberal, will be able to ignore.

One thing which could bring it all to naught would be backing away from our present stand...On maintenance of this stance depends framework of our future relations with Canada.[22]

Whether or not there was the conspiracy of forces that Diefenbaker saw in his darkest moments, or hinted at from the platform, there was no doubt that the Kennedy administration looked forward to a new Canadian government not led by John G. Diefenbaker. As the campaign opened, Washington kept its powder dry and watched events to the north with unusual care.

Butterworth reminded Washington on February 2 that the Rostow memorandum was still "hanging over our heads, and Diefenbaker or someone else may decide to try to make political hay of it at any time. It is probably a good thing that he doubtless knows that the Liberals are aware of his possession of it and the manner of his acquisition since, in essence, failure to return to such an invited guest a personal, confidential paper would be difficult for Diefenbaker to explain to the Canadian public."[23] Embassy officers reported discussion of the memorandum in their presence by Grattan O'Leary and the Liberal editor of the Winnipeg *Free Press*, Shane McKay, at the end of January, as evidence that its existence must have been fairly widely known.[24] But Butterworth implied that if the memo was still hanging over Kennedy's head, it was also hanging over Diefenbaker's. The prime minister knew the risks of using it.

Before his second winter campaign could begin, Diefenbaker flew to London for three days in late February to be invested as an honorary freeman of the City of London, the first Canadian prime minister to receive this honour. He enjoyed the interlude as a brief escape from political turmoil, a soothing balm for his bruised ego – and a burst of glowing and uncritical publicity that could not have been better timed. On Sunday, February 23, he read the lesson at the City Temple, paid a short visit to Sir Winston Churchill, and met Harold Macmillan for the first time since the collapse of Britain's negotiations to enter the Common Market. Next day, he and Olive rode in a royal landau, under escort by mounted outriders of the RCMP, to the Guildhall to receive the freedom of the city before an appreciative audience of 1100 guests. The Lord Mayor good-naturedly referred to Diefenbaker's three Indian chieftainships in wishing him "the sharp eyes of the eagle, the wariness and strength of the walking buffalo, and the joyous speed and abandon of the many spotted horses" during the coming election campaign. Diefenbaker responded gratefully for "the greatest civic distinction to which any man or woman can

Duncan Macpherson, Toronto *Star*, 1963

"Somebody up there doesn't like us"

aspire...To be of London is to share in a stream of history that has enriched a quarter of the world's population within the Commonwealth and free men everywhere." Afterwards, the Diefenbakers were honoured guests at a Mansion House banquet featuring nine wines. "He raised a glass to his lips to respond to the frequent toasts," wrote Charles King of Southam Press, "but apparently enjoyed the hospitality less than other guests." The party returned overnight to a chilly Ottawa dawn.[25]

The Chief had been unsettled by jokes and gossip about his strained appearance and shaking hands, and in a gesture reminiscent of Dwight Eisenhower's 1956 campaign, he released a medical certificate at the end of February signed by two Toronto physicians testifying that he was in excellent health. "At no time," they affirmed, "during this or at past examinations has there been evidence of any chronic illness." The Winnipeg *Free Press*, among other papers, published a photograph of the medical certificate.[26]

"The 1963 election campaign," Diefenbaker recalled, "was one of the more uplifting experiences of my life...There was no question that everyone was against me but the people, and that unless I could find a way to get the message across, I would be lost."[27] So – inspired by Harry Truman's 1948 "Give 'em hell!" campaign – he decided to conduct a whistle-stop election, travelling as much as possible by train, stopping briefly at the little towns to mingle with the crowds that appeared in bitter cold to greet him. At Capreol, Ontario, on February 28, Diefenbaker spent twenty minutes on the station platform as the temperature hovered at –22F. When his train arrived in Prince Albert on March 2 – delayed by unscheduled stops at Hague, Rosthern, and Duck Lake – Diefenbaker descended to a home town welcome from the mayor and five hundred citizens. The more sedate and "prime ministerial" speaking style of 1962 was discarded for the evangelist's tones of 1958, mingling nostalgia, scorn, and humour with hints of paradise and hellfire. The ridicule was mostly reserved for Mike Pearson and the Liberals, since Diefenbaker knew that Wallace McCutcheon and the State Department were measuring every speech for signs of excessive or provocative outbursts of anti-Americanism.[28]

The prime minister felt alone on the campaign trail – and most of the time he was alone. Davie Fulton had gone to British Columbia; Donald Fleming was not running, although he stayed in Ottawa to manage cabinet business until April 8; Douglas Harkness was running, but at odds with his leader; George Hees had retired and departed the country for the duration; Pierre Sévigny fought the election as an independent Conservative; Ernest Halpenny had retired; and other ministers were tied down in tight contests in their own constituencies.

As usual, Diefenbaker had one speech – with infinite variations of order, emphasis, and anecdote – for six weeks of campaigning. It was fully elaborated at his Prince Albert nominating meeting on March 2 before an audience of a thousand. He recalled elections from his youth at Fort Carlton, when candidates of both parties travelled together to speak from the same platform – and the occasion, perhaps apocryphal, when the Conservative fell ill and the Liberal delivered both speeches. (The story was familiar, so applause and laughter smothered the punch line.) He spoke to those in his audience "whose fathers and mothers came to this country, came here as pioneers, came here to build a Canada, came here to join with all the races of men. One of my reasons for being in public life and I've said it from the earliest days, was the opportunity to be able to do something in order to bring about in this nation without regard to racial origin, while preserving the constitutional rights of the initial and primary races of this country...equality of opportunity, to remove discrimination whatever one's racial origin may be, to give to Canadians as a whole a pride of being Canadians, to remove that stigma that in the past existed that blood count constituted something in the nature of citizenship."

In the last election, the Liberals had claimed that Canada "was on the road to ruin...They downgraded Canada. They undermined Canada. They did it deliberately in order to destroy." In doing so, he said, they provoked the foreign exchange crisis that the Diefenbaker government had acted decisively to overcome. "And today Canada, as a result of our action, has the largest foreign exchange amount it has ever had in the history of this nation." His government had enriched prairie farmers by selling grain to China on credit, and China had repaid its debts on time.

Diefenbaker explained his defence policy as one that changed to suit rapidly changing circumstances. Why should he be criticized for that when Britain and the United States followed the same shifting policy? When Canada agreed to accept two Bomarc missile units, the United States planned to build thirty or forty launching sites to protect their Strategic Air Command bases. Now there were only six: two in Canada and four in the United States.

> We thought at the time the Bomarc was established, was set, that we'd meet the problem of the bomber. However, more and more it's becoming known and apparent that such a system is no longer effective.
>
> The people of Canada are being fooled, or an attempt is being made to fool them, by the Opposition...
>
> And the other day, the other day, the Secretary of Defense of the United States, Mr. McNamara, said, well, we're keeping these Bomarcs, in effect not

because they are any good, but after all, we paid for them. Ah...I wonder why it is these facts are concealed from the people. Mr. Pearson says: Well, we have commitments. I say to him, there are no commitments that this Government has failed to carry out. Agreements entered into when one state of fact exists, are they to be maintained regardless of changing conditions?

...

What did Mr. Pearson say? He said – Oh... I wish the Government would be consistent. These are his words, and I am quoting you. "In my view we should get out of the whole Bomarc operation." That's two years and a half ago. "The Bomarc operation...not only do we not think it is an effective weapon; our objection is the kind of defense it is, that kind of defense strategy it represents which we do not think will be effective, however effective the weapon may be." Work that out; play that on your ukulele!

First he says it is no good, and then he says however good it is and however effective, we don't believe in it. And then he went on to say this – just like in the old crown and anchor game, you pay your money and you take your choice. (Laughter) All right...(laughter). "If the United States wishes to continue that kind of protection with the Bomarc, let the United States do so and let us withdraw from that kind of continental defense." Now he says, "Canadians, we never break our commitments." I agree with that. We never have...

This is another one. I simply use his quotations to support the stand that we have consistently taken...

..."The Ottawa Government should end its evasion of responsibility by discharging its commitments. It can only do this by accepting nuclear warheads." Well, he told us all the time *not* to do that...Then he really came out with one..."You can only do this by accepting nuclear warheads," I said to myself, that sentence can't finish there. Because I know him. (Laughter.) I know him..."We would accept them. Then having accepted them, we would re-examine at once the whole basis of the Canadian defense policy so as to make it more realistic and effective for Canada than the present one." (Laughter.)

...They shouldn't be playing politics such as Mr. Pearson's been playing with an issue such as that, that affects the lives, the hopes, and the future of mankind. (Applause.)

That's the view we take...We're going to set out in detail at the earliest opportunity this whole question in simple form...

Insofar as Canadian soil is concerned, I set this forth before and I again set it forth. We shall place ourselves in a position, by agreement with the

United States, so that if war does come, or emergency takes place, we shall have available to us readily accessible nuclear weapons. But in the meantime we shall not have Canada used as a storage dump for nuclear weapons. (Applause...Hear! Hear!)[29]

If the government's policy was confusing, Diefenbaker had demonstrated – to the delight of his partisan audience – that the Liberal policy was equally if not more confusing. Both Diefenbaker and Pearson were hapless dancing puppets in this game. The grand folly of nuclear deterrence meant, for Canada, a defence that could be no defence, and a policy that defied logic. There was no more sense to be made of it.

Diefenbaker disposed easily of Robert Thompson. The Social Credit leader, he suggested, wanted to get rid of him because Thompson knew there were no Social Credit votes in the west as long as he remained prime minister.

Diefenbaker was exhilarated by the fight. "You know," he told his Prince Albert audience, "in nineteen hundred and forty-eight they said of Harry Truman, he had no chance in the election. All the press said that, or at least 90%. All the Gallup polls said that. Only one person believed that Harry Truman would win and that was his wife. I have my wife and an awful lot of others across Canada!"[30] As his train arrived in Winnipeg, the *Free Press* reported that the prime minister's weekend in Saskatchewan had been "a tonic" for him. "The two days of uncritical acclaim from the people in 'small-town Saskatchewan' unquestionably has strengthened him for the campaign which he gets underway in earnest in a Winnipeg rally tonight."[31]

Only four major newspapers supported the Conservatives in 1963: the Ottawa *Journal,* the Winnipeg *Tribune,* the Victoria *Colonist,* and Beaverbrook's Fredericton *Gleaner.* But as Diefenbaker moved slowly through the small towns to rallies in the big cities, he grew more and more convinced that "the people" were indeed on his side. The crowds were big and enthusiastic and laughing with him. Mike Pearson and his team – despite their appearance of solidity and efficiency, and the promise of an activist government and reconciliation with the United States – could not ignite the same passions. And in mid-March they made a damaging error. Diefenbaker put it down to "the Liberal high command," who "seemed to mistake our country for the United States":

Their Madison Avenue techniques came a cropper with their colouring books, white pigeons that flew off never to be seen again, and that never-to-be-forgotten "truth squad." Poor Judy LaMarsh! I had much fun with her in Moncton and Halifax. She had a specially designated table right down at the front of the hall so she could hear everything. Although the people thought she was a great joke, they also were offended by the impudence of those who had sent her to challenge the truth of my every statement. The Liberals quickly got the message and ended the Truth Squad in two days. Had they kept her on, however, we might well have picked up several extra constituencies.[32]

For Diefenbaker, mistaking Canada for the United States meant introducing too-slick electoral techniques, turning politics into a professionally managed game, and paying more attention to opinion in the big cities and the Oval Office than in Duck Lake. The Chief himself, as a keen student of American electoral politics, had made his own contributions in earlier years to the shift in campaign techniques, and this time he had no hesitation in comparing himself to Abraham Lincoln and Harry Truman. His real objection was not to American models and American influences, but to American influences of a certain kind: too much eastern sophistication, too much comfort with power, too many displays of arrogance, too close an association with the Kennedys and the eastern liberal establishment. The trouble for him was – as the polls showed – that John Kennedy was a real and powerful competitor for the allegiance of Canadians, and the beneficiary in this election was bound to be the Liberal Party.[33]

But Diefenbaker's emotional campaign, coupled with the general confusion about nuclear weapons and the American relationship, had stopped the Liberals cold. Their support in the polls fell, while Conservative strength held steady and Créditiste sentiment grew in rural Quebec.[34] Liberal expectations of a parliamentary majority faded. In desperation, Keith Davey and Walter Gordon persuaded Pearson to promise that a new Liberal government would begin its term with "sixty days of decision." Pearson was worn out, ill, and depressed, and by the end of March he wondered whether he could finish the campaign.[35] Diefenbaker gained renewal in his own exhausting journeys, soaking up strength from his audiences as he played endlessly on his simple themes.

President Kennedy did not want to assist Diefenbaker's re-election, but in what Theodore Draper described as "the almost chaotic state of the leadership circles in Washington," the right hand often did not know what the left hand was doing. At the end of March, the US Defense Department offered Diefenbaker a gift by releasing the transcript of secret testimony that Defense Secretary McNamara had given earlier in the month to the House Appropriations Subcommittee. In it, McNamara imprudently declared that the remaining Bomarc missile sites were expensive and ineffective, but once established, could be maintained at little cost. "At the very least," he testified, "they could cause the Soviets to target missiles against them and thereby increase their missile requirements or draw missiles onto these Bomarc targets that would otherwise be available for other targets." Too late, the White House ordered a clarification explaining that the statement did not refer to the two dispersed Canadian sites – but the damage was done. Diefenbaker pounced: "The Liberal party would have us put nuclear warheads on something that's hardly worth scrapping. What's it for? To attract the fire of the intercontinental missiles. North Bay – knocked out. La Macaza – knocked out. Never, never, never, never has there been a revelation equal to this. The whole bottom fell out of the Liberal program today. The Liberal policy is to make Canada a decoy for intercontinental missiles."[36]

While the White House sought to maintain its public show of neutrality throughout the Canadian election, Kennedy could not restrain his private feelings. After the January 30 press release, Pearson remained fearful that another ill-considered effort to help him might backfire, and his fears were well founded. In late March, while Pearson was addressing a Canadian Legion meeting in Edmonton, he received a message on the platform that there was a telephone call for him from the White House. Pearson's press spokesman Richard O'Hagan called back on the janitor's telephone to discover that the messenger was Max Freedman, the Washington correspondent of the Winnipeg *Free Press* and a close friend of the president. He had just had a private dinner with Kennedy, and he insisted that he must speak to Pearson. O'Hagan brought the demand onstage to Pearson. Knowlton Nash recounts the story:

> Mystified and alarmed, knowing what Diefenbaker might do with such information, Pearson followed the janitor to a basement office. Nervously, he picked up the phone. They spoke for fifteen minutes, with Freedman enjoying his role as middleman between Kennedy and Pearson, passing on the highlights of his conversation with the president that night and some of Kennedy's suggestions. "For God's sake, tell the president not to say anything," Pearson said. "I don't want any help from him. This would be awful."...
>
> "This was a narrow escape," Pearson later said, "since I knew there were people abroad in this land who would...insist that it was a deep dark American plot to take over the country via Pearson and the Liberals. To my relief, it never was reported; the janitor said nothing about the call."[37]

With Pearson's fresh warning (and the McNamara testimony) in mind, Kennedy's national security adviser McGeorge Bundy took renewed precautions on April 1 in a memorandum to the secretary of state and the secretary of defense:

> During this climactic week of the Canadian election campaign it is likely that intensified efforts will be made to implicate the United States in one way or another, especially by accusing us of trying to influence the outcome. The President wishes to avoid any appearance of interference, even by responding to what may appear to be untruthful, distorted, or unethical statements or actions.
>
> Will you, therefore, please insure that no one in your Departments, in Washington or in the field, says anything publicly about Canada until after the election without first clearing with the White House. This applies to all contacts with the press regardless of the degree of non-attribution.[38]

Bundy must have been thinking of at least two provocative incidents. One concerned the suspicious opening of an American diplomatic pouch in the Ottawa post office.[39] The other involved that familiar hot potato, the Rostow memorandum. On March 27 Charles Lynch of Southam Press reported in the Vancouver *Province* and the Ottawa *Citizen* that Prime Minister Diefenbaker had in his possession an uncomplimentary presidential briefing document from President Kennedy's 1961 visit to Ottawa.[40] By the time the *Citizen* used the story, two paragraphs had been added quoting Diefenbaker in Kelowna, British Columbia, as saying that the story was "completely false...I don't know where that story came from...I have to repudiate it."[41] The State Department informed the American Embassy in Ottawa that it should respond to inquiries with a standard line: "We do not intend to comment on any speculative newspaper stories during a Canadian election campaign," but it was watching every move with care.[42]

On April 1 Lynch published a second story on the document, indicating that Diefenbaker had confirmed its existence. "Sources" added that he was unlikely to use it in the closing days of the election campaign. On the White House copy of this report, there is a handwritten note to McGeorge Bundy: "Pretty clear use of the 'push' document without 'using' it."[43] That view was confirmed in a dispatch from Butterworth the next day, reporting that Lynch had indicated that his source was Diefenbaker himself.[44] Butterworth wondered why there had been no editorial comment in Canada, and concluded that "this is simply too hot a story to handle since it involves question good faith in personal relations between Canadian Prime Minister and Chief of State of Canada's major ally." As a result, the public had been left with an impression that there had been an American threat to "bring economic pressure on Canada in effort get nuclear warheads on Canadian soil. Moreover no one has publicly asked why...there has not been explanation how document acquired or why it was not promptly returned. We are now getting worst of both worlds."

The State Department commented to Bundy that Butterworth wanted consideration of an American response. But State's inclination was to do nothing "unless Mr. Diefenbaker makes use of it in the next three days." Any American statement "would have to be very carefully weighed at the highest level, since any action would cause a sensation in Canada, with unpredictable results."[45] Over the next few days the White House considered several possibilities: publication of the full document, continuing refusal to comment, or a conditional "no comment at this time," which might imply a clarification after the election. Bundy's White House aide considered that Diefenbaker's most likely move on his "crooked path" would be to make selective references to part of the document on the evening of Friday, April 5. They would likely be sufficiently misleading to confirm the impression that the memo referred to pressures on Canada to accept nuclear weapons for storage. To respond in time, Washington would have to intervene before the Saturday morning newspapers went to press. The "tentatively agreed policy of this government" was to release the document from the White House "with a very brief comment designed to note in low key the unethical conduct of the Canadian Government in retaining and then disclosing the document," but the author urged instead a policy of "no comment at this time." Even a "gently chiding" release might be counterproductive in Canada, while a temporary "no comment" would confirm American neutrality in the election and also create "an air of mystery, as though we had a load of dynamite which we could easily detonate if we were not so determined to stay out of the campaign, especially in its closing hours."[46] By this time all the variations on Washington's "non-intervention" were being weighed as forms of intervention, calculated not to assist Diefenbaker and not to harm Pearson. For the moment, the White House simply waited.

Diefenbaker made no mention of the document on April 5, but by Saturday morning the story was blossoming. Peter Trueman of the Montreal *Star* and George Bain of the Toronto *Globe and Mail* both reported from Washington that the document had been written by Walt Rostow for the president and that it "contained at least one pencilled notation in the margin in the president's own hand." Bain identified the comment as: "What are we to say to the...on this point?" while Trueman quoted the words as: "What do we do with the...now?" (Both papers politely excised the epithet.) Bain said that the document contained no threats, and that "the Canadian government's purpose in retaining the document seems to have been to use it as a diplomatic lever." Washington's complaint was that there had been "a serious breach of diplomatic courtesy...in making use of a mislaid private document." The existence of the memorandum, he said, "did enter into diplomatic communications, perhaps through the United States ambassador having been informed."[47]

After these reports, the White House adopted another line of response: selective but full confidential briefings for a few correspondents, but no public statements. The first result was a dispatch by the New York *Times*'s James Reston, published in the Montreal *Star* (but not in the *Times*) on election day, April 8. It reported that Washington "is full of rumors that the prime minister's staff has been using a secret United States document as an instrument in his campaign for re-election." Reston said that a Washington *Post* reporter had told his paper that the missing phrase from Saturday's stories (supposedly in the president's handwriting) was "S.O.B." But "the report of Presidential anger seems to most observers here to be unlikely," since Washington's annoyance with Diefenbaker had arisen only recently over the issue of nuclear arms. That subject "was not in controversy then." "Besides," Reston added, "if anybody in Canada can read President Kennedy's handwriting, it is more than anybody in Washington has been able to do. In this city, most people find it almost impossible even to decipher his signature." What was true was that "Canadian-American relations have been poisoned by one incident after another." And "the very fact that Mr. Diefenbaker could have threatened to use the working paper in the 1962 election has inevitably entered into estimates here of the working relations between the two governments." Diefenbaker's office had refused to comment to the New York *Times* about any marginal comments on the memo by the president. In Washington, Reston judged, there was only one general conclusion: "The document should, as a matter of diplomatic courtesy, have been returned to the State Department."[48]

In the end, it seemed, the prime minister's surreptitious use of the Rostow memorandum in the last week of the election campaign was of no noticeable benefit to him. Washington, in its response by proxy, managed to make its effective point that Diefenbaker was the one who had committed the diplomatic offence. For those who noticed, the contretemps probably served to harden existing political commitments, both for and against the prime minister. He was either a courageous white knight or a blackguard. And Kennedy had not used the expletive deleted.[49]

On the last weekend of the campaign another unusual incident caused disturbance for Walton Butterworth and Mike Pearson, but it came too late to make any impact on the vote. On April 6 the Vancouver *Sun* published a story by the Southam reporter Bruce Phillips suggesting that "the Conservatives have a document so hot even they are afraid to use it, a document purporting to be a letter from American Ambassador Walton Butterworth to Liberal chieftain Pearson telling him the Conservatives are unfit to govern Canada." The party, Phillips said, had had the letter for "about two weeks," but had been "uneasy about using it because they did not know where the splinters would hit when the explosion came." The letter, dated January 14, offered congratulations to Pearson for his speech advocating the acceptance of nuclear warheads for Canadian weapons. Butterworth, he said, had learned of the existence of the letter and had called the cabinet secretary, Robert Bryce, to deny having written it. Pearson, too, vehemently denied its authenticity. Phillips reported that the letter "came into the hands" of George Drew in London, who forwarded it to Canada, but he explained nothing more about its provenance.[50] The case looked suspiciously like that of the Rostow memorandum. Had the government provided this document, too, to a friendly reporter for use without attribution?

What made the incident more outrageous for Butterworth was that the letter was a forgery. Using it was a kind of dirty trick unfamiliar in Canadian politics or in the recent history of Canadian-American relations. Butterworth asked the State Department to pursue the issue with Canada, but in the aftermath of the election, Washington decided to let the matter rest "and hopefully disappear with other flotsam and jetsam cast up by the campaign." Butterworth accepted the decision but protested to the State Department that it was mistaken: "What concerns me...is lest this be an indication that the Department is reverting to its old ways of treating Canada like a problem child for whom there was always at the ready a cheek for the turning...I do hope that in future we will deal with Canada with considered care and courtesy but in a more normal, matter-of-fact manner, and with due regard to the importance of obtaining quids for quos."[51]

Diefenbaker's account of the incident was disingenuous. Afterwards, in the memoirs, he wrote as though the letter had not been used in the campaign, and regretted that "not using it constituted a major political error." He claimed to have "confidential knowledge, which will be revealed in due course, that it was a true copy," but there appears to be no documentary evidence for the claim. Diefenbaker reproduced the entire letter in the memoirs and noted that after receiving it in late March he consulted Howard Green and Gordon Churchill about establishing its authenticity. Since there was no time to establish whether or not it was a forgery, he reported an honourable decision not to use it.[52]

The record, all of it available to Diefenbaker, looks less edifying. The letter, in photostat and postmarked March 20, 1963, was originally mailed to George Drew in London from an English address. Drew called Grattan O'Leary to warn him he had a "hot document," and dispatched it that day to Diefenbaker. Soon afterwards the prime minister met O'Leary and urged him to publish it in the Ottawa *Journal*. Drew had warned Diefenbaker that the letter "could be of vital importance if its authenticity were verified, and it could be extremely dangerous if by any chance it is an attempt to plant something which could obviously boomerang very badly." O'Leary thought it was a forgery and refused to publish it; Camp shared his scepticism. Diefenbaker kept the letter and discussed it with Allister Grosart, who passed on the story to the publisher of the Winnipeg *Tribune*, Ross Munro. Munro called Butterworth, who called Bryce to make his denial. And Bryce relayed the report back to Diefenbaker on his campaign train in western Canada.

Meanwhile, Diefenbaker had brought Howard Green and Gordon Churchill into his secret. He proposed to Green that he should return to Ottawa to "call in the Ambassador and ask him who wrote the letter. Howard was disturbed by the suggestion. I then suggested that he secure examples of signatures of the Ambassador, to which he replied that that would arouse suspicion." Another dead end. Diefenbaker "thus turned the investigation over" to Gordon Churchill. Formally, Diefenbaker had taken his distance. What followed was publication in a small Manitoba newspaper, from which Bruce Phillips picked up the story for Southam News.

Later the RCMP examined the copy and determined that there were no typewriters in Butterworth's office to match the one used in the letter. There were other anomalies, too. Diefenbaker believed that the RCMP commissioner had given Butterworth sufficient notice of his search to remove the incriminating machine, and he continued to insist that the letter was genuine. The point of this insistence, in face of the evidence, is obscure, unless Diefenbaker felt an unacknowledged responsibility for use of the letter – and an inability to admit he could have been wrong.[53]

The Diefenbakers returned as usual to home ground in Prince Albert for election day, while the Pearsons remained in Ottawa. As the count moved westwards that evening, Liberal hopes for a majority were raised and then lowered. Newfoundland delivered all seven of its seats to Pearson, but Diefenbaker held his ground in the Maritime provinces. In Quebec the Créditistes retained twenty seats, while the Liberals gained only twelve and the Conservatives lost six. In Ontario the Liberals picked up eight ridings from the Tories – not an overwhelming shift. At the Manitoba border Pearson had 119 seats (only thirteen short of an absolute majority), but there his bandwagon stalled. In seventy western and northern races, he won only ten, while Diefenbaker took forty-seven (for a loss of only two seats). At the final count Diefenbaker had 95 seats to Pearson's 129. Social Credit and the NDP held the balance, with twenty-four and nineteen seats, respectively. The Liberal Party had consolidated its strength in the cities, while Diefenbaker's Tory party settled more firmly into its rural and western strongholds. Only Quebec broke the national pattern, where Social Credit lost some areas of rural strength but achieved 15 percent infiltration into Montreal in several working-class neighbourhoods.[54]

Diefenbaker told a television interviewer on election night that the result reminded him of 1925, when Prime Minister King had lost by a plurality to Arthur Meighen's Conservatives, but "had decided, as was his right, to meet Parliament on the basis that no party had a majority."[55] That seemed only a bit of mischievous talk designed to keep the Liberals on edge. By the next day Churchill, Hamilton, Grosart, McCutcheon, Frost, and others were urging the government's resignation, and Diefenbaker accepted the choice. He was ready to face the Liberals as opposition leader, and nursed his resentments for later use. As he prepared for his flight to Ottawa on April 10, he told a Saskatchewan friend: "I went down there to see what I could do for the common people and the big people finished me – the most powerful interests." But he made no public statement about his intentions, beyond indicating that he would "watch eventualities."[56]

On April 12, in mysterious circumstances, six Créditiste MPs delivered a sworn affidavit to the governor general and to Mike Pearson declaring that the Liberal Party had the right to form the next government and promising their voting support to that government. Pearson had his absolute majority. Diefenbaker concluded that "there were no further eventualities for me to wait upon," and arranged to meet Pearson to agree upon the transfer of power. At noon on Monday, April 22, John G. Diefenbaker was succeeded as prime minister by Lester Bowles Pearson.[57]

FOR THE NEXT FEW WEEKS JOHN AND OLIVE WERE PREOCCUPIED WITH THE MOVE from 24 Sussex Drive to Stornoway, the house provided for the leader of the opposition, taking two of their household staff with them. On the evening before their move, Diefenbaker told his brother, "Olive made a discovery. We thought we had emptied every drawer and for some reason she looked at the desk in my room on which the TV was placed and found two extra drawers in the back of the desk which I had completely forgotten about which revealed quite a number of letters which would not have been fitting for our successors to read."[58] The move was trying. Diefenbaker wrote: "I am hoping we can go West because there is quite a bit of furniture that should be shipped down here as 'Stornoway' is anything but equipped. We have had to buy a washing machine, dryer and all the kitchen equipment and there will be about $1000.00 in odds and ends of furniture that we will have to purchase. The only room that is properly equipped is my office and library which Olive has fixed up most attractively...It is almost six years since I had my hands on the wheel of a car so I will have to take some lessons before I get a license. I simply can't exist by depending on taxis." Within a few weeks, Olive had taken her driving test and acquired a licence, "so we will be able to get around a lot easier than we have since moving," but in July "she was fortunate that she wasn't injured when the car went over the sidewalk into a plate glass window. She was very calm about it." Subsequently, the Diefenbakers were provided with a chauffeur, who took delivery of their new Buick Wildcat from General Motors in Oshawa on October 4. "It is a Canadian-made car," John told Elmer, "and while we would have preferred a better Buick felt that we must not purchase a car manufactured outside Canada."[59]

The Diefenbakers returned from a short trip to Saskatoon and Prince Albert in mid-May to find their surroundings more comfortable. "While we were away," John wrote, "the staff at the house worked very hard and got everything in readiness. As soon as some of the furnishings that we had shipped from Prince Albert arrive here it will become very homelike." Ten days later he was still adjusting to the life of an ordinary citizen: "Olive is still working on the house. Some of the furniture came from Prince Albert although the cost was very high. The freight on the bedroom suite was $400.00 and the cost of moving from 24 Sussex to our present address was over $650. A third-rate plumber did some work for us and charged us at the rate of $4.50 per hour. All these charges are far beyond anything that could have been imagined a few years ago." Diefenbaker paid them out of his own pocket.[60]

The adjustment of routine was substantial but less trying. "It is far less work being Leader of the Opposition than Prime Minister," he wrote on May 24, "and I am getting a great deal of rest and also more reading done than has been possible."[61] Diefenbaker observed the NATO ministerial meeting in Ottawa in May with resentment. "We invited them but the new Government does the entertaining and is receiving the applause. Lord Home went out of his way yesterday to build up Mr. Pearson by saying, in effect, that he became Prime Minister because he wanted Canada to be a good ally. Several of my colleagues are most annoyed at this because I refrained at all times from making political speeches in London that would criticize the Government or assist the Opposition."[62]

As the new Pearson government adjusted to office, settled its commitment to take nuclear warheads for Canadian weapons, appointed the Royal

Commission on Bilingualism and Biculturalism, stumbled through its first budget debate, and confronted a disturbing wave of terrorist bombings in Montreal, Diefenbaker was preoccupied with his own position in the party and the country. Pearson regarded his opponent with distaste: "There is certainly going to be lots of unpleasantness in the House," he wrote to his son on May 26. "D. is very nasty and cannot conceal his frustrations. He misses the pomp and prestige of office greatly and obviously."[63] Diefenbaker's former newspaper supporters kept up their complaints. At the end of May he told Elmer: "The 'Globe & Mail' and 'Telegram,' and to a lesser extent until today, the 'Gazette,' are spending their time in personal criticism, for certain of the big interests have determined that there must be a change of the leadership of the Conservative Party." Diefenbaker saw this criticism as a continuation of the winter conspiracy: "It is more than a coincidence that Davie Fulton was here on Monday and this is the third time that such a visit has been followed by an article by Arthur Blakely. However, I have got no intention whatsoever of falling in line with their plans and schemes. They should have learned that many years ago."[64] A week later he reported further: "Dave Walker gave a dinner on Wednesday night for the Conservative members of the Senate and the House of Commons and he made a typically frank speech except he told them they would not have been there if it had not been for me, much to my embarrassment. However, when speaking I pointed out that I had no intention of falling in line with the desires of the Liberal Party to get me out of the leadership with an assist from a few of my former colleagues."[65]

During the next six months there were frequent calls in the party – centred in Ontario and Quebec – for a leadership review. Diefenbaker put them down at first to the inspiration of Davie Fulton who, he believed, "is doing his best to bring about a Convention – under cover work by him always seems to come to light!" Just before a meeting of the Conservative executive in October, Diefenbaker received reports that George Hees's aide, Mel Jack, was coordinating efforts to remove him from the leadership by the spring of 1964, while "Fulton and his people" continued their activities. "I am more definitely set than ever before against resigning no matter what they may do," he told Elmer. "It is going to be a big fight and when these great and powerful financial interests determine a course of action they exert a tremendous influence. I beat them before and intend to do so again." In November the Chief commented publicly that "you don't have leadership conventions unless there is a vacancy. I am the leader and there is no vacancy." Within the organization, he strengthened his own position by installing Gordon Churchill as national director and the former MP Richard Thrasher as national secretary.[66]

Dalton Camp told the party executive in October: "I supported the Conservative Party and its Leader, Mr. Diefenbaker, because I believed them to be right in all the issues vital to the country. Indeed, the greater the issue, the more right they were. Far from apologizing for my personal stand, I exult in it. In fact, I celebrate it with each passing day." The leader had distinguished himself in the campaign. "Men in adversity do not always react the same. Thus, one of the prime qualities of leadership is personal courage. Those of us who saw Mr. Diefenbaker at close range during the campaign could not help but admire his courage, and could not help but be inspired by it. From the time he set out, we at Headquarters heard from him neither complaint, nor criticism, nor any discouragement. Even had he been wrong in what he stood for, it would have been a distinct privilege to have been associated with such courage."

Now Camp declared that the party, "singularly blessed by the remarkable incompetence of those who succeeded us in office," must seize its chances. That meant, paradoxically, engaging in "free expression and fresh thought within the Party itself...In the process of making a god of our Leader, we made sheep of ourselves...A healthy candor and a free exchange of thoughts are needed – should be encouraged – and must, in my opinion, be the purging influence resolving our present unresolved business. But I am not prepared to listen to those who would speak on Friday and leave us on Saturday, unless we do as we're told." This was a call to the faithful as skilfully ambiguous as one from Diefenbaker himself. The Chief took particular note of one paragraph, in which Camp called on the executive "to reunite this Party in mind and spirit. Surely, there must be more inviting targets on which to fix our aim than on one another. I would rather fight Grits than Tories...it is only self-inflicted wounds that are slow to heal and that can be mortal."[67]

For two weeks in September Olive and John travelled to Italy, Egypt, and Israel, with brief stopovers in Greece and Switzerland, enjoying the privileges of an elder statesman and opposition leader. They were accompanied by Diefenbaker's Commons colleague and physician, Dr P.B. Rynard. The trip was refreshing, and the leader returned to Ottawa for the reopening of parliament determined to confront both Liberal and Conservative opponents. Two provincial elections offered him mixed signals about the state of the party. In Ontario, John Robarts's Conservatives received an overwhelming mandate despite the active participation of federal Liberal ministers in the campaign, while in British Columbia Davie Fulton's Tories faced what Diefenbaker called "a frightful defeat" at the hands of W.A.C. Bennett's Social Credit Party, winning no seats and only 11 percent of the popular vote. In Diefenbaker's view that left Fulton with idle hands, which he would undoubtedly turn to the fight against the federal party leader. Diefenbaker thought he could handle that. The Ontario result, along with his own large correspondence, gave him hope that there was "a widely felt antagonism" to the Pearson government. The Chief planned to recommence war on two fronts, with speaking engagements across the country leading up to the annual meeting of the party in Ottawa in January 1964.[68]

At the end of October, Peter C. Newman's book *Renegade in Power: The Diefenbaker Years* was published to widespread publicity and immediately became a bestseller. Diefenbaker denied having read it, but told Elmer on October 31 that the book was "a terrible piece of muckraking and slander. I am considering commencing action for libel. It is full of falsehoods. I am told that some wealthy people in high places provided the finances for its publication and there is some evidence to support this fact."[69] Two advisers provided him with commentaries on the book, both emphasizing the inappropriate depiction of Diefenbaker as a "renegade" – by definition, "one who has deserted party or principles." "In the case of the Right Honourable Leader of the Opposition," one declared, "his principles have followed a strong, clear line from his first entry into politics until now. There has been no deviation. The title is part of the Liberal Party policy followed in the case of every Conservative Leader, of character assassination." But the other saw advantage in the name: "The book publishers – McClelland and Stewart – have added the title for box office purposes...As 'renegade' is a fighting word, the Conservatives will get all the benefit from having their supporters worked up to anger. In short, John Diefenbaker will enjoy a fresh windfall of sympathy votes...The immediate advantage to the Conservative Party is that Newman's book has brought John Diefenbaker to front page attention on a scale far beyond anything that could be contrived." The critic noted that – although the book contained "pure inventions of the kind dreamed up in after-hours drinking in the press gallery" – it portrayed Diefenbaker as "an extremely human person, a vivid and alive personality, and the recognizable hero of the Canadian scene." The story made him "the true Alger-series hero – poor, decent origins; family long associated with Canadian history; lost in the blizzard with Uncle Ed!...it is the legendary material that will get into the school books of future generations of Canadians." The legislative record was impressive, and the claim that Diefenbaker was indecisive merely showed that Newman "does not understand the process of decision in a parliamentary democracy." The public, the commentator thought, would absorb the legend and reject the author's bias; the book was based on "hearsay and guesswork, and...backstairs gossip"; its claims were unsubstantiated.[70]

Diefenbaker, too, was offended by the title. "Never has such an epithet been used in connection with one who has occupied the position of Prime Minister," he wrote in his random speech notes. "I leave the judgement of my course and my actions to the Canadian people. They will decide – you will decide whether that epithet 'renegade' is one that can fittingly be applied to one who has devoted his life without thought of reward to the service of this country. Like George Washington I say that my only regret is that I have only one life to give to my country. But my reputation I have always preserved intact...Sometimes these things hurt."[71] Elmer comforted him with lashing insults against Newman, and reported that he was spreading the word against the author. While visiting the University Hospital in Saskatoon, he had told a woman who wanted the book that it was "published by the Liberal Party as vile propaganda and the proceeds are to be used as campaign funds for the Liberal Party. I don't want you to waste your money." The woman had replied: "I am so glad you told me that." Elmer judged that "a person might as well fight back all the way." A week later he added: "We'll have to see that a decent book is written in your favor. I have quite a few notes – I jot them down when I think about them. These notes are not in order, but when I get them to-gether, I'll send you some more material."[72]

Diefenbaker consulted David Walker about whether he might have a case for libel, but decided instead to maintain his public silence and let his friends fight the battle of publicity. He was most satisfied by Michael Wardell's long "Reply to Newman" in the Fredericton *Daily Gleaner*. "The book is a sparkling affair that is already a best seller, and deservedly," wrote Wardell, "but it seems, in a way, an exercise in schizophrenia. Between the first part of the book and the rest of it there is a marked disconnection of thought and expression. The first part is a masterful historical summary of the formative years of Diefenbaker, from his beginnings as a small-town lawyer...to his becoming Prime Minister of Canada in 1957. The remainder of the book is a tirade of denunciation, execration and scarification. There are no contrasts of lights and shades; only bitter unrelieved black...The result is so patently biased, so unfair, and so reckless as to defeat its own ends, and bring sympathy to the subject rather than censure." Wardell shared the Chief's conviction that reporters, including Newman, and the CBC had seen the Conservative government through the eyes of the Liberal Party, and had thus been engaged, in Newman's words, in "an unpatriotic conspiracy, probably Liberal-inspired." Despite them all, Diefenbaker's policies had proved to be "good, solid, common sense." Wardell concluded with a call for loyalty: "If I were a Conservative politician, which I am not, I would stake my faith in Diefenbaker. I would expel the traitors from my Party, I would turn my back on the faint hearts, and I would go forward with my trust in the only man who can hope to lead my Party to victory. And I would bring these great issues to the test next spring."[73]

Renegade in Power was the first and most successful of a new Canadian genre, the journalist's dramatic summary of a political era. As much as anything Diefenbaker himself could do, the book helped to create the legend of a Canadian folk hero.

George Grant gave philosophic weight to the Diefenbaker legend when he published his *Lament for a Nation: The Defeat of Canadian Nationalism* in the spring of 1965. In counterpoint to Creighton's *Macdonald*, which had celebrated Canada's beginning, Grant lamented its end. For Grant, the dream of a North American alternative to American liberal, corporate society had been impossible. Diefenbaker was the nation's last, half-blind defender, an inadequate tragic hero acting with courage and instinctive wisdom in a hopeless cause. Paradoxically, *Lament for a Nation* made Diefenbaker a historical figure of consequence and – perhaps surprisingly – gave inspiration to a new generation of intellectual nationalists who made their influence felt in all three national parties during the decade that followed. In Grant's prose the legend had taken wing.

As he was mythologized, so he was demonized. In 1964, wrote John Saywell, Canada was a country divided over language and regionalism, in which traditions, loyalties, and views of the nation were in conflict. Parliament was wounded and, in the eyes of many, antiquated; and yet, puzzlingly, the men in it "were of an unusually high calibre. To resolve the paradox many observers were forced to conclude that the political and parliamentary process lay at the mercy of one man, whose natural desire to return to office and whose simplistic view of the nation's problems threatened to do irreparable damage to his party, if not to his country."[74]

As the year began, Diefenbaker toured the country denouncing Liberal approaches to national unity, pleading that Canada was one nation, not two. An element in that campaign was his effort to silence Conservative critics of his own leadership before the annual meeting of the party association at the beginning of February. In mid-January a Quebec constituency association circulated a letter to all constituency associations urging support for a leadership convention in 1964; and in Toronto, John Bassett and others promoted a vote of confidence in the leader to be conducted by secret ballot at the annual meeting. Diefenbaker's approach to criticism was almost the same as it had always been. He expected loyalty. He did not engage in extended negotiation with his opponents, but appealed beyond them to the broader party he had created, talking in vague terms of "the Toronto clique," or "the financial interests," or "the Warwicks of the Conservative Party" who opposed him. He did not attempt to organize or direct his own campaign of support, beyond falling in with one crucial encounter arranged by David Walker and Ted Rogers. Just before Christmas in 1963 he accepted an invitation to dinner at the Rogers home, where John Bassett would also be present. He told Elmer that "I am not looking forward to it in sweet contemplation. However, if I see him and there is no change in his attitude I will feel that I have done everything possible." That meeting led to another, private one in early January, which Diefenbaker thought had "turned out very well...Time will tell but I am hopeful that after the Annual Meeting the Telegram may decide to come back to the Progressive Conservative party. If it does that will be beneficial."[75]

The meeting apparently resulted in a real and crucial compromise. When Diefenbaker addressed the annual meeting on February 4, 1964, and called for the expected vote of confidence in his leadership, he told delegates that he was ready to accept a secret ballot if that was what they wished. The same day the lead editorial in the *Telegram*, titled "Day of Decision," called for an overwhelming vote of confidence in Diefenbaker – "whether it is a standing show of hands or a secret ballot."[76] Those two changes of position weakened the opposition to Diefenbaker. The motion for a secret ballot was defeated by three to one, and the motion of confidence, in an open vote, carried almost unanimously. About thirty opponents, including Douglas Harkness and J.M. Macdonnell, stood prominently together to register their dissent amid taunts from the leader's supporters. More abstained from voting. Diefenbaker thought he had disposed of the challenge for good, but that was clearly wishful thinking. "We cannot believe," commented the *Globe and Mail*, "that it is the end of the story, that a great party has really resigned itself to go into the next election behind a man who has proved he cannot lead." Even the *Telegram* remained sceptical of a leader who still failed to appreciate that "the job of restoring the party's fortunes demands conciliatory gestures on both sides." But Michael Wardell's Fredericton *Gleaner* judged that the endorsement of Diefenbaker was a "big decision, a noble, correct and triumphant one."[77]

To avoid damaging defections from the Quebec wing of the party, Diefenbaker attended a meeting of the Quebec caucus the next day and endorsed Léon Balcer as his Quebec lieutenant and "provincial leader of the federal party in Quebec." Balcer, he roundly declared, was a modern George-Etienne Cartier to his own Macdonald, and he would live in history. When the House of Commons opened two weeks later, Diefenbaker had rearranged the party's seating to place Balcer beside him on the front bench. But he denied that Balcer held the position of deputy leader or chief lieutenant. Balcer expressed his puzzlement to reporters.[78]

As a further symbol of reconciliation, the annual meeting elected Dalton Camp as the new president of the party, succeeding Diefenbaker's critic Egan Chambers. In his acceptance speech, Camp declared that the national association must be "in the service of the Parliamentary Party. Their policy must be our policy. And their leadership is ours, to be sustained and championed, supported and upheld." That was, precisely, the view of John Diefenbaker, who knew that his strongest supporters were in the parliamentary caucus.[79] But under Camp's inspiration the party was also thinking ahead, planning for renewed communication between party and leader – which he promised would be "cordial...confidential...candid" – and for a policy conference modelled on the Liberal Party's 1960 Kingston conference.

Paralleling Diefenbaker's political activity, the legend-making proceeded. In March the CBC presented Douglas Leiterman's hour-long profile *The Chief*, an engagingly sympathetic portrait of Diefenbaker in his home-town surroundings of Prince Albert, or fishing in deerstalker cap and dufflecoat, wry, witty, and unpretentious, the man of the people he had always declared himself to be. The film was an early and outstanding example of the techniques of *cinema vérité* then being pioneered by Canadian filmmakers with their new, lightweight cameras, telephoto lenses, and compact sound equipment. Leiterman said that the image of Diefenbaker had "the ring of truth," and his audiences believed it. The image contrasted vividly with the picture of attractive but bumbling incompetence and disorder conveyed by D.A. Pennebaker's film *Mr. Pearson*, which was temporarily withheld from showing on the CBC later in the year amid accusations of improper news management against the Liberal government.[80]

Prime Minister Pearson opened the 1964 session of parliament with emphasis on his party's plans for parliamentary reform, cooperation with the provinces, and "full partnership" among English- and French-speaking Canadians. Diefenbaker criticized the cabinet for irresolution, incoherence, and creeping centralization.[81] On February 25 the government scraped through a vote on a Conservative amendment by a vote of 128 to 120, when three Social Crediters and two New Democrats gave the cabinet its slight margin. For two months the House occupied itself with petty and raucous debate on interim supply, the estimates, and an unexciting budget, with repeated conflict over the timetable. The press blamed both the government for poor management and the opposition leader for persistent obstruction – which Diefenbaker denied as "a baseless and empty alibi."[82] He was enjoying the combat and hoping to defeat the government.

The issue that preoccupied the House for most of the year, perturbed the country, and brought fresh disturbance to the Conservative Party was put on the agenda by Pearson in May. He chose the annual convention of the Royal Canadian Legion in Winnipeg to announce that his government would propose a Canadian flag "designed around the Maple Leaf." Legion members were not appeased by his assurance that the Union Jack would remain as a symbol of the monarchy and membership in the Commonwealth, and they booed him lustily. The press in English-speaking Canada interpreted the prime minister's decision primarily as a bow to French-speaking sensitivities, either endorsing it as an act of statesmanship or denouncing it as craven pandering. In the face of widespread criticism – including Joey Smallwood's ultimatum that the Union Jack or the Red Ensign must share equal place as Canada's second flag – the government introduced two balanced resolutions on May 27: one provided for a maple leaf flag, along with maintenance of the Union Jack as the royal and Commonwealth flag of Canada; the other declared "O Canada" the national anthem and "God Save the Queen" the royal anthem of Canada. That compromise alienated some Quebec members of the Liberal caucus and antagonized the Créditistes, while failing to satisfy traditionalist Tories. The government was probably saved from initial defeat by the Speaker's decision to split the flag resolution into two separate votes.

The party leaders established their positions in three days of debate in mid-June. Prime Minister Pearson reiterated his faith in a maple leaf design; Diefenbaker denounced the proposal as a source of disunity and a distraction from "the chaos and confusion of the government," and called for a national referendum; Tommy Douglas appealed for calm and delay; and Réal Caouette praised Pearson's courage and opposed the Union Jack. Diefenbaker and many members of his caucus confirmed their position as die-hard supporters of the Red Ensign, and when debate was resumed in August it was clear that they were prepared for an endless filibuster. Léon Balcer and his Quebec colleagues sought some middle ground, and after a month of futility the parties agreed to refer the issue to a committee of fifteen to report within six weeks. Diefenbaker warned that his party would insist on unlimited debate on the committee's recommendation unless it reported virtually unanimously – but that seemed impossible because four of its Conservative members were committed to the Red Ensign.[83]

With the flag debate temporarily sidetracked, the House had a productive autumn, adopting a non-partisan redistribution bill and several major reforms in House of Commons procedure and organization. In October Diefenbaker and his colleague Erik Nielsen – a tough and honest Yukon lawyer who had entered the House in 1957 – led attacks on the government with charges that it had assisted the secret departure from the country of the longshoremen's union leader Hal Banks (who was being sought on criminal charges), and that Banks had contributed to Liberal campaign funds. The minister of justice and Liberal House leader, Guy Favreau, stumbled in defending the government's case. At the end of November, once again, Nielsen and Diefenbaker pounced on Favreau. The minister, they said, had failed to consult his legal officers before deciding not to prosecute a senior ministerial staff member for offering a bribe to obtain bail for the Montreal drug dealer Lucien Rivard; and Favreau had not informed Pearson of involvement by his own parliamentary secretary. Nielsen had prepared carefully and informed Favreau of his concerns in advance, in the hope of avoiding a partisan attack on the minister, but Favreau had taken no action. Once questions were asked, Pearson agreed to establish a judicial inquiry and dismissed the persons implicated, but he left Favreau dangling by failing, day after day, to correct a misstatement he had made about when Favreau informed him of the affair. Finally he did so, not in the House, but in a letter to Mr Justice Frédéric Dorion, the chairman of the inquiry.

Simultaneously, the Conservatives and the NDP raised serious charges of impropriety against two more Quebec ministers, René Tremblay and Maurice Lamontagne. They were politically crippled, but Pearson kept them in cabinet for another year. In January 1965 Pearson dismissed Yvon Dupuis, his minister without portfolio, who had been charged with accepting a bribe. The Liberal cabinet was shaken by these repeated indications of scandal and incompetence, all of them implicating Québécois ministers and all of them handled ineptly by Prime Minister Pearson. The leader of the opposition relished the atmosphere of attack, and – in Liberal eyes – enhanced his reputation as an evil genius.[84]

Pearson, who had always disliked the parliamentary battle, was driven to distraction by Diefenbaker's unyielding pursuit. In discouragement, Pearson let what now seemed to be his hatred of Diefenbaker carry him too far. On December 4, 1964, Diefenbaker received a letter from the prime minister, delivered at home by special messenger. It opened portentously:

> In discharge of my constitutional duty as Prime Minister, I am writing this letter to you as a Privy Councillor and former Prime Minister.
>
> I have been much concerned, not only about allegations made recently in a particular case, the Rivard case, but, even more, about an attitude toward the operation of the law that certain evidence in this case discloses. This

attitude is not widespread but the Rivard case illustrates the need to take thorough action to remove it.

The problem has not sprung up suddenly. In order to assess the need for corrective action, I have asked for a full report of instances in the last ten years or so in which political intervention was involved in investigations. This information will enable me to see how such matters could and should be dealt with.

One case (the Munsinger case) has given me very grave concern. It affects the security of the country. In 1960–61, a Minister who occupied a position of great responsibility in the Government was involved in a liaison which clearly endangered security.

I have been greatly disturbed by the lack of attention which, insofar as the file indicates, this matter received. The Minister was left in his position of trust.

I have decided that I cannot, in the public interest, let the matter lie where it was left and that I must ask the R.C.M. Police to pursue further enquiries.

I recognize that the file before me may not disclose all the steps that were taken. In view of this, it is my duty to write to you about the matter in case you might be in a position to let me know that the enquiries were pursued and the safeguards that were taken reached further than the materials before me would indicate. That material now indicates that the Minister of Justice brought the matter to your attention and that no action was taken.

Because national security is involved, this is the most serious and disturbing of the matters that have been brought to my attention. But I assure you that all incidents during the last ten years are being thoroughly examined and will be followed up without fear or favour if and when the evidence requires it.

If there is further information you can provide about the Munsinger case, I will be grateful if you will let me know.[85]

Pearson told Bruce Hutchison in February 1965 that he had called in the commissioner of the RCMP and asked to see "all the files you have on every MP since 1956."[86] The fishing expedition was a violation of cabinet convention and political decency unprecedented in Canadian history. Diefenbaker's excesses were matched by this one. Pearson's letter to Diefenbaker, reporting his discovery of the Munsinger file and his "very grave concern" about the apparent lack of attention Diefenbaker had given it, contained an implied threat that the information might be used against the ex–prime minister. Pearson's purpose – as he admitted to Hutchison – was "that if he was aware that I knew about the affair he might take it a little easier on us."[87] In his memoirs, Diefenbaker characterized the letter accurately as "an attempt to blackmail Her Majesty's Loyal Opposition into silence on the scandals rocking his government."[88]

Diefenbaker – who was ill in bed when he received the letter – consulted his House leader, Gordon Churchill, about it and decided that he would confront Pearson in person. One week later, on December 11, 1964, he met the prime minister in his East Block office. Pearson recalled: "He rushed over and started to wave his fists at me and said that he had a scandal on me too. That he knew all about my days as a Communist. I laughed in his face and said, 'Oh, you mean that testimony to the McCarran Committee by that deranged woman in Washington. Well, there's nothing to that. I remember at the time Dean Acheson sent a man up here to tell me about it and I told him to go ahead and publish it.' Well Diefenbaker was pretty deflated so I asked him if he'd been involved any further in the matter on which I'd seen the file and he said no. So I said, give it to me in writing. But of course he never has."[89]

Diefenbaker's account of the conversation is consistent with Pearson's, but he describes its ending in scornful terms.

> I remember that Pearson got to his feet. He walked over to me and, in his most ingratiating way, said: "We should not talk to each other like this, John." I rejoined: "I didn't write the letter that you sent to me, Mike." I added, "And neither did you." Mr. Pearson admitted that the letter had been drafted for him. He then added, "You know I am not a politician. I am a diplomat." I replied that I had heard a diplomat defined "as a person who lies away from home." I turned to leave and added, "You are no diplomat." I heard no more about the Munsinger case until January 1966.[90]

The two leaders were engaged in more than parliamentary combat: They were locked in distrust, contempt, and hatred, and that mutual obsession infected their followers and embittered the atmosphere of the House of Commons. For Diefenbaker, his old suspicion and jealousy of the urbane diplomat had deepened after Pearson had displaced him in power. Pearson, he believed, had gained power through an unfair conspiracy and had demonstrated his incompetence in office. He deserved to be removed. In a fair electoral battle, Diefenbaker was confident that Canadian voters would restore him to his rightful place.

Through the autumn the House committee on the Canadian flag conducted its contentious – and sometimes hilarious – proceedings, examining a large number of designs. The Conservative members of the committee, Diefenbaker admitted, were "badly out-manoeuvred." By the end of October the committee had discarded Pearson's three-maple-leaf design (Diefenbaker called it the "Pearson pennant") and opted for George Stanley's striking single red leaf with red bands. Diefenbaker commented that it was a flag Peruvians would salute. When the report was returned to the House, the opposition leader and his largely English-speaking caucus maintained their refusal to limit debate. Almost three dozen Conservative members wished to record their attitudes in a lost cause. Léon Balcer and the Quebec Conservatives, on the contrary, favoured a new flag without the Red Ensign, and warned that Tory opposition to it would devastate the party in Quebec at the next election. On December 11 he proposed that Pearson should use closure to end the debate, and a few days later the prime minister did so, leaving the Conservative Party deeply riven. Long after midnight on December 15, 1964, the House adopted the flag resolution, as partisans on one side of the House sang "O Canada" and those on the other sang "God Save the Queen." As the debate concluded, Diefenbaker told Pearson: "You have done more to divide Canada than any other Prime Minister."[91]

The Conservative Party found temporary relief for three days in September 1964, when politicians, academics, and critics of every political stripe gathered for Dalton Camp's party conference on Canadian goals in Fredericton, New Brunswick. The leader attended briefly to insist upon his friendship for intellectuals; Marshall McLuhan offered cryptic comments on the need for charismatic leadership to match the celebrity of the Beatles; and other participants offered Quebec everything and nothing. The historian W.L. Morton

Duncan Macpherson, Toronto *Star*, 1964

"**If he says he's the Leader of the Opposition, humour him.**"

warned Quebeckers that a decision to separate from Canada should be met by "every means including force if necessary," while Claude Ryan doubted whether that approach would attract support in the province. Davie Fulton proposed constitutional reform to assert the equality of the two language groups; and Montreal lawyer Marc Lalonde believed that a firm commitment to federalism in Ottawa would easily vanquish the separatists and semi-separatists. The conference offered a feast of ideas, but little evidence of a clear direction for the Conservative Party. Diefenbaker congratulated Camp for "one of the most beneficial conferences that have taken place in many years," and thought that the party should follow up with a new platform. He was disappointed that two caucus committees on policy had produced "very little of a constructive nature."[92]

The flag debate typified Conservative woes. In mid-January 1965 the eight-member Quebec caucus, under Léon Balcer's leadership, met in Montreal to consider its position in the party, and next day Balcer wrote at its direction to Camp asking him "to convene a meeting of the national executive...in order to fix a date for a national convention to decide upon the leadership of the party." Balcer told Camp that the crisis involved more than the flag.

> On every issue touching the taproots of Confederation, the hopes and aspirations of French Canada have been distorted, mis-represented and ignored. The repatriation of our Constitution; the opting-out formula; the B. and B. Commission; federal-provincial relations and even the Canada Pension Plan – each of them have been subjected to narrow, parochial, unreasoning criticism of the kind to which great issues should not be subjected. Our concern is not for criticism, or even opposition, to any of these, but to the disturbing pattern which the across-the-board opposition has revealed.
>
> It is our firm conviction, reached after the most careful consideration, that the Conservative Party can no longer carry on as a great national party under its present leadership and the policies which that leadership have engendered.

Balcer struck at Diefenbaker's jugular by asserting that the party had adopted policies that were "the direct antithesis of the great work of union wrought by Macdonald and Cartier – the first Canadians to master the art of governing this difficult country of ours." He called for the executive meeting to be held before the House reconvened on February 16, and noted that the Quebec caucus had already made a public announcement of its request.[93]

Camp faced what he described to Diefenbaker as "a cruel dilemma." Everyone he consulted thought that the Liberal government could and should be defeated; but equally everyone was aware of the public division in the Tory party. "All propose one or other ultimate solution to it, involving the leadership, but these taken together are mutually contradictory."[94] To confront the dilemma, Camp wrote to members of the national executive enclosing Balcer's letter, asking them to tell him at once whether they favoured an early meeting to consider Balcer's request. When 60 percent of the executive indicated their support, Camp called a national executive meeting for Saturday, February 6, 1965.[95]

During the last ten days of January the leader of the opposition was away from Ottawa, first in Prince Albert and then, for four crowded days, in London attending the funeral of Sir Winston Churchill. Camp did not consult Diefenbaker before calling the executive meeting, but explained his decision in a memorandum and an interview with the leader on February 2. Camp noted the extreme divisions between French- and English-speaking elements in the party, "agitation and unrest" among young members, a withdrawal of support for the federal party by the Ontario organization ("including its leadership"), shortages of candidates and funds, and the continued unrelenting opposition of the press. But he thought the executive retained "a strong sense of mutual confidence and solidarity among its non-Parliamentary members" and would not support Balcer's proposal for a leadership convention. He hoped that it might somehow find a solution that would retain the pride and vitality of the party – without suggesting what it might be. He passed on some harsh personal comments to Diefenbaker: "The most helpful thing I believe I could tell you is that a number in the Party fear what they take to be your 'political memory'; others admire your courage and your stalwart defense of what you think is right, but they also fear what they take to be an inflexibility of mind and an inflexibility in personal relationships. Someone said to me that 'the difference in the Conservative Party between loyalty and subservience had never been learned.'"[96] Salvaging the party's pride, it seemed, would have to involve someone's resignation. Probably nothing could save party unity.

Diefenbaker's staff members Burt Richardson and Tom Van Dusen counselled attack.[97] Richardson told Diefenbaker that Camp had committed "an act of perfidy" by calling the meeting of the national executive, designed "to assert power within the party, bringing the leader and all elements under the control of this clique." He suggested a number of countermeasures: a press campaign indicating that "the Chief is on the warpath, ready to strike"; an order to Camp to "recant and denounce the clique"; a meeting of the parliamentary caucus before the executive meeting to declare its support for the leader; a grassroots campaign to launch "a deluge of mail and messages" in his favour; and a public statement by Diefenbaker declaring his intention to fight. Richardson identified the rebels as "the Quebec group" and "the Toronto Turks," and doubted that they controlled the national executive. In any case, "the real power of the leader lies in the grass roots voters and in the caucus." The executive should be told by its parliamentary members that "whatever leader the party has, he must have loyalty...Above all, the leader should not resign at this time, as public opinion is beginning to accept the inevitability of John Diefenbaker being Prime Minister again."[98]

With only four days before the executive meeting, Diefenbaker and his supporters could hardly mount the campaign Richardson called for. But they did arrange a caucus meeting for February 5; and Diefenbaker – who was now receiving signals of a precipitate collapse in support among the faithful – engaged in a frenetic series of telephone conversations and personal encounters to measure his chances and rally his troops. Balcer announced his intention to boycott the caucus meeting, and plans for a motion to expel him from caucus were discussed. But Diefenbaker was also talking once more of his own retirement.[99]

By the time caucus gathered on February 5, Diefenbaker had put those thoughts behind him. He foresaw an early election, and called for a unified campaign aimed at victory. "I am not leading the Conservative Party into the wilderness," his notes declare. "I intend to lead this party to another task ordered by Canada's destiny. I am reminded of the motto of Count Frontenac: 'I will answer the enemy from the mouths of my cannon.'" If there was any fighting in the ranks, "it must stop now...Ferment inside a Party is a sign of life. But ferment carried on when the time comes for political battle is something else. It is treachery. I have, therefore, an assignment for those who have been outspoken around the campfires in the bivouac. As the battle approaches, let them make clear where they stand...I myself have caused some ferment in the Party, as rank and file supporter in my time. I have always given the Leader under whom I have served, my complete loyalty and support. I expect no less today as Leader."[100]

The caucus meeting continued for four hours, as supporters and critics had their say. David Walker, Allister Grosart, Erik Nielsen, and Terry Nugent led for the defence. But, as Peter Newman reported, "Diefenbaker, for the first time, was the subject of open laughter in the inner circles of his own party" when his old friend Senator Walker declared: "He's an honest man who ran an honest government, and I can say that nobody's ever found John Diefenbaker out."[101] A motion of confidence in Diefenbaker's parliamentary leadership was adopted by standing vote, and the leader left the meeting in high spirits. Others reported that "about a dozen" members had remained seated.[102]

Next morning, after Diefenbaker and Camp had breakfasted together to discuss the day's proceedings, 116 members of the national executive met in a warehouse room on the top floor of the party's new headquarters. Camp explained that Balcer and Diefenbaker would speak before lunch, and that afterwards a questionnaire would be distributed asking for advice on the issues in dispute. Diefenbaker had agreed with Camp that this would allow members to express their opinions, but would leave the secret results available only to the party president and himself. Balcer spoke for a few minutes, simply reading his previous letter to Camp and thanking all those present for attending in such large numbers. Diefenbaker, with Olive close by, spoke for almost an hour and a half. He denounced those who had opposed him in 1956, who had continued, privately and publicly, to oppose him ever since. They were "termites" pursuing their own ambitions. "Those who have ambition," he said, would have their opportunity in due course, but he recalled that Gladstone had won his last election at eighty-four. "You who have ambitions," he mocked, "should not be other than hopeful."

Diefenbaker surveyed his battlefronts and his enemies old and new. President Kennedy, he noted, had attempted to stop Canadian grain shipments to China, had stimulated the exchange crisis of 1962 to aid the Liberals, and had intervened in Canadian affairs in 1963. "The termites" accused Diefenbaker of being anti-Quebec: Was he responsible for the party's record in Quebec from 1921 to 1940? Was he the one who boycotted caucus? Was he the one now "termiting across the country"? In 1922 he had defended French language education in Saskatchewan in the Boutin case. Was he responsible for the Liberal provincial victory or the separatist tide in Quebec? He believed in one Canada. Had he leaked Davie Fulton's views on constitutional amendment to the Montreal *Gazette?*

As for himself, "I have no personal ambition. I have had everything. I don't care how you vote, but put yourself in my position. If you vote against me you are voting for the pattern of Liberalism. I want to know if you want that...If you want a Convention, have it. Get rid of me...They offered me the Chief Justiceship of Canada" – but he would say more about that another time. He recalled the lamentable records of Manion, Bracken, and Drew in Quebec. He played out his themes, returning again and again to Balcer, to Fulton, defying the meeting to "call your convention...go to work and do some defending and fighting...Do what you will. I don't come to you as a suppliant."[103]

When the meeting adjourned for lunch, Diefenbaker emerged to tell reporters that it was a fine meeting and that he had proposed "new ideas to strengthen the party." (He had called for two new party committees.) Nearly half the delegates left the building for lunch, while Diefenbaker ate sandwiches with those who remained. "In the old days," reported the Toronto *Star*, "all the delegates would have stayed to lunch and the chance of a word with The Chief."[104]

Dalton Camp opened the afternoon session by reading the questions proposed for the secret questionnaire: Should there be a leadership convention? Should the leader resign? Should there be a policy advisory committee? Should the party fully accept the new Canadian flag?[105] Diefenbaker "suddenly became very agitated," whispered to Gordon Churchill, exchanged notes with Olive and with David Walker, and then stood to complain that the national executive was an advisory body that could not pass judgment on the leader. He rejected inclusion of the second question. After a confused debate, five officers of the association withdrew to consider the problem. They returned fifteen minutes later to announce a unanimous decision to let the question stand. Now there was an angry impasse, broken by a motion from Erik Nielsen to delete the second question: a procedural motion that was, in effect, a veiled vote of confidence to be decided by a standing count. This, said the *Star*, was "the kind of question the rebels feared because some members dared not stand openly against the leader."

> About half of the delegates rose in favor of deleting the resignation question. When those opposed to the deletion stood up, Quebec and Ontario were almost unanimous and even one Saskatchewan delegate surprisingly joined them.
>
> The rebels were so surprised that they omitted to keep count but they accepted later that the margin at most was 55 to 52 and one delegate was sure it was only 53–52.[106]

The association's officers, who had proposed the question, had not voted. Eddie Goodman protested, but Camp insisted that they would not do so. "How can you not vote in favour of your own ballot when you got us here and presented it to us?" Goodman asked. Camp did not answer – and the question was deleted.[107]

Before the questionnaires were returned, other members of the executive spoke. Davie Fulton admitted to his ambition on behalf of, and his loyalty to, the party. He recalled that he had remained in the 1963 cabinet until after the election defeat, denied any improper conduct, and asked the executive to look forward, not back, in considering the party's needs.[108] J.M. Macdonnell, aged eighty-one and still "ramrod proud," also rose and looked directly at

Diefenbaker as he spoke: "It is possible that I qualify for this term 'termite,' since a year ago I was among the few who stood up against the leader. But since, in addition to being a termite, I am also an octogenarian, I doubt if I qualify for the leader's suggestion that all termites are moved by personal ambition."[109] At the end of debate John Diefenbaker returned to the microphone with a quieter call for party unity in the coming battle against the Grits. The questionnaires were returned to the national president for counting, and the meeting adjourned. Diefenbaker told reporters, "We have been able to bring about a sense of agreement as to the course to be followed in the days and weeks ahead," and asserted that there had been no challenge to his leadership. "There being no challenge, I didn't meet it...A national leadership convention is held only when there is a vacancy, and I can tell you there is no vacancy at this time." Dalton Camp offered more soft soap: "It was a family meeting in an appropriate spirit of the family home...We accomplished a good thing today." The results of the balloting, he explained, would be conveyed to Mr Diefenbaker in confidence, solely as advice.[110]

Camp announced the next day that the proposal for a leadership convention had been rejected by the meeting. The *Globe* reported that "the voting figures were not officially disclosed, but are believed to have been 55–52 ...Although the majority was narrow, it probably secures Mr. Diefenbaker's position for the foreseeable future." Balcer responded that the announcement "is in conflict with the general trend of yesterday's meeting," and asked to see "the complete figures and the voting slips on which they are based." Newman commented that Diefenbaker had been "cruelly wounded" by the meeting, and could "no longer count on the public affection which nurtured him." The Toronto *Star* spoke editorially of his "unshakeable will to power" as leader of a party "confused, divided and without hope." Many of those who opposed a leadership convention, it judged, had done so "not in support of Mr. Diefenbaker, but in fear that the Liberals would call an election while the Conservative party was helpless in a bitter leadership fight." Now Diefenbaker would lead the party into another general election against a Liberal government "racked by scandal," while many good Conservatives stood aside.[111] A few weeks later one Conservative MP from Quebec, Rémi Paul, left the caucus to sit as an independent; and in April Léon Balcer followed.

On February 17 Diefenbaker spoke to the people on television: "I have been maligned. I have been condemned. No one since the days of Macdonald has gone through the like...They say they want to remove me...I have been told...in the last few days that if I remain as Leader of the Conservative Party, support for the Party by certain interests will end. My friends, they believe they will succeed in this way. I will follow the will of the people. Will it be the will of the People or those that are all powerful?"[112]

Despite his bravado, Diefenbaker was worn down by his struggle, and Olive encouraged him to retire. In March he met with a small group of his closest supporters, apparently intent on making a voluntary departure. He told them of his intention to go. But the story was leaked and Diefenbaker – typically torn by conflicting advice – impulsively reversed himself. "I was so aroused by the necessity of denying to the press my decision to retire," he put it in his memoirs, "that I decided not to retire."[113] Diefenbaker's demons would not let him go by his own choice.

The demoralized Conservative Party could do little to hide its disarray except to attack the government, which was in its own state of chaos. Pearson pursued his quest for accommodation with the new Quebec, while his office remained disorganized and his Quebec ministers unusually accident-prone. After long and contentious debate, the Canada Pension Plan and legislation to permit Quebec to opt out of federal social programs were adopted during the winter. While the Dorion inquiry continued, the government faced new embarrassment when the key figure in the scandal, the narcotics dealer Lucien Rivard, escaped from Bordeaux jail by climbing over the wall from the prison yard where he was watering the skating rink on a warm evening in early spring. That permitted Diefenbaker to accuse the cabinet once more of "slack or careless administration of justice and law enforcement." Although Rivard had been held in a provincial jail, Diefenbaker accused the federal minister of negligence: "such a disregard of political morality on the part of this government as to shock the public conscience."[114]

In April the government began a new session of parliament by outlining plans for generous new public assistance programs, inevitably described as the Canadian version of President Johnson's "Great Society." Diefenbaker attacked the preview as "a catchall of promises," renewed his criticisms of the government's moral laxity, and challenged the proposed Fulton-Favreau formula for constitutional amendment as unworkable. At the very end of the session in June, the cabinet received Judge Dorion's report, which found that there had been a conspiracy to obstruct the course of justice in the Rivard affair, and that Guy Favreau, as minister, had failed to exercise proper discretion by neglecting to consult his legal officers when he learned of the bribe attempt. The cabinet went through a day of distressed consultation before the prime minister announced that Favreau had resigned as minister of justice but would remain in cabinet in another portfolio. The minister's prestige was destroyed, and the prime minister's half-measure gave the leader of the opposition more evidence for his claim that this was a weak and negligent government.[115]

The Conservative Party's never-ending domestic strife meant that its popularity in the polls declined steadily during the winter and spring of 1965. Mike Pearson dreamed of a majority government to finish his work of accommodation and social reform; and he dreamed, too, of a time when he would be free of the malign force across the aisle of the House. His advisers urged him to go to the electorate before Diefenbaker retired, both to conquer and to drive him out of politics. But the Rivard report, and a summer railway strike, gave Pearson pause through July and August. Finally, in early September, after polling his cabinet, Pearson announced an election for November 8, 1965, and appealed for a majority government. Diefenbaker echoed widespread editorial sentiment by denouncing the dissolution, but declared in predictable phrases that "we have an appointment with destiny and I say, forward in courage and faith." His wounded forces, reluctant, fatalistic, or bitterly loyal, gathered round him for one last crusade.

Diefenbaker talked of elections in the language of military campaigns, and he might have imagined himself, in 1965, as Laurence Olivier's Henry V encouraging his yeoman army on the eve of Agincourt. To his followers, though, he was no Olivier or Henry, the companion leader of the team, but a manic wanderer standing alone and surveying the hostile country beyond, his guides clustered separately behind him in anxious conclave about where he might be leading them. By the autumn of 1965 there was scarcely any national organization left; in Quebec there was hardly a party at any level.

During the first meeting of the Conservative campaign committee, Richard Thrasher took Eddie Goodman aside to ask him if he would run the campaign. Apart from supporting Léon Balcer at the February executive meeting, Goodman had taken no part in politics since the cabinet split of 1963. In Diefenbaker's eyes he was one of the Toronto conspirators. Goodman was incredulous. "How can you run an election campaign," he asked, "when the leader doesn't speak to the campaign chairman? Dief would never agree to this." Thrasher replied that Diefenbaker, who had been under pressure from Gordon Churchill and Allister Grosart, would accept him. Others had refused the job, and no one else could do it. Goodman reflected, consulted, and accepted, knowing that he was one of only a few – Camp and Brunt had been others – who could stand up to the Chief. He approached their first meeting "with a mixture of amusement and trepidation." Diefenbaker greeted him coldly, confirming that he had accepted Thrasher's advice that Goodman was "the best man under the circumstances." When Goodman asked for Diefenbaker's "absolute confidence...throughout the campaign, both in my loyalty and my judgment," Diefenbaker replied, "I have always found you forthright if sometimes mistaken, and I certainly accept your promise to do your best." But he asked for a delegate at headquarters for the duration. Goodman exploded: "Mr. Diefenbaker, there will be only one person reporting to you at my headquarters. Me. In one breath you tell me you trust me and in the next you ask for a personal agent." Diefenbaker backed off, then asked for a guarantee that Lowell Murray would not enter headquarters. Goodman agreed, but consulted Murray privately throughout the campaign.[116]

Diefenbaker then produced a copy of the discredited US Senate committee testimony of the spy Elizabeth Bentley accusing Pearson of wartime Soviet espionage, suggesting that it offered ammunition for the campaign. Goodman told him firmly that "we had quite enough material to make Pearson's leadership look bad without resorting to this type of scurrilous innuendo." Diefenbaker dropped the subject.[117]

Goodman's objective was to reunite the party and "bring back the dissidents of 1963 and 1964": to do what the Toronto *Star* had said could not be done under Diefenbaker's continuing leadership. The miracle was occurring. George Hees, Davie Fulton, Dalton Camp, and George Hogan were all candidates. The *Telegram*, too, had renewed its loyalty. The premier of Manitoba, Duff Roblin, was on the point of declaring his candidacy, but refused the final jump when Diefenbaker neglected to encourage him. At national headquarters, Flora MacDonald and James Johnston provided energy and ideas, and a fresh crew of young aides provided muscle.[118]

There was a lively spirit of gallows humour among the national organizers. Two stories especially became part of Diefenbaker lore. As they patched together the official version of a party program, Allister Grosart and Jim Johnston bantered about a winning election slogan; and a decade later Johnston explained the incident to Diefenbaker.

> One afternoon I said to Grosart that we had to answer the query of the public, why had our government lost its 208 seats. We were searching for a concise answer to that one...I said to him...what we should be doing by election day was getting the issue down to one point, "Give the old bugger another chance."
>
> So there were your friends laughingly treating you with affectionate disrespect.[119]

Johnston repeated the line to Goodman and others, and it was instantly transmitted across town to the prime minister's office. "This made me feel very badly," Johnston told Diefenbaker, "as I hated the thoughts of the Grits laughing at something like this, when it had all been said in good fun at the beginning...But...no offense was meant. It also summed up precisely what we were fighting for – another chance."[120]

Peter Newman reported the second story, perhaps from an account by Lowell Murray:

> On October 2, when the Conservative campaign seemed to be going well and it looked as if Diefenbaker might have a chance of winning, Goodman looked around his subalterns, most of whom had at one time or another opposed the Prince Albert politician, and said: "You know if Dief wins, there'll be the biggest political bloodbath this country has ever seen, and much of that blood is now running in the veins of those in this hotel room." The remark was greeted with shrieks of laughter and the assembled company immediately began to plan how they would act on election night following a Diefenbaker victory. It was agreed that Goodman would go on national television ("After all, I'll be something of an architect") and apologize to the people of Canada for having played such a monstrous practical joke on them. Then the entire Tory headquarters crew would join hands and leap off the roof of the Chateau Laurier.[121]

The party's electoral program was a patchwork put together by Alvin Hamilton and James Johnston, from speeches of Diefenbaker and Hamilton, vetted by the Union Nationale leader Daniel Johnson. It was an extension of Diefenbaker's earlier, progressive, and welfarist manifestos, with the added promise of "a great national conference on confederation." That commitment could not conceal the party's unresolved constitutional dilemma: How could Diefenbaker's belief in "one Canada" be reconciled with the recognition of "two founding nations," one of them represented by a French-speaking province, which was now promoted by the Laurendeau-Dunton ("B & B") Commission and endorsed by the Pearson government? The program offered the promise of "unity in equality between the two basic races of Canada, with every Canadian, regardless of race or creed, having equality in citizenship and equality of opportunity...The dismantling, piece-by-piece, of our country must stop. Canada cannot exist without Quebec, nor can we visualize Quebec without Canada." The message was confusing, and did not seem to be aimed at French-speaking voters. It became somewhat less mystifying when the Ontario premier, John Robarts, declared himself in favour of a constitutional conference to discover what it was that all provinces, including Quebec, wanted from a renewed confederation.[122]

But the party program was an irrelevance. For those who had returned to the fold, the election was an occasion to repair the foundations and prepare for life-after-Diefenbaker. Surely the campaign would be lost, and the leader would accept the final verdict of his jury or be forced to retire. The potential successors would re-establish their credentials and return to the House of Commons. For Diefenbaker, the election became an occasion for nostalgia, justification, historical redemption, and – as the campaign progressed – even for conquest of the Liberal foe. The leader found resonance in two issues, and repeated the themes with his singular passion. Above all he denounced the Liberal scandals: conflict of interest, dubious connections, a weak prime minister who would not confront the rot in his own administration, a cabinet that let criminals water hockey rinks on warm spring evenings. Because the subjects of scandal were almost all Québécois, the scandals blended vaguely into the second theme: national unity and the place of Quebec in Canada. The implication of some ugly racial defect among Pearson's Quebec ministers lay just below the surface, to be absorbed by Tory audiences outside Quebec. The Pearson government, through Diefenbaker's eyes, became an undifferentiated "galaxy of wrongdoers" undermining the moral fabric of the country.

Conservative advertising (for the first time since 1957) emphasized the strength of the team and played down the role of the leader. The provincial Tory premiers, Robert Stanfield, John Robarts, and Duff Roblin, declared their support and provided assistance. But John Diefenbaker inevitably dominated the campaign. He opted once more for a whistle-stop journey by train, crisscrossing the provinces to stop in scores of cities and small towns. His audiences were large and enthusiastic, laughing at his jokes and applauding his denunciations, enjoying the performance of a great political entertainer. Their warmth did not necessarily translate into votes, for they knew his record in office, but the campaign could be savoured for its own professional skill. Ben Malkin of the Montreal *Gazette* probably expressed the sentiments of many who watched him on that journey.

> He remains the very model of an opposition leader on the campaign trail – filled with scorn for the incompetents in government, ready to be charitable toward the malcontents within his own party should they wish to return to the fold, gaily scattering vague jelly-like promises across his campaign trail. He does so well in this role, that I think he is unwise to work so hard to relinquish it in favor of playing a part that has, in the past, proved a little beyond his special gifts.[123]

534

When the Diefenbaker train reached the prairies in early October, the leader indulged himself shamelessly in sentiment and nostalgia. With Elmer at his side, he took reporters by car to the homestead near Borden, Saskatchewan, to show them the decaying family shack and relate his stories of prairie fire, deadly blizzards, cheating grain buyers, and visits by the Métis fighter Gabriel Dumont. "I have these views," he told his companions, "and you've got to go back to see where they were formed...They were not always the right views, perhaps, but they were formed of the pioneer tradition."[124] Newman wrote that Diefenbaker "moves like a legend over the land...He is the political poet who can evoke the glories of a simpler past when the Red River carts still creaked along the Battleford trail and buffalo bones littered the horizonless prairie...On other occasions, Diefenbaker gives tongue to the sense of affront felt by the inhabitants of the small, flat Prairie towns who feel themselves overwhelmed by the alien world they never made. The mood at these whistle-stops is one of joyful defiance; pride in the fact that this singular politician reflects and champions their lonely way of life." But the crowds that greeted him, Newman reported, were mostly elderly, and the landscape was changing: "The legend of John Diefenbaker is being tested for the last time."[125] For George Bain of the *Globe*, the Chief seemed "like an old man dreaming dreams."[126]

Mike Pearson had always been a reluctant campaigner, and this time the effort, for him, was especially repugnant. While Diefenbaker met the voters face to face, Pearson stayed behind in Ottawa, attempting to establish the image of a responsible prime minister occupied with matters of state. (By November there were signs at every Diefenbaker rally declaring: "He cared enough to come.") Pearson's campaign was half-hearted and unconvincing, no match for the beguiling storytelling and high spirits of his opponent. The Liberal Party could find no compelling theme; its campaign amounted to an appeal for majority government and a warning against the destructive potential of Diefenbaker in power. In mid-campaign the Liberals were embarrassed by more reports of criminal links in Quebec, and by sensational charges, immediately denied, that J.W. Pickersgill had participated in arranging payoffs for the six Social Crediters who had supported a Pearson government in 1963. The electorate was disinclined to give Pearson his majority, and equally disinclined to think of Diefenbaker's restoration. The whole exercise, aside from the diverting political theatre, seemed pointless.[127]

While the Montreal *Gazette* lamented editorially that the public in 1965 were sheep without a shepherd, it praised their mature scepticism in demanding "what they are not being given – competent leadership for the balanced reconciliation of a diverse country." The *Globe and Mail* came cautiously back to the Tories through a process of elimination. By 1965, it judged, the Liberals had lost popular respect and the Conservatives had learned from their errors. "The party admitted it needs a leader. The leader has admitted he needs a party. There is, at least, ground for hope." But not too much. In Saskatchewan, Diefenbaker had the satisfaction of seeing both the *Leader Post* and the *Star-Phoenix* abandon their Liberal traditions to support the Conservatives. Elsewhere, there were editorial calls for a Liberal minority government and the departure of both party leaders. Nothing in the campaign pointed to any breakthroughs.[128]

On November 8 the electorate chose the status quo. The cities remained Liberal, the English-speaking countryside remained Conservative. Few ridings changed hands. Pearson picked up only two seats for a total of 131 – still two short of an absolute majority. Diefenbaker held what seemed to be his core support with ninety-seven seats. Excluding Quebec, Diefenbaker held a lead of fourteen seats over Pearson. The voters had delivered their conditioned verdict on both party leaders. Neither one of them could achieve a majority.

WHEN THE NEW PARLIAMENT MET IN JANUARY 1966 THERE WERE FRESH – OR RESurrected – faces on both sides of the aisle. The Liberal caucus was bolstered by the presence of the "three wise men" from Quebec – Jean Marchand, Gérard Pelletier, and Pierre Elliott Trudeau – and by the return of Robert Winters. The Diefenbaker front bench was reinforced by Davie Fulton, George Hees, and Richard Bell. Dalton Camp, Richard Thrasher, and George Hogan had all lost their contests. Pearson was demoralized by his failure to achieve a majority, and soon after the election he accepted the resignation of Walter Gordon as minister of finance in penance for the stalemate. Mitchell Sharp replaced Gordon at Finance, and Robert Winters became minister of trade and commerce. The government lost much of its reformist energy. Lamontagne and Tremblay departed to the back benches, and Lucien Cardin, who had replaced Favreau as justice minister the previous July, emerged as the senior Québécois minister. He was the most bitter antagonist of Diefenbaker in Liberal ranks – and thus a primary target of the Chief's own poisoned barbs.

Soon after the election Cardin made himself vulnerable by admitting on television that a Vancouver postal clerk, George Victor Spencer, had been dismissed from his job on suspicion of spying for the Soviet Union. He had not been charged with any offence, but had lost his pension, had no means of appeal, and would be under RCMP surveillance for the rest of his life. (He was then dying of cancer.) When the new House met, Diefenbaker and the New Democratic Party pressed the government for a public inquiry into what seemed a fundamental abuse of Spencer's rights. Cardin refused, and the intensity of the opposition's attacks increased. Pearson, who was both uneasy about the apparent invasion of rights and nervous about his political weakness, agreed to consider an inquiry. But he told the House in February that he had examined the file and decided it was unnecessary. Twice during parliamentary exchanges on the case in January and February, Pearson made veiled allusions to "other security cases" in the past that "might throw light on our security methods generally." Cardin, too, warned Diefenbaker about neglected security cases during his prime ministership.[129]

On March 4, 1966, the opposition's demands for an inquiry sharpened, and Diefenbaker extended the range of innuendo. He accused Pearson of creating "a labyrinth of deception" in the Spencer case, and suggested a pattern of impropriety on security matters stretching back to 1944.

> Mr. Diefenbaker: Yes, I want to cover that period. I want to see it fully investigated. The Prime Minister laughs, but I want to see as well that we make available to the commission meeting behind closed doors the revelations that have found their way to Washington and have there been placed in evidence that was taken in that body on security. We are not getting the facts.[130]

This was a reference to the old charge that Pearson had been a Soviet agent. By reviving it, Diefenbaker threw Pearson a defiant challenge and recalled their angry interview of December 1964. Each of the leaders felt secure in his own righteousness; each believed the other vulnerable. The combat was not rational. "I ask the government," Diefenbaker railed, "what are you going to do in this connection? What action are you going to take? Why will you not set up a royal commission now behind closed doors?...The assumption put forward that these things have happened over the years is of primary importance as a basis upon which to demand that there be such a commission."[131] The minister of justice faced the same withering contempt.

> Mr. Diefenbaker: I again impress on the government the need of action. I know the Minister of Justice is not acquainted with these things. He is seldom before the courts at any time, according to what I am told. Yet he is able to tell us that he knows everything has been well done. It is not enough, sir. There has been too much concealment and deception practised on this house in the last few weeks in this connection.[132]

Lucien Cardin responded in kind. He had "dared to criticize the untouchable one because of his attitude as prime minister" in 1962; and he believed "that every word I said at that time was right." Today Diefenbaker, "with his vicious attacks on individuals, his irresponsible accusations and insinuations in this house, is proving me to be right day by day." The leader of the opposition had learned nothing. "He is still blasting his way through paper walls and open doorways. He is blasting himself out of the leadership of his party and out of parliament and maybe, Mr. Chairman, when that is done we will be able to do some work in this chamber." Cardin asked Diefenbaker whether he believed "that the performance he has put on this afternoon is going to add any dignity or prestige to parliament? This is stirring up hostility in the house far beyond what is normal and necessary in debates."

> I am willing to listen to hon. members on all sides of the house who bring forward criticisms and constructive advice on the difficult problems concerning the administration of security matters. But a while ago the right hon. gentleman was accusing us of hiding the truth, of hiding evidence...Well, I can tell the right hon. gentleman that of all the members of the House of Commons he – I repeat, he – is the very last person in the house who can afford to give advice on the handling of security cases in Canada.

> Some hon. Members: Hear, hear.

> Mr. Cardin: And I am not kidding.

> Some hon. Members: Hear, hear.

> Mr. Diefenbaker: And again applause from the Prime Minister. I want that on the record.

> Mr. Cardin: I understand the right hon. gentleman said he wants that on the record. Would he want me to go on and give more?

> Some hon. Members: Go on. He wants it.

> Mr. Cardin: Very well.

> Some hon. Members: Hear, hear.

> Mr. Cardin: I want the right hon. gentleman to tell the house about his participation in the Monseignor case when he was prime minister of this country.

Some hon. Members: Hear, hear.

Mr. Diefenbaker: I am not worried. Have your commission look into it. Put it on the agenda.[133]

The incident passed, and Cardin moved on to other matters. But he had set the bait for the public and the press. What was "the Monseignor case"? What was Diefenbaker's involvement? Cardin stuck to his position that an inquiry in the Spencer case was unacceptable and unnecessary.

Later in the day his defences collapsed. David Lewis of the NDP told the House that he had spoken with Spencer's solicitor and learned that Spencer wanted an inquiry into "the nature of his dismissal and the unfair deprivation of his benefits." He closed his remarks with a motion to reduce the ministry's estimates by $17,000, the same amount as Cardin's salary, as an indication of lack of confidence in the minister.[134] Under sudden threat of defeat in the House, Prime Minister Pearson replied that this was the first indication he had had that Spencer was dissatisfied with his treatment, and offered – if he could confirm that claim in a telephone conversation with Spencer – to establish an inquiry into the fairness of the civil servant's dismissal. Three days later the inquiry was established.[135]

The leader of the opposition could not resist the temptation to taunt the minister. Lucien Cardin had vowed that there would be no inquiry, and had tried to blackmail the opposition. Now "common sense has taken the place of stubborness and absolute stupidity." The minister had inevitably been embarrassed: "There he stands, naked and unashamed, deprived of every argument he brought before this house." Diefenbaker assured members, in response to Cardin's accusation, that there had been no breach of security or danger to national security in any case under his administration.[136]

Pearson's unexpected reversal in the Spencer case prompted a cabinet crisis and a caucus revolt. Cardin threatened resignation, and Jean Marchand, Léo Cadieux, and J.-J. Côté, fed up with the humiliation of French-speaking ministers, warned Pearson that they would join him if he departed. Desperate manoeuvres went on in caucus to save the government, and at last Cardin agreed to stay. On March 10, acting on his own initiative, he called a press conference to elaborate on his charges against Diefenbaker. The old affair, he suggested, was "in some ways" worse than the Profumo case, which had brought down Prime Minister Macmillan in 1963. Cardin said that "Olga" Munsinger had been a spy before coming to Canada in 1951; that she had created security risks by associating with Conservative ministers; that Diefenbaker and Fulton knew of the case but had not referred it to their legal officers; and that she had left the country and died in East Berlin in 1961. Cardin explained that he was engaged in a dirty war: "There is a working arrangement," he claimed, "not only between the Prime Minister, myself and the members of the cabinet, but also all the MPs, and what we're going to do is to fight and fight hard, and, if we have to, use the same methods that are being used and have been used against us for the past three years."[137]

This outburst brought parliament to the point of breakdown. When the government proposed another judicial inquiry into the minister's accusations, the Conservatives promised to paralyse House business unless Cardin made specific charges and named the suspect ministers. Otherwise, all of Diefenbaker's ministers came under suspicion. Within days, Robert Reguly of the Toronto *Star* had located the mystery woman, alive, in Munich; and she named Pierre Sévigny and George Hees as her former ministerial acquaintances. Press, public, and back-benchers angrily denounced the excesses of political vengefulness in Ottawa, and the leaders themselves drew back with alarmed appeals for restraint and sanity. On March 14 the government proposed a judicial inquiry into all the statements made by the minister of justice regarding the Munsinger affair, the security implications of the case, the actions of ministers, and any other relevant matters, to be conducted by Mr Justice Wishart Spence of the Supreme Court of Canada. A public inquiry now seemed to be the only way of removing the conflict from the House; and by framing it in terms of Cardin's statements, the cabinet seemed to be partially restoring the balance and putting the minister's acts under independent scrutiny along with those of the previous government. Reluctantly, all parties agreed to the proposal. But in principle – as Diefenbaker, Fulton, Nielsen, and Douglas made clear in their remarks – a judicial inquiry into the political decisions of ministers undermined the principles of parliamentary government. An investigation arising from a sweep through the confidential records of previous governments was even less tolerable. The political discretion of John Diefenbaker and Davie Fulton was not a proper subject of scrutiny by a justice of the Supreme Court. The fate of politicians lay, properly, in the hands of the voters (and eventually, the historians) – but not the judges. The *Globe and Mail* commented that the terms of reference of the inquiry were "vague, vengeful, prosecutory...setting a precedent for endless witch-hunts as government succeeds government in Canada. The high office of the Prime Minister itself – that office which Mr. Pearson himself holds – is in the dock."[138]

As prime minister, Mike Pearson was primarily responsible for this collapse of civility. He had called for the RCMP files, kept them in his possession, informed his justice ministers of their contents, allowed his ministers to use their knowledge to threaten the opposition leader with exposure, made the same threats himself, encouraged Cardin to make his careless charges, kept him in the cabinet after he had done so, and created a Star Chamber inquiry intended to convict and destroy the career of an ex–prime minister. But Pearson had been sorely provoked, over the years since 1958, by an opponent zealous to crush his arch-competitor. The two leaders had jointly poisoned the political atmosphere. After Munsinger, there was not just a political standoff: Diefenbaker and Pearson, in destructive symbiosis, had forever discredited themselves. There were widespread calls for their retirement from public life; and within the parties, there were fresh and more profound tremors of discontent.[139]

After receiving evidence from the RCMP commissioner in a secret hearing without the presence of counsel for any of the Conservatives who were, in effect, on trial by public inquiry, Mr Justice Spence presided over three months of reckless political inquisition. Early in the inquiry he released a "handy document" summarizing the secret RCMP report on Gerda Munsinger, while admitting it was not evidence before the hearing. After two months of hearings, Diefenbaker, Fulton, and their lawyers withdrew from further participation in protest over their restricted access to evidence and over the content of the judge's warning about what he intended to deal with in his findings. On September 23 the Spence report was published. It pronounced Gerda Munsinger a serious security risk; held that Pierre Sévigny had made himself a security risk by his affair with her, although the judge found "no scintilla of evidence" of disloyalty in his actions; censured Diefenbaker for his failure to dismiss Sévigny and for other lesser offences; and chastised Fulton and Hees for separate indiscretions. The judgments were political rather than legal. Spence found all the actions of Pearson and Cardin affecting the case to be normal and justified. Conservatives and fair-minded observers of all political colours responded in anger that the inquiry had been a politically inspired vendetta designed to bring down the Tory leader. The inquisitor had fulfilled his tainted mandate. The mud was bound to stick. The *Globe and Mail* judged that – despite general recognition of the commission's impropriety – Canadians would be left with the belief "that they have, in the handling of the Munsinger affair, been wretchedly served by Mr. Diefenbaker, Mr. Fulton and Mr. Sévigny."[140]

THE CHIEF KNEW THAT THE CHALLENGE TO HIS LEADERSHIP WOULD BE RENEWED before the party's annual meeting of 1966. In the immediate aftermath of the 1965 election, the meeting of the national executive in January offered him no embarrassments. Diefenbaker favoured an early annual meeting, before his opponents could gather strength; but his supporters in Saskatchewan planned a celebratory dinner in Saskatoon on the March date that was proposed, and refused to yield. The possibility of a spring meeting slipped away.[141] Next there was talk of a date in June, but Diefenbaker vetoed that when he found himself embroiled in the Spence inquiry. Eventually a date in mid-November was agreed upon.

Meanwhile the Chief was consolidating his strength in the national office. Richard Thrasher had departed for his losing election bid, and Eddie Goodman had returned to Toronto after the campaign. James Johnston stayed on, and gradually, on the leader's urging, took on the duties of national director. By spring he was given the title. Johnston had few personal contacts in the party, except through Diefenbaker.[142] In April, as part of his effort to assert full control on behalf of the leader, Johnston dismissed Flora MacDonald from headquarters, where she had assumed more and more general duties since her original appointment as a typist in 1957. In 1966 she was an influential member of the organization, with especially strong ties among progressive, and mostly anti-Diefenbaker, elements across the country. The firing preoccupied the Conservative caucus meeting the next day. At the end of a heated debate dominated by George Hees and several Maritime and prairie members, caucus appointed a special committee to review the decision. Diefenbaker told them that he had full confidence in Johnston and would not reverse his decision; and the committee – with no means of controlling party headquarters – concurred in the decision. For critics of the leader, Johnston's appointment and MacDonald's departure marked another hardening of the lines between Diefenbaker loyalists and rebels.[143]

The party president, Dalton Camp, had performed his domestic peace-keeping role adroitly for sixteen months. Camp's ability to sense the moods of the national party was unsurpassed, and in the aftermath of the 1965 election he knew that the "gathering restlessness" would soon bring "conspiracies of Catilinian proportions." He suggested delicately to Diefenbaker in November that it would be reasonable to consider "at his leisure...the appropriate time for the party to choose a successor" sometime before the next general election. Diefenbaker responded predictably.

> Ah – the leader sighs, after not so long a pause – but you see there *are* no successors. He would illustrate by example. Fulton? Fulton had ditched himself, against all advice, by accepting the provincial leadership in British Columbia. He had no judgement. Fulton could never lead this party.

Hees? Hees had been like a son to him. But he had destroyed himself, running off with Bassett in 1963. Had he stood fast, he would be the next leader of this party. But not now. Not ever.

McCutcheon? A snort for McCutcheon's qualifications.

Who is there? The premiers? He had asked all of them – Robarts, Roblin, Stanfield – asked each of them to come and take their place in Parliament. He had even told Roblin, before the last election, there would be possibilities for him if he would come in – that was as far as he could go, you see – but, no, none of them would come forward.

There is no one, the leader says, sorrow in his voice, because, you see, no one can lead this party until he has sat in Parliament.[144]

When Camp next met Diefenbaker at the leader's call in March 1966, he found himself, unaccountably, in the presence of Richard Jackson of the Ottawa *Journal.* As the party leaders tore at each other daily in the House, Diefenbaker wished to initiate the party president into some secrets. From a bottom drawer he pulled a file containing the congressional committee testimony of Elizabeth Bentley about Pearson's wartime associations in Washington, and passed it across the desk. Camp read, and waited to learn the meaning of the occasion. Diefenbaker told Camp that he had a duty to remain leader just as long as Pearson was prime minister of Canada.[145]

There was clearly nothing Camp could do to persuade Diefenbaker to make a gracious and voluntary exit at a time of his own choosing. So in May 1966 – knowing the explosive content of the leadership issue – he spoke to a private meeting of Tories at the Albany Club in Toronto to propose an ingenious means of defusing the timebomb. The party, he believed, must have a new leader before the next election, which meant a convention by the spring of 1968. To reach that point, Camp suggested a procedural reform in the party to give its members a regular means of reassessing the leadership. The next annual meeting after an election in which the party had not gained power, he proposed, should face an automatic ballot on whether or not to hold a leadership convention. For 1966, Camp intended to soften any direct challenge to Diefenbaker by making leadership review the issue in his own contest for re-election as party president. Over the summer he found widespread support for his approach, and on September 20 he made it public in an address to the Toronto Junior Board of Trade. While Camp argued his case in general terms and did not attack Diefenbaker directly, his target and his objective were obvious. "Where the leader does not know the limits of his power," he argued, "he must be taught, and when he is indifferent to the interest of his party, he must be reminded." Canadian parties could no longer remain "huddled about obsolete political platforms, debating the past, divided on their leadership and leaving their future to the fate of accident." The *Globe and Mail* applauded Camp's courage, but the *Telegram* – while admitting he was "a doughty fighter" – considered him "badly overmatched" in another contest with the Chief and imprudent in his timing: "This is no time for Mr. Camp to lead a new rebellion. Mr. Diefenbaker has earned the right to decide for himself when he should step down."[146]

Two days before Camp's speech, Diefenbaker had shown his own confidence at a seventy-first birthday party in his parliamentary offices by reminding reporters of John A. Macdonald's last campaign at the age of seventy-six. In one year, he boasted, he would again occupy the prime minister's office on the floor below. Afterwards, he asked his aide Greg Guthrie: "Do you think I overdid it? Do you think I rubbed it in enough?"[147]

For six weeks Camp engaged in a national campaign for leadership review as the first stage in renewing the party system for a more democratic age. Beyond the call for review, his prescriptions were vague, but leadership was the compelling issue. Provincial party associations in Prince Edward Island, Quebec, and British Columbia voted in favour of reassessment; a ginger group of a dozen Conservative MPs declared themselves in support of Camp; and an editorial review of Canadian newspapers large and small, prepared in October for Diefenbaker, revealed fifty-nine in favour of a leadership review and only ten opposed.[148]

When Diefenbaker addressed a closed Conservative meeting at the Albany Club soon after Camp had launched his public campaign, he was challenged by an Ontario minister, Allan Lawrence, who suggested that a leadership convention might unite the party. Jim Johnston worried that this kind of "blunt impertinence" was wearing Diefenbaker down; he was "losing his genius for wisecracks and good repartee." A battle of resolutions swept party meetings across the country, as Camp, Diefenbaker, and their respective advocates manoeuvred for strength at the annual meeting. Frequently, Camp and Johnston – both noticeably balding – were mistaken for one another, sometimes under threat of violence from their own supporters. Erik Nielsen matched Diefenbaker's rhetoric in his defence by describing Camp's supporters as the Bay Street barons and crown princes of privilege, "petty little men" intent on disembowelling a great national party. Diefenbaker's loyalists – who included up to seventy members of the parliamentary caucus – arranged for the Toronto lawyer and former MP Arthur Maloney to contest the party presidency against Camp; and Johnston issued an agenda for the annual meeting without consulting Camp or other members of the national executive. It called for elections on the final day of meetings instead of the first day, in the expectation that a voice-vote declaration of confidence in Diefenbaker on the first day would dispose of the leadership issue. But at the executive meeting on the eve of the annual meeting, Camp's supporters overruled the Johnston agenda and restored the election of officers to a place before the leadership vote. By this time the dissidents included the two leading officers of the Ontario party association, Elmer Bell and Eddie Goodman; Senator McCutcheon, who had performed invaluable fundraising for the party during the 1965 election; and, it appeared, the three Tory premiers Robert Stanfield, John Robarts, and Duff Roblin.[149]

John Diefenbaker remained intransigent. He wanted to see Dalton Camp defeated, and he refused any efforts of compromise. When Johnston offered him a draft statement for delivery to the Ontario party meetings at the end of October which promised his retirement once the centennial celebrations of 1967 had ended, he baulked. "I can't read that," he insisted. "It's fine, but I can't read it. I told them that we would not discuss leadership. Besides, I can't make myself a lame-duck leader over such a long period." When Johnston spoke once on the telephone to Camp about reconciliation over the agenda, Diefenbaker pronounced the conversation a grievous error. While the leader still dreamed of defeating the government and leading another victorious campaign before centennial year, Johnston saw disaster ahead. Aside from Diefenbaker himself, he sensed, the loyalists in the House were growing weary of the battle. In the last days before the annual meeting, the infighting came

Duncan Macpherson, Toronto *Star*, 1966

down to a war of tactical advantage between Camp's allies in the association and Johnston's staff in the national office. Camp's forces won all the preliminary battles.[150]

As Diefenbaker prepared for his opening speech on November 14, he was advised by staff and friends to take all possible positions: to promise retirement, to fight on, to call for an immediate leadership convention, to ask for an immediate vote of confidence. Johnston pleaded with him not to provoke his opponents with any more mention of Gladstone and Macdonald hanging on in their old age, to which the Chief retorted with a glare: "I'll talk about Sir John if I like...Don't give me any of that stuff."[151]

Two hours before the convention opened in the ballroom of the Château Laurier hotel, the front rows of seats were occupied, mostly but not entirely by young supporters of Dalton Camp. Soon the room was overflowing. Diefenbaker deferred his arrival until the preliminary speeches were finished, taking his seat onstage in what had become a "continual roar" of voices. As Joel Aldred rose to introduce the leader, Johnston revealed to Camp that the timing was perfect: he had secretly arranged with the CBC to begin a direct television broadcast at that moment. The result turned out bittersweet for the loyalists. "It was this manoeuvre – although we could not have anticipated its importance at the time – which took that dreadful evening into Canadian living-rooms. It let the nation see, as no one could ever describe it, the method by which the old Chief was attacked. From coast to coast, they saw it while it was happening, live, in their capital city."[152]

Diefenbaker – the acknowledged master of his crowds – spoke in desperation to a cold and mostly silent audience. "Throughout his address," Arthur Blakely wrote in the Montreal *Gazette*, "they were well-mannered, aloof, and hostile. They sat on their hands whenever one of the chief's infrequent sallies started a round of applause. They converted into utter fiascos, by the simple device of doing nothing, the attempts to give Mr. Diefenbaker standing ovations at the beginning and end of his speech."[153] As Diefenbaker turned in anger on Dalton Camp, seated nearby on the platform beside him, demanding to know when and why Camp had betrayed his loyalty to the party leader, there were boos and cries of derision. Diefenbaker was shaken. The audience was not listening; he had no hope of controlling it. "Is this a Conservative meeting?" he cried in anguish. "No leader can stand if he has to turn around to find who's tripping him from behind." He cut short his words and turned from the rostrum, his face inflamed and his eyes darting wildly in distress. Johnston was quickly at his side, while the room broke into uproar and members of the platform party fled in disorder and embarrassment. "I'll quit tomorrow morning," he told the national director. "I'll resign in the morning. I told you what I would do if there was any widespread showing against me...I'm getting out." As they struggled out of the ballroom to the elevators, Diefenbaker was surrounded by delegates who had failed to get into the auditorium, most of them his supporters. They cheered him and wished him well.[154]

Diefenbaker's team spent a late night calculating how to break up the party, leaving a small rump of dissident MPs behind while the loyalists regrouped in a new party. Next day, as delegates continued to flow into Ottawa, the Diefenbaker forces took heart that the previous night's display would boomerang against Camp. Registration continued during the day in increasingly chaotic and uncertain conditions, in which both sides could register delegates without proper checking of credentials. Diefenbaker stayed away, only later slipping in a side door to meet groups of delegates privately.

The crucial vote on the party presidency came that afternoon. Camp and Maloney delivered their campaign speeches to a chastened audience. The most memorable lines were uttered by the challenger:

> I have no obligation to our national leader, I have no obligation to him whatsoever except one, which by reason I suppose of my Renfrew County upbringing is really to me, terribly important. And that is the single obligation that we all owe, each and every one of us to the man we picked as leader, loyalty and respect.
>
> That means among other things that in regard to the Right Honourable John George Diefenbaker, sometime Prime Minister of Canada, present leader of the opposition and the national leader of the Conservative Party of Canada, when he enters a room, Arthur Maloney stands up! When the day comes that he decides to lay down the mantle of leadership which we gave him, he will do so in a blaze of glory.[155]

Afterwards delegates dispersed to their provincial meeting rooms to cast their votes for president, and early that evening the result was conveyed to John and Olive by telephone. Camp had won, by a vote of 564 to 502. And in added rebuke, delegates had elected Flora MacDonald as national secretary of the party.[156]

After four years of scattered combat, Diefenbaker's legions had at last been outnumbered. But he had one final redoubt. The loyal core of his caucus gathered that evening in the parliamentary office of the whip, Eric Winkler, to demonstrate their support for Diefenbaker. The fantasy of a new party had faded, but seventy-one MPs signed a declaration of loyalty requesting Diefenbaker to remain as leader of the party. The signatories included seven ex-ministers, among them George Hees. A week later the caucus purged six of its members – who had not signed the pledge – from the party's national executive. The Tories, Bruce Hutchison commented in the Winnipeg *Free Press*, were performing "high tragedy reduced to low farce."[157]

With Maloney's defeat in the vote for president, Johnston and his national office staff abandoned management of the annual meeting and left its direction to Camp and Goodman. Diefenbaker's supporters lost interest in the proceedings, and when delegates straggled into the hall on November 16, no one was clear what would happen. Goodman introduced debate on the leadership resolutions – which, it was easily agreed, would be decided by secret ballot. As the discussion began, Diefenbaker arrived in the Château lobby, where his supporters mobbed him noisily. "I saw none of those people," Diefenbaker recalled, "who had jeered me down so short a time before." He did not enter the meeting hall, but encouraged his friends with the stoic lines of the Scots ballad: "Fight on, my men./ I am wounded but I am not slain./ I'll lay me down and bleed awhile/ and then I'll rise and fight again."[158] Inside the meeting, the dissidents were now in a majority on the floor, and the simple motion of confidence in the leader proposed earlier by Goodman's resolutions committee was amended to read: "That this party expresses its support of the Right Honourable John G. Diefenbaker, its national leader, and acknowledges its wholehearted appreciation of his universally recognized services to the party; and in view of the current situation in the party, directs the National Executive, after consultation with the national leader, to call a leadership convention at a suitable time before January 1, 1968." The resolution was adopted by a resounding vote of 563 to 186.[159]

CHAPTER 14

"An Old Man
Dreaming Dreams"

1967-1979

After November 15, Diefenbaker was deluged with messages of sympathy, delivered by telegram, telephone, letter, or by "tear-stained visitors," almost all of them assuming he would immediately resign as leader of the party. Liberal MPs, who only months before had shown their contempt and hatred for him in the House, let him know of their respect and avoided mention of his embarrassments in debate. Paul Martin told Jim Johnston: "We've had plenty of differences, but I just want you to know that I don't think he should ever have had to take that."[1]

Diefenbaker did not resign, but consulted endlessly with his advisers Jim Johnston, Gordon Churchill, Alvin Hamilton, Waldo Monteith, David Walker, and others. Loyalists and dissidents alike, in caucus and national executive, were concerned to hold the party's remnants together. As centennial year began with no word from Diefenbaker about his plans, MPs reported growing dissatisfaction in the constituencies. Johnston expected mass desertions, and shared the opinion of Churchill and Monteith that Diefenbaker should bow out in favour of an interim leader. The right occasion seemed to be a free-time CBC broadcast on "The Nation's Business" scheduled for January 18. On the day before, Diefenbaker called Johnston in to say that "the time had come for him to speak. He had been silent, and the party had been floundering." Davie Fulton was the only candidate for the leadership who had made his intentions clear, and the Chief was not about to let Fulton succeed him. Johnston went home to draft a resignation statement hedged with qualifiers, and returned the next morning to find Diefenbaker and his staff preparing a different speech. "Don't you see that once I say I am going, I have no more power left to hold this party together? I must stop Fulton." Diefenbaker gleefully seized Johnston's statement for his archives, but when Churchill and Monteith arrived he took it from his briefcase and read it to them. They laughed. As Diefenbaker finished, Johnston grabbed the page and tore it to pieces. "Here, that's mine!" Diefenbaker shouted. "You can't do that. You've destroyed the evidence."[2]

Diefenbaker taped the broadcast in ebullient mood. He thanked the "thousands of Canadians" who had recently sent him warm messages, deplored the divisions in the party provoked by Dalton Camp, and called for an immediate leadership convention to be made up entirely of democratically elected constituency delegates. He would not allow the party to become "the plaything or the puppet of a powerful few." He left his own future typically obscure. "I know that some will interpret what I am saying as being a swan song. Let me say at once – this is no swan song. Those who will interpret it that way do not know me. I have never in the past, and I shall not now, desert the course of a lifetime, of at all times upholding principle and standing for those things which in my opinion are good for Canada, for the people of this nation – never forgetting the humblest of our people."[3] What did he mean? What his aides in the studio could see was that "half the staff in the control room was in laughter." What he had done was to force Dalton Camp to react to the unexpected – if any surprise from the Chief could be called unexpected. Camp announced a meeting of the party's executive committee for January 28 and suggested that the convention would take place in the autumn.

Diefenbaker had not reopened the fight against a leadership convention, but his allies hoped to command a majority in the executive meeting and so to confine his opponents at every turn. They failed to do so. Camp had persuaded Eddie Goodman to become chairman of the convention and the planning committee, which allowed Camp to step out of Diefenbaker's focus and to canvass his own prospects as a potential candidate. When the meeting opened, Camp vacated the chair, the meeting transformed itself into the convention committee, and Goodman was confirmed as chairman. Roger Régimbal, a Quebec MP supported by the Diefenbaker lobby, was elected co-chairman. The meeting agreed that delegates should be elected from constituencies on the basis of the new, 1965 redistribution, which would require several months of reorganization and unsettle entrenched local executives. Diefenbaker's demand that delegates-at-large should be excluded was rejected. But there was no agreement on a convention date. Johnston, in consultation by telephone with Diefenbaker, who was away on a fishing holiday in Florida, gained agreement that the date should be "not later than September," to be confirmed after Goodman met with Diefenbaker on his return. Two weeks later the committee settled on an early September gathering in Toronto.[4]

Under Goodman's sure touch, the convention planning committee worked in astonishing harmony for five months, satisfying the pro-Diefenbaker faction with its even-handedness. The spirit of cooperation was undoubtedly aided by the general assumption that Diefenbaker – although he had made no commitment – would not himself be a candidate. But with Diefenbaker there was always ambiguity. When the convention committee met in Victoria in June, it faced potential deadlock over the issue of the leader's place on the program and the closing time for nominations. The Chief wished to address delegates on the opening night of the convention. Goodman was willing – as long as Diefenbaker himself was not a candidate for the leadership; so he planned that nominations should close that afternoon. Diefenbaker protested that he had a right to address the convention as leader without revealing whether or not he would be a candidate for his own succession. Under threat from the pro-Diefenbaker members of the committee that they would resign at once if his request were rejected – and that Diefenbaker, too, would instantly vacate the leadership – Goodman and the committee made a partial concession. Above all, they were concerned to restore the party's public reputation for fairness and unity after the discords of the previous years. Diefenbaker would go onto the opening night program whether or not he was a candidate, but nominations would still close before he spoke. For two months Diefenbaker grumbled and threatened in private, until Goodman, after consultation, gave way just two weeks before the convention. Nominations would not close until the morning after Diefenbaker's address. He would be allowed to keep both country and party in suspense until the last possible moment. It was not clear whether this was, for Diefenbaker, a small private war of personal dignity or part of some larger tactical campaign for advantage. Perhaps he did not know himself.[5]

Through the genial summer of centennial year and Expo 67, the Conservative Party prepared, in relaxed mood, for its convention of renewal. Davie Fulton and George Hees had been declared candidates, running hard, since February. Michael Starr, Wallace McCutcheon, and Alvin Hamilton soon joined the field. In June Donald Fleming came in: "running backwards," as James Johnston put it, apparently prodded out of retirement by Diefenbaker's encouragement. The three Tory premiers, John Robarts, Duff Roblin, and Robert Stanfield, seemed to be out of the race. Dalton Camp remained an enigma: He showed some preference for Stanfield or Roblin, but did not rule himself out, and kept a shadow organization at the ready. Diefenbaker talked privately with Stanfield about what might have become an endorsement, but that apparently came to nothing because the Chief expressed doubts about the Nova Scotia premier's stance on the "two nations." After a landslide provincial electoral victory in May, Stanfield became the focus of increased speculation throughout

June. Roblin and Camp played coy until mid-July, when Stanfield entered the race and Camp chose to support his old Maritime compatriot. Two weeks later Roblin, after months of indecision, announced his candidacy as well. With their reputations unsullied by the prolonged civil wars of the federal party, the two premiers quickly came to the front in the race for delegate support. Diefenbaker himself made no preparations for a campaign, although two young enthusiasts, Keith Martin and Bill Hatton, created a skeletal Youth for Dief organization to show their affection for him at the convention. But if Diefenbaker wished to find a challenge in the contest, he could find it in the presence of his nemesis Dalton Camp as chief strategist and speechwriter for Robert Stanfield.[6]

Diefenbaker preferred silence on the leadership contest, as his friends provided him with daily accounts of the latest gossip. A series of events during the summer – all of them welcomed and encouraged by the Chief – contributed to the growing Diefenbaker legend. On July 21 he attended the dedication of Diefenbaker Lake, the vast reservoir created on the South Saskatchewan River above Saskatoon by completion of the Gardiner Dam – the two names now twinned forever on the landscape as they had been in political combat over thirty years. In Regina in August, the leader dedicated the old family homestead building, which had been moved by Ross Thatcher's provincial Liberal government to a new site at Wascana Centre on the grounds of the provincial legislature. Saskatoon gave his name to a city park. And just before the leadership convention, RCA Victor released a long-play recording of Diefenbaker in reminiscence, reading his "I am a Canadian" pledge from his Bill of Rights speech, chuckling and telling anecdotes about his heroes John A. Macdonald, Wilfrid Laurier, Winston Churchill, and R.B. Bennett. The advance order, RCA reported, was the largest in Canadian history.[7]

Goodman, Régimbal, and Camp, hoping to supplement the leadership contest with some policy discussion that would restore the party's credit among the thinking classes, planned a policy conference to precede the convention. It took place at Montmorency Falls, Quebec, at the beginning of August, under the chairmanship of the Ontario minister of education, William Davis. The conference, Goodman felt, was "almost a resounding success." Just two weeks after Charles de Gaulle made his triumphal progress between Quebec City and Montreal along the *chemin du roy* and startled Canadians with his cry from the balcony of Montreal City Hall, "Vive le Québec...Vive le Québec *libre!*" the Conservative meeting threw the party into the maelstrom.

> The conference [Goodman explained] accepted the concept of *deux nations* not in the sense of two political states, but as a recognition of the country's

two founding peoples: an English community and French community with distinct cultural and linguistic backgrounds. It was an effort to show Quebec that the Progressive Conservative Party was sympathetic to its legitimate aspirations to maintain the existence of Canada's French culture. Unfortunately, these ideas are difficult to express, but easy to distort. The accusation was made by some of the delegates at Montmorency, led by Dick Bell in a spirited debate with Marcel Faribault, that we were advocating two sovereign states, or separate political status for Quebec. This was the beginning of an issue that was to be shrewdly manipulated by Pierre Trudeau and the Liberals to defeat the Tories in 1968.[8]

Before Pierre Trudeau seized upon it, "two nations" was an alarm signal for John Diefenbaker. He denounced the party's use of the phrase at a press conference on September 1. "When you talk about special status and Two Nations, that proposition will place all Canadians who are of other racial origins than English and French in a secondary position. All through my life, one of the things I've tried to do is to bring about in this nation citizenship not dependent on race or colour, blood counts or origin."[9] Two days before the formal opening of the convention, Goodman's policy committee endorsed the Montmorency resolution for recommendation to the convention.

BECAUSE HE COULD NEVER BRING HIMSELF TO OFFER HIS RESIGNATION FROM THE leadership of the Progressive Conservative Party, Diefenbaker brought turmoil to his party and disenchantment to his country. For years he filled the air with vague and reckless talk of conspiracies, dark networks of enemies who were working to dismantle Canada or destroy its independence – first in league with Washington, then in league with Quebec, always in league with the Liberal Party. He made the paranoid style dominant in Canadian politics as it had not been since the days of William Aberhart and Mitchell Hepburn; and by the time of the 1966 annual meeting of the party, he found the very conception-point of conspiracy in the mind of Dalton Camp.

For Diefenbaker, Camp remained thereafter the fount of evil – and the source of the Chief's own justification. The campaign to destroy John Diefenbaker – which reached its dramatic climax in Camp's orchestration of the 1966 defeat – was, after all, the campaign to destroy Diefenbaker's Canada. Personal and national destiny had become one. In the twilight of his life, Diefenbaker had unexpectedly claimed a destiny he had glimpsed in his youth and then lost for decades. After 1957, when the nation responded to his beguiling call, he had found it again. "One Canada" from sea to sea, Macdonald's and Cartier's political nation, was to be fulfilled a century later at the hands of their authentic heir. It must not be destroyed, by Pearson, by Kennedy, by Camp, by anyone. Of course Diefenbaker could not abandon his destiny; of course he could not abandon his leadership of the Progressive Conservative Party of Canada. What was at stake was not a personal career but a nation. So far had hubris taken him.

As the party conflicts and the election campaigns revealed, Diefenbaker had many followers in his mission. Some, like Arthur Maloney, were by 1967 followers out of decent loyalty. Some, in the caucus, were followers who knew their political lives depended on the Chief's presence. Some were admirers – worshippers even – who had been inspired by Diefenbaker in 1958 and had kept the faith. Some – westerners, maritimers, those marginalized by region, race, national origin – were followers because he was one of them. Some were new loyalists won by the persistence and courage of this man under siege. Some were followers because – despite or apart from policy – they found something unbearably smug and arrogant in the Liberal Party, or because they resented its complacency. Some were followers because they possessed the darker prejudices Diefenbaker's words and silences called forth. Some shared his bitterness. By 1967 it was difficult for Canadians – Conservatives or not – to remain indifferent to the man. The followers who remained with him had made an emphatic choice, as had those who departed to another party or another faction. At the leadership convention John Diefenbaker would draw attention, perhaps for the last time, to the strengths he had added to the party and the divisions he had created within it.

OLIVE AND JOHN ARRIVED AT THE ROYAL YORK HOTEL ON THE DAY BEFORE THE convention, to be greeted by a crowd of several hundred reporters and spectators, including "eight middle-aged to elderly women with Diefenbaker placards in a kick-line. One of the women held a rose between her teeth." Close by, James Johnston was confronted by another band of "little old ladies supporting Mr. Diefenbaker," who mistook him for Dalton Camp and threatened him with physical violence. Diefenbaker – once settled into the vice-regal suite – began to receive a stream of candidates, each of them seeking credit in reconciliation with the old Chief. Eventually all but McCutcheon and Fulton made calls on the leader. He lectured them on the evils of a "two nations" policy – and said nothing definite about his own intentions. On Thursday morning, September 7, the Toronto *Star* reported that he had told Duff Roblin he would walk out of the convention if it endorsed the idea of "two nations." The organizers made their final preparations for the televised opening and

Diefenbaker's address at Maple Leaf Gardens – and crossed their fingers about what he might say. No one knew whether he would announce his own candidacy.[10]

Maple Leaf Gardens was decked out in blue banners and portraits of all the Conservative leaders since Confederation when Eddie Goodman opened proceedings with his greeting, "Good evening, sports fans," on Thursday evening.[11] Goodman and John Robarts welcomed the audience; and then, to the chairman's surprise, there was a flurry at the other end of the arena. "The doors at the back of the Gardens suddenly swung open, and behind a swirl of pipers John and Olive Diefenbaker marched in...It was too late for officialdom to stop the display. Goodman was one of the few who seemed to appreciate the irony of it all, and a grin sneaked across his face. He had tried hard to keep Diefenbaker from speaking on the convention's opening night. But he had lost, and now the old Chief had arrived with his army of pipers, and on national television too."[12] This was the work of the Youth for Dief delegates, whom Diefenbaker had embraced in delicious good humour. Once the hall had settled, Goodman introduced two keynote speakers, Alberta's promising new Tory leader, Peter Lougheed, and the French-speaking co-chairman, Roger Régimbal. But they were only a sideshow. The crowds awaited the Chief. Anticipating the occasion, the *Globe and Mail* asked the drama teacher and producer Eli Rill to describe it through professional eyes. His report was head-ed: "Is Dief Another Barrymore?" "He came on stage with what they revere in the acting profession, the thing they called simply presence – the air of hold-ing an audience's attention just by being there. And, as any performer does, he made it clear that he could rise above his material, his script – even when he had written the script himself. What he was saying was of less value than how he said it."

The supporting cast "faded into the background after the star appeared...But what chance did they have – they were up against the shades of Garrick and Booth and Barrymore." The doubters soon "fell victim to the magnetism, the projection, the charisma (as the U.S. political mind-benders are calling it now) of Diefenbaker playing front and centre." Diefenbaker accepted a presentation painting, and stepped to the podium.

> He started low-key, a shade solemn, not to make too sudden a shift from a gift-laden lady's recital of the history of an obscure painter in water colors. His words, he said, would be inadequate. But he was Mark Antony over Caesar's body, re-shaping a mixed collection of emotions and attitudes into a unified, loud-voiced People's Party, "for all Canadians" – and conceivably

all for Diefenbaker. With jabbing, emphasizing, accusing finger and head-thrusts that gave no hint of galloping old age, he built towards a passion suitable for defending the Monarchy.

He quoted Scripture, touched lightly on his party's support of manly sports, invoked the unpolitical name of Bobby Hull. Then he continued his overt wooing of French Canada – low and vibrant at first, then building to a reverberant punch line – "I shall never agree to second-class citizenship for 6,000,000 people!"[13]

He plunged on, the spellbinder stilling the applause-mad audience time and again, holding them in check, playing them like a lyre, his tune a nostalgic paean of East York, Don Mills, all of Canada. When a rhetorical question drew an unexpected answer from the gods, he jumped on it like a tiger, used it to tease still another accent for his thesis. Now he crouched in defiance of the charge that he was growing old. Now, with fist clenched like any melodramatic ham, he turned the jaded gesture into significance.

His jowls quivered, as he repudiated the disaster-bound course of the Liberal government.

Now he switched to schoolmaster tones and quoted poetry supporting the One Nation policy. Speaking of devotion and dedication to fighting for those things "I have fought for all my life," he intoned the great line, "I am still here!"

We listened, and listened, but he did not finish the drama – a drama that has been longer than the Oresteia and Hardy's The Dynasts combined. He left us longing for the final curtain – a cliff-hanger if ever there was one. The rest was silence, though Hamlet was not dead. Or was he? Was Lear dead – or was he still raging on the heath, conducting the winds and hurricanes as though they were the Ottawa Symphony?

And Mr. Diefenbaker spoke, from time to time, in French. Nobody would mistake him for Mounet Sully reciting Racine or Corneille. His accent, quite simply, is agonizing, sometimes reducing the words to gibberish. But by God, we listen, doubly riveted – by the rolling waves of sound, and by the suspense of wondering whether it will mean anything.[14]

The speech was a dramatic triumph for the old stager, but it left the national audience puzzled. It had expected a farewell. Next morning a banner headline in the Victoria *Daily Colonist* read: "He wouldn't say yes/ He wouldn't say no."[15] As the nomination lists for the leadership contest were about to close at 10 am, John Diefenbaker issued a brief statement:

Last evening I stated I could not consider being a candidate for the leadership of the Progressive Conservative Party of Canada if this Party Convention accepts the TWO NATION concept as approved of by the Sub-Committee and by the Policy Committee.

I remain unchanged and unswerving in my opposition to that concept.

The TWO NATION Policy is not to come before the Convention until Saturday morning and as nominations close at ten o'clock this morning my name is being placed in nomination.[16]

He had no chance of re-election. But he would keep his party in turmoil to the end – and he would go down fighting.

The same morning the *Globe and Mail* called the "two nations" resolution "a landmark of clarity." The words that offended Diefenbaker read: "That Canada is and should be a federal state; that Canada is composed of the original inhabitants of this land and the two founding peoples (deux nations) with historic rights, who have been and continue to be joined by people from many lands; that the Constitution should be such as to permit and encourage the full and harmonious growth and development in equality of all Canadians." The *Globe* commented: "The Canadian who can find in it the seeds of our national disruption, the Canadian who can come away from it convinced that it was concocted with diabolical cunning, is quite a fellow. In fact, he is the fellow that John Diefenbaker is seeking to join him in his cockeyed campaign to have the words deux nations expunged from the record before the convention ends. And, of course, the old chief is finding support. His stock has never been higher – out in Social Credit country. Telegrams have been pouring in – from the Nineteenth Century."[17]

Eddie Goodman knew that Diefenbaker's nomination spelled trouble: not because he might win, but because he was provoking division at the very moment when the party hoped to regain popularity with a fresh image of unity and reconciliation. Soon after the Chief's nomination, Gordon Churchill called to ask for a meeting with Goodman and Davis. "Benny," Churchill said to Goodman, "I want you to know that when Bill Davis puts his report to the plenary session Dief and his supporters are going to vigorously oppose the *deux nations* resolution." Churchill, accompanied by the Chief's friend Joel Aldred, met with Goodman and Davis that afternoon to argue that the resolution would open the way to special status for Quebec. Goodman and Davis could not persuade them that this was a misconception. In frustration, Goodman told them that he had "no intention of letting you fellows destroy this convention and the party." He would ask Davis simply to table the policy report without comment or debate, and move on. There would be no vote to adopt or reject it. Churchill, whom Goodman accepted as "a man of good, if often mistaken, intentions," agreed.

When Davis presented the report to the convention on Saturday for tabling, only one delegate – Diefenbaker's spirited advocate Charlotte Whitton – demanded the right to speak. Goodman ordered her microphone turned off, and for a few moments she mouthed silent imprecations until the audience began to boo. "I made a point of order," Goodman remembered, "stopped the discussion, Whitton screamed 'Fascist' and the crisis was averted."[18]

After a dull round of nominating speeches and addresses from all the candidates – including Diefenbaker – on Friday evening, delegates trooped to the floor for the balloting on Saturday afternoon. Goodman's importation of American voting machines, intended to speed up the balloting, caused interminable confusion instead. Lines of delegates snaked slowly forward for the first ballot as the temperature in the Gardens rose to steamy heights. Diefenbaker boasted to reporters from a box seat about the disputed policy resolution: "They didn't dare bring that before the convention...They had it all arranged. It was going to be done well. It was going to be put through, and everyone was going to look happy...Principles must never be subverted in the hope of political gain."[19] He sat for a while with the ex-leader John Bracken. The Toronto *Star*'s Dominique Clift told Jim Johnston: "I've got a theory why he's doing it. You *anglais* are funny. You are all masochists. Dief knows what they did to John Bracken, and now they are doing it to him. He wants Bracken there beside him so everybody can see what's gone on before." He was joined in his box during the day by his brother, Elmer; his step-daughter, Carolyn Weir, and her son John; and by Helen Brunt, Joel Aldred, and the Paul Lafontaines. Others moved in and out during the voting.[20]

Finally, the first ballot results were announced. With more than 2200 votes cast, Robert Stanfield was in the lead with 519. Duff Roblin and Davie Fulton were second and third, with 349 and 343 votes. George Hees was next, with 295. Diefenbaker followed in fifth place, with 271 votes. He looked pained and "sank a little deeper into his chair, his tremor more intense." He took a short walk with Olive, returned to his seat, and huddled in conversation with Gordon Churchill. He did not withdraw. On the second ballot, as Stanfield and Roblin both gained votes, Diefenbaker remained in fifth place with a reduced count of 172. This time, "he went for another walk, then holed up with his advisers, and without Mrs. Diefenbaker, in a small room guarded by police. The rumor spread quickly through the halls that he was writing his resignation, and would announce it when he emerged." Instead he returned to his seat and voted for a third time. That ballot left Stanfield and Roblin in their steady climb, with Stanfield in the lead. Diefenbaker – still in fifth place – fell to 114. Olive had earlier donned dark glasses, and now "the first few trickles of tears" ran down below them. The Diefenbakers, Walker, Churchill, and Johnston rose to leave with a police escort, a few voices calling after them, "Don't go, John." Half a block from Maple Leaf Gardens, Johnston left the limousine to return to the arena with Diefenbaker's scrawled note of withdrawal from the race.[21]

It had been a hard day. At the Royal York an aide told reporters that Diefenbaker would not appear again that evening. But less than two hours later, as voting began on the fifth and final ballot – between Stanfield and Roblin – the Diefenbakers took their seats again at the Gardens. When Stanfield's victory was declared, the Diefenbakers applauded and walked together to the podium. Eddie Goodman introduced the Chief as "the greatest Canadian of the century." Diefenbaker offered his congratulations to Stanfield, pleaded for loyalty to the new leader, and echoed R.B. Bennett's retirement statement from 1938: "Don't, as the fires of controversy rage around your leader, add gasoline to the flames." In parting he left two more barbed reminders to those who followed.

> My course has come to an end. I have fought your battles, and you have given that loyalty that led us to victory more often than the party has ever had since the days of Sir John A. Macdonald.
>
> In my retiring, I have nothing to withdraw in my desire to see Canada, my country and your country, one nation.

But it was, even so, a gracious departure. "A little of the bitterness showed through," wrote George Bain, "and the short farewell just missed nobility. But it took great courage just to stand there and deliver it at all, for it had been an awful day for him." As he left the arena and returned to his hotel suite – the burdens relinquished – he had time for conversations with clusters of admirers who would not easily let him pass.[22]

JOHN DIEFENBAKER WAS NO LONGER LEADER OF HIS PARTY, AND DESPITE HIS PUBLIC concession, he was bitter. His resentment was focused on his successor, Robert Stanfield – who had commented lightly as he began his acceptance speech, "Personally, I'm determined to get along with that fellow Camp."[23] When Diefenbaker and Stanfield met privately at the Royal York Hotel two days later, Diefenbaker began by telling him he was "deeply concerned" by those words. Stanfield responded that he had been under strain, and that after Diefenbaker's withdrawal he had heard that the Chief had advised his supporters to vote for Roblin. Diefenbaker did not deny the story. Next Diefenbaker expressed concern that when the reporter Gordon Sinclair had asked Stanfield: "Are you going to kick him out of Stornoway at once?" Stanfield had answered: "Well, Stornoway is the home of the Leader of the Opposition." Stanfield apologized for having made a thoughtless reply, and insisted he would not rush the Diefenbakers out of the house. Diefenbaker challenged Stanfield about new arrangements for his office and staff, and received what he thought was a "noncommittal" reply. In a long memo after the meeting, Diefenbaker described it – perhaps generously – as "cool and reserved," although he noted that Stanfield "did indicate that he was firmly attached to me."[24] An hour later, in a telephone conversation with Gordon Churchill, Diefenbaker said: "He came to see me a little while ago. It is obvious that he does not want me in the House and it is also obvious that I get out of my office at once although he did not say so. It was also obvious that I should get out of the house."[25]

Diefenbaker's bile rose as he talked further with his supporters during the day. To one friend he reflected that the remark about Camp was "a deliberate slap. I don't know whether I should have gone back there at the end or not." He commented to Churchill about George Bain's commentary: "You will have to get the 'Globe & Mail.' It said my speech at the end was quite remarkable. It just stopped short of nobility. Now what kind of bastardy is that." Next day Diefenbaker wrote: "The press have slain me and now they have mutilated me."[26]

But there were unusual efforts to show him kindness. On his seventy-second birthday on September 18, as he was moving out of the leader's parliamentary offices, the staff gave him a birthday party at the home of his assistant Tom Van Dusen. Diefenbaker told stories to the four youngest Van Dusen children, sang several verses of "an interminable western ballad," and stayed until late in the evening. Two nights later, the parliamentary press gallery entertained him at an unusual retirement dinner, where he told them that he would never speak in the House again. The vow lasted until late in November.[27]

Diefenbaker and Olive made a brief visit to Saskatchewan, where his Prince Albert supporters put on a "Carry on, John" rally that attracted fifteen hundred locals. The mayor presented Diefenbaker with a mounted northern lake trout weighing fifty pounds and labelled "You've tackled many big ones, Keep Going." Despite the crowds and the affection, the Chief was unresponsive, still bitter and irritable. He left Prince Albert to attend similar events in Regina and Moose Jaw.[28] Diefenbaker returned to Ottawa and his new corner office in the Centre Block, looking out to the northwest across the Ottawa River to the Gatineau Hills beyond Hull. There he hung his giant bluefish and his print of the naval battle from the war of 1812, trophies of his encounters with John Kennedy. Later – when it became clear that Robert Stanfield had decided to keep Dalton Camp at a distance as a signal of reconciliation with the Diefenbaker loyalists – the Chief placed prominently in his outer office a *Telegram* cartoon of Camp slinking silently away from Ottawa. The national archivist agreed to take Diefenbaker's papers and records in temporary storage, while two padlocked filing cabinets of his confidential papers remained close by him in his office. He talked of writing his memoirs. During the autumn the Diefenbakers bought their own home in Rockcliffe Park and transformed the basement recreation room into a miniature historical museum decorated with Macdonaldiana, gifts from his foreign visits, Indian headdresses, and the brilliant gowns marking his many honorary doctorates.

The stream of public events flowed on without him. The old man appeared regularly in the House for the daily Question Period and then withdrew, taking no part in his own party's deliberations in caucus. He had his friends and loyalists still, but hardly felt himself a member of the party that had repudiated him. In November the Ontario premier John Robarts hosted his Confederation of Tomorrow conference of the provinces, and unknowingly began a twenty-five-year cycle of constitutional negotiations. Stanfield won a by-election to parliament in the same month – but Diefenbaker refused to escort the leader as he took his seat in the chamber, and instead stayed away from the House that afternoon. On December 15 Mike Pearson announced his own decision to retire from politics.

When the new leader of the Liberal Party, Pierre Elliott Trudeau, dissolved the House in April 1968 for a June general election, Diefenbaker belatedly accepted nomination in Prince Albert, where his re-election was a certainty. He remained barely on speaking terms with Stanfield. Diefenbaker and Trudeau – both dissidents by nature, both scrappers, both favourites of the media – established an immediate relationship of wary mutual respect. Trudeau endorsed Diefenbaker's commitment to one nation, and the Chief found perverse comfort in a Prince Albert campaign that was as personal and devoid of association with his national party as in the old days. He wished for Stanfield's failure. But throughout the west the Conservative Party needed the Chief's candidacy – however cool he might be to the new leadership and its policies.

For six weeks during the campaign the Diefenbakers occupied a suite in the Flamingo Motel in Prince Albert – where John, during Olive's absences,

561

exchanged mildly racy jokes with his cronies about Gerda Munsinger and her two ministerial friends, and Olive soothed his frequent fits of distemper. His loyal Prince Albert associates Dick Spencer, Max Carment, Ed Topping, Glen Green, and Art Pearson organized the campaign in a newly enlarged constituency, and found busywork for the sixteen-year-old Youth for Dief refugee Sean O'Sullivan, whom Diefenbaker had unaccountably imported from Hamilton for the duration of the campaign. In Spencer's eyes, O'Sullivan provided the Chief with adoration, and spoke the words of pain about his rejection that Diefenbaker himself could not express. For the local campaign workers, O'Sullivan's most useful function was to persuade a contemptuous Chief of the value of promotional "bumperschtickers." As usual, Elmer was present for the duration, "getting on Dief's nerves," O'Sullivan remembered, "and driving Olive crazy...Dief gave Elmer money and Elmer's task during the campaign was to buy King Edward cigars and pass them out on the Indian reserves on behalf of his brother."[29]

Diefenbaker campaigned slowly in his riding, chatting at lunch counters, attending baseball games, casually visiting voters' homes to drink too much tea and coffee. In his speeches he relentlessly attacked "two nations," even though no party was committed to the doctrine he imagined, but he gradually added lines that challenged Trudeau's unspecified policies. As the campaign neared its conclusion, Stanfield sought Diefenbaker's support at a rally in Saskatoon, an appearance that might somehow distinguish Diefenbaker's commitment to one Canada from that of Trudeau and the Liberals. Diefenbaker refused, and instead devised an awkward meeting at Saskatoon airport and a joint tour of the Western Development Museum – where they argued over "two nations." That evening Stanfield told his audience impatiently that he had never been an advocate of "two nations" or "special status" for Quebec. "My impression of the encounter," Diefenbaker's constituency president, Dick Spencer, wrote about the meeting with Stanfield, "was that it was a mean-spirited affair on Dief's part, embarrassing and dangerous to his legend. I knew in my heart that Dief and Mrs. D. couldn't help themselves, such was the anger and the hurt the very mention of Stanfield's name could summon. But how much more sensible and honourable a course it would have been to excuse themselves from the Saskatoon rendezvous and stay home with us. It was time for the campaign of 1968 to draw to a close." Only in two last-minute visits to rallies in Manitoba did Diefenbaker overcome his resentments and offer overt support for the leadership of his successor.[30]

Across the nation, the wave of adolescent Trudeaumania swept away opposition. On election night, the Chief revelled in Stanfield's humiliation.

*Diefenbaker and Donald Fleming lost the 1948 leadership contest on the
first ballot to George Drew, the premier of Ontario. On the platform, from
left to right, Diefenbaker, Edna, George Drew, Fiorenza Drew, Donald Fleming.*

*Diefenbaker maintained his law partnership in Prince Albert, mostly
in absentia, with John Cuelenaere and Roy Hall until the mid-1950s.
(Saskatchewan Archives: Star-Phoenix Collection)*

In December 1956 Diefenbaker easily won his third run for the leadership against his parliamentary colleagues Donald Fleming and Davie Fulton, shown here raising the victor's hands in triumph. (World Wide Photos)

Olive Diefenbaker was at John's side to celebrate his election as leader of the party. (Canada Wide)

Following the 1957 general election victory, Diefenbaker took three reporters to Lac La Ronge for a day of fishing. From left: Mark Harrison of the Toronto Star, Diefenbaker, Clark Davey of the Globe and Mail, and Peter Dempson of the Toronto Telegram. (Canada Pictures Ltd.)

On October 14, 1957, Queen Elizabeth II presided over a ceremonial meeting of her Privy Council for Canada before opening parliament that afternoon. (National Film Board)

*On April 1, 1958, Elmer and John posed happily as the telegrams poured
in after Diefenbaker's overwhelming general election victory.*

In Ceylon during his 1958 Commonwealth tour, Diefenbaker briefly took a ride on an elephant.

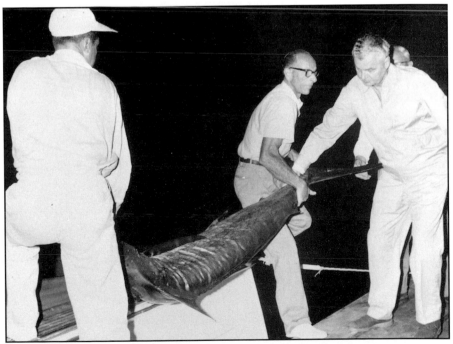

Bringing ashore the marlin, January 1961. This catch became the object of half-serious repartee between President Kennedy and Prime Minister Diefenbaker in February and May 1961. (Roy Bailey)

Diefenbaker received the Freedom of the City of London during an early interlude in the 1963 Canadian general election campaign. (Central Press Photos, London)

Diefenbaker turned on the party president, Dalton Camp, to accuse him of betrayal at the 1966 annual meeting of the Conservative Party. At this meeting, the party agreed to hold a leadership convention in defiance of Diefenbaker's wishes. (Canada Wide)

At Maple Leaf Gardens in September 1967 Diefenbaker made his last stand as leader of the party, challenging the phrase "deux nations" as the translation of "two founding peoples" in a convention resolution.

The House of Commons was not in session when Diefenbaker posed for his last formal portrait shortly before his death in August 1979. (Canadian Press)

In the Maritime provinces the party made gains, but in Quebec and Ontario it met disaster, and in the west it lost twenty seats. Diefenbaker gloated as his enemies Dalton Camp, Wallace McCutcheon, Marcel Faribault, Jean Wadds, Richard Bell, and Duff Roblin went down in their constituencies. The party won a total of seventy-two seats, twenty-five fewer than the Chief had delivered in 1965. But Diefenbaker won his own seat by 8600 votes over his NDP challenger. "The Conservative Party," he said on national television, "has suffered a calamitous disaster." The old man's eyes that evening "were more than twinkling, they were dancing. It was triumph. And Olive felt imperial. What a night for the two of them!"[31] The Diefenbakers returned to Ottawa reinvigorated by the party's failure.

JUSTIFIED AND WITHOUT OBLIGATION TO HIS PARTY, DIEFENBAKER RANGED FREE IN the new House of Commons, sometimes accepting the party line, sometimes ignoring it with impunity. Behind him he had a loyal claque of old Diefenbaker loyalists. Stanfield's caucus had even less representation from the cities of the nation, from the educated and the affluent, than Diefenbaker's after 1965. Stanfield's advocate Heath Macquarrie thought that the new leader had "a dozen to twenty supporters in caucus, plus the Nova Scotians – less than thirty altogether."[32] He would be forced once more to seek reconciliation with his opponents in the party; and he did so, gradually and patiently. He consulted Diefenbaker from time to time and – despite frequent provocations – always treated him with courtesy and respect. Diefenbaker was reluctant to admit it.

Towards the Chief's supporters in caucus Stanfield offered a similar display of confidence. Often they did not return it, regarding his tolerance as a sign of fatal weakness. The differences were revealed most dramatically in debate on Trudeau's official languages bill in early 1969. The legislation established French and English as equal languages in federal departments and agencies; proposed the creation of "bilingual districts" where federal services would be available in both languages; and created a new office of language commissioner responsible to parliament. The measure was as profound an assertion of Canadian values as Diefenbaker's Bill of Rights had been. But given the confusing debate on "two nations" that had preceded it, and the battle that was under way in Quebec over independence, the measure was controversial and easily distorted in English-speaking Canada. In the west, polls showed opposition as high as 70 percent. Robert Stanfield declared his support in principle, but many of Diefenbaker's loyalists in caucus, under the strident leadership of the Albertan Jack Horner, announced their more passionate opposition. In May 1969 Diefenbaker joined the opponents in a mean House of Commons speech describing the proposed language commissioner as a "commissar," a "dictator." He dared Tory MPs to reject the advice of their leader and oppose the bill. On second reading, seventeen Conservatives, including Diefenbaker, voted against the bill and fourteen abstained. Stanfield carried only forty of his members with him. The next day, in caucus, the leader angrily denounced the rebels for forcing a recorded vote. "Their stupidity," he said, "was exceeded only by their malice. There are some things in a political party one simply does not do to one's colleagues." He supported the bill because he sought the survival of a nationwide party, and he would countenance no further disobedience. The revolt collapsed under this show of firmness: the party united on all its proposals for amendments, and on third reading the bill passed on a voice vote. Diefenbaker's claque might be a nuisance and an embarrassment, but the challenge to Stanfield's leadership was hollow.[33]

There was one more brazen act in the summer of 1970, when Horner called a meeting of prairie Tory MPs for Saskatoon in August. Ostensibly the meeting would discuss agricultural policy; the real theme was Stanfield's leadership. Diefenbaker and more than a dozen of his colleagues attended, dodging reporters and acting suitably conspiratorial. "Stanfield," reported Anthony Westell in the Toronto *Star*, "had to spend the next week, when he should be undermining the government, hushing and shushing his own people, cooling off the row." A few days later, in a visit to Alberta, he declared Horner and his group "very stupid" for holding the meeting behind his back.[34] Diefenbaker was no longer a prime instigator of mischief, but he was loath to discourage anything that made life difficult for his Tory foes. In September he called reporters to his office to tell them he would not attend his party's caucus when it discussed the Saskatoon meeting and the issue of unity because the meeting had not been secret. "A closed meeting," he insisted, "is not a secret meeting." He added gratuitously that Dalton Camp was again trying to dominate the party. "Psychologists," he told them, "have long since determined that nothing is more disturbing for the human mind than for a person to have his victim still around after an assassination."[35]

Like other ex–prime ministers, Diefenbaker enjoyed foreign journeys as a reminder of the privileges of power. He travelled in these years to Taiwan as the guest of the Chinese nationalist government, where he was entertained by Chiang Kai-shek; and in 1969 he drew headlines during a visit to the Soviet Union in the company of Joel Aldred. In Moscow he met with a Soviet deputy premier and, according to his own account, discussed the damming of the Bering Strait "to divert the warm Gulf Stream into the Arctic waters and make the Arctic coast habitable"; the construction of domed cities in the Canadian north "similar to some in the USSR with populations of 500,000 to 1,000,000"; and a scheme to heat the waters of Hudson Bay with nuclear energy to make Churchill, Manitoba, a year-round port. He discussed wheat purchases from Canada with the head of the Soviet grain agency; and in Kiev he declared Ukraine an independent state free of the Soviet Union and called for the establishment of a Canadian consulate-general in the Ukrainian capital. The Soviets seemed to treat these diverting fancies calmly.[36]

In 1970 Diefenbaker marked two notable anniversaries. On March 26 he celebrated the thirtieth anniversary of his entry into the House of Commons along with the Liberal solicitor general George McIlraith. Prime Minister Trudeau presented Diefenbaker with a blue carnation and McIlraith with a red one. Diefenbaker responded: "I have been to the mountaintops and I have been down in the valley. I do not want to mention personal matters, but on an occasion like this, I am filled with emotion. I do want to say that one's happiness is greatly increased by having a wife to support, to stand and to counsel." He added, "I am not passing that on to the Prime Minister by way of a suggestion, but I say to him that if he would follow my advice in that connection he would be amazed at the transition which would take place." He warned the House that a Jewish congregation had presented him with a plaque of the Tree of Life and predicted he would live as long as Moses. That, he pointed out, was one hundred and twenty years.[37] In September he celebrated his seventy-fifth birthday, in the afternoon at home with friends, in the evening at a reception in the Railway Committee Room of the House of Commons, where he was presented with a briefcase by his parliamentary colleagues. He took the briefcase home and slid it under a bed, where it rested for months until he opened it one day to discover that it contained hundreds of mint dollar bills.

Diefenbaker continued to rise early during this parliamentary term, to take a brisk morning walk, and to arrive at his office before 8 am. His days were still filled with movement and unexpected shifts of schedule, as he took telephone calls, greeted visiting friends, reporters, and gangs of invading school children, sat in the House for Question Period (where he could conjure up a noisy round of desk-thumping and insults at the flick of a phrase), and casually misplaced letters by throwing them into desk drawers out of reach of his secretaries. He brought two of the Youth for Dief disciples of 1967 into his office as staff assistants, first Keith Martin and later Sean O'Sullivan, to learn disorder at the hand of a master.

Full of good intentions, he began a desultory effort to put thoughts on paper for his memoirs. Harold Macmillan encouraged him and explained how he had organized his own massive and graceful volumes; John Gray of the

Macmillan Company of Canada gently prodded in the background; and for several months two academics taped his recollections while they tried to make sense of the vast and disorderly bulk of the Diefenbaker Papers stored in the Public Archives.[38] But he was easily drawn back to his daily diversions and travels, and told visitors how the crowds that greeted him everywhere indicated he could make a successful return to power if he had the chance. After two years the first enterprise to produce his memoirs faded, and a succession of new literary advisers came briefly to his aid: Burt Richardson, Michael Wardell, Tom Van Dusen, Greg Guthrie, and finally John Munro and John Archer, who began to publish the memoirs with the first volume, *One Canada: The Crusading Years*, in 1975, when Diefenbaker reached the age of eighty. The second and third volumes followed in 1976 and 1977. In the meantime, Diefenbaker's supporters Tom Van Dusen, Robert Coates, and James Johnston published their own anecdotal accounts of his now-legendary career, honouring the heroic battles of his later years and denouncing the infamies of Dalton Camp.[39] Diefenbaker's brother, Elmer, faithful, dependent, and infuriating to the last, died in 1971.

Diefenbaker could never escape for long the demons of resentment that haunted him in his last years. His mind worked steadily on schemes petty and grand, ludicrous and sublime, to achieve final revenge on his foes and redemption for himself. The audiences that greeted him with affection and curiosity in his unending journeys across the nation, the many awards he received for humanitarian service, the admiring attention he gained from young people who visited his office to hear his hoary anecdotes as fresh revelations of his spirit and humour, the plaques and geographical names and statues that began to give physical dimension to his memory, all pleased and comforted him. The legend – which he absorbed and transformed into his own memory of events – became one private means of dealing with his political failures and disappointments. The factual record – as others might recall or rediscover it – lost its substance. The legend became, for him, the Truth. It had a dark as well as a light side – and the dark side was as important as the light in his private scheme of self-justification. The dark side was the record of conspiracy and betrayal by his enemies and opponents, never justifiable and never fair. If there were failures to admit, then they were not personal failures but failures imposed by malign forces always beyond his control. He was both the hero and the victim of his destiny, and somehow beyond personal responsibility.

In the autumn of 1972 his envied political opponent Mike Pearson, who had retired to write and teach a seminar at Carleton University, published the first, widely acclaimed volume of his memoirs, *Mike*. Soon afterwards Pearson fell ill with cancer, and just after Christmas he died. His coffin stood for twenty-four hours in the hall of honour of the Parliament Buildings, where 12,000 people came in the December cold to revere his memory. The next day his funeral took place at Christ Church Cathedral, where the Very Rev. A.B. Moore saw him off gently with the words of a Chinese poet, "mak(ing) his way into the distance...playing his flute as he goes."[40] John Diefenbaker was there to reflect on time's inexorable passage. Afterwards, he walked back to his office with a reporter and was asked whether, in death, he had kind words for Lester Bowles Pearson. Diefenbaker looked down for a long time in silence and at last shook his jowls and looked up: "He shouldn't have won the Nobel Prize."[41]

Mike Pearson had departed quietly, playing the flute as he went; but John Diefenbaker had something grander in mind to mark his own farewell. In the 1960s he had discussions with the University of Saskatchewan about placing his personal papers in a special collection there, but the university was reluctant to take on a collection so large and so expensive to maintain. When Diefenbaker was elected chancellor of the university in 1969, however, he announced at the installation ceremony that he was donating his papers to the university. The gift could not be refused, and in the succeeding years plans were developed, with support from both the provincial and federal governments, to establish the Diefenbaker Centre as his prime ministerial archive and museum. It was located on the high bluff above the South Saskatchewan River, and opened under its first director, John Munro, soon after Diefenbaker's death. In its plan the centre owed inspiration to the Truman Library in Independence, Missouri. The Truman Library has its Oval Office, meticulously copied from the White House and furnished with Harry Truman's office effects; the Diefenbaker Centre has not only the prime minister's East Block office but the cabinet room as well, furnished as they were from 1957 to 1963 with Canadian relics. The centre was intended to live not only as a Diefenbaker archive, but as a focus for the study of prairie history.[42]

After 1968, Diefenbaker fought three more federal elections in his Prince Albert riding. By 1972 he had grown genuinely contemptuous of the rich and dilettantish playboy Pierre Trudeau – an attitude that sat more comfortably with Diefenbaker than his ambiguity of 1968. Now he could endorse his successor without reserve as a leader who would respect parliament and Canadian tradition. He fought the 1972 summer campaign with his old verve and aggression, attending political events in his own constituency and beyond on thirty-nine days. For his constituency president, Dick Spencer, there was one briefly alarming evening when Diefenbaker erupted fire over the presence in the constituency of Peter Newman: "You know he wants to destroy me! He's a dangerous man...He's tried before, you know. What did you tell him?" Eventually reassured, the Chief sank into his chair with resigned sighs of "Ah, well...Ah, well." On the hustings he still enchanted the crowds – this time, dropping down into small prairie towns by helicopter. Diefenbaker coasted again to a comfortable victory, and watched the national returns with incredulity as Trudeau lost his majority and ended just a hair's breadth ahead of Stanfield, 109 seats to 107. The NDP held the balance with thirty-one seats. "Dief was more at home in his own Tory Party that night," reflected Spencer, "than he had been for some time." And yet: "I do not know what was the greater, Dief's satisfaction with the humbling of Pierre Elliott Trudeau or his relief that Stanfield had been denied power. I know the latter condition pleased Olive immensely...Now Dief saw another charismatic Canadian political leader wretchedly pulled from giddy heights down to the moor below. It was strangely satisfying." Diefenbaker could look forward to yet another campaign.[43]

In 1974, at age seventy-eight, Diefenbaker was nominated, for the first time since 1957, without Olive at his side. She was in an Ottawa hospital, but sent a telegram promising to be in the constituency before long. The national campaign went badly for Stanfield from the beginning, as Trudeau campaigned vigorously against the Conservative call for price and wage controls. As so frequently before, Diefenbaker rejected his party's program and went his own way. By election day the result was predictable: a new Liberal majority, 141 seats to 95. Diefenbaker's majority increased to over eleven thousand. For Robert Stanfield, this looked like the end of the road.[44] Two years later he was succeeded at a leadership convention by the unlikely choice of Joe Clark, one of those young students first drawn to a career in the Conservative Party by the inspiration of John Diefenbaker's 1957 election campaign. Another one, Brian Mulroney, would drive Clark out and succeed him in 1983.

Diefenbaker took the draft manuscript of the second volume of his memoirs to Barbados for a month-long Christmas holiday in 1975, but that interlude was cut short when Olive, now seventy-three years old, suffered a mild stroke and partial paralysis. The couple returned to Ottawa, where Olive gradually recovered movement on her left side.[45] On January 1, 1976, Diefenbaker was named a Companion of Honour in the Queen's New Year's Honours List, becoming one of a distinguished company that cannot exceed sixty-five members. Diefenbaker acknowledged the honour and told reporters that "it is a designation by the Queen herself and not based on a recommendation by the prime minister." The *Globe* commented that "Canadians of all political faiths will applaud...With a lesser man than Mr. Diefenbaker there might be reason to worry that this recognition by the Monarch might be a rite of passage from the political melee into the more gentle twilight of mellow nostalgia. But of John Diefenbaker we need have no such fear."[46]

When Diefenbaker travelled to London at the end of March for the ceremony of presentation at Windsor Castle, Trudeau injected his own, Diefenbaker-like, note of mischief by dropping the comment that it was he who had recommended Diefenbaker for the honour. The Chief – taking genuine or mock offence: Who could tell? – insisted that the queen had made her own choice, and that Trudeau had done no more than act as formal intermediary to discover whether he would accept.[47]

For Diefenbaker, the London trip was another memorable interlude. He stayed with his old political opponent and friend Paul Martin, who was now Canadian high commissioner. Despite their long competition, the two had always respected each other for their shared political vocations and talents. He was entertained – or better, he entertained – at a small luncheon hosted by the Commonwealth Parliamentary Association, "bantering quietly" with Martin and provoking his hosts to gusts of uproarious laughter with his anecdotes. That evening, Martin held a larger and equally convivial dinner in Diefenbaker's honour.[48] On April 1 he spoke to a lunch of four hundred guests at the Dorchester, telling old stories: "The sort of cracker-barrel stuff Dief has been giving Canadian audiences for years," reported George Bain in the Toronto *Star*, "requiring the occasional growl and subtle inflection to put it over, and going over here on Park Lane as it does in Lilac, Sask." Diefenbaker told his audience of the shortest judgment he'd ever heard, in a civil suit against a man who had made a final plea: "As God is my judge, I am not guilty." The judge had replied: "He's not. I am. You are." And he recalled that he had once been introduced by a Ford dealer in British Columbia who droned on interminably while searching for his name and then, "his eyes brightening like those of a politician who suddenly remembers a constituent," he announced: "And now, without further ado, I give you John Studebaker."[49]

The next day, Diefenbaker talked with Harold Macmillan, Edward Heath, and Margaret Thatcher, and spent "a fabulous evening" at Windsor Castle. Diefenbaker told the press that the queen "laughs at some of my cock-eyed stories. And last night she was in an almost ecstatic mood."[50]

He was also, good-humouredly, thinking about his own mortality. He commented to a reporter that early in 1975 someone from the Department of External Affairs had come to see him because "they thought I was going to die" and wanted to discuss funeral arrangements. "And I said, 'Hightail! Get!' and that's not regarded as appropriate language in certain circles in External

Affairs. I wasn't particularly enamored of the craving desire to get information about my funeral. Some people had no sense of humor. They thought I was terrible."[51] His visitor – in fact from the secretary of state's department – was Graham Glockling, the director of special events.

> When I took over state funerals as part of my portfolio in Secretary of State, I looked into files and there wasn't an awful lot there, quite frankly. And I thought, God, this is no way to run a railway or a funeral. So I was chatting to a few people and I said, it's a pity the incumbent couldn't have some input into this. A couple of people said, why don't you try it out for size. I thought, well, Diefenbaker's the most likely one...So I went over there. He was actually quite tickled at the whole idea...his words were something like, I'm so grateful that the government thinks enough of me to let me have a hand in the planning. I didn't want to tell him it wasn't the government, it was me. I just wanted to make my life easier.[52]

The project was titled Operation Hope Not, recalling the code-name of the planning committee for Winston Churchill's state funeral. (But Churchill himself was not a participant in the planning, and made only one suggestion: "Remember, I would like lots of military bands at my funeral." There were nine.[53]) Diefenbaker and Glockling completed the plan after several months, and Glockling filed it away.

During 1976 Olive partially recovered from her stroke, but she was weak and continued to suffer from the arthritis that had long pained her. In October she was hospitalized with a heart attack, but was released from hospital in December to spend Christmas at home. On December 22 she died. The funeral took place on Christmas Eve at the First Baptist Church in Ottawa, and she was interred in Beechwood Cemetery, beside the plot reserved for John. Another memorial service was held for her at St Alban's Cathedral in Prince Albert. The many public reflections on her life were warm and heartfelt. The Ottawa *Citizen* commented: "The serenity which marked her life and death was not a mere social grace. It was a tranquillity born of deep faith combined with extraordinary strength of character. She allowed her example to speak for her, the example of a woman who had no doubts about her role as the wife of a public figure. Her graciousness was the outward sign of the inner confidence, and it was more eloquent than mere declarations of philosophy. She was a radiant lady whose presence illuminated the places where she walked." The *Globe and Mail* said: "As the wife of a Prime Minister, she was a graceful and serious enthusiast. As the wife of a politician, she was a staunch and demanding ally. As a woman, she was an unapologetic defender of the value of supportive partnership between husband and wife, and Canadians responded with widespread respect." The Toronto *Star* spoke of her "calming influence on her mercurial husband."[54] The comments only hinted at the powerful influence Olive had had on her husband. Her public grace concealed a stern character, more forceful, more austere, more censorious than his own. At first she had been uneasy in her political role, but soon she was his closest confidante and firmest support. Later, in his adversity, she had reinforced rather than allayed his suspicions and his hatreds. For John, the death of this strong and loving partner of twenty-three years was a loss he could never overcome. For months he was in helpless despair, comforted intermittently by his faith.

He was still thinking – more frequently now – of his own approaching death. Aside from some troubled questions about the heavenly arrangements for Edna's and Olive's presence beside him, his preoccupations were worldly. He was concerned to set the final building stones of his legend properly in place. In the autumn of 1978 he proposed to his aides that he should be buried not in Beechwood Cemetery in Ottawa, but on the Saskatoon bluffs beside the Diefenbaker Centre, with Olive at his side. He approached Graham Glockling to reopen the file. The new proposal would require substantial fresh planning, including approval from the University of Saskatchewan, declaration of the site as consecrated ground, the transfer of Olive's remains to Saskatoon, and the provision of a funeral train for the long journey from Ottawa to Saskatoon. The Chief proposed that the train "should stop at some places along the route: Fort William, where my people came on foot from Winnipeg; Winnipeg, where they came in 1813 with the Red River Settlement; Watrous in Lake Centre constituency, as they elected me there in 1940; then Saskatoon." There were a thousand details besides. Glockling "just went ahead and changed the plans and the rest is history."[55]

In the summer of 1976 Joe Clark had replaced Robert Stanfield as leader of the Tory party. Clark was on Diefenbaker's blacklist as an exponent of the leadership review in 1966, and the Chief's distaste for him never wavered. But Diefenbaker was also increasingly alarmed by what he saw as the authoritarian and centrist tendencies of the Trudeau government. After some delicate probing by the Prince Albert constituency association about the Chief's intentions, Diefenbaker let them know in early April 1978 that he wished to stand again for parliament. On April 19 he was nominated at a small convention that was addressed by one of his younger party favourites, the Toronto mayor David Crombie. Diefenbaker delivered a strong speech full of sarcasm towards the

Liberal government – and then waited a full year for the general election.[56]

The Chief had outlasted many of his old Prince Albert cronies. By 1979 Art Pearson, Ed Topping, and Fred Hadley had passed on. Dick Spencer was left to run his campaign, along with Max Carment, Glen Green, and Harry Houghton. This time Diefenbaker imported another young acolyte from Ottawa, Michael McCafferty, who faithfully did his chores and endured the old man's frequent rages. John Munro, Diefenbaker's ghostwriter and the prospective director of the Diefenbaker Centre, was also present from time to time. Mary Carment and Lily Spencer managed the committee rooms. Spencer tried to keep Diefenbaker close to home and under careful watch, "so that he could be assisted and protected." He was often confused and seemed to manage best in short discussions of single issues or in face-to-face encounters with individual voters.

Early in the campaign, disaster struck. During the night of April 13, 1979, Diefenbaker apparently suffered a small stroke, fell from his bed, hit the bedside table, and blackened an eye. McCafferty, hearing the disturbance from the next room, struggled to get him back to bed. Next day he could not rise, and went through spells of jumbled and senseless talk. Dr Glen Green cared for him, and the confusion soon passed. Green and McCafferty told the press Diefenbaker was suffering from flu, had fallen in the night, and would spend the weekend in bed, but a Canadian Press report from Ottawa asserted that Diefenbaker was in a coma and would leave the race. Green vehemently denied the story. Spencer continued his account: "By Monday night Dief had regained normal awareness and began a steady recovery. Diagnosis of the malaise was no longer relevant. Our problem was now a political one. If John Diefenbaker did not recover completely, we would be running a candidate 'without all his marbles,' as one reporter harshly put it, or we would be forced to withdraw him, risking incredible damage to his legend."[57]

For five days Diefenbaker's four close friends cosseted and sheltered him from the press and the curiosity seekers, feeding him light foods until one of them complained that "this god-damned squirrel food isn't enough!" and Diefenbaker himself took "a huge breakfast of bacon and eggs, toast, jam and coffee in the hotel dining room Tuesday morning." The next day he was out on the street campaigning and putting the lie to all the gossip about a wild and incontinent interlude. He told a press conference he had had "a touch of flu" and a good rest. Now he wanted to talk about Pierre Trudeau again.[58]

For the rest of the campaign his aides watched him solicitously as he suffered repeated spells of anger, panic, and despair. The campaign did not pick up pace, and the NDP offered a firm and convincing challenge in the person of Stan Hovdebo, a young farmer and teacher. Diefenbaker's team began to fear defeat and humiliation, and stepped up their advertising under the slogan "Diefenbaker, Now More Than Ever." At the end they brought in the premier of Alberta, Peter Lougheed, for a crisp final rally attended by – among others – Peter Newman. ("I'm glad he came along," Diefenbaker commented afterwards.) The rally gave new confidence to the team. Diefenbaker remained tired and distracted: "His shakes had increased. His darting eyes and thin wisps of grey, wavy hair shooting out from above his ears gave him an amazed and comic look."

On election night the Tory campaign rooms in Prince Albert overflowed with national reporters and television crews, all there to observe Dief's last hurrah. As Joe Clark's Conservatives claimed a national minority victory, John Diefenbaker won his own seat for the thirteenth consecutive time, with a majority of more than four thousand votes. Diefenbaker spent the early evening in his committee rooms, and thanked his audience one last time: "If it wasn't for you, I wouldn't be here. It's my last campaign. I really mean that. I'm glad I stayed this time." Then he went upstairs to his room for a glass of beer with a friend, and declined the usual invitation to a late election-night supper at the Glen Greens.[59]

Diefenbaker returned to Ottawa for the swearing-in of the new Conservative government in melancholic mood. He was glad to see the Trudeau Liberals gone, but he could not rally much enthusiasm for Joe Clark and his team of young upstarts. Old grudges lasted forever. Flora MacDonald had sat next to him for much of the time in the House after her entry to the chamber in 1972, but he had not spoken a word to her since her firing from the national office in 1966. At the governor general's garden party following the swearing-in ceremony – where MacDonald had become secretary of state for external affairs – Diefenbaker responded to her efforts at reconciliation: "You! You! He should never have made you foreign minister! Minister of health, perhaps, or postmaster general; but never foreign minister!" He turned and stomped away, never to speak to her again.[60]

The House did not sit that summer. Diefenbaker returned once more to Prince Albert and came back to Ottawa in the heat of late July. He fussed with further changes in his funeral arrangements and his will, and arranged for a series of formal portraits in the House of Commons and his parliamentary office. On August 1 he wrote to his assistant Keith Martin and his friend Senator David Walker, assigning general responsibility for the funeral arrangements jointly to them and offering his latest thoughts on the display of his open casket at stops along the route of his final journey by train across the nation.[61] But he was planning a trip to the Yukon in late August for the opening of the Dempster highway, and in September to the People's Republic of China. On August 15 he appeared for a whimsical ceremony at the National Press Club to shoot the first ball on a new snooker table. On August 16, 1979, in the early morning, he died alone in his study at home.[62]

CHAPTER 15

A Burial
on the Prairie

T HE CASKET WAS MOVED WITHOUT CEREMONY TO THE HALL OF HONOUR OF parliament during the evening of Thursday, August 16, 1979. There John Diefenbaker's body lay in state in an open casket throughout the day and evening on Friday and Saturday, and again on Sunday morning, August 19. Ten thousand Canadians filed silently past the bier. At Diefenbaker's insistence, both the Red Ensign and the Canadian flag were draped on the coffin, the Red Ensign overlapping and obscuring the bottom of the maple leaf flag. On the day of his death the leader of the opposition, Pierre Trudeau, told reporters that Diefenbaker "had a vision of Canada that animated him and that gave him the ability to communicate with the people of Canada...I was struck by his vigorous defence of human rights and individual liberties. The Bill of Rights remains a monument to him...We were friends because we understood each other." The NDP leader Ed Broadbent commented that Diefenbaker was "the outstanding character in the House of Commons...Throughout his life he never forgot his humble beginnings."[1]

On Sunday afternoon the funeral cortege formed under the Peace Tower and the casket, borne by RCMP pallbearers, was carried through the great doors to a general salute. With a mounted RCMP escort, two fifty-man contingents of ceremonial guards, two military bands, and forty-nine honorary pallbearers, the procession slow-marched for almost a mile from Parliament Hill to Christ Church Cathedral for an interfaith service for the dead. Twelve hundred mourners in the body of the cathedral, and several hundred more in an adjoining hall, heard Psalms 23 ("The Lord is my shepherd") and 121 ("I will lift up mine eyes unto the hills"), Ecclesiasticus 44 ("Let us now praise famous men"), John Bunyan's great hymn "To be a pilgrim," the Russian "Kantakion of the departed," and Mendelssohn's "Then shall the righteous shine forth," sung by Diefenbaker's Prince Albert friend Jon Vickers. The service closed to

Julia Ward Howe's "Battle Hymn of the Republic" and the departing strains of Handel and Bach. At the cathedral door there was another general salute, a piper's lament, and a nineteen-gun salvo from the guns of the Royal Canadian Horse Artillery.[2]

From the cathedral the cortege moved to Ottawa railway station, where there was more band music and another nineteen-gun salute as the special train (three engines, the funeral car draped inside in black, five passenger cars, a lounge car, and a diner) pulled away to the west. On the train were eighty-four passengers, including an official party, family, friends, security staff, and thirty-eight journalists. Ceremonial stops to view the closed coffin had been planned for Sudbury, Winnipeg, and Prince Albert; but as the train moved west it was greeted everywhere by crowds along the tracks, and additional stops were added on the way, at Kenora, Melville, and Watrous. In Prince Albert, as the train pulled in on Tuesday afternoon, the overpass bridge was crowded and several thousand citizens filled the station square behind a guard of honour of the North Saskatchewan Regiment.

"Two nights and two days across three provinces," wrote Joan Hollobon of the *Globe and Mail*, "in a train that became an isolated world of memory and compressed emotion, have produced a new portrait of John Diefenbaker. He is still a man of many contradictions, but it is a kinder, gentler, even nobler portrait than that of the jowl-shaking thunderer of political vituperation." It was a portrait painted by Canadians along the journey's path. "Workmen holding hard hats in their hands as the train went by. Old men standing at attention. Women waving. Young people. They all saw John Diefenbaker as a fighter for the underdog, an honest man sincere in his convictions and in his vision of Canada." On the train were his personal staff, Bunny Pound, Betty Eligh, and Keith Martin, "in whom he inspired a fierce, protective loyalty" despite all his fits of temperament. "No one was fooled. Both the public and those close to the Chief recognized the flaws – the egotism, the flamboyance and histrionics, the long, bitter political memory. But we all have flaws, they seemed to say. They simply chose, for these few days, to honor the best that was as real a part of the man as the worst."[3]

From Prince Albert the funeral train moved slowly down the familiar railway line, the population of farms, villages, and towns spread out in quiet honour along the right of way, waving, smiling, crying, saying goodbye for the last time in what had become a long festival of national communion. At Saskatoon there was more ceremony as the draped casket was carried to a lying-in-state in Convocation Hall of the university; and then, on Wednesday, August 22, another procession on foot carried the coffin to graveside on the hilltop above the

South Saskatchewan River. Olive's coffin lay draped in black for reburial beside John's, his own still covered with a maple leaf flag overlain with the Red Ensign, and, cushioned at the foot, the medal of John's Companionship of Honour. Indians from the Mosquito Band sang a wailing honour song, a piper played another lament, and a trumpeter intoned the last post. Prime Minister Joe Clark delivered the eulogy at graveside, his voice carrying gently into the prairie wind. He called John Diefenbaker "the great populist of Canadian politics," a man deserving celebration for "the frontier strength and spirit of an indomitable man, born to a minority group, raised in a minority region, leader of a minority party, who went on to change the very nature of his country and to change it permanently," the advocate of social justice and human dignity for all Canadians.[4] In the late afternoon, John and Olive were committed to the prairie earth.

There was talk across Canada in those days – as John Gray of the Ottawa *Journal* reflected – about the death of John Diefenbaker. "They talked," he wrote, "in offices, on the street, over store counters."

> It was not grief or remorse which animated them; it was more a kind of affection. They talked casually about John, or the Chief, or the Old Man, as though they had known him for most of their lives, which in a way they had.
>
> With the exception of a few special policy initiatives, nobody will ever hold up the Diefenbaker government as a model of governance.
>
> For all his virtues, the man himself could be vindictive and vengeful. He operated largely on intuition and had little consistent or coherent political philosophy.
>
> But he had a passionate idea and ideal of the country and he was a fervent if sometimes erratic nationalist...
>
> In the end, his stature flowed from what he was personally, or what he seemed to be (in considerable measure the image he assiduously created), rather than from any record of achievement...
>
> To the outsiders of the world, and most of us are, there was something splendid about a man who held on. He seemed blessed with a kind of fearless independence, and people trusted that.[5]

What was his legacy? Diefenbaker broadened the Conservative Party and restored it as a national movement representing all regions of the country. He offered Canadians, briefly, an expansive sense of collective possibilities. He established compassion, fairness, and equal justice as principles of national policy. But his political career ended in failure. His one great talent – as a plat-form performer of undeniable genius – was also a seductive deceiver, both of himself and of his audiences. It disguised his weaknesses of character and polit-ical skill – his insecurity, indecisiveness, lack of trust, erratic and uncontrolled temperament, disorganization, unreflectiveness, and unrestrained zeal for power. His legend was bigger and more generous than the man. For Diefenbaker himself, it seemed finally to offer a substitute for the failures he could not face. Yet he had a stubborn pride, and his long life turned into epic. For Canada at mid-century, it was an undoubted act of virtue to embrace the legend of a leader who preached dignity and equality for all its citizens.

<hr/>

THE GRANITE GRAVESTONE CHOSEN BY JOHN DIEFENBAKER LIES FLAT ON THE GROUND and bears only his own and Olive's names and dates of birth and death. By Diefenbaker's choice, it is identical in style to the simple gravestone of Sir Winston Churchill at Bladon cemetery in Oxfordshire.[6]

The costs of the state funeral were estimated by staff in the secretary of state's department at from $200,000 to $500,000. Another federal official gave a figure of $485,000, including $100,000 or more for the special train. By any reckoning this was the most lavish of all Canadian state funerals, far surpassing in cost those of Georges Vanier in 1967 ($14,000), Mike Pearson in 1973 ($15,000), and Louis St Laurent in 1973 ($32,000). Three previous state funer-als had involved the use of funeral trains: for Mackenzie King, to Toronto in 1950; for Georges Vanier, to Quebec City in 1967; and for Vincent Massey, to Port Hope in 1968. Pearson's casket was carried twenty-four miles by hearse to his burial ground in Wakefield, Quebec.[7]

John Diefenbaker's last will and testament was dated August 7, 1979. In it he named Senator David Walker, Joel Aldred, Mr Justice Edward Hughes, and Dr Lewis Brand as his executors, and Thomas Van Dusen, Major Greg Guthrie, and Keith Martin as his literary executors. Diefenbaker had received by bequest from his brother the 240 acres of homestead lands of his mother and father and his uncle Edward, and he bequeathed these to the University of Saskatchewan, to be maintained in their existing state "so that future genera-tions will be enabled to view homestead life in general as it was in the pioneer days." Rental proceeds from the lands were to be used by the university for arthritis research. Diefenbaker directed that a cairn should be erected on the section once owned by his uncle, "who was my teacher in Halcyonia public school from 1906–1909 during the homestead days."

Diefenbaker's home in Rockcliffe Park was offered in his will to the government of Canada, on condition that it be established as a historical museum displaying "documents, letters and pictures of the pioneer days of the prairies, of the settlement of Canadians of all racial origins, which will emphasize my lifetime devotion that all Canadians, regardless of racial origin (subject to constitutional rights) shall be equal." After negotiation, Ottawa declined Diefenbaker's offer, the house was sold, and the proceeds were applied to his estate. His Prince Albert house had previously been given to his home city, also to be used as a museum. But he decided not to be buried in Prince Albert, because the city had not given his name to the new bridge spanning the North Saskatchewan River.

The will revealed that John and Olive had been made beneficiaries of a $475,000 trust fund established after 1960, whose creation he had apparently not learned of until 1973. Neither John nor Olive had received any benefit from the fund during their lives, and Diefenbaker directed that its proceeds should be divided among the Diefenbaker Centre, the city of Prince Albert, and an educational program to be conducted by the Diefenbaker Centre under direction of the literary executors. All of Diefenbaker's movable property, "including books, pictures, letters, papers and documents of all kinds," were bequeathed to the University of Saskatchewan for storage and exhibition in the Diefenbaker Centre. There were a number of smaller bequests to family and staff, churches, the masons, and various charities in Ontario, Manitoba, and Saskatchewan.[8]

Disputes over the powers of the literary executors and the secret trust fund first emerged on the funeral train in what Geoffrey Stevens described as "a seething conspiracy which floated across the Prairies on a cloud of alcohol after historian-ghostwriter John Munro wondered aloud why the hitherto unknown trust fund wasn't larger than it apparently was." A week later the controversy continued at the press conference called by the executors to explain the will. David Walker and Joel Aldred criticized the press for its reporting of the trust fund, and John Munro for having revealed it. Stevens wondered why Diefenbaker had been so incurious about the fund's existence, but concluded that the dispute was probably best forgotten.[9]

But it was not forgotten. In September, Canadian Press reported that in addition to the $475,000 available from the original trust fund, there might be a further $125,000 plus interest in a second fund referred to in a memo written by Olive, dated February 8, 1963, and discovered in the safe in Diefenbaker's office after his death.[10] The Diefenbaker Papers later revealed a confusing series of letters and memoranda from the 1960s containing veiled references to the trust fund (or funds), and indicating a certain confusion or indifference on Diefenbaker's part to the whole matter — although he had known of the fund's existence. The dispute between executors and literary executors about the capital and its disposition eventually reached the courts, and it was not settled definitively until May 1981, when the Ontario Supreme Court ruled that the will had given the literary executors only one function. Their task was to arrange for distribution of copies of Diefenbaker's memoirs to schools across Canada. The residue of the estate was subsequently allocated according to Diefenbaker's wishes.[11]

On August 16, 1994, on the fifteenth anniversary of John Diefenbaker's death, almost two hundred persons with links to the funeral and Diefenbaker's last journey gathered for a reunion in the Railway Committee Room of the Centre Block, hosted by the state funeral directors, Hulse, Playfair & McGarry. The guests included senators and MPs from all parties, members of the Chief's staff, Jon Vickers, Joe Clark, and Ed Schreyer, and some of the RCMP officers who had hoisted the coffin onto and off the train in 1979. The evening featured reminiscences formal and informal, including a film of the late Sean O'Sullivan performing a wickedly accurate parody of a Diefenbaker speech. It was the first – and perhaps the last – occasion of its kind in Ottawa.[12]

Notes

Full citations for secondary sources are given in the Bibliography, and short references only are used in the notes.

Abbreviations

CC Cabinet Conclusions, Canada
FRUS *Foreign Relations of the United States*
JGD John G. Diefenbaker
JGDI John G. Diefenbaker interview
JGDP John G. Diefenbaker Papers, Diefenbaker Centre Archives
OC 1 *One Canada: Memoirs of the Right Honourable John G. Diefenbaker: The Crusading Years, 1895-1956*
OC 2 *One Canada: Memoirs of the Right Honourable John G. Diefenbaker: The Years of Achievement, 1957–1962*
OC 3 *One Canada: Memoirs of the Right Honourable John G. Diefenbaker: The Tumultuous Years, 1962–1967*

Chapter 1 A Prairie Youth

1   See *OC 1*, 9–68. There may have been ten homes altogether. Nicholson writes that the family also lived in Port Elgin, Ontario, in 1897. Nicholson, *Vision*, 16
2   *OC 1*, 12–13
3   Ibid., 13–14; *The Globe*, November 6, 1900. The returning veterans of the South African Corps were members of the Royal Canadian Regiment, who had left for war in October 1899. Many other local units, including the 48th Highlanders, marched with them in the welcoming parade. Although the main ceremonies took place at the armouries on University Avenue, the parade did pass the city hall en route. Some of Diefenbaker's memories of his early life seem to have been stimulated by photographs; there is one elegant studio portrait of John and Elmer in their sailor suits "about 1902."
4   *OC 1*, 14
5   Ibid., 10
6   Ibid., 14–15.
7   *OC 1*, 1–2. Diefenbaker knew that the account of his ancestry in the memoirs was wrong, since he had learned that a cousin, George Brandt of Waterloo, Ontario, had given the correct one to reporters in 1958. Brandt's story was confirmed through records in the Waterloo County Registry Office by a reporter for the Hamilton *Spectator*. By placing the family's arrival one generation earlier, Diefenbaker seemed to be sustaining the story he had used in his campaigns for the leadership, emphasizing both the length of his Canadian ancestry and the possibility that the Diefenbakers had arrived in Canada via the United States as "Pennsylvania Dutch."

There were Diefenbakers of American origin in the Hawkesville area, but they were apparently unrelated. On the spelling of his name, Diefenbaker notes only that his grandfather retained the original spelling throughout his life. Hamilton *Spectator*, December 20, 1958

8   *OC 1*, 7

9   JGDI, December 11, 1969

10   *OC 1*, 7

11   Ibid., 8, 18. In a 1958 interview with Pierre Berton, Barbara Moon, James Bannerman, and Hugh MacLennan, Diefenbaker said that his father was "a great student" of history, no disciplinarian, and "quite an accomplished musician," who encouraged his students to enter public service. But he refused to say whether William had advised him to enter law or politics, or to comment on the balance between his mother and his father. When Barbara Moon asked what William was like as a father, Diefenbaker replied testily: "I have said it was a normal home. If you think I am going further than that, your questions in that direction do not merit the answer that you want." "Verbatim Proceedings...February 10, 1958," JGDP, VII/85/A/772.1, 49923–51, esp. 49924–27

12   *OC 1*, 7–9, 17–18

13   Ibid., 9

14   See Nicholson, *Vision*, 15.

15   See, for example, Nicholson's comments, which were based on interviews in the late 1950s with John, Elmer, and Mary Diefenbaker. Nicholson, *Vision*, 15

16   JGDI, December 11, 1969

17   *OC 1*, 2–5

18   Ibid., 10–15, esp. 15

19   Ibid., 16

20   Ibid., 18; note from Elmer, undated, in JGDP, V/3, 1349–52; William A.R. Thomson, *The Macmillan Medical Cyclopedia*, 918; JGDI, December 11, 1969. Consumption was the popular name for pulmonary tuberculosis. There is no subsequent family record of William's illness, and the following year seems to have been an extraordinarily active one for the whole family. It may be that the diagnosis, or John Diefenbaker's memory of it, or the accepted family story was incorrect.

21   Quoted in Nicholson, *Vision*, 16

22   *OC 1*, 19–20

23   Ibid., 20–21

24   Ibid., 22; note from Elmer, undated, in JGDP, V/3, 1349–52

25   *OC 1*, 23

26   Ibid., 23–24, 34. Diefenbaker also describes this schoolhouse home in "My First Prairie Christmas," *Reader's Digest*, December 1976, 49–52

27   *OC 1*, 31–32

28   Quoted in Nicholson, *Vision*, 17. See also *OC 1*, 35–40; JGDI, December 11, 1969. In the memoirs, Diefenbaker mistakenly places registration of the homestead in the autumn of 1905, after a visit to the land. The Dominion Lands Office records show that this actually occurred in 1904. William Diefenbaker's shortage of capital was common among homesteaders. Most immigrants were forced to seek second, paying jobs or to barter their skills in order to raise the estimated $1000 (or its equivalent in kind) needed to develop a quarter section. See Archer, *Saskatchewan*, 78, 100.

29   *OC 1*, 38–39

30   Ibid., 39; Archer, *Saskatchewan*, 133–38; Smith, *Prairie Liberalism*, 3–24

31   *OC 1*, 40–41

32   The memoirs suggest that this move took place in August 1906, while Edward Diefenbaker (in a brief biographical note prepared at John's request in May 1959 and edited in John's handwriting) says that it occurred in October. *OC 1*, 40; Ed. L. Diefenbaker, "Biography," JGDP, III/96, 66981–91, esp. 66983

33   *OC 1*, 41. Nicholson estimates the cost of materials for the house at $250. He adds that "its sufficiency as a home is perhaps best described by the fact that a tenant of the homestead in later years used it as a grain store." Diefenbaker suggests in the memoirs that he and his father built a one-room shack on the land in the summer of 1905 and apparently added to the building in 1906. Nicholson says that the shack was built in 1906 and then enlarged. In 1965 the Saskatchewan government moved the building to Wascana Centre in Regina as a historic site. *OC 1*, 39–40; Nicholson, *Vision*, 18

34   *OC 1*, 41–42; JGDI, December 11, 1969

35   *OC 1*, 42–43. Elmer remembered that his mother produced about ten pounds of butter per week and sold the surplus: "It fetched fourteen cents a pound, commanding a premium of two cents on account of its high quality." Quoted in Nicholson, *Vision*, 18

36   Archer, *Saskatchewan*, 140–41

37   Ibid., 141

38   *OC 1*, 49; Archer, *Saskatchewan*, 141

39   *OC 1*, 43

40   Ibid., 44

41   The writer was Lila A. Pope, who provided Diefenbaker in the 1970s with three short, undated reminiscences of Borden and the Halcyonia school. They can be found in JGDP, XIV/1/A/3. The description also appears in her contribution to the Borden and District local history, *Our Treasured Heritage*, 395.

42   JGDI, December 11, 1969

43   Ibid.

44   The chronicler Lila Pope, writing in 1980 about the Halcyonia school, wrote of this episode: "Fortunately John suffered no worse than frost bitten toes, or we might never have had him for our Prime Minister." JGDI, December 11, 1969; *OC 1*, 49–51; *Our Treasured Heritage*, 395

45   *OC 1*, 51

46   Ibid., 51–52

47   Ibid., 45–52

48   *OC 1*, 32, 44–54, 65; JGDI, December 11, 1969; Nicholson, *Vision*, 19. In his 1958 interview with Berton, Moon, Bannerman, and MacLennan, Diefenbaker said that, despite his father's small income, "in those days there was no book of any importance in history or biography or the like that was not bought." But he could not remember any book that had particularly influenced him, beyond an encyclopedia of biography. He had never read fiction or science, and could think of no title that he specially treasured. He refused to answer questions about his reading of the Bible on the ground that "that is very much my personal life, and something that I would prefer not to discuss." Several times he referred with admiration to the exploits of Gabriel Dumont, "this Indian fighter, the greatest of them all," whose story "has to be written." "Verbatim Proceedings...February 10, 1958," JGDP, VII/85/A/772.1, 49923–51, esp. 49930–35, 49944, 49948

49   *OC 1*, 67

50   Ibid., 66–68

51   *OC 1*, 41, 68; Garrett Wilson and Kevin Wilson, *Diefenbaker*, 12. The Wilsons note that William's "ability to acquire government employment so readily must indicate well-established credits with the Liberal Party, given the politics of the day." William kept his homestead land and eventually willed it to John and Elmer. On his father's death, John transferred his share to Elmer, and inherited it again on Elmer's death in 1971. William rose gradually from the position of gauger to preventive officer to assistant appraiser. In 1925 John wrote in his father's name to the provincial minister of public works, the Liberal A.P. McNab, noting his employment record in the Customs Office, by inference making the case for an increase in salary. Although Customs was a federal department, Diefenbaker seemed to expect that the appeal would make its way up Liberal patronage channels from Regina to Ottawa. Since John's political affiliation was already Conservative in this most partisan province, his covering note to

William bore a conspiratorial tone. "I was afraid to be more definite," John wrote, "as if the letter got into some one else's hands it might be hard to explain." In 1933, with Conservative governments in both Regina and Ottawa, Diefenbaker made a direct and urgent appeal to Premier Anderson to intercede on William's behalf to prevent his compulsory retirement at the age of sixty-five. "You will appreciate my position in this matter," Diefenbaker explained. "Those of the opposite political Faith are commencing to pour ridicule on me now and will continue so to do. Surely under the circumstances of this case and of the service which I have rendered for the Party something can be done towards preventing his retirement...Anything you can do will be appreciated." Anderson and other Saskatchewan Conservatives successfully intervened, and William remained in the public service until July 1937, when he retired at the age of sixty-nine. JGDP, V/30, 20250, 20273–74, 20278–90

52　*OC 1*, 71–73. If his estimates are correct, in 1910–12 John and Elmer were earning at an annual rate above that of their father. He records that, in July 1912, at the height of the land boom, he and Elmer were able to buy lots in River Heights on margin, as their father had done earlier on Victoria Avenue. When the boom collapsed in October 1912, all three lost their investments.

53　*OC 1*, 69; Nicholson, *Vision*, 21. Nicholson describes the bank as the Northern Grain Bank.

54　*OC 1*, 65

55　Ibid., 66

56　Telegram, Elmer to John Diefenbaker, June 17, 1957, JGDP, V/3, 1634

57　Nicholson, *Vision*, 14. A childhood acquaintance, C.J. Golding, wrote in 1980 that John had boarded on his family's farm in the summer of 1914 "while he was doing harvest work for a neighbouring bachelor." The date may actually have been 1913. Golding recalled that "Mr. Diefenbaker slept in the granary with me and at that time he told me he would be prime minister of Canada some day." *Our Treasured Heritage*, 123

58　*OC 1*, 75–76; JGDI, December 11, 1969. The Saskatoon *Daily Phoenix*'s account of the cornerstone laying makes no mention of Laurier's conversation with a newsboy. Nicholson quotes Diefenbaker as saying that "he paid me a dime, five times the price of a paper." The story was immortalized in 1972 when a plaque was placed on the Canada Building, opposite the entrance to the old Canadian National station in Saskatoon, quoting from the Joseph Schull biography of Laurier about the meeting of the prime minister and the newsboy. In 1990 the legend turned to bronze on the same site, when the *Star-Phoenix* donated a statue of Prime Minister Laurier and Master John Diefenbaker by the sculptor Bill Epp. Schull's source for the story was probably Diefenbaker. *Daily Phoenix*, July 30, 1910; Nicholson, *Vision*, 20–21

59　Quoted in Nicholson, *Vision*, 20. In his address to a civic reception in the Saskatoon ice rink that evening, Laurier spoke memorably about his desire to unite Canadians of all races and origins: "My days now must be short. You can see my hairs are grey, and I cannot hope to live many years; but when I am gone I want to feel sure that it will have to be admitted by my bitterest enemy that during fourteen years at least Canada made progress as she never made it before, united people, upon all races which have been brought here...In addition to this, when my last day comes, if my eyes can close on a policy, if I can look upon them as true Canadians, all preserving the pride of their race, but putting the pride of Canada first, I will feel that my life has not been lived in vain and I shall die happy." *Daily Phoenix*, July 30, 1910. These words may have been an early source of Diefenbaker's public attitudes.

60　A program for the Third Annual Elocution and Oratory Contest of the Saskatoon Collegiate Institute, April 1, 1912, lists John G. Diefenbaker's proposed speech on "The Progress of Canada during the Past Century." The student newspaper for May 1912 notes that he participated but did not win. Doris C. Haynes's 1967 memoir is the source of the story that Diefenbaker forgot his lines. JGDP, II/8, 6097a; XIV/1/A/3

61　*OC 1*, 70–71; JGDI, December 11, 1969. In 1969 he told a student that he wanted to become prime minister because "I felt the challenge of being able to do something to ensure that whatever racial origin, creed or colour they might be, all Canadians should be equal subjects, with equal constitutional rights. This came about as I saw people from all parts of the world coming into western Canada, most of them feeling, with reason, that those of other origins than English, in a citizen sense, or of French, were hyphenated Canadians. I decided I was going to do my part to bring about one Canada, and that became the subject of my continuous advocacy, both in the Saskatoon Collegiate Institute and University of Saskatchewan. I have pursued my objective. It took me almost half a century to bring about the enactment of the Bill of Rights in 1960." JGDI, December 11, 1969

62 Kerr and Hanson, *Saskatoon*, 84–86

63 *OC 1*, 77–78

64 Ibid., 78. His lecture notebooks, on the other hand, suggest a conscientious and orthodox undergraduate, dutifully recording without comment or question the outlines of the lectures he attended. See, for example, lecture notebooks, JGDP, II/9, 10, 7335–8054

65 *OC 1*, 78, 83

66 Ibid., 80–81

67 Some of his university notebooks and essays are preserved in his papers at the Diefenbaker Centre. They appear to be incomplete. His notes for Economics 17 (Canadian Economic History) include materials on statistics and statistical method, the history of banking and banking in Canada, and introductory sociology. They contain little Canadian economic history. See also Wilson, *Diefenbaker*, 15–16.

68 *OC 1*, 78, 82–83. The Wilsons, however, suggest that Diefenbaker was leader of the opposition in the mock parliament of 1914–15, that the debates were non-partisan, and that he appeared as head of "an untitled party," not the Conservative Party.

69 The dispute is recounted in Wilson, *Diefenbaker*, 13–15, from records in the Department of Education archives. The Diefenbaker Papers contain the daily register of attendance for the Wheat Heart School District for the year ending December 31, 1914, in which John Diefenbaker has signed the monthly attendance report from May through September, and Edward L. Diefenbaker has signed the reports from October through December. JGDP, II/12, 9963–74

70 *OC 1*, 81–82. The story of the incident passed down in one family, whose two boys were members of Diefenbaker's class that summer, is slightly different. A great niece, Cynthia (Krivoshein) McCormack, writes: "Some of the books say he was outside shooting – that is the part my Krivoshein relatives deny. The talk around the table was that 'J.D.' was *inside* the school shooting out the windows – my great uncles were outside to run and pick up what was shot. The bounty then was one cent for gopher tails and two cents for crows' feet." Cynthia McCormack to author, May 10, 1992

71 Kerr and Hanson, *Saskatoon*, 147–59

72 His papers record courses in economic history; money, banking and taxation; municipal and company law; sales law; and contracts and jurisprudence. Academic notebooks, JGDP, II/8,9,10

73 *The Sheaf*, April 1915; *OC 1*, 82–83

74 The John A. Hertel Company, *Canadian Bulletin No. 10*, July 7, 1915, JGDP, II/9, 8086–87; Wilson, *Diefenbaker*, 17. The saturated village was apparently Watrous.

75 *OC 1*, 84–85; The John A. Hertel Company, *Field Echoes and Pointers to Success*, December 24, 1915, JGDP, II/9, 8088; Wilson, *Diefenbaker*, 16–19.

76 Wilson, *Diefenbaker*, 19. Mighton later practised law in North Battleford.

77 Elmer to JGD, July 13 and 19, 1915, JGDP, V/3, 1393, 1389

78 Academic notebooks, JGDP, II/8,9,10; JGD to Mary Diefenbaker, April 16, May 16, 1916, JGDP, V/32, 248, 245; Certificate of Military Qualification, "Probationers," 27 May 1916, JGDP, II/12/166, 10024; *OC 1*, 85; Wilson, *Diefenbaker*, 19–20. There is no apparent basis for the claim made in the memoirs that "there was, I fear, no lack of evidence to show that commissions were excessively handed out on the basis of political and personal friendship. I had to wait for mine." The commission was issued nine days after Diefenbaker wrote his examinations.

79 *OC 1*, 85–86; Wilson, *Diefenbaker*, 20; JGD to Col. Edgar, DOC, MD No. 12, Regina, August 21, 1916; telegram, DOCMD12 to JGD, August 22, 1916; Saskatoon *Star-Phoenix*, August 26, 1916, JGDP, II/13/167, 10025–26, 10029

80 JGDP, II/13/167, 10170–72. Hugh Aird and Allan McMillan had been classmates of Diefenbaker in high school and university, took officers' training with him, and were also articling law students. McMillan was killed in action and Aird was wounded. "Sadie" was Sadie Bridgeman, a sister of Mary Diefenbaker.

81 JGDP, II/13/167, 10172–75

82 Diary, September 14, 16, 18; Capt. E.H. Oliver to Mrs Diefenbaker, September 18, 1916, ibid., 10177–78; II/12/166, 10034

83 Diary, September 20–October 6, 1916; JGD to Mary Diefenbaker, September 21, 1916; White Star Line Passenger List, SS *Lapland*, From Halifax, NS, to England, September 23, 1916, JGDP, II/13/167, 10178–83; V/1, 243; II/12/166, 10036–39; *OC 1*, 86–87; Wilson, *Diefenbaker*, 20–21

84 Diary, October 3–6, JGDP, II/13/167, 10182–83; *OC 1*, 86

85 *OC 1*, 88–89

86 Ibid., 89–90

87 JGDI, November 28, December 12, 1969; Biographical sketch, nd, JGDP, II/2, 803–05; Nicholson, *Vision*, 22; Newman, *Renegade*, 47

88 Diary, October 6–November 4, 1916, JGDP, II/13/167, 10183–91

89 Diary, November 5–10, 1916; Charing Cross Hotel pamphlet and ticket stub 4617, "H.M. Forces, Officer on leave, Charing Cross to Shorncliffe, First Class 11/8," ibid., 10192–93, 10063–119

90 Diary, November 13–16, 1916, ibid., 10194–95

91 Diary, November 17–26, ibid., 10195–98

92 Diary, December 6–12, ibid., 10200–02

93 Diary, December 18–29, ibid., 10204–08. The February 1917 order for Lieutenant Diefenbaker's return to Canada is addressed to him at the 19th Reserve Battalion. Ibid., II/12/167, 10122

94 Diary, December 29, 1916–January 1, 1917, JGDP, II/13/167, 10207–08; *OC 1*, 89

95 Diary, February 7–20, 1917, JGDP, II/13/167, 10166–69

96 Ibid., II/12/167, 10124–33. In an interview in 1969, Diefenbaker told the author: "I tried my best. They wouldn't have it and they sent me back. Then – after about six months, not that long, five months – I then tried to get into the RAF and I thought I was going to be alright there...but that was out because...there was a recurrence of the haemorrhage when I got up...when I got up to 5000 feet I started to bleed." This account appears to have been a brief flight of fancy. JGDI, December 12, 1969

97 Board of Pension Commissioners for Canada to JGD, April 9, 1918; certificate issued with War Service Badge to JGD, May 25, 1918, JGDP, II/13/167, 10142, 10138–39

98 In the First World War the Canadian Army acknowledged 15,500 "neuropsychiatric disabilities," including 9000 cases defined as "shell shock and neurosis." The terms were imprecise, as they remained by 1940. General E.L.M. Burns wrote of the army's straightforward approach to human behaviour in 1914–18: "At that time a man did what he was told, encouraged by the kindly admonitions of his sergeant or sergeant-major – or else. If he reported to the medical officer with nothing visibly the matter with him, he was malingering, a crime under the Army Act." Terry Copp and Bill McAndrew add chillingly that "it seems plausible that at least some of the 25 Canadians and 346 British soldiers executed for cowardice or desertion were dysfunctional psychoneurotics." They comment on the approach of medical boards at the opening of the Second World War, taking up where they had left off in 1918: "If the medical board had doubts about an individual's mental fitness its job was to reject him, not to diagnose him."

The Canadian government's neuropsychiatric advisers in 1939 were concerned above all to confront "the pension question": "After World War 1 large numbers of veterans received pensions on the basis of neuro-psychiatric disability. There was a strong belief that such pensions, by formally recognizing the existence of a psychoneurosis, reinforced the condition instead of helping to cure it." By that reasoning, the Pension Board's rejection of the Diefenbaker claim in 1918 could be regarded as therapeutic.

Dr Colin Russel, who had been a leading neuropsychiatrist in the First World War at the Ramsgate Special Hospital for Nervous Cases, held that all "fear reactions" could be handled successfully with "rest, food and an understanding appreciation." For him the more serious problem was "a large class, which became larger, the further one got away from the front, who exhibited all the evidences of conversion hysteria – the so-called shell shock." He believed that this hysteria was caused by "extraordinary suggestibility" or the lack of "high moral standards." During the Second World War, as one of the Canadian Army's leading consultants, he treated such cases with electric shock, psychotherapy, reclassification, or reassignment. His patients from 1940 to 1942 displayed "a wide variety of symptoms – strong fear reactions, chronic headaches, enuresis, gastric illness, uncontrollable restlessness, exaggerated physical weakness, muscle tics, obsessions, phobias – the list was almost endless." Alarming numbers of British and Canadian soldiers who had not faced combat were invalided out in 1940–41 with "gastric, mental and nervous problems." There were more than 100,000 cases in the British Army. Diefenbaker seems to have marched in a large shadow army. See Copp and McAndrew, *Battle Exhaustion*, 13–17, 67–68.

99   "Officer's Declaration Paper, Canadian Over-seas Expeditionary Force...Certificate of Medical Examination, August 26, 1916," contained in Lieutenant J.G.B. Diefenbaker's military personnel file (MPF)

100 "Medical Case Sheet, 26/11/16, Crowborough Camp," MPF

101 The diagnosis was "ametropia"; it was treated with corrective lenses. Casualty and hospitalization records, Lieutenant J.G.B. Diefenbaker, C.M.S. (196th Bn.); "Medical Case Sheet, 26/11/16, Crowborough Camp," MPF

102 The full case description reads: "This officer suffered a great deal from symptoms of weakness and partial loss of compensation before enlistment. Immediately after enlistment he was given ten days leave owing to heart trouble and weakness. He cannot double, climb a hill or do physical training owing to dyspnoea difficulty in breathing and general weakness. He has a blowing systolic refurgitant _____ [unintelligible word] considerable cardiac hypertrophy. Diffuse apex beat. Weak sight corrected by glasses. Weak physique, and has dyspnoea upon exertion." "Medical Case Sheet, 26/11/16, Crowborough Camp," MPF

103 *Macmillan Medical Dictionary* (1906, 1958), 226, 294

104 "Proceedings of a Medical Board, Saskatoon, 27th day April 1917," MPF

105 DOC, MD #12, to Adjutant-General, Canadian Militia, Ottawa, May 25, 1917; DOC, MD #12, to Secretary, Militia Council, Ottawa, August 29, 1917, MPF

106 "Medical History of an Invalid," August 4, 1917, MPF. It is clear from later correspondence that Diefenbaker's previous medical records from England were not available to the medical board in Saskatoon in August. They were finally forwarded from Canadian militia headquarters on October 30, 1917, after Diefenbaker had been retired. DOC, MD #12, to Secretary, Militia Council, Ottawa, September 28, 1917; Adjutant-General, Canadian Militia, to GOC, MD #12, October 9, 1917; Cablegram, Records Ottawa to Canrecords London, October 6, 1917; Adjutant-General, Canadian Militia, to GOC, MD #12, October 30, 1917, MPF

107 Ibid.

108 "Medical History of an Invalid," October 10, 1917, ibid. The *Oxford Companion to Medicine* describes one type of valvular heart disease as "incompetence," when a defective valve fails to prevent retrograde flow. *Black's Medical Dictionary* suggests that "the detection of valvular disease unfits a person for entrance upon any public service, and renders him subject, if he becomes a candidate for life assurance, either to refusal or to a heavily increased premium." For treatment, *Black's* continues, "the subject of such disease must lead a quiet and well-regulated life, avoiding, as far as may be, excitement, worry, and sudden strains,

although methodical attention to business, and even hard, steady work, are quite well done." *Oxford Companion to Medicine* (1986), 1416, 1522; *Black's Medical Dictionary* (34th ed., 1984), 438–40

109 DOC, MD #12, to Secretary, Militia Council, Ottawa, October 26, 1917, MPF

110 Adjutant-General, Canadian Militia, to DOC, MD #12, November 13, 1917, ibid.

111 In Pearson's case, the affliction was described as "neurasthenia." See the account in English, *Shadow*, 42–47.

112 Taylor, *English History*, 70

113 *OC 1*, 87; the story was also recounted in JGDI, December 12, 1969.

114 Diary, November 30, December 6, 8–12, 1916, February 10, 1917, JGDP, V/13, 10198, 10200–03; JGDI, December 12, 1969. Diefenbaker also said in the 1969 interview that he had heard parliamentary speeches at the time by Winston Churchill, Sir John Simon, Asquith (while still prime minister), Arthur Balfour, Stanley Baldwin, and Ramsay MacDonald.

115 Wilson, *Diefenbaker*, 24; *OC 1*, 92

116 "Robert Service," JGDP, XIV/1. The manuscript is described by Diefenbaker in a covering memo of May 1965 as "personal notes I made on Robert Service in February of 1918." This appears to be Diefenbaker's earliest remaining reference to Olive Freeman.

117 *The Sheaf*, April 1919

118 Seven persons received the degree of Bachelor of Laws. They included Emmett Hall, who had articled with Diefenbaker at Lynd and Yule. The convocation program noted that sixty-six former students of the university had been killed, died of wounds, or were missing in action. J. Kelso Hunter to JGD, September 28, 1918; Law Society of Saskatchewan, Law Examinations, nd, 1919; University of Saskatchewan, Eighth Annual Convocation, May 1, 1919, JGDP, I/26, 7308, 7313, 9997–10007; *OC 1*, 91–92, 96–97; Wilson, *Diefenbaker*, 24, 26

Chapter 2 Choosing a Party

1 *OC 1*, 96–97; Wilson, *Diefenbaker*, 26–29

2 Diefenbaker's lease on the property commenced on August 1, 1919, for a seven-month term at a nominal rent of one dollar. In 1971 the local Lions' Club built and furnished a replica of the office building, although on a different site. Michael Stechishin completed his articles with Diefenbaker in 1921 and then practised law in Yorkton. In 1940 he was appointed to a district court judgeship. JGDP, I/26, 8749–50; *OC 1*, 97–98, 101–02; Wilson, *Diefenbaker*, 27–33

3 Wilson, *Diefenbaker*, 4–5

4 JGDP, I/26, 6704–25; *OC 1*, 98–100; Wilson, *Diefenbaker*, 1–9; Saskatoon *Star-Phoenix*, August 8, 1919; *Wakaw Recorder*, August 13 and October 22, 1919. The uncertain or casual spelling of Ukrainian names in Saskatchewan in 1919 was reflected in seven versions of the name of the accused in court documents, letters, and newspaper reports: Chernyski, Charnecki, Czerneski, Charnecky, Chenoski, Cheniski, Chernesky.

5 This account of an acquittal on his birthday is related by Newman, Nicholson, and Diefenbaker himself. Newman, *Renegade*, 47–48; Nicholson, *Vision*, 22; *OC 1*, 98–100. Apparent confirmation of that date appears in the Diefenbaker Papers on two photocopies of the *Wakaw Recorder*'s story of the trial, dated in handwriting "Sept 18 1919"; but this is actually the *Recorder* story of October 29. The formal charge on the trial day is dated October 23, 1919, and other correspondence confirms that the trial occurred in late October. Emmett Hall also notes in his oral history interview for the Diefenbaker Centre that the trial did not occur on Diefenbaker's birthday. The author and date of the handwritten dating of the story are not clear. See JGDP, I/7/A/135, 6736–37, 6747, 6751–52; XVIII/OH/41 (Acc. 126), May 19, 1986.

6 The original of Hall's note is in the Diefenbaker Papers, JGDP, I/7/A/135, 6750; a slightly edited version appears in Wilson, *Diefenbaker*, 7.

7 Wilson, *Diefenbaker*, 8

8 JGDP, I/8/A/154,155, 8170, 8197–202; Wilson, *Diefenbaker*, 33–34; *OC 1*, 101–02

9   Manager, Bank of Montreal, Wakaw to JGD, June 7, 1920; JGD to manager, June 9, 1920, JGDP, I/8/A/155, 8194–95

10   JGDP, I/8/A/154, 8170; Wilson, *Diefenbaker*, 34–37

11   *OC 1*, 134–35

12   Aileen Stobie Baldwin, quoted in Holt, *Other*, 100; see also 99–100; *OC 1*, 134.

13   The Freemans were United Empire Loyalists descended from Mayflower Pilgrims who had emigrated to Massachusetts Bay in 1620. Her grandfather, who was also a Baptist minister, was one of the founders of Acadia University, and her father was an Acadia graduate. See the biographical sketch of Olive by John H. Archer in *OC 3*, xv–xxiii.) The date when John re-established contact is not clear. Soon after his election to the House of Commons in 1940 he was corresponding with Olive's brother Hal, who taught at McMaster University in Hamilton. Hal mentioned Olive, invited John to visit "one or both," and offered Diefenbaker tuition in French. Diefenbaker commented: "Your offer to coach me in French is very gratifying to me. It has always been my opinion that, in order to make an effective member, one should know the French language to the extent of at least being able to follow the debates, and, when I see you, I will go over this matter with you." There is no record that anything came of this. Hal and Gertrude Freeman to JGD, nd, 1940; JGD to Hal Freeman, May 4, 1940, JGDP, II/11, 9074–75

14   Holt, *Other*, 74–75

15   Ibid., 103

16   Holt writes that Beth was buried in "the wedding gown she had made for her marriage to John Diefenbaker. That was her last wish" (ibid., 103–04). Holt's source for this story was Dorothy Cleveland Little, the daughter of the Newells' neighbours who had nursed Beth until her death. Emmett Hall, however, rejects the claim "that there was any serious relationship" between Diefenbaker and Newell. He recalled in 1986 that Beth Newell suffered from tuberculosis "as early as the fall of 1918 and was practically confined to her bed." Mrs Newell, he said, occasionally telephoned him "to provide Beth with some company – this was the extent of JGD's association with her as well." JGDP, XVIII/OH/41

17   In the memoirs, Diefenbaker recounts the story of an auto race from Prince Albert to Saskatoon in which his competitor, an "eccentric Hungarian," drove off a Saskatchewan river ferry into the river. When the man surfaced above his car and shouted "Damn, hell, what you believing in! Don't worry, J., I standing on the cushion," Diefenbaker says he "laughed until the haemorrhaging that I had suffered overseas began again. Back in hospital for a major operation, I had a narrow escape." He does not date this incident. *OC 1*, 135–36; Wilson, *Diefenbaker*, 41

18   *Boutin et al. v. Mackie*, (1922) *2 Western Weekly Reports* 1197 (Sask.); *OC 1*, 120–21; Wilson, *Diefenbaker*, 37–39; *Le Patriote de l'Ouest*, May 1922

19   Diefenbaker discusses the early years of his legal career in chapters six and seven of his memoirs, *OC 1*, 93–124. For accounts of some of his major cases, see Wilson, *Diefenbaker*, passim.

20   *OC 1*, 102–03; Wilson, *Diefenbaker*, 40–41

21   *OC 1*, 136–37

22   Wilson, *Diefenbaker*, 39–42; *OC 1*, 137

23   *OC 1*, 74–75

24   Ibid., 75; JGDI, December 11, 1969

25   *OC 1*, 75; JGDI, December 10, 1969

26   Subsequently, he blamed the electoral frauds of 1917 on the Conservative minister of the interior, Arthur Meighen, who was also sponsor of the Wartime Elections Act. Meighen, he claimed, had directed the chief electoral officer to shift overseas votes among designated constituencies to assure the election of Unionist candidates. Diefenbaker said in 1969 that his source for this claim was a senator, who told him that he had personally delivered the message from Meighen to the chief electoral officer. The issue was raised at the Liberal Convention of 1919, and Meighen did not deny the accusation. In 1969 Diefenbaker

commented: "I don't claim to be pious or anything of the kind, but that's wrong, no matter how you look at it." JGDI, December 11, 1969

27 *OC 1*, 91, 126–27

28 *OC 1*, 132–33; JGDI, December 10, 1969. In the more vivid language of the interview, Diefenbaker's story was: "I came back on the Monday and said, 'Who in the hell did this? Here's your bloody papers and it's all over with.'"

29 Wilson, *Diefenbaker*, 51

30 JGDI, December 10, 1969

31 Wilson, *Diefenbaker*, 50–52

32 Ibid., 52–53

33 *OC 1*, 140

34 Ibid., 58–64, 139–41; Wilson, *Diefenbaker*, 50–55

35 Prince Albert *Herald*, October 15, 1925, quoted in Newman, *Renegade*, 49

36 JGDI, August 14, 1969

37 *OC 1*, 141–43; Newman, *Renegade*, 49–50

38 *OC 1*, 143

39 Ibid., 141

40 Ibid., 140–41; Wilson, *Diefenbaker*, 52–53

41 *OC 1*, 143. There is no published record that he visited Wakaw. The local newspaper supported the Liberal Party, despite threats from Conservative advertisers that they would boycott its pages if it did so. Wilson, *Diefenbaker*, 54

42 Quoted in Wilson, *Diefenbaker*, 54

43 *OC 1*, 143–44. Nevertheless, as compared with the 1921 results, Conservative candidates on the prairies shared votes lost by the Progressives with the Liberals and polled more votes in total than either the Liberals or Progressives. See the *Reports, Chief Electoral Officer, Fourteenth General Election*, and *Fifteenth General Election*, 360–90, 429–532.

44 *Herald*, December 1, 1925; Wilson, *Diefenbaker*, 55

45 Diefenbaker writes: "The Conservative Party, as such, decided not to run a candidate in that by-election, but they did not want Mr. King to go unopposed. I received a telegram suggesting that an Independent candidate run. I was standing, this telegram in hand, looking out from my window at the traffic on Central Avenue below. It was a cold, blustery day in January 1926. Across the street I saw Dave Burgess. I sent one of my staff to ask him to come up. I knew Burgess well, and respected his ability. His war record in the Royal Flying Corps was outstanding. When he came into my office I said, 'You have often told me that you'd like to be in Parliament. Well, how about running as an Independent?' Without hesitation, he agreed to do so. It was: 'Dave Burgess, M.C., for M.P.' King, of course, was a shoo-in; to defeat the Prime Minister in a by-election is almost an impossibility." There is no record in the Diefenbaker Papers of this telegram. Liberal newspapers noted during the contest that "the witness to Mr. Burgess' nomination paper was formerly employed in the office of J.G. Diefenbaker, Conservative candidate on October 29," and reported local gossip that a federal party emissary had visited Prince Albert carrying "a little black bag" containing "a round sum to support any candidate who would allow his name to go forward." But later in the year the Toronto *Telegram* reported that the decision not to nominate formally against King was taken on federal orders and against the instincts of the local party. In that case, the Burgess nomination might suggest local defiance. The paper also noted that in the general election of September 1926, Arthur Meighen did not speak in Saskatchewan and left Diefenbaker to fight King alone in Prince Albert. "Why was King let down so easy?" the *Telegram* asked. "That is one of the mysteries of the late debacle in the west." *OC 1*, 160–61; Saskatoon *Phoenix*, February 9, 1926; Toronto *Telegram*, October 21, 1926

46 Wilson, *Diefenbaker*, 55–56; *OC 1*, 144

47 Quoted in Wilson, *Diefenbaker*, 66

48 *Phoenix*, February 17, 1926; *OC 1*, 145–48; Wilson, *Diefenbaker*, 56–57

49   Gray, *Bennett*, 263–64; *OC 1*, 146–54

50   *OC 1*, 148

51   Ibid., 151–53

52   *Herald*, August 9, 1926; Wilson, *Diefenbaker*, 57–59

53   "An appeal to base prejudice," *Phoenix*, August 12, 1926

54   JGDI, June 27, December 11, 1969; *OC 1*, 148–50

55   Quoted in *OC 1*, 149

56   "Prince Albert's Conservative Candidate," *St. Peter's Messenger*, Meunster, August 11, 1926.
      Diefenbaker's companions on the platform, Strong and MacDougall, had been the two main
      speakers at the banquet honouring him in Prince Albert on December 1, 1925. See *Herald*,
      December 1, 1925.

57   Quoted in *OC 1*, 149; Wilson, *Diefenbaker*, 58

58   The source of Diefenbaker's claim may have been an advertisement in the *Ukrainian Voice*
      of August 16, 1926, over the name of F.W. Wright, the official agent for W.L. Mackenzie King.
      The advertisement quoted a Conservative candidate in Ontario as saying that "no person
      not of British birth should be given a right to vote in Canada," and interpreted this to mean
      that the Meighen government, if re-elected, would remove that right from all naturalized
      Canadians. This piece of electoral hyperbole may have been matched (or surpassed) by
      Diefenbaker's imaginative leap from the removal of voting rights to deportation one by one.
          The campaign was crude in other ways as well. Diefenbaker later charged that agents of
      the provincial police, acting under political direction, had attempted to set him up for
      charges on a liquor offence during the campaign. He said that while being driven to a pub-
      lic meeting in Parkside, he discovered a bottle of illegal home-brew on the seat beside his
      travel bag. He threw the bottle away. That evening, he said, all the cars outside the meeting
      hall were searched by special detectives of the liquor squad, and one officer confessed to
      him: "I should tell you that they wanted me to plant liquor on you there and I refused...I was
      directed by the inspector of police to do that." After the Conservatives came to power in
      September 1930, Diefenbaker said that he gained access to the attorney general's files and
      discovered that the liquor police had been in Parkside that night. Diefenbaker asked that
      one member of the police force (by then, the RCMP) should be dismissed for his responsi-
      bility in the affair, but the minister of justice refused and had him transferred instead to the
      National Parks service. Wilson, *Diefenbaker*, 58; JGDI, June 27, 1969; and *Herald*, August 31
      and October 1, 1926

59   The vote in Prince Albert constituency was King, 8933; Diefenbaker, 4838. *OC 1*, 153–54;
      Wilson, *Diefenbaker*, 59; Newman, *Renegade*, 50

60   *OC 1*, 154; Wilson, *Diefenbaker*, 59

61   Gray, *Bennett*, 279–85; *OC 1*, 155–56

62   Quoted in Gray, *Bennett*, 284

63   *OC 1*, 155–57, 161–62

64   The short but spectacular history of the Klan in Saskatchewan is recounted in Robin, *Shades*,
      1–86; Kyba, "Ballots and Burning Crosses," and Calderwood, "Rise."

65   Robin, *Shades*, 59

66   The statistics are cited in detail, ibid.

67   J.F. Bryant to R.B. Bennett, March 16, 1928, Bennett Papers, 24954–55; Robin, *Shades*, 60–61

68   J.G. Gardiner to W.L. Mackenzie King, August 23, 1927, quoted in Robin, *Shades*, 62

69   W.L.M. King to J.G. Gardiner, August 30, 1927, quoted ibid., 64

70   Ibid., 63–65

71   "Platform adopted at the Saskatchewan Conservative Convention. At Saskatoon. March 14th
      and 15th, 1928," Bennett Papers, 24974–77. Bryant, in his first letter to Bennett reporting
      reassuringly on the convention, quotes a slightly different version of the resolution. J.F.
      Bryant to R.B. Bennett, March 16, 1928, ibid., 24954–57

72   J.F. Bryant to R.B. Bennett, March 16, 1928, ibid. See also Wilson, *Diefenbaker*, 77–79.

73 See, for example, A.G. MacKinnon to R.B. Bennett, March 28, 1928; J. Harvey Hearn to R.B. Bennett, March 28, 1928; J.J. Leddy to R.B. Bennett, March 28, April 12, April 17, 1928; M.A. MacPherson to R.B. Bennett, April 7, 1928; J.A.M. Patrick to R.B. Bennett, April 21, 1928; M.J. Perkins to R.B. Bennett, May 23, 1928, Bennett Papers, 25003–06, 24987–90, 24992–93, 25019–20, 25029–33, 24994–5001, 25035–38, 25074–76

74 J.F. Bryant to R.B. Bennett, May 31, 1928, ibid., 25113. Soon after the convention, one of the absconding Klan officials, Pat Emmons, was arrested in the United States, waived his rights under extradition, and was returned to Regina and Moose Jaw, where he was tried on charges of fraud and misappropriation of funds. Emmons testified that he had met with J.T.M. Anderson to coordinate Klan and Conservative Party campaigns against the Liberal government, and that Anderson had tried to seize control of the Klan. The criminal charges were dismissed, but the political evidence intensified the party conflict. Emmons followed up by publishing affidavits about his meetings with Conservative leaders and speaking at a noisy public meeting in Regina. He was then hustled secretly out of the country. Although R.B. Bennett suggested to Anderson that he should sue to clear his name, Anderson neither sued nor denied that he had met with Emmons. Conservatives complained, with good reason, that the affair had been orchestrated by the Gardiner government. F.R. MacMillan to R.B. Bennett, May 7, 1928; R.B. Bennett to J.T.M. Anderson, June 20, 1928, ibid., 25056–57, 25130; Robin, *Shades*, 73–78

75 See especially R.B. Bennett to J.J. Leddy, November 6, 1928, Bennett Papers, 25187. Bennett advised Leddy to accept the situation "with equanimity," and remembered what he saw as a similar example of political prudence or cynicism: "You will, perhaps, recall that it was the Liberal Party that came to power through the Manitoba school issue in 1896, and Sir Wilfrid Laurier was content to retire behind the lines of *torres vidras* [sic]. Might it not be well for us to emulate the example of so great a tactician?" Bennett's allusion was to Wellington and the Peninsular War. Torres Vedras was the solid British defensive line before Lisbon where the French under Massena approached and then turned back in October 1810, marking the turning point in the war.

76 J.F. Bryant to R.B. Bennett, April 11, 1928, ibid., 25014–18; Robin, *Shades*, 300 n120. The other possibility was that MacKinnon's name appeared on the typed list, but was omitted at the platform when the names were read to the convention. Dr J.F. Leddy, the son of J.J. Leddy, who became president of the University of Windsor, recalled being told emphatically by his father that Diefenbaker had played a part in blackballing the two Catholic nominees at the convention. Private information

77 J. Harvey Hearn to R.B. Bennett, March 28, 1928, Bennett Papers, 24988

78 Wilson, *Diefenbaker*, 79

79 Ibid.; McLeod, "Politics," 139–40

80 J.J. Leddy to R.B. Bennett, October 29, 1928, Bennett Papers, 25185–86; Regina *Morning Leader*, October 19, 1928; Wilson, *Diefenbaker*, 81

81 *OC 1*, 157

82 *Morning Leader*, October 22, 1928; Wilson, *Diefenbaker*, 81–83; *OC 1*, 157–58. Diefenbaker's account of this incident in the memoirs is drained of all content; without any mention of the nature of his questions, it becomes a long and amusing anecdote about Gardiner's agility in evading answers. This notable gap is perhaps an indication of Diefenbaker's subsequent unease about the attitudes of the Saskatchewan party in the late 1920s – and his own role in it.

83 The by-election result was Liberal 2764, Conservative 2705. Manitoba *Free Press*, October 26, 1928; Ward and Smith, *Gardiner*, 98; Wilson, *Diefenbaker*, 82

84 Quoted in Wilson, *Diefenbaker*, 83

85 Ward and Spafford, *Politics*, 114–23; Archer, *Saskatchewan*, 209–12

86 Wilson, *Diefenbaker*, 84–85

87 *OC 1*, 150–51. The memoirs offer two more insights into Diefenbaker's state of mind about the Klan and its attitudes. He admits that he was once consulted briefly by J.J. Maloney about

the Klan's legal affairs; and he speculates that, if he had won the seat in 1929 and become attorney general, he probably would have supported the Conservative government's legislation to ban a Catholic presence in public schools. "That would have been my destruction. I would have been irredeemably associated in the public mind with the religious and racial bigotry of the period." *OC 1*, 151. By good fortune, he implies, his ambivalent relationship to the Klan was in fact forgotten. In an undated, tape-recorded dictation from the 1960s, Diefenbaker makes the unsubstantiated claim that "I took a strong stand against the activities of the Ku Klux Klan which at that time was flourishing and had for a year or so earlier." "Dictation found on a tape purchased by Mr. Garnet C. King of Perth, Ontario, and presented to Mr. Diefenbaker on July 21st, 1970," JGDP, XIV/1/A/3

88 Ward and Spafford, *Politics*, 120–23; Wilson, *Diefenbaker*, 85; Archer, *Saskatchewan*, 211–12

89 T.C. Davis to J.G. Gardiner, October 29, 1936, Gardiner Papers, 41289, quoted in Ward and Smith, *Gardiner*, 146–47

90 Wilson, *Diefenbaker*, 48

91 Ibid., 49

92 The Prince Albert *Daily Herald* reported that Cousins had died in his sleep and that "the doctor stated that death was due to natural causes, probably the result of being gassed during the war." *Daily Herald*, June 9, 1927; *OC 1*, 137; Wilson, *Diefenbaker*, 65

93 An outline of Elmer's career can be traced in the Diefenbaker Papers. One of his enterprises, for which John acted as lawyer and financial guarantor, was the Acme Storage Company. From May 1931 until January 1933 this company held a franchise as the Prince Albert beer bottle exchange. The business was a financial failure and folded in dispute among the three partners after it lost the city franchise. See JGDP, I/1/A/1, 44–84.

94 Wilson, *Diefenbaker*, 65

95 *OC 1*, 137

96 Holt, *Other*, 106

97 Quoted ibid., 108

98 Ibid, 109–10. Much of Holt's information about Edna and the Diefenbaker family in this period comes from Edna's niece Sheila Brower, who became a frequent visitor in the Diefenbaker homes from 1927 onwards and remained a close and fascinated observer of family relationships throughout her aunt's life. In Edna's later life she confided at length in Sheila.

99 Ibid., 111

100 Ibid.; Wilson, *Diefenbaker*, 69; JGD to William Diefenbaker, July 19, 1928, JGDP, V/1, 6; Holt and the Wilsons say that both William and Mary made the trip, but John's postcard to William suggests, "You are lucky you didnt come along. Nearly froze to death last evg. Between tires and bad roads have not had such a wonderful trip."

101 Holt, *Other*, 113–14

102 Quoted ibid., 117

103 See ibid., 118

104 Ibid., 119

105 Ibid., 120

106 Betty Andrews Davis, quoted ibid., 121. She was the wife of Ted Davis, the new editor of the Prince Albert *Herald*.

107 Ibid., 127

108 Ibid., 124–33. There is no direct evidence of the reasons why John and Edna had no children, and no basis, even, for plausible speculation. Holt intimates that John's preoccupation with his political career meant that he would not accept the distractions of raising a family; but in the absence of firm evidence, there is no way of telling whether such suggestions on his part were statements of intention or rationalizations.

109 Wilson, *Diefenbaker*, 60–65; Saskatoon *Star-Phoenix*, September 22, 1927

110 *R. v. Olson*, (1929) 1 *Western Weekly Reports* 432, 23 *Saskatchewan Law Reports* 321, 51 *Canadian Criminal Cases* 122, (1929) *Dominion Law Report* 300 (CA); Wilson, *Diefenbaker*, 70–73

111 Wilson, *Diefenbaker*, 95. "One of the enduring legends of the Saskatchewan bar," they write, "is of E.C. Leslie, K.C., opening a case in the Court of Appeal: 'My Lords, this is an appeal from a judgment of Mr. Justice Taylor. But there are other grounds.'"

112 Wilson, *Diefenbaker*, 100

113 *Daily Herald*, November 22, 1929; *Star-Phoenix*, March 4, 1930; JGD case notebook, JGDP, I/7, 8486–502; Diefenbaker & Elder to minister of justice, telegram, undated; undersecretary of state to John J. Diefenbaker [sic], March 4, 1930, ibid., 8560–61; Wilson, *Diefenbaker*, 89–109

114 *R. v. Wysochan* (1930) 54 *Canadian Criminal Cases* 172 (Sask. CA)

115 *Morning Leader*, March 19, 1930, quoted in Wilson, *Diefenbaker*, 114

116 The case is reported on the front page of the *Star-Phoenix*, March 21, 1930.

117 The Diefenbaker Papers contain a transcript of the appeal judgment, as well as correspondence and telegrams to the minister of justice seeking a stay of execution and petitioning for a new trial on evidence of Wysochan's intoxication. But W.G. Elder wrote to Diefenbaker on June 17, 1930: "I have absolutely no hope whatsoever of any consideration at the hands of the Department. However, for your personal information I might say that after speaking to a great number of people...I have somewhat changed my mind in respect to the case. I don't think that we should lose any sleep over the matter whatever." Elder apparently accepted Wysochan's guilt. See JGDP, I/9, 9528–31, 9535–36, 9549, 9552; Wilson, *Diefenbaker*, 110–24.

Chapter 3 A Provincial Life

1 Archer, *Saskatchewan*, 211–15; Smith, *Prairie Liberalism*, 195–99; Ward and Smith, *Gardiner*, 107–21, 143–44

2 Wilson, *Diefenbaker*, 125–26

3 *OC 1*, 156–61. In the late winter of 1930 Diefenbaker made an insurance claim seeking compensation for absence from his office from February 13 to March 13, 1930, supported by a medical certificate, on the ground that he had suffered an "attack of influenza" resulting from exposure, and noting that he had had no illness lasting more than two weeks in the previous five years. The record does not make clear whether this was the same illness Diefenbaker referred to in the memoirs, where he reported that "my haemorrhages had recurred, and the doctors ordered me to take a long rest." JGDP, II/10/135, 8597–606; *OC 1*, 156

4 *OC 1*, 160–61; Wilson, *Diefenbaker*, 126–27; Courtney, *Voting in Canada*, 18. W.D. Cowan served one undistinguished term in the House, where he spoke occasionally against bankers, freetraders, socialists, Liberal immigration policies, and the absence of federal aid to Saskatchewan. He said in June 1931 that despite hardship, the typical Saskatchewan resident was still "cheery and goodhumoured. If he has nothing but oatmeal porridge he is content." The maverick Liberal back-bencher J.-F. Pouliot referred to Cowan as "the nightshirt from Long Lake" and told the House that Cowan had received a salary of $2170 in 1929 as treasurer of the Saskatchewan Klan. Cowan responded later that he did not mind Pouliot's teasing and promised he would stand one day at the pearly gates in a Klan outfit and pull Pouliot in, out of gratitude for Pouliot's criticism of the farmer-labour group in the House. *Debates*, March 24, 1931, 242–53; June 12, 1931, 2589–92; March 28, 1933, 3498–501

5 *Report of the Royal Commission to Inquire into Statements Made in Statutory Declarations and Other Matters, 1930; The Saskatchewan Record*, published by the Liberal-Conservative Party of Saskatchewan, April 1931; Wilson, *Diefenbaker*, 127–32; *OC 1*, 129–30

6 Wilson, *Diefenbaker*, 131–32

7 Archer, *Saskatchewan*, 213–19; Friesen, *Canadian Prairies*, 382–406

8 JGDP, II/10, 8302–505; Wilson, *Diefenbaker*, 139; JGDI, August 14, 1969. The Diefenbaker Papers suggest a certain lack of order, or casualness, in the financial records of the Diefenbaker law office. In 1935, 1936, 1937, and 1938, for example, Diefenbaker either submitted inconsistent federal and provincial income tax returns or resubmitted revised statements. His net taxable income for 1936 was shown on various forms as $3546, $3935, $4568, or $3537.

9   JGDI, August 14, 1969; JGDP, I

10   JGD to the Manager, Banque Canadienne Nationale, Prince Albert, May 12, 1933, March 29, 1935, JGDP, II/10/131, 8214–15, 8220

11   Wilson, *Diefenbaker*, 149

12   *OC 1*, 138; Wilson, *Diefenbaker*, 150–51

13   Holt, *Other*, 139–40; Wilson, *Diefenbaker*, 148

14   Holt, *Other*, 140–44; Wilson, *Diefenbaker*, 153–54. Holt gained her information and comments on these relationships from Sheila Brower, Mary Louise (Connell) Hose, Helen Brunt, Emmett and Belle Hall, Priscilla McCloy, and Molly Parrott, among others.

15   Holt, *Other*, 155

16   Ibid., 150–51; JGDP, II/10/135, 8606

17   From the mid-1920s to the 1940s, for example, Diefenbaker was a member of the Prince Albert Canadian Club, the Young Men's Chamber of Commerce, the Kiwanis Club, the Prince Albert Horticultural Society, the Benevolent and Protective Order of Elks, the Loyal Orange Lodge, the Shriners, and was a modest contributor to a wide range of local charities. He was an elected member of the Senate of the University of Saskatchewan from 1932 to 1938, and was active in the Canadian Bar Association throughout this period.

18   Wilson, *Diefenbaker*, 151

19   Quoted ibid., 155–56

20   In his memoirs Diefenbaker said that civic bonds with a face value of $100 were being bought "for twenty-five dollars or less" by "members of the Davis clique," who naturally opposed him in the election because he wanted the city to buy up the discounted bonds. But he reflected on his defeat: "Of course, had I won in 1933, I would not have been in a position to accept the leadership of the provincial Conservative Party in 1936...In retrospect, there seems almost a logic which was not apparent at the time." By 1975 the invisible hand guiding Diefenbaker's career seemed as sure in hindsight as the one guiding Mackenzie King's. Wilson, *Diefenbaker*, 156; *OC 1*, 168–69

21   Wilson, *Diefenbaker*, 156–57

22   Ibid., 157–58; Ward and Smith, *Gardiner*, 165–72. The Conservative Party lost seats disproportionately in the three-way fight: the Liberals won 48 percent of the popular vote, the Conservatives 27 percent, and Farmer-Labour 24 percent.

23   *OC 1*, 162; JGDI, December 10, 1969

24   *OC 1*, 162

25   Ibid.

26   JGDI, December 10, 1969

27   Ibid.

28   Ibid.

29   Ibid.

30   The occasion for Diefenbaker's conversation with Bennett over Stevens's future is uncertain; Diefenbaker suggested that it was in October 1934, apparently just before Stevens's resignation. In 1934 Diefenbaker had no reason to notice, but the secretary of the price spreads commission and eventual author of the commission's report was a young External Affairs officer named L.B. Pearson. *OC 1*, 163–64; English, *Shadow*, 168–69; JGDI, December 10, 1969

31   *OC 1*, 162–63

32   The genesis of the speeches is traced in the J.W. Dafoe Papers, Grant Dexter to J.W. Dafoe, January 4, 1935; Dafoe to Chester Bloom, January 11, 1935; Bloom to Dafoe, January 14 and January 30, 1935; Dexter to George Ferguson, May 11, 1935; Bloom to Dafoe, September 18, 1935. See also the *Canadian Annual Review, 1935–36*, 3.

33   JGD to Robert Weir, January 10, 1935, JGDP, II/1/25, 455–56

34   Ibid.

35   See J.W. Dafoe to John A. Stevenson, May 17, 1935; Grant Dexter to Dafoe, May 20, 1935; Dafoe to Tom King, May 30, 1935; Dexter to Dafoe, June 3, 1935, Dafoe Papers.

36 JGD to Senator Huey P. Long, January 22, 1935, JGDP, II/11/141, 9150

37 JGD to D.L. Burgess, March 26, 1935, ibid., 9021

38 Friesen, *Canadian Prairies*, 399–400; Ward and Smith, *Gardiner*, 182–88

39 According to the memoirs, Diefenbaker "was in line" for appointment to the Saskatchewan Court of King's Bench in 1935, but, in the absence of a vacancy, Bennett sounded Diefenbaker out during the election campaign on a district court judgeship. Diefenbaker was not interested. *OC 1*, 164, 169; Wilson, *Diefenbaker*, 178

40 Prince Albert *Daily Herald*, July 23, 1935; Wilson, *Diefenbaker*, 178

41 *OC 1*, 164. J.M. Barrie, in a rectorial address at St Andrew's University in 1922 entitled "Courage," said: "Courage is the thing. All goes if courage goes." Diefenbaker was also on the platform for Bennett's campaign speech in Saskatoon the next night, September 26, 1935. JGDP, II/11/142, 9233, 5812

42 Ward and Smith, *Gardiner*, 189–94; Wilson, *Diefenbaker*, 178–79

43 Courtney, *Voting in Canada*, 18–19; Wilson, *Diefenbaker*, 179; Ward and Smith, *Gardiner*, 193–94

44 Gardiner's labyrinthine negotiations with King over the appointment are laid out in Ward and Smith, *Gardiner*, 195–202.

45 "Excerpts from Speech delivered by Rt. Hon. R.B. Bennett March 4, 1938 to the Conservative Conference at Ottawa," JGDP, II/1/26, 516–18. The caption is in Diefenbaker's handwriting.

46 JGDI, December 10, 1969. A slightly different wording appears in the Diefenbaker memoirs. *OC 1*, 164–65

47 *OC 1*, 166; JGDI, December 10, 1969

48 Wire, JGD to R.B. Bennett, January 26, 1939, JGDP, II/1/25, 461

49 Quoted in Wilson, *Diefenbaker*, 137

50 Wilson, *Diefenbaker*, 137–38

51 Quoted ibid., *Diefenbaker*, 164. Cookson later served for seventeen years as the Regina chief of police.

52 Ibid., 165

53 Ibid.

54 Ibid., 166

55 According to Arthur Cookson, the boy's first lawyer, Alfred Svoboda, who was displaced by John Diefenbaker at the request of Bohun's father, had refused to give up the shirt to Diefenbaker for use in the trial. Ibid., 170

56 Winnipeg *Free Press*, October 2, 1933

57 Quoted in Wilson, *Diefenbaker*, 171–72

58 *Daily Herald*, February 22, 1934; Wilson, *Diefenbaker*, 172

59 Wilson, *Diefenbaker*, 172–73; *Daily Herald*, March 8 and 9, 1934

60 *Daily Herald*, November 4–9, 1935; Wilson, *Diefenbaker*, 180–89

61 Saskatoon *Star–Phoenix*, December 2, 1935

62 Ibid., February 12 and April 28, 1936; Wilson, *Diefenbaker*, 185–89

63 Regina *Daily Star*, February 5, 1936, quoted in Wilson, *Diefenbaker*, 202

64 *R. v. Harms*, (1936) 2 *Western Weekly Reports*, 114 (Sask.); *Daily Star*, February 5 and 6, 1935; Wilson, *Diefenbaker*, 190–202

65 *Daily Star*, April 20, 1936; Wilson, *Diefenbaker*, 203

66 Wilson, *Diefenbaker*, 204

67 Regina *Leader*, May 14, 1936

68 JGD to R.L. Hanbidge, October 2, 1936, JGDP, II/3/38.4, 2908–10. In the memoirs, Diefenbaker wrote that "I did not have it in mind to become Party Leader, nor did I campaign in any way for the office. But as President, it was difficult to resist the demands of E.E. Perley, M.P. from Qu'Appelle, and of R.L. 'Dinny' Hanbidge from Kerrobert, and of other leading Conservatives that I allow my name to go forward." *OC 1*, 166. The source of the claim seemed to be this letter to Hanbidge of October 2; Diefenbaker ignored or missed evidence from later in the month that he had, indeed, sought the leadership.

69   In *The Other Mrs. Diefenbaker*, Holt wrote that Diefenbaker, at a dinner party in the fall of 1936,
      "was effusive about Hitler's leadership, his ability in restoring Germany's economy. He
      described the German dictator as a 'spellbinder,' referring to the opening of the Games,
      Hitler's showcase of the triumphs of Naziism, and the supremacy of the pure Aryan race."
      She suggests that Edna silenced Diefenbaker, and told him later of critical press reports about
      Nazi atrocities. Holt, *Other*, 153–54

70   There are a number of items from the "Vimy and Battlefields Pilgrimage, July 1936" in the
      Diefenbaker Papers. Diefenbaker's presence in Berlin is recorded in postcards to Edna on
      August 9, 1936, and to his father on August 12, 1936. The speech was made in Melfort,
      Saskatchewan, on March 1, 1937; the reference to the Nazi system appears in a letter to Laura
      S. Martin of April 9, 1940; and the exchange with Franz Rosenow of Berlin occurred from
      October 21, 1936, to April 21, 1937. See JGDP, II/13, 15, 18674–91; 11694; 9179–80; 9243–48;
      Melfort *Journal*, March 2, 1937.

      In the memoirs, Diefenbaker wrote that he attended the Games and "saw Hitler, Goering,
      Goebbels, and Dr. Funk. They were within thirty or forty feet of me. I saw at first hand the
      curse of militarism renewed in the German people." *OC 1*, 201.

      In June 1937 the *Western Producer* published a letter from one O. Reidell, alleging that
      Diefenbaker had attended a rally of the Nazi party in Nuremberg in September 1936 and
      that he maintained "regular and intimate" contact with the Nazis. Diefenbaker wrote to
      Reidell and the newspaper denying the allegations and threatening legal proceedings in the
      absence of retractions. Diefenbaker said that he had no doubt Reidell "is but a tool for
      others who will remain anonymous, using him for the propagation of false propaganda."
      Reidell withdrew his charges, and the *Western Producer* published Diefenbaker's letter on June
      24, 1937, along with an editorial note saying that "we regret most sincerely the contribution
      we made to spreading this canard and that, having discussed the matter with Mr.
      Diefenbaker, we do not believe there is a scintilla of evidence to support the charges made by
      Mr. Reidell." *Western Producer*, June 3 and 24, 1937; JGDP, II/7/97, 5525–26; II/16/234,
      12147–56; Wilson, *Diefenbaker*, 215–16

      In June 1937 Prime Minister King was received by Adolf Hitler in Berlin, and the editor
      of the *Western Producer* commented to Diefenbaker that "I would imagine now, after Mr.
      King's long interview with Hitler, that anybody who was going to use this material against
      you is going to run into a boomerang." A.P. Waldron to JGD, July 6, 1937, JGDP, II/7/97, 5526

71   R.L. Hanbidge to JGD, September 25, 1936, JGDP, II/3/38.4, 2903–04

72   JGD to R.L. Hanbidge, October 2, 1936, ibid., 2908–10

73   See, for example, JGD to Mr & Mrs William Roberts, Zealandia, October 21, 1936, ibid., 2924;
      Wilson, *Diefenbaker*, 209–13.

74   Saskatoon *Star–Phoenix*, October 29, 1936; see also Regina *Leader Post*, October 29, 1936; *Daily
      Star*, October 29, 1936.

75   *Daily Star*, October 29, 1936

76   J.F. Anderson to JGD, August 10, 1937, enclosing a copy of his letter to R.B. Bennett, JGDP,
      II/3/33.2, 1598–600

77   JGD to J.F. Anderson, August 11, 1937; copy, J. Earl Lawson, MP, to H.E. Keown, August 10,
      1937, JGDP, II/3/33.2, 1601, 1604

78   Just after the election, Diefenbaker wrote to an Ontario MP: "I put in about seventeen
      months without any salary and am naturally very discouraged. I received no assistance from
      the East, other than generous personal help from Mr. Bennett." Within days of the 1938
      defeat, the provincial party office received a contribution of $5000 from Ottawa. JGD to
      Denton Massey, MP, June 19, 1938, JGDP, II/15/218, 11627–28; *OC 1*, 176

79   *OC 1*, 174. The deposits of twenty-two candidates cost Diefenbaker $2200. In a letter written
      in early April, Diefenbaker said: "I am hopeful that the Conservatives will have about 35
      candidates in the field." JGD to R.W. Ward, Edmonton, April 8, 1938, JGDP, II/1/1, 2

80   Smith, *Prairie Liberalism*, 233–43

81 Edmonton *Journal*, April 27, May 27, 1938; *Today and Tomorrow* 3, May 12, 1938; Helen Orpwood, "The Saskatchewan Election," *Canadian Forum*, August 1938, 136–37; *Free Press*, May 17 and 19, 1938; *OC 1*, 174–76; Wilson, *Diefenbaker*, 217–21

82 Regina *Leader Post*, May 19, 1938, quoted in Smith, *Prairie Liberalism*, 239

83 Wilson, *Diefenbaker*, 217–22; *OC 1*, 173–77

84 Smith, *Prairie Liberalism*, 239–43; Wilson, *Diefenbaker*, 221; *OC 1*, 176

85 JGD to G.S. Thorvaldson, June 18, 1938, JGDP, II/1/23.2, 360–62

86 JGD to E.E. Perley, June 17, 1938, ibid., 343

87 Diefenbaker quickly and graciously acknowledged such indications of support. He had already taken note of the significance of Hnatyshyn's commitment to the party when he wrote to E.E. Perley in February 1938 that Hnatyshyn "has done much to alter the antagonistic attitude towards the Conservative Party which has heretofore characterized the Ukrainian people in this Province." JGD to E.E. Perley, MP, February 9, 1938; John Hnatyshyn to JGD, June 11, 1938; JGD to John Hnatyshyn, June 10 and June 18, 1938, ibid., 501, 10788–89, 10815

88 *OC 1*, 173–74; Wilson, *Diefenbaker*, 221; JGD to Alex H. Reed, December 9, 1938; JGD to J.H. Currie, June 6, August 30, 1939, JGDP, II/3/33.2, 1669–71, II/4/40, 3403, 3407

Chapter 4 Seats of the Mighty

1 *OC 1*, 177

2 Quoted in Holt, *Other*, 173. Holt also reports that Diefenbaker's Prince Albert friend and political supporter Violet Chisholm recalled his expressed intention to leave politics after the 1938 defeat. Ibid., 174

3 These signs were evident to her maid Florence Pelletier and her niece Sheila Brower, among others. In his memoirs Diefenbaker notes only that "my wife was not well." *OC 1*, 176–77

4 See Holt, *Other*, 175–83.

5 See JGD to Château Laurier, wire, June 17, 1938; Château Laurier to JGD, wire, June 17, 1938; JGD to R.F. Pratt, June 18, 1938; R.F. Pratt to JGD, June 20, 1938; JGD to J.R. MacNicol, June 20, 1938, JGDP, II/1/26, 354–55, 357, 359, 366.

6 J.R. MacNicol to JGD, June 21, 1938, ibid., 372

7 JGD to A.E. Whitmore, June 15 and June 22, 1938; JGD to M.A. MacPherson, June 22, 1938; JGD to Mrs W.M. Roberts, June 25, 1938; JGD to J.R. MacNicol, June 27, 1938; J.R. MacNicol to JGD, June 27, 1938; H.A. Stewart to JGD, June 27, 1938; JGD to H.A. Stewart, June 30, 1938; George McLean to JGD, June 28, 1938; JGD to George McLean, June 29, 1938, JGDP, ibid., 292–93, 375, 387, 373, 390–92, 401–03

8 The vote was Manion 830; MacPherson 648; Harris 49; Massey 39. Lawson had withdrawn after the first ballot. See Granatstein, *Survival*, 10–17; *OC 1*, 177–79; Courtney, *Selection*, 187–88.

9 E.E. Perley, MP, to JGD, May 12, 1939; Arthur Kendall to JGD, May 12, 1939; JGD to John R. Anderson, June 6, 1939, JGDP, II/1/26, 591–92, 599–600

10 George W. McLean and Mrs A.R. Robinson to JGD, nd; JGD to Mrs A.R. Robinson, June 6, 1939; W.B. Kelly to JGD, June 5, 1939; JGD to W.B. Kelly, June 8, 1939; JGD to John R. Anderson, June 6, 1939, ibid., 595–600

11 *OC 1*, 180–81

12 Saskatoon *Phoenix*, June 16, 1939; *OC 1*, 181–83; Wilson, *Diefenbaker*, 231–32; JGDI, August 14, 1969. Kelly, the president of the constituency association, perpetuated the local party's historic link with the Ku Klux Klan. In the late 1920s he had been the Kligrapp (or branch president) of the Imperial unit of the Klan. Wilson, *Diefenbaker*, 231–32. He was Diefenbaker's official agent during the 1940 campaign.

During the 1956 leadership contest, Diefenbaker gave a slightly different story of the nominating convention to the Toronto *Globe and Mail*: "Now, he recalls with feelings of dismay at the close call, that he had gone to Imperial just to thank the voters who had vainly cast their ballots for him in the provincial election. His late wife, Edna, was with him, quite pleased at the thought that politics was being relegated to the background in their life." *Globe and Mail*, November 12, 1956. His arrival at a federal nominating convention, and his subsequent nomination, were entirely unexpected. Here was a double twist: Not only was the story of the accidental nomination fanciful but in 1956 he feigned dismay that if he had not made the trip to thank his constituents, he would not have become an MP, and by implication would not have been a candidate for the leadership. The fates were obviously with him. His mention of Edna's feelings sustains the view that one reason for his show of reluctance was his need to persuade her to accept his continuing political career.

13   *OC 1*, 182–83; JGDI, August 14, 1969; and see, for example, copious correspondence and campaign materials in the file "Conservative Party: National – Organization, Lake Centre," from June 16, 1939, to September 1, 1939, JGDP, II/1/27, 604–762.

14   *OC 1*, 179–80

15   E.E. Perley to JGD, June 23, 1939; Arthur Kendall to JGD, July 20, 1939, JGD to R.C. Manion, July 20, 1939, JGDP, II/1/27, 632, 687–88, 621

16   JGD to A.E. Whitmore, July 27, 1939; JGD to Major G. Dunn, August 29, 1939; J.M. Robb to JGD, September 16, 1939, JGDP, II/1/27, 543–45

17   Granatstein, *Survival*, 30–35

18   Diefenbaker was acting as respondent in the case on behalf of the crown in an action to compel officials and ministers to carry out the law for the benefit of subjects. After winning at trial and appeal, Diefenbaker lost the case in the Supreme Court on a split decision. *E. Swain et al. v. R. Ex relatione Adolph Studer*, (1941) *Supreme Court Records* 40; *OC 1*, 183

19   *OC 1*, 183–84

20   The case is recounted in Wilson, *Diefenbaker*, 232–48; *OC 1*, 183–84; Holt, *Other*, 186–90. See also the Prince Albert *Herald* and Saskatoon *Star-Phoenix*, October 6 and December 5, 1939, February 13–19, 1940; Prince Albert *Herald*, October 17, 1940; Saskatoon *Star-Phoenix*, October 18, 1940; *R. v. Emele*, (1940) 2 *Western Weekly Reports*, 545, 74 *Canadian Criminal Cases* 76 (Sask. CA).

21   Quoted in Wilson, *Diefenbaker*, 233

22   Ibid., 246

23   Diefenbaker dates the second trial incorrectly; it took place on October 16–17, 1940. *OC 1*, 184; Prince Albert *Herald*, October 17, 1940; Saskatoon *Star-Phoenix*, October 18, 1940; Wilson, *Diefenbaker*, 252–59

24   JGD to R.J. Manion, wire, January 29, 1940, JGDP, II/1/27, 549

25   The proposal for a coalition was made without notice at the Conservative caucus meeting on January 26, 1940, by Earl Rowe, MP. It received unanimous approval and was publicly announced by Manion immediately afterwards. This caucus also reaffirmed the party's opposition to conscription for overseas service. Granatstein notes that, since the prospect of a winning alliance with Duplessis in Quebec was already gone, the decision "can only be interpreted, therefore, as reflecting a Conservative desire to maintain national unity and as a reaction to what was believed to be the mood of the electorate." Granatstein, *Survival*, 42–47

26   *OC 1*, 184–92; Wilson, *Diefenbaker*, 249–52; JGD to W.B Scarth, April 4, 1940; JGD to G.S. Thorvaldson, April 4, 1940; JGDP, II/1/27, 563, 565

27   "John Diefenbaker," mimeo, nd, JGDP, II/1/27, 804–05. Brownridge had joined the Diefenbaker office as an articling student, but his duties in 1939–40 were mostly political.

28   *OC 1*, 187–88; Wilson, *Diefenbaker*, 250–51

29   *OC 1*, 191–92; Wilson, *Diefenbaker*, 251–52; Holt, *Other*, 191–92

30   Mary F. Diefenbaker to JGD, April 1, 1940, JGDP, V/1, 543. Mary's spelling, punctuation, and syntax have been left (in this and other letters) as in the originals, except that periods in the middle of sentences, where the sense seems to indicate, have been replaced by commas.

31   William T. Diefenbaker to JGD, April 1, 1940, JGDP, V/1, 55–60

32 Keegan, *The Second World War*, 64–81
33 James Sinclair's recollections of the meeting are recounted in Holt, *Other*, 192–93.
34 Quoted ibid., 193
35 Ibid., 194–95
36 Interview with Clyne Harradence, November 3, 1991. According to Harradence, who packed the boxes in Prince Albert in the 1950s, Diefenbaker left most of the files untouched both in Prince Albert and Ottawa.
37 Nicholson, *Vision*, 28
38 Ibid.
39 R.A. Bell to JGD, March 29, 1940, JGDP, III, 305
40 J.M. Robb to JGD, March 28, 1940, ibid., 555
41 JGD to Mary F. Diefenbaker, April 2, 1940, JGDP, V/1, 304
42 Mary F. Diefenbaker to JGD, April 10, 1940, ibid., 311–12
43 Ottawa *Evening Citizen*, May 13 and 14, 1940
44 JGD to Mary F. Diefenbaker, May 15, 1940, JGDP, V/1, 316–A–B–C
45 Mary F. Diefenbaker to JGD, May 24, 1940, ibid., 317–19. The reference to "hunks" is garbled. "Bohunk" was an insulting western Canadian epithet for Poles or Slavs, undoubtedly familiar to Mary Diefenbaker. But in this context it is confusing and seems to mean "Huns," the common pejorative term for the German enemy. The Grits were the Liberal enemy. William Diefenbaker might have cringed at his wife's references to the "cruel, bloodthirsty nation" of his ancestors, who would get what was coming to them in the end. If her comments reflected a deeper attitude, as the letters suggest, they may help to explain John's unusual sensitivity over his German surname.
46 *OC 1*, 193–94
47 *Evening Citizen*, June 13, 1940
48 House of Commons, *Debates*, May 27, 1940, 238–39; *OC 1*, 220–21
49 "Report to the House," Special Committee on the Defence of Canada Regulations, August 1, 1940, JGDP, III/89, 72083–91. In the cabinet reorganization that followed the death of Norman Rogers, Ilsley become minister of finance on July 8, 1940.
50 *OC 1*, 195. In the memoirs Diefenbaker does not mention the content of the speech.
51 *Debates*, June 13, 1940, 748–51
52 The Liberal member for Parry Sound, Arthur Slaght, another nominee to the special committee, also spoke in favour of the death penalty for spies and saboteurs. *Evening Citizen*, June 13, 1940; "Report to the House," Special Committee on the Defence of Canada Regulations, August 1, 1940, JGDP, III/89, 72083; "An Act Respecting Treachery," typewritten draft, containing handwritten comments and amendments in Diefenbaker's hand, ibid., 71956–63. Diefenbaker spoke in the House in the bill's support. *Debates*, July 25, 1940, 1938–40
53 Granatstein, *Survival*, 58–62; Granatstein, *Canada's War*, 98–99; Pickersgill, *Mackenzie King Record 1*, 102
54 For Diefenbaker's comments on the House of Commons and its members during the 1940s, see *OC 1*, 193–272.
55 *Debates*, February 28, 1941, 1141. In their leaderless and discouraged condition, Conservative MPs even canvassed the possibility of Bennett's resurrection as party leader. H.A. Bruce wrote twice to Bennett in the autumn of 1940, seeking his agreement to return and noting that George McCullagh, publisher of the *Globe and Mail*, believed that Bennett was "the one man to strike terror in the heart of Mackenzie King." Bruce gave up his quest after Lord Beaverbrook told him in January 1941 that Bennett "has settled down in England and made his home in its countryside. And there he means to abide." H.A. Bruce to Rt Hon. R.B. Bennett, December 6, 1940; Beaverbrook to H.A. Bruce, January 4, 1941, Bruce Papers
56 See, for example, his contribution to the debate on the throne speech, *Debates*, November 19, 1940, 224–29. One of his views – in favour of the death penalty for treason – was consistent

with his wartime patriotism and anxiety over subversion, but perhaps surprising in light of his later opposition to the death penalty. See the *Debates*, July 25, 1940, 1938–40.

57 Ibid., January 30, 1942, 180–87

58 Ibid., February 25, 1942, 835–39

59 For Diefenbaker's speech on amendment of the Mobilization Act to permit, but not to require, compulsory overseas service, see ibid., June 15, 1942, 3329–35.

60 Ibid., July 2, 1942, 3888

61 Ibid., July 2, 1942, 3888–91

62 *OC 1*, 197

63 Ibid., 199–200. As happens frequently in the memoirs, Diefenbaker personalizes this encounter. But H.A. Bruce reported the outburst, second hand, to Beaverbrook as though it had been an attack on Hanson, or the Conservative caucus, rather than on Diefenbaker: "One day at a private meeting arranged between Mr. Hanson and two of his colleagues with King and four of his Cabinet...he suddenly got into a rage and shouted hysterically, almost in tears – 'You are always talking about Churchill – What has he done that I have not done. I trust in God, follow my conscience and work day and night,' and ended by saying, 'I hate you Hanson, I hate you.' It is only fair to say that some of his colleagues who were present were heartily ashamed of his exhibition of temper and petulance." H.A. Bruce to Beaverbrook, June 25, 1941, Bruce Papers

64 *OC 1*, 200

65 Ibid., 207

66 Ibid., 6, 208. This was a family story told to John by his mother. In the memoirs Diefenbaker refers to the loyal soldier both as his grandfather and his great-grandfather.

67 Pickersgill, *Mackenzie King Record 1*, 405–06

68 *OC 1*, 208; *Debates*, 4782–89

69 Mary F. Diefenbaker to JGD, March 22, 1941, JGDP, V/1, 199–203

70 William T. Diefenbaker to JGD, March 27, 1941, ibid., 82–86

71 William T. Diefenbaker to JGD, March 20, 1941, ibid., 80

72 William T. Diefenbaker to JGD, May 13, 1942, ibid., 356–61

73 Mary F. Diefenbaker to JGD, May 15, 1942, ibid., 367–68

74 Granatstein, *Survival*, 68–69

75 Ibid., 70–72

76 See Graham, *No Surrender*, 95

77 Granatstein, *Survival*, 73–81. Meighen's words are from a letter to Murdoch MacPherson, August 7, 1941.

78 Graham, *No Surrender*, 97–107; *OC 1*, 249–50; Granatstein, *Survival*, 82–96; JGDI, November 14, 1969

79 Pickersgill, *Mackenzie King Record 1*, 277–78

80 For the York South campaign, see especially Graham, *No Surrender*, 107–31; Granatstein, *Survival*, 94–112.

81 Pickersgill, *Mackenzie King Record 1*, 348

82 Quoted in *OC 1*, 251. King's statement does not appear in the House of Commons *Debates*. But at one point during the evening session the Speaker commented, "There should be less conversation in the chamber...I ask hon. members to refrain," to which the MP then addressing the House responded: "Apparently the election returns are on the minds of all hon. members rather than what I am trying to say." As a matter of course, the *Debates* did not record parliamentary banter. It could be that King said something like this; or perhaps Diefenbaker's reference in his memoirs is based on King's own entry in his diary, as it appeared in the *Mackenzie King Record*. See the *Debates*, February 9, 1942, 425.

83 Diefenbaker's emerging vision was reflected later that year in his address accepting nomination at the party's leadership convention in Winnipeg.

84 Granatstein, *Survival*, 114–15; Graham, *No Surrender*, 132

85 *Debates,* June 10, 1942, 3244; July 2, 1942, 3329–35; Granatstein, *Survival,* 115–19

86 Granatstein, *Survival,* 119–25

87 For a detailed account of the conference's background, genesis, and proceedings, see ibid., 125–35.

88 Ibid., 134

89 Meighen to H.R. Milner, October 17, 1942, quoted in Granatstein, *Survival,* 135

90 Ibid., 136–37

91 The insight about Meighen's purpose is that of Roger Graham in his *No Surrender,* 139.

92 Meighen to Bracken, November 17, 1942, quoted ibid., 142

93 Ibid., 144

94 David J. Walker to JGD, October 10, 1942, JGDP, III/72, 58535

95 "George McG" to JGD, November 20, 1942, ibid., 58546–53

96 Ottawa *Citizen,* December 8, 1942. The editor of the Winnipeg *Free Press,* John W. Dafoe, reported his account of the fix (as told to him "right from the horse's mouth") in a letter to his Ottawa correspondent Grant Dexter. In his telling, the arrangement involved the withdrawal of Murdoch MacPherson's candidacy but not those of Diefenbaker and Green, who "wd be allowed to submit their names but the machine wd see to it that their votes did not amount to anything...My informant tells me they think the thing is as good as settled, saving the remote possibility of a blow-up at the convention. Meighen has figured out that there will not be time to organize a bolt, as the delegates will arrive uninformed and will be taken into camp by the managers." According to Dafoe, MacPherson was furious about this prearrangement. He subsequently decided to repudiate it and accept nomination. J.W. Dafoe to Grant Dexter, November 28, 1942, Dexter Papers

97 "George" to JGD, Monday (undated), JGDP, III/72, 58502–05

98 Granatstein, *Survival,* 144–46

99 Diefenbaker's account recalls that David Walker's remarks were spontaneous and that his words were: "What are you doing here? You're not a Conservative. You're just like the camel who got into the Arab's tent," and to the audience: "You can boo. You don't bother me." *OC 1,* 254. Walker's doubts about Diefenbaker's candidacy meant that he came to Winnipeg prepared to nominate Sidney Smith for the leadership. He remained ready to do so until the last-minute nomination of Bracken, and Smith's decision not to contest it. The description of Howard Green's collapse is by Evelyn S. Tufts, quoted in Granatstein, *Survival,* 147–48. See also Graham, *No Surrender,* 149–50; Newman, *Renegade,* 58–59; JGDI, June 27, August 14, 1969.

100 The first quotation is from Evelyn S. Tufts, quoted in Granatstein, *Survival,* 148; the second is from Newman, *Renegade,* 59.

101 Convention address (mimeographed), JGDP, III/72, 58506–23

102 Granatstein, *Survival,* 148–50; Graham, *No Surrender,* 150–51

103 He said in 1969: "Of course there never was any chance for me being elected. I had no campaign in forty-two whatever. I just turned up, and I had a lot of votes!" JGDI, June 27, 1969

104 But Diefenbaker was lukewarm about the change of party name, which he believed unnecessary – or perhaps irrelevant. He noted that it had previously called itself the Liberal-Conservative Party, the National Liberal-Conservative Party, and the Conservative Party – until 1940, when it campaigned as the National Government Party. "I have always," he wrote, preferred the name Conservative." JGDI, June 27, December 11, 1969; Leonard W. Fraser to JGD, December 16, 1942, Donald M. Fleming to JGD, December 18, 1942, JGDP, III/72, 58636–37; *OC 1,* 254–55

105 *OC 1,* 254

106 Granatstein, *Survival,* 153–55; *OC 1,* 256–57; Pickersgill, *Mackenzie King Record 1,* 477

107 *OC 1,* 257. Granatstein writes that "the results of this informal poll are unknown." Granatstein, *Survival,* 154

108 JGDI, August 14, 1969. Diefenbaker suggested that Earl Rowe was the leader of "that group

from Toronto" who opposed him. He told this story in the aftermath of his 1967 leadership defeat, which may add to its sardonic tone. As with his other defeats, he rationalized this one in retrospect by suggesting that success would mean that "King would have walked all over me," presumably crushing his prospects for the permanent leadership. In his memoirs he told the same story in somewhat less detail, noting similarly that "Fate moves in its peculiar way." *OC 1*, 258. His claim to have displayed his vote for Graydon was substantiated by Rodney Adamson, who wrote in his diary that evening: "At 8.30 Caucus reconvenes and Gordon is chosen leader by one vote over John Diefenbaker. John voted for Gordon and Gordon voted for himself. This is a swell situation." Rodney Adamson, Diary, January 27, 1943, Adamson Papers; also quoted in Granatstein, *Survival*, 155

109 See, for example, Mary F. Diefenbaker to JGD, "Just a line to let you know that everything is O.K. only we cant get anything done. The garden is not plowed yet, and the storm windows are still on, and the big man of the house sits on his back bone and wonders, waiting for some one to come and begg to have the work to do. he just sits looking at his hands and saying over and over, my hands has been so bad, so bad. he is going to see the Dr today, and for the life of me I cant see there is anything to trouble about"; also Mary F. Diefenbaker to JGD, March 19 and June 20 (no year), JGDP, V/1, 160–62, 174–76, 189–91.

110 William T. Diefenbaker to JGD, March 14, 1944, ibid., 118–23

111 Mary F. Diefenbaker to JGD, March 19 (no year), ibid., 189–91

112 Mary F. Diefenbaker to JGD, April 19, 1944, ibid., 391–93

113 Mary F. Diefenbaker to JGD, May 2 (1944), ibid., 394–96

114 JGD to Elmer Diefenbaker, May 5, 1944, JCDP, V/3, 1456. The incident is also described in Robertson, *More*, 236–37.

115 Incomplete traces of this incident, and of Elmer's military career, appear in the Diefenbaker Papers, but there are no references to it in any remaining correspondence from either John or Elmer Diefenbaker. In 1946 Elmer was granted a 5 percent disability pension for partial deafness, which was increased in 1964 to a rate of 30 percent disability ($54 per month) and in 1966 to 40 percent (or $80 per month). The previous pattern of John's care for Elmer suggests that he acted for Elmer in seeking the pension. JGDP, V/43, 28796–945

116 "Certified Copy of Registration of Death," March 22, 1945, JGDP, V/14, 9309

117 What follows is based upon evidence in the Diefenbaker Papers, the Adamson Papers, the Bruce Papers, Holt, *Other*, and Robertson, *More*.

118 See, for example, Mary F. Diefenbaker to JGD, February 8 [1942], in which she comments: "Glad to hear Edna was feeling so much better." JGDP, V/1, 326–30

119 In February 1941, for example, their mutual friend and fellow MP Rodney Adamson recorded in his diary that "Mrs. Diefenbaker is soothed down over dinner at Government House." Diary, February 19, 1943, Adamson Papers

120 Sheila Brower told Holt that Diefenbaker could not distinguish green from brown, and thus needed help coordinating the colours of his clothing. Holt, *Other*, 249; Robertson, *More*, 236

121 See Holt, *Other*, 183-84

122 Diary, May 13, 1942, Adamson Papers. Adamson recorded the intimacies of his own life in the diary with unusual frankness; he was one of the Diefenbakers' close friends and seemed to have no conceivable reason for commenting inaccurately about what Edna told him.

123 Ibid., May 21, 1943

124 Ibid., February 7, 1944

125 This episode is related in Holt, *Other*, 242–50. It is based on Holt's interviews with Sheila Brower, Priscilla McCloy, Virginia O'Brien, and Dorothy Fraser.

126 Ibid., 250–51. Clyne Harradence also mentions this incident in his oral history interview for the Diefenbaker Centre. JGDP, XVIII/OH/45, November 17, 1985

127 Howland's first letter in the Diefenbaker files is dated July 10, 1945, but he begins it by commenting that "I think we are becoming regular correspondents." A telegram and a second letter remain, dated respectively in July 1945 and on February 27, 1946. According to

Holt, Diefenbaker's secretary in Prince Albert received correspondence in the office about Edna's illness in this period, and recalls that Diefenbaker sometimes destroyed such letters. JGDP, V/10, 9139–40, 9145; Holt, *Other*, 256–63

128 Dr Goldwin W. Howland to JGD, July 10, 1945, JGDP, V/10, 9140. In this letter Howland does not offer a diagnosis, but in a letter of February 1946 he writes of "an extreme case of an obsession." The electroconvulsive therapy she received in that month – a short series of five treatments – suggested a diagnosis of mild rather than severe depression, or some other relatively mild mental condition. It is not clear from the available record why Howland described this as one of his "hardest cases." Dr Goldwin W. Howland to JGD, February 27, 1946, ibid., 9145

129 See below, Edna to JGD (undated), from Homewood Sanitarium.

130 JGD to Edna Diefenbaker, April 25, 1945, JGDP, V/10, 7076. Newsreels of the audience at the opening ceremony show Diefenbaker in the audience, glowing in self-awareness.

131 Goldwin W. Howland to JGD, July 10, 1945, JGDP, V/10, 9140

132 Diefenbaker was apparently planning to see Edna soon after this letter, but later in the month Howland wired him to suggest that he should postpone a visit until August 1. Telegram, Dr Goldwin W. Howland to JGD, July 20, 1945, JGDP, V/10, 9139

133 Wilson, *Diefenbaker*, 172

134 Dr Goldwin W. Howland to JGD, July 10, 1945, JGDP, V/10, 9140

135 Electro shock therapy, or electroconvulsive therapy (ECT), was a controversial treatment for a range of mental disorders including schizophrenia and depression, introduced in Italy in 1938 and widely practised in North America by the mid-1940s. The treatment consisted of short bursts of electric current applied through electrodes on the temples to induce convulsions. Patients were given muscle relaxants and anesthetized before treatment. They suffered varying degrees of memory loss, but usually recovered memory over time. ECT was used in varying clinical circumstances and without generally accepted controls, more frequently in private psychiatric hospitals than in public ones. The records of its success tended at this time to be anecdotal and impressionist rather than scientific. There were immediate and continuing questions over its long-term effects, both beneficial and damaging, and over the ethics involved in its use. Since its physical effects were unknown, and its psychological effects unpredictable, the use of ECT on humans was, in effect, a dubious form of experimentation. The practice later came under intensive critical study among psychiatrists. By the 1970s, despite more limited and controlled application, it remained a subject of professional controversy. See, for example, *Electroconvulsive Therapy: Task Force Report 14* (American Psychiatric Association, September 1978); Peter Roger Breggin, *Electro-Shock: Its Brain-Disabling Effects*.

136 Edna Diefenbaker to JGD (undated), JGDP, V/10, 7077–85

137 Bruce makes reference to Edna's illness and her presence at Guelph in letters to Diefenbaker on January 10, February 21, and April 5, 1946. The originals do not appear in the Diefenbaker Papers, but copies can be found in the Bruce Papers. Bruce's interest was prompted both by his friendship with Diefenbaker and by his role as an informal medical adviser.

138 Dr Goldwin W. Howland to JGD, February 27, 1946; The Homewood Sanitarium to JGD, March 31, 1946, JGDP, V/10, 9145, 9151; H.A. Bruce to JGD, April 5, 1946; H.A. Bruce to Miss Gladys Dudley, April 10, 1946, Bruce Papers; Holt, *Other*, 261. The Diefenbaker Papers do not reveal who authorized the use of ECT, or even whether specific consent was sought. Edna's letter (quoted above) seems to suggest her willingness to receive shock therapy as a means of escaping from hospital. Dr Howland wrote in February 1946 that "she is getting her own way" in receiving the treatments, but added that "I, personally, am pleased she is going to take them...the main hope is in shock treatment." The treatment was bound to be frightening for the patient, and probably a matter of confusion for a medical layman like her husband.

The accounts for Edna's six months in Homewood Sanitarium amounted to $8.50 per day for regular care and treatment, plus sundry personal expenses, plus $37.50 for electro shock treatment. At an estimated $300 per month, the bills reached close to $2000.

139 Dr Glen Green, JGDP, XVIII/OH/37, February 20, 1986

140 The McGregor quotation is from Holt, *Other*, 265–66.

Chapter 5 New Name, Old Party

1 Diefenbaker had known Bracken since his own first year at the University of Saskatchewan in 1912, when Bracken had joined the faculty briefly as professor of field husbandry. Diefenbaker recalled in his memoirs: "I followed his career. I watched him on the stump; he had an amazing capacity for meeting people. I do not think I have ever known anyone more effective with a farm audience. He understood their problems, and the farmers knew it. No one in public life knew more about agriculture, both theoretical and practical. John Bracken was a man of good character; his word was his bond. He was also blessed with a wonderful wife who ably assisted him through his years of public service." *OC 1*, 256. But privately, in retrospect, Diefenbaker's memories were less generous, hinting at a long memory of grievance from the period of Bracken's choice as leader.

2 The occasion referred to was apparently at Manitou Beach, Watrous, on August 7, 1943. In the memoirs Diefenbaker mistakenly identifies the location as "a small town between Regina and Moose Jaw." The meeting was widely advertised, but there seemed to be no newspaper reports of the incident. *OC 1*, 256; M.L. Hargreaves to JGD, August 26, 1943, and enclosures, JGDP, III/13/147, 9139–43

3 Pickersgill, *Mackenzie King Record 1*, 478

4 Granatstein, *Survival*, 155–58

5 Ibid., 165–67. The members of the proposed national organization committee were to be Henry Borden as chairman, J.H. Gundy (who was already Bracken's finance chairman), E.W. Bickle (Drew's fundraiser), James S. Duncan, Alex McKenzie (Drew's chief organizer), and Richard Bell.

6 Richard Bell, "Problems of Organization," nd [1944], quoted in Granatstein, *Survival*, 159

7 Pickersgill, *Mackenzie King Record 1*, 564–603, 630–36; Granatstein, *Survival*, 163–65; Granatstein, *Canada's War*, 249–93

8 Granatstein, *Canada's War*, 276

9 House of Commons, *Debates*, February 4, 1944, 188

10 *OC 1*, 152–53

11 Diary, July 26, 1944, Adamson Papers

12 *Debates*, July 27, 1944, 5460

13 Diary, July 27, 1944, Adamson Papers

14 Herbert Bruce's comment about a bribe was judged unparliamentary by the Speaker, and when Bruce refused to withdraw the charge, he was named and suspended from the House for the day. *Debates*, July 31, 1944, 5677; H.A. Bruce to Gordon Graydon, July 20, 1944, Bruce Papers; Toronto *Globe and Mail*, August 10, 1944; Granatstein, *Survival*, 169

15 *Debates*, July 28, 1944, 5527–28

16 Quoted in Granatstein, *Survival*, 173

17 *Debates*, February 10, 1944, 365

18 Ibid., July 10, 1944, 4668

19 Granatstein, *Survival*, 177–78

20 Diary, July 24, 1944, Adamson Papers

21 *Debates*, July 10, 1944, 4672–73. Diefenbaker's speech appears in the *Debates*, July 10, 1944, 4667–72.

22 Ibid., July 10, 1944, 4673

23 The complex story of the conscription crisis is told, *inter alia*, in Dawson, *Conscription*; Stacey, *Arms*; Ward, *Party Politician*; Pickersgill and Forster, *Mackenzie King Record 2*.

24 Ward, *Party Politician*, 170

25 *Debates*, November 23 and December 5, 1944, 6539–43, 6805–10. Diefenbaker shared the party's view that conscription should apply to Pacific as well as European service. But by the time of the June 1945 general election, with the European war at an end, his keenness on compulsory assignment in the Pacific theatre had cooled to match the sentiments of prairie voters. He wrote in his memoirs that 7000 envelopes containing "highly decorative literature for distribution in my constituency," calling for the transfer of Canada's European forces to the Pacific, were summarily destroyed as soon as he had read the message. *OC 1*, 258–59

26 Granatstein, *Survival*, 183–84; *Canada's War*, 389–94

27 Granatstein, *Canada's War*, 404

28 *Mackenzie King to the People*, 126, quoted in Granatstein, *Canada's War*, 408

29 Quoted in Williams, *Conservative Party*, 169

30 Quoted in Granatstein, *Canada's War*, 405

31 Some of his campaign material mentions that he had seconded a House motion to make all home service conscripts available for Pacific service. *OC 1*, 258–59; JGDI, August 14, 1969; Typescript, "May I review some salient matters..." undated, JGDP, III/45/498, 35395

32 A handwritten memo on "the Elbow Dam," apparently in Elmer's handwriting, proposes a slightly different slogan: "It will be a dam site surer and sooner, if you re-elect John Diefenbaker." *OC 1*, 260–61; JGDI, August 14, 1969; Memo, "Publish an elaborate pamphlet..." undated, JGDP, III/84/1048, 67001–04

33 Diefenbaker received financial support for his campaign from his friends David Walker and Bill Brunt in Toronto and Mickey O'Brien in Vancouver. Walker was especially helpful, providing a cheque for $1000 and covering the cost of Diefenbaker's recorded radio addresses. J.F. Anderson to JGD, May 21, 1945; "List of meetings to be held week of May 28th, 1945"; "Week of June 4th/45"; Notice of radio addresses, May–June 1945; David J. Walker to JGD, May 31, 1945; Memo, "Cheques handed by Mr. Diefenbaker to his Official Agent, August 3, 1945," JGDP, III/45/498, 35408–09, 35424, 35434, 35401, 35426, 35439

34 Pickersgill and Forster, *Mackenzie King Record 2*, 399

35 *OC 1*, 263

36 *Public Opinion Quarterly* 9 (summer 1945): 234

37 Williams, *Conservative Party*, 169–70, 199; Granatstein, *Canada's War*, 409–10; *OC 1*, 260–63

38 *OC 1*, 263

39 Fleming, *Near 1*, 107–08, 111–12, 135. Fleming himself was a vain and ambitious MP, but he was also an accurate witness who could honestly report in his memoirs that caucus members described him as an "Eager Beaver" because of his capacity for work and his tenacity in debate.

40 Fulton interview, September 24, 1993

41 See my *Diplomacy*, 129–30.

42 Pickersgill, *Mackenzie King Record 3*, 136. These events are treated at length in the King diaries and in my *Diplomacy*, 94–136.

43 *Debates*, March 21, 1946, 135–40

44 Ibid., March 21, 1946, 137–38

45 Pickersgill, *Mackenzie King Record 3*, 156–57; Smith, *Diplomacy*, 135

46 *Debates*, April 2, 1946, 510–11. The bill was the product of a compromise in the Liberal cabinet, fashioned by Mackenzie King and Paul Martin, which established Canadian citizenship but maintained that "a Canadian citizen is a British subject." That offended some nationalists, both French- and English-speaking, but was necessary to assure the support of many Liberals. Diefenbaker criticized the bill for requiring that British and Commonwealth immigrants would have to apply for citizenship through citizenship courts like all other immigrants, and Martin subsequently altered the draft to allow British subjects to file directly for citizenship with the secretary of state. See Martin, *Very Public 1*, 445–53.

47 *Debates*, April 2, 1946, 511. Diefenbaker's phrase, "unhyphenated Canadians," probably had

an American source as well. Decades before, Woodrow Wilson had attacked immigrants as "hyphenated Americans"; and in the 1920 presidential campaign, the Democratic vice presidential candidate, Franklin Roosevelt, had appealed to xenophobic voters with the claim that his party wanted "all-American votes only." Roosevelt's family was already long enough established in America to remove him from the hyphenated class. See Cook, *Eleanor Roosevelt 1*, 280.

48 *Debates*, May 3, 1946, 1177. Despite suggestions in his memoirs that he had been an advocate of the Japanese Canadians in the House during their wartime internment, this appears to be the first parliamentary reference Diefenbaker made to their plight. His postwar intervention was less troublesome in caucus than it would have been in wartime, when west coast MPs were fanatically committed to expulsion and internment; but Diefenbaker was careful to limit his protest at this time to the government's attempt to arrange deportations. Nevertheless, even in 1946 members of the Conservative caucus from British Columbia, including Davie Fulton, took a less critical position.

49 *Debates*, May 6, 1946, 1310–14

50 Ibid., May 6, 1946, 1311; Martin, *Very Public 1*, 450–51

51 *Debates*, May 6, 1946, 1311–12

52 *Globe and Mail*, May 10, 1946; Winnipeg *Free Press*, May 20, 1946; Martin, *Very Public 1*, 448–51. Diefenbaker persisted at third reading of the citizenship bill by seeking to attach another amendment requiring a House of Commons resolution favouring a bill of rights, to be examined by a select committee "properly representative of the entire population of Canada." The proposed amendment was ruled out of order by the Speaker, a ruling sustained on Diefenbaker's appeal to the House. *Debates*, May 16, 1946, 1575–79

53 See Berger, *Fragile Freedoms*, 170–75.

54 *Debates*, May 16, 1947, 3148–49

55 Ibid., May 16, 1947, 3149–59

56 Ibid., 3158–59

57 "The Week on Parliament Hill," May 20, 1947, JGDP, III/66, 52755–56

58 Elmer Diefenbaker to JGD, May 24, 1947, JGDP, III/3/29.5, 1472–76, esp. 1472–73. Elmer continued the letter with a three-page description of his latest venture as salesman for a pipe with a built-in lighter, previously unknown in Saskatchewan. "Once it catches on it will move," he assured John, although "I went out with it yesterday but had trouble making appointments, but those who saw it really talked." He was also selling wagons and kiddy cars, thanks to an agency arranged by Bill Brunt which "has great possibilities."

59 JGD to Glen How, July 14, 1947; JGD to H.R. Harrison, August 5, 1947, JGDP, III/3/29.5, 1558, 1556; Belliveau, "Diefenbaker," 51–55

60 The committee did, however, recommend that the existing limitation on appeals to the Supreme Court of Canada requiring that cases must involve monetary disputes should be removed. Diefenbaker believed that this change would mean that the "need for a bill of rights while not remote would be materially reduced." JGD to H.R. Harrison, August 29, 1952, JGDP, III/4/29.11, 2366; Belliveau, "Diefenbaker," 54–55

61 These included A.R.M. Lower, F.R. Scott, and Eugene Forsey. They differed, however, over whether a federal statute would be sufficient, and whether it would apply to provincial as well as federal actions.

62 Belliveau, "Diefenbaker," 59. This is the form that Diefenbaker's bill took, when it became law ten years later.

63 *Debates*, July 10, 1946, 3328–29

64 Ibid., 3328

65 *OC 1*, 240–47

66 See Ward and Smith, *Gardiner*, 284–86.

67 *OC 1*, 261–2. Diefenbaker mistakenly suggests that Gardiner was responsible for a small revision of constituency boundaries before the 1945 general election, intended to ensure

his defeat in that election. But that change actually occurred as part of the major readjustment of 1947, described by Diefenbaker as a "Jimmymander."

68   Boundary adjustments were also made, it appeared, to reduce electoral prospects for four other prominent Conservatives: Davie Fulton in British Columbia, John Bracken in Manitoba, J.M. Macdonnell in Ontario, and George Black in the Yukon. Black did not contest the 1949 election, while Bracken and Macdonnell were defeated.

69   *Debates,* July 14, 1947, 5598-99

70   Ibid., July 15, 1947, 5667

71   Ibid., 5669-70. Diefenbaker was defensive when asked why he had signed the subcommittee report recommending the boundary changes. "There is a fine question," he replied, "I have heard that before. It was once raised as a defence by a highwayman who stuck a gun into the face of a victim and said, 'Your money or your life'; and then afterwards said, when charged, 'Why did he consent?'" The subcommittee, he suggested, had responded to some of his complaints and threatened that it would revert to the original scheme if he did not sign; so he did. Ibid., July 14, 15, 1947, 5600, 5646-47, 5664-67

72   The Conservatives had conducted their own gerrymander in 1932, as Diefenbaker pointed out, when Mackenzie King's Prince Albert boundaries had been altered by the Conservative majority. King had pleaded with Prime Minister Bennett for fairness then, just as Diefenbaker did with King now. Ibid., July 15, 1947, 5643-45, 5667-69

73   Holt heard the account of Diefenbaker's apology from Walter Tucker. Holt, *Other,* 279

74   *OC 1,* 262

75   See, for example, Hugh C. Farthing to H.A. Bruce, July 29, 1948; H.A. Bruce to Hugh C. Farthing, August 10, 1948, Bruce Papers. On Bracken's decision to resign, see also Perlin, *Tory Syndrome,* 64; Fraser, *"Blair Fraser Reports",* 14-16.

76   JGD to David J. Walker, July 13, 1948, JGDP, III/72, 58673-74. Diefenbaker's isolation in the caucus is reflected in this comment. He seemed to know nothing of the advice to retire then being offered to Bracken by Davie Fulton, Richard Bell, and J.M. Macdonnell. See Fraser, *"Blair Fraser Reports",* 14-16.

77   JGD to M.J. O'Brien, July 23, 1948; JGD to David Walker, August 4, 1948, JGDP, III/73, 58699, 58722

78   JGD to David Walker, August 28, 1948, ibid., 58843

79   JGD to J.F. Anderson, September 16, 1948, ibid., 58996

80   JGD to J.F. Anderson, September 16, 1948, ibid., 58996; Hugh C. Farthing to H.A. Bruce, September 10, 1948, Bruce Papers

81   JGD to J.F. Anderson, July 30, 1948, JGDP, III/73, 58717

82   Hugh C. Farthing to H.A. Bruce, September 10, 1948, Bruce Papers

83   David Walker to JGD, August 13, 1948, JGDP, III/75, 60565

84   *Globe and Mail,* September 11, 1948. Parliament had recently adopted the Combines Investigation Act, which Diefenbaker had criticized for what he saw as its excessively lenient penalties for corporate lawbreakers.

85   Toronto *Star,* August 31, 1948

86   *Globe and Mail,* September 14, 1948

87   Toronto *Star,* September 21, 1948

88   *Globe and Mail,* September 18, 1948

89   Ibid.

90   R.J. Gratrix to W.R. Brunt, August 31, 1948; JGD to Mary F. Diefenbaker, September 17, 1948, JGDP, III/73, 58890; V, 419-20

91   David J. Walker, quoted in the Toronto *Star,* September 17, 1948

92   *Globe and Mail,* September 18, 1948. In the following days there were press reports that two pro-Diefenbaker delegates had been omitted from the Ontario list of delegates-at-large. But Diefenbaker himself took the high road and "dissociated himself from charges that the convention was being 'fixed.'" *Globe and Mail,* September 20, 1948. In retrospect, Diefenbaker

charged that the national director of the party, Richard Bell, had acted improperly in select-ing delegates-at-large: "His attitude to me in the forty-eight convention in the choice of del-egates was just unbelievable, totally biased, prejudiced and without any compunction as to the need of maintaining reasonable fairness." JGDI, August 14, 1969. In his memoirs, Diefenbaker suggested that the convention organizers were "one hundred per cent dedi-cated to ensuring that Drew would be the Leader," and that delegates-at-large were selected solely to assure Drew's victory. "Anyone suspected of supporting me was removed from the list of authorized delegates-at-large. For that purpose, there were people stationed outside my hotel suite taking down the names of my visitors. This created needless bad feelings between my supporters and Drew's." *OC 1*, 267. There were 311 delegates-at-large, 237 ex officio delegates, and 765 riding delegates named to the convention. "Proposed Rules for the Conduct of the Election of Leader – Progressive Conservative National Convention – 1948," JGDP, III/73, 59540–43

93 Toronto *Star*, September 24, 1948; Ottawa *Citizen*, October 1, 1948
94 Toronto *Star*, September 29, 30, 1948
95 Ibid., September 25, 1948
96 Ibid., September 29, 1948
97 Nellie L. McClung to JGD, September 22, 1948. Diefenbaker replied that he was "deeply honoured" by her letter. JGDP, III/73, 59054–55
98 A.R.M. Lower to JGD, September 29, 1948, ibid., 59125
99 J.B. McGeachy, "PCs in Convention," *Globe and Mail*, October 1, 1948
100 Ottawa *Citizen*, October 1, 1948
101 Ibid.
102 *Globe and Mail*, October 1, 1948; Winnipeg *Tribune*, October 1, 1948
103 *Tribune, Globe and Mail, Citizen*, October 2, 1948
104 *Citizen*, October 2, 1948. The information that Diefenbaker's ancestry was Dutch rather than German apparently came from Diefenbaker himself. He might equally have taken Mr Dooley's advice to call himself Anglo-Saxon: "An Anglo-Saxon is a German that's forgot who was his parents." See Moynihan, *Pandaemonium*, 12. The Dutch label (as in "Pennsylvania Dutch," who were German in origin) was an ingenious means of dealing with what was still a political liability in Canada: a name that was neither British nor French. The Dutch, who were heroic allies to Canada during the war and already popular postwar immigrants, were surely next best in the Canadian ratings.
105 *Tribune* and *Citizen*, October 2, 1948
106 The convention had voted in favour of outlawing the party.
107 *Citizen*, October 2, 1948
108 Ibid.
109 *Tribune*, October 4, 1948
110 *Citizen*, October 4, 1948
111 Ibid.
112 *OC 1*, 268. Diefenbaker failed to say that this coolness might have been a response to his own display of pique at the convention. According to Donald Fleming, "Diefenbaker and his wife made a conspicuous departure from the platform in very bad taste soon after the result of the balloting was announced." Fleming, *Near 1*, 148
113 Paul Martin to JGD, October 7, 1948, JGDP, III/73, 59294
114 Bill Archer to JGD, October 7, 1948, ibid., 59290-91
115 Davie Fulton to JGD, October 7, 1948, ibid., 59284-87
116 Davie Fulton to JGD, October 7, 1948, ibid., 59282-83
117 G.S. Thorvaldson to David J. Walker, October 6, 1948, ibid.
118 JGD to Bill Archer, October 14, 1948; JGD to A.R.M. Lower, October 8, 1948, ibid., 59292, 59126
119 JGD to Jack Anderson, October 7, 1948, ibid. These figures suggest that Diefenbaker was

hoping for something close to a dead heat between himself and Drew on the first ballot, and the need for a second ballot after the elimination of Fleming on the first.

120 *Globe and Mail*, October 8, 1948
121 JGD to the editor, *Globe and Mail*, October 15, 1948
122 See, for example, Graham, *Frost*, 135–37. Drew entered the House through a by-election in the Ottawa region constituency of Carleton on December 13, 1948. At least one Conservative friend of Diefenbaker referred to Drew privately as "Georgie Porgie." Evelene Blakely to Edna Diefenbaker, July 12, 1949, JGDP, V/53, 34153
123 Grant Dexter, *Mr. Drew in Action*, quoted in Williams, *Conservative Party*, 212
124 Fleming, *Near 1*, 172
125 Bothwell et al., *Canada*, 116–17; OC 1, 268–69
126 Williams, *Conservative Party*, 173–74, 212
127 Ibid., 174; *OC 1*, 268
128 Bothwell et al., *Canada*, 117
129 James McCook, quoted in Williams, *Conservative Party*, 175
130 Perlin, *Tory Syndrome*, 53; Williams, *Conservative Party*, 180–81
131 Williams, *Conservative Party*, 179–80. In later editions the last line read "Vote St. Laurent."
132 *OC 1*, 271
133 Ibid., 260–61
134 Ibid., 262
135 Bothwell et al., *Canada*, 117; *OC 1*, 262, 271; Williams, *Conservative Party*, 181–84
136 Edna indicates, in her letters from this time, that John was writing regularly to her as well as forwarding Hansard and newspapers. But these letters do not survive in the Diefenbaker Papers.
137 Edna to JGD, undated, JGDP, V/10, 7046–47
138 Edna to JGD, undated, ibid., 7056–59
139 Edna to JGD, undated, ibid., 7069–72
140 Edna to JGD, undated, ibid., 7091
141 Quoted in Holt, *Other*, 281
142 Nicholson, *Vision*, 29
143 Holt dates this move indefinitely in "late 1946 or early 1947," but it seems to have been later. Holt, *Other*, 272–75
144 Van Dusen, *The Chief*, 8–9
145 The reporters included Frank Swanson of the Ottawa *Citizen*, Arthur Blakely of the Montreal *Gazette*, and Peter Dempson of the Toronto *Telegram*. Holt, *Other*, 273–77; Dempson, *Assignment Ottawa*, 88
146 The words are those of Frank Swanson, quoted in Holt, *Other*, 273
147 Frank Swanson also testified to the plentiful presence of liquor and wine at these parties, and insisted that Diefenbaker had "the odd drink" of scotch, despite his claims to be a teetotaller. Dempson, on the other hand, wrote that "Diefenbaker himself would wander among the guests with a glass of sherry in his hand, but I can't recall ever seeing him take a sip." Dempson, *Assignment Ottawa*, 88; Holt, *Other*, 274
148 Kate Aitken to Mrs John G. Diefenbaker, enclosing a transcript of her CFRB program, September 21, 1948, JGDP, V/53, 34148–50
149 Dempson recalled one disturbing encounter in the late 1940s when he interrupted a private argument in the MP's office. Diefenbaker revealed that Edna wanted him to accept an offer to become counsel for a major oil company at a salary five times that of an MP, and asked Dempson for his opinion. Dempson faltered at this invitation to intrude in a personal dispute. He thought Diefenbaker should accept, but knew he would not do so. "Well, I finally blurted out, it's an attractive offer. Financially, you'd be far better off. But I'm afraid you wouldn't be happy, leaving public life." Diefenbaker "snorted" his agreement and announced that he would reject the offer. Dempson, *Assignment Ottawa*, 84–85

150 Holt reported that James and Kathleen Sinclair and Alvin Hamilton, among others, noticed Edna's jealousy. Edna's reference to John's secretary reads: "Who is your Stenographer you never said if you can have Mr. Gratrix or not." Holt, *Other*, 312; Edna to JGD, undated, JGDP, V/10, 7069–72

151 Edna to JGD, all undated, JGDP, V/10, 7087–90, 7094–101

152 F. Lennon, The Battle Creek Sanitarium, Battle Creek, Michigan, to JGD, February 28, 1950, JGDP, V/14, 9155–A. The correspondence in the Diefenbaker Papers is incomplete and there is no indication of the outcome of his inquiries. The Battle Creek "San" is the subject of T. Coraghessan Boyle's 1993 comic novel, *The Road To Wellville*, and the film of the same name.

153 Stephen Smith, "Cornflakes, love and money," Toronto *Star*, July 24, 1993

154 Mary F. Diefenbaker to JGD, undated (dated by archivist April 1950), JGDP, V/1, 422–23

155 Mary F. Diefenbaker to JGD, June 1, 1950, ibid., 424–25

156 See, for example, Holt, *Other*, 291–92. There is evident heaviness or swelling in Edna's neck in photographs from the summer and autumn of 1950.

157 JGD to Herbert A. Bruce, September 6, 1950, Bruce Papers

158 Edna Diefenbaker to Mary F. Diefenbaker, September 19, 1950, JGDP, V/1, 428

159 See Holt, *Other*, 295–98.

160 In Vancouver, he told his niece Sheila that Edna was being treated for shingles. Holt, *Other*, 297–98

161 JGD to Mary F. Diefenbaker, November 13, 1950, JGDP, V/1, 431

162 Holt, *Other*, 297–99; JGD to Mary F. Diefenbaker, November 13, 1950, JGDP, V/1, 431–32

163 JGD to Mary F. Diefenbaker, November 13, 24, 26, 1950, ibid., 431–39

164 JGD to Mary F. Diefenbaker, November 24, 1950, ibid., 433–34; JGD to Edna, November 15, 1950, quoted in Holt, *Other*, 298

165 Ibid.

166 The quotation is from JGD to Louis Breithaupt, January 22, 1951, JGDP, III/59, 47417–18; Holt, *Other*, 300–03.

167 Holt, *Other*, 303–04

168 Percy Philip to Edna Diefenbaker, January 31, 1951, JGDP, V/53, 34253

169 Dave Walker to Edna Diefenbaker, Saturday, undated, ibid., 34196–98

170 Martin, *Very Public 2*, 288–89; see also Holt, *Other*, 308–10.

171 Diefenbaker had also told his sister-in-law Susan Brower that his distraction over Edna's illness made it impossible for him to focus on anything else. Diefenbaker relates his story of the incident in *OC 1*, 111–16; Holt's account, based on interviews with Susan Brower, is in Holt, *Other*, 304–07.

172 Prince Albert *Daily Herald*, February 10, 1951 (also quoted in Holt, *Other*, 321–22). For the Laing, Green, and Gardiner tributes, see the *Debates*, February 7 and 9, 1951, 158, 161, 241. The "unelected member" is referred to by Douglas How of Canadian Press in the Ottawa *Citizen*, February 8, 1951; the "gay and lovable personality" is described by Margaret Aitken of the *Telegram*, both quoted in Holt, *Other*, 319, 323.

173 Holt, *Other*, 327–28; Saskatoon *Star-Phoenix*, February 10, 1951

174 Holt, *Other*, 323–24

175 Interment Order No. 15304, Woodlawn, City of Saskatoon, February 9, 1951, JGDP, V/unnumbered

Chapter 6 The Big Fish

1 *OC 1*, 112–14; Holt, *Other*, 329–30

2 Quoted in Holt, *Other*, 129–30

3 *OC 1*, 114, 116

4 Ibid., 115

5 Ibid., 116

6   See, for example, the account of Donald Fleming in *Near 1*, 178–85.

7   House of Commons, *Debates*, May 21, 1951, 3253

8   Fleming, *Near 1*, 208

9   Ibid., 212

10   Diefenbaker mentions several of these factors in *OC 1*, 271. Blair Fraser's phrase appears in a profile in his column in *Maclean's*, December 1, 1953, reprinted in Fraser, *"Blair Fraser Reports"*, 53–62.

11   *OC 1*, 271

12   In 1953, aside from a hectic ten-week period of election campaigning, Diefenbaker made more than thirty speeches in Saskatchewan, Manitoba, and Ontario to service clubs and PC associations. In August 1953 he was made Chief Eagle by the Duck Lake Indian band. Diefenbaker pocket diary for 1953, JGDP, III/24/312, 17217–310

13   *OC 1*, 271–72

14   House of Commons, *Debates*, June 30, 1952, 3983. Fleming calculated that the townships removed from the riding had given Diefenbaker 3447 votes in 1949, compared with 1166 Liberal and 2049 CCF ballots. Ibid., 3977

15   *OC 1*, 272–76

16   George Whitter to JGD, June 17, 1966, JGDP, XIV/1

17   Ibid. Although Diefenbaker received this account from Whitter in 1966, presumably in response to a request for information for his memoirs, it is not mentioned in *One Canada.*

18   The record does not make clear whether there were two separate fishing trips. It is possible that Whitter's memory confused the chronology and that there was only one trip, to both Waskesiu and Lac La Ronge, as Elmer's letter suggests. *OC 1*, 272–73; Elmer Diefenbaker to Mary F. Diefenbaker, July 26, 1952, JGDP, V/31, 20451

19   Brunt arranged with Diefenbaker's Toronto friend George Johnston to provide Elmer with a $500 honorarium for several weeks in the constituency. "I have never met anyone," Brunt wrote to Elmer, "who has the happy faculty that you have for being able to go into a Riding, size up the situation and then be able to tell a prospective candidate just what his chances are of being elected." As late as April 15, 1953, Diefenbaker was still seeking guidance from friends in Lake Centre and had not ruled out renomination there. W.R. Brunt to Elmer Diefenbaker, October 29, 1952; JGD to Gus Mackay, April 15, 1953, JGDP, III/50/544, 39817–18, 39822

20   R.G. Green to JGD, February 10, 1953, JGDP, III/15/187, 10885–88

21   The formal nomination meeting of the Prince Albert PC Association took place on May 16, 1953, at Diefenbaker's request. The local Conservative Orest Bendas noted that, although press reports said the nomination meeting was organized by the Diefenbaker Clubs, it was officially a Conservative nominating convention. Diefenbaker "did not try to separate himself completely from the party." That was a matter of both courtesy and prudence. *OC 1*, 273–74; Prince Albert *Daily Herald*, November 28, 1952; Memo, "Executive meeting held at this office Nov. 26, 1952," JGDP, III/15/187, 10872; JGD to M.J. O'Brien, February 19, 1953; JGD to George Drew, April 8, 1953, JGD to Gus Mackay, April 15, 1953, JGDP, III/75/958.12, 61076; III/79/969.7, 62677; III/50/544, 39822; III/24/312, 17247–60; XVIII/OH/749

22   JGD to Olive Palmer, quoted in Spencer, *Trumpets*, 9

23   See Fleming, *Near 1*, 223–31, esp. 225.

24   Ibid., 227. The other Conservative members of the committee were Rodney Adamson, Davie Fulton, Douglas Harkness, J.R. Macdonnell, and George Pearkes.

25   The classic account of the Liberal Party in this period of dominance is Whitaker's *Government Party.* See especially chapter 5, "The Government Party Fulfilled, 1945–58," 165–215. For the 1953 campaign, see Camp, *Gentlemen*, 133–39; *OC 1*, 274–75; Fleming, *Near 1*, 238–41.

26   *OC 1*, 275

27   Camp, *Gentlemen*, 136

28   George Whitter to JGD, June 17, 1966, JGDP, XIV/1

29   Diefenbaker pocket diary for 1953; "John Diefenbaker – Ontario Itinerary," July 6–9, 1953; "John Diefenbaker – Ontario, Nova Scotia, New Brunswick Tour," July 25–31, 1953, JGDP, III/24/312, 17264–84; III/49/539, 39220, 39254–55; Spencer, *Trumpets*, 10–16

30   Spencer, *Trumpets*, 15

31   Quoted ibid., 15

32   *OC 1*, 274–75; Holt, *Other*, 332

33   Marjorie (Bunny) Pound, JGDP, XVIII/OH/83.1–4, 84.1–2, July 11, 14, 1986; May 19, July 7, 1989. Camp reports one disconcerting occasion in the winter of 1955–56 when Diefenbaker, still a back-bencher, rebuked him for an imagined slight in failing to find Olive a place at a banquet headtable. "I know how these things happen," Diefenbaker told Camp. "But I want you to know, you see, there will never be a next time. That's all. If my wife can't be there, then I won't be there. Is that clear?" Camp excused himself, thinking "What a strange man." Camp, *Gentlemen*, 195–96

34   JGD to Roy Hall, February 16, 1953; JGD to Clyne Harradence, May 22, 1954, JGDP, I/18/13.5, 16730, 16733; Royal Bank, Watrous to JGD, June 22, 1956, ibid., III/32, 23869–70; XVIII/OH/83.1–4, 84.1–2; XVIII/OH/45. Harradence had run as a Liberal candidate in the 1956 provincial election and believed that this may have been a factor in Diefenbaker's reluctance to sort out his position in the law firm.

35   JGD to E. Cathro, December 1, 1955, JGDP, I/6, 6133

36   J.V. Clyne, *Jack of All Trades*, quoted in the *Globe and Mail*, October 26, 1985

37   Ibid.

38   Fleming, *Near 1*, 242

39   Ibid., 243

40   Ibid., 244

41   *OC 1*, 270

42   Its members were identified by Tom McMillan as Ellen Fairclough, George Nowlan, Clair Casselman, Earl Rowe, J. Waldo Monteith, J.M. Macdonnell, R.W. Mitchell, Léon Balcer, R.A. Bell, and the journalist Grattan O'Leary. Tom McMillan, "The 1956 Conservative Leadership Convention," unpublished paper

43   Camp, *Gentlemen*, 145

44   Ibid., 140–48; Perlin, *Tory Syndrome*, 53–54

45   Bruce Hutchison to Grant Dexter, April 7, 1955, Hutchison Papers

46   Bruce Hutchison to Grant Dexter, July 1, 1955, ibid.

47   W.L. Morton wrote that "beneath the surface, vague discontent and flickering uneasiness were stirring and taking form as criticism of the government." Morton, *Kingdom of Canada*, 507

48   See Kilbourn, *PipeLine*, passim; Bothwell and Kilbourn, *C.D. Howe*, 283–316; Fleming, *Near 1*, 297–321. The financial scheme that allowed construction to proceed (involving initial government ownership of the northern Ontario section of the pipeline) was devised by Howe's deputy, Mitchell Sharp.

49   Davie Fulton noted his coordinating role with Stanley Knowles in an interview with the author, September 24, 1993.

50   Hampden was one of the five members of the English parliament whose aborted arrest in the House of Commons by Charles I led to the English Civil War. He was one of Diefenbaker's heroes.

51   *Debates*, May 25, June 4, 1956, 4344-52, 4661-62; Fleming, *Near 1*, 303–12; Kilbourn, *PipeLine*, 111. Fleming denied suggestions that the incident had been planned and intentionally provoked as "a wicked collection of falsehoods in every particular."

52   *Debates*, May 17, 1956, 4031–44. One of Diefenbaker's frequent correspondents on the pipeline issue was the Toronto advertising executive George Johnston, who criticized the official Conservative tactic of cooperation with the CCF and suggested that an alternative line running partly through the United States could be built quickly and without public

subsidy. Diefenbaker followed Johnston's advice about seeking information from other American gas distribution companies. Johnston seems to have influenced Diefenbaker's tentative approach in his speech of May 17. George Johnston to JGD, February 23, 1956, JGDP, III/68/911, 54925–27

53 Interview with Davie Fulton, September 24, 1993. Diefenbaker's brief but melodramatic account of the pipeline debate in his memoirs does not mention his reluctance to support the party's tactics. Instead, he emphasizes the comparison to the Long Parliament's defiance of Charles I that was implied in his remark about John Hampden; and he gives credit to the "valiant fighters" Drew, Fleming, Fulton, Green, and Coldwell. Fleming comments pointedly that, on an occasion when the CCF leader M.J. Coldwell, George Drew, Fleming himself, and other members stepped into the aisle to protest against an outrageous ruling by the Speaker, "At no time did John Diefenbaker leave his seat." *OC 1*, 245–47

54 JGD to J.M. Cuelenaere, June 30, 1956, JGDP, I/18/13.5, 16694; Kilbourn, *PipeLine*, 136

55 Those present at the drafting of Drew's letter of resignation, according to two of the participants, were Grattan O'Leary, J.M. Macdonnell, Léon Balcer, Earl Rowe, George Nowlan, Bill Rowe, Ellen Fairclough, Fiorenza Drew, and Dr Ray Farquarson (Drew's physician). Stursberg, *Leadership Gained*, 5–7; Camp, *Gentlemen*, 205–11; Fleming, *Near 1*, 322–23; O'Leary, *Recollections*, 114–16; *OC 1*, 276

56 George Pearkes to JGD, September 22, 1956, JGDP, III/74/950, 59686–87

57 David J. Walker to JGD, September 24, 1956, JGDP, III/74/951.1, 59804–05

58 "I have to go along with the gang, Benbo," Hees told Eddie Goodman. Hees brought with him the useful support of John Bassett and the Toronto *Telegram*, and the organizing talents of Eddie Goodman. As Dana Porter, the provincial treasurer of Ontario, pointed out to Diefenbaker, the Ontario government had supported Liberal policy on the natural gas pipeline as a participant and as a beneficiary. Diefenbaker's relative passivity during the parliamentary struggle may thus have been a factor in Frost's decision to support him for the leadership; it may even have been one of Diefenbaker's own calculations during the debate. Goodman, *Life*, 72–75; Dana Porter to JGD, December 10, 1956, JGDP, III/74/14.5, 60259–60; Charlotte Gobeil, Interview with John Bassett, Political Memoirs, CTV, January 3, 1993

59 Memo, "For your information when calling Mr. Alex McKenzie," nd, JGDP, III/74/14.5, 59696; Goodman, *Life*, 72–76; Fleming, *Near 1*, 324–26; Stursberg, *Leadership Gained*, 12–13; Peter Stursberg, "Desperate Search on for Tory Candidate to Oppose Diefenbaker," Toronto *Star*, October 11, 1956

60 Nicholson reported that the Old Guard had also approached a British Conservative MP and expatriate Canadian, the notoriously pompous Sir Beverley Baxter, to come home to the leadership campaign. After these efforts had failed, party president Léon Balcer announced his own candidacy in late November, but withdrew it a few days later. Patrick Nicholson, "Old Guard Can't Stop Diefenbaker," Winnipeg *Tribune*, November 14, 1956; Windsor *Daily Star*, November 23, 1956; Winnipeg *Tribune*, December 3, 1956

61 Telegram, Gordon Churchill to JGD, October 3, 1956; "Summary of meeting of supporters of candidature of John Diefenbaker for leader of Progressive Conservative Party," nd, JGDP, III/74/14.5, 59866, 59721–22

62 Leadership announcement, nd, JGDP, III/74/14.5, 59706

63 "Summary of meeting of supporters of candidature of John Diefenbaker for leader of Progressive Conservative Party," nd, JGDP, III/74/14.5, 59721–22

64 Sévigny wrote long letters to Diefenbaker offering his opinions on a wide range of subjects such as sincere leadership, Quebec's dislike of British domination, avoiding military support for the UN in the Middle East, a distinct Canadian flag, the priority of provincial rights, useless government spending, and opposition to dictatorship. He gave no indication of any activity to recruit Diefenbaker delegates in Quebec. Pierre Sévigny to JGD, November 16 and November 27, 1956, JGDP, III/74/14.5, 60036–40, 60108–10; Fleming, *Near 1*, 326–27

65 Fulton recalled that "this was my first overt action which brought me into conflict with John, and he could never understand why I had run...I think he was very disappointed: he had counted on my support. Whether my running was an error or not is very difficult for me to judge...But unfortunately he held it against me, there's no question about that." E.D. Fulton, interview with author, September 24, 1993; Stursberg, *Leadership Gained*, 14

66 "Diefenbaker Leads Field as Tory Leader in Poll," Canadian Institute of Public Opinion, November 24, 1956

67 "Wars May Come and Go/ Party Lines Hold Firm," Canadian Institute of Public Opinion, December 1, 1956

68 Bothwell et al., *Canada*, 127–29; English, *Worldly*, 107–45

69 The Egyptian government identified the Canadian forces with the British invasion army, at least partly because of the unit's name. Extended negotiation resulted in a compromise, under which Canada would provide technical and logistical support units, while the entire UNEF operation would remain under command of the Canadian general E.L.M. Burns. The Queen's Own returned from their way station in Halifax to home base in Calgary. Pearson reflected that the Egyptian reaction was "entirely predictable...In retrospect, this was not an unfriendly gesture on Nasser's part, it was just being sensible." Pearson's biographer John English suggests that the affair strengthened Pearson's interest in a distinctive Canadian flag. Pearson, *Mike 2*, 261–71; English, *Worldly*, 141

70 *Debates*, November 29, 1956, 139–44; *OC 1*, 280–81. Diefenbaker's reference to his earlier proposal for a UN peacekeeping force was subtly misleading. In January, Diefenbaker had mentioned "something in the nature of an international force" to stand between the Arabs and Israelis, as suggested in reports of talks between President Eisenhower and Prime Minister Eden. Pearson, in reply, did not reject, but endorsed, the idea: "If that proposal were made...and if it became a matter for United Nations consideration, I am sure this country as well as other countries would want to do what they could to carry it into effect." But he added that no such proposal had been made to the UN or the Canadian government, and that he was reluctant to commit the government's hand in advance. This was diplomatic discretion rather than rejection. *Debates*, January 31, 1956, 723; February 1, 1956, 775–77

71 *Debates*, November 29, 1956, 139–44

72 Fleming, *Near 1*, 327; *Globe and Mail*, November 30, 1956; Winnipeg *Tribune*, December 3, 1956; Winnipeg *Free Press*, December 4, 1956

73 Camp, *Gentlemen*, 232

74 Goodman, *Life*, 76–77. Camp recalled that the Diefenbakers occupied a single room rather than a suite. Camp, *Gentlemen*, 254

75 On Camp's advice, O'Leary had been bumped from his original position as keynote speaker to make way for Premier Robert Stanfield, the party's new political hero from Nova Scotia. The change turned out for the best, in Camp's view, because "O'Leary could not have done both the eulogy of Drew and the keynote address." Coincidentally, Camp ghostwrote the Stanfield speech. Camp, *Gentlemen*, 233–37

76 Ibid., 235–37

77 See, for example, Ted Rogers to JGD, September 25, 1956, JGDP, III/74/14.5, 59826–29; Camp, *Gentlemen*, 233; Sawatsky, *Mulroney*, 41–47. Diefenbaker's own insecurity was echoed among the nineteen delegates and alternates who attended the convention from Prince Albert. According to Dick Spencer, they had "nagging fears that somehow the westerners and their candidate might be outfoxed in the capital." Spencer, *Trumpets*, 18

78 Camp, *Gentlemen*, 233, 238

79 Quoted in Stursberg, *Leadership Gained*, 15. Diefenbaker no doubt knew of Bell's role some weeks earlier in the "Stop Diefenbaker" discussions, and thus believed he had reason to doubt Bell's neutrality. Bell insisted that he "preserved a total impartiality and judicial approach as chairman." Films of Diefenbaker's nomination speech show Bell sitting, stony-faced and motionless, as others on the platform applauded Diefenbaker's conclusion.

80　Sévigny, *This Game*, 37–41, esp. 41; Stursberg, *Leadership Gained*, 16–21; Camp, *Gentlemen*, 238–40; Meisel, *Election 1957*, 31–33; *OC 1*, 278–79. Pierre Sévigny saw Diefenbaker's refusal to alter his plans as a sign of "terrible indecision," while Churchill saw it as a sign of "courage and determination." In his memoir, Sévigny wrote that Diefenbaker had invited him to second the nomination; the indecision came when Diefenbaker subsequently opted for Pearkes and failed to tell Sévigny. Sévigny insisted later that, when confronted with the dispute, Diefenbaker could not make up his mind, and finally left the decision to others. But Churchill and Hees credited him with decisiveness. Perspective, in this case, was all. Sévigny claimed that the choice cost Diefenbaker sixty votes or more at the convention, which seems doubtful. Meisel could find no plausible explanation for Diefenbaker's gratuitous alienation of Quebec delegates.

81　Camp, *Gentlemen*, 28–30

82　Camp, the professional, judged that the speech had a "curious abjectness," that it was "a poor speech, poorly organized and poorly spoken." But he recognized that Diefenbaker had nourished long-starved hopes. J.B. McGeachy, *Financial Post*, December 22, 1956; Sévigny, *This Game*, 41–42; Fleming, *Near 1*, 328–29; Camp, *Gentlemen*, 247–48; Toronto *Telegram*, December 14, 1956; *Globe and Mail*, December 15, 1956

83　The *Globe and Mail* reported that Diefenbaker received 102 votes from Quebec delegates, or one-third of the total, but that seems doubtful. In a frank letter to Diefenbaker written shortly after the convention, Fleming attributed the figure to George Hees and called it "utterly preposterous...My best information is that neither you nor Davie obtained more than about a score of votes in Quebec." Fleming, *Near 1*, 329; Sévigny, *This Game*, 42–43; Camp, *Gentlemen*, 250–52; *Globe and Mail*, December 15, 1956; "Acceptance Speech by Mr. Diefenbaker"; Donald Fleming to JGD, December 27, 1956, JGDP, XII/120/F/390

Chapter 7　On the New Frontier

1　Camp, *Gentlemen*, 254

2　Ibid., 255

3　Fleming, *Near 1*, 329–30

4　Ibid., 332–34

5　Interview with Richard Bell, October 11, 1969. Drew convinced Bell that he should stick around to help pick up the pieces, by running for parliament in 1957.

6　Toronto *Globe and Mail*, December 15, 1956

7　Camp, *Gentlemen*, 241

8　George Bain, "Minding Your Business," *Globe and Mail*, January 10, 1957. Bain seemed to be responding to Peter Stursberg's report, "A Lone Wolf Takes Over the Tory Party," in the Toronto *Star*, December 15, 1956. Stursberg also reported doubts among Conservative MPs about "his quality of leadership" and "his ability as an administrator." For Stursberg, Diefenbaker after 1948 had been "irascible and erratic...not a deep thinker...superficial and petty." He concluded, however, that Diefenbaker's caucus critics recognized that the man might change, "the dark shadows should disappear," now that his ambition had been achieved.

9　Prince Albert *Herald*, December 29, 1956; Spencer, *Trumpets*, 20–21. For an analysis of Diefenbaker's appeal as a charismatic leader, whose personal qualities resonate among distressed or expectant followers, see Courtney, *Selection*, 168–72.

10　In the memoirs, Diefenbaker wrote: "What I did not need was a National Headquarters full of people whose chief desire was to torpedo me so as to bring about a new leadership convention as quickly as possible." This was a curiously suspicious attitude for a new leader; but as he had admitted, his previous relations with the party office had been unfriendly. *OC 2*, 6

11　Camp, *Gentlemen*, 256–60, esp. 260. In an interview after his retirement, Churchill said that he had had "a desk-banging argument" with Diefenbaker in January 1957, after which he wished to have no part in the election campaign. (If his recollection was correct, this would have been before the creation of the triumvirate.) Diefenbaker had persuaded him to continue, Churchill said, "because Mr. Diefenbaker respected a man who would stand up to him." Despite their disagreements, Churchill recalled that their political views coincided "90% of the time." Churchill did not mention the subject of the January disagreement. Gordon Churchill interview with W.F.W. Neville, July 7, 1970

12   The tale is told at length in Camp, *Gentlemen*, 256–77, and Diefenbaker's words are as reported by Camp. Camp's objection to Grosart was based on a "superficial" judgment that Grosart was "incompetent in matters of advertising" and an opportunist: "While I marvelled at his toughness, accommodated by a masculine, roguish charm, I considered him cynical and uncommitted. Politics on that basis was impossible to me. I wanted the Conservative Party to become an effective, efficient political instrument – such as could bring down a Liberal government." Ibid., 259. In one of his most blatant efforts to rewrite history, Diefenbaker claimed in the memoirs that Camp had played no part in the 1957 campaign: "At that time, I knew nothing of him whatever...In 1957...he was nothing." *OC 2*, 29. This was just one indication of the rage Diefenbaker felt over the campaign, eventually successful, to remove him from the leadership after the 1965 election.

    Diefenbaker's apparent indecision about the party's electoral management may have been affected by his effort to recruit a former Conservative Party stalwart, Mel Jack, as his executive assistant or campaign manager. Jack had been fired from the leader's office in 1954 by George Drew, and had been taken into the civil service through the good offices of Walter Harris and J.W. Pickersgill. When Diefenbaker sought him out, Jack responded that he would accept "if it can be arranged without sacrificing my present economic position with regard to earnings, pension and security of employment." That would involve a firm contract, a pension, and a salary of $10,000 to $12,000 per year. For the depression-formed lawyer, that was too high a price. After the 1957 Conservative victory, Jack became George Hees's executive assistant and was credited with much of Hees's success in that portfolio. Melville R. Jack to JGD, February 14, 1957, JGDP, IV/8/333.8 Misc.,6377; Nicholson, *Vision*, 40–42

13   Charlotte Whitton to JGD, January 15, 1957, JGDP, XII/7/A/172

14   Pierre Sévigny to JGD, April 4, 1957, JGDP, IV/19/391.5 Que. Sévigny's letter was in response to a curt letter from Diefenbaker in which he said: "I am very anxious to have you announce your candidacy now... Please let me hear from you by return." Sévigny subsequently decided to run, but lost his contest in 1957. JGD to Pierre Sévigny, April 2, 1957, ibid.

15   Fleming, *Near 1*, 337–38; *OC 2*, 9

16   JGD to Mary F. Diefenbaker, January 2, 1957, JGDP, V/1, 560

17   Nicholson, *Vision*, 37–38

18   House of Commons, *Debates*, March 15, 1957, 2349

19   Ibid., 2350

20   L.B. Pearson to JGD, March 29, 1957, JGDP, IV/29/861 Egypt, 20685

21   "Statement by John G. Diefenbaker, Q.C., M.P.," April 4, 1957, ibid., 20698; *Debates*, April 4, 1957, 3058–59

22   Mike Pearson to JGD, April 3, 1957, JGDP, IV/29/861 Egypt, 20690. Pearson seems to have dated the note for the previous day.

23   See, for example, Toronto *Star*, April 5, 1957

24   JGD to Mrs R.C. McFaul, April 8, 1957, JGDP, IV/29/861 Egypt, 20702

25   *Debates*, April 10, 1957, 3358–59

26   Ibid., April 12, 1957, 3466

27   Ibid., 3492–93

28   Ibid., 3493–502

29   For example, Diefenbaker received and filed the May 1957 bulletin from Ron Gostick's extremist "Canadian Intelligence Service," titled "Does Responsibility for Norman Tragedy Point at Pearson and St. Laurent," and a long letter from Edith Dickey Moses in South

Carolina, who condemned American fellow-travellers on the basis of the Senate subcommittee hearings and concluded: "I have just gone over the Norman record...And I personally have not the slightest doubt that he was a Communist. With his background I consider it sheer stupidity for your government to have sent him to Egypt. And if Lester Pearson were not white-washing this I am sure more shocking information would come out." "Does Responsibility for Norman..." *Canadian Intelligence Service* 7 (May 1957); Edith Dickey Moses to JGD, April 14, 1957, JGDP, IV/17/*352 EA, 11242; IV/29/861 Egypt, 20716–19

30 R. Donellan to JGD, April 14, 1957, JGDP, IV/29/861 Egypt, 20723–24

31 M.W.M., "Memorandum for Mr. Diefenbaker: Re Norman Case," May 7, 1957, JGDP, IV/17/*352 EA, 11229–32

32 There is now a large literature on Herbert Norman and "the Norman affair," but the evidence remains ambiguous, as it tends to be in Cold War intelligence cases in the absence of documents from the Soviet archives. See, for example, "The Strange Case of Mr. Norman," *U.S. News & World Report*, April 26, 1957; Bowen, *Innocence Is Not Enough*; Barros, *No Sense of Evil*; English, *Shadow*, 301–02; English, *Worldly*, 164–82. On the strictly domestic, political aspects of the affair, English judges that "the Norman controversy illuminates a great deal about Pearson, the Liberal government, and their times." Pearson, he suggests, was a decent man who preferred to keep such issues out of "party politics." In the United States, Norman would have been hounded out of public life, but in Canada "Pearson and his colleagues kept matters to themselves." "McCarthyism's failure in Canada may be the victory of élitist tendencies in Canadian political life in the post-war period. It was also, however, the victory of civility and decency." English, *Worldly*, 181–82

33 Creighton, *John A. Macdonald: The Young Politician*; *John A. Macdonald: The Old Chieftain*

34 Fleming, *Near 1*, 335

35 M.W. Menzies to Dr Glen Green, December 1, 1956; June Menzies to JGD, January 6, 1957; JGD to June Menzies, January 17, 1957; M.W. Menzies to JGD, January 22, 1957; JGD to M.W. Menzies, January 29, 1957; Donald Eldon to Derek Bedson, January 30, 1957; M.W. Menzies to JGD, February 11, 1957; telegram, JGD to M.W. Menzies, February 26, 1957, JGDP, XIII/284/E/88, 179377–419; IV/1/201, 497–509; see also *OC 2*, 10–13; Bothwell et al., *Canada*, 186–88; Meisel, *Election 1957*, 42–44. After the 1957 general election, Menzies became an adviser in the prime minister's office, where he remained until 1959.

36 M.W. Menzies to JGD, January 22, 1957, JGDP, OF/271/333.8 M and Mc

37 This is particularly obvious, for example, in Diefenbaker's marked copies of Menzies's letter of March 28, 1957, and his memo on national policy of April 6, 1957. M.W. Menzies to JGD, March 28, 1957; "Memo for Mr. Diefenbaker," April 6, 1957, JGDP, IV/22/*391.8, 14965–71, 14788–807

38 "Memo for Mr. Diefenbaker: National Policy," April 6, 1957, ibid., 14788–807, esp. 14788–90

39 Menzies proposed, for example, immediate completion of the Pine Point railway to the south shore of Great Slave Lake; paving of the Mackenzie and Alaska highways; completion of the Stewart–Cassiar highway to bypass the Alaska panhandle in northern British Columbia; a railway from Prince George, British Columbia, to Whitehorse, Yukon; a carefully planned system of "development roads" in the territory; improved air, radio, and telephone services in the north; and major federal initiatives to provide hospital, education, and social services for the new province. M.W. Menzies, "Memo for Mr. Diefenbaker: National Policy," April 6, 1957, ibid., 14792–800

40 This is especially evident in Menzies's comments to Diefenbaker on policy discussions in the National Campaign Committee on April 7 and 8, 1957. M.W. Menzies, "Memo for Mr. Diefenbaker," April 10, 1957, ibid., 14943–47; see also Meisel, *Election 1957*, 41–44

41 On the Ontario bargain, see Graham, *Frost*, 329–35.

42 Camp, *Gentlemen*, 277–79

43 JGD to Elmer Diefenbaker, April 11, 1957, JGDP, V/3, 1608–09

44 JGD to Elmer Diefenbaker, April 11, 13, 14, 1957, JGDP, ibid., 1610–13. In April, Diefenbaker

expressed guilty concern that his response to a letter of congratulations had not been received: "I cannot understand this as I wrote you a personal letter in long hand. I don't know what happened. Yours is not the only case. There are at least half a dozen others who have told me they did not receive the replies that I wrote which were all sent at about the same time. These letters may have been misplaced in a group." JGD to Charles Peters, April 11, 1957, ibid., IV/3/284, 2045

45 JGD to Elmer Diefenbaker, March 29, April 10, April 11, April 13, April 14, and May 5, 1957, JGDP, V/3, 1604–05, 1608–13, 1619

46 JGD to Elmer Diefenbaker, nd, February 1957, ibid., 1595–98

47 JGD to Elmer Diefenbaker, February 22, 1957, ibid., 1599–602

48 JGD to Elmer Diefenbaker, March 29, 1957, ibid., 1604

49 JGD to Elmer Diefenbaker, April 14, 1957, ibid., 1613

50 JGD to Elmer Diefenbaker, April 11, 1957, ibid., 1610–11

51 Spencer, *Trumpets*, 27–30

52 *Globe and Mail*, April 25, 1957

53 Ibid., April 26, 1957

54 Graham, *Frost*, 331–33

55 M.W. Menzies to JGD, April 19, 1957, JGDP, IV/22/*391.8, 14817–20. Finlayson was Bracken's and Bennett's former private secretary.

56 "Major Campaign: Speech No. 1..." JGDP, XXI/17/589. The impact of those words, repeated endlessly in the 1957 campaign, is reflected in phrases that still echoed after thirty years in the political rhetoric of Brian Mulroney and Preston Manning.

57 Ibid.

58 This campaign included Newfoundland, which Diefenbaker visited during the week before the Massey Hall meeting. In summary, his itinerary was as follows: April 15–17: Newfoundland; April 18–24: Prince Albert; April 25–26: Ontario; April 27: Quebec; April 28–May 4: PEI, Nova Scotia, New Brunswick; May 5–7: Quebec; May 8–13: Ontario; May 14–16: Manitoba; May 17: Saskatchewan; May 18: Alberta; May 19–24: British Columbia; May 25–26: Alberta; May 27: Saskatchewan; May 28–29: Ontario; May 30–31: Quebec; June 1: New Brunswick; June 2–4: Nova Scotia; June 5–7: Ontario; June 8: Saskatchewan. "Itinerary – John Diefenbaker – 1957"; "Itinerary...May 25th...June 7th," JGDP, IV/4/*304–1957, 2732–38, 2799–801, 2822

59 Diefenbaker wrote to Elmer that "the travelling accommodations are very good. We have an exceptionally fine private railway car complete with porter and cook." JGD to Elmer Diefenbaker, April 29, 1957, JGDP, V/3, 614

60 Diefenbaker told Elmer at the end of April that the Gallup Poll showed an increase in Conservative support in Ontario in the previous month of 6 percent, and gave the party more potential votes than the Liberal Party for the first time since 1935. JGD to Elmer Diefenbaker, April 29, 1957, ibid., 1614

61 "Spread Too Thin," *Globe and Mail*, May 14, 1957

62 "Canadian National Election, June 10, 1957," Despatch: Embassy, Ottawa, 980, May 16, 1957, USNA, State/3210/742.00/1–757

63 Diefenbaker told his mother that he had visited his father's old school in Greenwood. "They had the pay book there and also the reference to the hiring." JGD to Mary Diefenbaker, May 28, 1957, JGDP, V/1, 585; *Globe and Mail*, May 14, May 28, May 29, 1957

64 Dempson, *Assignment*, 92

65 Meisel, *Election 1957*, 151

66 Ibid., 156–57

67 Winnipeg *Free Press*, April 30, 1957, quoted in Meisel, *Election 1957*, 157

68 Nicholson, *Vision*, 50–52; Meisel, *Election 1957*, 94, 185; *OC 2*, 33

69 Meisel, *Election 1957*, 160–62, 179, 186, 188. St Laurent's letter was sent on National Liberal Federation letterhead to service members on lists available to all parties.

70 Quoted in Levine, *Scrum Wars*, 209

71 Dempson, *Assignment*, 94; Colin Wright interview with Peter Dempson, December 16, 1970. The reporters' estimates also appear in Dempson. He used the figure of ninety-seven in the interview; in his book, he records Diefenbaker's guess as "between ninety-five and one hundred and five seats."

72 Churchill commented on the affair, and reproduced his second memorandum, in "Recollections and Comments on Election Strategy," *Queen's Quarterly*, winter 1970, 499–511. The Robinson articles appeared in the Toronto *Telegram* in September 1954. See also Meisel, *Election 1957*, 166–68.

73 Churchill, "Recollections," 502

74 Ibid., 503

75 Meisel, *Election 1957*, 172–73

76 *Globe and Mail*, May 31, 1957; "Donald Fleming Itinerary," JGDP, IV/4/*304–1957, 2765

77 The fullest, though self-centred, account is in Sévigny, *This Game*. William Hamilton reported to Diefenbaker that Léon Balcer had agreed that Hamilton should take responsibility for seven predominantly English-speaking ridings on Montreal Island, where "six good candidates have been nominated." Hamilton recognized that the attitude of Quebec delegates to the leadership convention "represents a genuine resistance to your leadership," but he estimated that Diefenbaker would draw suporters to the party in about ten seats, most of them on Montreal Island. He also urged that Balcer "should continue as provincial leader in Quebec despite his ill-considered observation at the convention." Diefenbaker expressed his gratitude for Hamilton's advice. The "Comité des Bleus" was formed before the leadership convention of 1956 by Paul Lafontaine (a former Conservative organizer from the Bennett period) and others, including Norman Genser, René Duranleau, Alphonse Patenaude, Wilfred Dufresne, MP, Harry and Josie Quart, Marcel Faribault, and Pierre Sévigny. It was strongly opposed to the influence in the Quebec party of the Union Nationale and Léon Balcer. William Hamilton to JGD, December 27, 1956, January 17, 1957; JGD to William Hamilton, January 16, 1957, JGDP, IV/19/391.5; "Du: Comité des Bleus pour Diefenbaker"; Paul E. Lafontaine to JGD, February 7, 1957; Norman N. Genser to JGD, June 17, 1957, ibid., XII/94/E/104.1

78 "A Crucial Election," *Globe and Mail*, June 8, 1957

79 "Today's Big Opportunity," ibid., June 10, 1957

80 The papers he sampled were the *Globe and Mail*, the Montreal *Gazette*, and the Ottawa *Journal*. Beck, "Election of 1957," quoted in Meisel, *Election 1957*, 237

81 Meisel, *Election 1957*, 190

82 Telegram, Ottawa to secretary of state, 623, June 5, 1957, USNA, State/3210/742.00/1–3155

83 George Hogan, "Election Predictions," nd, JGDP, IV/4/304–1957

84 Goodman, *Life*, 85

85 JGD to Elmer Diefenbaker, June 4, 1957, JGDP, V/3, 1628–31

86 JGD to Elmer Diefenbaker, June 2, 1957, ibid., 1622–27. A.V. Svoboda was a member of the National Campaign Committee from Saskatoon. By the end of the campaign, Elmer had received at least $2000 in cash for his campaign work, paid by W.R. Brunt and Alastair Grosart from funds raised by Brunt. Brunt reported raising $7200 from national contributors, which was applied to the Prince Albert campaign. W.R. Brunt to E.C. Gerry, March 4, 1957; W.R. Brunt to Arthur Pearson, April 2 and April 15, 1957; W.R. Brunt to JGD, June 9, 1957, ibid., XII/96/F/31, XII/108/F/155

87 Spencer, *Trumpets*, 36–37; *OC 2*, 33; Prince Albert *Herald*, June 10, 1957

88 Nicholson, *Vision*, 52

89 Spencer, *Trumpets*, 37–39; Nicholson, *Vision*, 52–55; Dempson, *Assignment*, 94–95; *OC 2*, 33–34

90 *Globe and Mail Magazine*, June 29, 1957; Nicholson, *Vision*, 52–53

91 The manuscript speech can be found in the Diefenbaker Papers, headed "Very important – keep" and undated. Diefenbaker wrote in his memoirs: "It was suggested that, whatever the

outcome, I should be prepared to go on national television and radio, and that it would be wise to prepare a couple of speeches, one in the event that we won, and one in the event that we lost. I said, 'One. We're not going to lose.'" JGDP, IV/4/304–1957; *OC 2*, 33

92   Ibid.
93   Spencer, *Trumpets*, 39–40
94   Ibid, 40
95   *Globe and Mail*, June 12, 1957
96   *OC 2*, 34
97   Dempson, *Assignment*, 95. The other two reporters on the trip were Clark Davey of the *Globe and Mail* and Mark Harrison of the Toronto *Star*. Duff Roblin later remembered that Diefenbaker caught the largest fish on the second day, but he spoke of lake trout rather than pickerel. Patrick Nicholson, who was not present, wrote that Diefenbaker had "landed the paltry catch of two jackfish, one about two pounds and the other a throw-back." Duff Roblin to JGD, June 11, 1965, JGDP, XII/87/D/176; Nicholson, *Vision*, 55
98   Quoted in Levine, *Scrum Wars*, 209

Chapter 8 Rt Hon. John George Diefenbaker

1   Quoted in Levine, *Scrum Wars*, 209–10
2   Nicholson, *Vision*, 55; Newman, *Renegade*, 97; *OC 2*, 36
3   Cabinet Conclusions (CC), 18, June 13, 1957. The agriculture minister, James Gardiner, and one other minister advocated this view. Nicholson, *Vision*, 55–56; Pickersgill, *Seeing Canada Whole*, 476; *OC 2*, 36
4   CC, 32–57, June 13, 1957
5   Ibid.
6   Nicholson, *Vision*, 55
7   Ibid., 56
8   Telegram, Elmer Diefenbaker to JGD, June 17, 1957, JGDP, V/3, 1634. Diefenbaker's friend Eugene Forsey would have exploded at Elmer's suggestion that Olive was "the first lady of the nation," an Americanism that ignored Canada's separation of head of state from head of government.
9   Gordon Churchill, memorandum "For Professor Neville," July 23, 1970
10   Nicholson, *Vision*, 56–57; Fleming, *Near 1*, 341–43; *OC 2*, 37–49; interview with Davie Fulton, September 24, 1993
11   Interview with Davie Fulton, September 23, 1993. Diefenbaker later invited Stanley Knowles, the CCF's expert on parliamentary procedure, to take the speakership; but he, too, refused the offer. Diefenbaker's third choice was Roland Michener, who accepted the invitation just before the opening of parliament in October. See *Debates*, October 15, 1957, 31.
12   *OC 2*, 42; Fleming, *Near 1*, 342–44; Gordon Churchill, memorandum "For Professor Neville," July 23, 1970; Goodman, *Life*, 86–87. The reference to "certain people" is by Churchill.
13   *OC 2*, 37–49; Fleming, *Near 1*, 344–45; Goodman, *Life*, 86; Ministry list (untitled, nd); R.B. Bryce, "Memorandum for Mr. Diefenbaker: Re: Ministerial portfolios," June 19, 1957; "Appointments," June 21, 1957, JGDP, XII/2/A/20, XII/96/F/33, XII/1/A/18
14   George Drew to JGD, June 21, 1957, JGDP, XII/7/A/225
15   Fleming, *Near 1*, 345
16   The prime minister reported to cabinet on his return that he had enquired in London about British practice and had been assured that St Laurent's account was correct. He thus suggested it should apply in Canada. The rationale was that new administrations should not have access to the potentially embarrassing secrets of previous ones. The practice seemed to be a mutually beneficial rule of prudence. CC, 34–57, June 21, 1957; 42–57, July 6, 1957
17   Cabinet document 115/57, June 21, 1957; press release, June 22, 1957, JGDP, XII/1/A/18
18   CC, 35–57, June 22, 1957. The rule for lawyers was that their names should be removed from partnerships, although they might still be separately identified as counsels to their firms.

19   CC, 35–57, June 22, 1957. These two paragraphs are blanked out of the public record of cab-
      inet decisions on national security grounds. The Diefenbaker Papers contain the texts of the
      departmental recommendations to cabinet, background papers, and the interim agreement
      as it had previously been approved by the Liberal cabinet in February. It is reasonable to
      assume that cabinet extended the agreement as recommended, pending the completion of
      a "permanent arrangement." RBB, "Memorandum for Mr. Diefenbaker," June 21, 1957,
      accompanying "Memorandum for the Minister," June 20, 1957, Department of External
      Affairs; "Memorandum for Cabinet: Canada–United States Agreement on Overflights," June
      19, 1957, Minister of National Defence; and appendices, JGDP, XII/1/A/18
20   CC, 35–57, June 22, 1957
21   CC, 37–57, June 25, 1957. Howard Green took the chair as acting prime minister during
      Diefenbaker's absence in London.
22   Fleming, *Near 1*, 346
23   Livingston T. Merchant to Julian L. Nugent, June 18, 1957, USNA, State/3210/ 742.00/
      6–1857
24   CC, 35–57, June 22, 1957
25   Robinson, *Diefenbaker's World*, x
26   Diefenbaker's suspicion may have been exaggerated, but there was something in it that was
      widely recognized. The American ambassador, for example, commented on the expected
      change of government in the abbreviated prose of a cable to Washington on June 11: "Senior
      civil servants with 22 years under Liberal administration have close familiarity with Liberal
      policies and developed almost automatic reflex to individual Ministers and Cabinet plan-
      ning and prejudices. On basis their experience and feeling for Liberal policies they were
      frequently able and willing on their own initiative to express government thinking and to
      take decisions or implement routine projects in both domestic and foreign field without
      prior reference to Cabinet. This situation suddenly changed by election. Senior civil servants
      are now ignorant of future government's thinking." Telegram, Ottawa to secretary of state,
      640, June 11, 1957, USNA, State/3210/742.00/6–1157
27   JGDI, December 10, 1969
28   Ibid.
29   Newman, *Renegade*, 100; JGDI, December 10, 1969; John G. Diefenbaker, "I Am a Canadian,"
      RCA Victor Recording CC–1027, nd. The only sources for Churchill's words were the recol-
      lections of Olive and John Diefenbaker.
30   JGDI, December 10, 1969
31   Ibid.
32   Confidential information
33   Later, Diefenbaker suggested that he had mentioned the desirability for Canada of a shift
      of 15 percent of Canada's trade with the United States to the United Kingdom, but in the
      conference he apparently made no reference to this figure, either as example or target. JGDI,
      December 10, 1969; CC, 42–57, July 6, 1957: Toronto *Telegram*, June 28, 1957; Toronto *Star*,
      June 29, 1957
34   *The Times*, July 8, 1957
35   Ottawa *Journal*, July 8, 1957; see also Nicholson, *Vision*, 59–60. The *Globe and Mail*'s head-
      line on the same day was almost identical. The Privy Council Office later prepared a
      "Reference file on Statements and Comments concerning the '15% Diversion' as referred
      to by the Prime Minister in his return from the July 1957 Commonwealth Prime Ministers'
      Conference." April 22, 1960, JGDP, XII/100/F/76
36   Winnipeg *Tribune*, July 9, 1957; Lethbridge *Herald*, July 11, 1957. It is not evident that
      Diefenbaker was aware of Duncan's statement. However, the *Tribune* editor, Carlyle Allison,
      was a political friend who might have mentioned it in conversation with the party leader.
      Two days after Diefenbaker's comment, Duncan, who was then chairman of Ontario Hydro,
      wrote to Diefenbaker to urge him on. Duncan noted that he had created the Dollar-Sterling

Trade Board in 1949, made up of prominent Canadian businessmen, with the same object of encouraging more purchases from the sterling area and fewer from the United States. He told Diefenbaker that he had two proposals to stimulate inter-Commonwealth trade. When Diefenbaker responded with interest, Duncan wrote again to suggest that a major trade delegation should be sent to England "headed by a senior Minister," and that government departments and companies should be directed to switch purchases to the United Kingdom and sterling area. Duncan's chief concern was that British industry had neglected its trading opportunities in Canada and that it had to be pushed and jollied into seeking out orders and meeting them on time. John Bassett added his support for the trade delegation, and the proposal resulted in a mission headed by Gordon Churchill in November 1957 that included Duncan among its members. Diefenbaker was grateful for Duncan's advice and assistance, but he was advised not to seek Duncan's support in the 1958 election campaign because of his anti-labour reputation as a "high hat" at Massey-Harris and Ontario Hydro. James S. Duncan to JGD, July 8 and August 27, 1957; John Bassett to JGD, September 25, 1957; Kingsley Graham to JGD, February 11, 1958, JGDP, VI/229/313.312, 188479–80; VI/475/721.2, 368779–83, 368760–62; VI/475/721.1 Churchill, 368600

37 Ottawa *Journal*, July 23, 1957
38 CC (UK), 54 (57), 1, July 9, 1957
39 Ibid., 56 (57), 7, July 23, 1957
40 Ibid., 62 (57), 2, August 27, 1957
41 Ibid.
42 Ibid.
43 CC, 61–57, 6, August 30, 1957
44 CC, 67–57, September 20, 1957
45 Fleming, *Near 1*, 382–84. In his memoirs, Diefenbaker suggests that the deputy minister of trade and commerce, Mitchell Sharp, was overheard discussing the British proposal on a TCA flight to Toronto shortly afterwards, that this was reported back to the prime minister, that Robert Bryce talked to Sharp at Diefenbaker's direction, and that Sharp "immediately resigned" from the civil service as a result. But Diefenbaker dates the incident in April 1958, when Sharp actually did leave his position. By that time, the British proposal had been public knowledge for six months and no indiscretion seems likely. In the cabinet minutes for the previous October 3, however, Diefenbaker is reported as referring to a "leak" of the proposal "some weeks before," which may refer to his claim about Sharp. But if this was the reason for Sharp's resignation, the six-month time lapse needs explanation. In his memoirs, Sharp says that his decision to resign was his own and that it was taken because he believed neither Churchill nor Diefenbaker would trust him. The direct evidence of this distrust, he suggests, was disagreement over three policy issues (not including the British offer) and advice from a Conservative minister about the prime minister's attitude to him. Sharp does not mention any indiscretion involving the British offer. In correspondence with the author, Sharp says that "I was not asked to resign at any time by anyone. I took the initiative when I received an offer of employment from Brazilian Traction, Light and Power Company...I did talk to a friend about the proposal by the British government of a free trade agreement with Canada which I didn't consider as a secret. I am not certain now whether Bryce spoke to me about the matter, but if he did, I didn't tell him I was considering resignation, which took place many months later, after the 1958 general election." *OC 2*, 52–53; Sharp, *Which Reminds Me*, 68–77; Sharp to author, February 14, 1995
46 Gordon Churchill had told a British cabinet minister that he and Sidney Smith, the new secretary of state for external affairs, opposed Canadian rejection of the offer. CC (UK), 69 (57), 4, September 19, 1957
47 Lloyd, *Canada in World Affairs*, 66–70; Fleming, *Near 1*, 388–89; Montreal *Gazette*, September 30, 1957; Toronto *Star*, September 30, 1957
48 Harold Macmillan to JGD, August 29, 1957, JGDP, XII/8/A/282.1

49 Macmillan's offer to recommend Diefenbaker's appointment came on September 4. Diefenbaker accepted at once, and his office showed eagerness to make use of the title as quickly as the UK order-in-council could be issued – if possible by his sixty-second birthday on September 18. The appointment was not quite managed by that day, but the prime minister nevertheless wrote to his mother that "there are no more honors to acquire for me since the Queen made me an Imperial Privy Councillor yesterday." Diefenbaker had previously been supplied by External Affairs with a memorandum setting out how quickly previous prime ministers had been named to the UK Privy Council. Prime minister of the United Kingdom to the prime minister of Canada, September 3, 1957, September 12, 1957; JGD to James Thomson, acting high commissioner for the United Kingdom, September 12, 1957; James Thomson to JGD, September 14, 1957; telegram, secretary of state for commonwealth relations to high commissioner for the United Kingdom, Ottawa, No. 1553, September 19, 1957; JGD to Mary F. Diefenbaker, September 17, 1957; memorandum, "Appointment of Canadians to the Privy Council of the United Kingdom and Designation of the Members of the Privy Council of Canada," July 25, 1957, JGDP, XII/8/A/282.1; V/1, 614–17; VI/337/380/U57.5

50 CC, 73–57, October 3, 1957. The communiqué, as finally agreed, did not mention the target.

51 Montreal *Gazette*, November 22, 1957

52 *U.S. News and World Report*, April 18, 1959; Ottawa *Journal*, April 21, 1958

53 Fleming, *Near 1*, 386–91; *OC 2*, 73–74; CC, 72–57, 73–57, October 3, 1957. As late as May 18, 1958, Diefenbaker was still rehearsing his arguments in a memorandum noting George Drew's comments on the subject:

> George Drew phoned me and said there cannot be any free trade because it could not be achieved until the pound would be fully convertible.
>
> There can only be free trade when the United Kingdom could buy from us. Free trade means freedom to sell as well as to buy.
>
> Whatever the arguments used in favour of the proposition, we are not in a position to consider it until Great Britain removes its quotas and assures convertibility.
>
> The offer that was made should not have been revealed as negotiations are difficult unless they can be secret.

JGD, memorandum, "British Free Trade Offer, So-Called," JGDP, VI/478/722.1

54 CC, 38–57, June 27, 1957

55 Fleming, in his diligence, counted the cabinet meetings and told us in his memoirs that "I never went to one of them unprepared." Fleming, *Near 1*, 345

56 CC, 45–57, July 11, 1957

57 CC, 73–57, October 3, 1957

58 R.B. Bryce, "Memorandum to the Prime Minister: Canadian Security Policy," and attachments, July 10, 1957, JGDP, XII/1/A/18

59 "Cabinet Directive; Security Screening of Government Employees, Circular No. 29," December 21, 1955, 2, ibid.

60 Ibid., 4

61 Ibid., 17

62 Bryce, "Memorandum to the Prime Minister: Canadian Security Policy." The Security Panel, Bryce explained, was set up in 1946 to advise the cabinet and coordinate procedures. The spur was the revelation of spying contained in information brought to the government by the defecting Soviet cypher clerk, Igor Gouzenko. The panel was entirely made up of civil servants, under Bryce's chairmanship, and consisting as well of the undersecretary of state for external affairs, the deputy ministers of defence, defence production, citizenship and immigration, and the RCMP commissioner. In practice, much of the panel's work after 1953 was carried out by a subpanel, also made up entirely of permanent officials.

63   For later references to the Security Policy, see below, 347–49, on the RCMP's "homosexual project"; and 520–22, 536–41 on Diefenbaker's charges against L.B. Pearson in 1964–66.

64   DRCB, "Cabinet Positions to Be Filled," "Parliamentary Assistant Positions to Be Filled," August 1, 1957; "Cabinet Ministers Positions to Be Filled," nd, and accompanying JGD hand-written notes, JGDP, XII/2/A/20; Fleming, *Near 1*, 370; *Globe and Mail*, August 8 and August 20, 1957

65   For example, on August 12, 1957, Diefenbaker received a statement signed by twenty-four Canadians and Americans "presently spending vacations on Grand Manan, New Brunswick," expressing their "fervent hope" that he could retain the services of Pearson "in the interests of world peace and international goodwill." A secretary replied laconically on the prime minister's behalf that "Mr. Diefenbaker will bear in mind your suggestion in his discussions with his colleagues." JGDP, VI/119/312.2

66   D. Leo Dolan to JGD, November 3, 1957, JGDP, VI/315/352/E/98

67   Diefenbaker told his mother: "I think I really hit the jack-pot in getting President Sidney Smith of Toronto to take over the Ministry of Secretary of State for External Affairs. I did not find the job too hard; it was most enjoyable but there was no way I could attend the United Nations and still remain the Prime Minister so I had to find someone to take over from me." Diefenbaker appointed a back-bencher to the Senate in order to precipitate a by-election in the Ontario riding of Hastings-Frontenac, which was won by Smith in November 1957. *OC 2*, 45–46; JGD to Mary F. Diefenbaker, September 11, 1957, JGDP, V/1, 608

68   Ottawa *Journal*, September 13, 1957; Lloyd, *Canada in World Affairs*, 16–18; *OC 2*, 45–46; Robinson, *Diefenbaker's World*, 37

69   Montreal *Star*, September 13, 1957; *Globe and Mail*, September 13, 1957; New York *Times*, September 13, 1957; Lloyd, *Canada in World Affairs*, 17–18

70   Address by the Prime Minister of Canada...at Dartmouth College, Hanover, New Hampshire, September 7, 1957, "Great Issues in the Anglo-Canadian-American Community," JGDP, XXI/18/619

71   Robinson, *Diefenbaker's World*, 7

72   Thompson and Randall, *Canada and the United States*, 196–98; Jockel, *No Boundaries*, 91–117

73   "Aide Memoire: Integration of Operational Control of Canadian and Continental United States Air Defence Forces in Peacetime," June 12, 1957, JGDP, XII/117/F/335

74   Ibid.

75   CC, 32–57, June 13, 1957

76   Minutes, House of Commons Special Committee on Defence, 1963, 510

77   Minister of National Defence, "Memorandum to Cabinet: Integration of Operational Control of Canadian and Continental United States Air Defence Forces in Peacetime," July 22, 1957; "Aide Memoire: Integration of Operational Control of Canadian and Continental U.S. Air Defence Forces in Peacetime," July 23, 1957, JGDP, XII/117/F/335

78   CC, 52–57, July 31, 1957

79   CC, 52–57, July 31, 1957; "Joint Statement by the Secretary of Defence of the United States and the Minister of National Defence of Canada," August 1, 1957, JGDP, XII/20/A/556; Montreal *Gazette*, August 2, 1957

80   CC, 34–57, June 21, 1957; 35–57, June 22, 1957

81   JGD to Elmer Diefenbaker, nd, 1957; JGD to Elmer Diefenbaker, July 3, 1957, JGDP, V/3, 1646–50

82   Nicholson, *Vision*, 60–62. When the children had gone to bed, he told the Nicholson parents a joke he claimed to have told Kwame Nkrumah, the president of Ghana, about a tribal chief complaining to his slaves that the missionary they were boiling would not be edible: "You shouldn't have put him in the cauldron; he's not a boiler, he's a Friar." Diefenbaker did not report Nkrumah's reaction.

83   JGD to Mary F. Diefenbaker, July 23, 1957, JGDP, V/1, 595

84   Newman, *Renegade*, 102

85 JGD to Mary F. Diefenbaker, August 6 and August 20, 1957; JGD to Elmer Diefenbaker, July 7 and December 6, 1957; Dr D.M. Baltzan to JGD, November 4, 1957, JGDP, V/1, 597–600, 602; V/3, 1650–51, 1706–07; XII/36/C

86 JGD to Mary F. Diefenbaker, August 23, 1957, JGDP, V/1, 603

87 JGD to Mary F. Diefenbaker, September 19, 1957, ibid., 618–19

88 JGD to Mary F. Diefenbaker, September 29, 1957, ibid., 621

89 JGD to Mary F. Diefenbaker, September 28, 1957, ibid., 620

90 Elmer Diefenbaker to Mary F. Diefenbaker, October 14, 1957, JGDP, V/31, 20485–500

91 CC, 70–57, September 26, 1957

92 Elmer Diefenbaker to Mary F. Diefenbaker, October 16, 1957, JGDP, V/31, 20493–500

93 House of Commons, *Debates*, October 14, 1957, 5–6; Nicholson, *Vision*, 73–75; Newman, *Renegade*, 103–05

94 The next day the prime minister announced the appointment of a royal commission on energy, to be chaired by the Toronto businessman Henry Borden. The Gordon Commission on Canada's economic prospects had recommended creation of a national energy board to supervise the transmission and export of Canadian oil and gas, and the Conservative Party had favoured such a body since 1955. But cabinet agreed that the speech from the throne should contain no reference to such a body "since there was, at present, no vestige of a plan to bring in legislation establishing this authority. The proposal had not received sufficient study." Instead, cabinet agreed on a diversion. Questions were expected in the House concerning improprieties in financing the Northern Ontario Pipeline (an Ontario crown corporation), and at least one purpose behind the royal commission was to avoid such embarrassment to the Frost government. Cabinet noted that "the establishment of such a Royal Commission would have the effect, among others, of foreclosing all discussion in the House of Commons on the trans-Canada pipeline and of removing the possibility of a vote on this particular issue...No mention should be made of the proposed Royal Commission in the Speech from the Throne, as otherwise its subject matter could be brought up in the House." The terms of reference were quickly drafted and approved by order-in-council on October 15, "since the matter might be raised the following day by Mr. Coldwell in the House." Whether this favour to Frost was the result of overt negotiation is uncertain. CC, 76–57, 77–57, 79–57, October 10, 11, 15, 1957; McDougall, *Fuels and the National Policy*, 80–83

     Cabinet avoided another potential difficulty in this session by deciding against the routine appointment of a House standing committee on privileges and elections, since "the setting up of this committee might cause embarrassment to some members of the government whose election expenses had been higher than the average." CC, 74–57, October 4, 1957

95 CC, 80–57, October 19, 1957

96 Virtually the entire legislative program was adopted in the following three months.

97 *Debates*, October 15, 1957, 44

98 JGD to Mary F. Diefenbaker, October 22, 1957, JGDP, V/1, 626–27

99 JGD to Mary F. Diefenbaker, November 23, 1957, ibid., 632

100 Ibid.

101 JGD to Mary F. Diefenbaker, December 14, 1957, ibid., 637–40

102 JGD to Mary F. Diefenbaker, December 29, 1957, ibid., 641; Newman, *Renegade*, 105

103 The issue arose at the second meeting of cabinet on June 22, 1957, in discussion of the parliamentary schedule. The cabinet minutes reported: "There were those who felt that it was important to hold an early session in September with a view to implementing some of the more important pledges the Conservative Party had made during its electoral campaign, and then seek dissolution in order to have general elections in the Fall of this year. However, because the visit of the Queen to Ottawa would be robbed of the greater part of its significance if she did not open the first session of the new Parliament, and because it would be

virtually impossible to hold a short session between September 28 and October 11, the consensus...was that there was no alternative but to agree that the first session should be convened to meet on October 14th...This, of course, ruled out the possibility of holding general elections prior to the Spring of 1958." CC, 35–57, June 22, 1957

104 Eugene Forsey, "Letter to the editors," Ottawa *Journal,* August 9, 1957; Forsey to JGD, October 30, 1957, JGDP, VI/93/304, 80197–98. The *Journal* omitted the paragraph quoted here.

105 Forsey to JGD, October 30, 1957, JGDP, VI/93/304, 80197–98

106 JGD to Eugene Forsey, November 8, 1957, ibid., 80200

107 JGD to Mary F. Diefenbaker, January 15, 1957, JGDP, V/2, 645

108 JGD to Mary F. Diefenbaker, January 31, 1958, JGDP, V/2, 652

109 JGD to Mary F. Diefenbaker, January 1958 (nd), ibid., 647–49

110 JGD to Mary F. Diefenbaker, January 31, 1958, ibid., 652

111 English, *Worldly,* 199–201; Pickersgill, *Seeing Canada Whole,* 483–85; Nicholson, *Vision,* 77–81; *OC 2,* 80–83

112 *Debates,* January 20, 1958, 3514–20

113 Nicholson, *Vision,* 79; *OC 2,* 81–82; Fleming, *Near 1,* 445–47

114 Fleming, *Near 1,* 447

115 *Debates,* January 20, 1958, 3521–23

116 M.W. Sharp, "Canadian Economic Outlook for 1957," JGDP, IV/2/*201, 793–838; also in VII/282/E/73, 177734; Nicholson, *Vision,* 64–72; Sharp, *Which Reminds Me,* 72–74. The first copy in the Diefenbaker Papers is heavily marked in Diefenbaker's hand and appears to be the one used by the prime minister in the House; it has no cover page. The second, containing underlinings of key sections (many of them the same passages), appears to be the copy given by Nicholson to Diefenbaker. It includes a cover page with the designation "secret" on it. When the opposition challenged Diefenbaker in the House for making improper use of a confidential document, he responded that his copy lacked a cover page indicating its secrecy. This seems to have been a white lie. The copy tabled by the prime minister in the House after referring to the document also had no cover page.

117 Nicholson approached Tom Bell, MP, the parliamentary secretary to Gordon Churchill, and asked whether the department had on file an annual forecast of employment or economic prospects for 1957 that he might see. At a regular meeting with Mitchell Sharp in September 1957 (also attended by Bell), Churchill asked Sharp whether there was such a document. Sharp said there was and called his office to deliver copies, which he gave to Churchill and Bell. When Churchill suggested that he might make public the contents, Sharp protested that the report was labelled "secret" and contained confidential advice to the previous government. If such documents were to be made public, he pointed out, civil servants would tailor their content to suit the views of the ministry rather than offering their frank advice. Sharp asked whether the government intended to publish any advisory documents prepared for them since taking office, and when pressed for an example, "I referred to the report prepared for the government on the implications of the 15 per cent shift in imports from the United States to the United Kingdom advocated by Prime Minister Diefenbaker, a report that was highly critical of Diefenbaker's idea." The discussion ended and Sharp comments: "I thought I had convinced him that the outlook report should not be published, and perhaps I did convince him." Bell apparently delivered a copy of the report to Nicholson thereafter. Nicholson, *Vision,* 66; Sharp, *Which Reminds Me,* 72–74

118 Sharp, "Canadian Economic Outlook for 1957," 1–12

119 Nicholson, *Vision,* 69–70

120 Ibid., 70–71

121 *Debates,* January 20, 1958, 3524–30. Although Diefenbaker's target in the House was the Liberal opposition, this was also an implicit denunciation of the senior civil servants who had prepared and recommended the report to their ministers. They were now advisers to his own government: Mitchell Sharp in Trade and Commerce, Kenneth Taylor in Finance,

Robert Bryce in the Privy Council Office. Within a week Taylor had prepared a memorandum pointing out that the economic forecasts in the Sharp document were accurately reflected in Walter Harris's budget speech of March 14, 1957, and that Harris's budget appeared to officials as a reasonable response to the then-current situation. He added that he thought it unlikely that Harris had ever seen a copy of the report. "The number of such reports being prepared and circulated is large and their volume is a bit frightening," he told Donald Fleming. "For your information I attach four such reports that have reached my desk in the past three weeks."

Robert Bryce gave Diefenbaker a copy of this memorandum on January 28, 1958, adding his own judgment that Harris's budget forecasts were even more cautious than those in the Sharp report. Bryce quietly warned the prime minister that his arguments might be shown up: "It is possible that the Liberals may yet work over this material themselves and use it in rebuttal either in the House or outside." RBB, "Memorandum for the Prime Minister Re: Trade and Commerce Outlook paper and its relation to the budget," January 28th 1958, enclosing K.W. Taylor to Mr Fleming, Memorandum, January 27, 1958, JGDP, XII/34/B/125; *OC 2*

122 Fleming, *Near 1*, 447
123 Quoted in Stursberg, *Leadership Gained*, 88
124 *Debates*, January 21, 1958, 3572
125 Fleming, *Near 1*, 447–48
126 *Globe and Mail*, February 1, 1958
127 *Debates*, February 1, 1958, 4199–202; *OC 2*, 82–84. Diefenbaker sought the advice of ministers and Conservative MPs in early January on the most desirable election date. More than a dozen responses are noted in his papers, including replies from J.M. Macdonnell, George Pearkes, Sidney Smith, and Davie Fulton: several favoured an immediate dissolution, and only one MP proposed an election date as late as September. Their calculations were entirely political; none suggested any constitutional limits hindering the prime minister from seeking a dissolution of parliament at any time. A number of the letters appear in JGDP, VI/93/304–1958; Sidney Smith to JGD, January 27, 1958, ibid., XII/123/F/436

Chapter 9 Visions, Dreams, and Fallen Arrows

1   Stursberg, *Leadership Gained*, 94
2   *OC 2*, 84
3   Winnipeg *Free Press* and *Globe and Mail*, February 13, 1958. The Winnipeg meeting was described in many accounts, including Stursberg, *Leadership Gained*, 93–94, 97–98; Nicholson, *Vision*, 82–83; *OC 2*, 84–85
4   Quoted in Stursberg, *Leadership Gained*, 98
5   Goodman, *Life*, 90
6   Quoted in Stursberg, *Leadership Gained*, 94
7   Quoted ibid., 95
8   Newman, *Renegade*, 99–119, esp. 113
9   Gordon Churchill to JGD, nd, JGDP, VI/94/304–1958.2
10 English, *Worldly*, 201–02
11 *Globe and Mail*, March 28, 1958
12 Stursberg, *Leadership Gained*, 94
13 Diefenbaker's words are quoted in Newman, *Renegade*, 114–15.
14 The slogan was first used by a Conservative candidate in Vancouver, John Taylor, in his successful 1957 campaign. Allister Grosart noted its effect and appropriated it for Diefenbaker's national campaign in 1958, when its impact was much greater. Interview with Gowan T. Guest, August 6, 1994; Fleming, *Near 1*, 454
15 JGD to Duff Roblin, February 23, 1958, JGDP, VI/94/304–1958.1. Three Rivers was the home riding of Premier Duplessis, and of Diefenbaker's minister Léon Balcer.

16 Marion Wagner to Derek Bedson, March 6, 1958, JGDP, VI/94/304–1958.2, 81635–36

17 *Globe and Mail*, April 1, 1958. The Diefenbakers' Prince Albert house was occupied by tenants. On Olive Diefenbaker's back, see telegram, Jim Nelson to Art Burns, March 24, 1958, JGDP, VI/94/304–1958.2, 81365.

18 "Draft for T.V. Acceptance Speech, March 31, 1958, Saskatoon," JGDP, VI/95/304–1958.4, 81825–29. A typewritten excerpt from Lincoln's first inaugural speech containing the words used by the prime minister is located in Diefenbaker's "Lincoln file." JGDP, VII/154/A/1386, 94147. The plea comes in a passage in which Lincoln speaks of the dangers of "hot haste" and "precipitate action" by southern opponents of the Union, and urges upon them calm and self-restraint. If Diefenbaker intended to compare his own situation, after a massive nationwide victory, to that of Lincoln on the verge of civil war in 1860, he was indulging in somewhat curious fantasy. The allusion may suggest Diefenbaker's continuing sense that the forces opposing him were intransigent and threatening, however much "the people" supported him. Diefenbaker had been coupled with Abraham Lincoln in many introductions during the campaign, and supporters had provided him with books about the American president, one of which he dipped into while awaiting the results that afternoon. Peter Newman reports: "He was, once again, trying to read the Abraham Lincoln biography, but still couldn't summon much interest in it." Newman, *Renegade*, 117

19 Telegram, JGD to Hon. Lester B. Pearson, April 1, 1958, JGDP, VI/95/304–1958.5, 82142

20 Richard Nixon to JGD, April 1, 1958, JGDP, XII/A/306

21 JGD to Richard Nixon, April 10, 1958, ibid.

22 JGD to Colin B. McKay, April 9, 1958, JGDP, VI/95/304–1958.5 NB, 82082

23 JGD to Elmer Diefenbaker, April 6, 1958, JGDP, V/3, 1731–34

24 JGD to Colin B. McKay, JGDP, VI/95/304–1958.5 NB, 82082

25 Telegram, JGD to new Conservative MPs, April 1958, JGDP, VI/94/304–1958.2, 81777

26 Patrick Nicholson mentions "Noel Dorion, a former General President of the Bar of Quebec; Jacques Flynn, grandson of the last Conservative premier of Quebec; Yvon Tassé, prominent Quebec City engineer; André Gillet, mayor of St. Michel; Jean-Noel Tremblay, brilliant young intellectual and a professor at Laval University; Charles-Edouard Campeau, Montreal town planner." Nicholson, *Vision*, 101. Other prospects among English-speaking members included Egan Chambers and John Pratt.

27 William Hamilton to JGD, April 14, 1958, JGDP, VI/119/312.2, private

28 Diefenbaker rid himself of Courtemanche to the Senate within two years (soon after that he was forced to resign in scandal), and appointed Comtois lieutenant governor of Quebec in 1961. He died in a fire that destroyed the vice-regal residence. Patrick Nicholson reports Comtois's habit of reading the newspaper and solving crossword puzzles during cabinet meetings. Nicholson, *Vision*, 100

29 On the other hand, the government extended its courtesy to French-speaking members of the new House by installing a system of simultaneous translation. This encouraged participation in debates by French-speaking MPs by making their speeches accessible to the almost wholly unilingual majority of English-speaking members.

30 Quoted in Stursberg, *Leadership Gained*, 103

31 A select committee on estimates had existed since 1955; the Diefenbaker government made it a standing committee. The government also enlarged membership in some other committees to accommodate its gaggle of back-benchers. The estimates committee was given sixty members, veterans affairs forty, and several other committees between thirty-five and sixty members. The prime minister argued that these changes, particularly the creation of an estimates committee, were intended to "make parliament...more effective" as an agency of review. That purpose was also served by the appointment of an opposition member as chairman of the public accounts committee, and the extension of powers to call for persons, papers, and records to all standing committees of the House. These reforms were imitations of existing practices at Westminster. The opposition parties supported the changes. CC,

30–58, April 15, 1958; House of Commons, *Debates*, May 12, 1958, 8; May 30, 1958, 679–703

32 Quoted in Stursberg, *Leadership Gained*, 103

33 Harkness is quoted ibid., 104; Fleming, *Near 1*, 457–58.

34 CC, 21–58, February 5, 1958

35 CC, 39–58, May 2, 1958

36 CC, 41–58, May 7, 1958. These cabinet minutes refer only to the Breughel, although previous and later cabinet records suggest that the May 7 decision involved both the Breughel and the Monaco.

37 CC, 48–58, May 27, 1958

38 CC, 68–58, July 14, 1958; CC, 80–58, August 9, 1958. Ellen Fairclough argued that the agent had acted in good faith in making the Monaco purchase, that this should be confirmed, and that the necessary supplementary funding of $22,000 should be requested from parliament to make up the deficiency in the purchase fund. The cabinet preferred to let the agent sue for his commission. The Opposition criticized the cabinet for its reversal during discussion of the National Gallery estimates for 1959 and 1960, and quoted the comments of a member of the board of trustees, the artist Lawren Harris, who said that dealers throughout the world were now suspicious of deals with the National Gallery. "Conservative governments," he asserted, "have never shown any interest whatever in art." *Debates*, February 23, March 12, 13, 1959; June 17, 1960, 1364, 1903-05, 1915-21, 5070-71

39 Fleming, *Near 1*, 467; Newman, *Renegade*, 134–35

40 *Debates*, May 12, 1958, 5–6

41 Fleming, *Near 1*, 489–93; *Debates*, June 17, 1958, 1230–77

42 Fleming, *Near 1*, 497. The prime minister's economic adviser, Merril Menzies, learned of the conversion loan from Diefenbaker only on the morning of its announcement, when Diefenbaker told him he was "extremely concerned" about it. Another ministerial aide consulted by Menzies, Roy Faibish, wrote at the time that Diefenbaker was "disturbed and somewhat confused." Menzies "was literally staggered...because essentially this was a program that greatly intensified the restrictive policies that both Mr Fleming, the minister of finance, and Mr Coyne, the governor of the Bank of Canada, believed in so strongly, and were pursuing by various means." Menzies presented a memo to the prime minister the next day outlining his concerns about the conversion's severely restrictive effects, while Faibish expressed similar concerns to his minister, Gordon Churchill. "Canada Conversion Loan," M.W. Menzies to JGD, July 15, 1958; memorandum, Roy Faibish to Alvin Hamilton, July 16, 1958, JGDP, VI/284/E/97, 179749–53, 179754–57; Stursberg, *Leadership Gained*, 117–19

43 Fleming, *Near 1*, 497–501, esp. 498, 500. The CBC broadcast was preceded by a display of prime ministerial fury, when the camera spilled film on the studio floor. Diefenbaker, "ever ready to suspect sabotage by the CBC or the civil service," was calmed by apologies from the CBC president, Alphonse Ouimet, and delivered his remarks flawlessly. Afterwards, when Ouimet said to him, "You didn't seem to be angry," he was tartly rebuked by the prime minister: "I'm not angry at the people of Canada." Ibid., 500

44 Churchill is quoted in Roy Faibish's memorandum to Alvin Hamilton, July 16, 1958, JGDP, VI/284/E/97, 179754–57.

45 Fleming, *Near 1*, 501

46 Stursberg, *Leadership Gained*, 118–19, esp. 119; see also Bothwell et al., *Canada*, 205–08.

47 Fleming, *Near 1*, 504–05; CC, 79–58, 82–58, 83–58, 85–58, 86–58, 90–58, August 8, 13, 14, 19, 22, 29, 1958

48 Fleming, *Near 1*, 509–20; *OC 2*, 200–01; JGDP, XII/104/F/91.1, F/91.2

49 JGD to Mary F. Diefenbaker, April 29, May (undated), May 20, June 3, 14, 21, July 5, 15, 1958, JGDP, V/1, 674–79, 686–87, 689, 702, 708–11, 726, 731

50 JGD to Mary F. Diefenbaker, September 17, October 1, 10, 1958, ibid., 770, 772, 783

51 JGD to Mary F. Diefenbaker, October 2, 18, 22, 1958, ibid., 775, 789–94, 795

52 JGD to Mary F. Diefenbaker, August 31, 1958, ibid., 763–66

53 JGD to Mary F. Diefenbaker, September 19, 1958, ibid., 771. For the moment, Diefenbaker seemed less interested in his father's family – perhaps because his uncle, Ed Diefenbaker, showed slight interest in his pre-eminence. His uncle, who lived in retirement in Regina, was "apparently...so busy it is impossible for him to write," and could not visit Mary in hospital because "apparently he has got such important matters that require his undivided attention that he just can't get away." The prime minister was offended when Ed did write, asking him to stop sending copies of Hansard "as it causes too much work for the mailman! What an excuse!" Diefenbaker sent Ed a copy of an August 1958 personal profile in the *Saturday Evening Post*, but told his mother, "I don't know whether he will even read it. He doesn't write any more as I told him to be more careful in the way he writes as I can't read his scribble." By the summer of 1959, however, Ed had made amends by providing the prime minister with a sixteen-page, handwritten "Biography of the Hon. J.G. Diefenbaker" recalling the homesteading years from 1905 to 1910. JGD to Mary F. Diefenbaker, June 3, July 16, August 24, 1958, ibid., 689, 736, 760; Ed. L. Diefenbaker, "Biography of J.G. Diefenbaker," May 1959, ibid., XII/82/D/48

54 R.B. Bryce to J. Léger, September 4, 1957; memo, D.R.C. Bedson to William Hamilton, December 4, 1957; Allan K. Hay to JGD, May 14 and May 27, 1958, Press Release Concerning Prime Minister's Summer Residence (first draft), June 19, 1959, JGDP, VI/120/313.5, 101974, 101973, 101971, 101970, 101961. Bryce noted that the house had been rented during the summer of 1957 by the director of the National Gallery, Alan Jarvis.

55 JGD to Mary F. Diefenbaker, May 18, 1958, ibid., V/1, 682

56 Ibid.

57 Robinson, *Diefenbaker's World*, 20–21

58 *Debates*, November 13, 1957, 1059–62

59 Ibid., 1060

60 Robinson, *Diefenbaker's World*, 21

61 Ibid., 22

62 McLin, *Canada's Changing Defense Policy*, 47–48

63 Ibid., 48; *Debates*, May 19, 1958, 52

64 "Agreement between The Government of Canada and The Government of The United States of America concerning the Organization and Operation of the North American Air Defence Command (NORAD), Signed at Washington, May 12, 1958," JGDP, XII/20/A/556, 1–2

65 Ibid., 3–4

66 *Debates*, June 10, 1958, 994–95

67 Ibid., 999

68 *Globe and Mail*, June 11, 1958

69 *Debates*, June 10, 1958, 999–1006, esp. 1000

70 Ibid., 1003

71 McLin, *Canada's Changing Defense Policy*, 56; Robinson, *Diefenbaker's World*, 23

72 The government's own confusion about the integrated command was reflected in its uncertainty over when, and whether, Canadian fighter squadrons actually came under NORAD control. Diefenbaker distinguished between "command" – which he insisted remained Canadian – and "operational control" – which fell under NORAD; and on June 10 he said that no Canadian squadrons had yet been assigned to NORAD. The chairman of the chiefs of staff, General Foulkes, and the secretary of cabinet, Robert Bryce, could not establish clearly what effect the agreement had on Canadian squadrons, but said (in Foulkes's words, "not to confuse the issue further") that an order-in-council should allocate them to NORAD. The order was adopted in July 1958. General Charles Foulkes, "Memorandum to the Minister, Assigned Forces," June 11, 1958; R.B. Bryce, "Memorandum for the Prime Minister, Re: Allocation of Forces to NORAD," July 11, 1958, JGDP, XII/20/A/556

73   Gowan Guest was a young lawyer and active Conservative from Vancouver; James Nelson had been the Ottawa bureau chief of United Press and president of the parliamentary press gallery.

    Olive and John both offered advice to Elmer as he prepared for this adventure, and John provided castoff clothing for ceremonial dinners. "The Dress suit has been sent to you," he wrote to his brother on October 15. "Please look *inside* the inside pocket and remove the ticket showing my name on it (if there is one) before you send it to the Tailor. Tell him that you have grown since it was made for you so that it doesn't get out as to the origin of the suit...You will have to get another suit (and a good one) – not one which costs $25 on sale! (As Uncle Ed says Ha! Ha!)." JGD to Elmer Diefenbaker, October 15 (1958), JGDP, V/4, 1872–75. Diefenbaker later dated this 1959, which appears to be incorrect.

74   Robinson, *Diefenbaker's World*, 55–56

75   Ibid., 56–57

76   Ibid., 59–60

77   Ibid., 60

78   High Commission, Ottawa, to Commonwealth Relations Office, No. 1140, 20 October 1958, PRO, PREM 11/2606. These dispatches were routinely copied to the prime minister's office and to Buckingham Palace. The final judgment, that Diefenbaker did not intend to engage in serious political discussion, was wrong, as his pointed conversations later proved. He did not believe that he needed advice from External Affairs to guide him.

79   High Commission, Ottawa, to Commonwealth Relations Office, No. 1084, 3 October 1958, ibid.

80   This was a trip Diefenbaker had hoped to make in December 1957 at the time of the NATO Council meeting in Paris.

81   Robinson, *Diefenbaker's World*, 63–64

82   *Daily Express*, November 5, 1958. The *Express* had a large circulation, and tirelessly boosted Beaverbrook's special cause of Commonwealth free trade. But it had little political influence. See also the *Globe and Mail*, November 5, 1958.

83   Quoted in Canadian High Commission, London, to External Affairs, Telegram 4172, November 4, 1958, 2, JGDP, XII/112/F/214

84   *Daily Express*, November 5, 1958

85   The first meeting, on October 31, was a private one between the two leaders, after which Macmillan prepared his own notes. The record of the second meeting, on November 3 – which included officials – was kept by the British and cleared with Basil Robinson. It covered a sweeping nine-point agenda, including de Gaulle's NATO proposal, arms sales to Israel and the Middle East balance of power, Pakistan, the presence of British troops in Jordan, Cyprus, the law of the sea, potential BOAC landing rights in Toronto, Commonwealth trade, and Diefenbaker's promotion of a world food bank. Diefenbaker also met privately with the British foreign secretary, the Earl of Home, for a still more detailed exchange on November 4, mostly on Asian and Chinese affairs. Home advised Diefenbaker to reassure Pakistan, India, Ceylon, and Malaya about the US desire for peace, and to encourage firmness against Chinese pressures. "Note by the Prime Minister of his conversation with Mr. Diefenbaker on Friday, October 31, 1958"; "Record of a meeting held at 10 Downing Street...on Monday, 3rd November 1958 at 11 am..."; "Record of conversation between the Secretary of State and Mr Diefenbaker on November 4, 1958," PRO, PREM 11/2606

86   Macmillan to JGD, November 4, 1958; Macmillan to JGD, November 6, 1958, ibid.

87   See Robinson, *Diefenbaker's World*, 64–69.

88   Robinson noted that Diefenbaker could have been briefed as effectively on European military matters "from sources within the Canadian official family," but often preferred to hear from "distant, or at least different, voices." Ibid., 67–68

89   Ibid., 64–67

90   Ibid., 67; telegram, Macmillan to JGD, November 6, 1958, PRO, PREM 11/2606

91 "Itinerary, 2 (F) Wing, Grostenquin, 6–7 Nov 1958," JGDP, XII/42/B/366

92 *OC 2*, 101

93 Ibid., 100

94 Ibid., 103

95 Diefenbaker had insisted that the official tour should be limited to Commonwealth countries, and he took naturally in his speeches to the evangelist's role as advocate of the Commonwealth's values. He saw the multiracial association as the external counterpart of his own, ideal Canada. In Kuala Lumpur, for example, he said: "As I move around this Commonwealth...I feel that we have been able to achieve that which never before in history has been attained. It used to be said...that unless you belong to the same race or unless you have affinities in religion or unless you inhabit a given area where you have similar geographic or historical backgrounds, you have the beginnings there of strife. We in this Commonwealth have proven the contrary. Diverse in every way, we have been able to bring about the feeling of comradeship and brotherhood which I have felt everywhere I have been. We can see eye to eye; we have a common heritage; we have a common objective – the maintenance of peace in freedom. Let us march forward together in the future as we have in the past." "A New Concept of the Commonwealth," November 28, 1958, DEA *Statements and Speeches*, 59/13

96 Robinson, *Diefenbaker's World*, 74

97 *OC 2*, 103–05

98 JGD to Macmillan, November 15, 1958, PRO, PREM 11/2606. According to Robinson, Diefenbaker was notably influenced in his judgments of Ayub Khan by the positive views of the Canadian high commissioner, Herb Moran.

99 Macmillan to JGD, November 23, 1958, JCDP, XII/35/B.152.1

100 The words are from his typewritten "Notes for Prime Minister's Report to Parliament on his World Tour, 1958," which were not delivered to the House. JGDP, XII/125/F/495

101 Robinson, *Diefenbaker's World*, 73

102 Ibid., 74. Meanwhile, British diplomats around the world were watching Diefenbaker's progress from their typically lofty heights. The British high commissioner in Ottawa, Joe Garner, replying to a long report on the tour from the Commonwealth Relations Office, commented: "On the whole, given Mr. Diefenbaker's passion for publicity and his desire to hit the headlines, his public remarks on the tour, though occasionally framed in somewhat blunt language have been a good deal better than one might have expected and I have no doubt that some of this is a reflection of the guidance he received in London." Garner wondered whether Diefenbaker might more wisely have stayed at home: "He has really had no rest or respite since the election campaign in the middle of last year and has been living on his nerves ever since. A period of relaxation at home in which he could have had time to ponder on some of the big problems that face him might have been more helpful before the Parliamentary melee begins again in January." Joe Garner to Sir Gilbert Laithwaite, Commonwealth Relations Office, November 27, 1958, PRO, PREM 11/2606

103 Robinson, *Diefenbaker's World*, 75

104 *OC 2*, 110

105 Robinson, *Diefenbaker's World*, 77

106 *OC 2*, 111

107 Ibid., 111–14; Robinson, *Diefenbaker's World*, 78–80

108 Robinson, *Diefenbaker's World*, 79

109 R.H. Scott to Sir Gilbert Laithwaite, CRO, December 5, 1958, PRO, PREM 11/2606

110 Quoted in Robinson, *Diefenbaker's World*, 80; *OC 2*, 114–15

111 Nash was the New Zealand prime minister. G. Mallaby to Sir Gilbert Laithwaite, CRO, January 8, 1959, PRO, PREM 11/2606; see also *OC 2*, 118–19; Robinson, *Diefenbaker's World*, 82–83. Robinson wrote that Diefenbaker and Menzies "were anything but soulmates" despite their shared loyalty to the Commonwealth, that neither one liked listening to the other, that

Diefenbaker "felt uncomfortable in the presence of Menzies' polished wit and jovial sophistication," and that Menzies was perhaps jealous of Diefenbaker as a rival Commonwealth leader. At the Commonwealth conference of 1957 Menzies had been reported as making a slighting comment about Diefenbaker, and Robinson speculates that his hospitality in 1958 may have been intended to make up for that. Ibid., 81–82

112 Mallaby to Laithwaite, CRO, January 8, 1959; Robinson, *Diefenbaker's World*, 82

113 *OC 2*, 119–20

114 The source and precise nature of these reports is not clear: perhaps it was Howard Green, perhaps William Brunt, who briefed Diefenbaker regularly by telephone. Patrick Nicholson to JGD, December 3, 1958, JGDP, XII/117/F/331

115 *Globe and Mail*, January 13, 1959

116 McLin, *Canada's Changing Defense Policy*, 60–67. The saga of the Arrow from inspiration to demise has spawned an unusual mythology, sustained over forty years by an endless flow of newspaper and television features, a cult literature, and a play featuring an on-stage model of the aircraft. Thirty years after its destruction, tales were still told of phantom sightings of the doomed prototypes. The Arrow seems as deeply lodged in English Canadian memory as the Canadian Pacific Railway or the Calgary Stampede. See, for example, Dow, *The Arrow*; Shaw, *There Never Was an Arrow*; Stewart, *Shutting Down the National Dream*; and Campagna, *Storms*.

117 *Debates*, June 28, 1955, 5380

118 McLin, *Canada's Changing Defense Policy*, 68

119 CC, 67–57, September 20, 1957

120 CC, 82–57, October 24, 1957. Diefenbaker himself did not participate in this meeting with company officials.

121 CC, 83–57, October 25, 1957

122 CC, 85–57, October 29, 1957. These development costs would be added to the $226 million committed by the end of the 1957–58 fiscal year.

123 CC, 85–57, October 29, 1957. The prime minister mentioned the need "to deal appropriately, and in time, with the question of the money supply"; others called for added funding for low-cost housing, beyond the $150 million already committed.

124 George Pearkes to JGD, January 27, 1958, JGDP, VI/94/304–1958.2, 80913–14

125 McLin, *Canada's Changing Defense Policy*, 73–74; Campagna, *Storms*, 93. The prospect of foreign purchases would mean a longer production run and substantial reductions in unit costs, which might make the Arrow a reasonable gamble. But apparently Pearkes was already too late with his request. Campagna quotes a Department of Defence Production memo suggesting that "by April 1958 it was accepted in Canada that, in the interests both of technical interworking and economy, the only sensible thing to do was to extend" the semi-automatic ground environment (SAGE), its communications systems, and the Bomarc sites north of the border. Campagna, *Storms*, 87

126 The relevant documents are "Minister's memorandum," August 22, 1958 (Cab. Doc. 247–58); CC, 86–58, August 22, 1958; CC, 92–58, September 3, 1958; CC, 94–58, September 7, 1958; CC, 95–58, September 8, 1958; CC, 96–58, September 21, 1958; CC, 97–58, September 22, 1958.

127 CC, 89–58, August 28, 1958

128 CC, 89–58, August 28, 1958

129 CC, 89–58, August 28, 1958

130 CC, 92–58, September 3, 1958. The comparative figures were:

Arrow with Astra–Sparrow	$1,261.5 million
Arrow with US missiles	$ 896.0 million
US F–106 substitute	$ 559.0 million
Bomarc (240 missiles)	$ 520.3 million

The Arrow estimates excluded development costs of approximately $400 million before September 1, 1958.

131 CC, 94–58, 95–58, September 7 and September 8, 1958

132 CC, 89–58, August 28, 1958

133 CC, 92–58, September 3, 1958

134 Bryce acknowledged the point of David Golden, the deputy minister of defence production, that the purchase of American aircraft would be "a slap in the face to the Canadian industry," but responded: "I think that can be answered best if the numbers to be bought are so small that the cost of the Canadian planes are [sic] obviously out of all proportion to the U.S. planes even if the 105 is a somewhat better plane." Confidential information. American development of the F–106 was cancelled a few months later.

135 CC, 94–58, September 7, 1958

136 CC, 95–58, September 8, 1958. At this meeting Pearkes suggested that employment might be maintained for two years at Avro if twenty pre-production and forty-eight production aircraft were built, all of them to go into service in five squadrons.

137 The interview was requested by Crawford Gordon. Diefenbaker apparently did not tell cabinet that his meeting with Gordon on September 17 had been belligerent, but he later insisted that it began that way. "Crawford Gordon was a noisy fellow, who thought when I saw his physical dimensions that fear should overwhelm me," Diefenbaker said in 1970. But "it was really nothing...he swept in and was blatantly noisy and he swept out." In the memoirs, Diefenbaker denies rumours of "a nasty personal confrontation." Gordon, he suggests, began the meeting "in a blustering fashion" by pounding his fist on the prime minister's desk, but was calmed by Diefenbaker's warning of possible injury. Nevertheless, Diefenbaker writes that the company's reaction was "extreme," "strongly worded," and intransigent. Since the issue before cabinet at this point was immediate cancellation, another way of reading the interview is to see it as an interim triumph for Gordon. At the next cabinet meeting, Diefenbaker proposed six months more life support for A.V. Roe. JGDI, May 27, 1970; OC 3, 37–38

138 CC, 96–58, September 21, 1958

139 CC, 96–58, 97–58, September 21 and September 22, 1958

140 In the memoirs, he calls the September decision "what amounted to a six-month formal notice so that they might adjust gradually to their new situation." OC 3, 37

141 Press release, "Revision of the Canadian Air Defence Programme," Office of the Prime Minister, September 23, 1958. JGDP, XII/29/B/9

142 Ibid.

143 M.W. Menzies, "Memorandum for the Prime Minister: The Arrow Program," September 23, 1958, JGDP, VI/55/171

144 Blair Fraser, "Backstage at Ottawa: What Led Canada to Junk the Arrow," Maclean's, October 25, 1958

145 Globe and Mail, September 25, 1958

146 Saskatoon Star-Phoenix, September 25, 1958

147 "Avro Chief Still Expects Green Light," Globe and Mail, September 25, 1958; Crawford Gordon, "...statement to avert misinterpretation of the new defence policy," September 24, 1958, appended to J.N. Kelly to Leslie M. Frost, January 13, 1967, Frost Papers

148 "Statement by Crawford Gordon...to Annual Meeting of Shareholders, October 27, 1958: The Arrow and Iroquois Programs," JGDP, VI/55/171, 47089–93. Gordon quoted a recent speech by Air Marshal C.R. Slemon, the Canadian deputy commander of NORAD, on the continuing need for manned interceptors "for as long as the manned bomber is part of the threat." He reported that three Arrows were then being test flown, and a fourth was about to fly. Gordon wrote to Diefenbaker enclosing a copy of the statement, but received no reply.

149 See, for example, Dorothy J. Westlake to JGD, September 26, 1958; F.E. Hyde to JGD, October 10, 1958; Keith Spicer to JGD, December 15, 1958, JGDP, VI/54,55/168. On

December 15 the *Globe* repeated its editorial view that "the brilliant team of scientists" at A.V. Roe "must not...be broken up."

150 CC, 129–58, December 22, 1958. Diefenbaker warned publicly of the effects of Avro's lobbying when he told the House on January 19, 1959: "Let me make this matter perfectly clear. Lobbies will have no effect on the decision that this government makes on the question of defence." *Debates*, January 19, 1959, 57. This seems, in retrospect, not so much an admonition to avoid lobbying as a warning that Avro's fate had already been sealed.

151 CC, 22–59, February 14, 1959; Fleming, *Near 2*, 13–16. The preparations leading to February 17 included further meetings of the military chiefs of staff – who indicated their preference for an American aircraft to replace the Arrow – and the cabinet defence committee, production of additional summary documents for ministers, and continuously changing estimates of cost prepared in the Departments of Defence and Finance. Confidential information

152 CC, 23–59, February 17, 1959. The draft seems to have been written by Robert Bryce. Two days later, on February 19, Diefenbaker said he was still considering his statement, and sought ministerial advice. He asked that a committee consisting of Donald Fleming, George Pearkes, Davie Fulton, Sidney Smith, and Raymond O'Hurley meet that afternoon to prepare a final revision. CC, 24–59, February 19, 1959

153 Diefenbaker's statement included no analysis of the Arrow's costs, beyond the assertion that they were too high when considered as part of a larger defensive package that now included Bomarc-SAGE. Ministers' estimates of costs fluctuated according to what items were included in the calculation. In September 1958 Pearkes quoted a figure of $12.6 million per aircraft to cabinet. By January 1959, with less expensive armament, he used a figure of $7.8 million per aircraft, and a few weeks later the Department of Defence Production suggested a cost of $7.7 million per plane. But these two estimates included $300 million to complete the development phase of twenty aircraft – most of it already committed – which almost doubled Avro's figures for production of ninety-two operational aircraft. In October 1958 Avro offered Pearkes a fixed-price contract for delivery of these ninety-two planes at $3.75 million each – which meant savings of several hundred million dollars over estimates of the previous August, and annual production costs that would never come close to the figure cited in cabinet in September of $400 million. Avro also proposed an advanced schedule that would commence delivery of operational aircraft in September 1960 rather than spring 1961. Diefenbaker later used figures of $9 million or $7 million per plane, but never argued that cost alone was the decisive factor in the cancellation.

154 *Debates*, February 20, 1959, 1221–24. Diefenbaker may have been unaware at this time that the Bomarc B planned for use in Canada could not be fitted with non-nuclear warheads. In the memoirs he suggests that "no information was given us that the United States would abandon, or had abandoned, its plans to manufacture a conventional warhead for the missile." His statement that "the full potential" of the weapons required arming with nuclear warheads was worthy of Monty Python: without the warheads they had no potential. In any case, his commitment to acquiring warheads seemed unambiguous in the February 20 statement; and he reiterated his position in a CBC interview with Tom Earle that evening. *OC 3*, 44; see also Fleming, *Near 2*, 18–19.

155 The notes are filed in JGDP, XII/29/B/9.

156 Telegram, Crawford Gordon to JGD, February 20, 1959, JGDP, XII/1/A/11

157 *OC 3*, 41

158 *Globe and Mail*, February 21, 1959. There were further editorials on February 23 and 25 emphasizing the need to salvage Avro's technical capacities and to reach "a genuine sharing of defense production" with the United States – without which the *Globe* foresaw that "we stand to lose our economic independence, our political independence, without the Communists so much as striking a blow." John Bassett's Toronto *Telegram* gave the prime minister's decision unequivocal support, while other papers widely praised Diefenbaker for a courageous and wise choice and, like the *Globe*, urged him to pursue a substantial Canadian

role in an integrated system of defence production. One of the rare dissenting voices was that of Tim Creery on the CBC's "Capital Report," who suggested that the preoccupation with jobs and production sharing avoided discussion of the government's policy. "I believe," he said, "we are going headlong into a type of defense integration with the United States which, besides its damaging effects on our own independence, may not even be the most effective role which Canada can play in working for a peaceful world." *Telegram*, February 21, 1959; "Press Views on the Arrow and Defense," *Globe and Mail*, February 25, 1959; transcript, "Capital Report," February 22, 1959

159 Telegram, Leslie Frost to JGD, February 21, 1959, JGDP, XII/1/A/11. Frost's report that he learned of the decision in the legislature is contained in his personal memorandum, "The Diefenbaker Days," nd, 9, Frost Papers

160 The pilot was J.A. McCurdy, who later served as lieutenant governor of Nova Scotia from 1947 to 1952. He received the McKee Trophy for 1959 in commemoration of that flight. Pearkes told the House that "a replica of the Silver Dart flew a short distance this afternoon before it met with a slight accident." *Debates*, February 23, 1959, 1278

161 CC, 25–59, February 23, 1959

162 The minister of defence production, Raymond O'Hurley, opened the House that day with a general statement on negotiations for defence production sharing. His statement was vetted in advance by the prime minister, who deleted the opening paragraph from the draft. It read: "The growing integration of the defence of North America and the cost and complexity of modern defence equipment is making it more and more difficult for Canada to develop and produce major weapon systems on a strictly independent basis. Accordingly, Canadian work in the design, development and production of defence equipment will have to be closely integrated with the major programs of the United States. It is gratifying to report that the United States Government recognizes this and is working out with us, design, development and production sharing agreements." *Debates*, February 23, 1959, 1269–70; confidential information

163 *Debates*, February 23, 1959, 1271–78, esp. 1278

164 Ibid., February 23, 1959, 1288

165 Ibid., 1295

166 Ibid., 1296

167 Ibid., 1306. Leslie Frost believed, on the contrary, that the order to stop work left "really no option but for the company to immediately post notices in their plants telling the workers to go home." His advice, from J. Grant Glassco of Clarkson, Gordon, was that the government's contract with Avro "permitted the orderly termination of the contract over a period of some six months or so, allowing the workers to make their arrangements for new employment and indeed permitting government forces and agencies to come into play...It would have meant that the workers would have time and opportunity to adjust their lives instead of being given a lump sum of money and turned out on the street." Leslie M. Frost, "The Diefenbaker Days," 9–10, Frost Papers

168 It is not clear whether Diefenbaker participated in or was aware of this decision, which seems to have been taken in the defence and defence production departments, perhaps for security reasons related to the high performance of the aircraft. There is no evidence, as some critics have suggested, of a vengeful plot to blot out the physical and historical record of the plane. But Diefenbaker did hold a grudge against Avro. Later in the year he asked O'Hurley to investigate rumours about Avro's financial practices, and in August he wanted Sir Roy Dobson, the managing director of Avro's British parent, Hawker Siddeley, to declare that the CF–105 had been inadequate and deserved cancellation. Confidential information

169 Frost, "The Diefenbaker Days," 10

Chapter 10 "History Is a Hanging Judge"

1 JGD to Elmer Diefenbaker, February 27, 1959, JGDP, V/3, 1809

2 JGD to Mary F. Diefenbaker, February 16, 1959, ibid., V/1, 815

3   JGD to Mary F. Diefenbaker, March 12, 1959, ibid., 828
4   JGD to Mary F. Diefenbaker, April 29, 1959, ibid., 847–48
5   JGD to Mary F. Diefenbaker, June 7, 13, 1959, ibid., 856, 874
6   Fleming, *Near 2*, 39–49
7   Blair Fraser, *Maclean's*, March 14, 1959, reprinted in Fraser, *"Blair Fraser Reports"*, 62–72
8   Roy Faibish, quoted in Stursberg, *Leadership Gained*, 177–78. Faibish was Alvin Hamilton's executive assistant.
9   George Hees, quoted ibid., 180; see also Newman, *Renegade*, 140–41.
10   Many of his brief handwritten notes on cabinet discussions are preserved in the Diefenbaker Papers. See also Alvin Hamilton's comment in Stursberg, *Leadership Gained*, 179–80.
11   See the comments of Alvin Hamilton and Davie Fulton in Stursberg, *Leadership Gained*, 176, 178–79. Hamilton commented: "I can honestly say that, during the five and a half years that I spent as a minister, I don't recall a single instance of him interfering with any of my departmental responsibilities." But when Hamilton made thoughtless public comments, as he sometimes did, Diefenbaker showed his rage.
12   Interview with E.D. Fulton, September 24, 1993
13   Interview with Gowan Guest, August 6, 1994; Stursberg, *Leadership Gained*, 181–82. The only specific directive that Guest could recall was that anyone who had been a pallbearer at Edna's funeral should have automatic and instant access to the prime minister. Guest circulated a memo to staff on the organization of the office into seven sections in January 1959, "in order that better service can be provided to all concerned." It urged them to refer matters directly to those responsible, "rather than through other persons." This seems to have been the first document to inform the two dozen staff members what their respective duties were. Gowan T. Guest, "Re: Organization of the Prime Minister's Office," January 28, 1959, JGDP, XII/70/C/340
14   Gowan T. Guest, "Memorandum to: The Prime Minister, Subject: Office Organization," July 10, 1959, JGDP, XII/38/B/263; Stursberg, *Leadership Gained*, 181–82. Guest's proposal was that George Hees's executive assistant, Mel Jack, should become the permanent executive assistant to Diefenbaker, but he remained the indispensable *éminence grise* behind George Hees.
15   Gowan T. Guest to JGD, August 4, 1960, JGDP, XII/5/A/98; interview with Gowan Guest, August 6, 1994. Guest and his wife remained friends of the Diefenbakers. Soon afterwards, when visiting Vancouver, Diefenbaker, still the debt-fearing prairie lawyer, expressed fatherly shock that Guest had taken a $12,000 mortgage as partial payment for a house.
16   See Newman's *Renegade*, 273–75; M.W. Menzies, "Memorandum for the Prime Minister," April 15, 1958; "Memorandum for the Prime Minister," May 10, 1959, JGDP, XII/37/B/214. Diefenbaker abruptly recalled Menzies from his civil service position to assist him in the 1962 election campaign. Menzies unhappily resigned his career job to satisfy Diefenbaker, and after the election joined a Winnipeg economic consulting firm.
17   See, for example, Dempson, *Assignment*, 99–109; Stursberg, *Leadership Gained*, 156–58; Levine, *Scrum Wars*, 209–23; Newman, *Renegade*, 314–34.
18   Victor Mackie in Stursberg, *Leadership Gained*, 157
19   Dempson, *Assignment*, 108–09; Nicholson, *Vision*, 104–05; Levine, *Scrum Wars*, 218. Shortly afterwards, Conservative headquarters announced that it had paid the costs of the Department of Transport flight to the Yukon. King was the object of greater prime ministerial fury on another occasion in 1962.
20   James Oastler, quoted in Newman, *Renegade*, 315
21   Dempson, *Assignment*, 102–05
22   Nicholson, *Vision*, 105
23   In February 1961 Diefenbaker was furious over suggestions made by the *Globe and Mail*'s Philip Deane at a Toronto dinner hosted by Oakley Dalgleish that Diefenbaker had interfered personally in the work of the Canadian delegation to the United Nations. In a draft

memo to Dalgleish, Diefenbaker described the charge as an "unmitigated falsehood" and "downright prevarication." Whether or not the memo was delivered, the publisher quickly learned of Diefenbaker's displeasure and let the prime minister know that Deane "was no longer in his employ." In this case Deane was not the apostate (he had never been an intimate), but the *Globe and Mail* was. Draft memo, JGD to Mr Oakley Dalgleish, February 26, 1961; Senator L.P. Beaubien to JGD, March 7, 1961, JGDP, XII/56/C/124

24 The quotation is from the transcript of a tape recording made by Michael Wardell of the Fredericton *Gleaner* on November 20-21, 1970, and passed on to Diefenbaker at that time. JGDP, XIV/E/219. Despite their close friendship from 1956 to 1962, Diefenbaker does not mention Bassett in his memoirs for this period. Bassett became *persona non grata* when the *Telegram* turned against Diefenbaker during the 1963 election campaign. Polite relations were soon restored, but Diefenbaker was offended by Bassett's failure to stand up for him at the 1966 annual meeting of the Progressive Conservative Party, and this time there was no reconciliation. The final volume of the memoirs makes only slighting references to Bassett.

25 John Bassett to JGD, December 20, 1957, JGDP, VI/312.2.02–Bassett, 102742

26 John Bassett to JGD, May 22, 1958, ibid., 102731

27 John Bassett to JGD, March 23, 1959, ibid., 102727

28 See, for example, Peter Dempson's "Two Years...Onward and Upward," *Telegram*, May 9, 1959.

29 Bassett quotes Beaverbrook in the Wardell tape. In his letter to Diefenbaker, he set out these reasons (and others) in more diplomatic language. He believed he could "make a more useful contribution to the maintenance of the political ideas and ideals which you represent and in which I so strongly believe" by staying where he was as publisher of the *Telegram* and chairman of the new television station recently granted a private broadcasting licence by the Board of Broadcast Governors – the new authority created by the Diefenbaker government in 1958. Diefenbaker had already been criticized for conferring the favour of the TV licence – although there was never evidence to suggest interference in the BBG's choice. A copy of Bassett's letter of November 16, 1960, appears with the Wardell transcript. A few weeks later, Bassett sought and received Diefenbaker's permission to establish three "Diefenbaker Scholarships" at the University of New Brunswick, to be awarded to students from Israel "in recognition of your services to your country and also of your appreciation and understanding of the aspirations of Israel, where you are remembered as a honored visitor." John Bassett to JGD, December 7, 1960; JGD to John Bassett, December 16, 1960, JGDP, VI/312–2.02–Bassett, 102694, 102693

30 Members of the two new governing boards were appointed by orders-in-council in November 1958. Under the guidance of George Nowlan, cabinet agreed to avoid excessive partisanship and to select members by region. Diefenbaker's preferences were only evident in two (or perhaps three) of the fifteen appointments to the Board of Broadcast Governors, including his longtime friend Carlyle Allison (editor of the Winnipeg *Tribune*) as a full-time member and his Prince Albert supporter and friend Dr Mabel Connell as a part-time member. The CCF constitutional expert Eugene Forsey was also named a part-time governor. Among the nine part-time members appointed to the board of the CBC, only one – the broadcaster and former Conservative MP Kate Aitken – was suggested by Diefenbaker. Conrad, *Nowlan*, 217–18; "Background and History of the Canadian Broadcasting Corporation Board of Directors," February 1961, JGDP, XII/51/C/76

31 Conrad, *Nowlan*, 219–25. Diefenbaker does not mention the affair in his memoirs.

32 CC, 57–59, April 21, 1959

33 Michael Wardell, "John Bassett at Toronto...November 20/21, 1970," JGDP, XIV/E/219. Bushnell replied to Bassett after reading the text of Barkway's broadcast, "He most certainly did not pull any punches"; but he added that "Barkway was about the only person who took this severely critical tone" on the issue...Too bad you had not heard 'the other side.'" Bassett copied the letter to Diefenbaker with the suggestion that "one of these days when you have a little more time, I would like to have a serious talk with you about the CBC and how, I

believe, the real problem with regard to a general anti-government feeling can, perhaps, be solved." Diefenbaker replied: "I shall be looking forward to that serious talk of which you write." Bassett's solution probably referred to more effective control of management by the CBC board, which was later sought by the government. In mid-April a *Telegram* editorial returned to the attack, charging that "the CBC has maintained a strong editorial bias which can be described as anti-government." John Bassett to JGD, April 3, 1959, enclosing copy of E.L. Bushnell to Bassett, April 1, 1959; JGD to John Bassett, April 8, 1959, JGDP, VI/312.2.02–Bassett, 102724–26; editorial, *Telegram*, April 14, 1959

34   *Debates*, June 23, 1959, 5041; Gowan T. Guest, "Private Memorandum for The Prime Minister and Minister of National Revenue only," June 24, 1959, enclosing "Draft Statement," nd, JGDP, XII/2/A/25. Diefenbaker also received ("for the P.M.'s future reference") a list of fees paid by the CBC to all speakers, commentators, and panelists during 1958, containing over three hundred names of journalists, broadcasters, and academics. There is no indication that Diefenbaker made any direct use of the information, but it remained in his confidential files. G.G. to Mr. Hetherington, "Earnings of Speakers...on all programs 1958," nd, ibid.

35   According to W.L. Morton, a member of the CBC board during the dispute, the phrase "heads will roll" originated with Nowlan's combative assistant (and intimate friend) Ruby Meabry, who had telephoned Bushnell on her own initiative in the hope of spiking the program's criticisms of the government. Knowlton Nash suggests that the words came originally from Diefenbaker himself. After Diefenbaker's defeat in 1963, Meabry became one of Diefenbaker's secretaries as leader of the opposition. Colin Wright, "Summary of an interview with Professor W.L. Morton," February 26, 1971; Conrad, *Nowlan*, 225–29; Levine, *Scrum Wars*, 222–23; Dempson, *Assignment*, 105–08; Peers, *The Public Eye*, 193–200; Nash, *Microphone Wars*, 294–300; *Telegram*, June 22, 24, 25, 1959. In 1961, during the absence of both Diefenbaker and Nowlan, ministers agreed to recommend creation of a cabinet committee "to assist Mr. Nowlan in investigating the programming of the CBC." But nothing came of the proposal on their return. CC, 32–61, March 14, 1961

36   Horwood, *Joey*, 239

37   CC, 34–59, 35–59, 36–59, 37–59, March 11, 12, 13, 14, 1959; Fleming, *Near 2*, 32–33; Newman, *Renegade*, 163–70; Conrad, *Nowlan*, 223–24; Pickersgill, *The Road Back*, 52–57

38   Fleming, *Near 2*, 34; Newman, *Renegade*, 167–70; *Debates*, March 16, 1959, 1959–62; interview with E.D. Fulton, September 24, 1993

39   *Debates*, March 16, 1959, 1959

40   See, for example, Fleming, *Near 2*, 34. L.B. Pearson, who was embarrassed by Smallwood's actions and the support they received from his Newfoundland MPs, did not explicitly reject the Diefenbaker government's decision.

41   *OC 2*, 316–20, esp. 320; Horwood, *Joey*, 234–48; Stursberg, *Leadership Gained*, 222–24; interview with E.D. Fulton, September 24, 1993

42   Fleming, *Near 2*, 31–33

43   *Debates*, March 25, July 14, 15, 1959, 2215–16, 5985–6019, 6028–67; Fleming, *Near 2*, 34–38

44   Robinson, *Diefenbaker's World*, 89–91; *OC 2*, 45–46; Fleming, *Near 2*, 26–27

45   JGD to Elmer Diefenbaker, March 20, 1959, JGDP, V/3, 1811–14

46   The previous three paragraphs are based upon Dempson, *Assignment*, 103–05; Robinson, *Diefenbaker's World*, 93; Fleming, *Near 2*, 27–30. Fleming saw his rejection as the turning point of his career. Afterwards it was downhill all the way.

47   Robinson, *Diefenbaker's World*, 93; Newman, *Renegade*, 340–46

48   Diefenbaker's account of the appointment differed notably from this one. He insisted that the idea was his own, inspired by seeing Vanier at an honorary degree ceremony at Université de Montréal in June 1959. "No one," wrote Diefenbaker, "had suggested his name to me." According to Diefenbaker, the intermediary in his approach was Cardinal Léger. The claim seems specifically intended to deny Bassett's role, but the record refutes it. Editorial, *Telegram*,

December 4, 1958; John Bassett to JGD, December 23, 1958; Michael Wardell, "John Bassett at Toronto...November 20/21, 1970, 7–8, JGDP, XII/4/A/61, XIV/E/219; *Telegram*, June 10, 1959; *OC 2*, 60–61; Robinson, *Diefenbaker's World*, 81; Dempson, *Assignment*, 109; Fleming, *Near 2*, 81–83; Newman, *Renegade*, 232

49 Elizabeth R to JGD, May 13, 1959; JGD to Mary F. Diefenbaker, June 18, July 2 and 7, 1959, JGDP, XII/87/D/167; V/1, 877, 886, 890–91; Fleming, *Near 2*, 55–59

50 JGD to Mary F. Diefenbaker, June 14, 18, 20, July 2, 7, 9, and 24, 1959; JGD to Elmer Diefenbaker, July 18, 1959, JGDP, V/1, 875, 877, 878–81, 886, 890–91, 894–97, 909, 906–07. On July 8 the Diefenbakers incurred the wrath (or ridicule) of the press by offering only tea and lemonade to several hundred guests at a humid reception marking the end of a long parliamentary session. The *Globe and Mail* reported that this was "almost unheard of" in Ottawa, except at parties hosted by the Indian and Pakistani high commissions. But the story added that, at a large buffet supper for the queen in Montreal two weeks earlier, the Diefenbakers had offered only orange juice. Diefenbaker told reporters that "he thought it was a good idea and would continue with it." George Nowlan was not impressed: when he could not get a cool gin and tonic, he spat out an oath and departed. Allister Grosart told a reporter that Diefenbaker had responded to his plea to serve alcohol with twinkling eyes: "Give them hot tea; it will be good for them." *Globe and Mail*, July 9, 1959; Stursberg, *Leadership Gained*, 158–59

51 For these two paragraphs, see JGD to Mary Diefenbaker, July 17, August (nd), September 9, October 16 and 21, 1959; February 26, May 7, June 3, November 11, 1960, JGDP, V/1, 908, 928–31, 932, 945–46, 958, 1032, 1071–72, 1139. Diefenbaker did not actually receive the Freedom of the City of London until a brief visit in late February 1963, after his government's defeat in the House of Commons

52 A.R.M. Lower to JGD, July 9, 1957, JGDP, XII/5/A/122

53 *Globe and Mail*, April 25, 1958

54 Bora Laskin, "Constitutional Power Respecting a Bill of Rights for Canada," June 27, 1958, JGDP, VII/68/A/551.2, 39812–20. Diefenbaker marked his copy of this document with frequent underlinings and marginal comments.

55 Interview with E.D. Fulton, September 24, 1993; *OC 2*, 255–56; *Globe and Mail*, September 6, 1958

56 McWhinney, "Bill of Rights," *CAR 1960*, 260

57 *Globe and Mail*, September 8, 1958

58 Ibid., September 11, 1958

59 Goodman monitored the debate and kept in touch with the prime minister on the subject throughout the winter. See E.A. Goodman to JGD, January 13, March 9, 1959; JGD to E.A. Goodman, March 13, 1959, JGDP, VI/366/413.1, 286137, 285461–62.

60 Bora Laskin, "The Proposed Bill of Rights," December 10, 1958; E.A. Goodman to JGD, January 13, 1959, JGDP, VII/68/A/551.2, 39835–49; VI/366/413.1, 286137–38

61 McWhinney, "Bill of Rights," 262

62 *Globe and Mail*, September 9, 1959

63 F.R. Scott to JGD, December 21, 1959, JGDP, VI/366/413.1, 285648–49

64 *OC 2*, 256–57; JGD to F.R. Scott, December 22, 1959, ibid., 285647

65 *Debates*, July 1, 1960, 5643–50, esp. 5645, 5649–50

66 Ibid., July 7, 1960, 5939. Diefenbaker used his old poetic licence about his mother's name.

67 Ibid., July 1, 1960, 5643; *OC 2*, 258

68 *Debates*, August 4, 1960, 7552–53; *Globe and Mail*, August 5, 1960

69 *Globe and Mail*, August 11, 1961. Diefenbaker also used the ornamental copy of the Bill as the frontispiece to the second volume of his memoirs.

70 *OC 2*, 264–65

71 Bill C–79, "An Act for the Recognition and Protection of Human Rights and Fundamental Freedoms," sections 2, 6(5)

72   *OC 2*, 262–63

73   See above, 258–60. In April 1966, when preparing for hearings of the Spence commission of inquiry, Diefenbaker prepared a memorandum for file which briefly recalled his practice in security matters. Robert Bryce, he wrote, would bring specific security cases to him for review, but he denied having seen any reference to "the Cabinet Directive of 1952" [sic]: "The Clerk of the Privy Council would outline the case and his views and I would be shown the documents in the particular case. After discussion, I would give suggestions as to what course should be followed that, in my opinion, would protect the security of the State while at the same time assuring to the maximum degree consistent with national security the fundamental rights of the individual." JGD, Memorandum, April 24, 1966, JGDP, XIV/E/172

74   Don Wall to Security Panel, May 12, 1959, CSIS, AIR 91–088, quoted in Robinson and Kimmel, "Queer Career," 319–45, esp. 332

75   J.M. Bella to RCMP commissioner, April 29, 1959, CSIS, AIR 92–008, quoted ibid., 334

76   Ibid., 342. Fleming, who was by now justice minister, attended this meeting, along with Bryce, Robertson, Harvison, Pelletier, and Wall.

77   Ibid., 339–42

78   Victims of the purge included an assistant undersecretary of state for external affairs, who had worked closely with the prime minister during his first three years in power. He resigned from the public service in 1960, and subsequently had a distinguished private career. Another was a Canadian ambassador in Moscow, who was fired in 1960. Diefenbaker may have been referring to these cases in his 1966 memorandum when he mentioned "two cases involving Embassy representatives of the U.S.S.R." [sic]. JGD, Memorandum, April 24, 1966, JGDP, XIV/E/172; *Globe and Mail*, April 25, 1992; Robinson and Kimmel, "Queer Career," 335; Sawatsky, *For Services Rendered*, 172–74

79   Interview with E.D. Fulton, September 24, 1993

80   JGD, Memorandum, April 24, 1966, JGDP, XIV/E/172

81   JGD, Confidential memorandum, "Re: Gerda Munsinger," April 26, 1966. The person referred to was apparently Willie Obront, a Montrealer of dubious reputation. See also *OC 3*, 176.

82   E.D.F. to prime minister, nd, JGDP, XIV/E/145

83   JGD, "Memorandum re: Interview with Col. Sévigny," December 21, 1960, JGDP, XIV/15/E/172

84   JGD, "Misc.," handwritten memorandum, nd, 1966, JGDP, XII/122/F/420

85   *CAR 1960*, 75–78, 83–85

86   *Debates*, January 18, 1960, 68–73, esp. 73

87   Ibid., February 1, 1960, 547

88   Toronto *Star*, February 2, 1960

89   H.E. Davies to JGD, November 19, 1959, JGDP, XII/8/A/282.3

90   *Debates*, January 29, 1960, 491

91   Ibid., February 5, 1960, 759

92   Robinson, *Diefenbaker's World*, 123. Diefenbaker's personal account of the 1960 and 1961 Commonwealth conferences is in *OC 2*, 208–21.

93   Telegram, Robert Menzies to External Affairs, No. 62, April 6, 1960, JGDP, XII/100/F/69. Diefenbaker marked these passages in the telegram.

94   George Ignatieff to External Affairs, No. 1115, April 11, 1960, JGDP, XII/100/F/69

95   Robinson, *Diefenbaker's World*, 124

96   The cabinet held a lengthy and inconclusive discussion of the subject on April 11. According to the minutes, Diefenbaker told cabinet that its division "showed how difficult it was to reach a wise and agreed decision on this matter. It would be necessary to move forward gradually." CC, 47–60, April 11, 1960

97   Robinson indicates that this summary is based on his diary notes taken from April 5 to 11, 1960. Robinson, *Diefenbaker's World*, 124

98   *Debates*, April 11, 1960, 3087–89; Robinson, *Diefenbaker's World*, 125–26

99   CC, 51–60, April 20, 1960

100 Robinson, *Diefenbaker's World*, 126

101 "Draft Answer to Possible Question on South Africa," nd, JGDP, XII/41/B/337

102 *Debates*, April 27, 1960, 3339

103 Robinson, *Diefenbaker's World*, 126–27

104 *Evening Standard*, April 29, 1960; *Daily Express*, April 30, 1960

105 "Meeting of Commonwealth Prime Ministers: Final Communiqué," May 13, 1960, JGDP, XII/55/C/110

106 *Debates*, May 16, 1960, 3900

107 Handwritten notes, nd, JGDP, XII/100/F/69. The text Diefenbaker used in the House on May 16 was largely written by Basil Robinson, and reflected the more cautious position of the Department of External Affairs. See JGDP, XII/41/B/337.

108 Diefenbaker returned to the subject at the next cabinet meeting, suggesting that "the Canadian people should somehow be made aware of the implications for Canada of forth-coming changes in the composition of the Commonwealth. The U.K. allowed free migra-tion of peoples, and as a result large-scale immigration of non-white people had already occurred and was continuing." CC, 58–60, 59–60, May 14, 16, 1960

109 Harold Macmillan to JGD, August 3, 1960, JGDP, XII/6/A/149

110 Basil Robinson to USSEA, November 3, 1960, DEA, file 50085–J–40, vol. 1, quoted in Robinson, *Diefenbaker's World*, 175

111 Macmillan, *Pointing the Way*, 293

112 Robinson, *Diefenbaker's World*, 175–76. Robinson commented that the case exemplified "the difference between his approach and that of St Laurent and Pearson. They would have been scouting for common ground with other governments, perhaps New Zealand and India, searching for compromises that might become solutions. Diefenbaker was certainly inter-ested in what others were thinking and planning, but the ambiguity in his own thinking and his concern to avoid political trouble at home deterred him from active consultation."

113 HCG, "Memorandum to the Prime Minister," December 30, 1960; HCG, "Memorandum to the Prime Minister," January 16, 1961, JGDP, XII/55/C/110

114 Robinson, *Diefenbaker's World*, 177–78

115 Creighton had served, at Diefenbaker's nomination, as a member of the British commission on the future of the Central African Federation, and thus had recently informed opinions on southern Africa. There had been intense public debate on South Africa in Canada, and Diefenbaker had received a large correspondence on the issue, including a resolution of the Board of Evangelism and Social Service of the United Church of Canada opposing read-mission and a statement from Patrick Nicholson urging a "bold acceleration" of South Africa's policy of creating Black homeland states, which he saw as "the germ of an accept-able solution to the Commonwealth problem." D.G. Creighton, "Should the Republic of South Africa be readmitted to the Commonwealth?" nd, JGDP, XII/54/C/109.1; "Canada Must Reject Apartheid," *Telegram*, January 21, 1961; United Church of Canada, "Canada, South Africa and the Commonwealth Conference"; Pat Nicholson, Memorandum, March 1, 1961, JGDP, XII/76/C/404

116 RBB, "Memorandum: Prime Minister," nd, JGDP, XII/76/C/404

117 Robinson, *Diefenbaker's World*, 179–80; JGD, "Memorandum for Cabinet: Memorandum for Saturday February 11, 1961," JGDP, XII/76/C/404; George Drew, Memoranda to JGD, February 23, 24, and 27, 1961, JGDP, XII/55/C/110. The Diefenbaker memorandum con-tains the prime minister's brief handwritten notes of views expressed at the meeting.

118 "Press Conference with the Rt. Hon. John G. Diefenbaker...at London Airport," March 7, 1961, JGDP, XII/55/C/110

119 Robinson, *Diefenbaker's World*, 181–82

120 RBB, "Memorandum for the Prime Minister: Re: South African issue," March 9, 1961, JGDP, XII/55/C/110

121 Ibid.

122 RBB to JGD, March 10, 1961, JGDP, XII/55/C/110

123 "Press Conference: Mr. R.B. Bryce and Mr. G.S. Murray," March 10, 1961, JGDP, XII/55/C/110

124 JGD, "Points for Preliminary Discussion on South African Membership," March 12, 1961, JGDP, XII/55/C/110; Robinson, *Diefenbaker's World*, 182–84

125 "Press Conference, The Hon. E. Davie Fulton and Mr. R.B. Bryce," March 13, 1961, JGDP, XII/55/C/110

126 Robinson, *Diefenbaker's World*, 184

127 "Meeting of Commonwealth Prime Ministers: Draft of Paragraphs for Communique," March 13, 1961; JGD, "Points for Further Statement on South Africa," March 14, 1961, JGDP, XII/55/C/110; XII/76/C/404; Robinson, *Diefenbaker's World*, 184–85

128 Diefenbaker added his questions and Verwoerd's answers in handwriting to his copy of the revised draft communiqué. "Meeting of Commonwealth Prime Ministers: Communique: Revised draft of passage on South Africa's racial policy," 3:30 pm, March 14, 1961, JGDP, XII/55/C/110; see also Robinson, *Diefenbaker's World*, 185; "Press Conference, The Hon. E. Davie Fulton and Mr. R.B. Bryce, March 14, 1961," JGDP, XII/55/C/110

129 Diefenbaker's and Fulton's handwritten notes appear on pages headed "Mr. Macmillan." Ibid., XII/55/C/110

130 Robinson, *Diefenbaker's World*, 185

131 Macmillan's full account of the meeting appears in his *Pointing the Way*, 285–300.

132 Robinson, *Diefenbaker's World*, 186

133 "Draft of Communiqué: 15th March, 1961," JGDP, XII/55/C/110

134 Macmillan suggests that he "induced" Verwoerd to withdraw the application by making clear that if the issue were forced to a vote, "the result...would be an almost overwhelming vote against." Macmillan, *Pointing the Way*, 299

135 In his background press briefing, Davie Fulton told Canadian reporters that "the reason why South Africa withdrew its application for membership was because they found that insistence by the other members of the Commonwealth on a declaration of principle, first, and second, on a declaration that South Africa's policies were inconsistent with these principles, was felt by South Africa to be unacceptable." JGD, "Mr Verwoerd Mar 15/61," JGDP, XII/55/C/110; Robinson, *Diefenbaker's World*, 186; "Supplementary Press Briefing – March 15, 1961, Hon. E. Davie Fulton and Mr. R.B. Bryce," JGDP, XII/55/C/110

136 "Press Conference – Right Hon. John G. Diefenbaker...March 16, 1961," JGDP, XII/55/C/110

137 *Debates*, March 17, 1961, 3079–83, esp. 3082–83; *OC 2*, 217–18; Robinson, *Diefenbaker's World*, 188. The draft text was written by Basil Robinson and Geoffrey Murray on the overnight return flight from London to Gander, and refined by Diefenbaker on the last leg to Ottawa. As an example of Diefenbaker's extended prose on a single subject, it was unusually precise and coherent.

Chapter 11 "Hazard...Our Constant Companion"

1 JGD to Mary F. Diefenbaker, January 4, 1960, JGDP, V/1, 1002

2 House of Commons, *Debates*, January 14, 15, and 28, 1960, 1–3, 43–74, 435; *Saturday Night*, February 20, 1960, 33; *CAR 1960*, 3–5. The Cross column is in the Diefenbaker Papers, XII/50/C/59.

3 Newman, *Renegade*, 378–79; *Globe and Mail*, June 17, 19, and 24, December 23, 1961

4 *Le Devoir*, September 14, 1960, quoted in *CAR 1960*, 61

5 The *Globe and Mail* reported in a front-page story in December 1959 that Pearkes was "fatigued by the pressures of the toughest portfolio in the Government," and remained "only because Prime Minister Diefenbaker hasn't settled on anyone to succeed him." *Globe and Mail*, December 19, 1959

6   "Notes on Cabinet Organization," August 24, 1960, JGDP, XII/51/C/65
7   JGD, Memoranda, "Cabinet Changes Proposed by Jim Oastler, August 18," "Cabinet Suggestions by Senator Thorvaldson," August 27, 1960, JGDP, XII/51/C/66
8   *Globe and Mail*, October 12, 1960; JGD, Memorandum, "Rearrangement of Cab," nd, JGDP, XII/51/C/66; *CAR 1960*, 61–63
9   CC, 22–60, February 6, 1960
10   RBB, "Memorandum for the Prime Minister: Re: Cabinet procedures," February 9, 1960, JGDP, XII/96/F/33
11   The cabinet committee on finance and credit, which dealt with the finance minister's borrowing plans, worked efficiently under Fleming's guidance. In August the *Globe and Mail* reported that "top civil servants" were complaining about Diefenbaker's failure to fill over two dozen senior vacancies, while overlooking many obvious internal candidates. Fleming, *Near 2*, 150–51; *Globe and Mail*, August 26, 1960
12   Horne, *Macmillan 1957–1986*, 233
13   Quoted in *CAR 1960*, 100
14   "Remarks by the Rt. Hon. John G. Diefenbaker...at Washington Airport on arrival June 3, 1960," JGDP, XII/42/B365
15   JGD, "Toast to the President – Dinner, Friday night," JGDP, XII/42/B/365
16   H.B. Robinson, "Briefs for Prime Minister's Visit to Washington, June 3, 1960"; JGD, Memorandum, "Can US Relations," nd, JGDP, XII/112/F/212, XII/42/B/365; CC, 68–60, 72–60, 73–60, June 6, 14 and 15, 1960
17   CC, 72–60, 73–60, June 14 and 15, 1960. Exercise "Sky Shield" would involve the suspension of private and commercial air traffic in North America for several hours, a simulated attack by 250 aircraft to be met by 1000 interceptors, and emergency operations by the two governments. A previously planned operation, "Sky Hawk," had been cancelled in 1959 in the absence of Canadian agreement. This time the Canadian cabinet accepted a smaller exercise within North American radar range, but noted the risks: "Aircraft might stray beyond the intended range, or the Soviets might regard the exercise as sufficient provocation to lead them to carry out their threat of attacking American bases without warning." Cabinet also noted "an article in the current issue of Maclean's magazine which asserted that Canada was controlled by the United States."
18   J.J.S. Garner to JGD, enclosing "Message from the Rt. Hon. Harold Macmillan..." September 15, 1960, JGDP, XII/77/C/435
19   JGD to Harold Macmillan, September 17, 1960, ibid.
20   "Memorandum for the Prime Minister: Comments on Khrushchov's Speech to the U.N.," September 23, 1960, ibid.; Robinson, *Diefenbaker's World*, 152
21   Robinson, *Diefenbaker's World*, 153
22   H.B. Robinson diary, quoted in ibid., 154
23   "Address by the Prime Minister...John G. Diefenbaker, before the United Nations General Assembly, September 26, 1960," JGDP, XII/77/C/435
24   *CAR 1960*, 126–27; Arnold Heeney to JGD, September 27, 1960; Foreign Language Press Review Service, Department of Citizenship and Immigration, "Comments on PM Diefenbaker's UN Speech," October 1960, JGDP, XII/77/C/435, XII/113/F/229; Robinson, *Diefenbaker's World*, 154–55
25   Robinson, *Diefenbaker's World*, 156
26   Horne, *Macmillan 1957–1986*, 278–79; Robinson, *Diefenbaker's World*, 155; JGD to Elmer Diefenbaker, September 29, 1961, JGDP, V/4, 2019
27   Robinson, *Diefenbaker's World*, 154–55; Horne, *Macmillan 1957–1986*, 278–79
28   Basil Robinson, Memo for file, November 9, 1960, quoted in Robinson, *Diefenbaker's World*, 165–66
29   Diefenbaker reported his "wonderful visit" in a letter to his brother the same day. JGD to Elmer Diefenbaker, January 17, 1961, JGDP, V/4, 2063

30 JGD, "Memorandum Re: Visit with President Eisenhower, Washington, January 17, 1961," JGDP, XII/86/D/149. Sometime later, perhaps in the preparation of his memoirs, Diefenbaker wrote five foolscap pages of similar reminiscences about his encounters with Ike, from their first meeting – "First showed friendship at the Church Service in Paris in Dec 1957 (NATO meeting) when he got up from his place by himself and came over to the right aisle and shook hands with Olive and me"; to the opening of the St Lawrence Seaway in 1959 – "he took Olive and I back to Montreal by helicopter. I got in back seat but security guards said 'No' – no one must sit behind him"; to their joking discussion in New York in September 1960 over whether Nixon should have agreed to the television debates with Kennedy – "I opposed – (a) Poker Game – (b) Why advertise your political opposition...After a while in came Howard Green and C.A. Herter...and Pres. said John agrees with your view." JGD, "Eisenhower," nd, JGDP, XIV/14/E/119

31 Dwight Eisenhower to JGD, January 18, 1961, JGDP, XII/7/A/232

32 Richard Nixon to JGD, January 16, 1961, JGDP, XII/9/A/306

33 JGD, "Memorandum Re: Conversation with Arnold Heeney," January 17, 1961, JGDP, XII/86/D/149

34 Quoted in Robinson, *Diefenbaker's World*, 168

35 Ibid., 169

36 Livingston Merchant (the US ambassador-designate to Canada), who was then undersecretary of state for political affairs, was a helpful intermediary. Ibid.

37 Nash, *Kennedy and Diefenbaker*, 63–65. The official transcript reporter spelled the name "Diefenbacher." The two "old friends" had only once shaken hands.

38 *Debates*, February 8, 1961, 1852; Nash, *Kennedy and Diefenbaker*, 64. Knowlton Nash commented: "ABC-TV news referred to the Canadian prime minister as 'Diefenbacon,' the *Washington Post* called him 'Diffenbaker,' and United Press called him 'Fiffenbaker.' Even the American ambassador to Canada always called him 'Diefenbacker.'"

39 Dean Rusk, "Memorandum for the President, Subject: Prime Minister Diefenbaker's Visit..." February 17, 1961, Kennedy Papers, POF/113/Canada/Security 1961

40 JGD, "Notes for Conference in Washington with President Kennedy," February 20, 1961, JGDP, VII/260/A/2347; Robinson, *Diefenbaker's World*, 170–71

41 Robinson, *Diefenbaker's World*, 171–73

42 The print was framed and on the prime minister's wall for Kennedy's visit to Ottawa in May 1961. *OC 2*, 168; Robinson, *Diefenbaker's World*, 199; Nash, *Kennedy and Diefenbaker*, 113

43 Robinson, *Diefenbaker's World*, 172–73; *Debates*, 2220–21; Nash, *Kennedy and Diefenbaker*, 91–100; *OC 2*, 167–69

44 Nash, *Kennedy and Diefenbaker*, 99

45 Robinson, *Diefenbaker's World*, 191–92

46 Ibid., 192–93; *Debates*, April 19, 1961, 3795

47 Robinson, *Diefenbaker's World*, 194; Nash, *Kennedy and Diefenbaker*, 104

48 Robinson, *Diefenbaker's World*, 194–95

49 Livingston Merchant to secretary of state, May 11, 1961, No. 893; "Triangular Proposition: F101B–Pinetree–F104G (To be raised only at Canadian initiative)," May 12, 1961, Kennedy Papers, POF/113/Canada Security, JFK Trip to Ottawa, 5/16–18/61; Robinson, *Diefenbaker's World*, 195–96

50 Robinson, *Diefenbaker's World*, 196

51 SecState WashDC to The White House, May 15, 1961, Kennedy Papers, NSF/Canada: General:05/15/61–05/30/61, 4485

52 Kennedy had managed to disguise that he suffered from Addison's disease, a painful degenerative disease affecting the spinal cord. It was obvious from his appearance that he was taking frequent injections of cortisone, purportedly to deal with the pain of a war time injury; and he took various other medications "prescribed and unprescribed, each day, sometimes every hour." The Kennedy biographer Richard Reeves added that he had

"persistent venereal disease, a very uncertain stomach that restricted him to a bland diet all his life, some deafness in his right ear, and a baffling range of allergies that sometimes laid him out." By contrast, the hypochondriacal Diefenbaker – although also partially deaf – was in thriving good health. Reeves, *President Kennedy*, 42–44, 120

53   Ibid., 120

54   *Debates*, May 17, 1961, 4962–65, esp. 4965; Nash, *Kennedy and Diefenbaker*, 124–25

55   This account is based primarily on Robinson, *Diefenbaker's World*, 198–209, and follows consistently the lines proposed in the American briefing documents, especially the main collection of briefing papers in the Kennedy Papers, POF/113/Canada Security, JFK trip to Ottawa/5/61 (B).

56   The original and one photocopy of the memorandum are filed separately in the Diefenbaker Papers. The original is unblemished, but the photocopy contains Diefenbaker's double underlinings wherever the word "push" appears. There are numerous copies, with appended comments, in the Kennedy Papers for 1962. WWR, "Memorandum to the President: What we want from the Ottawa trip," May 16, 1961, JGDP, XII/88/D/204, XII/85/D/113

57   Robinson, *Diefenbaker's World*, 206–07

58   Merchant to secretary of state, May 19, 1961, Kennedy Papers, NSF/18/Canada: General: 05/15/61–05/30/61, Embtel 923

59   JGD to Elmer Diefenbaker, May 18, 1961, JGDP, V/4, 2135

60   Diefenbaker spoke of that "callow young man" to the diplomat George Ignatieff, who is quoted in Nash, *Kennedy and Diefenbaker*, 130. Less than a month later the US Treasury Department briefly held up delivery of grain-unloading equipment needed for ships transporting Canadian grain from Vancouver to China, but exempted the equipment from the US Trading with the Enemy Act on representations from the US Embassy in Ottawa and the Canadian ambassador in Washington. Diefenbaker later claimed that he had berated and threatened Kennedy in a telephone conversation until the unloaders were released, and that this "was the end of any friendly personal relationship between President Kennedy and myself." Diefenbaker's secretary, Bunny Pound, and State Department officials doubted the accuracy of Diefenbaker's account of the incident. On June 8, 1961, Diefenbaker told the House of Commons that the dispute had been settled by diplomatic means, and that "such cooperation is an example to all the world." *OC 2*, 179–81; Nash, *Kennedy and Diefenbaker*, 132–35

61   The prime minister also sent Elmer a cheque, presumably to cover the funeral expenses. JGD to Elmer Diefenbaker, August 5, 1960, JGDP, V/4, 2003

62   The four were William, Edna, Edward – and Mary still to come. Diefenbaker neglected to mention that Edna had been buried deep so that his own body could lie above hers; the capacity was thus six. JGD to Elmer Diefenbaker, July 23, 1960, ibid., 2000

63   JGD to Elmer Diefenbaker, August 26, 1960, ibid., 2010

64   Dr D.M. Baltzan to JGD, December 1, 1960, JGDP, XII/49/C/36

65   Prince Albert *Herald*, February 21, 1961; *Globe and Mail*, February 22, 1961; Saskatoon *Star-Phoenix*, February 23, 1961; Regina *Leader Post*, February 22, 1961; *The Scotsman*, March 11, 1961

66   JGD to Elmer Diefenbaker, April 1, 1961, JGDP, V/4, 2117

67   *CAR 1960*, 6–7; *Debates*, February 19, 20, March 1, 2, 3, 1960, 1231–33, 1241–44, 1608–25, 1648–69, 1687–708

68   Diefenbaker briefly noted the comments of fourteen ministers and recorded nothing beside Fleming's name – whose assumption, as minister of finance, that there would be a budget can probably be taken for granted. Two ministers, Maclean and Fairclough, seemed to suggest a dissolution without a budget, while most others favoured a budget in March. JGD, Handwritten notes, "Secret Discussion Budget, February 9, 1960," JGDP, XII/51/C/65

69   *CAR 1960*, 7; Fleming, *Near 2*, 145–46

70 Fleming, *Near 2*, 146, 151–65

71 Charles Lynch, quoted in Fleming, *Near 2*, 166

72 Diefenbaker told his brother: "There have been all kinds of alibis for the outcome in Saskatchewan and no doubt there will be a number who will join with the Star-Phoenix in condemnation of me in connection with the deficiency payments decision. I believe that the medical doctors, by their lobby against the Medical Act, made that subject the issue to the exclusion of almost all others." JGD to Elmer Diefenbaker, June 13, 1960, JGDP, V/4, 1979

73 Fleming, *Near 2*, 217–21

74 Ibid., 221–23; CC, 107–60, September 7, 1960

75 Three of the seats had previously been Conservative and one Liberal. In Niagara Falls, Judy LaMarsh held the seat for the Liberals; in Peterborough the "New Party" candidate Walter Pitman took an old Conservative riding; in Henri Courtemanche's former riding of Labelle the Liberal candidate won; and in the New Brunswick seat of Royal, Hugh John Flemming claimed the government's only victory.

76 Fleming, *Near 2*, 243–49; *Debates*, December 20, 1960, 999–1017

77 Diefenbaker's retrospective view in his memoirs was that Coyne "apparently belonged to the economic school which had considered that the only way out of the Great Depression was to have more depression, and that the only way to cure unemployment was to create more unemployment." Coyne, he asserted, had conducted "a political campaign against my government. He was an unregenerate Grit." *OC 2*, 270–77; Fleming, *Near 2*, 304

78 The chartered banks were alarmed by the rate because they were limited by statute to a maximum 6 percent rate on their commercial loans. Donald Fleming to JGD, August 10, 1959, JGDP, VI/75/231, 66060–61

79 Telegram, Norman R. Whittall to JGD, August 13, 1959; Norman R. Whittall to JGD, August 13, 1959, ibid., 66063–67

80 Gowan Guest to Donald Fleming, August 15, 1959, ibid., 66073

81 Leslie M. Frost to JGD, August 20, 1959, ibid., 66054–56

82 Fleming, *Near 2*, 304–05

83 J.E. Coyne, Memorandum: "Speeches," nd, 1961, JGDP, XII/56/C/118.2; Fleming, *Near 2*, 305

84 *CAR 1960*, 9–10

85 *Globe and Mail*, March 23, 1960

86 Fleming, *Near 2*, 305–08; *CAR 1960*, 69–70

87 W.E. Rowe to Donald M. Fleming, December 1, 1960, copied to JGD, JGDP, VII/70/A/575.1

88 The royal commission was chaired by Hon. Dana Porter, chief justice of Ontario, and reported after the Conservative government had lost power in 1963. Among other things, it recommended legislative redefinition of the relationship between the bank and the government, one later adopted by the Pearson government. Fleming lamented in his memoirs: "Had we had such legislation in effect in 1960 and 1961 the so-called Coyne affair would never have arisen." CC, 149–60, December 6, 1960; Fleming, *Near 2*, 290–91

89 At its meeting on November 21, 1960, the board of directors gave its unanimous support for Coyne's Calgary speech of October 5. "Living within our means by expanding our means to live better," and his Toronto speech of November 14: "Foreign debt and unemployment." J.E. Coyne, Memorandum: "Speeches," nd, 1961, JGDP, XII/56/C/118.2

90 J.E. Coyne, "Living within Our Means by Expanding Our Means to Live Better," a speech to the Annual Meeting of the Canadian Chamber of Commerce, October 5, 1960, JGDP, VII/70/A/575.1

91 Fleming, *Near 2*, 308–09

92 J.E. Coyne, Memorandum: "Speeches," nd, 1961, JGDP, XII/56/C/118.2

93 Quoted in the Vancouver *Sun*, March 23, 1961

94 *Debates*, March 15, 1961, 3014, also quoted in Fleming, *Near 2*, 310–11

95 Fleming, *Near 2*, 312–13

96   Ibid., 313
97   Ibid., 313–14
98   CC, 35–61, March 23, 1961; Fleming, *Near 2,* 314
99   Fleming, *Near 2,* 314–15; CC, 35–61, March 23, 1961
100 Fleming, *Near 2,* 315–19; CC, 37–61, March 30, 1961
101 Fleming, *Near 2,* 318; CC, 37–61, March 30, 1961
102 Donald Fleming to JGD, handwritten note, March 30, 1961, JGDP, XII/56/C/118.2
103 Fleming, *Near 2,* 319; CC, 47–61, 48–61, April 28, May 1, 1961
104 Fleming, *Near 2,* 319–20; CC, 60–61, May 27, 1961
105 Fleming, *Near 2,* 320
106 Ibid., 320
107 Ibid., 320–21; CC, 64–61, June 8, 1961
108 Fleming, *Near 2,* 322–23
109 J.E. Coyne to Donald M. Fleming, June 9, 1961, JGDP, XII/56/C/118.2
110 J.E. Coyne to Donald M. Fleming, June 9, 1961, ibid. Fleming expressed surprise that Coyne claimed to favour such a change: "If he had been advocating such a course he had totally succeeded in keeping me in the dark about it." He added: "Had it been in effect there would never have been a Coyne case." But the extraordinary lack of communication between minister and governor, and the failure on both sides to clarify the relationship in private discussion before the breakdown, does not suggest that the law would have made any difference. Under the Pearson government, the Bank of Canada Act was amended to this effect. Coyne's other two letters of June 9 dealt with the pension by-law and a 1961 proposal for a bond issue. Fleming, *Near 2,* 322–23
111 Fleming added: "In the light of what was about to transpire it might have been politically better in the end for all concerned if we had agreed and allowed Coyne to fill out his term to its end. I doubt, however, if we could have honourably justified that course at the time." The minister was carrying the case almost entirely alone, without consulting the prime minister about tactics; Diefenbaker seemed, to this point, almost a bystander. Probably a prime minister in confident control of his cabinet could, if he wished, have reversed the decision, avoided a public fight with the governor, and come to a settlement. Coyne gave his own account of these discussions in a letter to Fleming of June 13. Fleming, *Near 2,* 323; J.E. Coyne to Donald M. Fleming, June 13, 1961, JGDP, XII/56/C/118.2
112 Fleming, *Near 2,* 323–25; J.E. Coyne to Donald M. Fleming, June 13, 1961, JGDP, XII/56/C/118.2
113 J.E. Coyne, "Press Statement," June 13, 1961, JGDP, XII/56/C/118.2
114 Fleming, *Near 2,* 325. The statement was almost three times the length of Coyne's.
115 *Debates,* June 14, 1961, 6314–16
116 Ibid., 6326–57
117 Editorial, "Mr. Coyne's Masters Speak Their Piece," Montreal *Star,* June 15, 1961
118 Montreal *Gazette,* June 15, 1961
119 Diefenbaker was not in the House at the time, and Fleming believed that he was bound by the cabinet's previous decision not to refer the bank's annual report to committee. When the prime minister returned, Fleming told him of the refusal and, according to Fleming, "he saw no reason to alter our planned strategy." Diefenbaker recalled: "My own view was that we should have agreed. However, once Mr. Fleming had taken his position there could be no change; certainly I was not going to countermand him on this issue. Had we set up the committee of the House of Commons, we could have destroyed Coyne for all time." Fleming called this a "barefaced attempt to escape responsibility...Diefenbaker presided day after day at the cabinet meetings where all the decisions were taken. Never did he voice the opinion that Coyne should have had a hearing before a parliamentary committee." This was another point in the saga at which tactical skill and self-confidence would have reduced the government's exposure to criticism. Fleming, *Near 2,* 330–31, 344; *OC 2,* 275; *Debates,* June 26, 1961, 7047–61

120 Fleming, *Near 2*, 334–35

121 Pickersgill commented on the issue afterwards in at least three places. He told Peter Stursberg in 1975: "Once it had become a political issue, once it was clear that in my opinion he was being done the grossest injustice, I saw no reason whatever for concealing my support of him and going to see him and talk to him. There was nothing improper about it. I had a perfect right to do it." He denied Fleming's charge of collusion (also made to Stursberg) in a letter to Fleming in 1982, and added: "It was only after the government asked Coyne to resign that we discussed the matter at all. I felt, at that stage, when I had learned about the issue over the pension, that I was quite justified as a friend in giving him my views on the matter as it had then developed." In his 1994 memoir, he reviewed his role in the debate, and repeated his denial of Diefenbaker's claim that he had written parts of Coyne's letters during the affair.

Bruce Hutchison's papers show that Coyne met secretly with Pearson at least once in April 1960 to discuss his views on policy at the reporter Grant Dexter's home. But Hutchison reports that Coyne's views were "too hair-raising for comfort," and that "it is easy for Mike to refuse Jim's counsel." In Hutchison's view, Coyne was much closer to the Tories than to the Liberals in policy, and offered Diefenbaker an excellent cover: "If I were Dief I wouldn't fire Jim. I would encourage him to go on and develop his ideas to their ultimate logic, which is sheer protectionism. If he would give his blessing to some thimble-rigging of the tariff, import controls etc., the government would have the blessing of the most respected public servant in the country. What could be sweeter?" Hutchison believed that Pearson had no coherent economic policy, and probably saw more consistency in Conservative policy than there really was. Stursberg, *Leadership Gained*, 234; Fleming, *Near 2*, 726–27; Pickersgill, *Seeing Canada Whole*, 549–53; Bruce Hutchison to Grant Dexter, April 16, 1960; Bruce Hutchison to Victor Sifton, April 18, 1960, Hutchison Papers, I.B

122 Besides his press statement and letter to Fleming dated June 13, 1961, Coyne's other releases included statements or letters (some of them accompanied by bank documents) on June 15, 19, and 26, July 6 (two statements), 8, 10, and 11, 1961. JGDP, XII/56/C/118.2

123 *Debates*, July 5, 1961, 7563

124 Ibid., 7574–75

125 Ibid., 7589–90

126 The quotation is from Erskine May's *Parliamentary Practice* (16th edition), referred to by H.W. Herridge. In the United States, he noted, bills of attainder were unconstitutional. *Debates*, July 5, 1961, 7591–92

127 *Debates*, July 5, 1961, 7593; GTG, Memorandum To: The Prime Minister, July 15, 1959, JGDP, XII/118/F/356

128 During his appearance before the Senate committee, Coyne identified the adviser "in whom he places reliance" as the former governor of the bank, Graham Towers. *Debates*, July 5, 1961, 7592–95; *Proceedings of the Standing Committee on Banking and Commerce*, Senate of Canada, July 10, 1961, 49–50

129 "Statement by J.E. Coyne, Governor of the Bank of Canada," July 6, 1961, JGDP, XII/56/C/118.2

130 *Debates*, July 7, 1961, 7685

131 Ibid., 7693

132 Pearson insisted on answering that he did not favour the pension. Ibid., 7694–95

133 Judith Robinson, "Diefenbaker...with a difference," *Telegram*, July 10, 1961

134 *Debates*, July 7, 1961, 7707–08

135 *Globe and Mail*, June 13, 1961

136 *CAR 1961*, 18; Newman, *Renegade*, 421–22

137 JGD, "Memorandum: Re: Coyne in Senate Committee," July 12, 1961, JGDP, XII/56/C/118.2

138 "Statement by J.E. Coyne," July 13, 1961, ibid.

139 On the recommendation of the Porter Royal Commission on Banking and Finance, the Bank

of Canada Act was amended in 1967 to incorporate this understanding in law. "Statement by Louis Rasminsky, Governor of the Bank of Canada," July 31, 1961, JGDP, VI/6/231.1, 66210–213; Fleming, *Near 2*, 345–47

140 Ottawa *Journal*, July 18, 1961; Fleming, *Near 2*, 347–48

141 JGD to Elmer Diefenbaker, July 15, 1961, JGDP, V/4, 2182

142 *CAR 1961*, 70–74

143 Quoted in Smith, *Gentle Patriot*, 80–81

144 *CAR 1961*, 81–86

145 These included, in 1961, the Glassco Commission on government operations, the O'Leary Commission on publications, the McPherson Commission on transportation, the Porter Commission on banking and finance, the Hall Commission on health services, the Bladen Commission on the automotive industry, and the Gill Commission on unemployment insurance. The *Globe and Mail* likened the commissions to a psychiatrist's couch on which ministers could relieve their tensions and "go away refreshed, having banished from their minds whatever was bothering them." *Globe and Mail*, July 24, 1961

146 When he met a delegation from the Voice of Women, the prime minister pointed out to them that their anti-war campaigning mirrored Soviet propaganda, but he was also influenced by the strength of their national support. CC, 84–61, 89–61, 90–61, 91–61, 92–61, 93–61, 96–61, 98–61, July 24, August 17, 21, 22, 23, 25, and 31, September 6, 1961; Fleming, *Near 2*, 370–74; JGD to Elmer Diefenbaker, September 14, 1961, JGDP, V/4, 2213; JGD, "Memorandum: Re: Meeting with 'Voice of Women' Delegation," September 27, 1961, JGDP, XII/78/C/445

147 *CAR 1961*, 20

148 *Debates*, May 6, 1961, 4445–55

149 JGD, "Secret, Re PC party," handwritten notes, July 30, 1961, JGDP, XII/35/B/137

150 Fleming, *Near 2*, 428–30

151 On December 22 Diefenbaker received a telegram from J.M. Macdonnell regretting that he had not denied the rumours of a change in Finance, and indicating that Fleming's removal would be regarded with "positive alarm" by "leading business men." Ibid., 430–31; telegram, J.M. Macdonnell to JGD, December 22, 1961, JGDP, XII/60/C/178

152 *Telegram*, Ottawa *Citizen*, December 21, 1961; *Globe and Mail*, December 22, 1961

153 Ottawa *Citizen*, *Telegram*, December 27, 1961; Toronto *Star*, December 29, 1961; Fleming, *Near 2*, 433–37. Newman wrote in *Renegade in Power* that Fleming had only won the battle by capitulating on an expansionist, pre-election budget for 1962. Fleming described this account as "probably the one farthest removed from the truth." Newman, *Renegade*, 188–89; Fleming, *Near 2*, 434

154 Fleming, *Near 2*, 435

155 Alternatively, Fulton is placed in Health and Welfare – which would apparently have meant dropping Waldo Monteith. JGD, Memorandum (handwritten), December 27, 1961, JGDP, XII/51/C/66

156 Fleming's naiveté in the memoirs seems unusal for someone who so distrusted Diefenbaker. An alternative explanation could be that Fleming, who saw himself as the best English-speaking friend of Quebec in cabinet, realized but could not admit that he had frustrated Diefenbaker's plan and thus prevented the elevation of Noël Dorion to a senior ministry.

157 *Globe and Mail*, December 30, 1961; Ottawa *Citizen*, December 29, 1961; Toronto *Star*, December 29, 1961

158 *Debates*, February 22, 1962, 1138–41

Chapter 12 A Government Disintegrates

1 Macmillan's conversations on the subject with Kennedy were confirmed by George Drew in a confidential discussion with the British cabinet secretary, Sir Norman Brook, on May 4. Drew reported to Diefenbaker that Macmillan was convinced that "unless there could be

some form of economic and trade unity established throughout Europe within ten years, it would be impossible for NATO to stand together and Russians would be able to walk in." A strong Europe, on the other hand, "with an expanding economy working in some form of cooperative association will provide a better market for Canada, the Commonwealth and USA than would be the case if Europe and Britain were weakened through the present divisions becoming permanent." Telegram, Drew to JGD, May 5, 1961, 1690, JGDP, XII/81/D/37

2 Drew's contacts with Beaverbrook and his special interest in the views of the *Daily Express* are noted, for example, in Diefenbaker's memo of a telephone conversation with Drew on June 10, 1961, and in telegrams from London in November 1961 and April 1962. JGD, "Confidential Memorandum Re: Conversation with Hon. George Drew from London Saturday June 10, 1961..."; Drew to External, 4042 Emergency, November 11, 1961; Drew to JGD, 1564 Emergency, April 30, 1962, JGDP, XII/111/F/200; XII/81/D/37

3 Diefenbaker gave the same message, in what seemed more sarcastic terms, to the UK high commissioner three days later. The French government confirmed to Canada that it would insist on "stringent" terms for UK entry, which would include the application of the common tariff to "all countries not themselves members of the common market." JGD, "Confidential Memorandum Re: Telephone Conversation with Prime Minister Macmillan, June 9, 1961..." JGDP, XII/86/D/149; JGD, "Memorandum Re Conversation with Sir Saville Garner...June 12th 1961..."; NAR, "Memorandum for the Prime Minister: The United Kingdom and the European Common Market," June 14, 1961, ibid., XIV/8/D/15.2

4 *Sunday Telegraph,* June 11, 1961, quoted in telegram, Drew to JGD, June 11, 1961, JGDP, XII/54/C/108

5 That point was emphasized in an accompanying "Paper for Mr. Diefenbaker." The Canadian government was soon awash in documents laying out the details of current Canadian trade with the United Kingdom. In 1960 Canadian exports to the United Kingdom amounted to $915 million. About $300 million of this trade would be unaffected by application of the EEC common tariff, while another $500 million would be "especially vulnerable" through the loss of free entry or preference. But actual estimates of Canadian loss remained highly speculative and subject to exaggeration. As Duncan Sandys told Diefenbaker in July 1961, joining the Common Market "would not change the eating habits of the English people." Harold Macmillan to JGD, July 3, 1961, JGDP, XII/111/F/200; "Possible British Accession to the EEC – Trade Effects," nd, 1961, ibid., XII/81/D/37; JGD, "Conversation of the Prime Minister with the Rt. Hon. Duncan Sandys..." July 15, 1961, ibid., XIV/8/D/15.2

6 Harold Macmillan, "Paper for Mr. Diefenbaker," July 3, 1961, JGDP, XII/111/F/200

7 Robertson attended a meeting of the cabinet committee on the subject to express his opposition to the government's public line at about the same time. RBB, "Memorandum for the Prime Minister: Re: Sandys' visit next week," July 4, 1961, JGDP, XII/81/D/37; Robinson, *Diefenbaker's World,* 212–14

8 Robinson, *Diefenbaker's World,* 214–15; JGD, "Conversation of the Prime Minister with the Rt. Hon. Duncan Sandys – Ottawa – July 14, 1961," JGDP, XII/54/C/108; Fleming, *Near 2,* 387–88

9 "Message from the Rt. Hon. Harold Macmillan, M.P. to the Rt. Hon. John G. Diefenbaker, Q.C., M.P.," July 26, 1961, JGDP, XII/81/D/37

10 "Remarks by the Honourable George Hees at the Commonwealth Conference on the Question of the U.K. Move into the European Common Market," September 1961, JGDP, XII/111/F/200; Fleming, *Near 2,* 391

11 "Text of Press Communiqué issued at close of Commonwealth Economic Consultative Council Meeting in Accra, September 15, 1961," JGDP, XII/81/D/37

12 Ottawa *Citizen,* September 15, 1961; *Financial Times,* September 22, 1961. Donald Fleming denounced Young's report as Liberal propaganda, but his own account of the meetings sustains Young's interpretation. The *Financial Times* article is included in full in a dispatch from the Canadian High Commission in London to Ottawa that Diefenbaker extensively

marked. He triple-circled the description of Canadian pleadings as "violence." Fleming, *Near 2*, 389–96; telegram, London to External, 3443, September 22, 1961, JGDP, XII/81/D/37

13 JGD, "Thoughts on ECM," nd, JGDP, XII/54/C/108

14 The press comments were reported in dispatches from the Canadian High Commission in London to Ottawa. High Commission to External, 4042 Emergency, November 11, 1961, JGDP, XII/81/D/37; High Commission to External, Scan No. 46, November 13, 1961, ibid., XII/81/D/39. See also the *Globe and Mail*, November 11, 1961.

15 Drew instructed a senior officer, Benjamin Rogers, to attend the November meeting "at very short notice" in his place. Two weeks later, in a personal message to the prime minister, Drew reported that he would certainly attend Heath's next briefing "as I have finally thrown off the severe chest cold which has been bothering me for more than two weeks." JGD to high commissioner, London, PMO 106/12, November 13, 1961; Drew to JGD, 4043 Emergency, November 12, 1961; Drew to JGD, 4220, November 24, 1961, JGDP, XII/81/D/37; Robinson, *Diefenbaker's World*, 216; Benjamin Rogers to author, July 28, 1995

16 Diefenbaker's notes from an informal meeting of ministers on March 23, 1962, record criticisms of the government's stance by Churchill, Flemming, Starr, Halpenny, Walker, O'Hurley, Dinsdale, Monteith, Fairclough, and probably Nowlan. After the meeting, Ellen Fairclough wrote Diefenbaker to add her comment that the effects of British entry on Canadian exports would not be felt for ten years, "by which time we surely would have taken action to counteract them. Why knock our own blocks off over a hypothetical situation?" JGD, "Ministers' Meeting – March 23, 1962, Re Common Market"; Fairclough to JGD, March 23, 1962, JGDP, XII/54/C/108

17 Horne, *Macmillan, 1957–1986*, 447; CC, 7–63, January 29, 1963; *OC 2*, 202–06. Diefenbaker later claimed that de Gaulle insisted to him in November 1958 that Britain would not get into the Common Market and that he had reported the conversation to Macmillan, without any response. Diefenbaker said he had repeated de Gaulle's warning to the Commonwealth prime ministers at their meeting in September 1962, but Edward Heath, "flushed with anticipated success," would not believe it. Since the formal British application for entry was not made until October 1960, warning of what amounted to a French veto in 1958 seems unlikely. Such a conversation could have occurred when de Gaulle visited Canada in the spring of 1960. JGDI, December 10, 1969; *OC 2*, 205

18 Leslie Frost to JGD, July 21, 1961, JGDP, XII/61/C/189

19 Leslie Frost to JGD, November 8, 1961, Frost Papers (also quoted in Graham, *Frost*, 403)

20 He did find his appointment as a member of the Privy Council, which was made formal in December 1961, "very pleasing...more than anything else in fact." Leslie Frost to JGD, October 7, 1961, JGDP, XII/4/A/89; Graham, *Frost*, 403–05

21 Leslie Frost to JGD, February 19, 1962, JGDP, XII/12/F/395

22 Dalgleish suggested a royal commission on tax structure; and for the short term, a tax holiday for new businesses, tax incentives for research, added depreciation allowances for new capital assets produced in Canada, and a 50 percent tax reduction on profits of new export businesses. Oakley Dalgleish to JGD, February 13, 1961, JGDP, XII/89/E/23

23 Frost to JGD, February 19, 1962, JGDP, XII/12/F/395. Frost wrote again the next day to point out that the "Liberal brain trust," including Walter Gordon and Mitchell Sharp, was preparing a platform that would capitalize on the report of Gordon's royal commission on Canada's economic prospects, "which no doubt will have its own appeal. I would not underestimate this. He has already committed himself to a book and as well a number of articles and speeches which your advisers should take apart at once and study." Leslie Frost to JGD, February 20, 1962, JGDP, XII/12/F/395

24 JGD, "Strictly Confidential Memorandum," February 23, 1962, JGDP, XII/89/E/23; JGD to Leslie Frost, February 25, 1962, Frost Papers

25 He gave credit for assistance to Harry Edmison, George Gathercole, Ray Farrell, Wallace McCutcheon, and Harry Price, and noted that they made use of Dalgleish's letters and "read

Walter Gordon's book and speeches, and we are therefore indebted to him for anything that there is good in his emanations." The mention of Gordon may have been a slip, since Gordon – as Pearson's chief policy adviser and a candidate in the coming election – had already declared himself dedicated to Diefenbaker's defeat. Ten days later Frost supplied Donald Fleming with supplementary thoughts for his budget. The editor of the the *Telegram*, Burton Richardson, also gave Diefenbaker a brief, upbeat outline of an electoral program at the same time. Leslie Frost to JGD, March 23, 1962; Leslie Frost to Donald Fleming, April 4, 1962; Burt Richardson to JGD, March 28, 1962, JGDP, XII/12/F/395

26　JGD to Leslie Frost, March 24, 1962, ibid.

27　Oakley Dalgleish to JGD, April 10, 1962, JGDP, XII/89/E/23

28　Among Diefenbaker's last-moment acts were references to committee of proposals to end closure and to create an independent electoral boundaries commission. Both were promises from the 1957 campaign that had been neglected for five years; neither could be achieved in the short 1962 session. House of Commons, *Debates*, January 22, 1962, 57–75; January 23, 1962, 82–90

29　CC, 141–61, December 28, 1961; 14–62, February 6, 1962; *Debates*, February 6, 1962, 573

30　The memo is unsigned. It may have been from John Fisher or Allister Grosart. "Confidential," January 6, 1962, JGDP, XII/70/C/344

31　Fleming, *Near 2*, 472–86; *Debates*, April 10, 1962, 2688–718; *CAR 1962*, 3–9

32　Those present included Dalton Camp, Finlay MacDonald, George Hogan, Eddie Goodman, Roy Faibish, Bill Wylie, Roy Deyell, and Lowell Murray. Grosart reported the party's electoral prospects to Diefenbaker after this meeting, estimating that it had 137 safe seats and ten "probables." This was an optimistic account of what he had heard. Interview with Dalton Camp, February 4, 1969; "Notes of a Meeting – January 22, 1962: Where Do We Stand?" JGDP, XII/40/B/294.2

33　JGD to Elmer Diefenbaker, March 23, 1962, JGDP, V/4, 2427–28

34　JGD to Chief Justice C.C. Miller, March 24, 1962, JGDP, VI/126/1936.2

35　Diefenbaker's draft reply appears in the same file. Eugene Forsey to JGD, March 21, 1961, JGDP, XII/61/C/185

36　Diefenbaker used it especially when speaking to ethnic audiences and in Quebec. Among those who encouraged him to use the theme were Gordon Chown, MP, and Jack Cauley. Chown wrote that "we can push the Liberal Party out to the extreme left; hold ourselves out as the champions of competitive enterprise; and leave the New Party image in the public mind as 'left of left,' thereby implying that their political philosophy will expedite our country to the path of Communism." The Liberal candidates and advisers Diefenbaker linked to the wartime administration were Walter Gordon, Mitchell Sharp, C.M. Drury, Maurice Lamontagne, and Tom Kent. Only Sharp had actually been a civil servant in that period. Gordon Chown to JGD, May 26, 1961; Jack Cauley to JGD, December 29, 1961, JGDP, VI/93/1434C, VI/60/432; *Debates*, January 22 and 23, 1962, 73, 85–89; *Globe and Mail*, January 25, March 9, 1962

37　Hamilton's committee consisted of Gordon Churchill, Don Johnson, Merril Menzies, Roy Faibish, and John Fisher. Alvin Hamilton to JGD, September 21, 1961, JGDP, OF/1315/Election; Carrigan, *Canadian Party Platforms*, 261–70, 286; *CAR 1962*, 10–12

38　"Itinerary – Prime Minister John Diefenbaker – 1962," JGDP, VI/96/1509.1, 82484–97, 82579–93, 82619, 82629–39; ibid., 1509.2, 82786–91, 82861–67

39　The American record of the incident is contained in a seven-page letter from Merchant to the acting secretary of state, George Ball. Merchant delivered the letter by courier to Ball "in the belief that you will want to discuss its contents with the President at the earliest possible opportunity." Livingston Merchant to George Ball, May 5, 1962, Kennedy Papers, NSF: Canada: General: Rostow Memorandum 05/16/61 and Related Materials, 05/61–05/63, Mandatory Review Cases NLK–94–9, NLK–94–11

40　McGeorge Bundy, "Personal – Eyes Only Memorandum for...George W. Ball, the Under

Secretary of State," May 8, 1962; telegrams, Ball to ambassador, Ottawa, May 8, 1962, 1080, 1081, Kennedy Papers, NSF: Canada: Rostow Memorandum 05/16/61 and Related Materials, 05/61–05/63, Mandatory Review Cases NLK–94–9, NLK–94–11

41 Telegram, Merchant to acting secretary of state, May 9, 1962, 1148, Kennedy Papers, NSF: Canada: Rostow Memorandum...Mandatory Review Case NLK–94–11

42 Robinson diary, May 9, 1962, quoted in Robinson, *Diefenbaker's World*, 268–69

43 Merchant to secretary of state, May 13, 1962, 1164, Kennedy Papers, NSF: Canada: Rostow Memorandum...Mandatory Review Case NLK–94–11

44 This was not accurate. At least three others on the prime minister's staff – the unnamed aide who delivered the memo, his secretary, Marion Wagner, and his foreign affairs adviser, Basil Robinson – knew of it; and Robinson had also discussed the matter confidentially with Norman Robertson, Robert Bryce, and the Canadian ambassador in Washington, Ed Ritchie. Robinson, *Diefenbaker's World*, 267–70

45 Ibid., 270

46 Fleming, *Near 2*, 487–501; *OC 3*, 117–25; CC, 49–62, 50–62, May 1 and 2, 1962

47 *OC 3*, 124–25

48 Robinson, *Diefenbaker's World*, 266

49 JGD, Memorandum: "To do – Sunday, May 20, 1962," JGDP, XIV/9/D/17

50 Neil S. Crawford, "Memorandum to the Prime Minister," May 3, 1962, JGDP, XII/66/C/290.2

51 *OC 3*, 127–28; Fleming, *Near 2*, 502–03

52 Diefenbaker responded to the strippers: "I was raised on a homestead in Saskatchewan; that is why I know what those things are." *CAR 1962*, 16–17

53 Charles Lynch, quoted in *CAR 1962*, 17

54 *Globe and Mail*, May 7, 12, 14, 28, 30, and 31, June 4, 5, 6, and 8, 1962

55 Ibid., June 8, 1962; *CAR 1962*, 18–19

56 Walter Gray, "The Week That Counts," *Globe and Mail*, June 11, 1962; *CAR 1962*, 19–21

57 *Globe and Mail*, June 15, 1962

58 Ibid., June 5, 1962

59 Montreal *Gazette*, May 28, 1962

60 For the results, see *CAR 1962*, 22–27; the reference to Macdonald is in the *Globe and Mail*, June 22, 1962.

61 "Daily Transactions Affecting Exchange Fund Owned Reserves," August 23, 1962, JGDP, XII/107/F/147.2; Fleming, *Near 2*, 516–20; *OC 3*, 131–34; CC, 57A–62, June 20–24, 1962. There were eight separate meetings of cabinet, plus meetings of the special committee. No secretaries attended, and no records were kept, until Fleming presented Bryce with a brief statement on the emergency program after the last meeting, held at the prime minister's home on Sunday, June 24, 1962. This statement alone appears in the official record.

62 *OC 3*, 121

63 Ibid., 132–33. Fleming's view was that the exchange reserves "could not be expected to survive more than a few days." He reported that the exchange fund reached its lowest point of $1100 million on June 24. Fleming, *Near 2*, 517

64 CC, 57A–62, June 20–24, 1962; *OC 3*, 132–36; Fleming, *Near 2*, 518–24; *CAR 1962*, 28–29, 184–87

65 Leslie Frost to JGD, June 22, 1962, JGDP, XII/61/C/189

66 Telegrams, Leslie Frost to JGD, June 25, 1962, ibid.

67 On July 2 Macmillan wrote again to express satisfaction that the financial community had acted rapidly to assist Canada, to note that Britain had provided one-third of Canada's $300 million draw on IMF funds as well as $100 million in bilateral credits, and to offer a gentle reminder that Diefenbaker had said that the import surcharges would be withdrawn as soon as possible. Harold Macmillan to JGD, June 24, July 2, 1962, JGDP, XII/8/A/282.3

68 Davie Fulton to JGD, June 29, 1962, JGDP, XII/61/C/190

69 Interview with E.D. Fulton, September 24, 1993

70   W.F.W. Neville, "Memorandum of a meeting with Hon. Gordon Churchill, 7 July 1970," 4

71   Churchill was not precise about when Diefenbaker first raised the matter of resignation, although he seemed to place it in the first six weeks after the election. Churchill described this period as "the most difficult of my life," when the prime minister was still "visibly shattered" by the election results. Churchill recalled that Diefenbaker talked "almost every other day" about resignation, "and several times in cabinet." W.F.W. Neville, "Memorandum of a meeting with Hon. Gordon Churchill..." 4–5

72   Oakley Dalgleish to JGD, July 6, 1962, JGDP, XII/56/C/122

73   *OC 3*, 139–40

74   Frost also sent a copy of his letter to Dalgleish, noting that he had "endeavoured to put things on the line and I hope it works, particularly for his sake to say nothing of the country." Leslie Frost to JGD, July 12, 1962, JGDP, XII/61/C/189; Leslie Frost to Oakley Dalgleish, July 12, 1962, Frost Papers

75   JGD, "Memorandum," July 16, 1962, JGDP, XII/61/C/189

76   Diefenbaker had telephone conversations on July 17 and 19 with Frost and on July 21 with Dalgleish; Frost recorded a summary of his reasons for refusal in a memo headed "Don't want to!" and dated August 1962. JGD, "Note," July 21, 1962; "Memorandum," July 21, 1962, ibid.; Leslie Frost, "Don't want to!" August 1962, Frost Papers

77   Leslie Frost to JGD, July 18, 1962; JGD, "Note," July 21, 1962, JGDP, XII/65/C/261; Leslie Frost, "The Diefenbaker Days," 13–15, Frost Papers; Graham, *Frost*, 407–08; *OC 3*, 139–40

78   JGD to Elmer Diefenbaker, July 14, 1962, JGDP, V/5, 2549–50

79   *OC 3*, 140–41; JGD to Elmer Diefenbaker, July 26, 1962, JGDP, V/5, 2564–65

80   *OC 3*, 141. The cabinet met at Sussex Drive from July 25 until it resumed meeting on Parliament Hill on August 29.

81   Marjorie (Bunny) Pound, Oral History, July 7, 1989, JGDP, XVIII/OH/83.3

82   In particular, Alvin Hamilton had been hospitalized for several weeks after the election. JGD to Elmer Diefenbaker, August 11 and 14, 1962, JGDP, V/5, 2596–97, 2598–99

83   Quoted in Fleming, *Near 2*, 526

84   Ibid., 526–27; *OC 3*, 142

85   JGD, "Memorandum Re: Discussion with Hon. E. Davie Fulton, Tuesday, August 7, 1962," JGDP, XII/61/C/190; interview with Hon. E.D. Fulton, September 24, 1993; *OC 3*, 143–44

86   *OC 3*, 141–48; *CAR 1962*, 31–33; Fleming, *Near 2*, 527–31; Conrad, *Nowlan*, 266–68

87   Sévigny, *This Game*, 225

88   *CAR 1962*, 32

89   *OC 3*, 141

90   Robinson was puzzled why, if Diefenbaker was convinced that de Gaulle would veto Britain's application, he spent so much energy opposing it. *OC 2*, 92–93, 205; Horne, *Macmillan 1957–1986*, 355–57; Robinson, *Diefenbaker's World*, 279–82; CC, 73–62, 73A–62, 74–62, 75–62, 80–62, August 30 and 31, September 3, 5, and 21, 1962

91   JGD, "Memorandum for Wednesday August 8," August 5, 1962; JGD, "Memorandum to: Hon. M.W. McCutcheon, C.B.E.," August 25, 1962; MWM, "Memorandum to: The Prime Minister," September 4, 1962; JGDP, XII/51/C/66; XII/65/C/261

92   *Debates*, September 27, 1962, 7–9; *OC 3*, 148–50

93   Smith, *Gentle Patriot*, 109

94   JGD to Leslie Frost, October 7, 1962, JGDP, XII/61/C/189

95   *OC 3*, 150–51; Conrad, *Nowlan*, 272–76

96   Sévigny, *This Game*, 232

97   Interview with Hon. E.D. Fulton, September 24, 1993; W.F.W. Neville, "Memorandum of a meeting with Hon. Gordon Churchill, 7 July 1970"

98   W.F.W. Neville, "Memorandum of a meeting with Hon. Gordon Churchill..." Sévigny also commented on this "drinking group," whose personally labelled bottles were kept in a cupboard and "reserved for the owner's particular use." Sévigny, *This Game*, 227

99   HCG, "Memorandum for: The Prime Minister," October 22, 1962, JGDP, XII/88/D/204;
     Reeves, *President Kennedy*, 333–425

100 Quoted in Robinson, *Diefenbaker's World*, 284

101 Ibid., 284–85; Nash, *Kennedy and Diefenbaker*, 181

102 Robinson, *Diefenbaker's World*, 285

103 Horne, *Macmillan 1957–1986*, 362–67; Nash, *Kennedy and Diefenbaker*, 182

104 The words are those of Macmillan's diary, commenting on the American ambassador's briefing
     on Monday morning. The ambassador, David Bruce, had been told by the State Department
     to carry a revolver that day, which he did. Horne, *Macmillan 1957–1986*, 364–65

105 HCG, "Memorandum for: The Prime Minister," October 22, 1962, JGDP, XII/88/D/204

106 Ibid.

107 Diefenbaker noted in handwriting at the top of the memo: "Seen first at meeting with Mr
     Merchant and ministers 5.30 pm. Delivered to me at home at 7 pm *after* broadcast of Pres
     Kennedy." Robinson confirms from a confidential source (perhaps Bryce or Robertson) that
     Diefenbaker did not receive the memo before Merchant's visit, although Bryce had seen it
     and did not think the proposal was acceptable. Diefenbaker claims in the memoirs that he
     talked to the president some time after meeting with Merchant and engaged in an argument
     over UN onsite inspection, the alert status of NORAD units, and the absence of consulta-
     tion. But the conversation (if there was one) did not, apparently, occur that day, as
     Diefenbaker implies. HCG, "Memorandum for: The Prime Minister/Cuba," JGDP,
     XII/88/D/204; Robinson, *Diefenbaker's World*, 286–87; *OC 3*, 82–83

108 This account is based on reports of the meeting by Douglas Harkness and Livingston
     Merchant; Merchant spoke later about the meeting with Basil Robinson. D.S. Harkness, "The
     Nuclear Arms Question and the Political Crisis which Arose from It in January and February,
     1963," August 19–27, 1963, Harkness Papers; Livingston T. Merchant to Secretary of State
     Rusk and the Under Secretary of State (Ball), memorandum, nd, 441, *FRUS, 1961–1963*,
     1190–91; Robinson, *Diefenbaker's World*, 285–86

109 John F. Kennedy to JGD, October 22, 1962, JGDP, XII/88/D/204

110 "Memorandum from Livingston T. Merchant to Secretary of State Rusk..." nd, 441, *FRUS
     1961–1963*, 1190–91; Robinson, *Diefenbaker's World*, 285–86; Harkness, "Nuclear Arms
     Question," 7–9

111 "Notes used by Prime Minister for address in the House on the Kennedy announcement of
     the 'quarantine' of Cuba – October 22, 1962," JGDP, XII/56/C/120; *Debates*, October 22,
     1962, 805–07

112 Ghent-Mallet and Munton, "Confronting Kennedy," 85

113 "Memorandum...Merchant to...Rusk," nd, 441, *FRUS, 1961–1963*, 1190

114 DEF CON 5 was normal; DEF CON 3 indicated "very serious international tension"; DEF
     CON 1 meant war. The Canadian equivalent of DEF CON 3 was known as READY. Harkness,
     "Nuclear Arms Question," 9–10; Ghent-Mallet and Munton, "Confronting Kennedy," 86

115 Harkness, "Nuclear Arms Question," 10; *Globe and Mail*, January 2, 1963

116 Harkness, "Nuclear Arms Question," 11; CC, 93–62, October 23, 1962

117 The only limitations short of full alert were that no personnel on leave were recalled, but no
     active personnel were granted leave. Harkness, "Nuclear Arms Question," 11–12

118 Diefenbaker's memoirs leave the impression that the conversation took place on the evening
     of October 22, which seems wrong. Robinson places it in the late afternoon of October 23,
     but confirms the substance of Diefenbaker's account from notes taken by Diefenbaker's
     secretary, Bunny Pound. *OC 3*, 82–83; Robinson, *Diefenbaker's World*, 288

119 Harkness, "Nuclear Arms Question," 12–13. Whether, or to what extent, Diefenbaker was
     aware of the unauthorized involvement of Canadian forces in the military alert is not clear.
     Bryce believed (according to Robinson) that "Diefenbaker had a pretty good idea of what
     was going on and preferred to let it happen in a less than formal way." In his memoirs,
     Diefenbaker claimed that he did not believe "the popular notion that...Mr. Harkness, under

the influence of the Canadian military and the United States Pentagon, engaged in a clandestine authorization of a full alert on 22 October." Canadian military activity, at sea as well as in NORAD, was more extensive and more closely integrated with American operations than even Harkness recorded; and there seems little doubt that Diefenbaker had an inadequate understanding of the degree or consequences of the operational integration resulting from the existence of the NORAD and NATO commands. These issues are examined in detail in Haydon, *1962 Cuban Missile Crisis*. See also *OC 3*, 88; Robinson, *Diefenbaker's World*, 288.

120 Robinson adds that Diefenbaker came to Pearson's office to seek his advice, and agreed that Pearson should ask questions in the House to elicit the prime minister's jointly prepared response. Diefenbaker, however, opened the day with a statement that incorporated Pearson's advice without acknowledgment, and without giving Pearson a chance to speak. Pearson's secretary told Robinson that he was "angry about being double-crossed and his regard for Diefenbaker sank even further." *Debates*, October 23, 1962, 821; Robinson, *Diefenbaker's World*, 289, 334

121 CBC transcript, nd, JGDP, XII/56/C/120

122 *Debates*, October 25, 1962, 911–13; the draft texts, with Diefenbaker's revisions, are in JGDP, XII/56/C/120.

123 *Washington Post*, October 27, 1962

124 Reeves, *President Kennedy*, 410–26; Robinson, *Diefenbaker's World*, 290–91

125 Orme Dier to Basil Robinson, January 25, 1987, quoted in Robinson, *Diefenbaker's World*, 291–92

126 Reeves, *President Kennedy*, 410–26

127 "Statement by the Prime Minister, Sunday, October 28, 1962," JGDP, XII/56/C/120

128 Harkness, "Nuclear Arms Question," 13

129 Ibid., 13–14; CC, 96–62, October 30, 1962; *OC 3*, 90, 93–94; Robinson, *Diefenbaker's World*, 297–98. Diefenbaker suggested that the renewed negotiations gave Canada the chance to "raise questions concerning the working of NORAD" and the meaning of consultation in periods of crisis, but there is no indication that these issues were discussed. The standby proposal for storing warheads in the United States was outlined in a memo from Green to Diefenbaker on October 26, and suggested that "nuclear warheads would be brought into Canada only on a finding by Cabinet that an emergency exists and a concomitant request to the United States Government to provide the warheads." HCG, "Memorandum for: The Prime Minister: Provision of Nuclear Warheads," JGDP, XIV/17/E/222.9

130 Harkness, "Nuclear Arms Question," 14–17; Robinson, *Diefenbaker's World*, 298–300; *OC 3*, 106–07

131 *Globe and Mail*, November 9, 1962; Toronto *Star*, November 9, 1962

132 George Hogan to JGD, November 8, 1962, JGDP, XII/62/C/215

133 George Hogan, "The Conservative Party and the United States," November 8, 1962, ibid. The confusion of Diefenbaker's political constituency was illustrated by the (Liberal) Toronto *Star*'s editorial, "Ready, Aye, Ready," which congratulated the prime minister for having done none of the "foolish and mischievous" things that Hogan suggested. Toronto *Star*, November 9, 1962

134 JGD, "Strictly Confidential Memorandum: Re: Telephone Conversation with George Hogan, Friday Nov 9th. 1962 Regarding Speech in Toronto Nov. 8th. – Cuba &C"; unsigned handwritten memos, JGDP, XII/62/C/215; *Debates*, November 9, 1962, 1451

135 Harkness, "Nuclear Arms Question," 16–17

136 W.W. Butterworth to Department of State, December 17, 1962, 442, *FRUS, 1961–1963*, 1191–92; O.W. Dier, "Call by Ambassador Butterworth on the Prime Minister," December 18, 1962, JGDP, XIV/19/F/5

137 *OC 3*, 94–95; Harold Macmillan to JGD, November 30, 1962; Derick Amory to JGD, December 5, 1962, JGDP, XII/8/A/282.3

138 The phrase was provided to Diefenbaker by his new executive assistant, Burt Richardson,

who had joined him from the *Telegram* to replace John Fisher – who was about to become commissioner for the 1967 centennial. Richardson preceded Diefenbaker to Nassau by one day and reassured the prime minister in a telephone message: "Regardless of what the doctrinal professors of the State Department and External Affairs say, Kennedy is anxious to improve relations with you." There was scant evidence for this belief. *OC 3*, 95; B.T. Richardson, "Memorandum to: The Prime Minister," December 20, 1962, JGDP, XIV/19/F/5

139 Diefenbaker said in the memoirs that he told Kennedy he would soon have proposals to discuss with him. The official Canadian minute of the meeting does not mention the subject, but Diefenbaker's own memorandum for file, written in Nassau, does so. There is no record of any response from the president. *OC 3*, 98–99; "Bahamas Meetings – December 21–22, 1962, Specific points discussed with President Kennedy at Luncheon Meeting December 21"; JGD, "Memorandum Re: Discussions with President Kennedy, Nassau, Bahamas – December 21, 1962," December 23, 1962, JGDP, XII/66/C/291

140 Diefenbaker's own records of the meetings, along with the delegation's memoranda and draft communiqués, appear in JGDP, XIV/9/D/17, XII/66/C/291, and XII/113/F/222.

141 JGD, "Draft statement on meeting in Nassau with President Kennedy and Prime Minister Macmillan," January 21, 1963, JGDP, XII/66/C/291; *OC 3*, 105–06; *Debates*, January 21, 1963, 2898–99

142 JGD to Elmer Diefenbaker, January 2, 1963, JGDP, V/5, 2724. In mid-January Olive was examined at the Montreal Neurological Institute and provided with a back brace. JGD to Elmer Diefenbaker, January 11, 1963, ibid., 2725

143 Robinson, *Diefenbaker's World*, 302–03

144 Transcript of a press conference with General Lauris S. Norstad, January 3, 1963, JGDP, VI/2/108 (Norstad)

145 *Le Devoir*, January 5, 1963

146 Harkness, "Nuclear Arms Question," 18

147 Ibid., 19

148 English, *Worldly*, 249–51; Pearson, *Mike 3*, 69–72; Robinson, *Diefenbaker's World*, 304

149 Harkness, "Nuclear Arms Question," 20. Diefenbaker offered a variation of the point to Finlay Macdonald in a telephone conversation on January 14: "In 1878 Macdonald was in the same position. The Grits announced on a Thursday that they were in favour of free trade. Sir John changed his speech around and went to the country...I am trying to work out a Declaration of National Idealism somewhat as I made at the conclusion of my Bill of Rights speech – 'I am a Canadian...' About 8 lines." On the other hand, Diefenbaker recorded another telephone conversation with John Pallett on the same day in which he blamed Norstad for his indecision: "We would have made an announcement if it had not been for Norstad. There is American domination again. The attitude Kennedy took to Macmillan in the Bahamas was simply to push him." JGD, "Conversation with Finlay Macdonald," January 14, 1963; JGD, "Telephone conversation with John Pallett," January 14, 1963, JGDP, XII/71/C/354; VII/73/A/610.4

150 E.A. Goodman to JGD, January 15, 1963, JGDP, XII/71/C/354; Goodman, *Life*, 94–101; *OC 3*, 153–55. Diefenbaker had the chutzpah to declare in his memoirs that he was "entirely satisfied" with the defence resolution and that he agreed with Goodman's approach to it. But he added delphically: "It is of significance that Goodman was John Bassett's lawyer and George Hees's principal backer, a powerful man within the Toronto Tory hierarchy with a considerable influence over Ontario's Premier, John Robarts."

151 Harkness, "Nuclear Arms Question," 21–23

152 Ibid., 23–24

153 Fleming, *Near 2*, 581–82; Harkness, "Nuclear Arms Question," 26–29. Fleming described it as "a momentous document," and prided himself that he had "kept the original in a secret place these twenty years."

154 Fleming, *Near 2*, 583. Harkness's account is generally similar, although he adds some personal exchanges not reported by Fleming. Fleming suggests that there was no further discussion of the memo, while Harkness recalls that cabinet discussed it the next morning in the absence of the prime minister and that the "great majority" of ministers accepted it. When that was reported to Diefenbaker by Fleming, he maintained his defiance. Harkness, "Nuclear Arms Question," 29–31

155 Ibid., 32

156 Fleming, *Near 2*, 583–84; Robinson, *Diefenbaker's World*, 156; *Debates*, January 25, 1963, 3125–37

157 Harkness, "Nuclear Arms Question," 32–36

158 *Globe and Mail*, Ottawa *Citizen*, January 26, 1963

159 Harkness, "Nuclear Arms Question," 35–44; *Debates*, January 28, 29, 1963, 3157–58, 3203–06

160 Fleming, *Near 2*, 592–94

161 "United States Information Service Special: United States and Canadian Negotiations Regarding Nuclear Weapons," January 30, 1963, JGDP, VII/75/A/612; Robinson, *Diefenbaker's World*, 306–09

162 NAR, "Memorandum for the Prime Minister," January 30, 1963, JGDP, XII/104/F/100; Robinson, *Diefenbaker's World*, 306–07

163 Fleming, *Near 2*, 588–89

164 Ibid., 589; Harkness, "Nuclear Arms Question," 46

165 *Debates*, January 31, 1963, 3289–305, 3313–28; Harkness, "Nuclear Arms Question," 46–47; Fleming, *Near 2*, 589–90. Under House procedures there was no appeal against Speaker's rulings, but the three opposition parties combined to defeat the government by 122–104 and to overturn the rule.

166 *Debates*, January 31, 1963, 3313–28; Harkness, "Nuclear Arms Question," 47–48

167 Telegram, Canadian Embassy, Washington, to External Affairs, 351 emergency, February 1, 1963, JGDP, VII/75/A/612; Washington *Post*, New York *Times*, January 31, 1963. The Bundy story became the official American line on February 7, when Bundy telephoned the Canadian ambassador, Charles Ritchie, to say that "the President knew nothing in advance about the State Department release of January 30 which triggered the currrent controversy. Bundy said 'it was a case of stupidity and the stupidity was mine.'" A memorandum from Bundy to Kennedy on February 14, 1963, confirms this, speaking of "my obvious error in giving telephone clearance, even under the pressure of time, without giving you a whack at it." Ross Campbell for NAR, "Memorandum for the Minister," February 7, 1963, JGDP, XIV/9/D/17; McGeorge Bundy, "Memorandum for the President," February 14, 1963, Kennedy Papers, NSF: Canada: General: 02/01/63–02/14/63, Mandatory Review Case NLK–87–215

168 Harkness, "Nuclear Arms Question," 48–51. According to Harkness, the nine were Balcer, Fleming, Hugh John Flemming, Halpenny, Harkness, Hees, McCutcheon, Nowlan, and Sévigny.

169 Ibid., 51–52; Fleming, *Near 2*, 594–95

170 Harkness, "Nuclear Arms Question," 52

171 The quotation is from a memorandum by Carlyle Allison, recording the events of the weekend, which he sent much later to Diefenbaker. Carlyle Allison to JGD, April 26, 1971, JGDP, XIV/9/D/17

172 Harkness, "Nuclear Arms Question," 52–53; *OC 3*, 5–6. In the memoirs, Diefenbaker mentions only that "a prominent journalist" had baited Harkness. The prime minister's informant was probably Carlyle Allison, who also provided Diefenbaker with the tip about further resignations. Diefenbaker was "effusively" thankful for the information. Carlyle Allison to JGD, April 26, 1971, JGDP, XIV/9/D/17

173 *OC 3*, 160. The account that follows is drawn chiefly from the memoirs, Diefenbaker's notes made during the meeting, another (and fuller) handwritten summary (perhaps by Gordon Churchill), Harkness's essay, Fleming's detailed record, and Patrick Nicholson's *Vision* (which

was based on copious leakage). There were no officials present, and no formal record was kept.

174 Peter Newman gave that version of the story from his cabinet sources. Newman, *Renegade*, 475

175 *OC 3*, 160–64; JGD, "Meeting, Feb 3/63" (handwritten notes, including Bell's draft of cabinet resolution), JGDP, XIV/17/E/222.12; "Meeting of Ministers, February 3rd, 1962" (sic) (handwritten notes, unsigned), ibid., XIV/17/E/222.8; Harkness, "Nuclear Arms Question," 54–59; Fleming, *Near 2*, 597–601; Nicholson, *Vision*, 230–36; Douglas S. Harkness to JGD, February 3, 1963 (and covering "Memorandum to the Prime Minister"), JGDP, XIV/17/E/222.12. Diefenbaker told Fleming that Fulton made a second visit that night (which Fulton denies) to tout his own qualifications as prime minister. Two documents in the prime minister's files suggest that there was only one visit, by Fulton and Hees together. JGD, "Saturday, February 2, 1963" (sic), February 10, 1963; "Chronology of Events re Crisis," nd, JGDP, XIV/17/E/222.11; XIV/14/E/143

176 Fleming, *Near 2*, 601. Fleming's doubts about who controlled the succession were sound. Once Diefenbaker had resigned, the selection of a new prime minister would lie with the governor general, whose duty would be to find a candidate most likely to command support in the House. He was not obliged to consult Diefenbaker, and would almost certainly have sought advice from other ministers who were opposed to Fleming. The most likely temporary favourite seemed to be Nowlan.

177 CC, 10–63, February 4, 1963; Fleming, *Near 2*, 601–02; *OC 3*, 165

178 *Debates*, February 4, 1963, 3377, 3395–409; *CAR 1963*, 299–301

179 Nicholson, *Vision*, 227–30, 236

180 Michael Wardell, "Chateau Laurier. February 6, 1963," JGDP, XIV/9/D/17

181 Nicholson, *Vision*, 239

182 *Debates*, February 4, 1963, 3410–14

183 Wardell, "Chateau Laurier," JGDP, XIV/9/D/17

184 Nicholson, *Vision*, 242–46. Wardell's account from Robert Thompson was not inconsistent, although Wardell heard it only after the government defeat. Nicholson's remarkable part in this affair is explained by Diefenbaker as the result of his ambition for a senatorship, which he now hoped to secure from a new prime minister as the reward for his king-making role. The prospect of an appointment under Diefenbaker had certainly been discussed, and Nicholson's name went before cabinet at the meeting in September 1962 when Grattan O'Leary and Allister Grosart were made senators. Nicholson's appointment, however, was not confirmed. Diefenbaker wrote that "he would have received this elevation in due course." His disenchantment may have followed that disappointment. Wardell, "Chateau Laurier," JGDP, XIV/9/D/17; *OC 3*, 166; CC, 82–62, September 24, 1962

185 "Chronology of events re crisis," JGDP, XIV/14/E/143; Nicholson, *Vision*, 247–49

186 Nicholson, *Vision*, 249–50; Fleming, *Near 2*, 604–05

187 *Debates*, February 5, 1963, 3431

188 Ibid., 3438–48

189 Nicholson, *Vision*, 256–60; Fleming, *Near 2*, 607

190 *Globe and Mail*, February 6, 1963

191 *Telegram*, February 6, 1963

192 The account is by Dalton Camp, quoted in Stursberg, *Leadership Lost*, 72

193 The account of the caucus meeting is based on *OC 3*, 171–72; Harkness, "Nuclear Arms Question," 68–71; Fleming, *Near 2*, 609–14; Nicholson, *Vision*, 261–63; Stursberg, *Leadership Lost*, 71–77; *Globe and Mail*, Toronto *Star*, February 7, 1963. The reports vary somewhat in detail and chronology, but are consistent in their accounts of the powerful mood of the occasion. Harkness wrote that the meeting "was an outstanding example of the working of mass psychology and the influence of crowd emotion to cause men to agree to a course of action which they knew to be wrong and which they had previously decided against. It was again an

example of a failure in human courage when the pressure was extreme. Had the half dozen or more ministers who had decided to resign done so, I believe the Caucus would have seen the impossibility of the situation and agreed to Diefenbaker resigning."

Chapter 13 A Leader at Bay

1   "The Sacrifice Was Too Great," *Telegram*, February 7, 1963
2   "A Matter of Morality," *Globe and Mail*, February 8, 1963
3   Wallace McCutcheon to JGD, February 6, 1963, JGDP, XIV/E/222.10 Defence (Haslam). The concluding warning proved empty. There were no further negotiations with the United States on warheads during the election campaign. On February 11 George Nowlan established the same position in public, telling the Halifax *Chronicle Herald* that he would "quit the cabinet immediately if an anti-American election program were presented by his party."
4   E.A. Goodman to JGD, February 5, 1963, JGDP, OF/1326/Ontario–Political 1963
5   Stursberg, *Leadership Lost*, 78–79; Goodman, *Life*, 102–03
6   Stursberg, *Leadership Lost*, 80–85; Sévigny, *This Game*, 284–86. Hees must have been subject to further persuasion during the week. Richard Bell told Stursberg: "I heard that John Bassett threatened to expose him with something that was subsequently exposed. I was told soon afterwards that there was this scandal in the background of which I then knew nothing. This story moved around amongst ministers, idle gossip, no proof, no nothing. Frankly none of us believed that George would have gone out except under very heavy, almost irresistible, pressure." The reference was to Hees's involvement with Gerda Munsinger, which was known to the RCMP security service and probably to Diefenbaker and Fulton. Diefenbaker later believed that Bassett also knew the story and had threatened Hees that he would spill it if Hees did not resign. Bassett denied the accusation. Diefenbaker makes only veiled reference to this story in his memoirs.

> During the 1963 campaign, I was asked over and over again: "Why did George Hees resign?" "What happened between the Wednesday, when he came out of the caucus and announced to the press, 'We're all together,' and Saturday morning when he resigned?" I could have told the Canadian people, and possibly I should have. I have said it was an error, not of the head but of the heart. Had I revealed what I knew, this would have brought harm to the innocent members of families. Prime Ministers, according to the late Earl Attlee, have to be butchers; I never reached the point where I could do anything that might bring harm or hurt to the innocent. Sir John Macdonald once said, "Be to our faults a little blind, and to our virtues always kind."

There is nothing in the papers to suggest that Diefenbaker had any proof of his implied accusation. Stursberg, *Leadership Lost*, 79–80, 86; *OC 3*, 177

7   JGD, Memorandum, February 18, 1963, JGDP, XIV/E/222.10 Defence (Haslam). Sévigny's account is consistent with this story. Burt Richardson reports that he had been warned earlier by Hees's executive assistant, Mel Jack, "that something was going on," but he may or may not have told the prime minister what to expect. *OC 3*, 174–75; Stursberg, *Leadership Lost*, 83–85; Sévigny, *This Game*, 285
8   Stursberg, *Leadership Lost*, 83–87. Sévigny had a sarcastic comment about others who had not resigned: "There were a lot of cabinet ministers resigning each night around 11 o'clock, after the tenth whiskey. One of them was McCutcheon. The next morning he would appear with his face red as a beet and carry on. He resigned more often at night than he did in the morning. Many ministers talked about resigning, some of whom denied it since, but I know damn well that they did. One of them was Léon Balcer." Ibid., 87
9   JGD to Elmer Diefenbaker, February 8, 1963, JGDP, V/5, 2758
10 Helen Brunt to Olive and John, nd, JGDP, V/28, 18670–72
11 JGD to Elmer Diefenbaker, February 20, 1963, JGDP, V/5, 2793–94

12 JGD to Elmer Diefenbaker, February 22, 1963, ibid., 2795

13 Press release, January 14, 1963; Dalton Camp to JGD, nd, unsigned, JGDP, IX/38/B/87.1; XII/97/F/37

14 George Hogan to JGD, February 20, 1963, JGDP, OF/765

15 *OC 3*, 178–79

16 *CAR 1963*, 303

17 *OC 3*, 178–79

18 *Newsweek*, February 18, 1963

19 Ibid., 33

20 Dalton Camp, memo to constituency presidents, February 13, 1963, JGDP, VII/291/F/48

21 *OC 3*, 107

22 "Telegram from the Embassy in Canada to the Department of State," February 3, 1963, 445, *FRUS, 1961–1963*, 1196–99

23 W. Walton Butterworth to William R. Tyler, February 2, 1963, Kennedy Papers, NSF: Canada: Rostow Memorandum...Mandatory Review Case NLK–94–11

24 Ibid.

25 Toronto *Star, Telegram*, and Winnipeg *Tribune*, February 25, 1963; Toronto *Star*, February 26, 1963

26 W. Keith Welsh, MD, and T. Albert Crowther, MB, "To whom it may concern," February 19, 1963, JGDP, VII/291/F/55; Winnipeg *Free Press*, March 1, 1963

27 *OC 3*, 178, 182

28 Calgary *Herald*, February 25, 1963; Montreal *Star*, March 1, 1963; Prince Albert *Herald*, March 2, 1963; *OC 3*, 183–86. In the memoirs Diefenbaker notes that "my message throughout was consistently pro-Canadian; charges that I was on an anti-American rampage were patently false. Indeed, for the reasons earlier explained, I did not give the weight it deserved to United States interference in our affairs."

29 *Globe and Mail*, March 4, 1963. The main defence portion of the speech was transmitted to the State Department and the White House from the Ottawa embassy the same day. In his covering letter, Butterworth quoted Diefenbaker's assertion that "we shall not have Canada used as a storage dump for nuclear weapons." Telegram, Ottawa to secretary of state, 1124, March 4, 1963, Kennedy Papers, NSF: Canada: General

30 *Globe and Mail*, March 4, 1963

31 Winnipeg *Free Press*, March 4, 1963

32 *OC 3*, 188–89. See also English, *Worldly*, 262; LaMarsh, *Memoirs*, 36–44.

33 In March the State Department told the White House that a Canadian Gallup Poll showed that 54 percent of Canadians believed the prestige of (and respect for) the United States in Canada had grown in the previous year, whereas only 20 percent felt that way in polls conducted in 1957 and 1961. The Canadian Institute of Public Opinion explained that they "believed the results are largely a reflection of President Kennedy's actions regarding Cuba and his personal popularity." William H. Brubeck, "Memorandum for Mr. McGeorge Bundy, The White House," March 15, 1963, S/S 3942, Kennedy Papers, NSF: Canada: General

34 In January 1963 Gallup showed the Liberals at 47 percent, the Tories at 32 percent, the NDP at 10 percent, Social Credit and others at 11 percent. By March the standings were Liberals, 41 percent; Tories, 32 percent; NDP, 11 percent; Socred and others, 16 percent. In early April support for the Liberals and the Tories remained as in March, while NDP support had grown to 14 percent and Social Credit/other had fallen to 13 percent. On March 8 Daniel Johnson told Diefenbaker that "Réal's support is at its highest peak right now; a vote tomorrow would return 50–55 Socreds." Another poll published by the *Telegram* on March 30 showed the Liberals and Conservatives in virtually a dead heat nationally (at 38 to 36 percent), with wide regional variations. *CAR 1963*, 34–35; Daniel Johnson to JGD, March 8, 1963, JGDP, XII/115/F/281

35 English, *Worldly*, 263–64

36 Theodore Draper, "McNamara's Peace," *New York Review of Books*, May 11, 1995, 7–11, esp. 8; McNamara and Diefenbaker, quoted in Nash, *Kennedy and Diefenbaker*, 292–93; Lyon, *Canada in World Affairs*, 202–07

37 Nash, *Kennedy and Diefenbaker*, 278–79

38 McGeorge Bundy, "Memorandum from the President's Special Assistant for National Security Affairs (Bundy) to Secretary of State Rusk and Secretary of Defense McNamara," April 1, 1963, 446, *FRUS, 1961–1963*, 1199–1200

39 Department of External Affairs to Embassy of the United States of America, No. 35, March 29, 1963, enclosure No. 3 to Embassy's A–890, Ottawa embassy to secretary of state, April 2, 1963, Kennedy Papers, NSF: Canada: General

40 Vancouver *Province*, Ottawa *Citizen*, March 27, 1963

41 Ottawa *Citizen*, March 27, 1963

42 Telegram, State to Amembassy Ottawa, Amconsul Vancouver, March 27, 1963, 1001, 34, Kennedy Papers, NSF: Canada: General: Rostow Memorandum...

43 Telegram, Ottawa to secretary of state, April 1, 1963, 1267, ibid.

44 Telegram, Butterworth to secretary of state, April 2, 1963, 1271, ibid.

45 William H. Brubeck, "Memorandum for McGeorge Bundy, The White House, Subject: Diefenbaker's 'Secret Document,'" April 3, 1963, ibid.

46 L.J. Légère (Niccolo), "Memorandum for Mr. Bundy, Subject: Diefenbaker 'Secret Document,'" April 4, 1963, ibid., Mandatory Review Case NLK–94–9. There was calculation in the proposal that any release should come from the White House rather than the State Department: "We ought to finesse the January 30–associated 'U.S. State Department' out of the act and capitalize on the President's popularity in Canada. Naturally this in no way reflects on State, but is merely tactical in the light of circumstances."

47 Montreal *Star*, *Globe and Mail*, April 6, 1963; telegram, Butterworth to secretary of state, April 6, 1963, 1292, Kennedy Papers, NSF: Canada: General: Rostow Memorandum...

48 Montreal *Star*, April 8, 1963

49 A second article in the *Globe and Mail* by George Bain (apparently based on a briefing by Kennedy's press secretary, Pierre Salinger) on April 12 offered a full and accurate account of the entire story, including the point that it seemed to be the use of the word *pushed* that had upset Diefenbaker. Bain reported that "although efforts to uncover the actual words of a pencilled notation on the paper in the president's handwriting have been unsuccessful, it can be reported with assurance that it was not of an offensive nature. When the story became a repeat sensation in the last week of the campaign, there was talk here that the president had pencilled in something like: 'What do we say to the A.O.B. (sic) about this?' Because of reluctance here to talk about the document at all, or anything else relating to Canada, during the campaign, this could not be proved or disproved at the time. But it was not so." No one in Washington could be entirely sure whether there was a handwritten comment, since Diefenbaker had possession of the original document. But Bain and his sources were correct: There was no handwritten comment. Knowlton Nash wrote that Kennedy said to Ben Bradlee: "At the time, I didn't think Diefenbaker was a son of a bitch. I thought he was a prick"; and to Hugh Sidey of *Time*: "That's untrue...I'm not that stupid...And besides, at the time I didn't know him so well." After the change of government in April 1963, the US administration discussed whether any effort should be made to retrieve the original document from Diefenbaker, but decided that would be fruitless. When Pearson met Kennedy for the first time as prime minister at Hyannis Port in May 1963, the subject was raised during "an informal group conversation after dinner," and on Pearson's inquiry, Basil Robinson asserted that he had seen the document and that it had "no handwritten comment on it." Telegram, Butterworth to secretary of state, April 12, 1963, 1322, Kennedy Papers, NSF: Canada: General: Rostow Memorandum...; "Memorandum of Conversation: Subject: Memorandum prepared by Mr. Rostow," May 10, 1963, ibid., POF: Canada: Security, 1963; Nash, *Kennedy and Diefenbaker*, 288–89

50 Vancouver *Province*, April 6, April 8, 1963; telegram, Butterworth to secretary of state, April 7, 1963, 1294, Kennedy Papers, NSF: Canada: General: Rostow Memorandum...

51 Telegram, Rusk to Amembassy Ottawa, April 12, 1963, 1033, Kennedy Papers, NSF: Canada: General: Rostow Memorandum...Mandatory Review Case NLK 94–11; "Telegram from the Embassy in Canada to the Department of State," April 15, 1963, 447, *FRUS, 1961–1963*, 1200–01

52 *OC 3*, 8–10

53 Nash gives a full account of the chain through which the letter passed, and the remaining evidence can be found scattered in Diefenbaker's own files. Drew's covering letter to Diefenbaker is in the papers, although its letterhead has been roughly torn from both pages. There are also several of Diefenbaker's own memos on the affair. No copy of the offending letter can be found in the Diefenbaker Papers. On May 27, 1963, in the face of Liberal protests, Gordon Churchill read the letter in the House of Commons. Nash, *Kennedy and Diefenbaker*, 285–87; George Drew to JGD, date removed; JGD, "Memorandum Re: Phone Conversation with George Drew, March 25, noon, from Nanaimo"; MW to JGD, nd, re telephone call from Bryce; JGD, "Interference of the Americans in Canadian politics in the election," JGDP, XII/88/D/202; XII/58/C/155; XII/88/D/204; XII/95/E/127; *Debates*, May 27, 1963, 318–22

54 *CAR 1963*, 35–39

55 *OC 3*, 189

56 Ibid., 191; Leslie Frost to JGD, April 11, 1963, JGDP, XII/36/B/166

57 "A Son Excellence Le Gouverneur Général du Canada," April 12, 1963, JGDP, XII/41/B/335; *OC 3*, 192–95

58 JGD to Elmer Diefenbaker, April 26, 1963, JGDP, V/3, 2897

59 JGD to Elmer Diefenbaker, May 1, June 7, July 27, October 3, 1963, ibid., 2909–10, 2946, 3030, 3126–27

60 JGD to Elmer Diefenbaker, May 13, 23, 1963, ibid., 2927, 2932

61 JGD to Elmer Diefenbaker, May 24, 1963, ibid., 2933–34

62 JGD to Elmer Diefenbaker, May 23, 1963, ibid., 2932

63 Quoted in English, *Worldly*, 268

64 JGD to Elmer Diefenbaker, May 31, 1963, JGDP, V/3, 2937

65 JGD to Elmer Diefenbaker, June 7, 1963, ibid., 2946

66 *CAR 1963*, 40–41; JGD to Elmer Diefenbaker, July 27, October 22, 25, 1963, JGDP, V/3, 3030, 3146, 3157

67 Dalton K. Camp, "Remarks...to the Executive Officers of the Progressive Conservative Association of Canada," October 26, 1963, JGDP, IX/38/B/87.1

68 *OC 3*, 204–06; JGD to Elmer Diefenbaker, September 10, 18, October 2, 25, 1963, JGDP, V/3, 3090, 3094, 3124, 3157

69 JGD to Elmer Diefenbaker, October 31, 1963, JGDP, V/3, 3166

70 "Renegade in Power," October 28, 1963; "The Diefenbaker Years: Commentary on Peter Newman's 'Renegade in Power...'" November 4, 1963, JGDP, IX/16/A/548.1

71 JGD, nd, ibid.

72 Elmer Diefenbaker to JGD, November 11, 17, 1963, JGDP, V/3, 3178–85, 3189–95

73 JGD to Brigadier Michael Wardell, November 22, 1963; Michael Wardell, "The Editorial Page...Reply to Newman," Fredericton *Gleaner*, November 16, 1963, JGDP, IX/16/A/548.1. Another of Diefenbaker's friends, Gowan Guest, contributed a measured review of the book to the *Commentator* in December 1963. Guest noted: "For the author to fail to emphasize the twinkle in the eye, the gesticulations with the anecdotes, and the hearty guffaw is to deprive the man of one of his essential characteristics. For him to pass over as lightly as he does the sympathetic understanding of John Diefenbaker for the private sufferings of people he comes to know is to distort one of his most attractive traits." *Renegade*, Guest judged, "has no sympathy for John Diefenbaker...Nevertheless, it is a book which no sophisticated Canadian

should fail to read and a book which no politically interested Canadian can fail to find absorbing from dedication to index." Gowan T. Guest, "Perspicacity without Perspective," *Commentator,* December 1963, 17–18

74 *CAR 1964,* 3

75 JGD to Elmer Diefenbaker, December 17, 1963, January 4, 1964, JGDP, V/3, 3234; V/6, 3241

76 *Telegram,* February 4, 1964

77 Diefenbaker told his brother on January 25 that if the motion to hold a secret ballot carried, he would at once announce his resignation as leader since "I do not intend to be the Leader of a Party and be subject to continuing sniping from the minority." Apparently he thought better of that threat in the ten days that followed. *Globe and Mail, Telegram,* February 5, 1964; *CAR 1964,* 9–10; *OC 3,* 220–21; JGD to Elmer Diefenbaker, January 25, 1964, JGDP, V/6, 3278

78 *CAR 1964,* 10; *OC 3,* 221

79 Dalton K. Camp, "Acceptance Speech..." February 4, 1964, JGDP, IX/38/B/87.1; *OC 3,* 218–20

80 Dalton K. Camp to JGD, March 30, 1964, JGDP, IX/38/B/87.1; Douglas Leiterman, "Television Journalism," *Globe and Mail,* June 25, 1964; *CAR 1964,* 439–40

81 House of Commons, *Debates,* February 20, 1964, 42–66

82 Quoted in *CAR 1964,* 21

83 *Debates,* June 15–17, 1964, 4306–09, 4317–32, 4347–52, 4357–60; *CAR 1964,* 22–29

84 For accounts of the scandals, see Gwyn, *Shape of Scandal,* passsim; *CAR 1964,* 38–44; English, *Worldly,* 279–83; Nielsen, *The House,* 133–50.

85 L.B. Pearson to JGD, December 4, 1964, quoted in *OC 3,* 267–68

86 Hutchison, "A conversation with the prime minister," February 11, 1965, Hutchison Papers

87 Ibid.

88 *OC 3,* 269

89 Hutchison, "A conversation with the prime minister"

90 *OC 3,* 269–70

91 *Debates,* December 11, 14, 1964, 10965, 11075, 11136, 11139; *OC 3,* 225–26; *CAR 1964,* 33–38

92 *CAR 1964,* 90–93; JGD to Dalton K. Camp, October 17, 1964, JGDP, IX/38/B/87.1

93 Léon Balcer to Dalton K. Camp, January 15, 1965; press communiqué, January 14, 1965, JGDP, XII/93/E/98

94 Dalton K. Camp, "Memorandum to: The Rt. Hon. John G. Diefenbaker..." February 1, 1965, JGDP, XIV/16/E/193

95 Dalton K. Camp to executive officers of the Progressive Conservative Association of Canada, January 19, 1965; Dalton K. Camp, "Memorandum to: The Rt. Hon. John G. Diefenbaker..." February 1, 1965, JGDP, XII/93/E/98; XIV/16/E/193; Toronto *Star,* January 25, 1965

96 Dalton K. Camp, "Memorandum to: The Rt. Hon. John G. Diefenbaker..." February 1, 1965, JGDP, XIV/16/E/193

97 As leader of the opposition, Diefenbaker had three assistants: Richardson, the former editor of the *Telegram;* Van Dusen, who had been Michael Starr's executive assistant from 1957 to 1963; and Greg Guthrie, a former journalist and military officer.

98 Burt Richardson, Memorandum, February 2, 1965, JGDP, XII/93/E/98

99 TVD, "Caucus. 1. Motion to expel Balcer," nd, JGDP, VII/169/A/1580, 104216–18; Diefenbaker dictated at least six memoranda on the crisis on February 4, in two of which he indicated that he might retire. Erik Nielsen told him "that would be a terrible calamity, we would have no one to lead us in the election. I said I was not going to be used in an election campaign and be thrown out after." Diefenbaker set two conditions for himself. He would not accept any kind of veto imposed by the Quebec caucus; and he would not continue as leader "if John Robarts and the Organization in Ontario are going to be against me." These memos are filed in JGDP, XII/93/E/98.

100 "Memorandum, re PC Caucus February 5/PC National Executive February 6," February 4, 1965, JGDP, XII/93/E/98

101 Toronto *Star*, February 10, 1965

102 *CAR 1965*, 10–11

103 This account of Diefenbaker's speech is based on the detailed notes of Davie Fulton. E.D. Fulton, "Executive Meeting, PC Ass'n. 6/2/65," Fulton Papers

104 Toronto *Star*, February 8, 1965

105 The questionnaire was headed: "Letter of advice to the National Leader...intended to serve solely as advice to the National Leader...to be communicated to him by the National President." JGDP, IX/64/B/630

106 The published accounts differ over whether the vote was on a Nielsen or a Goodman motion, and whether the vote was 55–52, 57–55, 53–52, or 52–50. Toronto *Star*, February 8, 1965; *CAR 1965*, 11–12; Goodman, *Life*, 104–05

107 Goodman, *Life*, 105

108 E.D. Fulton, "Executive Meeting, PC Ass'n," February 6, 1965, Fulton Papers

109 Quoted by Peter C. Newman in the Toronto *Star*, February 10, 1965

110 *Globe and Mail*, February 8, 1965

111 Ibid.; Toronto *Star*, February 8, 10, 1965

112 Quoted in *CAR 1965*, 14

113 *OC 3*, 240

114 *CAR 1965*, 15–16; *Debates*, March 3, 1965, 11931–43

115 Gwyn, *Shape of Scandal*, 222–37; Nielsen, *The House*, 133–43; *OC 3*, 231–35

116 Murray had been Davie Fulton's executive assistant, and was then in the same position with Wallace McCutcheon. He remained close to Fulton, and was thought to be one of Peter Newman's confidants about the cabinet crisis of 1962–63. For an account of these events in 1965, see Goodman, *Life*, 106–12.

117 Ibid., 112–13

118 Ibid., 112–17; Newman, *Distemper*, 358–60; Toronto *Star*, October 2, 1965

119 Johnston was an economist who had worked as an editorial writer for the *Financial Post*, editor of the Stratford *Beacon-Herald*, and publisher of the Aurora *Banner*. He joined party headquarters for the 1965 campaign. This account was part of a commentary on the 1965 campaign written for Diefenbaker as he wrote his memoirs in 1974. It seemed intended to persuade Diefenbaker that the jibe was not part of a campaign of subversion which, in retrospect, he perceived among traitors to his cause at national headquarters. Newman and Goodman also tell the story with slight variations. James Johnston to JGD, "Memorandum: Recollections of 1965 General Election Meetings, E.A. Goodman letter and Newman's 'Distemper of our Times...'" December 3, 1974, JGDP, XIV/1/A/13; Johnston, *The Party's Over*, 41–42; Newman, *Distemper*, 360; Goodman, *Life*, 116–17

120 James Johnston to JGD, "Memorandum..." JGDP, XIV/1/A/13

121 Newman, *Distemper*, 360

122 Carrigan, *Canadian Party Platforms, 1867–1968*, 320–23; Johnston, *The Party's Over*, 42; Johnston to Diefenbaker, "Memorandum..." JGDP, XIV/1/A/13; *OC 3*, 254–56; *CAR 1965*, 101

123 Montreal *Gazette*, September 29, 1965

124 *Globe and Mail*, October 11, 1965

125 Toronto *Star*, October 12, 1965

126 *Globe and Mail*, October 13, 1965

127 English, *Worldly*, 306–11; *CAR 1965*, 86–95; Newman, *Renegade*, 355–57, 365–74

128 Montreal *Gazette*, October 11, 1965; *Globe and Mail*, October 30, 1965; *CAR 1965*, 85–86

129 *Debates*, January 31, February 23, 28, 1966, 426, 1681–83, 1877–90; *OC 3*, 270–71

130 *Debates*, March 4, 1966, 2206

131 Ibid.

132 Ibid., 2209

133 Ibid., March 4, 1966, 2211

134 Ibid., 2227–31

135 Ibid., March 4, 7, 1966, 2241–44, 2293–98

136 Ibid., March 7, 1966, 2298–99

137 *CAR 1966*, 13–14; *Globe and Mail*, March 9, 1966; Van Dusen, *The Chief*, 175–76

138 For discussion of the Spence Commission's creation and terms of reference, see the *Debates*, March 14, 1966, 2613–31, 2663–82; March 15, 1966, 2685–702; Nielsen, *The House*, 54–59; English, *Worldly*, 350–57; *OC 3*, 266–73; *Globe and Mail*, March 16, 1966; Van Dusen, *The Chief*, 178–82.

139 *CAR 1966*, 12–17; Newman, *Distemper*, 387–406

140 The inquiry and the Spence report are reported at length in Van Dusen's *The Chief*, 165–229. See also *CAR 1966*, 32–33; *OC 3*, 272–73. Diefenbaker's main files on the inquiry are contained in JGDP, VII/214,216/A/1991.2,1991.10; XII/86/D/141,142; XII/122/F/420; and XIV/14,15/E/145,172. The Fulton Papers contain full files of the inquiry in volumes 108 and 109.

141 Johnston, *The Party's Over*, 72–74

142 Ibid., 89

143 "Report of General Caucus of April 20th 1966"; "Report of Special Committee of Caucus," May 4, 1966; JGD, "Memorandum re: Miss Flora MacDonald," JGDP, XII/80/D/30, XII/119/F/384; Johnston, *The Party's Over*, 82–83

144 Camp, *Points of Departure*, 16–17

145 Ibid., 18

146 *Globe and Mail*, *Telegram*, September 22, 1966; Goodman, *Life*, 124–25; Johnston, *The Party's Over*, 110–19; *OC 3*, 273; *CAR 1966*, 41–43

147 Johnston, *The Party's Over*, 112–13

148 *CAR 1966*, 43–44; "A Record of Editorial Opinion Regarding Mr. Camp's Stand," nd, JGDP, IX/38/B/87.2

149 Johnston, *The Party's Over*, 118–34; *CAR 1966*, 44–46

150 Goodman, *Life*, 124–31; Johnston, *The Party's Over*, 124–46

151 Johnston, *The Party's Over*, 152

152 Ibid., 154–55

153 Montreal *Gazette*, November 16, 1966. Nicholson reported that Camp's organizers had "drilled, rehearsed and positioned an effective commando force" in the hall, with detailed instructions to avoid applause and to heckle and boo frequently. Diefenbaker repeated this account in his memoirs. Orillia *Packet-Times*, November 24, 1966; *OC 3*, 276–77

154 Johnston, *The Party's Over*, 154–55; *OC 3*, 276–78. Diefenbaker's outline notes for the speech were contained in four brief pages, in which he reasserted his commitment to "the fundamentals on which Sir John A. Macdonald laid the cornerstone": equality of opportunity through public education; medicare; assistance to free enterprise and the elderly; and promotion of agricultural and resource sales. The notes conclude with a promise to "transfer the mantle of leadership and responsibility" to any younger leader who commits himself to fulfil these pledges and fights "to prevent this great Conservative Party from becoming one of reaction and inaction." Most of the message was never delivered. JGD, "Notes for opening speech," November 13, 1966, JGDP, XII/119/F/381

155 Quoted in *OC 3*, 279

156 Johnston, *The Party's Over*, 157–62; *CAR 1966*, 47

157 *OC 3*, 301; Johnston, *The Party's Over*, 162; Winnipeg *Free Press*, November 26, 1966

158 There are several variations. Diefenbaker identifies the author as "Sir Andrew Barton, an Elizabethan soldier." The lines appear as "Johnnie Armstrong's Last Goodnight" in Dryden's *Miscellanies* of 1702: "Fight on, my merrie men all,/ I'm a little wounded, but I am not slain;/ I will lay me down for to bleed a while,/ Then I'll rise and fight with you again." *OC 3*, 279–80

159 "Resolution passed – Conservative Party Annual Meeting, November 16th – Carried. 563–186," JGDP, VII/193/A/1819; Johnston, *The Party's Over*, 163–65; *CAR 1966*, 47–48

Chapter 14 "An Old Man Dreaming Dreams"
1   Johnston, *The Party's Over*, 166–67
2   Ibid., 172–74
3   Quoted ibid., 175; *CAR 1967*, 24–25
4   Goodman, *Life*, 132–34; Johnston, *The Party's Over*, 177–80; *CAR 1967*, 24–25; James Johnston, Memorandum for executive committee meeting, January 25, 1967, JGDP, VII/193/A/1819, 122386–90
5   Diefenbaker's threat was that he would refuse to provide a message or a picture for the conference program, and would not attend the convention, unless his demand was met. JGD to E.A. Goodman, June 21, 1967; E.A. Goodman to JGD, July 19, 1967; E.A. Goodman to JGD, August 21, 1967; "Johnston Message Re Leadership Convention Nomination Times Memo," August 1967, JGDP, XIV/18/E/225, XII/91/E/52, XII/120/F/391; Johnston, *The Party's Over*, 180–89
6   Diefenbaker had also made some desultory efforts over the winter to interest the mayor of Montreal, Jean Drapeau, in contesting the leadership as his chosen successor. Drapeau was grateful to Diefenbaker for promoting Expo 67 for Montreal, but he was not interested in the Tory leadership. *CAR 1967*, 24–32; Johnston, *The Party's Over*, 191–216; JGD, "Re Mr Stanfield," May 16, 1967, JGDP, XIV/16/E/210
7   *CAR 1967*, 179; Vancouver *Province*, August 29, 1967; "I am a Canadian," RCA Victor CC–1027
8   Goodman, *Life*, 135–36
9   Quoted in Van Dusen, *The Chief*, 245–46
10 Toronto *Star*, *Globe and Mail*, September 7, 1967; Johnston, *The Party's Over*, 225–29; *CAR 1967*, 34–35; Goodman, *Life*, 136 37
11 Goodman, *Life*, 137
12 Johnston, *The Party's Over*, 228
13 In his concentration on the flow of language, Rill missed Diefenbaker's meaning here. The six million he referred to were not French-speaking Canadians, but Canadians from neither the English- nor French-speaking charter groups.
14 *Globe and Mail*, September 9, 1967
15 Victoria *Daily Colonist*, September 8, 1967
16 JGD, press statement, September 8, 1967, JGDP, XII/121/F/392. Diefenbaker's assistant Tom Van Dusen had prompted the Youth for Dief organizers to obtain nomination papers for him in August, and found the necessary twenty-five delegate signatories before Diefenbaker himself indicated his willingness to stand. Van Dusen, *The Chief*, 244–52
17 "The Charade Is Recognized," *Globe and Mail*, September 9, 1967. After his Thursday speech, Diefenbaker had received a telegram of support for his "two nations" stance from the Social Credit premier of Alberta, Ernest Manning, and a similar telephone call from the Social Credit attorney general of British Columbia, Robert Bonner. Van Dusen, *The Chief*, 251
18 Goodman, *Life*, 137–38; *Globe and Mail*, September 11, 1967
19 *Globe and Mail*, September 11, 1967
20 Johnston, *The Party's Over*, 239–40
21 Ibid.
22 *Globe and Mail*, Fredericton *Daily Gleaner*, September 11, 1967
23 Quoted in Stevens, *Stanfield*, 195. Diefenbaker remembered the words as "I think I can get along with this fellow, Camp."
24 JGD, "Memorandum Re: Conversation with Premier Stanfield, Royal York Hotel, Monday, September 11, 12.00 noon to 12.30 noon," JGDP, XII/121/F/392
25 JGD, "Memorandum Re: Phone conversation with Hon. Gordon Churchill, Winnipeg, Monday, September 11, 1.25 P.M.," ibid.
26 JGD, "Memorandum Re: Phone conversation with Mayor McFarland, Picton, 1.10 P.M., Monday, September 11, 1967"; JGD, "Memorandum Re: Phone conversation with Hon.

Gordon Churchill...”; JGD, memorandum, September 12, 1967, JGDP, XII/121/F/392, IX/41/B/165

27 Van Dusen, *The Chief,* 253–54

28 Spencer, *Trumpets,* 126–27

29 Ibid., 114, 129–36; O'Sullivan, *Both My Houses,* 28–30

30 Spencer, *Trumpets,* 140–43

31 Ibid., 143–44

32 Quoted in Stevens, *Stanfield,* 228

33 Ibid., 229–34; *CAR 1969,* 8–11

34 Toronto *Star,* September 10, 1970; Stevens, *Stanfield,* 234–35

35 *Globe and Mail,* September 10, 1970

36 Toronto *Star,* October 16, 20, 1969, November 26, 1989

37 Ibid., March 26, 1970

38 Harold Macmillan to John Gray, October 9, 1969, enclosing JGD to Harold Macmillan, October 2, 1969, and Harold Macmillan to JGD, October 9, 1969 (copies in the author's possession). The two academics were W.F.W. Neville and the author, assisted by John O. Stubbs and Colin Wright. The interviews are those referred to in this text as JGDI, 1969 and 1970.

39 Van Dusen, *The Chief;* Coates, *The Night of the Knives;* Johnston, *The Party's Over*

40 English, *Worldly,* 391–92

41 The reporter was Stewart McLeod, who told this story at the fifteenth anniversary celebration of the Diefenbaker funeral train, held in August 1994 in the Railway Committee Room of the House of Commons.

42 Hayden, *Seeking a Balance,* 249. In cooperation with the National Archives, a major project of reorganizing and classifying the Diefenbaker Papers for public use was begun in 1980. It was completed, after a series of financial vicissitudes, in 1994. The centre's initial financing by governments and university did not survive the economy drives of the 1980s, and by 1995 it was being funded by a private foundation, the Diefenbaker Society. The society raises a substantial part of its annual income from participation in the Western Canada Lottery, which would have shaken – or tickled – John Diefenbaker's Baptist soul.

43 Spencer, *Trumpets,* 146–64

44 Ibid., 165–71

45 Ottawa *Journal,* January 2, 1976

46 “One of the Queen's men,” *Globe and Mail,* January 2, 1976

47 Toronto *Star,* March 30, 1976. Diefenbaker's annoyance with Trudeau for suggesting a Canadian role in the affair may have reflected embarrassment over a distant incident. In 1959, when Vincent Massey retired as governor general, Diefenbaker was consulted by the queen about awarding Massey a retirement honour. Diefenbaker replied that during his prime ministership, as had been the custom since 1939, no Canadians should receive United Kingdom honours. Massey did not receive his reward. In the second volume of the memoirs, which he was completing at the time of his award, Diefenbaker commented that he had been “obliged to advise the Queen” not to honour Massey, and added somewhat curiously: “I personally was in the position where I might have received high and prestigious honours, but I made it clear I could not accept them. For example, in 1958 when I was in Malaya, Prime Minister Tunku Abdul Rahman offered me his country's highest decoration. I automatically turned it down.” If Trudeau had graciously suspended Canadian policy to recommend or concur in Diefenbaker's Companion of Honour, Diefenbaker might not have wished to be reminded of his own decision. *OC 2,* 59

48 Toronto *Star,* March 31, 1976

49 Ibid., April 2, 1976

50 *Globe and Mail,* April 3, 1976

51 Ibid.

52 Quoted in Stephen Smith, "Interview with Graham Glockling," March 1995, in author's possession.

53 Gilbert, *Never Despair,* 1347

54 Ottawa *Citizen,* December 24, 1976; *Globe and Mail,* Toronto *Star,* December 23, 1976

55 "Memo to Mr. Diefenbaker: Re Burial – in Saskatoon," September 11, 1978; "Rough Notes re Funeral of Mr. Diefenbaker," November 24, 1978; "Re Funeral arrangements," November 30, 1978, JGDP, XII/82/D/56; Smith, "Interview with Graham Glockling," March 1995. The reference to the order of precedence in heaven for two wives is from Spencer, *Trumpets,* 175.

56 Spencer, *Trumpets,* 174–78

57 Ibid., 180–81

58 Ibid., 181–82

59 Ibid., 188–91

60 Flora MacDonald, Goodman Lecture, University of Western Ontario, September 28, 1994

61 JGD to Keith Martin; JGD to Senator David Walker, August 1, 1979, JGDP, XII/82/D/56

62 Ottawa *Citizen,* August 16, 1979; O'Sullivan, *Both My Houses,* 159–60

Chapter 15 A Burial on the Prairie

1 Ottawa *Citizen,* August 16, 1979; *Globe and Mail,* August 18, 1979; Brian McGarry, "Rt. Hon. John Diefenbaker Funeral," Hulse, Playfair & McGarry files

2 "Order of Service, State Funeral, John G. Diefenbaker, 1895–1979," August 19, 1979

3 *Globe and Mail,* August 23, 1979

4 Ibid.

5 Ottawa *Journal,* August 18, 1979

6 Diefenbaker first raised the question of a gravestone modelled on that of Churchill in a memorandum about his will written in March 1969, and he repeated his preference when he met the director of special events in the mid-1970s. JGD, "Confidential Memorandum," March 13, 1969, JGDP, XIV/8/D/13.2; Smith, "Interview with Graham Glockling," March 1995

7 Sean O'Sullivan put the total cost of the funeral at $1 million; and Robert Sheppard, writing on the occasion of Richard Nixon's funeral in 1994, used the same figure. The Diefenbaker funeral, he commented, was more elaborate than Nixon's. O'Sullivan, *Both My Houses,* 163; *Globe and Mail,* April 27, 1994; McGarry, "Rt. Hon. John Diefenbaker Funeral"

8 "The last will and testament of the Rt. Hon. John G. Diefenbaker, made this 7th day of August, 1979," JGDP, XII/83/D/67

9 *Globe and Mail,* August 28, 1979

10 Ibid., September 15, 1979

11 For early correspondence on the trust fund, see Henry Langford to Dr D.M. Baltzan, August 9, 1962; Dr D.M. Baltzan to Henry Langford, August 11, 1962, JGDP, XIV/18/E/232.3; Henry Langford to JGD, November 8, 1962; Dr D.M. Baltzan to JGD, January 11, 1963; K. Burn to JGD, September 15, 1967; JGD, "Note," September 20, 1967; JGD, "Re Senator Brunt Fund," nd, JGDP, XII/83/D/66, XII/29/B/11. In his 1970 interview with Michael Wardell, John Bassett mentioned occasions in 1957, 1958, and 1962 when he approached Diefenbaker with donations he had raised for Diefenbaker trust funds (the latter two each involving a cheque for $100,000 from Garfield Weston). Diefenbaker vehemently refused the gifts, and suggested that any donations should go directly into the party's accounts for its general use. Bassett said that Diefenbaker was "a man of incontestable probity" in financial matters, which seems to be true. Michael Wardell, "John Bassett at Toronto, Friday & Saturday, November 20/21, 1970," JGDP, XIV/16/E/219; *Globe and Mail,* May 16, 1981

12 Reception Program, August 16, 1994; Ottawa *Citizen,* August 17, 1994

Bibliography

A note on sources

The major primary source for a Diefenbaker biography must be the collections in the Diefenbaker Centre Archives at the University of Saskatchewan. These collections contain the public and personal papers of John Diefenbaker, and the private papers of his parents, William and Mary, his brother, Elmer, and his wives, Edna and Olive, arranged in twenty-two separate series. The papers in this large collection have been carefully organized and indexed by the archivists of the centre, and the relevant series have been reviewed for security clearance by the National Archives of Canada. Some documents have been withheld on security grounds, but the collection nevertheless offers a near-comprehensive record of the private life, legal practice, and public career of John Diefenbaker. Diefenbaker himself was a compulsive collector of records, including his own random notes, memoranda, letters, press clippings, speech texts, photographs, and reference materials, all of which now reside in the centre along with his books and collected artifacts. The centre also contains an extensive oral history series of taped interviews with Diefenbaker's friends and political associates, and a large photograph and slide collection. For the prime ministerial period, documents relating to most major subjects remain scattered in separate files and series that reflect the haphazard filing and numbering practices of Diefenbaker's office, and they must be searched out in the indexes under all related titles. The main files for the prime ministerial period are contained in series VI – Prime Minister's Office Numbered Correspondence; series VIII – Prime Minister's Office Unnumbered Correspondence; series XII – Personal and Confidential, 1957–79; and series XIV – Memoirs. For students of Canadian history, politics, law, foreign relations, prairie settlement, and political psychology, the centre is a vast treasure-trove of original materials.

The National Archives of Canada is a second essential source. It contains the cabinet records of the Diefenbaker government, departmental records, and the collected papers of many members of the King, St Laurent, Diefenbaker, and Pearson cabinets. The National Archives also has microfilm copies of the Diefenbaker Papers from the Diefenbaker Centre collection. The audio-visual division of the archives includes a large collection of radio and television tapes covering John Diefenbaker's political career.

In the United States, the most useful sources for the Diefenbaker period are the US National Archives in Washington, the John Fitzgerald Kennedy Library in Boston, Massachusetts, and the published volumes of *Foreign Relations of the United States*. Substantial parts of Kennedy's presidential papers dealing with the tempestuous relationship between Kennedy and Diefenbaker remain restricted on security grounds, but access to restricted materials can frequently (though slowly) be gained by "mandatory review" of the presidential papers in the Kennedy Library – a process still distinct from normal review under the US freedom of information law.

In the United Kingdom, cabinet and prime ministerial records are available in the Public Record Office. Access to minutes of the Commonwealth prime ministers conferences of 1960 and 1961 relating to South African membership in the Commonwealth, however, is unaccountably

672

closed until well into the twenty-first century, even though that dark phase of South African history has passed and the republic has re-entered the Commonwealth. For those meetings, the records available in the Diefenbaker Papers are sufficient to establish the Canadian position in detail.

Private papers consulted in other archival collections are listed below.

Interviews and correspondence
Agar Adamson, Robert Becker, Richard Bell, Ruth M. Bell, Ian Bickle, Pamela Branch, Jeffry V. Brock, Dalton Camp, Gordon Churchill, John G. Diefenbaker, E. Davie Fulton, Edwin A. Goodman, Gowan Guest, Christine Hammond, Douglas Harkness, Clyne Harradence, J. Francis Leddy, Cynthia McCormack, Flora MacDonald, Brian McGarry, Brian Mackey, Keith Martin, John A. Munro, Marjorie (Bunny) Pound, Peter Roberts, H. Basil Robinson, Benjamin Rogers, Mitchell Sharp, Marion Wagner, Lorne Whitty

Government documents
Audio-visual archives (National Archives of Canada)
Canada, Cabinet Conclusions (National Archives of Canada)
Canada, House of Commons, *Debates*
Proceedings of the Standing Committee on Banking and Commerce, Senate of Canada, July 1961
Department of External Affairs (DEA) files (National Archives of Canada)
Department of National Defence, Military Personnel Files (National Archives of Canada)
Foreign Relations of the United States (FRUS)
Privy Council Office (PCO) files (National Archives of Canada)
United Kingdom, Cabinet Conclusions (Public Record Office)
United Kingdom, Cabinet Office files (Public Record Office)
United States, Department of State files (US National Archives)

Personal papers
Rodney Adamson Papers (privately held)
Richard Bell Papers (National Archives of Canada)
R.B. Bennett Papers (National Archives of Canada)
Herbert A. Bruce Papers (Queen's University Archives)
J.W. Dafoe Papers (National Archives of Canada)
Grant Dexter Papers (Queen's University Archives)
John G. Diefenbaker Papers (Diefenbaker Centre Archives)
Leslie Frost Papers (Trent University Archives)
E. Davie Fulton Papers (National Archives of Canada)
R.B. Hanson Papers (National Archives of Canada)
Douglas Harkness Papers (National Archives of Canada)
Bruce Hutchison Papers (University of Calgary Archives)
John F. Kennedy Papers (Kennedy Library)
J.M. Macdonnell Papers (Queen's University Archives)
W.L. Mackenzie King Papers (National Archives of Canada)
L.B. Pearson Papers (National Archives of Canada)
John A. Stevenson Papers (Queen's University Archives)

Newspapers, journals, and magazines
Calgary *Herald*, Edmonton *Journal*, *Financial Post*, Fredericton *Gleaner*, Hamilton *Spectator*, Montreal *Gazette*, Montreal *Star*, Ottawa *Citizen*, Ottawa *Journal*, Prince Albert *Herald*, Regina *Daily Star*, Regina *Leader Post*, Saskatoon *Star-Phoenix*, Toronto *Globe and Mail*, Toronto *Star*, Toronto *Telegram*, Vancouver *Province*, Winnipeg *Free Press*, Winnipeg *Tribune*, *Daily Express*, *Financial Times*, *Manchester Guardian*, *The Times*, New York *Times*, Washington *Post*, *Canadian Forum*, *Canadian Historical Review*,

Commentator, Journal of Canadian Studies, Maclean's, Queen's Quarterly, Saturday Night, New York Review of Books, Newsweek, Time, US News & World Report

Books and articles

Archer, John H. *Saskatchewan: A History.* Saskatoon: Western Producer Prairie Books, 1980

Barros, James. *No Sense of Evil: Espionage, the Case of Herbert Norman.* Toronto: Deneau, 1986

Berger, Thomas R. *Fragile Freedoms: Human Rights and Dissent in Canada.* Rev. ed. Toronto: Clarke, Irwin, 1982

Black, Conrad. *Duplessis.* Toronto: McClelland & Stewart, 1977

Black's Medical Dictionary. 34th ed. New York: A. & C. Black, 1984

Borden History Book Committee. *Our Treasured Heritage: Borden & District.* Borden, 1980

Bothwell, Robert, Ian Drummond, and John English. *Canada since 1945: Power, Politics, and Provincialism.* Rev. ed. Toronto: University of Toronto Press, 1989

Bothwell, Robert, and William Kilbourn. *C.D. Howe: A Biography.* Toronto: McClelland & Stewart, 1979

Bowen, Roger. *Innocence Is Not Enough: The Life and Death of Herbert Norman.* Vancouver: Douglas & McIntyre, 1986

Breggin, Peter Roger. *Electro-Shock: Its Brain-Disabling Effects.* New York: Springer, 1979

Brennan, Patrick H. *Reporting the Nation's Business: Press-Government Relations during the Liberal Years, 1935–1957.* Toronto: University of Toronto Press, 1994

Camp, Dalton. *Gentlemen, Players & Politicians.* Toronto: McClelland & Stewart, 1970

— *Points of Departure.* Toronto: Deneau and Greenberg, 1979

Campagna, Palmiro. *Storms of Controversy: The Secret Arrow Files Revealed.* Toronto: Stoddart, 1992

Campbell, Robert M. *The Full-Employment Objective in Canada, 1945–85.* Ottawa: Economic Council of Canada, 1991

Carrigan, D. Owen. *Canadian Party Platforms, 1867–1968.* Toronto: Copp, Clark, 1968

Christian, William. *George Grant: A Biography.* Toronto: University of Toronto Press, 1993

Churchill, Gordon. "Recollections and Comments on Election Strategy." *Queen's Quarterly* 77 (winter 1970): 499–511

Clyne, J.V. *Jack of All Trades: Memoirs of a Busy Life.* Toronto: McClelland & Stewart, 1985

Coates, Robert C. *The Night of the Knives.* Fredericton: Brunswick Press, 1969

Conrad, Margaret. *George Nowlan: Maritime Conservative in National Politics.* Toronto: University of Toronto Press, 1986

Conway, J.F. *The West: The History of a Region in Confederation.* 2nd ed. Toronto: James Lorimer, 1994

Cook, Blanche Wiesen. *Eleanor Roosevelt*, vol. 1: *1884–1933.* New York: Penguin, 1992

Copp, Terry, and Bill McAndrew. *Battle Exhaustion: Soldiers and Psychiatrists in the Canadian Army, 1939–1945.* Montreal: McGill-Queen's University Press, 1990

Courtney, John C. *The Selection of National Party Leaders in Canada.* Toronto: Macmillan, 1973

— ed., *Voting in Canada: A Selection of Papers.* Toronto: Prentice Hall, 1967

Creighton, Donald. *The Forked Road: Canada 1939–1957.* Toronto: McClelland & Stewart, 1976

— *John A. Macdonald: The Young Politician.* Toronto: Macmillan, 1952

— *John A. Macdonald: The Old Chieftain.* Toronto: Macmillan, 1955

Dawson, R. MacGregor. *The Conscription Crisis of 1944.* Toronto: University of Toronto Press, 1961

Dempson, Peter. *Assignment Ottawa: Seventeen Years in the Press Gallery.* Toronto: General, 1968

Dewitt, David B., and David Leyton-Brown, eds. *Canada's International Security Policy.* Toronto: Prentice Hall, 1995

Diefenbaker, John G. *One Canada: Memoirs of the Right Honourable John G. Diefenbaker*, vol. 1: *The Crusading Years, 1895–1956.* Toronto: Macmillan, 1975

— *One Canada: Memoirs of the Right Honourable John G. Diefenbaker*, vol. 2: *The Years of Achievement, 1956–1962.* Toronto: Macmillan, 1976

— *One Canada: Memoirs of the Right Honourable John G. Diefenbaker*, vol. 3: *The Tumultuous Years,*

1962–1967. Toronto: Macmillan, 1977

— "My First Prairie Christmas." *Reader's Digest,* December 1976, 49–52

Dow, James. *The Arrow.* Toronto: James Lorimer, 1979

Egerton, George, ed. *Political Memoir: Essays on the Politics of Memory.* London: Frank Cass, 1994

Electroconvulsive Therapy: Task Force Report 14. New York: American Psychiatric Association, September 1978

English, John. *Shadow of Heaven: The Life of Lester Pearson,* vol. 1: *1897–1948.* Toronto: Lester & Orpen Dennys, 1989

— *The Worldly Years: The Life of Lester Pearson,* vol. 2: *1949–1972.* Toronto: Knopf Canada, 1992

Fleming, Donald M. *So Very Near: The Political Memoirs of Honourable Donald M. Fleming,* vol. 1: *The Rising Years;* vol. 2: *The Summit Years.* Toronto: McClelland & Stewart, 1985

Fraser, John, and Graham Fraser, eds. *"Blair Fraser Reports": Selections 1944–1968.* Toronto: Macmillan, 1969

Friesen, Gerald. *The Canadian Prairies: A History.* Toronto: University of Toronto Press, 1987

Ghent-Mallet, Jocelyn, and Don Munton. "Confronting Kennedy and the Missiles in Cuba, 1962." In Don Munton and John Kirton, eds. *Canadian Foreign Policy: Selected Cases,* 78–100. Toronto: Prentice Hall, 1992

— "Deploying Nuclear Weapons, 1962–63." In Munton and Kirton, eds. *Canadian Foreign Policy: Selected Cases,* 101–17

Gilbert, Martin. *Never Despair: Winston S. Churchill, 1945–1965.* Toronto: Stoddart, 1988

Glassford, Larry A. *Reaction and Reform: The Politics of the Conservative Party under R.B. Bennett, 1927–1938.* Toronto: University of Toronto Press, 1992

Goodman, Eddie. *Life of the Party: The Memoirs of Eddie Goodman.* Toronto: Key Porter, 1988

Grafftey, Heward. *Lessons from the Past: From Dief to Mulroney.* Montreal: Eden Press, 1987

Graham, Roger. *Arthur Meighen,* vol. 3: *No Surrender.* Toronto: Clarke, Irwin, 1965

— *Old Man Ontario: Leslie M. Frost.* Toronto: University of Toronto Press, 1990

Grant, George. *Lament for a Nation: The Defeat of Canadian Nationalism.* Toronto: McClelland & Stewart, 1965

Granatstein, J.L. *Canada 1957–1967: The Years of Uncertainty and Innovation.* Toronto: McClelland & Stewart, 1986

— *Canada's War: The Politics of the Mackenzie King Government, 1939–1945.* Toronto: Oxford University Press, 1975

— *A Man of Influence: Norman A. Robertson and Canadian Statecraft, 1929–68.* Toronto: Deneau, 1981

— *The Politics of Survival: The Conservative Party of Canada, 1939–1945.* Toronto: University of Toronto Press, 1967

Gray, Colin S. *Canadian Defence Priorities: A Question of Relevance.* Toronto: Clarke, Irwin, 1972

Gray, James H. *R.B. Bennett: The Calgary Years.* Toronto: University of Toronto Press, 1991

Gwyn, Richard. *The Shape of Scandal: A Study of A Government in Crisis.* Toronto: Clarke, Irwin, 1965

— *Smallwood: The Unlikely Revolutionary.* Toronto: McClelland & Stewart, 1968

Hayden, Michael. *Seeking a Balance: The University of Saskatchewan, 1907–1982.* Vancouver: University of British Columbia Press, 1983

Haydon, Peter T. *The 1962 Cuban Missile Crisis: Canadian Involvement Reconsidered.* Toronto: Canadian Institute of Strategic Studies, 1993

Hertel, John A., Company. *Canadian Bulletin No. 10.* Chicago: July 1915

— *Field Echoes and Pointers to Success.* Chicago: December 1915

Hill, Douglas. *The Opening of the Canadian West.* London: Heinemann, 1967

Holt, Simma. *The Other Mrs. Diefenbaker.* Toronto: Doubleday Canada, 1982

Horne, Alistair. *Macmillan 1957–1986,* volume 2 of the official biography. London: Macmillan, 1989

Horner, Jack. *My Own Brand.* Edmonton: Hurtig, 1980

Horwood, Harold. *Joey: The Life and Political Times of Joey Smallwood.* Toronto: Stoddart, 1989

Hutchison, Bruce. *The Unfinished Country: To Canada with Love and Some Misgivings.* Vancouver: Douglas & McIntyre, 1985

Jockel, Joseph T. *No Boundaries Upstairs: Canada, The United States and the Origins of North American Air Defence, 1945–1958.* Vancouver: University of British Columbia Press, 1987

Johnston, James. *The Party's Over.* Toronto: Longman, 1971

Kaplan, William. *State and Salvation: The Jehovah's Witnesses and Their Fight for Civil Rights.* Toronto: University of Toronto Press, 1989

Keegan, John. *The Second World War.* New York: Viking Penguin, 1989

Kent, Tom. *A Public Purpose: An Experience of Liberal Opposition and Canadian Government.* Montreal: McGill-Queen's University Press, 1988

Kerr, Donald, and Stan Hanson. *Saskatoon: The First Half-Century.* Edmonton: NeWest, 1982

Kilbourn, William. *PipeLine: TransCanada and the Great Debate, A History of Business and Politics.* Toronto: Clarke, Irwin, 1970

Kyba, Patrick. *Alvin: A Biography of the Honourable Alvin Hamilton, P.C.* Regina: Canadian Plains Research Center, 1989

— "Ballots and Burning Crosses – The Election of 1929." In Ward and Spafford, eds. *Politics in Saskatchewan*, 105–23

LaMarsh, Judy. *Memoirs of a Bird in a Gilded Cage.* Toronto: McClelland & Stewart, 1968

Legault, Albert, and Michel Fortmann. *A Diplomacy of Hope: Canada and Disarmament, 1945–1988.* Montreal: McGill-Queen's University Press, 1992

Levine, Allan. *Scrum Wars: The Prime Ministers and the Media.* Toronto: Dundurn Press, 1993

Lloyd, Trevor. *Canada in World Affairs*, vol. 10: *1957–1959.* Toronto: Oxford University Press, 1968

Lyon, Peyton V. *Canada in World Affairs*, vol. 12: *1961–1963.* Toronto: Oxford University Press, 1968

Macmillan, Harold. *Pointing the Way: Memoirs*, vol. 5: *1959–1961.* London: Macmillan, 1972

Macquarrie, Heath. *Red Tory Blues: A Political Memoir.* Toronto: University of Toronto Press, 1992

Martin, Lawrence. *The Presidents and the Prime Ministers: Washington and Ottawa Face to Face: The Myth of Bilateral Bliss, 1867–1982.* Toronto: Doubleday, 1982

Martin, Paul. *A Very Public Life*, vol. 1: *Far from Home.* Ottawa: Deneau, 1983

— *A Very Public Life*, vol. 2: *So Many Worlds.* Toronto: Deneau, 1985

McCourt, Edward. *Saskatchewan.* Toronto: Macmillan, 1968

McDougall, John N. *Fuels and the National Policy.* Toronto: Butterworths, 1982

McIlroy, Thad, ed. *Personal Letters of a Public Man: The Family Letters of John G. Diefenbaker.* Toronto: Doubleday Canada, 1985

McLeod, Keith A. "Politics, Schools and the French Language, 1881–1931," in Ward and Spafford, eds., *Politics in Saskatchewan*, 124–50

McLin, Jon B. *Canada's Changing Defense Policy, 1957–1963: The Problems of a Middle Power in Alliance.* Baltimore: Johns Hopkins Press, 1967

Meisel, John. *The Canadian General Election of 1957.* Toronto: University of Toronto Press, 1962

— ed. *Papers on the 1962 Election.* Toronto: University of Toronto Press, 1964

Menzies, Sir Robert Gordon. *Afternoon Light: Some Memories of Men and Events.* London: Cassell, 1967

Morton, W.L. *The Kingdom of Canada: A General History from Earliest Times.* Toronto: McClelland & Stewart, 1963

Moynihan, Daniel Patrick. *Pandaemonium.* New York: Oxford University Press, 1993

Nash, Knowlton. *Kennedy and Diefenbaker: Fear and Loathing across the Undefended Border.* Toronto: McClelland & Stewart, 1990

— *The Microphone Wars: A History of Triumph and Betrayal at the CBC.* Toronto: McClelland & Stewart, 1994

Newman, Peter C. *The Distemper of Our Times.* Toronto: McClelland & Stewart, 1978

— *Renegade in Power: The Diefenbaker Years.* Toronto: McClelland & Stewart, 1989

Nicholson, Patrick. *Vision and Indecision.* Toronto: Longmans Canada, 1968

Nielsen, Erik. *The House Is Not a Home: An Autobiography.* Toronto: Macmillan, 1989

O'Leary, Grattan. *Recollections of People, Press and Politics.* Toronto: Macmillan, 1977

Orpwood, Helen. "The Saskatchewan Election." *Canadian Forum*, August 1938: 136–37

O'Sullivan, Sean (with Rod McQueen). *Both My Houses: From Politics to Priesthood.* Toronto: Key Porter, 1986

Oxford Companion to Medicine. New York: Oxford University Press, 1966

Paltiel, K.Z. *Political Party Financing in Canada.* Toronto: McGraw-Hill, 1970

Pearson, Lester B. *Mike: The Memoirs of the Right Honourable Lester B. Pearson,* vol. 1: *1897–1948;* vol. 2: *1948–1957;* vol. 3: *1957–1968.* Toronto: University of Toronto Press, 1972, 1973, 1975

Peers, Frank W. *The Public Eye: Television and the Politics of Canadian Broadcasting, 1952–1968.* Toronto: University of Toronto Press, 1979

Perlin, George C. *The Tory Syndrome: Leadership Politics in the Progressive Conservative Party.* Montreal: McGill-Queen's University Press, 1980

Pickersgill, J.W. *The Road Back.* Toronto: University of Toronto Press, 1986

— *Seeing Canada Whole: A Memoir.* Markham: Fitzhenry & Whiteside, 1994

Pickersgill, J.W., ed. *The Mackenzie King Record,* vol. 1: *1939–1944.* Toronto: University of Toronto Press, 1960

Pickersgill, J.W., and D.F. Forster, eds. *The Mackenzie King Record,* vol. 2: *1944–1945;* vol. 3: *1945–1946;* vol. 4: *1947–1948.* Toronto: University of Toronto Press, 1968, 1970

Reeves, Richard. *President Kennedy: Profile of Power.* New York: Simon & Shuster, 1993

Reid, Escott. *Radical Mandarin: The Memoirs of Escott Reid.* Toronto: University of Toronto Press, 1989

Report of the Royal Commission to Inquire into Statements Made in Statutory Declarations and Other Matters, 1930. Regina: Liberal-Conservative Party of Saskatchewan, April 1931

Ritchie, Charles. *Diplomatic Passport: More Undiplomatic Diaries, 1946–1962.* Toronto: Macmillan, 1981

Robertson, Heather. *More than a Rose: Prime Ministers, Wives and Other Women.* Toronto: Seal Books, 1991

Robin, Martin. *Shades of Right: Nativist and Fascist Politics in Canada, 1920–1940.* Toronto: University of Toronto Press, 1992

Robinson, Daniel. "Planning for the 'Most Serious Contingency': Alien Internment, Arbitrary Detention, and the Canadian State, 1938–39." *Journal of Canadian Studies* 28 (summer 1993):5–20

Robinson, Daniel, and David Kimmel. "The Queer Career of Homosexual Security Vetting in Cold War Canada." *Canadian Historical Review* 75 (September 1994): 319–45

Robinson, H. Basil. *Diefenbaker's World: A Populist in Foreign Affairs.* Toronto: University of Toronto Press, 1989

Sawatsky, John. *For Services Rendered: Leslie James Bennett and the RCMP Security Service.* Toronto: Doubleday, 1982

— *Mulroney: The Politics of Ambition.* Toronto: Macfarlane Walter & Ross, 1991

Saywell, John T., ed. *Canadian Annual Review,* 1960–68. Toronto: University of Toronto Press, 1961–69

Sévigny, Pierre. *This Game of Politics.* Toronto: McClelland & Stewart, 1965

Sharp, Mitchell. *Which Reminds Me...A Memoir.* Toronto: University of Toronto Press, 1994

Shaw, E.K. *There Never Was an Arrow.* Toronto: Steel Rail, 1979

Sheaf. Saskatoon: University of Saskatchewan, April 1915, April 1919

Smith, David. *Prairie Liberalism: The Liberal Party in Saskatchewan, 1905–71.* Toronto: University of Toronto Press, 1975

Smith, Denis. *Diplomacy of Fear: Canada and the Cold War, 1941–1948.* Toronto: University of Toronto Press, 1988

— *Gentle Patriot: A Political Biography of Walter Gordon.* Edmonton: Hurtig, 1973

Speaight, Robert. *Vanier: Soldier, Diplomat and Governor General: A Biography.* Toronto: Collins, 1970

Spencer, Dick. *Trumpets and Drums: John Diefenbaker on the Campaign Trail.* Vancouver: Douglas & McIntyre, 1994

Stacey, C.P. *Arms, Men and Governments: The War Policies of Canada, 1939–1945.* Ottawa: Information Canada, 1970

Stevens, Geoffrey. *Stanfield.* Toronto: McClelland & Stewart, 1973

Stewart, Greig. *Shutting Down the National Dream: A.V. Roe and the Tragedy of the Avro Arrow*. Toronto: McGraw-Hill Ryerson, 1988

Stursberg, Peter. *Diefenbaker: Leadership Gained, 1956–62*. Toronto: University of Toronto Press, 1975
— *Diefenbaker: Leadership Lost, 1962–67*. Toronto: University of Toronto Press, 1976

Swainson, Neil A. *Conflict over the Columbia: The Canadian Background to an Historic Treaty*. Montreal: McGill-Queen's University Press, 1979

Tarnopolosky, Walter Surma. *The Canadian Bill of Rights*. 2nd rev. ed. Toronto: McClelland & Stewart, 1975

Taylor, A.J.P. *English History, 1914–1945*. Oxford: The Clarendon Press, 1965

Thompson, John Herd, and Stephen J. Randall. *Canada and the United States: Ambivalent Allies*. Montreal: McGill-Queen's University Press, 1994

Thomson, William A.R. *The Macmillan Medical Encyclopedia*. New York: Macmillan, 1906, 1959

Van Dusen, Thomas. *The Chief*. Toronto: McGraw-Hill, 1968

Waite, P.B. *The Loner: Three Sketches of the Personal Life and Ideas of R.B. Bennett, 1870–1947*. Toronto: University of Toronto Press, 1992

Ward, Norman. *A Party Politician: The Memoirs of Chubby Power*. Toronto: Macmillan, 1966

Ward, Norman, and David Smith. *Jimmy Gardiner: Relentless Liberal*. Toronto: University of Toronto Press, 1990

Ward, Norman, and Duff Spafford, eds. *Politics in Saskatchewan*. Toronto: Longmans Canada, 1968

Whitaker, Reginald. *The Government Party: Organizing and Financing the Liberal Party of Canada, 1930–58*. Toronto: University of Toronto Press, 1977

Whitaker, Reginald, and Gary Marcuse. *Cold War Canada: The Making of a National Insecurity State, 1945–1957*. Toronto: University of Toronto Press, 1994

Williams, John R. *The Conservative Party of Canada, 1920–1949*. Durham: Duke University Press, 1956

Wilson, Garrett, and Kevin Wilson. *Diefenbaker for the Defence*. Toronto: James Lorimer, 1988

Theses

Belliveau, Robert M. "Mr. Diefenbaker, Parliamentary Democracy and the Canadian Bill of Rights." MA thesis, University of Saskatchewan, 1992

Calderwood, William. "The Rise and Fall of the Ku Klux Klan in Saskatchewan." MA thesis, University of Saskatchewan, 1968

Gingrich, Stephen K. "Defence Production Sharing and Canada and the United States, 1957–1967." MA thesis, University of Western Ontario, 1990

Halabura, Gerald M. "Diefenbaker and Electoral Redistribution: Principle or Pragmatism?" MA thesis, University of Saskatchewan, 1992

Acknowledgments

This book had a long genesis. My father introduced me briefly to John Diefenbaker at a meeting of the Canadian Bar Association in Winnipeg in August 1942, and from then on I was aware of the activities of the MP for Lake Centre, Saskatchewan, as his parliamentary reputation grew on the prairies. By 1957, when he came to power, I was certain his life would offer rich material for inquiry. In that era of reawakened political interest, I watched his rise and fall with fascination.

I am grateful to Donald Creighton for setting the modern standard of Canadian political biography. His *John A. Macdonald* was published in the mid-1950s at the right moment to influence John Diefenbaker's vision of Canada and my interest in the biographical art.

In 1967, when Diefenbaker seemed on the point of retirement as leader of his party, I made known to him my interest in writing about his life and career. For three years after that, in extended personal interviews, negotiation, and ventures into his papers, I received a close education in his character which was later valuable in seeking to portray him. In 1970 – failing any agreement on the use of materials from his papers – this early project was abandoned. I doubted that I would return to it.

Almost twenty years later, the Diefenbaker Centre and the National Archives were well advanced in organizing the mass of the Diefenbaker Papers, but no one had yet ventured on a biography. I was drawn back to the subject, and with support from the Social Sciences and Humanities Research Council of Canada I began work on this book in 1989.

Over that long journey, I am obliged to many persons for support. In my research and interviews in 1969 and 1970 I was joined by W.F.W. Neville, with assistance from John O. Stubbs, Colin Wright, Arlene Davis, and Fran Cormode. I benefited from frequent discussion of the Diefenbaker government and its successors with Bernard Blishen, David Cameron, Bruce Hodgins, David Kettler, W.L. Morton, David Morrison, Joe Wearing, and Alan Wilson. T.H.B. Symons, president of Trent University, and T.E.W. Nind, dean of arts and science, gave their encouragement, as did John Gray and Diane Mew of the Macmillan Company of Canada. Dalton Camp gave generous interviews during his year as Skelton-Clark Fellow at Queen's University. John Diefenbaker's staff or former staff – Bunny Pound, Betty Eligh, Marion Wagner, Gerry Haslam, and Keith Martin – offered helpful insights about the Chief. Bill Neville and Colin Wright interviewed Gordon Churchill, Clark Davey, Peter Dempson, Norman DePoe, and Robert Blackwood, and made their interviews available to me. By the time I returned to the subject in 1989, I had moved to the University of Western Ontario, and I am grateful for advice and comment from Jack Hyatt, Don Avery, John McDougall, and Clark Leith, and for research assistance from Alison Bramwell and Tom Saunders. At the Diefenbaker Centre I found skilled support and help from the successive directors, John A. Munro, Elizabeth Diamond, Stan Hanson, and Bruce Shephard; from the archivists Steve Billinton, Fiona Haynes, and Joan Champ; from archival assistants Naoise Johnston and Chris Kitzan and research clerical assistants Katie Andrews and Michael St Denis; and from Centre staff members Helen Aikenhead and Pat St Louis. John Courtney, Gay and Fred Forster, David Smith, and Duff Spafford provided hospitality and helpful advice in Saskatoon. Robert K. Webb acted as my American intermediary in seeking mandatory review of documents at the Kennedy Library, and Suzanne Forbes was helpful there. The archival staff of the National Archives of Canada – particularly John Bell, Loretta Barber, and Bill Wood – were unfailingly obliging, as were archivists at the Queen's University Archives, the US National Archives, the Public Record Office at Kew, and the University of Calgary Archives.

For the use of papers and/or comment on the Diefenbaker period, I am grateful to Agar Adamson, Anthony Adamson, Blair Adamson, Ruth Bell, Admiral Jeffry V. Brock, George and Sheila Connell, John English, Davie Fulton, Eddie Goodman, Gowan Guest, Douglas Harkness, Clyne Harradence, Dr J.F. Leddy, Cynthia McCormack, Flora MacDonald, Brian McGarry, Desmond Morton, Peter Roberts, Basil Robinson, Benjamin Rogers, and Carolyn Weir. Many others volunteered their memories of encounters with John Diefenbaker in tones of affection, puzzlement, or sometimes outrage. For various acts of assistance I am grateful to Stevie Cameron, Stephen Clarkson, Margaret Doxey, John Gray, Jack McLeod, Bill Montgomery, and Mayling and John Stubbs. Bella Pomer has given wise professional counsel, Jan Walter has been a superb editor, and Rosemary Shipton an exemplary copy editor. My son, Stephen, has been a constant source of literary inspiration; and my wife, Dawn, as always, has given endless encouragement and advice as first reader and discerning critic. I am grateful to all of them.

DS
Port Hope, Ontario
August 1995

Grateful acknowledgment is made for permission to quote copyright material published by the following:

Deneau and Greenberg, for an extract from *Points of Departure* (1979), by Dalton Camp;

Doubleday, for extracts from *The Other Mrs. Diefenbaker* (1982), by Simma Holt;

General Publishing, for an extract from *Assignment Ottawa: Seventeen Years in the Press Gallery* (1968), by Peter Dempson;

Key Porter, for extracts from *Life of the Party: The Memoirs of Eddie Goodman* (1988), by Eddie Goodman;

Longman, for extracts from *The Party's Over* (1971), by James Johnston, and *Vision and Indecision* (1968), by Patrick Nicholson;

James Lorimer, for extracts from *Diefenbaker for the Defence* (1988), by Garrett and Kevin Wilson;

McClelland & Stewart, for extracts from *Gentlemen, Players & Politicians* (1970), by Dalton Camp; *So Very Near: The Political Memoirs of Honourable Donald M. Fleming* (1985), by Donald Fleming; *Kennedy and Diefenbaker: Fear and Loathing across the Undefended Border* (1990), by Knowlton Nash; *Renegade in Power: The Diefenbaker Years* (1989) and *The Distemper of Our Times* (1978), by Peter C. Newman; and *This Game of Politics* (1965), by Pierre Sévigny;

Macmillan, for extracts from *One Canada: Memoirs of the Right Honourable John G. Diefenbaker* (1975, 1976, 1977), by John G. Diefenbaker;

Prentice-Hall, for an extract from *Canadian Foreign Policy: Selected Cases* (1992), ed. by Don Munton and John Kirton;

University of Toronto Press, for extracts from *The Politics of Survival: The Conservative Party of Canada, 1939–1945* (1967), by J. L. Granatstein; *The Mackenzie King Record*, vol. 1 (1960), ed. by J. W. Pickersgill; *Shades of Right: Nativist and Fascist Politics in Canada, 1920–1940* (1992), by Martin Robin; *Diefenbaker's World: A Populist in Foreign Affairs* (1989), by Basil Robinson; and *Diefenbaker: Leadership Gained, 1956–62* (1975), by Peter Stursberg.

Index

687

The text of this book is set in ITC New Baskerville. This recent version, designed for ITC by M. Carter and J. Quaranta in 1978, is based on the classic eighteenth century design by Englishman John Baskerville. The Baskerville typeface of 1757 is known as a "transitional" face, embodying features of the old style along with the thick and thin lines of the modern style.

The headlines are set in Fashion Compressed No. 3, a typeface designed by Alan Meeks in 1986 for Letraset. It draws heavily on a traditional Italian face called Torino, designed in 1908 by Alessandro Butti.

Book design and typesetting by James Ireland Design Inc., Toronto